Penser une démocratie alimentaire
Thinking a food democracy

(Vol. 2)

Propositions Lascaux entre
ressources naturelles et besoins alimentaires

Lascaux proposals between
natural resources and food needs

Le Programme Lascaux (2009-2014) est dirigé par François Collart Dutilleul, Professeur à l'Université de Nantes.

Les travaux menant aux présents résultats ont bénéficié d'un soutien financier du Conseil européen de la recherche au titre du 7e programme-cadre de la Communauté européenne (7e PC/2007-2013) en vertu de la convention de subvention CER n° 230400.

Ces travaux ne reflètent que les opinions de leurs auteurs et l'Union n'est pas responsable de l'usage qui pourrait être fait des données figurant dans les publications.

Penser une démocratie alimentaire
Thinking a food democracy

(Vol. 2)

Propositions Lascaux entre ressources naturelles et besoins alimentaires

Lascaux proposals between natural resources and food needs

Sous la direction scientifique de
François Collart Dutilleul

Coordinateur éditorial
Thomas Bréger

Instituto de Investigación en Derecho Alimentario, 2014

INIDA
P.O. Box 161-2400 Desamparados,
San José, Costa Rica

c o n t a c t @ i n i d a . e u

w w w . i n i d a . e u

Penser une démocratie alimentaire (Vol. 2), Propositions Lascaux entre ressources naturelles et besoins alimentaires /
Thinking a food democracy (Vol.2), Lascaux proposals between natural resources and food needs

INIDA, Collection "ouvrages collectifs" (Serie obras colectivas), Vol. IV
1ère édition, 2014

ISBN : 978-2-918382-09-6

Cet ouvrage « Penser une démocratie alimentaire » a été réalisé grâce au soutien et à la collaboration des membres de « l'équipe Lascaux », en particulier de Claire BLANDEL, *de Sarah* TURBEAUX *et de Jean-Philippe* BUGNICOURT. *Le programme Lascaux tient également à remercier chaleureusement Marlen* LEON GUZMAN *et Hugo* MUÑOZ UREÑA *(Dir. Editions Inida) pour leur disponibilité et leur soutien constant aux projets menés par le programme.*

Sommaire

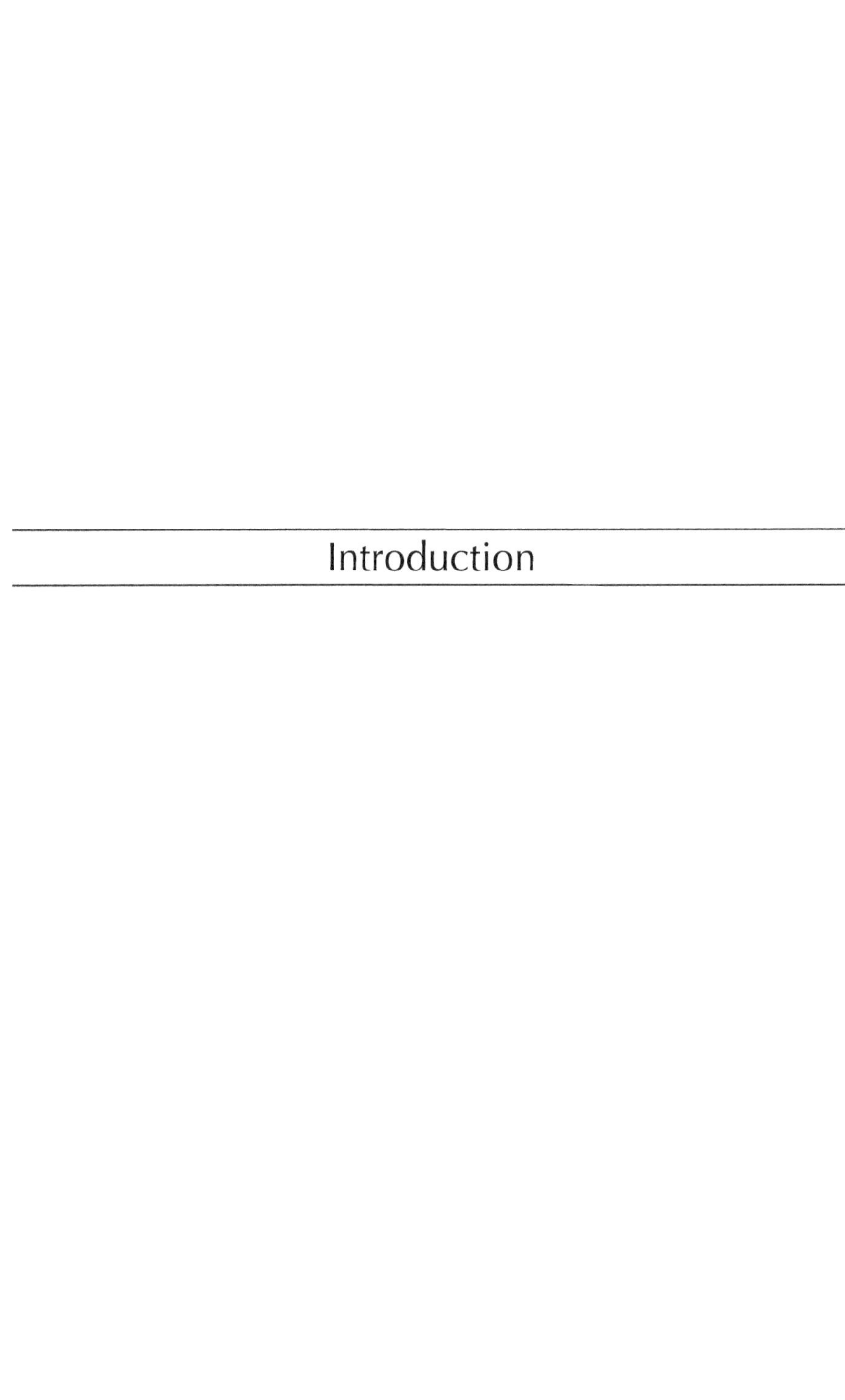

Introduction

Un nouvel horizon de recherche : Les moyens juridiques d'un ajustement des ressources et des besoins alimentaires

François COLLART DUTILLEUL *

Dans un premier ouvrage, les chercheurs du programme Lascaux ont mené des analyses avec leurs outils et leurs méthodes des sciences sociales. Ces travaux ont conduit à faire des propositions d'évolution du droit, notamment international. Ces propositions, publiées en français dans le premier volume[1], le sont de nouveau ici, en anglais. Mais ces évolutions, quelle que soit la valeur scientifique de leurs fondations et de leurs appuis, doivent être socialement acceptables et acceptées. Dans ce volume 2, les chercheurs se mettent alors à l'écoute de la société civile. Ils laissent parler et ils dialoguent avec des ONG, avec des organisations internationales, avec des syndicats, des *think tanks*, des entreprises, des citoyens. Il s'agit toujours de penser une démocratie alimentaire. Mais quelles sont les conditions juridiques d'une telle démocratie ? Quels verrous faut-il ouvrir ? Quels nouveaux principes doit-on forger ?

- Faut-il établir une « exception alimentaire » à la manière de « l'exception culturelle » ?
- Comment préserver l'accès des petits paysans à la terre, à l'eau, aux ressources de la biodiversité ?
- Peut-on laisser aux Etats un espace de souveraineté alimentaire dans la mondialisation du commerce ?
- Par quels moyens peut-on garantir les besoins fondamentaux des personnes dans un droit du marché encadré ?
- Comment assurer le respect des droits de l'Homme dans un monde gouverné par les libertés économiques ?
- Faut-il définir un nouveau contrat social pour préserver les ressources naturelles et nourrir une planète de plus en plus habitée ?

---

* Professeur à l'Université de Nantes. Directeur du programme Lascaux.

[1] *Penser une démocratie alimentaire* (dir. F. COLLART DUTILLEUL et coord. T. BREGER), vol. 1, Edicion INIDA, 2013.

- Est-il possible de coordonner les enjeux écologiques, alimentaires et démographiques de l'exploitation des ressources naturelles ?
- Est-il concevable d'élargir le droit des consommateurs-mangeurs à un droit des consommateurs-citoyens ?

Ce qui ressort de ce dialogue, centré sur la sécurité alimentaire dans le monde, c'est la volonté partagée de rechercher les moyens juridiques d'améliorer cette sécurité, de rendre plus effectifs les droits fondamentaux (en particulier le droit à l'alimentation) tant au Nord qu'au Sud, de garantir aux paysans des droits leur permettant de vivre et faire vivre leurs familles avec leur travail, de rendre le commerce international plus équitable et profitable aux pays en développement, de mettre le consommateur en situation de mieux choisir son alimentation afin de passer de l'état de mangeur à celui de citoyen.

Ce qui ressort de ce dialogue, c'est aussi la nécessité de penser un droit « *out of the box* », un droit qui sort du cadre étroit de la loi de l'offre et de la demande appliquée à la terre (accaparement des terres), à l'eau, aux matières premières agricoles (libéralisation du commerce international), un droit qui ne se réduit pas à équilibrer les forces en présence dans un marché qui ne devrait être que concurrentiel.

Il faut en effet permettre aux Etats comme aux diverses collectivités publiques, dans le cadre d'une démocratie alimentaire, de définir leur propre politique d'ajustement de leurs ressources naturelles avec le besoin fondamental de nourrir leur population. C'est pourquoi il est nécessaire de concevoir des moyens juridiques précisément adaptés à la mise en œuvre d'une telle politique.

Ce dernier constat a conduit à poser plus généralement la question de l'ajustement, par des politiques publiques appropriées, des ressources et des besoins. Cette question devra faire l'objet d'une seconde phase du programme Lascaux. Cette seconde phase visera la recherche d'un encadrement juridique permettant la mise en œuvre d'une loi économique et sociale à définir, appelée « loi d'ajustement des ressources et des besoins ». Cette loi, au sens juridique, social et économique, supposera des recherches étendues à l'ensemble des ressources naturelles (terre et agriculture, eau, énergie, forêt, sous-sol...).

En effet, nos « vies économiques » sont fondées sur une loi que l'on pourrait appeler « la loi d'ajustement des ressources et des besoins ». Cette loi des ressources et des besoins est en réalité une « loi de la vie ». On pourrait aisément la transposer à tous les êtres vivants.

Nous avons des ressources et des besoins et nos vies économiques consistent à les ajuster en permanence. Si nous n'avons pas assez de ressources, nous empruntons, ou bien nous demandons de l'aide ou déclarons un surendettement. Si nous avons trop de ressources, nous épargnons pour d'autres jours. Ainsi vivons-nous en visant cet ajustement. Au plan des individus, les ressources ajustées sont essentiellement financières.

La loi d'ajustement des ressources et des besoins est pareillement au cœur de la vie des entreprises. Une entreprise se gère en ajustant ses ressources et ses besoins. Cela a des effets positifs et négatifs. On peut raisonner sous l'angle des marchandises, sous l'angle du capital, sous l'angle du personnel. Quand une entreprise a besoin d'argent, elle lève des fonds pour ajuster, le cas échéant, ses ressources à ses besoins de fonctionnement ou de développement. Si elle a trop de salariés ou pas assez, elle licencie ou elle embauche ; elle ajuste ses ressources humaines à ses besoins. Au plan des entreprises, les ressources ajustées sont surtout des ressources financières et humaines. Mais certaines d'entre elles, eu égard à leur activité, utilisent ou prélèvent des ressources naturelles (agriculture, agroalimentaire, énergie, mines, forêts...) qu'elles peuvent surexploiter, tarir, endommager.

Dans quelle mesure les Etats et autres institutions territoriales peuvent-ils développer des politiques publiques d'ajustement de leurs ressources naturelles avec les besoins socio-économiques fondamentaux des populations dont ils ont la charge ? C'est précisément en y réfléchissant à l'égard du besoin de se nourrir, et donc de la sécurité alimentaire, que les difficultés sont apparues.

La première difficulté vient de ce que, dans la situation présente, la marge de manœuvre des Etats et des institutions territoriales est faible et cela pour plusieurs raisons :

- Tout d'abord, les ressources naturelles sont le plus souvent en dehors de l'emprise des institutions publiques dès lors qu'elles font l'objet, non de biens communs, mais d'une propriété privée qui confère au titulaire des prérogatives qui sont parfois qualifiées d'absolues. Cela tend à accentuer les disparités dans la valeur des terres, à accroître l'urbanisation et l'artificialisation des terres, à orienter la gestion foncière et des ressources dans le sens de valeurs marchandes.

- Ensuite, les institutions publiques sont dépendantes d'une organisation commerciale internationale qui les empêche d'intervenir sur les richesses produites à partir des ressources naturelles. En effet, le système de l'Organisation Mondiale du Commerce (OMC) laisse une marge de manœuvre très faible aux Etats qui voudraient réguler la circulation et la distribution des richesses produites au profit de leurs populations. En principe, les ressources naturelles ne sont saisies qu'à travers leur valeur marchande et les Etats ne peuvent freiner la libre circulation et le libre-échange des marchandises issues de ces ressources. Les Etats ne peuvent pas, sauf exceptions limitées, subventionner un produit, réglementer les prix, contingenter les importations ou les exportations. Le mouvement actuel, qui privilégie les accords commerciaux bilatéraux plutôt que les accords multilatéraux, va d'ailleurs dans le même sens. Or lorsque ces richesses produites sont précisément celles dont dépend la sécurité alimentaire d'un pays, celui-ci est privé d'un moyen déterminant si une crise survient.

- Enfin, les différentes tentatives de maîtrise des ressources naturelles au plan international ont montré leurs limites. Trois négociations internationales ont assez largement échoué depuis novembre et décembre 2009 : celle sur les effets du changement climatique, de Copenhague à Durban, qui concerne la protection des ressources, celle sur la sécurité alimentaire à la FAO, à Rome, qui concerne donc le premier des besoins fondamentaux des populations, et celle sur le commerce international des matières premières agricoles à l'OMC, à Genève et en décembre 2013 à Bali. Sans doute la négociation de Bali a-t-elle conduit à un résultat provisoire, permettant aux pays en développement d'approvisionner les populations pauvres en constituant des stocks alimentaires à des prix encadrés sans encourir de sanctions. Mais il s'agit d'un accord à la fois minimaliste et de faible portée. Aucune solution réellement efficace ne peut être pensée si on ne relie pas entre elles les trois négociations. Car c'est de ces trois négociations ensemble que peut résulter la possibilité d'un ajustement des ressources naturelles et des besoins sociaux au premier rang desquels le besoin alimentaire.

La seconde difficulté se manifeste dans les pays qui accueillent des investissements étrangers. Ces investissements se réalisent souvent par un accaparement des terres au détriment des populations locales, sans contreparties à la hauteur des besoins fondamentaux - au premier chef alimentaires - des populations et à des conditions environnementales non durables. Or les investissements internationaux dans les ressources naturelles des pays en développement sont en expansion considérable depuis les années 2008-2009. Ils conduisent à l'accaparement d'importantes surfaces de terres pour y réaliser des exploitations agricoles, minières, pétrolières ou forestières. Ils peuvent aussi viser l'exploitation de nappes phréatiques et, plus généralement, de l'eau. Ce phénomène de l'accaparement manifeste l'inadaptation des droits nationaux d'Etats économiquement faibles.

Il en résulte que, très limités dans leur pouvoir de gérer leurs ressources naturelles de manière ajustée aux besoins de la population, les Etats et autres institutions publiques des pays en développement sont particulièrement handicapés. En effet, ces pays stagnent avec une pauvreté qui persiste alors même qu'ils disposent de richesses importantes sur leur territoire. Sans doute les facteurs de cette stagnation sont-ils nombreux (climat, corruption, instabilité politique...). Mais il n'en demeure pas moins que des obstacles juridiques objectifs empêchent un tel ajustement même en l'absence de ces autres facteurs. Quant aux pays développés, ils sont tout aussi limités dans leur pouvoir d'agir, mais avec une portée et des conséquences évidemment différentes.

Ces dernières années, les crises de la finance et des économies ont montré les difficultés qu'avaient tant les Etats que les collectivités en difficulté à peser sur l'ajustement des ressources financières (crise financière et explosion des dettes souveraines) et humaines (crise économique et explosion du chômage). Mais la situation est encore plus calamiteuse pour les ressources naturelles face aux crises qui menacent diversement selon le degré de développement : réchauffement climatique, crise énergétique, évolution démographique, crise économique, crise alimentaire, appauvrissement de la biodiversité, dégradation des sols et des ressources en eau, pollution.

L'une des principales clés se situe en réalité à l'OMC qui, au plan international, est le lieu où se fait l'ajustement des ressources et des besoins par le commerce. Elle se situe aussi au cœur des accords commerciaux bilatéraux que l'Europe, en particulier, négocie avec des pays de tous les continents : le Canada, les Etats-Unis, la Corée, le Japon, la Chine... auxquels s'ajoutent tous les Accords de Partenariat Economique (APE) négociés avec les pays d'Afrique, Caraïbes et Pacifique (ACP). Mais l'ajustement par les règles du commerce international, qu'il soit d'origine multilatérale ou bilatérale, ne tient pas compte de toutes les particularités des Etats : situation économique et niveau de développement, situation géographique et climatique, situation énergétique, situation sociale... Le commerce transnational ne tient pas davantage compte des évolutions à venir en termes de disparités démographiques, de transition énergétique, de lutte contre le réchauffement climatique, de réduction des inégalités d'accès aux ressources naturelles et de réduction de la malnutrition ou de la pauvreté. Or ce sont là autant de facteurs qui sont déterminants pour la sécurité alimentaire.

Une autre clé se situe dans le droit des investissements internationaux qui relève de plus de 3000 traités bilatéraux ainsi que des règles de l'OMC[2] et des règles d'arbitrage de l'ONU (CIRDI)[3]. Ces droits pèsent lourdement face à la faiblesse des droits nationaux qui, dans les pays d'accueil, sont censés protéger l'accès à la terre, protéger l'environnement et protéger les intérêts des populations locales.

On voit ainsi que l'encadrement juridique propre à assurer la sécurité alimentaire et, partant, à garantir le premier des besoins fondamentaux, doit tenir compte de deux enjeux majeurs.

Le premier enjeu est relatif à une gestion mesurée des ressources naturelles et à l'adaptation de cette gestion aux effets du changement climatique. Cela suppose d'élaborer, par les moyens combinés des sciences naturelles et des sciences sociales, un « diagnostic » qui s'appuie sur le constat des changements environnementaux (climat, biodiversité, dégrada-

[2] Accord sur les mesures concernant les investissements et liées au commerce (MIC).

[3] Le CIRDI est la principale institution pour la résolution des différends internationaux relatifs aux investissements : https://icsid.worldbank.org/ICSID/

tions, pollution...), sur les indicateurs permettant de les « mesurer » afin d'apprécier la déperdition en ressources naturelles d'un territoire donné. Ce diagnostic est parallèlement établi en recherchant les causes, spécialement juridiques, de cette déperdition et, par voie de conséquence, du « capital » de ressources utilisables. Sous l'angle du droit, ce diagnostic doit impliquer l'ensemble des niveaux politiques, du local à l'international. Si le droit est toujours du côté des causes des problèmes, il est aussi du côté des solutions. En effet, le droit est un langage social qui à la fois porte les valeurs et véhicule les politiques publiques qu'une société définit pour elle-même. Il s'agit alors de définir l'encadrement juridique que nécessitent la coexistence de valeurs marchandes et non marchandes, une exploitation durable des ressources naturelles et un ajustement de ces ressources aux besoins socio-économiques fondamentaux.

Le second enjeu est relatif à la transition écologique, à ses risques, à ses opportunités et aux transformations sociales qu'elle implique. Car c'est là que se croisent et interfèrent les écosystèmes et les systèmes socio-économiques. Il s'agit alors de promouvoir des politiques publiques qui passent de la dimension d'aménagement du territoire et de la dimension de protection de l'environnement à une troisième dimension qui est celle de la gestion des ressources naturelles ajustée aux besoins. C'est par un tel ajustement qu'on peut en effet à la fois parler authentiquement de gouvernance des ressources et rechercher un degré élevé de cohésion sociale via une plus grande justice dans l'accès à ces ressources. Toute politique publique visant l'exploitation des ressources doit être attentive en particulier à la diversité des situations urbaines et rurales, aux mouvements de population des campagnes vers les villes, des phénomènes accrus d'émigration de populations pauvres du Sud vers le Nord. On retrouve ici ce qui caractérise les concepts « d'empreinte écologique » et de « dette écologique », mais utilisés positivement pour aider à la prise de décisions politiques. On ne peut pas durablement assurer la sécurité alimentaire sans une attention particulière à ces concepts.

Mais pour ouvrir les voies juridiques d'une gestion des ressources naturelles ajustées aux besoins, il faut évidemment déterminer des indicateurs scientifiques permettant de réaliser une évaluation des ressources naturelles disponibles sur un territoire politiquement organisé et, en parallèle, réfléchir au concept même de ressources naturelles. Il en va des ressources naturelles comme des ressources financières. Aucune politique n'est possible si on ne connait pas le capital dont on dispose.

Du côté des besoins, la notion de besoins alimentaires mérite tout autant d'être précisée et il faudrait plus largement se demander s'il est possible de concevoir les besoins fondamentaux par référence aux droits fondamentaux. En réalité, cette question des besoins fondamentaux doit être abordée de manière pragmatique. S'il est nécessaire de chercher à les définir, en particulier en droit international et pour l'application de ce droit, il ne faut pas chercher à trancher entre les définitions diverses existantes en économie, en droit, en psychologie, en anthropologie, en sociologie, car il ne saurait y avoir une définition universelle et imposée à tout le monde, à toutes les cultures, à tous les pays... Mieux vaut poser en principe qu'il appartient à chaque Etat ou institution en situation de développer des politiques publiques relatives aux ressources naturelles de définir les besoins à couvrir.

Mais si l'on s'en tient aux ressources et aux besoins alimentaires, comment faire, dans un contexte de contraintes écologiques, écosystémiques, économiques, sociales, démographiques, pour nourrir 9 milliards de personnes en 2050 ? Où situer le point d'équilibre, pour assurer la sécurité alimentaire entre l'auto-approvisionnement et le commerce, entre la nature et la technologie, entre les besoins du consommateur-mangeur et les attentes du consommateur-citoyen, entre l'encadrement juridique des marchés et le libre-échange ? Y a-t-il des références ou des modèles juridiques dans le monde ?

L'Islande a élaboré un projet de Constitution soustrayant les ressources naturelles (non encore appropriées) à la propriété pour en faire une détention du peuple islandais pour ses propres besoins. L'Equateur a modifié sa Constitution en 2008 pour reconnaître des droits effectifs à la nature. Le Québec a adopté une loi sur l'eau en 2009 qui soustrait l'eau à toute forme de propriété publique ou privée. La Nouvelle Zélande a adopté en 1991 une loi visant à réaliser l'ajustement des ressources naturelles et des besoins socio-économiques en établissant des règles de fond et des procédures spéciales. Mais l'exemple le plus abouti et le plus prometteur est sans doute la Charte de La Havane de 1948, signée par 53 pays mais qui n'a jamais été mise en œuvre pour des raisons tenant à la politique intérieure des Etats-Unis. Cette Charte aurait dû compléter le GATT et elle était de nature non seulement à humaniser la mondialisation, mais aussi à permettre aux Etats de déroger aux règles de libre-échange et de réaliser l'ajustement de leurs ressources naturelles et de leurs besoins en cas de difficulté et en fonction de leurs situations particulières. Elle a fait l'objet, dans le programme Lascaux, d'une des propositions d'évolution du droit international[4]. Cette Charte trop vite oubliée mérite d'être analysée de manière plus approfondie à partir de ses travaux préparatoires à rechercher dans les archives des Etats-Unis, dans celles de Cuba, dans celles de l'OMC/GATT à Genève et de la FAO à Rome.

Si la question d'un ajustement des ressources naturelles et des besoins alimentaires était surmontée, il serait alors possible d'aller plus loin et d'élaborer un cadre juridique théorique et pratique pour la reconnaissance innovante et originale d'une loi d'ajustement des ressources (naturelles) d'un territoire et des besoins (fondamentaux) des populations qui y vivent. Une telle loi pourrait s'inspirer de la doctrine de « l'économie substantielle » de l'économiste Karl Polanyi[5]. Nous connaissons assez bien l'encadrement juridique que requiert la mise en œuvre de la loi d'ajustement de l'offre et de la demande. Mais nous ne savons à peu près rien de ce que pourrait être un droit de l'ajustement des ressources naturelles et des besoins fondamentaux. C'est à cela que le programme Lascaux devrait désormais s'atteler.

---

[4] V. F. COLLART DUTILLEUL, Les voies d'amélioration de la sécurité alimentaire dans un contexte de mondialisation du commerce, in *Penser une démocratie alimentaire*, vol. 1, p. 213. La version anglaise de cette proposition du programme Lascaux est reproduite dans le présent ouvrage, v. *Infra*, p. 43.

[5] *La subsistance de l'Homme - La place de l'économie dans l'histoire et la société*, Flammarion, 2011, p. 56.

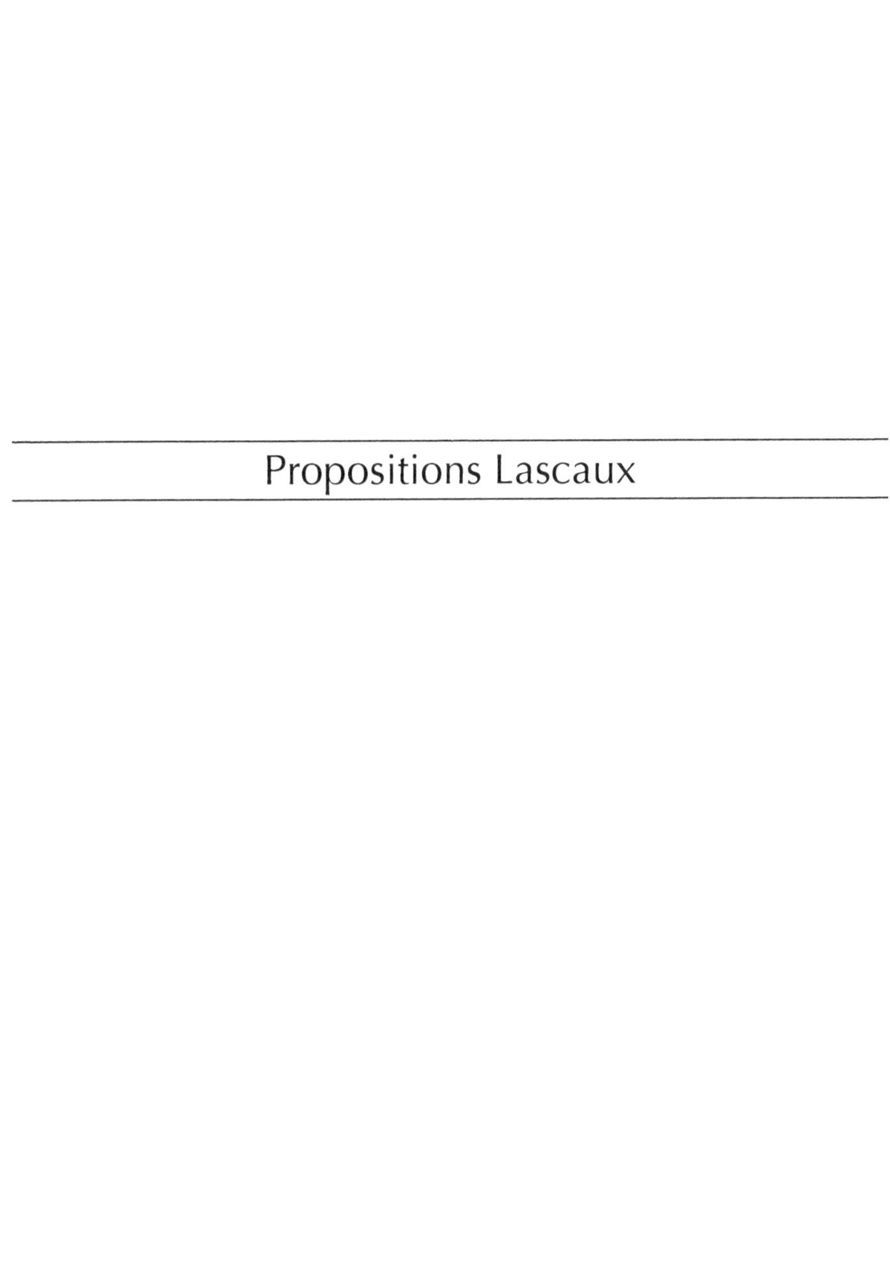

Propositions Lascaux

International recognition of an "exception for food" on the model of the "cultural exception"

François COLLART DUTILLEUL *

The recognition of a cultural exception dates from as far back as 1947 with the General Agreement on Tariffs and Trade (GATT), which constituted the first stage in the globalisation of trade founded on the principle of free trade but allowed for legal exceptions for certain cultural products, in particular for cinematographic films and national treasures.

This is still the case today with the World Trade Organisation (WTO), the successor to GATT. However, GATT was in reality only a part of a fuller international treaty which also was to provide for legal exceptions to free trade for "primary commodities": those of agriculture, forestry, fishing and minerals. This treaty was the Havana Charter, signed by 53 countries in March 1948. Because of a situation extraneous to the Charter, it has never been ratified or put into effect, unlike GATT itself. The result is that **"cultural exceptions" are recognised, while "exceptions for food" are not.**

With GATT, cultural exceptions only applied to trade in certain goods. Not all cultural products were concerned, nor were all the problems linked to the preservation of the world's cultural wealth. Hence the idea of completing the special rules of GATT with a wider international convention which would be politically significant and enshrine the sovereignty of States in the field concerned. These considerations led to the adoption by UNESCO on 20 October 2005 of the ***Convention on the Protection and Promotion of the Diversity of Cultural Expressions***.

With this in mind, how might one envisage a "***Convention on the achievement of food security and the preservation of agricultural diversity***" negotiated within the United Nations Food and Agriculture Organisation (FAO)? Such a convention ought to aim to achieve the three objectives contained within the FAO's definition of food security: Food security *"exists when all people, at all times, have economic, social and physical*

* Professor of Law at the University of Nantes, Director of the Lascaux programme (ERC). Contact: lascaux.recherche@univ-nantes.fr

access to sufficient, safe and nutritious food to satisfy their nutritional requirements and food preferences to enable them to lead an active and healthy life". This therefore means people should have access to sufficient food in both quantity and nutritive value, to healthy food and to the food of their choice. It is thus clear that, as for access to culture, access to food products which are standardised through the effects of globalisation is not enough. Each population and each individual should have access to food which corresponds to the agricultural, traditional, religious and gastronomic particularities of the place where they live. In the same way as it is not enough that the whole world has access to the same television series in order for each person's right to culture to be guaranteed. Therefore, **just as the protection of the diversity of cultural expressions is necessary, so is that of agricultural biodiversity.**

This parallel between the access to culture and the access to food justifies envisaging the exception for food by reference to the cultural exception. In the same way it justifies the proposal for an international convention on food security on the model of the Convention on culture. In order to outline these proposals and start a process of reflection towards this goal, it was thought best to see if a draft convention based on the text of the one designed to preserve cultural diversity would work.

We therefore propose the text below as an attempt to transpose the UNESCO Convention of 2005 to agriculture and food.

Convention on the Protection and Promotion of the Diversity of Cultural Expressions	Convention on the achievement of food security and the preservation of agricultural diversity[1]
The General Conference of the United Nations Educational, Scientific and Cultural Organization, meeting in Paris from 3 to 21 October 2005 at its 33rd session,	The General Conference of the United Nations Food and Agriculture Organization (FAO), ...
Affirming that cultural diversity is a defining characteristic of humanity,	*Affirming* that food security is a necessity for all humanity,
Conscious that cultural diversity forms a common heritage of humanity and should be cherished and preserved for the benefit of all,	*Conscious* that agricultural biodiversity forms a common heritage of humanity and should be cherished and preserved for the benefit of all,
Being aware that cultural diversity creates a rich and varied world, which increases the range of choices and nurtures human capacities and values, and therefore is a mainspring for sustainable development for communities, peoples and nations,	*Being aware* that food security is founded on agricultural biodiversity which creates a rich and varied world, increases the range of choices, guarantees diversity in forms of agriculture, expresses the capacities and know-how of successive generations of farmers, and therefore is a mainspring for sustainable development for communities, peoples and nations,

[1] This table is based on the main ideas in the Proposal for a "Convention on the achievement of food security and the preservation of agricultural biodiversity". The full Proposal is available in *Penser une démocratie alimentaire*, COLLART DUTILLEUL F. and BRÉGER T. (eds.), vol. 1, ed. Inida, San José, Costa Rica, 2013, p. 13.

Recalling that cultural diversity, flourishing within a framework of democracy, tolerance, social justice and mutual respect between peoples and cultures, is indispensable for peace and security at the local, national and international levels,	*Recalling* that food security, flourishing within a framework of democracy, tolerance, social justice and mutual respect between peoples and cultures, is indispensable for peace and security at the local, national and international levels,
Celebrating the importance of cultural diversity for the full realization of human rights and fundamental freedoms proclaimed in the Universal Declaration of Human Rights and other universally recognized instruments,	*Celebrating* the importance of food security for the full realization of human rights and fundamental freedoms proclaimed in the Universal Declaration of Human Rights, in the International Covenant on economic, social and cultural rights, and in other universally recognized instruments,
Emphasizing the need to incorporate culture as a strategic element in national and international development policies, as well as in international development cooperation, taking into account also the United Nations Millennium Declaration (2000) with its special emphasis on poverty eradication,	*Emphasizing* the need to incorporate food security as a strategic element in national and international development policies, as well as in international development cooperation, taking into account also the United Nations Millennium Declaration (2000) with its special emphasis on poverty eradication,
Taking into account that culture takes diverse forms across time and space and that this diversity is embodied in the uniqueness and plurality of the identities and cultural expressions of the peoples and societies making up humanity,	*Taking into account* that food and agriculture take diverse forms across time and space and that this diversity is embodied in the climates, the geography, the uniqueness and the plurality of the identities, religions and histories of the peoples and societies making up humanity,

Recognizing the importance of traditional knowledge as a source of intangible and material wealth, and in particular the knowledge systems of indigenous peoples, and its positive contribution to sustainable development, as well as the need for its adequate protection and promotion,	*Recognizing* the importance of traditional knowledge, and in particular the knowledge systems of indigenous peoples, as a source of intangible and material wealth, and its positive contribution to food security, the preservation of agricultural biodiversity and natural resources, and sustainable development, as well as the need for its adequate protection and promotion,
Recognizing the need to take measures to protect the diversity of cultural expressions, including their contents, especially in situations where cultural expressions may be threatened by the possibility of extinction or serious impairment,	*Recognizing* the need for and the legitimacy of taking measures to protect food security and agricultural biodiversity, especially in situations where they may be threatened,
Emphasizing the importance of culture for social cohesion in general, and in particular its potential for the enhancement of the status and role of women in society,	*Emphasizing* the importance of food security for social cohesion in general, and in particular its contribution to the enhancement of the status and role of women in agriculture and society,
Being aware that cultural diversity is strengthened by the free flow of ideas, and that it is nurtured by constant exchanges and interaction between cultures,	*Being aware* that food security cannot depend alone on self-sufficiency in food for each country, but that it is strengthened by the free flow of food products, and that it is nurtured by constant trade between countries,
Reaffirming that freedom of thought, expression and information, as well as diversity of the media, enable cultural expressions to flourish within societies,	*Reaffirming* that freedom of choice for food is an integral part of food security and that it entails giving consumers the information they need in order to exercise this freedom according to economic, dietary, social, environmental, cultural and religious criteria,

Recognizing that the diversity of cultural expressions, including traditional cultural expressions, is an important factor that allows individuals and peoples to express and to share with others their ideas and values,	*Recognizing* that the particularity and diversity of foods are important factors that allow individuals and peoples to express and to share with others their traditions and values,
Recalling that linguistic diversity is a fundamental element of cultural diversity, and reaffirming the fundamental role that education plays in the protection and promotion of cultural expressions,	*Recalling* that the diversity of food traditions and customs is a fundamental element of food sovereignty, and reaffirming the fundamental role that smallholdings play in the protection and promotion of agricultural diversity and in the effectiveness of humanity's right to food,
Taking into account the importance of the vitality of cultures, including for persons belonging to minorities and indigenous peoples, as manifested in their freedom to create, disseminate and distribute their traditional cultural expressions and to have access thereto, so as to benefit them for their own development,	*Taking into account* the importance of the vitality of agriculture for all, including for women, persons belonging to minorities and indigenous peoples, as manifested in their freedom to protect, grow and consume their traditional food and to have access thereto, so as to benefit them for their own development,
(...)	
Recognizing the importance of intellectual property rights in sustaining those involved in cultural creativity,	*Recognizing* the importance of intellectual property rights in sustaining those involved in the improvement of the security and diversity of food supplies,
Being convinced that cultural activities, goods and services have both an economic and a cultural nature, because they convey identities, values and meanings, and must therefore not be treated as solely having commercial value,	*Being convinced* that foodstuffs and agricultural raw produce have a fourfold nature: economic, social, environmental and cultural, because they convey identities, values and meanings, and must therefore not be treated as solely having commercial value,

Noting that while the processes of globalization, which have been facilitated by the rapid development of information and communication technologies, afford unprecedented conditions for enhanced interaction between cultures, they also represent a challenge for cultural diversity, namely in view of risks of imbalances between rich and poor countries,	*Noting* that the processes of globalization, which have been facilitated by the rapid development of technologies in food production, represent a challenge for food security, in particular in view of risks of imbalances between rich and poor countries and of the scientific and social debates of which such technologies are the object,
(...)	
Referring to the provisions of the international instruments adopted by UNESCO relating to cultural diversity and the exercise of cultural rights, and in particular the Universal Declaration on Cultural Diversity of 2001,	*Referring* to the provisions of the international instruments relating to food security, the right to food, the protection of biodiversity and the preservation of natural resources,
Adopts this Convention on 20 October 2005.	*Adopts* this Convention on ....
I. Objectives and guiding principles	**I. Objectives and guiding principles**
Article 1 – Objectives	**Article 1 – Objectives**
The objectives of this Convention are:	The objectives of this Convention are:
(a) to protect and promote the diversity of cultural expressions;	(a) to protect and promote the basic right to food and to guarantee food security throughout the world;
(b) to create the conditions for cultures to flourish and to freely interact in a mutually beneficial manner;	(b) to create the conditions for diverse forms of agriculture to flourish;
(c) ...	(c) ...

(d) ...	(d) ...
(e) to promote respect for the diversity of cultural expressions and raise awareness of its value at the local, national and international levels;	(e) to promote respect for agricultural biodiversity and the preservation of natural resources, and raise awareness of their value at the local, national and international levels;
(f) to reaffirm the importance of the link between culture and development for all countries, particularly for developing countries, and to support actions undertaken nationally and internationally to secure recognition of the true value of this link;	(f) to reaffirm the importance of the links between agriculture, food security and development for all countries, particularly for developing countries, and to support actions undertaken nationally and internationally to secure recognition of the true value of these links;
(g) to give recognition to the distinctive nature of cultural activities, goods and services as vehicles of identity, values and meaning;	(g) to give recognition to the distinctive nature of agricultural and food activities, goods and services as being essential for human life and as vehicles of identity, values and meaning;
(h) to reaffirm the sovereign rights of States to maintain, adopt and implement policies and measures that they deem appropriate for the protection and promotion of the diversity of cultural expressions on their territory;	(h) to reaffirm the sovereign rights of States to maintain, adopt and implement policies and measures that they deem appropriate for guaranteeing food security on their territory;
(i) to strengthen international cooperation and solidarity in a spirit of partnership with a view, in particular, to enhancing the capacities of developing countries in order to protect and promote the diversity of cultural expressions.	(i) to strengthen international cooperation and solidarity in a spirit of partnership with a view, in particular, to enhancing the capacities of developing countries to guarantee the security of their food supplies.

Article 2 – Guiding principles	**Article 2 – Guiding principles**
1. Principle of respect for human rights and fundamental freedoms	1. Principle of respect for human rights and fundamental freedoms
Cultural diversity can be protected and promoted only if human rights and fundamental freedoms, such as freedom of expression, information and communication, as well as the ability of individuals to choose cultural expressions, are guaranteed. No one may invoke the provisions of this Convention in order to infringe human rights and fundamental freedoms as enshrined in the Universal Declaration of Human Rights or guaranteed by international law, or to limit the scope thereof.	Food security can be protected and promoted only if human rights and fundamental freedoms, such as the right to food and water, as well as the ability of individuals to choose their food, are guaranteed. No one may invoke the provisions of this Convention in order to infringe human rights and fundamental freedoms as enshrined in the Universal Declaration of Human Rights, the International Covenant on economic, social and cultural rights, or guaranteed by international law, or to limit the scope thereof.
2. Principle of sovereignty	2. Principle of sovereignty
States have, in accordance with the Charter of the United Nations and the principles of international law, the sovereign right to adopt measures and policies to protect and promote the diversity of cultural expressions within their territory.	States have, in accordance with the Charter of the United Nations and the principles of international law, the sovereign right to manage their natural resources in order to satisfy the basic needs of both present and future generations, and in consequence to adopt such measures and policies as they may deem appropriate to guarantee food security within their territory.

3. Principle of equal dignity of and respect for all cultures	3. Principle of equality and respect for all forms of agriculture and food
The protection and promotion of the diversity of cultural expressions presuppose the recognition of equal dignity of and respect for all cultures, including the cultures of persons belonging to minorities and indigenous peoples.	Food sovereignty presupposes the recognition of equality of and respect for all forms of agriculture and food.
4. Principle of international solidarity and cooperation	4. Principle of international solidarity and cooperation
International cooperation and solidarity should be aimed at enabling countries, especially developing countries, to create and strengthen their means of cultural expression, including their cultural industries, whether nascent or established, at the local, national and international levels.	International cooperation and solidarity should be aimed at enabling countries, especially developing countries, to create and develop the means required for their food security, including their agriculture and their agri-food industries, whether nascent or established, at the local, national and international levels.
5. Principle of the complementarity of economic and cultural aspects of development	5. Principle of the complementarity of economic and social aspects of development
Since culture is one of the mainsprings of development, the cultural aspects of development are as important as its economic aspects, which individuals and peoples have the fundamental right to participate in and enjoy.	Since agriculture is one of the mainsprings of development, the social aspects of development are as important as its economic aspects, which individuals and peoples have the fundamental right to participate in and enjoy.

6. Principle of sustainable development	6. Principle of sustainable development
Cultural diversity is a rich asset for individuals and societies. The protection, promotion and maintenance of cultural diversity are an essential requirement for sustainable development for the benefit of present and future generations.	Natural resources and agricultural biodiversity are rich assets for individuals and societies. Their protection is an essential requirement for sustainable development for the benefit of present and future generations.
7. Principle of equitable access	7. Principle of equitable access
Equitable access to a rich and diversified range of cultural expressions from all over the world and access of cultures to the means of expressions and dissemination constitute important elements for enhancing cultural diversity and encouraging mutual understanding.	Equitable access to a rich and diversified range of foodstuffs constitutes an important element for guaranteeing food security. Such equitable access should be able to be enjoyed both through short supply circuits and through international trade.
8. Principle of openness and balance	8. Principle of openness and balance
When States adopt measures to support the diversity of cultural expressions, they should seek to promote, in an appropriate manner, openness to other cultures of the world and to ensure that these measures are geared to the objectives pursued under the present Convention.	When States adopt measures to guarantee food security for their populations, they should take into account, in an appropriate manner, openness to other sources of food, regional, national, continental and international, and ensure that these measures are geared to the objectives pursued under the present Convention.

II. Scope of application	**II. Scope of application**
Article 3 – Scope of application	**Article 3 – Scope of application**
This Convention shall apply to the policies and measures adopted by the Parties related to the protection and promotion of the diversity of cultural expressions.	This Convention shall apply to the policies and measures adopted by the Parties in the aim of guaranteeing food security for their populations.
III. Definitions	**III. Definitions**
Article 4 – Definitions	**Article 4 – Definitions**
For the purposes of this Convention, it is understood that:	For the purposes of this Convention, it is understood that:
1. Cultural diversity	1. Food security
"Cultural diversity" refers to the manifold ways in which the cultures of groups and societies find expression. These expressions are passed on within and among groups and societies. Cultural diversity is made manifest not only through the varied ways in which the cultural heritage of humanity is expressed, augmented and transmitted through the variety of cultural expressions, but also through diverse modes of artistic creation, production, dissemination, distribution and enjoyment, whatever the means and technologies used.	In accordance with the FAO World Food Summit of 1996, "Food security" exists when all people, at all times, have economic, social and physical access to sufficient, safe and nutritious food to satisfy their nutritional requirements and food preferences to enable them to lead an active and healthy life.

2. Cultural content	2. Agricultural biodiversity
"Cultural content" refers to the symbolic meaning, artistic dimension and cultural values that originate from or express cultural identities.	The term *Agricultural biodiversity* "is a broad term that includes all components of biological diversity of relevance to food and agriculture. It encompasses the variety and variability of animals, plants and micro-organisms, at genetic, species and ecosystem levels, which are necessary to sustain key functions of the agro-ecosystem, its structure, and processes for, and in support of, food production and food security."
3. Cultural expressions	3. Food sovereignty
"Cultural expressions" are those expressions that result from the creativity of individuals, groups and societies, and that have cultural content.	The right of any contracting Party to implement agricultural and food policies or to take the necessary measures to guarantee food security on its territory, provided that such policies or measures are not applied in such a way as to constitute either an arbitrary or unjustifiable means of discrimination between countries with the same conditions, or a disguised restriction on international trade.
4. ...	4. ...
5. ...	5. ...

6. Cultural policies and measures	6. Agricultural and food policies and measures
"Cultural policies and measures" refers to those policies and measures relating to culture, whether at the local, national, regional or international level that are either focused on culture as such or are designed to have a direct effect on cultural expressions of individuals, groups or societies, including on the creation, production, dissemination, distribution of and access to cultural activities, goods and services.	"Agricultural and food policies and measures" refers to those policies and measures relating to food and agriculture, whether at the local, national, regional or international level that are either focused on agriculture and food as such or are designed to have a direct effect on food security and the implementation of the basic right to food, including on the production and distribution of, and access to, agricultural and food activities, goods and services.
7. Protection	7. Food availability
"Protection" means the adoption of measures aimed at the preservation, safeguarding and enhancement of the diversity of cultural expressions. "Protect" means to adopt such measures.	"Food availability" means the availability of food in sufficient quantity and appropriate quality, the provision of which is guaranteed by national production or imports (including food aid).
8. Interculturality	8. Food autonomy
"Interculturality" refers to the existence and equitable interaction of diverse cultures and the possibility of generating shared cultural expressions through dialogue and mutual respect.	"Food autonomy" refers to the proportion of the food supply for a State's population which is produced on the territory of that State.

IV. Rights and obligations of Parties	**IV. Rights and obligations of Parties**
Article 5 – General rule regarding rights and obligations	**Article 5 – General rule regarding rights and obligations**
1. The Parties, in conformity with the Charter of the United Nations, the principles of international law and universally recognized human rights instruments, reaffirm their sovereign right to formulate and implement their cultural policies and to adopt measures to protect and promote the diversity of cultural expressions and to strengthen international cooperation to achieve the purposes of this Convention.	1. The Parties, in conformity with the Charter of the United Nations, the principles of international law and universally recognized human rights instruments, reaffirm their sovereign right to formulate and implement their agricultural and food policies and to adopt measures to guarantee the security of food supplies for their populations and to strengthen international cooperation to achieve the purposes of this Convention.
2. When a Party implements policies and takes measures to protect and promote the diversity of cultural expressions within its territory, its policies and measures shall be consistent with the provisions of this Convention.	2. When a Party implements policies and takes measures to guarantee food security within its territory, its policies and measures shall be consistent with the provisions of this Convention.
Article 6 – Rights of parties at the national level	**Article 6 – Rights of parties at the national level**
1. Within the framework of its cultural policies and measures as defined in Article 4.6 and taking into account its own particular circumstances and needs, each Party may adopt measures aimed at protecting and promoting the diversity of cultural expressions within its territory.	1. Within the framework of its agricultural and food policies and measures as defined in Article 4.6 and taking into account its own particular geographical and climatic conditions, circumstances and needs, each Party may adopt measures aimed at guaranteeing food security within its territory.
2. Such measures may include the following:	2. Such measures may include the following:

(a) regulatory measures aimed at protecting and promoting diversity of cultural expressions;	(a) regulatory measures aimed at protecting and promoting agricultural biodiversity;
(b) measures that, in an appropriate manner, provide opportunities for domestic cultural activities, goods and services among all those available within the national territory for the creation, production, dissemination, distribution and enjoyment of such domestic cultural activities, goods and services, including provisions relating to the language used for such activities, goods and services;	(b) measures that, in an appropriate manner, provide opportunities for domestic agricultural and food activities, goods and services to be adequately represented, among all those available within the national territory, for their production, distribution, availability, and promotion by means of quality marks or geographical indications or labels, including provisions relating to the quality required for such activities, goods and services;
(c) measures aimed at providing domestic independent cultural industries and activities in the informal sector effective access to the means of production, dissemination and distribution of cultural activities, goods and services;	(c) measures aimed at providing domestic farmers and agri-food companies effective access to the means of production and distribution of agricultural and food activities, goods and services;
(d) measures aimed at providing public financial assistance;	(d) measures aimed at providing public financial assistance to farmers with the aim of enhancing national food security or preserving natural food resources and agricultural biodiversity;
(e) ...	(e) ...
(f) measures aimed at establishing and supporting public institutions, as appropriate;	(f) measures aimed at establishing and supporting public institutions engaged in agricultural, food and nutritional policies, as appropriate;

(g) measures aimed at nurturing and supporting artists and others involved in the creation of cultural expressions;	(g) measures aimed at nurturing and supporting farmers and particularly women involved in farming, as well as all those involved in agricultural food production;
(h) measures aimed at enhancing diversity of the media, including through public service broadcasting.	(h) measures aimed at promoting regional or national food and agricultural products, particularly by mentioning their geographical origin (the indication of origin) or a particular quality.
Article 7 – Measures to promote cultural expressions	**Article 7 – Measures to guarantee food security**
1. Parties shall endeavour to create in their territory an environment which encourages individuals and social groups:	1. Parties shall endeavour to create in their territory an environment which encourages individuals, farmers, firms and social groups:
(a) to create, produce, disseminate, distribute and have access to their own cultural expressions, paying due attention to the special circumstances and needs of women as well as various social groups, including persons belonging to minorities and indigenous peoples;	(a) to create, produce, distribute and sell their own production and enable the population to have access thereto, paying due attention to the circumstances and food needs of certain categories of consumers, i.e. children, pregnant women and the elderly, as well as various social groups, including persons belonging to minorities and indigenous peoples;
(b) to have access to diverse cultural expressions from within their territory as well as from other countries of the world.	(b) to give the whole population access to the diverse food and agricultural production from within their territory as well as from other countries of the world.

2. Parties shall also endeavour to recognize the important contribution of artists, others involved in the creative process, cultural communities, and organizations that support their work, and their central role in nurturing the diversity of cultural expressions.	2. Parties shall also endeavour to recognize the important contribution of farmers and all those involved in the productive process, of the firms and organizations that support their work, and their central role in feeding the population.
	3. Without prejudice to the provisions of articles 5 and 6, a Party may determine the existence of special situations in which food security, within its territory, is compromised or requires any urgent measures.
	4. Parties may take all appropriate measures in order to guarantee food security in the situations mentioned in paragraph 1, in conformity with the provisions of this Convention.
	5. Parties shall report to the World Food Security Committee of the FAO all measures taken to meet the demands of the situation, and the Committee may put forward appropriate recommendations.
Article 8 – Measures to protect cultural expressions	**Article 8 – Measures to protect agricultural biodiversity**
1. Without prejudice to the provisions of Articles 5 and 6, a Party may determine the existence of special situations where cultural expressions on its territory are at risk of extinction, under serious threat, or otherwise in need of urgent safeguarding.	1. Without prejudice to the provisions of Articles 5 and 6, a Party may determine the existence of special situations where vegetable or animal varieties destined for food on its territory are at risk of extinction, under serious threat, or otherwise in need of urgent safeguarding.

2. Parties may take all appropriate measures to protect and preserve cultural expressions in situations referred to in paragraph 1 in a manner consistent with the provisions of this Convention.	2. Parties may take all appropriate measures to protect and preserve such varieties in situations referred to in paragraph 1 in a manner consistent with the provisions of this Convention.
3. ...	3. ...
Article 9 – Information sharing and transparency	**Article 9 – Information sharing and transparency**
Parties shall:	Parties shall:
(a) provide appropriate information in their reports to UNESCO every four years on measures taken to protect and promote the diversity of cultural expressions within their territory and at the international level;	(a) provide appropriate information in their reports to FAO every four years on measures taken to guarantee food security within their territory and at the international level;
(b) designate a point of contact responsible for information sharing in relation to this Convention;	(b) designate a point of contact responsible for information sharing in relation to this Convention;
(c) share and exchange information relating to the protection and promotion of the diversity of cultural expressions.	(c) share and exchange information relating to food security.
Article 10 – Education and public awareness	**Article 10 – Education and public awareness**
Parties shall:	Parties shall:

(a) encourage and promote understanding of the importance of the protection and promotion of the diversity of cultural expressions, inter alia, through educational and greater public awareness programmes;	(a) encourage and promote understanding of the importance of the objectives of protecting agricultural biodiversity and preserving natural food resources and food security, inter alia by means of educational and public awareness enhancement programmes, and through the development of information enabling consumers to take account of such objectives in choosing the food they consume;
(b) cooperate with other Parties and international and regional organizations in achieving the purpose of this article;	(b) cooperate with other Parties and international and regional organizations in achieving the purpose of this article by drawing up common principles governing the information to supply to consumers;
(c) (...)	(c) (...)
Article 11 – Participation of civil society	**Article 11 – Participation of civil society**
Parties acknowledge the fundamental role of civil society in protecting and promoting the diversity of cultural expressions. Parties shall encourage the active participation of civil society in their efforts to achieve the objectives of this Convention.	Parties acknowledge the fundamental role of civil society in protecting agricultural biodiversity and the implementation of food security for everyone. Parties shall encourage the active participation of civil society in their efforts to achieve the objectives of this Convention.
Article 12 – Promotion of international cooperation	**Article 12 – Promotion of international cooperation**

Parties shall endeavour to strengthen their bilateral, regional and international cooperation for the creation of conditions conducive to the promotion of the diversity of cultural expressions, taking particular account of the situations referred to in Articles 8 and 17, notably in order to:	Parties shall endeavour to strengthen their bilateral, regional and international cooperation for the creation of conditions conducive to the protection of agricultural biodiversity, taking particular account of the situations referred to in Article 8, notably in order to:
(a) facilitate dialogue among Parties on cultural policy;	(a) facilitate dialogue among Parties on agricultural and food policy;
(b) enhance public sector strategic and management capacities in cultural public sector institutions, through professional and international cultural exchanges and sharing of best practices;	(b) enhance public sector strategic and management capacities in public sector institutions in charge of agricultural and food policy, through professional and international cultural exchanges and sharing of best practices;
(c) reinforce partnerships with and among civil society, non-governmental organizations and the private sector in fostering and promoting the diversity of cultural expression	(c) reinforce partnerships with and among civil society, non-governmental organizations and the private sector in fostering and protecting agricultural biodiversity and the diversity of food supplies, and guaranteeing food security throughout the world;
(d) promote the use of new technologies, encourage partnerships to enhance information sharing and cultural understanding, and foster the diversity of cultural expressions	(d) promote the use of new technologies and encourage partnerships to enhance information sharing, taking account of the social acceptability of such technologies in light of the cultures, needs, expectations and traditions proper to each country or people;
(e) ...	

Article 13 – Integration of culture in sustainable development	**Article 13 – Integration of food and agriculture in sustainable development**
Parties shall endeavour to integrate culture in their development policies at all levels for the creation of conditions conducive to sustainable development and, within this framework, foster aspects relating to the protection and promotion of the diversity of cultural expressions.	Parties shall endeavour to incorporate food and agriculture concerns in their development policies at all levels for the creation of conditions conducive to sustainable development and, within this framework, foster aspects relating to the protection of agricultural biodiversity and the guaranteeing of food security.
Article 14 – Cooperation for development	**Article 14 – Cooperation for development**
Parties shall endeavour to support cooperation for sustainable development and poverty reduction, especially in relation to the specific needs of developing countries, in order to foster the emergence of a dynamic cultural sector by, inter alia, the following means:	Parties shall endeavour to support cooperation for sustainable development and poverty reduction, especially in relation to the specific needs of developing countries, in order to foster the emergence of a dynamic food and agriculture sector by, inter alia, the following means:
(a) the strengthening of the cultural industries in developing countries through:	(a) supporting farms, operators and agri-food firms in developing countries through:
(i) creating and strengthening cultural production and distribution capacities in developing countries;	(i) creating and strengthening the production and distribution capacities of agricultural and food products in developing countries;
(ii) facilitating wider access to the global market and international distribution networks for their cultural activities, goods and services;	(ii) facilitating wider access to the global market and international distribution networks for their agricultural and food activities, goods and services;

(iii) enabling the emergence of viable local and regional markets;	(iii) supporting local and regional markets;
(iv) adopting, where possible, appropriate measures in developed countries with a view to facilitating access to their territory for the cultural activities, goods and services of developing countries;	(iv) adopting, where possible, appropriate measures in developed countries with a view to facilitating access to their territory for the agricultural and food products of developing countries;
(v) ...	(v) ...
(vi) encouraging appropriate collaboration between developed and developing countries in the areas, inter alia, of music and film	(vi) encouraging appropriate collaboration between developed and developing countries in the areas, inter alia, of productivity and quality of agricultural and food products;
(b) capacity-building through the exchange of information, experience and expertise, as well as the training of human resources in developing countries, in the public and private sector relating to, inter alia, strategic and management capacities, policy development and implementation, promotion and distribution of cultural expressions, small-, medium- and micro-enterprise development, the use of technology, and skills development and transfer	(b) capacity-building through the exchange of information, experience and expertise, as well as the training of human resources in developing countries in the public and the private sector relating to, inter alia, strategic and management capacities, policy development and implementation, promotion and distribution of agricultural and food products, small-, medium- and micro-enterprise development, the use of technology, and skills development and transfer;
(c) technology transfer through the introduction of appropriate incentive measures for the transfer of technology and know-how, especially in the areas of cultural industries and enterprises	(c) the transfer of technology and know-how through the introduction of appropriate incentive measures, especially in the areas of agriculture and agri-food industries and firms;

(d) ...	(d) ...
VII. Final clauses	**VII. Final clauses**
(...)	(...)

A fairer balance for international investments in farmland in developing countries

François COLLART DUTILLEUL [*]

International investments play a large part in globalising the economy. In developing countries, they can provide the means to exploit natural wealth. Such investments take the form of companies exploiting mines, forests or farmland. On one hand, they can promote the development of agriculture and better use of unexploited or underexploited land, provide work for the national population, and create wealth which benefits the host country. But they pose serious problems when they lead to the expulsion of local populations from their traditional lands and when they add up to no more than the seizure of natural resources for the benefit of the investors, without sufficient consideration or even the slightest consideration for the economy of the host country. In such cases the term 'grabbing' of land and natural resources is fully justified.

From the legal point of view, international investment and the land-grabbing which may result are governed by the national laws of the country in which the investment is made (investment law, agricultural law, land law, environmental law, etc.) and by bilateral treaties specially drawn up for such investments (the U.N. has inventoried over 3000 of these to date). Consequently, the issues raised call for specific analyses for each country, although general comments and observations may remain valid.

Concerning land law, many countries in which international investments pose problems have laws covering the acquisition and exploitation of land which are based on both customary and "modern" legal systems, functioning side by side. Customary law derives from the practices, rules and ancestral traditions of a community which has been settled on part of a territory since time immemorial. Modern law is based on land registry and private or public property deeds which are indexed, officially recognised and enforceable against all parties.

* Professor of Law at the University of Nantes, Director of the Lascaux programme (ERC). Contact: lascaux.recherche@univ-nantes.fr

In such countries, there are in fact three categories of particularly fragile populations:

- native or indigenous peoples who have lost control of their territory to the benefit of modern States which have gradually encroached on them;
- peasant farmers in developing countries who have no security of tenure on the land where they have lived for generations and from which they draw their livelihoods;
- women farmers, who in many countries, especially in Africa, work land which is owned exclusively by men.

A large number of adjustments would be needed, in several areas of law, to solve the problems encountered by these fragile populations, and so that international investments in the farmland of a developing country benefit the country and its population at least as much as the investors.

Two such adjustments deserve particular attention.

1) Collective ownership is the best means of avoiding discrimination between men and women regarding the ownership of land since, by hypothesis, the land then belongs to every man and woman. It is also the best means of providing security of tenure to organised communities which draw their livelihoods from common land/territory.

For this reason, in countries where traditional community-based occupation of lands and modern individual title deeds coexist, the official recognition of collective property deeds benefiting communities is a necessary element of any solution, whatever form it may take.

2) Any contract of investment in land should, in order to contribute effectively to the development of the host country, satisfy conditions which respect the principles or directives issued by the various international organisations, particularly the FAO.

A "set of clauses" stipulating the obligations and commitments of investors should therefore be drawn up, to be included in all investment contracts. Such obligations relate to:

- involving the population living on the land concerned in the negotiation and implementation of the contract in a way that is effective, public and transparent;

- carrying out, in public, a prior socio-environmental audit;
- employing local farm hands in preference to labour imported by the investor;
- growing a significant proportion of products which are useful for feeding the local population rather than for producing biofuels or raw materials for non-food use (textiles, etc.);
- selling the foodstuffs in the country of production rather than exporting them;
- using methods of working the land which preserve the environment and natural resources, in preference to methods which risk leaving the land exhausted when a long-term contract expires;
- a precise description of the investments made by the investor, with financial guarantees for meeting the commitments undertaken (for example, deposits or bank guarantees payable on first demand);
- financial and economic compensation which is precise, specifically included in the contract and significant for the host country;
- prohibiting selling the contract or sub-leasing the land without the agreement of the sovereign State and the guarantee that the commitments will be taken up by the new operator.

A set of such clauses could be formally included in the national laws on investments, and could also act as a “specification” for an international certification for “responsible or sustainable investment” which the FAO would implement and manage.

Putting international trade in agricultural products at the service of food security

François COLLART DUTILLEUL [*]

Background information...

During the Second World War, President Roosevelt organised three important international conferences designed to form the basis for building a peaceful world. According to him, a peaceful future would be conditioned upon the resolve to treat neither money, labour nor nature as commercial goods. Thus, some time before the conferences of Bretton Woods and Philadelphia, the Hot Springs conference on agriculture and food took place, with the aim of answering the question of how to imagine the post-war world so that each country would be able to develop its agriculture and feed its population. It was at Hot Springs that the creation of the FAO and of an organisation for international trade was decided. For Roosevelt, such an organisation presupposed that agricultural products would not be the object of a system of pure, untrammelled free trade. He therefore initiated the negotiation of an international charter with the aim of creating, within the U.N., an international organisation for trade and laying down rules governing the globalisation of commerce. The negotiation took place after his death and culminated in the signing of the Havana Charter in March 1948 by 53 countries. But since the United States did not ratify it, because of opposition in Congress to Roosevelt's successor President Truman, the other countries did not see the point of doing so either. Nevertheless, part of this Charter had already been implemented as early as autumn 1947, outside the U.N., by the 23 richest countries because they wanted to re-launch world trade without delay. This part of the Charter was given the name GATT. Now GATT was supposed to disappear the moment the whole of the Havana Charter was ratified. We know what became of that, however.

* Professor of Law at the University of Nantes, Director of the Lascaux programme (ERC). Contact: lascaux.recherche@univ-nantes.fr

The Havana Charter

In the Havana Charter was a chapter introducing a special system for international trade in primary commodities: the products of agriculture, fishing, forestry and mining – in other words, for all natural resources. This special system had several objectives, among which were food security, economic development, full employment and the preservation of natural resources.

The Havana Charter was thus intelligent in that it showed a way forward which combined international free trade and humanistic aims. For example, in case of a duly recognised problem of food security in connection with international trade in a primary commodity, the countries directly concerned by such a problem would be allowed to make an agreement providing for temporary measures departing from the rules of free trade. In this regard the Charter gave the FAO powers of initiative and expertise. We could probably not apply the same system today to maize and oil, rare earths or fishing quotas. Nevertheless, concerning agricultural products and the role of the FAO, the Charter is as relevant today as before.

The world has lost much in dropping this Charter for reasons to do with the internal politics of the United States, and things would doubtless be different today if it had been ratified. GATT and the WTO have shaped a globalisation process which has neither allowed the countries of the South to develop, nor ensured full employment or food security, nor preserved natural resources: all aims which the world is desperately pursuing without being able to find a way to negotiate successfully towards them.

Agricultural raw materials are not the same as other goods. They are the very basis of the nourishment of humankind. It is essential to design a free trade system for them which takes full account of States' public debt, of the 900 million people suffering from famine, of the growing numbers out of work or with no means of subsistence, of the future of our natural resources, and consequently of people's basic needs.

After a great deal of research on all five continents, we have concluded that the way towards achieving these objectives should be guided by a return to the spirit of the Havana Charter, as set out in its Chapter VI.

INTER-GOVERNMENTAL *AGRICULTURAL* COMMODITY AGREEMENTS[1]

SECTION A - INTRODUCTORY CONSIDERATIONS

Article 55

Difficulties relating to ***Agricultural*** Commodities

The Members recognize that the conditions under which some *agricultural* commodities are produced, exchanged and consumed are such that international trade in these commodities may be affected by special difficulties such as the tendency towards persistent disequilibrium between production and consumption, the accumulation of burdensome stocks and pronounced fluctuations in prices. These special difficulties may have serious adverse effects on the interests of producers and consumers, as well as widespread repercussions jeopardizing ***food security in any given country***. The Members recognize that such difficulties may, at times, necessitate special treatment of the international trade in such commodities through inter-governmental agreement.

Article 56

Agricultural and Related Commodities

1. For the purposes of this Charter, the term "***agricultural*** commodity" means any product of farm, forest or fishery, ***destined or potentially destined for food for humans***, in its natural form or which has undergone such processing as is customarily required to prepare it for marketing in substantial volume in international trade.

2. The term shall also, for the purposes of this Chapter, cover a group of commodities, of which one is ***an agricultural*** commodity as defined in paragraph 1 and the others are commodities, which are so closely related, as regards conditions of production or utilization, to the other commodities in the group, that it is appropriate to deal with them in a single agreement.

3. (...)

---

[1] This is the part of the original text of chapter VI of the 1948 Havana Charter concerned with "Primary Commodities" (art. 55 & foll.), **with our proposed modifications in bold italics**.

Article 57

Objectives of Inter-Governmental ***Agricultural*** Commodity Agreements

The Members recognize that inter-governmental ***agricultural*** commodity agreements are appropriate for the achievement of the following objectives:

(a) to prevent or alleviate the serious economic difficulties which may arise when adjustments between production and consumption cannot be effected by normal market forces alone as rapidly as the circumstances require;

(b) to provide, during the period which may be necessary, a framework for the consideration and development of measures which have as their purpose economic adjustments designed to promote the expansion of consumption or a shift of resources and man-power out of over-expanded industries into new and productive occupations, including as far as possible in appropriate cases, the development of secondary industries based upon domestic production of ***agricultural*** commodities;

(c) to prevent or moderate pronounced fluctuations in the price of ***an agricultural*** commodity with a view to achieving a reasonable degree of stability on a basis of such prices as are fair to consumers and provide a reasonable return to producers, having regard to the desirability of securing long-term equilibrium between the forces of supply and demand;

(d) to maintain and develop the natural resources of the world and protect them from unnecessary exhaustion;

(e) to provide for the expansion of the production of ***an agricultural*** commodity where this can be accomplished with advantage to consumers and producers, including in appropriate cases the distribution of basic foods at special prices;

(f) to assure the equitable distribution of ***an agricultural*** commodity in short supply.

SECTION B - INTER-GOVERNMENTAL *AGRICULTURAL* COMMODITY AGREEMENTS IN GENERAL

Article 58

Agricultural Commodity Studies

1. Any Member which considers itself substantially interested in the production or consumption of, or trade in, a particular primary commodity, and which considers that international trade in that commodity is, or is likely to be, affected by special difficulties, ***or that a food security risk in connection with that commodity exists***, shall be entitled to ask that a study of the commodity be made.

2. Unless the Organization decides that the case put forward in support of the request does not warrant such action, it shall promptly invite each Member to appoint representatives to a study group for the commodity, if the Member considers itself substantially interested in the production or consumption of, or trade in, the commodity. Non-Members may also be invited.

3. The study group shall promptly investigate the production, consumption and trade situation in regard to the ***agricultural*** commodity, and shall report to the participating governments and to the Organization its findings and its recommendations as to how best to deal with any special difficulties which exist or may be expected to arise. The Organization shall promptly transmit to the Members these findings and recommendations.

Article 59

Agricultural Commodity Conferences

1. The Organization shall promptly convene an inter-governmental conference to discuss measures designed to meet the special difficulties which exist or are expected to arise concerning a particular ***agricultural*** commodity:

(a) on the basis of the recommendations of a study group, or

(b) at the request of Members whose interests represent a significant part of world production or consumption of, or trade in, that commodity, or

(c) at the request of Members which consider that their economies ***or their food security*** are dependent to an important extent on that commodity, unless the Organization considers that no useful purpose could be achieved by convening the conference, or

(d) on its own initiative, on the basis of information agreed to be adequate by the Members substantially interested in the production or consumption of, or trade in, that commodity.

2. Each Member which considers itself substantially interested in the production or consumption of, or trade in, the commodity concerned, shall be invited to participate in such a conference. Non-Members may also be invited to participate.

Article 60

General Principles governing ***Inter-Governmental Agricultural*** Commodity Agreements

1. The Members shall observe the following principles in the conclusion and operation of all types of inter-governmental ***agricultural*** commodity agreements:

(a) Such agreements shall be open to participation, initially by any Member on terms no less favourable than those accorded to any other country, and thereafter in accordance with such procedure and upon such terms as may be established in the agreement, subject to approval by the Organization.

(b) Non-Members may be invited by the Organization to participate in such agreements and the provisions of sub-paragraph (a) applying to Members shall also apply to any non-Member so invited.

(c) Under such agreements there shall be equitable treatment as between participating countries and non-participating Members, and the treatment accorded by participating countries to non-participating Members shall be no less favourable than that accorded to any non-participating non-Member, due consideration being given in each case to policies adopted by non-participants in relation to obligations assumed and advantages conferred under the agreement.

(d) Such agreements shall include provision for adequate participation of countries substantially interested in the importation or consumption of the commodity as well as those substantially interested in its exportation or production.

(e) Full publicity shall be given to any inter-governmental ***agricultural*** commodity agreement proposed or concluded, to the statements of considerations and objectives advanced by the proposing Members, to the nature and development of measures adopted to correct the underlying situation which gave rise to the agreement and, periodically, to the operation of the agreement.

2. The Members, including Members not parties to a particular ***agricultural*** commodity agreement, shall give favourable consideration to any recommendation made under the agreement for expanding consumption of the commodity in question.

Article 61

Object of Inter-Governmental Agricultural Commodity Agreements

(…) ***An agricultural*** commodity agreement is an inter-governmental agreement:

(a) ***which involves*** the regulation of production or the quantitative control of exports or imports of a primary commodity and which has the purpose or might have the effect of reducing, or preventing an increase in, the production of, or trade in, that commodity; or

(b) ***which involves*** the regulation of prices; ***or***

(c) whose object is to reserve all or part of the domestic production of a primary commodity for populations which are victims of food insecurity.

(…)

Article 62

Circumstances Governing the use of ***Inter-Governmental Agricultural*** Commodity Agreements

The Members agree that ***inter-governmental agricultural*** commodity control agreements may be entered into only when a finding has been made through *an agricultural* commodity conference or through the Organization by consultation and general agreement among Members substantially interested in the commodity, ***or through the high-level Group of Experts on food security and nutrition of the United Nations Food and Agriculture Organization, that:***

(a) a burdensome surplus of a ***an agricultural*** commodity has developed or is expected to develop, which, in the absence of specific governmental action, would cause serious hardship to producers among whom are small producers who account for a substantial portion of the total output, and that these conditions could not be corrected by normal market forces in time to prevent such hardship, because, characteristically in the case of the primary commodity concerned, a substantial reduction in price does not readily lead to a significant increase in consumption or to a significant decrease in production; or

(b) widespread unemployment or under-employment in connection with ***an agricultural*** commodity, arising out of difficulties of the kind referred to in Article 55, has developed or is expected to develop, which, in the absence of specific governmental action, would not be corrected by normal market forces in time to prevent widespread and undue hardship to workers because, characteristically in the case of the industry concerned, a substantial reduction in price does not steadily lead to a significant increase in consumption but to a reduction of employment, and because areas in which the commodity is produced in substantial quantity do not afford alternative employment opportunities for the workers involved*; or*

(c) difficulties as described in Article 55, in relation to an agricultural commodity, have led to, or risk leading to, a state of food insecurity affecting a country, region, duly identified community or category of vulnerable persons, which would not, in the absence of specific government measures, be corrected by normal market forces.

Article 63

Additional Principles Governing ***Inter-Governmental Agricultural*** Commodity Agreements

The Members shall observe the following principles governing the conclusion and operation of ***inter-governmental agricultural*** commodity agreements, in addition to those stated in Article 60:

(a) Such agreements shall be designed to assure the availability of supplies adequate at all times for world demand at prices which are in keeping with the provisions of Article 57 (c), and, when practicable, shall provide for measures designed to expand world consumption of the commodity.

(b) Under such agreements, participating countries which are mainly interested in imports of the ***agricultural*** commodity concerned shall, in decisions on substantive matters, have together a number of votes equal to that of those mainly interested in obtaining export markets for the commodity. Any participating country, which is interested in the commodity but which does not fall precisely under either of the above classes, shall have an appropriate voice within such classes.

(c) Such agreements shall make appropriate provision to afford increasing opportunities for satisfying national consumption and world market requirements from sources from which such requirements can be supplied in ***the manner which is the most effective, the most capable of preserving natural resources and the most economical***, due regard being had to the need for preventing serious economic and social dislocation and to the position of producing areas suffering from abnormal disabilities.

(d) Participating countries shall formulate and adopt programmes of internal economic adjustment believed to be adequate to ensure as much progress as practicable within the duration of the agreement towards solution of the ***agricultural*** commodity problem involved.

Article 64

Administration of ***Inter-Governmental Agricultural*** Commodity Agreements

1. Each ***inter-governmental agricultural*** commodity agreement shall provide for the establishment of a governing body, herein referred to as a Commodity Council, which shall operate in conformity with the provisions of this Article.

2. Each participating country shall be entitled to have one representative on the Commodity Council. The voting power of the representatives shall be determined in conformity with the provisions of Article 63 (b).

3. The Organization shall be entitled to appoint a non-voting representative to each Commodity Council and may invite any competent inter-governmental organization to nominate a non-voting representative for appointment to a Commodity Council. ***The FAO shall be a non-voting ex-officio member of each Commodity Council.***

4. Each Commodity Council shall appoint a non-voting chairman who, if the Council so requests, may be nominated by the Organization.

5. The Secretariat of each Commodity Council shall be appointed by the Council after consultation with the Organization.

6. Each Commodity Council shall adopt appropriate rules of procedure and regulations regarding its activities. The Organization may at any time require their amendment if it considers that they are inconsistent with the provisions of this Chapter.

7. Each Commodity Council shall make periodic reports to the Organization on the operation of the agreement which it administers. It shall

also make such special reports as the Organization may require or as the Council itself considers to be of value to the Organization.

8. The expenses of a Commodity Council shall be borne by the participating countries.

9. When an agreement is terminated, the Organization shall take charge of the archives and statistical material of the Commodity Council.

Article 65

Initial term, Renewal and Review of *Inter-Governmental Agricultural* Commodity Agreements

1. ***Inter-governmental agricultural*** commodity agreements shall be concluded for a period of not more than five years. Any renewal of an ***inter-governmental agricultural*** commodity agreement, including agreements referred to in paragraph 1 of Article 68, shall be for a period not exceeding five years. The provisions of such renewed agreements shall conform to the provisions of this Chapter.

2. The Organization shall prepare and publish periodically, at intervals not greater than three years, a review of the operation of each agreement in the light of the principles set forth in this Chapter.

3. Each ***inter-governmental agricultural*** commodity agreement shall provide that, if the Organization finds that its operation has failed substantially to conform to the principles laid down in this Chapter, participating countries shall either revise the agreement to conform to the principles or terminate it.

4. ***Inter-governmental agricultural*** commodity agreements shall include provisions relating to withdrawal of any Party.

Article 66

Settlement of Disputes

Each ***inter-governmental agricultural*** commodity agreement shall provide that:

(a ***(i)***) any question or difference concerning the interpretation of the provisions of the ***inter-governmental agricultural commodity*** agreement or arising out of its operation shall be discussed originally by the Commodity Council;

(a (ii)) if the Commodity Council cannot resolve the issue within the terms of the agreement, it shall be deferred by the Council to a Conciliation Commission composed of five members, with the directors-general of the Organization and of the FAO nominating two each and

a President being chosen by common consent by the four nominated members. The Conciliation Commission shall decide matters on a simple majority of its members. It shall lay down its own procedure. It shall put forward a proposal for settling the difference, which the voting members of the Commodity Council shall examine in good faith. In case of disagreement over the competence of the Conciliation Commission, the Commission itself shall decide whether it is competent;

(b) if the question or difference cannot be resolved by the Council in accordance with the terms of the agreement, it shall be referred by the Council to the Organization, which shall apply the procedure set forth in Chapter VIII with appropriate adjustments to cover the case of non-Members.

SECTION C - MISCELLANEOUS PROVISIONS

Article 67

Relations with Inter-Governmental Organizations

1. With the object of ensuring appropriate co-operation in matters relating to intergovernmental ***agricultural*** commodity agreements, any intergovernmental organization which is deemed to be competent by the Organization, such as the Food and Agriculture Organization, shall be entitled:

(a) to attend any study group or ***agricultural*** commodity conference;
(b) to ask that a study of ***an agricultural*** primary commodity be made;
(c) to submit to the Organization any relevant study of ***an agricultural*** commodity, and to recommend to the Organization that further study of the commodity be made or that ***an agricultural*** commodity conference be convened.

2. Furthermore, FAO shall have the right to sit on the Councils responsible for managing inter-governmental Commodity Control Agreements, as stated in Article 64.3.

Article 67-1

Emergency measures

1. At the request of a Member and following the consent of the Director-general of the World Trade Organization, the Director-general of the United Nations Food and Agriculture Organization may authorize

that Member to take measures under Article 61 if such measures are approved by the high-level Group of Experts on food security and nutrition of the Committee on world food security of the FAO, and if they are:

a) necessary for the protection of the health and life of persons in cases of food insecurity duly noted by the Group of Experts; or

b) necessary for the preservation of exhaustible natural resources, where there is a serious risk of exhaustion which may eventually lead to or aggravate a state of food insecurity.

2. Such measures shall not be applied in such a way as to constitute a disguised restriction on international trade;

3. They shall be authorized for a limited period, which may not exceed one year, unless the situation is reexamined by the Group of Experts who then issue a further authorization.

4. They shall be publicized by the United Nations Food and Agriculture Organization.

5. The implementation of such measures shall be monitored and assisted by the United Nations Food and Agriculture Organization.

(...)

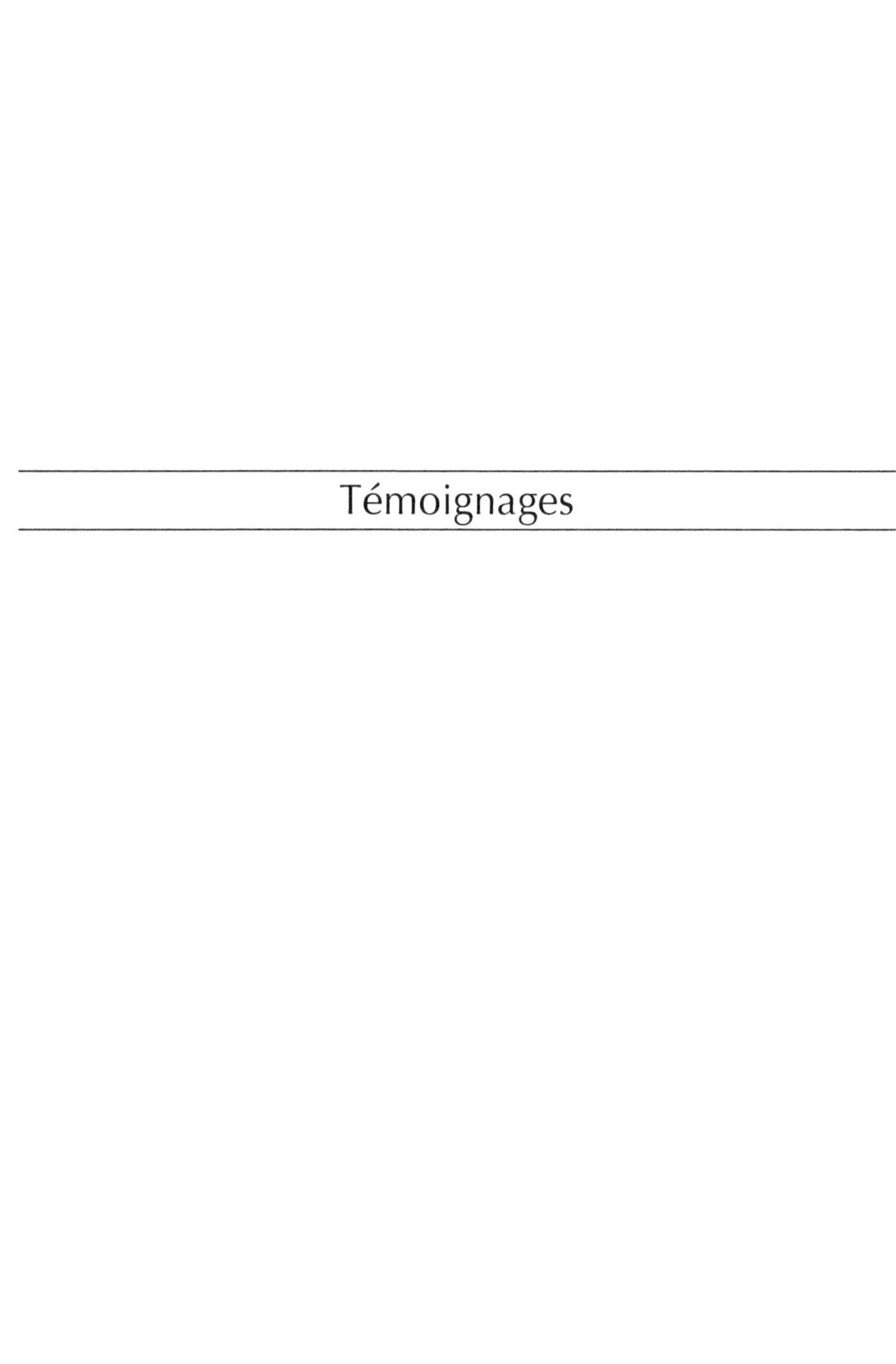

Témoignages

Thinking new ways for resistance

RAJAGOPAL P.V. *

In the large field of agriculture, land and food, there are three major actors in place.

The first set of actors is those systematically trying to deprive marginalized communities from their land and resources in the name of development and progress. This process began with the indigenous people, then with the nomads, the small shop keepers, etc.

The second set of actors is those trying, through their work and actions, to influence and reform the institutions, the policies and laws. In a globalizing world, these actors are essential, whether they are researchers, members of NGOs or civil society.

The third set of actors is those who are resisting this process of globalization, through non-violent protests. The underlying principle of this resistance is to that when choosing between silence and action and between violence and peace, one must opt for non-violent direct actions.

In a globalizing world, conflicts are inevitable but violence or non-violence is a choice. On one side, we need to effectively work on this choice, and on the other side, we need to put an end to the contradiction that exists regarding the amount of money spend on conflicts, military equipment instead of non-violence and peaceful measures. In most countries, there is no ministry for peace, no budget for non-violence programs.

One process of non-violent resistance is converting anger into positive actions. Today, because of unemployment, poverty and deprivation, there is a growing level of anger within many societies. But anger is not necessarily a bad element; it gives the society more energy and determination. Coordinating anger and converting it into non-violent actions is one of

* Fondateur et Président d'Ekta Parishad - Inde. Intervention de Rajagopal P. V. à l'occasion des Rencontres internationales du programme Lascaux « Penser une démocratie alimentaire », 25-27 novembre 2013 à Nantes.

the areas where NGOs such as Ekta Parishad[1] has been working for many years.

Another area of work is the conversion of difficulties into possibilities. Often, people say that mobilization is difficult because there are not enough resources. Therefore, it is important to analyze and understand the resources available within the society in order to convert the difficulties into possibilities. For example, a lot of poor people would say that they have to walk many kilometers to get drinking water or firewood. In terms of possibilities, this means that they have the capacity to walk. If they say they do not have enough food and they have to work under high temperatures, it means they are strong enough to survive difficult conditions. This is how Ekta Parishad managed to organize long marches with 25 000 people[2].

Another option is to create a "basket of success", that is to say bring people together to act successfully. There are several components to this basket. First of all, we need to realize the power of the poor. Generally, we look at poor people with the idea that they need to be helped. But in reality there is an inbuilt power among poor people in spite of the situation they live in. Then, we need to realize the power of the young. Young people have tremendous energy, which can be used to breathe new impetus and take action. There is also the power of solidarity. For example, during the great march organized in India, hundreds of thousands letters came to the Prime Minister, which eventually led to a change of policy from the government. Finally, another component is the power of non-violence. If people

---

[1] Ekta Parishad is a popular movement founded in 1991 in India and based on the gandhian principle of non-violent actions with the aim to help people to better control the resources that are essential to life: water, land and forest (http://www.ektaparishad.com/).

[2] In October 2007, 25 000 people representing communities from all over India participated in the march towards Janadesh, which proved to be the greatest non-violent movement for agrarian reform in the history of the country. Many victories were won, including the creation in 2007 of a National Committee for Agrarian Reform. Nevertheless, the situation remained extremely problematic for Indian farmers, which justified a new large-scale action in 2012. Over a whole year, until October 2th, 2012, marches were organized in different states - Madhya Pradesh, Chhattisgarh, Jharkhand, Orissa, Bihar, Uttar Pradesh, etc. - and in some particular states, the march culminated in a rally. During the last two weeks, more than 100 000 people walked more than 300 kilometers from Gwalior to the Parliament in Delhi (See « Ekta Parishad : Pour une nouvelle dignité paysanne » ; http://www.peuples-solidaires.org/ekta-parishad/).

can be trained, organized to protest non-violently, it can have a tremendous impact in terms of shift of policy.

In conclusion, in order to bring about change in a globalizing world where global forces are trying to grab land and resources, we need to innovatively think of new ways to encourage people to resist.

Les droits de l'Homme au service de la sécurité alimentaire

Olivier DE SCHUTTER *

Je voudrais peut-être commencer par un bref rappel d'ordre historique. Pendant des années le droit à l'alimentation a été présent, certes, dans les textes et figurait à l'article 25 de la Déclaration Universelle des Droits de l'Homme, mais il a été oublié, omis, et n'a pas été considéré comme un instrument utile pour les gouvernements tentant de réduire la faim et la malnutrition. Et même lorsque le Pacte International relatif aux droits économiques, sociaux et culturels a été adopté en 1966 (entrée en vigueur en 1976), le droit à l'alimentation demeurait relativement peu concret aux yeux des gouvernements et n'était pas invoqué lorsque l'on parlait de politique agricole et alimentaire.

Les choses ont changé à partir du début des années 1990, notament à la suite de travaux mettant en lumière que les progrès faits en matière de production agricole, l'augmentation de la disponibilité de calories par tête d'habitant, ne suffisaient pas à mettre fin à la faim dans le monde de manière durable. Les gouvernements ont dû se poser la question de savoir pourquoi les politiques misant sur l'augmentation de l'offre pour réduire la faim n'étaient pas effectives. Parmi les travaux qui ont inspiré leur réflexion, on trouve l'ouvrage de l'économiste indien Amartya Sen intitulé « Pauvreté et Famine : essai sur les garanties d'accès et la privation », dans lequel l'auteur examine les quatre grandes famines du 21ème siècle. Il démontre qu'elles ont eu lieu bien que les récoltes aient été bonnes, parce certains groupes de population ont perdu leur capacité à avoir accès à un revenu suffisant leur permettant d'acheter de la nourriture sur les marchés et que les gouvernements ne leur sont pas venus en aide. Amartya Sen montre ainsi que la question de la démocratie et de l'obligation pour les gouvernements de prendre des choix en fonction des besoins de la population est

* Rapporteur spécial des Nations Unies sur le droit à l'alimentation. Intervention d'Olivier DE SCHUTTER à l'occasion des Rencontres internationales du programme Lascaux « Penser une démocratie alimentaire », 25-27 novembre 2013 à Nantes.

tout à fait décisive pour la sécurité alimentaire et la réduction de la faim et de la malnutrition.

En 1976, lors du 2nd Sommet mondial sur l'alimentation, les chefs d'Etat et de Gouvernement ont adopté un plan d'action qui demandait aux organes compétents des Nations Unies de clarifier le contenu du droit à l'alimentation, dont on se rendait compte qu'il était particulièrement déterminant pour que les politiques de sécurité alimentaire réussissent et que les plus marginalisés bénéficient des efforts des gouvernements. Il ne suffit pas de produire plus, il faut encore prendre en compte les questions de justice distributive, de justice sociale.

Dans l'intervalle, les recherches du juriste norvégien Asbjørn Eide ont permis aux travaux menés à la suite du Sommet mondial sur l'alimentation de progresser assez rapidement. En 1980, Eide fut sollicité par le ministère norvégien des Affaires étrangères pour réfléchir à la manière dont les droits de l'Homme pouvaient être mieux pris en compte dans les politiques de coopération au développement en Norvège. Il s'est interrogé sur la manière de faire passer le message des droits de l'Homme dans ces politiques. Pour cela, il a examiné la manière dont les droits de l'Homme se rapportaient au marché et a abouti à la conclusion que ces droits imposaient trois types d'obligations aux gouvernements : une obligation de ne pas s'ingérer dans la jouissance des droits, une obligation d'intervenir pour protéger les victimes d'atteintes aux droits de l'Homme lorsque celles-ci sont causées par des acteurs privés et l'obligation de donner effet aux droits de l'Homme. Ce triptyque des obligations étatiques est apparu particulièrement utile à la clarification du droit à l'alimentation. En 1999, le Comité des droits économiques, sociaux et culturels adoptait ainsi l'Observation générale n° 12 sur le droit à l'alimentation en y impliquant ce schéma. Lorsque le Sommet mondial sur l'alimentation se réunit en 2002, des négociations furent lancées sur un autre texte étroitement lié à l'Observation générale n° 12, devenu par la suite les « directives volontaires à l'appui de la concrétisation progressive du droit à l'alimentation dans un contexte de sécurité alimentaire nationale ». Adopté par le Conseil de la FAO en 2004, ce texte est le premier à avoir été négocié selon un processus inter-gouvernemental et il clarifie dans le plus grand détail le contenu d'un droit économique et social. Ces directives volontaires continuent d'être régulièrement invoquées. En octobre 2014, lors de sa 41ème

session, le Comité de la sécurité alimentaire mondiale devrait procéder à un bilan de la mise en œuvre de ces directives volontaires. Les gouvernements devront alors s'expliquer sur le suivi qu'ils auront donné à ces dernières.

Aujourd'hui, les enjeux ne sont plus théoriques ; nous ne sommes plus dans la clarification de la signification du droit à l'alimentation. En revanche, la question de la mise en œuvre effective demeure, et deux trajectoires distinctes peuvent être identifiées.

Le premier modèle caractérise certains Etats où les juridictions ont joué un rôle tout à fait déterminant dans la mise en œuvre du droit à l'alimentation. A titre d'exemple, citons tout d'abord l'Afrique du Sud où une loi a été adoptée pour préserver les ressources halieutiques et éviter la surpêche. Cette loi prévoyait que les pêcheurs devaient obtenir des droits de pêcher pour éviter qu'ils n'épuisent les stocks de poissons disponibles. Mais cette loi ne prenait pas en compte les intérêts des petits pêcheurs artisanaux qui ne s'étaient pas enregistrés. Ceux-ci se sont alors plaints devant la juridiction nationale, avançant que le système de quotas n'avait pas été conçu pour eux. Les juridictions sont alors intervenues pour dire qu'il fallait remanier la loi de manière à prendre en compte les intérêts des pêcheurs traditionnels et rendre possible la poursuite de cette activité, essentielle pour la subsistance des populations vivant à proximité des côtes. En 2012, l'Afrique du Sud a ainsi adopté une version révisée de la loi.

Le second exemple concerne la Cour Suprême du Népal qui a réussi, par une ordonnance de 2008, à persuader le Gouvernement d'étendre un programme d'aide alimentaire à l'ensemble du territoire du Népal et non à quelques districts seulement.

Enfin, un troisième exemple est celui de la Cour Suprême indienne. En 2001, une coalition d'ONG indiennes constatent qu'au Rajasthan, l'un des Etats les plus pauvres de l'Inde, le Gouvernement n'intervient pas pour fournir une aide alimentaire à bas prix sur les marchés, et ce malgré l'existence de réserves alimentaires disponibles dans le pays. La Cour Suprême est alors intervenue pour ordonner au Gouvernement de libérer les stocks. Elle est même allée au-delà, délivrant chaque année depuis 2001 des ordonnances visant à améliorer sur toute une série de points les programmes sociaux que les différents gouvernements de l'Union indienne ont mis en œuvre pour protéger la population contre la faim et la malnutrition. Au total, la Cour Suprême est intervenue sur 8 programmes sociaux (sur la mise au travail des personnes sans autre source de revenus dans les zones rurales, sur l'aide aux femmes enceintes et allaitantes, sur les repas alimentaires dans les écoles, etc.) pour énoncer que ces programmes devraient être étendus à l'ensemble du territoire et améliorés dans leur mise en œuvre. Le juge s'est donc transformé en « ingénieur social », complétant le travail du législateur, sans tout à fait se substituer à lui. La Cour est soutenue par tout un réseau d'ONG, qui signale en retour tout manquement à la bonne mise en œuvre des programmes sociaux ayant valeur constitutionnelle. En septembre 2013, le National Food Security Act adopté par le Gouvernement indien traduit sous forme législative une série d'avancées jurisprudentielles permises par la Cour Suprême.

Le second modèle possible dans la mise œuvre effective du droit à l'alimentation est celui développé notamment en Amérique Latine et qui a démarré dans le milieu des années 2000. A la suite du Guatemala et du Brésil en 2005-2006, plusieurs Etats ont adopté une stratégie nationale visant à réviser le droit à l'alimentation à travers des lois-cadres définissant une structure institutionnelle garantissant la participation de la société civile à l'élaboration de cette stratégie, en collaboration avec différents départements ministériels. Le dernier exemple en date de cette vague de réformes législatives adoptées sur la base de ces lois-cadres est celui du Mexique. Avec l'arrivée à la présidence d'Enrique Pena Nieto, le Mexique a adopté une nouvelle initiative intitulée « La croisade contre la faim » qui repose sur un décret exécutif établissant un programme visant à éradiquer la faim. Sur le modèle de ce qui s'était déjà fait ailleurs en Amérique Latine et Centrale, cette initiative prévoit que les différents départements ministériels collaborent à travers des plans d'action développés et coordonnés par le ministère du Développement social. Ces plans d'action vont être inspirés par des initiatives locales, car toutes les communautés sont invitées à établir des comités afin d'identifier les priorités et les pistes d'amélioration pour la sécurité alimentaire au niveau local. Le Gouvernement fédéral s'engage par la suite à soutenir les initiatives locales.

Les avantages de ces stratégies nationales sont les suivants : elles permettent tout d'abord une coordination interdépartementale. La réalisation du droit à l'alimentation suppose que tous les ministères travaillent ensemble de manière coordonnée et harmonisée. Ensuite, ces stratégies sont adoptées sur une base participative. Ce sont les organisations de la société civile, les représentants des populations les plus pauvres qui vont identifier les obstacles que les personnes rencontrent dans l'accès à l'alimentation et qui vont formuler des recommandations que le gouvernement devra ensuite prendre en compte dans l'élaboration de ses stratégies. Etant co-auteurs de ces stratégies, cela permet également de s'assurer que les ONG en surveilleront la mise en œuvre. Ces stratégies obligent donc le gouvernement à rendre des comptes, à faire des rapports réguliers sur les progrès réalisés, à adopter des indicateurs permettant de s'assurer que le rythme est tenu. Ce sont des outils de gouvernance, une manière de rendre justiciable des droits qui sont à réalisation progressive.

La question qui continue de préoccuper les chercheurs est celle de savoir comment mesurer l'effectivité du droit à l'alimentation dans le succès des politiques de sécurité alimentaire. Si l'on mettait côte à côte une carte du monde montrant les progrès réalisés dans la réduction de la faim et la malnutrition et une autre identifiant les dispositifs institutionnels mis en place et les stratégies nationales ou lois-cadres adoptées, pourrait-on montrer une corrélation entre les deux ? Ce genre d'exercice est difficile à effectuer mais paraît essentiel. Certains pays ont fait des progrès sans se soumettre au contrôle de leur population, sans fonder leurs progrès sur le droit à l'alimentation (comme par exemple la Chine ou le Rwanda) ; certains autres possèdent, à l'inverse, des dispositifs intéressants sur papier mais n'avancent pas pour autant (comme par exemple le Guatemala, où le taux de mortalité infantile demeure très élevé, où la discrimination contre les populations autochtones est très forte et où l'inégalité dans l'accès à la terre demeure une source de conflits, et ce malgré l'adoption d'une loi-cadre en matière de droit à l'alimentation). Entre ces deux cas, il y a certains pays où le droit à l'alimentation a permis de faire des progrès importants, en favorisant la participation de la société civile à la définition des politiques, en soumettant le gouvernement à un certain contrôle de la part de l'opinion publique, en définissant la réalisation du droit à l'alimentation comme une priorité nationale, définie comme telle au plus haut niveau du gouvernement. Néanmoins, il reste, pour les juristes, tout un travail important à faire pour démontrer la valeur ajoutée du droit à l'alimentation dans le succès des politiques de sécurité alimentaire.

I.- Vers une nouvelle approche des ressources naturelles alimentaires

A) L'impact des transitions écologique, sociétale et alimentaire

Définitions des ressources naturelles et implications pour la démarche juridique

Edgar FERNANDEZ FERNANDEZ [*], Claire MALWE [**]
& Ioan NEGRUTIU [***]

La construction d'un droit dédié aux ressources naturelles nécessite de s'accorder préalablement sur les notions clés. A cet égard, les choix effectués ne seront pas indifférents ou dépourvus de conséquences : ils reflètent les valeurs considérées comme fondamentales dans nos sociétés. Bien que les choix de vocabulaire soient essentiellement des choix politiques, nous soutenons que le concept légal de « ressources naturelles » devrait satisfaire aux objectifs de maintien des systèmes supportant la vie sur Terre et de satisfaction des besoins fondamentaux humains.

En dépit de l'importance des concepts légaux et de celle des ressources naturelles pour le futur de l'humanité, les définitions des « ressources naturelles » dans les instruments légaux internationaux ou régionaux sont presque inexistants. La « Convention africaine sur la Conservation de la Nature et des Ressources naturelles » est l'une des rares à essayer de définir cette notion. Cependant, elle n'en donne pas une véritable définition, faute d'établir un critère afin de déterminer ce qui doit être ou non considéré comme une ressource naturelle. A la place, le texte de la Convention définit le concept en établissant une liste d'éléments qui, s'agissant des buts poursuivis par la Convention, seront considérés comme des ressources naturelles. Dans sa version originale (1968), la Convention disposait que le terme de ressources naturelles « signifie ressources naturelles renouvelables, c'est-à-dire les sols, les eaux, la flore et la faune » (article 3). Dans sa version modifiée (2003) [1], le texte dispose que, par l'expression « ressources naturelles », on entend « les ressources renouve-

[*] Chercheur invité au Collegium de Lyon. Chercheur associé à l'Institut Ouest : Droit et Europe de l'Université de Rennes 1.

[**] Chercheur invité au Collegium de Lyon. Maître de conférences à l'Université de Rennes 1, Institut du Droit Public et de la Science Politique (EA 4640).

[***] Biologiste, Directeur de l'Institut Michel Serres, ENS de Lyon.

[1] Convention africaine révisée sur la conservation de la nature et des ressources naturelles, adoptée le 11 juillet 2003.

lables, tangibles ou non tangibles, notamment les sols, les eaux, la flore et la faune, ainsi que les ressources non renouvelables » (article 5). Le Principe 2 de la Déclaration de Stockholm[2] fournit un autre exemple de « liste » de ressources naturelles : « les ressources naturelles du globe et particulièrement l'air, l'eau, le sol, la flore et la faune (...) ».

La Convention sur la Diversité Biologique (CDB)[3] ne définit pas les ressources naturelles, mais évoque deux concepts plus spécifiques : celui de « ressources biologiques » et de « ressources génétiques ». Selon l'article 2 de la CBD, le premier de ces termes « inclut les ressources génétiques, les organismes ou éléments de ceux-ci, les populations, ou tout autre élément biotique des écosystèmes ayant une utilisation ou une valeur effective ou potentielle pour l'humanité ». Le concept de « ressources génétiques » doit être entendu, pour sa part, comme « le matériel génétique ayant une valeur effective ou potentielle ». Cette approche utilitariste, qui a été qualifiée par certains auteurs de « restrictive »[4], semble s'inscrire dans une perspective économique du terme « ressources »[5]. En effet, la définition de « ressources naturelles » est principalement dépendante de la signification accordée au terme « ressources ». Pour ces commentateurs, l'approche qui justifie ces définitions devrait être questionnée car, « il est prudent de considérer que tous les éléments biotiques des écosystèmes ont une utilité ou un intérêt potentiels pour l'homme » et que « virtuellement, tout le matériel génétique a une valeur potentielle, au moins jusqu'à preuve du contraire »[6].

---

[2] Déclaration finale de la Conférence des Nations Unies sur l'environnement, Stockholm, 5-16 juin 1972.

[3] Convention sur la diversité biologique, 5 juin 1992 (1993) 1760 R.T.N.U. 79 (n° 30619).

[4] GLOWKA Lyle, BURHENNE-GUILMIN Françoise et SYNGE Hugh, *Guide de la Convention sur la Diversité Biologique*, Environmental Policy and Law Paper, n° 30, IUCN, Gland et Cambridge, 1996, p. 28.

[5] v. ROTILLON Gilles, *Economie des ressources naturelles*, La Découverte, Paris, 2005, p. 6.

[6] GLOWKA Lyle, BURHENNE-GUILMIN Françoise, et SYNGE Hugh, *op.cit.*, p. 22 et 28. All biotic components of ecosystems "have some kind of actual or potential value for human use", and "virtually all genetic material is potentially valuable at least until proven otherwise".

D'autres types de définitions des ressources naturelles peuvent également être trouvés dans des documents dépourvus de valeur juridique provenant d'organisations internationales et régionales. Nous en présenterons ici trois exemples : celle adoptée par l'Union internationale pour la Conservation de la Nature (IUCN), par l'Organisation mondiale du Commerce (OMC), ainsi que par la Commission européenne.

La définition des ressources naturelles retenue par l'IUCN est redondante, car elle reprend le terme de « ressource » sans le définir. Selon cette définition, les ressources naturelles sont « les ressources produites par la nature, communément subdivisées en ressources non-renouvelables, telles que les minéraux et les combustibles fossiles, et les ressources naturelles renouvelables qui propagent ou soutiennent la vie et se renouvellent naturellement par eux-mêmes lorsqu'ils sont correctement gérés, ce qui inclut les plantes et les animaux, ainsi que le sol et l'eau »[7].

L'OMC retient une véritable définition des ressources naturelles, mais celle-ci est très étroite car elle répond exclusivement à une approche commerciale. Dans son Rapport sur le commerce mondial 2010, dédié au commerce des ressources naturelles, l'Organisation définit les ressources naturelles, « aux fins du présent rapport » comme « les stocks de matières présentes dans le milieu naturel qui sont à la fois rares et économiquement utiles pour la production ou la consommation, soit à l'état brut, soit après un minimum de transformation »[8]. Cette définition montre que les stocks de matières qui existent dans la nature n'ont pas tous un intérêt pour l'OMC : seuls ceux qui deviendront des marchandises susceptibles d'être commercialisées sur les marchés sont inclus dans la définition retenue. Pour l'OMC, l'eau de mer ne constitue pas une ressource naturelle dès lors qu'elle est considérée comme étant d'une valeur intrinsèque et directe limitée pour la consommation et la production. Selon cette définition, l'air ne

---

[7] IUCN. *Publishing with IUCN: IUCN Definitions Glossary*; http://cmsdata.iucn.org/downloads/en_iucn_glossary_definitions.pdf, viewed on June 21, 2013. "Resources produced by nature, commonly subdivided into non-renewable resources, such as minerals and fossil fuels, and renewable natural resources that propagate or sustain life and are naturally self-renewing when properly managed, including plants and animals, as well as soil and water".

[8] World Trade Organization, World Trade Report 2010: Trade in natural resources, 2010, p. 46.

constitue pas non plus une ressource naturelle car les individus peuvent l'obtenir gratuitement, simplement en respirant. Les biens agricoles, ce qui inclut la nourriture, n'entrent pas non plus dans la catégorie des ressources naturelles pour plusieurs raisons : d'une part, « leur production nécessite d'autres ressources naturelles comme intrants, en particulier la terre et l'eau, mais aussi différents types d'engrais. Surtout, les produits agricoles sont cultivés, et non extraits du milieu naturel »[9]. Par exception, deux catégories de biens agricoles sont cependant considérés comme des ressources naturelles par l'Organisation mondiale du Commerce : il s'agit des produits de la pêche et des produits forestiers[10]. Finalement, les principaux groupes de produits considérés comme des ressources naturelles par l'OMC sont les produits de la pêche, les produits forestiers, les combustibles, les minerais et autres minéraux et métaux non ferreux[11]. Dès lors, la définition retenue par l'OMC des ressources naturelles ne s'inscrit pas dans la problématique du maintien des systèmes supportant la vie sur Terre et de la satisfaction des besoins fondamentaux. En effet, bien que leur gestion durable soit cruciale pour affronter ces deux défis, l'air et l'eau de mer ne sont pas considérés comme des ressources naturelles dans le cadre de cette définition. Ainsi que le mentionne l'Organisation des Nations Unies pour l'Alimentation et l'Agriculture (FAO), d'autres ressources essentielles (telles que le sol, l'eau, les ressources génétiques et la biodiversité), ne sont pas retenues par l'OMC[12]. En ce sens, le Professeur François Collart Dutilleul a porté ses critiques sur la définition retenue par l'OMC et considère qu'afin d'être plus conforme aux enjeux alimentaires, le concept de ressources naturelles devrait comprendre « la terre elle-même, les matières premières agricoles, l'eau et les ressources de la biodiversité »[13].

Le GATT contient une disposition spécifique (article XXg) dans laquelle il fait référence aux « ressources naturelles épuisables » : « rien

[9] *Ibid.*

[10] *Ibid.*

[11] *Ibid.*

[12] FAO, "Natural Resources and Environment: About the NR Department", http://www.fao.org/nr/aboutnr/en/, viewed on June 21, 2013.

[13] Collart Dutilleul François, "Law devoted to food issues and natural resources exploitation and trade", http://www.droit-aliments-terre.eu/documents/sources_lascaux/articles/2011/FCD_ENSLyon_05_2011_EN.pdf, viewed on July 9, 2013.

dans le présent Accord ne sera interprété comme empêchant l'adoption ou l'application par toute partie contractante des mesures : (...) (g) se rapportant à la conservation des ressources naturelles épuisables, si de telles mesures sont appliquées conjointement avec des restrictions à la production ou à la consommation nationales ». Bien que l'Accord ne donne aucune définition des ressources naturelles, l'Organe d'appel a précisé que les « ressources naturelles épuisables » ne sont pas seulement le pétrole, le minerai de fer et les autres ressources non biologiques mais également les ressources biologiques renouvelables[14].

La Commission européenne a, quant à elle, retenue une approche beaucoup plus large que celle utilisée par l'OMC pour déterminer ce qui peut être considéré comme une ressource naturelle. Dans deux communications relatives à l'utilisation des ressources naturelles, la Commission a fourni une liste d'éléments naturels qui sont inclus dans le champ de la notion. Bien qu'elle n'ait pas donné de définition de ce concept, il est possible d'observer qu'une approche utilitariste a prévalu dans la construction de ces deux listes dès lors que, dans les deux cas, il est fait référence aux ressources naturelles dont dépendent les économies et que les ressources sont considérées comme des « matières premières »[15]. Tout d'abord, dans sa communication du 21 décembre 2005 sur une « Stratégie thématique sur l'utilisation durable des ressources naturelles »[16], la Commission a indiqué que les ressources naturelles dont dépendent les économies incluent les matières premières comme les minéraux, la biomasse et les ressources biologiques ; les milieux comme l'air, l'eau et le sol ; les ressources dynamiques comme le vent, la géothermie, les marées et l'énergie solaire ; et l'espace (surface de la terre) ».

---

[14] World Trade Organization, *op.cit.*, p. 168. Selon l'Organe d'appel, « La biologie moderne nous enseigne que les espèces vivantes, bien qu'elles soient en principe capables de se reproduire et soient donc « renouvelables », peuvent dans certaines circonstances se raréfier, s'épuiser ou disparaitre, bien souvent à cause des activités humaines. Les ressources biologiques sont tout aussi « limitées » que le pétrole, le minerai de fer et les autres ressources non biologiques ».

[15] The Oxford in line dictionary defines "*raw material*" as "*the basic material from which a product is made*". http://oxforddictionaries.com/definition/english/raw-material?q=raw+material, viewed on June 25, 2013.

[16] COM(2005) 670 final of December 21, 2005.

D'autre part, dans sa communication du 26 janvier 2011 consacrée à l'Initiative - phare « une Europe efficace dans l'utilisation des ressources » de la Stratégie Europe 2020[17], la Commission a indiqué que les ressources naturelles englobent « les matières premières telles que les combustibles, les minéraux et les métaux, mais aussi les produits alimentaires, le sol, l'eau, l'air, la biomasse et les écosytèmes ».

En conclusion, les définitions actuelles des « ressources naturelles » répondent à une approche étroite et utilitaire qui n'apparaît pas adaptée aux objectifs de maintien des systèmes supportant la vie sur terre et de satisfaction des besoins fondamentaux. Afin de satisfaire ces deux objectifs, l'ensemble des éléments naturels, et pas seulement ceux qui peuvent être directement ou indirectement utilisés et consommés par l'homme ou qui ont une utilité actuelle et tangible pour l'homme, sont essentiels et devraient faire l'objet d'une protection. Pour cette raison, une définition, telle que celle qui suit, dégagée de toute perspective utilitariste, pourrait être adaptée aux objectifs ci-dessus mentionnés : « Ensemble constitué des éléments biotiques et non biotiques de la Terre, ainsi que des diverses formes d'énergie reçues (énergie solaire) ou produites sans intervention de l'homme (marées, vents) »[18]. Ceux-ci participent, directement ou indirectement, au maintien des fonctions, des cycles et des services des écosystèmes.

D'un point de vue écologique, on peut également considérer que les ressources naturelles sont des (flux de) matériaux et des services essentiels à la vie en général et à la vie et à la connaissance humaines en particulier. Les ressources biologiques, en tant que matériaux et processus générés par la vie, sont un composant essentiel des ressources naturelles. Plus spécifiquement, la ressource humaine est un composant constitutif des ressources biologiques et, en tant que tel, elle fait partie d'une diversité de réseaux de nourriture et d'énergie.

Selon cette définition, et en tant que construction et convention sociales, les ressources et l'environnement dans lequel elles s'insèrent, font

---

[17] COM(2011) 21 of January 26, 2011.

[18] GUNN S. William, MURCIA Colette, PARAKATIL Francis. *Dictionnaire des secours d'urgence en cas de catastrophe*, Conseil international de la langue française, France Editeurs, Paris, 1984, p. 112.

directement partie du contrat social. Pour Juliette Grange[19], l'objectif est de faire des ressources des « biens communs fondamentaux ». Selon elle, sont considérés comme biens fondamentaux communs à une nation, à un territoire : l'eau, l'air, diverses ressources naturelles / biologiques, les paysages, la sécurité sanitaire, la connaissance[20]. A ces biens, il faut reconnaître des formes de propriété sociale. Cela va dans le sens des traditions des communautés indigènes[21], pour lesquelles des liens forts avec le territoire ont toujours existé. Leurs territoires, en tant que systèmes socio-écosystémiques, sont vécus comme des « communs ». Dans cette conception, les ressources naturelles constituent un patrimoine : nature plus culture conditionnent continuellement « soutenabilité » environnementale, collectivité et diversité humaines. C'est tout l'intérêt de notre démarche et de cette mise au point. Elle permet de faire appel à l'outil juridique pour satisfaire à la fois la justice sociale par l'accès aux besoins fondamentaux, la responsabilité environnementale par la prise en compte des fonctions et des services écosystémiques et, éventuellement, l'acceptabilité culturelle elle-même au niveau sociétal.

---

[19] Juliette GRANGE, *Pour une philosophie de l'écologie* (Agora 2012).

[20] En droit français, il existe la notion de « patrimoine commun de la nation » article L. 110-1 et L. 210-1 du code de l'environnement. L'article L. 110-1 : « les espaces, ressources et milieux naturels, les sites et paysages, la qualité de l'air, les espèces animales et végétales, la diversité et les équilibres biologiques auxquels ils participent font partie du patrimoine commun de la nation ». L'article L. 210-1 : « l'eau fait partie du patrimoine commun de la nation. Sa protection, sa mise en valeur et le développement de la ressource utilisable, dans le respect des équilibres naturels, sont d'intérêt général ».

[21] CABALLOS MEDINA, Marcela et PETIT, Olivier, Conflicting rights and interests in indigenous territories. The implications of exploitation and conservation of natural resources. In : *Strategic Natural Resource Governance. Contemporary Environmental Perspectives*, Bruxelles, PIE Peter Lang, Coll Regional Integration and Social Cohesion, vol 10, 19-50, 2012.

Alimentación, buen vivir y derechos de la naturaleza: una breve mirada desde América Latina

Maria Valeria BERROS [*]

I.- Introducción

La presente contribución posee como objetivo presentar algunas perspectivas sobre la cuestión alimentaria que se han comenzado a traducir hacia el campo legal en recientes regulaciones latinoamericanas y que permiten ser enlazadas con el problema de la protección de la naturaleza y la satisfacción de necesidades socio-económicas fundamentales de las poblaciones. En este sentido pueden identificarse un conjunto de normativas que dan cuenta de la problemática alimentaria desde una ética que podría ser ubicada, dentro de los actuales debates de la filosofía ambiental, como no antropocéntrica y que recupera las cosmovisiones de los pueblos indígenas.

La tarea de revisión del vínculo entre naturaleza y sociedad, que es medular dentro de la filosofía ambiental, problematiza la construcción dicotómica moderna y hoy recibe traducción en el ámbito del derecho[1]. Se discute en términos de revisión del estatuto jurídico de la naturaleza y aparece como un planteo relevante el revisar la idea de naturaleza como objeto de explotación - aún con ciertos límites ya dispuestos que pueden ser visualizados en el derecho ambiental - y pensar el tránsito hacia la noción de naturaleza como sujeto de derecho o bien reflexionar sobre otro tipo de estrategias[2].

Este debate en la actualidad se encuentra con regulaciones relevantes en el contexto de América Latina que reconocen a la naturaleza

---

* Doctora en Derecho, FCJS, UNL. Docente de la Universidad Nacional del Litoral. Becaria Postdoctoral de CONICET. Argentina.

[1] BERROS, M. Valeria (2013) *"El estatuto jurídico de la naturaleza en debate (meulen en el mundo del derecho)"* en Revista de Derecho Ambiental Nro 36. Abeledo Perrot. Buenos Aires.

[2] OST, François (2003) A natureza à margen da lei. A ecologia à prova do direito Lisboa. Instituto Piaget.

en términos de sujeto de derecho, lo cual implica de modo concomitante una serie de revisiones entre las que aparece el tema alimentario. La reforma constitucional de Ecuador alude en su preámbulo a la decisión de construir una nueva forma de convivencia ciudadana en diversidad y armonía con la naturaleza para alcanzar el buen vivir. En Bolivia la carta magna reconoce la plurinacionalidad y postula construir el Estado Unitario Social de Derecho Plurinacional Democrático, y en el nivel legislativo se aprueba la Ley de Derechos de la Madre Tierra en 2010 y la Ley Marco de la Madre Tierra y Desarrollo Integral para el Vivir Bien en 2012. Estas normas marcan un quiebre importante respecto de la perspectiva occidental moderna sobre la cuestión de los recursos naturales, la naturaleza y la relación entre lo humano y lo no humano a partir de la asignación de categoría de sujeto de derecho a la Pachamama o Madre Tierra.

En la presente contribución el objetivo consiste en identificar cuáles han sido las referencias que sobre el tema alimentario se inscriben en los mencionados documentos legales a los efectos de presentar los aportes que se construyen desde perspectivas que recuperan tradiciones ancestrales, modos de vida y cosmovisiones indígenas. En primer término presentamos la noción de buen vivir o vivir bien y la configuración de la naturaleza en tanto sujeto de derecho para, luego, mostrar las referencias que se efectúan sobre el tema de la alimentación.

II.- El "buen vivir" o "vivir bien" como horizonte alternativo

Tanto en la reforma constitucional de Ecuador como de Bolivia aparece con un grado importante de centralidad la noción de "buen vivir" (sumak kawsay) o "vivir bien"[3] (sumaj kamaña, sumaj kausay, yaiko kavi

[3] La Ley Marco de la Madre Tierra y Desarrollo Integral para el Vivir Bien de 2012 realiza una definición en su art. 5: "*El Vivir Bien (Sumaj Kamaña, Sumaj Kausay, Yaiko Kavi Päve) es el horizonte civilizatorio y cultural alternativo al capitalismo y a la modernidad que nace en las cosmovisiones de las naciones y pueblos indígena originario campesinos, y las comunidades interculturales y afrobolivianas, y es concebido en el contexto de la interculturalidad. Se alcanza de forma colectiva, complementaria y solidaria integrando en su realización práctica, entre otras dimensiones, las sociales, las culturales, las políticas, las económicas, las ecológicas, y las afectivas, para permitir el encuentro armonioso entre el conjunto de seres, componentes y recursos de la Madre Tierra. Significa vivir en complementariedad, en armonía y equilibrio con la Madre Tierra y las sociedades, en equidad y solidaridad y eliminando las desigualdades y los*

päve) y ello es presentado en términos de alternativa al modo de vida actual, excediendo la cuestión meramente económica y, claro está, con diferentes matices[4]. Se trata de categorías que atraviesan ambos pactos constitucionales y se postulan como una forma de organización post neoliberal que si bien se vincula con la economía, trasciende dicho ámbito hacia lo social e incluye, verbigracia, la espiritualidad lo cual en general ha sido opacado al interior del mundo jurídico moderno[5].

Este paradigma alternativo se articula con el reconocimiento de la Pachamama como sujeto de derecho en la Constitución ecuatoriana y de la Madre Tierra reconocida también en esos términos por la legislación boliviana de 2010 y 2012 ya referenciadas. Estos documentos legales se desmarcan de la inspiración antropocéntrica que subyace a buena parte de las regulaciones legales, incluso las ambientales. Dentro del marco de las tres posturas que suelen presentarse desde la ética ambiental estaríamos ante manifestaciones que podrían enrolarse dentro del bio y eco-centrismo que se alejan del antropocentrismo más o menos acentuado que subyace al plexo normativo aún dedicado a la tutela ambiental[6]. Por el contrario, la mirada bio-céntrica considera que toda forma de vida es valiosa por sí misma, los seres vivos por el hecho de serlo poseen valor moral y deben ser respetados independientemente de la funcionalidad que pudieren poseer para la especie humana. Al interior de esta postura se advierten

---

mecanismos de dominación. Es Vivir Bien entre nosotros, Vivir Bien con lo que nos rodea y Vivir Bien consigo mismo".

[4] Sobre una genealogía del concepto puede verse: Paula Lucía AGUILAR, Pilar FIUZA, Mara GLOZMAN, Ana GRONDONA, Victoria HAIDAR, Pablo PRYLUKA (2013) *Hacia una genealogía del "Buen Vivir". Contribuciones desde el Análisis Materialista del Discurso.* Inédito.

[5] Por ejemplo, la Ley Marco de la Madre Tierra y Desarrollo Integral para el Vivir Bien de 2012 de Bolivia al referirse a los valores del vivir bien en tanto horizonte alternativo al capitalismo refiere en el art. 6 a: *"1. Saber Crecer: Vivir Bien, es crecer y compartir con espiritualidad y fe, en el marco del respeto a la libertad de religión y de las creencias espirituales de acuerdo a las cosmovisiones del pueblo boliviano, que promueve y construye vínculos edificantes, virtudes humanitarias y solidarias para llevar a cabo una vida armoniosa*".

[6] Para ampliar: ESQUIVEL FRIAS, E. (2006) *Responsabilidad y sostenibilidad ecológica.* Tesis Doctoral. Departamento de Filosofía y Letras. Universidad Autónoma de Barcelona y en Jeangène Vilmer, JB. (2011) *L'éthique animale.* Paris. PUF.

diferentes posiciones entre las que se destaca una que focaliza sobre la consideración moral de los animales no humanos[7] y otra que alude a la reverencia por la vida[8]. La perspectiva eco-céntrica considera el concepto de ecología de Ernst Haeckel y consolida la idea de mundo natural con un valor intrínseco que le es inherente. Se destacan aquí la "ética de la tierra" identificada con Aldo Leopold quien afirma que el humano es el responsable sobre lo que ocurre con la naturaleza y la "deep ecology" que se articula con la trayectoria del filósofo noruego Arne Naess quien construye la "Filosofía T" en la que la naturaleza se ubica como centro de la moral.

En el caso de estas reformas constitucionales, si bien pueden identificarse articulaciones con contenidos de estas éticas no antropocéntricas, es medular la revalorización de las cosmovisiones indígenas que conciben de manera diferente - y con una gran riqueza de matices - la relación entre lo humano y lo no humano.

En dichas normas que se encuentran atravesadas por el ensamblaje entre buen vivir o vivir bien y los derechos reconocidos a la naturaleza se encuentran diferentes referencias al tema alimentario que se presentan a continuación.

III.- Las referencias a la problemática alimentaria

Si pudiera realizarse un esquema en torno a los tópicos que sobre la cuestión alimentaria se encuentran en las regulaciones referidas podríamos destacar los siguientes: (i) el rol del Estado: como garante del derecho a la alimentación y de la soberanía y seguridad alimentarias, limitado en la cooperación internacional y tratados internacionales por el no perjuicio de la soberanía alimentaria, impulsando maneras locales de producir alimentos; (ii) la alimentación como parte integrante del buen vivir o vivir

[7] SINGER, Peter (1999) Liberación animal. Madrid: Trotta. Sobre el problema del especismo véase HORTA, Oscar (2004) *Una tipología del especismo. Criterios distintivos y significación moral en Ética ecológica. Propuestas para una reorientación*. RIECHMANN, J (coord.) Montevideo: Editorial Nordan Comunidad.

[8] En la reverencia por la vida puede subrayarse la obra de inicios del siglo XX de Albert Schweitzer que construye una tesitura basada en la voluntad de vivir que es atribuida a todo ser vivo y coloca a la reverencia por la vida como principio ético central.

bien, (iii) la alusión a la modificación genética de cultivos, (iv) la referencia a los latifundios.

Con respecto al primero de los temas (i), tanto en la Constitución de Ecuador (art. 3) como en la de Bolivia (art. 16) el Estado se compromete a asegurar el derecho a la alimentación y ello se dispone como uno de sus deberes primordiales, así como la necesidad de promoción de la soberanía alimentaria (art. 281 Constitución de Ecuador y art. 405 Constitución de Bolivia). Asimismo, en el caso de Ecuador se estipula en el art. 284 que la política económica posee entre sus objetivos asegurar la soberanía alimentaria (inc.3) y la política comercial también debe contribuir a que esta última se garantice (art. 304, inc.4).

Como parte de esa garantía se verifican también algunas limitaciones, por ejemplo, en el campo de la cooperación y/o negociaciones internacionales. Bolivia aclara en el art. 255 que las relaciones internacionales, la negociación, suscripción y ratificación de tratados internacionales debe regirse por el principio de seguridad y soberanía alimentaria para toda la población. En similar sentido, Ecuador plantea que la cooperación en el contexto latinoamericano será un objetivo estratégico para el Estado y allí deben intentar promoverse las políticas coordinadas de soberanía alimentaria.

Como se señaló en el apartado anterior la idea de buen vivir o vivir bien atraviesa las normas referidas y, por tanto, también se articula con el problema de la alimentación (ii). En la Constitución de la República del Ecuador dentro de los "Derechos del Buen Vivir" se afirma que *"Las personas y colectividades tienen derecho al acceso seguro y permanente a alimentos sanos, suficientes y nutritivos; preferentemente producidos a nivel local y en correspondencia con sus diversas identidades y tradiciones culturales. El Estado ecuatoriano promoverá la soberanía alimentaria"* (art. 14). Con ello se articula la idea de soberanía alimentaria con la de seguridad así como una manera de producir que acentúa el ámbito local y la recuperación de la diversidad y tradiciones culturales[9]. Esta recuperación

[9] Ello se refuerza en el art. 281 referido a la soberanía alimentaria que estima que *"La soberanía alimentaria constituye un objetivo estratégico y una obligación del Estado para garantizar que las personas, comunidades, pueblos y nacionalidades alcancen la autosuficiencia de alimentos sanos y culturalmente apropiado de for-*

también se encuentra en el caso de Bolivia que estima en el art. 24 de la mencionada Ley Marco de 2012 que estipula entre las orientaciones y bases para el Vivir Bien *"Inc. 5. Priorizar e incentivar la agricultura, pesca, ganadería familiar comunitaria y la agroecología, de acuerdo a la cosmovisión de cada pueblo indígena originario campesino y comunidad intercultural y afroboliviana, con un carácter diversificado, rotativo y ecológico, para la soberanía con seguridad alimentaria, buscando el diálogo de saberes"*.

A lo expuesto se suma que en la misma ley aparece la cuestión alimentaria con un grado importante de centralidad dado que se afirma que "Saber alimentarse" es medular, representa uno de los valores del vivir bien: *"Vivir Bien es alimentarse con calidad y productos naturales; saber combinar las comidas y bebidas adecuadas a partir de las estaciones del año, respetando los ayunos y ofrendando alimentos a la Madre Tierra"* (art. 6). Luego sigue un apartado expresamente destinado al "Saber alimentarse para vivir bien" (art. 13) y allí se alude a: el rol rector del Estado a través de sus políticas públicas y como garante del acceso a alimentos en cantidad y calidad; la prioridad del acceso a la tierra y al agua; el reconocimiento de la diversidad de maneras de producir y la protección de las variedades locales y nativas así como el fomento de las culturas y tradiciones alimentarias; la necesidad de implementar acciones para evitar la mercantilización del acceso a recursos genéticos y la privatización del agua; la priorización del abastecimiento interno; la revalorización de los sistemas de vida de los pequeños productores, naciones y pueblos indígena originario campesinos, comunidades interculturales y afrobolivianas; entre otros tópicos.

En relación a la intervención de la ciencia y tecnología en la modificación genética de cultivos en ambos Estados se visualizan claras referencias (iii). En el caso de Ecuador existe una prohibición constitucional en el art. 15 que determina *"Se prohíbe el desarrollo, producción, tenencia,*

---

ma permanente. Para ello, será responsabilidad del Estado: 1. Impulsar la producción, transformación agroalimentaria y pesquera de las pequeñas y medianas unidades de producción, comunitarias y de la economía social y solidaria... 6. Promover la preservación y recuperación de la agrobiodiversidad y de los saberes ancestrales vinculados a ella; así como el uso, la conservación e intercambio libre de semillas"

comercialización, importación, transporte, almacenamiento y uso de armas químicas, biológicas y nucleares, de contaminantes orgánicos persistentes altamente tóxicos, agroquímicos internacionalmente prohibidos, y las tecnologías y agentes biológicos experimentales nocivos y organismos genéticamente modificados perjudiciales para la salud humana o que atenten contra la soberanía alimentaria o los ecosistemas, así como la introducción de residuos nucleares y desechos tóxicos al territorio nacional" y en Bolivia la Ley de 2012 estima que debe eliminarse progresivamente los cultivos de organismos genéticamente modificados autorizados en el país (art. 24).

Por último, se determinan ciertas pautas sobre la distribución de tierras (iv). La Ley boliviana de 2012 alude a la necesidad de eliminar los latifundios así como la concentración de otros componentes de la Madre Tierra (art. 19, inc. 2). Luego se explicita la necesidad de una regulación y control de la extranjerización de la propiedad (art. 19, inc. 3) lo que puede ser conjugado con la promoción e incentivo de la agricultura familiar y periurbana en armonía y equilibro para el consumo familiar (art. 24, inc. 14). La Constitución ecuatoriana en similar sentido afirma que: *"Se prohíbe el latifundio y la concentración de la tierra, así como el acaparamiento o privatización del agua y sus fuentes"* (art. 282).

IV.- Reflexiones finales

Los documentos legales analizados se pueden presentar como la traducción jurídica de una búsqueda de maneras alternativas de vivir, que aquí se presenta como Buen Vivir o Vivir Bien en Ecuador y Bolivia respectivamente. Ello se conjuga con una concepción de naturaleza como sujeto de derecho que responde a cosmovisiones opacadas de pueblos indígenas y que puede dialogar con algunas elaboraciones de la ética ambiental en la búsqueda de alejarse del antropocentrismo moderno.

En este tránsito aparece un camino interesante en el que se ponen en discusión diferentes temas entre los cuales aparece el alimentario y se presentan varias de las problemáticas que se ligan a esta cuestión, desde el campo de negociaciones internacionales, hasta la existencia de latifundios, modificación genética de cultivos, modos de producción locales y recuperación de saberes en circulación, tradiciones y costumbres. Este conjunto de reglas que conforman pactos constitucionales recientes permiten también iniciar una apertura de diálogo con otras culturas, un diálogo que trate de aprender desde el intercambio entre lo diverso. Ello posee mucha riqueza en diferentes planos, entre éstos, el alimentario poniendo el acento en la necesidad de preservar los componentes de la Madre Tierra, de la Pachamama sin dejar de atender a las necesidades sociales.

Referencias bibliográficas

-AGUILAR, P.; FIUZA, P.; GLOZMAN, M.; GRONDONA, A.; HAIDAR, V.; PRYLUKA, P. (2013) *Hacia una genealogía del "Buen Vivir". Contribuciones desde el Análisis Materialista del Discurso.* Inédito.

-BERROS, M. Valeria (2013) *"El estatuto jurídico de la naturaleza en debate (meulen en el mundo del derecho)"* en Revista de Derecho Ambiental Nro 36. Abeledo Perrot. Buenos Aires.

-ESQUIVEL FRIAS, E. (2006) *Responsabilidad y sostenibilidad ecológica.* Tesis Doctoral. Departamento de Filosofía y Letras. Universidad Autónoma de Barcelona.

-HORTA, Oscar (2004) *Una tipología del especismo. Criterios distintivos y significación moral en Ética ecológica. Propuestas para una reorientación.* Riechmann, J (coord.) Montevideo: Editorial Nordan Comunidad.

-JEANGÈNE VILMER, JB. (2011) *L'éthique animale.* Paris. PUF.

-OST, François (2003) A natureza à margen da lei. A ecologia à prova do direito Lisboa. Instituto Piaget.

-SINGER, Peter (1999) *Liberación animal.* Madrid: Trotta.

Pour une démocratie socio-environnementale : cadre pour une plate-forme participative sur la « transition écologique » *

Catherine BADEL, Paul BARTH, Amandine BASSET, Olivier BASTIANELLI, Benjamin BENTI, Caroline BERGER, Chloé BERGER, Lily BICKERSTAFFE, Lucas BONNIN, Raphael BOURNHONESQUE, Baptiste BUSI, Victoire CARDOT, Sylvie CLAPPE, Nicolas DOLL, Mehdi DOUMANE, Ronan DUCHESNE, Valentine FEDERICO, Léa FRANÇOIS, Cassandre GAULTIER, Raphaël GAYET, Marine GROSLAMBERT, Noël HANNA KAZAKIAN, Louis JACOB, Agathe JASSON, Solène KNIPPING, Piero Lo MONACO, Paul MARCHAL, Mégane MISSAIRE, Jean-Louis PALGEN, Adèle PONTIES, Carine REY, Gaëtan RICHARD, Kévin SERMET, Victor VIRLOGEUX, Jérémie VIVIANI, Lelia YASSINE, Marie ZACHARY, Anthony ZIDANE ** et Ioan NEGRUTIU ***

Il se trouve autant de différence de nous à nous-mêmes que de nous à autrui.

Montaigne

Résumé

L'anthropocène triomphant actuel, avec ses forçages environnementaux et sociaux, est à l'origine de l'accélération des dégradations des milieux de vie sur Terre et de l'accentuation des tensions sociales et géopolitiques. Passer à un anthropocène de gestion équitable, informé et sobre vis-à-vis de toutes les ressources et dans tous les secteurs d'activité (*slow*

* Les auteurs remercient la Direction des Etudes de l'ENS et les responsables du Master BioSciences pour avoir soutenu la formation « Science et Société » et pour avoir encouragé le projet « transition écologique ». Nous avons bénéficié des conseils et de la collaboration de Jean-Pascal BASSINO, François COLLART DUTILLEUL, Edgar FERNANDEZ FERNANDEZ, Philippe FREMEAUX, Wojtek KALINOWSKY, Claire MALWE, Jean-Michel SALLES dans cette réflexion. Ioan NEGRUTIU remercie l'Institut Universitaire de France pour lui avoir permis de développer une interdisciplinarité alliant enseignement et recherche.

** Département de Biologie, Master BioSciences, ENS de Lyon.

*** Biologiste, Directeur de l'Institut Michel Serres, ENS de Lyon.

anthropocene), impose une analyse préalable sur l'ensemble des activités et des rapports humains. Cette transition dite « écologique », mais en réalité à la fois sociétale et écologique, est tout sauf un ajustement technique de secteurs dits prioritaires et technocratiques. Elle est avant tout culturelle, politique et philosophique au sens propre du terme. Elle est un horizon pour des trajectoires de développement humain, pour des constructions sociales et économiques, censées redéfinir socialement richesse, bien-être, travail etc. La dénomination « transition écologique » est largement véhiculée, mais ses bases conceptuelles ne sont pas entièrement acquises ni même élaborées. Dans ce contexte, les étudiants en première année de Master BioSciences à l'Ecole Normale Supérieure (ENS) de Lyon ont préparé une première étude analytique de ce changement radical et global de société pour mieux comprendre dans quelle société ils souhaitent vivre, en donnant du sens aux activités humaines présentes et à venir. Une trentaine de dossiers sur divers secteurs d'activités et acteurs de la société ont été produits et ont servi de support à cette synthèse. Plus largement, le but est de construire un socle conceptuel et une plate-forme de travail sur lesquels les questions de fond, mais aussi opérationnelles, peuvent être posées et étudiées en permanence. Cette démarche participative est ouverte à la collectivité sur le site http://institutmichelserres.ens-lyon.fr/.

Sommaire

1. Introduction – vous avez dit « anthropocène » ?

L'homme, espèce sociale et culturelle inédite, est capable de développer des technologies puissantes afin de transformer l'environnement, créant ainsi des conditions de travail et des modes de vie en constante évolution. Depuis la révolution industrielle, les activités humaines sont devenues le moteur prédominant des changements biosphériques. Elles constituent une sorte de force géophysique qui, pour certains, est définie par équivalence géologique comme l'époque appelée « anthropocène » et sa phase actuelle, la Grande Accélération (Steffen et al, 2011 ; Ellis *et al*, 2011). Pour d'autres - et par dérision -, la présence massive de déchets humains marque l'âge du « poubellien supérieur ». Des seuils considérés comme critiques ont été atteints, ou sont en passe de l'être, dans l'exploitation des ressources naturelles, mais également concernant le climat, les cycles de l'azote et du phosphore, la perte de biodiversité, le remaniement des paysages, l'acidification des océans et l'utilisation de l'eau douce (Rockström *et al*, 2009). Paradoxalement, la ressource humaine, en forte croissance, subit à son tour les effets des forçages mentionnés. Avec les travaux du Club de Rome et les observations satellitaires des années 1970, une prise de conscience du caractère fini des ressources planétaires a vu le jour, appelant à un changement de culture sociétale : « limiter, gérer, compenser », « *reduce, reuse, recycle* (les 3R) ». Cela nécessite une analyse systémique de nos modes de production, de consommation et de distribution des richesses, du sens même que nous donnons au développement économique et social, mais surtout un questionnement profond des rapports homme-nature. Cela représente donc une vaste entreprise, puisqu'il s'agit de s'attaquer aux contradictions sociales et écologiques de notre société afin : (1) d'intégrer les activités humaines dans les limites fonctionnelles de la biosphère ; (2) d'assurer une qualité de vie humaine durable, équitable et socialement juste. Les ingrédients, obstacles et enjeux qui contrarient ou favorisent ce changement profond, sont brièvement rapportés ci-après.

1.1 Concurrence débridée, compétitivité, productivisme – le carburant idéologique de la « Grande Accélération »

Le système capitaliste et son ordre social esquissé ci-dessus, est défini comme un régime économique ou un statut juridique « d'une société humaine caractérisée par la propriété privée des moyens de production et leur mise en œuvre par des travailleurs qui n'en sont pas propriétaires » (Larousse 2013). Dans ce cadre, la part des systèmes de crédit, l'évolution de la notion de profit, la globalisation et la généralisation du *low cost*, les dérégulations institutionnelles à grande échelle, ainsi que l'accélération des cycles d'innovations dans tous les domaines en contexte de croissance démographique, révèlent le rôle moteur que jouent dans la crise globale des facteurs comme la concurrence, la compétitivité, le productivisme et la surproduction, et ce que l'on appelle les avantages comparatifs (Schumpetter, 1939 ; Gadrey, 2013). Or, on est loin d'une concurrence parfaite qui intègre les coûts socio-environnementaux des activités économiques, ou d'une compétitivité définie comme « la capacité d'une nation à améliorer durablement le niveau de vie de ses habitants et à leur procurer un haut niveau d'emploi et de cohésion sociale » (Coutrot *et al*, 2012). Les conséquences directes sont connues : inégalités et pauvreté, aliénation par le travail, ainsi que chômage structurel.

On peut reprendre l'analyse autrement. La financiarisation de l'économie et sa concentration posent plusieurs problèmes de fond : confusion entre création de valeur et richesse, système de rente et compétition spéculative généralisés, hausse sans précédent de la productivité, elle-même source de surexploitation du travail, mais aussi des ressources naturelles (Gomez, 2013).

Pour tenter de sortir de ces difficultés, on peut observer comment la théorie économique fait appel aux processus de « concurrence » et de coopération à l'œuvre dans les écosystèmes (Tisdel, 2013). On retiendra que la compétition entre espèces et à l'intérieur de l'espèce opère pour les ressources essentielles et limitantes. Dans les systèmes biologiques, différents organismes entretiennent également des relations à bénéfice réciproque (les symbioses, par exemple) qui ont souvent évolué à partir de relations concurrentielles (parasitisme) et se sont révélées plus efficaces dans l'accès partagé aux ressources. L'asymétrie entre l'étude des relations de concurrence et de coopération en économie a peut-être conduit à des théories minimisant le rôle des mécanismes basés sur des associations à bénéfice réciproque. Il reste à analyser et à modéliser des stratégies et des solutions faisant appel à plus de solidarité et de coopération à tous les niveaux, en particulier au sujet de la gestion collective des ressources, en tant que biens communs (*v. section 2.6*).

1.2 Sémantique du changement : transition, transformation, conversion, révolution ?

Il est souhaitable que la remise en cause de nos modes de vie actuels se fasse d'une manière assumée, dans « un mélange de continuité et d'innovation » (Touraine, 2013). Transition, transformation et conversion sont des termes véhiculés actuellement avec la « transition écologique » comme formule prépondérante. La distinction de ces mots est essentielle (*Tableau 1*), puisqu'ils conditionnent à eux seuls la façon dont le changement doit être conçu et appréhendé.

	Conversion	**Transition**	**Transformation**
Définition	- Fait d'adopter une croyance religieuse que l'on considère comme la vérité. - Fait de changer sa conduite, son opinion pour une autre que l'on considère plus juste.	- Passage d'un état à un autre - Changement provisoire, menant à un nouveau stade	- Changer complètement - Donner une autre forme, une autre apparence
Mots / expressions reliés	- Changement d'avis - Conversion religieuse - Rendre plus simple et élémentaire	- Chose qui suit une autre - Chacun des états successifs d'une chose	- Donner une propriété nouvelle - Faire devenir autre

Tableau 1. Comparaison des termes « conversion », « transition » et « transformation » (recherches effectuées à partir du dictionnaire en ligne *sensagent.com*).

Ainsi, le changement devrait prendre en compte les contextes politiques, culturels et géographiques existants (on dit en biologie que tout processus est historiquement informé). Une composante « expérimentale » forte est donc à prévoir (sous forme d'essai-erreur), pour permettre l'apparition d'une diversité d'innovations et de solutions adaptées et adaptatives, suivie ou non de leur rétention sociétale. Ceci est d'autant plus probable que le changement se fera dans un cadre co-évolutionniste (Foxon, 2011) dans lequel écosystèmes, technologies, institutions, stratégies économiques et pratiques des usagers s'agenceront en permanence. La mise en cohérence des innovations à tous ces niveaux représente un filtre puissant, reliant progressivement des ensembles d'éléments hétérogènes dans de nouvelles configurations. Cette co-construction et sa progressivité semblent favoriser l'idée d'un processus de transition permettant de mieux comprendre la direction vers laquelle le changement s'opèrera.

Pour certains, cette perception n'est pas acceptable. Par exemple, pour Sandra Laugier, philosophe responsable de l'interdisciplinarité au CNRS, le fait d'envisager le passage d'un état stable à un autre est une « grave erreur » (Libération, juin 2013). Le changement devrait plutôt se faire dans un contexte de *transformation*. On donnerait ainsi une toute nouvelle forme au système actuel. Selon Patrick Viveret, la transformation est une mutation profonde, une totale métamorphose (Libération, septembre 2013). Jean-Philippe Magnen (2011) parle d'une nécessaire refonte globale et en profondeur de l'économie, qui passera certes par la conversion de certains secteurs, mais aussi et surtout par l'invention de nouveaux secteurs. L'économiste Nicholas Stern évoque, quant à lui, une mutation industrielle profonde pour le développement d'une économie à faible intensité carbone (Stern, 2007). Pour tous, le système actuel doit nécessairement être abandonné pour qu'un nouveau puisse émerger. Plus classiquement, la crise et le changement qu'elle appelle ne sont-ils pas du registre d'un renversement séculaire, d'une « démolition et reconstruction structurelles » (Braudel, 1979) ? Dans la même veine, Westley et coll. (2011) considèrent que des profondes transformations sont nécessaires et « *require radical, systemic shifts in deeply held values and beliefs, patterns of social behavior* (and technological innovation), *and multi-level governance and management regimes* ».

Il faut également noter le déroulement des « États Généraux de la Transformation Citoyenne » en Octobre 2013 et la mise en relation des plates-formes collaboratives. Parmi elles se trouve « Le Pacte Civique », lancé en 2011 pour « amorcer et accompagner dans la durée les transformations collectives et individuelles requises par les crises, dérives et fractures qui touchent notre société et notre démocratie » (http://www.pacte-civique.org/MarchE).

Pour mieux asseoir les analyses et les controverses futures sur la sémantique du changement, il est souhaitable d'intégrer les questions des rapports homme-nature afin de mieux comprendre les processus mis en œuvre.

1.3 Les rapports homme-nature comme humanisme contractuel et responsable

Les considérations ci-dessus nous incitent à mieux vouloir comprendre comment les sociétés s'inscrivent dans la nature, comment elles transforment les milieux pour les rendre plus habitables et pour qu'ils produisent plus de services. Les sociétés prélèvent les ressources pour les intégrer dans les processus qui sous-tendent leur fonctionnement. Les problèmes environnementaux sont à la fois économiques, sociaux et politiques. Descola (2011) considère que la nature est une production sociale et que l'opposition nature/culture n'est qu'une pure convention, déterminant ainsi notre perception du monde. Pour dépasser ce dualisme dans un contexte de crises multiples (dont celles de la démocratie représentative et de la citoyenneté), Juliette Grange (2012) propose une révolution écologique, un humanisme dont l'objectif est de faire des biens communs fondamentaux un Bien public dans le cadre d'une *Res publica* nationale, européenne, voire mondiale. Elle dit, « ce qui fait la valeur de l'environnement n'est pas seulement ce qu'il contient – la nature comme un ensemble de ressources, mais aussi les possibilités qu'il offre aux humains ». L'écologie et l'environnement font donc directement partie du contrat social, car il existe une nouvelle espèce de « nature » dépendante de l'humanité (créée par l'agriculture et l'industrie) par laquelle l'empreinte écologique et la justice sociale sont étroitement liées. Il s'agit de ne pas « sanctuariser la Nature, mais de considérer comme Bien premier des éléments garantissant les conditions d'une vie réellement humaine » ; c'est-à-dire les ressources, qu'il est de notre intérêt de préserver. En même temps, accéder à une forme de plénitude demande de bien comprendre et de hiérarchiser les besoins humains (Maslow, 2006) (v. *section 3.2*). C'est dans ce sens que l'éthique environnementale s'efforce de démontrer que les entités naturelles (communautés biotiques et écosystèmes) sont des « valeurs intrinsèques » (Larrère, 2013).

2. Faire rentrer l'économie dans les bio- et socio-sphères.

La société de consommation occidentale, dont l'essor de ses flux quantitatifs affecte tous les secteurs d'activités humaines, apparaît à travers notre regard comme une brève parenthèse dans notre évolution.

2.1 Consommation, forçages socio-écosystémiques, enjeux démographiques

La surconsommation, tout comme le ressenti d'un « droit naturel à l'abondance », et un mélange de volonté, de différentiation sociale, de rivalité mimétique et de libération individuelle (Baudrillard, 1970 ; Reich, 2007), sont à l'origine d'une aliénation par le travail, d'inégalités accrues et d'une dégradation des rapports sociaux.

Actuellement, 38 % de la production primaire planétaire sont utilisés par les activités et les besoins de 7 milliards d'êtres humains. Parmi les 62 % restants, seulement 10 % sont exploitables, car la régénération et la résilience des fonctions et services écosystémiques, dont fait partie la diversité biologique, consomment au moins la moitié de cette production primaire (Running, 2102 ; Barnosky *et al*, 2012). Plus de 8 milliards d'habitants sur la planète sont attendus d'ici 2030, ce qui aura pour conséquence d'augmenter les besoins en eau et en nourriture de 35 et 40 % respectivement (Global Trends 2012, www.dni.gov/nic/globaltrends). En conséquence, satisfaire les besoins vitaux des générations actuelles et à venir, tout en préservant les fonctions et les services des écosystèmes, semble irréalisable si les modèles de développement économique restent inchangés. Les pays les plus pauvres seront les premiers touchés par cette diminution des ressources alimentaires et en eau. En 2050, il est prévu que même les pays développés ne seront plus à l'abri de pénuries (Brown, 2014). Ainsi, les tensions pour l'utilisation des ressources naturelles seront plus que jamais exacerbées (par exemple, les conflits liés à l'eau et l'accaparement des terres ; Adams *et al*, 2003).

Le fait que la Terre ne puisse supporter l'augmentation de la consommation par habitant couplée à la croissance démographique fait aujourd'hui consensus. Tant que nous sommes dans une situation de dépassement écologique, la Terre peut être considérée comme surpeuplée (Brown, 2008). La maîtrise de la démographie, de la consommation et du réajustement des ressources sont donc des enjeux majeurs pour la transition écologique. L'agencement de nos villes, de nos modes de production d'énergies, de nourriture etc., doivent être repensés pour arriver à une consommation globale ne dépassant pas les seuils d'autosuffisance (v. *section 2.6*).

Les Nations Unies ont rappelé, lors de la conférence de Copenhague en 2009, qu'il était primordial de réduire la population de manière importante pour faire face à ces multiples enjeux. Mais, à notre avis, il faudra surtout lutter contre les inégalités, qu'elles soient alimentaires, sanitaires, sociales ou écologiques.

2.2 Croissance versus décroissance, les modèles fiables manquent toujours

La croissance est la variation positive de la production de biens et de services marchands dans une économie sur une période donnée (Clerc, 2013). Les modèles économiques qui utilisent de manière intensive les ressources physiques doivent être_repensés dans le sens d'un découplage en termes de production et de consommation. Ce découplage se décline chez les experts soit par la croissance durable (ou « verte »), soit par la décroissance. Dans les deux cas, des investissements publics et privés importants sont nécessaires à court terme pour restructurer l'économie et les infrastructures en particulier (le rapport Stern préconise d'utiliser 2 % du PIB annuellement à cet effet ; Stern 2007).

La croissance. La révolution industrielle verte reste un pari, car (1) son potentiel de croissance (bâtiments intelligents, transports et urbanisme, services, etc.) est considéré comme faible à court terme dans les pays développés et (2) la création nette d'emplois est jugée peu robuste à long terme (Clerc, 2013 ; Frémeaux et Lalucq, 2013 ; Tubiana, 2013). Par ailleurs, il ne faut pas oublier que les conditions sont très variables entre les pays en termes de base énergétique, d'empreinte environnementale, ainsi que dans la nature et les objectifs du contrat social à mettre en place. L'étude prospective concernant l'adoption du « facteur 4 » dans la diminution des émissions de gaz à effet de serre en France d'ici 2050 illustre la difficulté de la tâche (CLIP, 2012). Sur les cinq scénarios analysant les modes de vie et les comportements individuels associés (consumérisme vert, individu augmenté, dualité et sobriétés plurielles, écocitoyenneté, âge de la connaissance), aucun n'arrive à atteindre pleinement cet objectif lorsque l'on vise l'accès à une qualité de vie pour tous et une cohésion sociale satisfaisante, tout en préservant les services fondamentaux des écosystèmes.

La décroissance, concept politique, économique et social, récuse une croissance infinie sur une planète aux ressources finies. Les conséquences sociales et économiques de la décroissance sont à prendre en charge par les pouvoirs publics (Callenbach, 2011) : modes de production très économes en matières premières, réduction importante de la consommation et des inégalités sociales, passage d'une société de l'accumulation à une société de l'usage, etc. Le concept de la décroissance reste à élaborer et à argumenter davantage sur l'ensemble des processus socio-écosystémiques. La recherche d'une vision économique inspirée par des considérations liées aux fonctions et mécanismes performants à l'œuvre dans les écosystèmes (compétition, efficacité des ressources et efficacité énergétique, processus évolutifs coopératifs, etc) est une voie à privilégier (v. *section 1.1*). Dans cette recherche, le rôle des indicateurs socio-environnementaux et l'importance capitale de la gestion publique des *big data* (v. *section 2.4*) ne peuvent qu'être soulignés.

Dans l'ensemble, le changement de modèle de production d'une économie linéaire (matières premières – produits – déchets) à une économie circulaire s'impose, car il peut avoir un impact considérable sur le développement. Il s'agit d'instaurer un premier cercle vertueux (Rifkin, 2013 ; Guichardaz, 2013). L'Etat doit jouer un rôle majeur de par ses capacités de financement et d'investissement, de législation, d'infrastructures et de pédagogie. Les acteurs locaux doivent impérativement compléter et appuyer cette initiative, le cœur du concept d'économie circulaire reposant sur des réseaux locaux, innovants et efficaces, notamment par rapport aux problèmes d'externalités négatives (v. *section 3.3*).

Enfin, il faut rappeler que beaucoup d'activités humaines se déroulent en dehors des marchés (Dasgupta, 2010) et que l'espace de la marchandise et de la marchandisation peur être borné. Ensemble, ces deux aspects changent également la perception et le design du développement.

2.3 Pour la dignité, par le travail, le vivre ensemble

La production économique est gérée et organisée par le monde du travail : réorienter la production, c'est repenser le travail (par exemple, le sens même du travail, la part des formes d'économie sociale et solidaire) ou le réorienter (c'est-à-dire créer de nouveaux emplois dans des secteurs clefs de la transition ou procéder à la reconversion des emplois déjà existants). En effet, la transition écologique nécessite une adaptation massive de divers secteurs phares (Renner *et al*, 2008), tels que l'agriculture et l'agro-alimentaire, l'eau, la valorisation des déchets, les énergies renouvelables ou encore l'efficacité énergétique. Pour mieux anticiper les compétences requises et les besoins en formation (Pôle Rhone-Alpes, 2013), l'importance de l'information et des jeux de données est cruciale, notamment dans l'évaluation de la création nette d'emplois (c'est-à-dire la création soustraite à la destruction) dans un secteur donné et l'évaluation des effets sur d'autres secteurs (OIT, 2012).

Repenser le travail signifie aussi promouvoir la démarche du *care* : développer les liens sociaux malmenés, restaurer la dignité et la capacité d'agir des individus, la recherche d'un art de vivre ensemble, introduire du sensible et le souci d'autrui (Brugère 2010 ; Manifeste convivialiste, 2013). L'Economie Sociale et Solidaire (ESS) s'attache à intégrer ces dimensions. Son importance croissante s'est traduite par la création en 2012 d'une délégation du ministère de l'Economie et des Finances spécifiquement dédiée à ce domaine et par un projet de Loi cadre. L'ESS est constituée de l'Economie Sociale, regroupant les associations, mutuelles, coopératives et fondations, dont le but est de satisfaire un objet social défini par les adhérents, ainsi que de l'Economie Solidaire qui rassemble des organisations à forte utilité sociale et de services de proximité, comme les organisations caritatives et humanitaires ou les associations d'aide et de soin à la personne. Ces deux économies ne sont pas mutuellement exclusives, la plupart des structures se situent dans les deux catégories (Frémeaux, 2013).

2.4 Les incontournables Big Data

Les *big data* correspondent aux jeux de données colossaux générés ces dernières années et dont la quantité croît de façon exponentielle. Ils sont issus de notre usage d'Internet (par exemple, l'ensemble des contenus engendrés sur les réseaux sociaux et qui sont donc des données personnelles), par les services publics (par exemple, l'ensemble des données cartographiques d'un pays) ou encore par la communauté scientifique (notamment les données issues des techniques de séquençage de nouvelle génération). Il s'écoule autant d'informations en une heure aujourd'hui que durant toute l'année 2000. Et cela a un coût : Internet est en passe de franchir la barre symbolique des 10 % de demande mondiale en énergie (de Ravignan, 2013) et le stockage de ces données nécessite leur concentration dans des *data centres* inégalement répartis dans le monde. En même temps, on atteint actuellement des limites méthodologiques dans les capacités à explorer, exploiter et visualiser ces quantités d'informations. Néanmoins, le système de *big data* possède une capacité de transformation de nos sociétés hors du commun (Belliard, 2013) au niveau de l'économie et la productivité économique, de la gestion politique ou des innovations socio-environnementales. Par exemple, il est à l'origine d'outils permettant aux décideurs d'améliorer les flux matériels et monétaires en temps réel afin de mieux gérer et d'adapter les décisions aux territoires et aux habitants. Dans le cadre des projets Rifkin, le « cyberespace » favorise le développement d'immenses réseaux et génère de nombreux flux d'informations. Ces derniers permettent l'optimisation de la productivité des entreprises, de l'observation des comportements (des consommateurs comme des salariés), et de l'amélioration de notre impact environnemental en gérant autrement notre consommation d'énergie (le Master Plan dans la région Nord-Pas de Calais). Pour les plus idéalistes, ces flux iront jusqu'à permettre l'évolution vers une « civilisation empathique » et la libération vis-à-vis du monopole des entreprises dominantes (c'est le cas pour les imprimantes 3D, par exemple ; Rifkin, 2013 ; http://www.latroisiemerevolutionindustrielle ennordpasdecalais.fr/)

Cependant, le revers de la médaille du système des *big data* révèle plusieurs problèmes qui sont loin d'être résolus : la propriété, l'appropriation et l'usage des données (Guillaud, 2013), la complexité de la réglementation et son évolution, ainsi que les impacts environnementaux. Dans le monde scientifique, les *big data* représentent par exemple une « jungle à défricher » (Demarthon, 2012).

2.5 La gouvernance – redondances, lenteurs et casse-têtes institutionnels

Le passage à un autre modèle de société ne peut se faire sans des institutions porteuses de valeurs politiques, sociales et culturelles qui structurent les relations au sein des sociétés et qui définissent un but, un cadre, des stratégies et des outils pour leur réalisation. Les défis sont universels (l'accès équitable aux ressources, notamment énergétiques, la pauvreté, etc ; Ravillon, 2007 ; Shah, 2013), mais les instruments pour réaliser les changements peuvent être très différents. La « gouvernance de la transition » est également censée réunir des organisations expertes et des citoyens dans des configurations adaptées aux questions en débats et aux actions à mettre en place. Sur la base de la diversité des situations sociétales à laquelle nous serons confrontés, une co-occurence de processus de transition – transformation – conversion est envisageable (v. *section 1.2*). L'inventaire non exhaustif des programmes, initiatives et activités en cours ci-après permettrait de les apprécier dans leur diversité.

En ce qui concerne la gouvernance mondiale, les Nations Unies agissent pour une convergence des niveaux de développement de tous les pays. Le sommet de la Terre à Rio en Juin 2012 a énoncé un grand nombre d'engagements, tels que la mise en place d'une gouvernance internationale de l'environnement (Article 88) renforçant le Programme des Nations Unies pour l'Environnement (PNUE) en terme d'autorité mondiale, mais aussi l'établissement d'une gouvernance mondiale du développement durable (Article 84) et l'instauration d'un financement du développement durable par une Stratégie de Financement facilitant la mobilisation des ressources et leur bon usage (article 255) (http://www.uncsd2012.org/thefuturewewant.html).

En parallèle, les huit Objectifs du Millénaire pour le Développement ont été adoptés en 2000 avec pour ambition d'être atteints en 2015. Ces objectifs visent à : (1) réduire l'extrême pauvreté et la faim, (2) assurer l'éducation primaire pour tous, (3) promouvoir l'égalité et l'autonomisation des femmes, (4) réduire la mortalité infantile, (5) améliorer la santé maternelle, (6) combattre les maladies, (7) assurer un environnement humain durable, et (8) mettre en place un partenariat mondial pour le développement. Le rapport 2012 souligne les principales difficultés dans la réalisation de ces objectifs, dont les plus préoccupants restent la faim et la pauvreté dans le monde (http://www.un.org/en/development/desa/publications/mdg-report-2012.html).

La Conférence environnementale (Feuille de Route, 2012) qui s'est déroulée en France en Septembre 2013 est un exemple intéressant. Elle a réuni un grand nombre d'acteurs : représentants d'ONG environnementales, associations, organisations syndicales, employeurs, collectivités, ainsi que des parlementaires. Elle a produit une feuille de route pour la transition écologique qui fixe le programme de travail du Gouvernement. Dans un but de coordination, une Agence nationale de la biodiversité et un Conseil national de la transition ont été créés. Le problème majeur des propositions qui ont été annoncées est la mise en application et la coopération de toutes les parties. De plus, les calendriers de mise en place des mesures liées à l'environnement s'étalent parfois sur plusieurs décennies et ne reflètent pas l'urgence de la situation.

Au niveau local, les plans climat-énergie territoriaux (PCET ; http://www.pcet-ademe.fr) et les Agendas 21 de 1992 (http://www.un.org/french/ga/special/sids/agenda21/) décrivent les secteurs où le développement durable est applicable dans le cadre des collectivités territoriales. L'Agenda 21 formule ainsi des recommandations au sujet de la pauvreté, la santé, la pollution, le logement, la gestion des mers, des forêts et des montagnes, la gestion de l'agriculture, des déchets, etc. Parallèlement à ce plan d'action, une déclaration sur l'environnement et le développement énumère vingt-sept principes à suivre pour mettre en œuvre l'Agenda 21. Cette démocratie de construction dans la prise de décisions implique tous les types d'acteurs locaux dans une démarche de diagnostic et de délibération collective.

En recoupant l'ensemble de ces informations, il apparaît que les concertations internationales sur les objectifs/approches au niveau national restent fortement problématiques. De même, les initiatives permettant d'envisager une répartition équitable des ressources mondiales représentent sans doute la difficulté majeure dans la concrétisation des Objectifs du Millénaire. On peut donc légitimement s'interroger sur la volonté et la capacité réelles des institutions à gérer les crises actuelles et à préparer la transition.

2.6 Alertes des scientifiques et changement du statut des ressources

La recherche scientifique aide à une meilleure compréhension des phénomènes et processus œuvrant dans la société et l'environnement. On estime par exemple que 60 % des services des écosystèmes sont en train d'être dégradés ou sont utilisés de manière non durable (Speidel *et al*, 2009). En d'autres termes, les ressources sont plus rapidement consommées que la Terre ne les régénère : l'homme utilise le « capital » de la nature et pas seulement ses « intérêts ». En effet, la Terre a besoin d'un an et quatre mois pour régénérer notre consommation annuelle (Global Footprint Network data, 2008). Il en résulte une raréfaction de certaines ressources naturelles, comme par exemple les terres cultivables ou l'eau. Selon les estimations des Nations Unies de 2011 (Overshoot Index, 2011), tandis que certains pays comme le Gabon ont une autosuffisance[1] supérieure à 1 500 %, d'autres comme le Koweït, le Japon, l'Union européenne ou les Etats-Unis atteignent respectivement seulement 4,4 %, 14,2 %, 47,6 % et 53,7 % (et c'est le cas de la majorité des pays).

Ces analyses des changements environnementaux et écosystémiques ont donné aux scientifiques les arguments permettant d'anticiper des évolutions probables vers un monde plus pauvre en écosystèmes et en biodiversité, où la nourriture, la qualité de l'eau, les conditions sanitaires, et donc les conditions de vie seraient limitantes pour une humanité en croissance démographique. Le *Stockholm Memorandum* en 2011 (co-signé par une vingtaine de Prix Nobel) et le *Scientific Consensus on Maintaining Humanity's Life Support Systems in the 21st Century* en 2013 font appel à l'ensemble de la communauté internationale pour agir et traiter d'une manière coordonnée les cinq défis globaux suivants : (1) le dérèglement climatique, (2) la perte de diversité écosystémique et l'extinction accélérée d'espèces, (3) la pollution, (4) la croissance démographique et (5) la surconsommation des ressources. L'idée de la nécessité d'une approche intégrée est à retenir. Parmi les mesures avancées, on trouve notamment l'éducation et l'allocation équitables des ressources. Ce genre de consen-

---

[1] L'autosuffisance est « le rapport entre la surface du pays et la surface nécessaire pour subvenir à la consommation de ses habitants, calculée à partir de l'empreinte écologique des habitants ». Elle indique le seuil de régénération et de résilience des systèmes ressources.

sus permettrait à terme une gestion mondiale des ressources (Stiglitz, 2010).

L'égalité des ressources. Pour permettre à chacun de subvenir à ses besoins vitaux, il apparaît donc nécessaire de définir les ressources comme des biens communs, « aussi inaliénables et fondamentaux que nos droits et nos libertés » (Grange, 2012). Ces biens communs incluraient l'eau, l'air, le sous-sol, la biodiversité, mais aussi les lieux de vie non pollués, la sécurité sanitaire, les savoirs, la culture et les différentes formes de socialité. En partant de là, la liberté politique doit inclure la libre disposition des biens fondamentaux communs (considérés comme un Bien premier, Bien public) : la définition d'un bien commun est comprise « non comme un donné naturel, mais comme un idéal politique ». Prenons l'exemple de l'alimentation. La nourriture, de ressource locale elle est devenue marchandise privée trans-nationale. Il est temps de repenser son statut : un bien commun global (Vivero Pol, 2013)[2].

Plus généralement et en pratique, la force publique ne serait pas le gérant des biens communs, mais le garant de leur statut non appropriable et de leur gestion durable et équitable. En cela, référence est faite aux travaux de John Rawls et Amartia Sen : les biens fondamentaux, en tant que Bien public, doivent faire l'objet de législations, de revendications et de réflexions dans un cadre politique (v. *section 3.2*). Des comptes devront être rendus aux citoyens sur le choix des dépenses publiques, basé sur un effet redistributif incluant une protection sociale et une éducation de qualité. Cela ouvre la voie à une éthique de la redistribution.

3. Recadrage de la transition par les ressources, dénominateur socio-écosystémique de base

L'économie des ressources naturelles a toujours été au centre des préoccupations des économistes et tient une place centrale dans la transition écologique. L'enjeu de la préservation des ressources renouvelables et non-renouvelables est double, car il s'agit de concilier à la fois la qualité de vie des citoyens et la résilience des écosystèmes comme une assurance par rapport au présent et aux générations futures.

---

[2] V. *Infra*, Jose Luis VIVERO POL, "The commons-based international Food Treaty: A legal architecture to sustain a fair and sustainable food transition", p. 177 et ss.

3.1 Approche intégrée réunissant secteurs et acteurs

La gestion des ressources doit être envisagée à court, moyen et long termes. Il est clair que la transition sociétale et écologique doit embrasser tous les secteurs et activités humaines à la fois. Les mesures correspondantes concernent l'ensemble des acteurs : citoyens, industries exploitantes, pouvoirs politiques nationaux (ministères chargés de l'environnement et du développement durable) ou internationaux (OPEP, G20), organisations non gouvernementales de protection de l'environnement (Greenpeace, WWF), organisations intergouvernementales de protection de la santé humaine (FAO, OMS, CCNUCC) et de l'environnement (PNUE). Les actions entreprises par l'ensemble de ces acteurs sont différentes en fonction des ressources concernées, des territoires et de leur gouvernance, etc.

La démarche mettant l'accent sur les ressources permet d'intégrer tous les secteurs d'activités humaines pour rendre la transition cohérente. Les Conférences environnementales organisées en France en 2012 et 2013 (Feuille de Route, 2012) ne semblent pas avoir pris la mesure de la nécessité d'une démarche globale et intégrative. Leur organisation sous forme de tables rondes a traité cinq thèmes différents : la préparation du débat national sur la transition écologique, la reconquête de la biodiversité en France, la prévention des risques sanitaires environnementaux, le financement de la transition et de la fiscalité écologique, et l'amélioration de la gouvernance environnementale. La feuille de route a largement centré les objectifs sur la transition énergétique (v. aussi Schmid, 2013).

Pour illustrer notre démarche doublement intégrative sur les ressources naturelles, trois exemples ont été retenus dans le registre du droit, de l'intelligence territoriale et de la finance.

3.2 Le droit, charpente de la transition

La transition écologique pose la question de la gouvernance des ressources naturelles. Par le passé, leur gouvernance et leur distribution ont toujours contribué à mieux asseoir un contrôle politique et économique asymétrique. Entre acteurs publics, privés et communautaires, la position dominante des marchés se traduit aujourd'hui par la marchandisation de la gouvernance (avec des pratiques de privatisation et de commodification des ressources), illustration de l'organisation actuelle de l'économie globale (Maganda et Petit, 2012). La gouvernance est comprise ici comme « un réseau décisionnel basé sur une variété d'instruments et d'acteurs agissant à des multiples niveaux, ayant des stratégies et des buts différents, mais devant trouver des compromis assurant un développement basé sur une gestion soutenable et socialement équitable des ressources ». Ces compromis entre acteurs s'adressent à des questions de droits de propriété, droits de l'homme et droit de l'environnement. "*All persons have the right to a secure, healthy and ecologically sound environment. This right and other human rights, including civil, cultural, economic, political and social rights, are universal, interdependent and indivisible*" (1994, http://www1.umn.edu/humanrts/instree/1994-dec.htm). Dans cet ensemble de droits universels et naturels, le droit à la propriété reste paradoxal, dans le sens où il est le moins universel de tous, car tous les humains ne sont pas égaux devant (le droit à) la propriété, et où les rapports de force et les structures légales donnent souvent avantage à ce dernier au détriment des autres (Maganda et Petit, 2012).

Les questions que posent la transition sont celles (1) de la reconfiguration institutionnelle pour mieux assurer la légitimité, la transparence, l'équité et la justice dans l'accès aux ressources, (2) de l'évaluation objective des besoins vitaux par rapport à ceux jugés dispensables (superflus) en situation d'accès équitable (assez bien identifiés pour l'alimentation, la santé et l'hygiène, l'éducation ; Costanza *et al*, 2007 ; v. aussi Maslow, 2006) et (3) d'une limite à l'usage du droit à la propriété privée pour mieux gérer les communs au bénéfice des capacités écosystémiques de support de la vie. L'analyse d'Edgar Fernandez et Claire Malwé[3] indique que nous disposons de principes, d'outils et de dispositifs nous permettant de répondre à ces questions, mais que l'ensemble manque de cohérence et que leur mise en application est déficiente.

---

[3] V. *Supra* E. FERNANDEZ FERNANDEZ, C. MALWE et I. NEGRUTIU, « Définitions des ressources naturelles et implications pour la démarche juridique », *in* F. COLLART DUTILLEUL (dir), T. BREGER (coord.), *Penser une démocratie alimentaire* vol. 2, Edicion Inida, San José, 2014, p. 71 et ss.

3.3 Intelligence territoriale: où es-tu ?

La transition nécessite des politiques territoriales assurant une cohérence aux niveaux local et global. Cette « intelligence territoriale » correspond aux processus permettant « d'acquérir une meilleure connaissance du territoire », « d'agir de façon pertinente et efficiente », de « projeter, définir, animer et évaluer les politiques et les actions de développement territorial durable » et « de mieux maîtriser son développement » (http://www.collaboratif-info.fr/chronique/quest-ce-que-lintelligence-territoriale). Il est à noter que « l'appropriation des technologies de l'information et de la communication, et de l'information elle-même, est une étape indispensable ». Or, ce n'est pas ce que l'on observe : les villes autant que les campagnes développent des interactions globales, mondiales et généralisées plutôt que ciblées et orientées au niveau régional ou local (Seitzinger *et al*, 2012). De cette réorientation de l'utilisation territoriale découlent alors des problèmes environnementaux, sociaux ou économiques (Seto *et al*, 2011), mais aussi géopolitiques. L'urbanisation accélérée du monde, doublée par la pauvreté (Ravillon, 2007), apparaît plutôt comme une « bidonvillisation » du monde. Force est de constater que la dimension territoriale de la transition pose l'un des problèmes les plus critiques au développement durable, tel un talon d'Achille.

3.4 Aspects financiers: le crédit plutôt que l'impôt

Afin d'engager des changements stratégiques, l'argent recouvre un potentiel d'initiative et de déploiement quasi absolu, permettant d'agir sur des laps de temps très courts. En effet, il peut (ré)orienter la part des richesses crées à partir du capital économique, humain, social ou naturel. Les aspects financiers passent, par exemple, par :

- la fiscalité écologique qui permet d'intégrer aux marchés financiers les externalités négatives (dont la pollution), modifiant ainsi les comportements les plus polluants au profit d'alternatives ayant une empreinte environnementale plus faible ;
- la réforme des aides publiques qui favorisent les comportements polluants. Dans un rapport publié en 2012, le Centre d'Analyse stratégique listait les « aides publiques dommageables à la biodiversité » : celles favorisant la destruction et la dégradation des habitats, la su-

rexploitation des ressources naturelles, la pollution, ou l'introduction d'espèces invasives (http://www.strategie.gouv.fr/content/rapport-les-aides-publiques-dommageables-la-biodiversitéles-ressources).

- l'épargne et des actifs boursiers, dispositifs incitatifs sur des critères non-financiers pour les investisseurs dans le financement de projets à faible empreinte carbone ou en direction des entreprises ayant une meilleure performance environnementale.

Des architectures éco-financières centrées sur la transition ont été imaginées et alimentent concepts et solutions pratiques depuis quelques années (NEF, 2009).

3.5 D'autres secteurs en bref

L'agriculture (doublement verte, « agro-ruralisée », « écologiquement intensive », « à haute qualité environnementale ») doit conjuguer performances économiques, sociales et environnementales tout en assurant une sécurité et une démocratie alimentaire crédiblement durables. Dans le domaine de la santé publique se posent des questions sur l'hôpital-entreprise, la prévention, l'éducation et l'égalité d'accès aux soins pour tous. L'éducation et la culture ont été la toile de fond de cette analyse et engagent des valeurs et des identités, la conscience collective et les changements de mentalités, avec des chartes (Belgrade, 1975) et traités (Tbilisi en 1977) oubliés. L'impératif est de donner tout son sens à une éducation environnementale qui se cherche encore (Boyes et Stanisstreet, 2012 ; Rickinson, 2001). *Last but not least*, la transition énergétique qui occupe tous les esprits (Schmid, 2013) peut se résumer au dilemme suivant : *Energy is the one and only real limiting factor in the long run, because given enough energy there will always be enough natural non-energy resources extractable from the crust of the Earth* (Neumayer, 2000). En théorie, forcément.

4. Conclusion – une transition « toutes ressources » - centrée

Quels sont les changements majeurs à envisager afin de pouvoir assurer un cadre politique environnemental et sociétal cohérent permettant d'amorcer les transitions, transformations ou conversions analysées dans ce travail ?

Soixante propositions rassemblées par « Alternatives Economiques » (*Et si on changeait tout*, 2011) constituent une première base de réflexion et ont le mérite de pouvoir s'inscrire dans divers contextes socio-politiques, en suivant des priorités identifiées et des calendriers adaptés. Nous avons voulu compléter ce tableau. Les grands défis identifiés ici comprennent la réduction des inégalités sociales et écologiques, la ré-allocation et l'accès aux ressources, la transparence de l'information et des données, la démographie, la réappropriation du local et du collectif, l'éducation par et pour l'esprit critique, civique et écologique.

Les caractéristiques constitutives des écosystèmes éclairent les limites des activités humaines, en particulier lorsque les théories économiques dominantes, encore inspirées par des analogies mécanicistes (systèmes clos, processus réversibles, pas de temps courts, accumulation infinie de capital), tentent de les ignorer. A cela, René Passet (et depuis une vingtaine d'année, l'économie écologique) oppose la « bioéconomie » ou ses variantes, parfaitement insérée dans la biosphère, dans le sens où « les organisations économiques doivent en respecter les lois et les mécanismes régulateurs, en particulier les rythmes de reconstitution des ressources renouvelables » (http://biosphere.blog.lemonde.fr/2010/10/23/ladieu-a-la-croissance/).

Dans cet esprit, nous avons favorisé ici les approches visant l'interdépendance entre les systèmes économiques, politiques et sociaux, ainsi que le contexte spécifique environnemental, culturel et éthique. La problématique des ressources est apparue comme un élément transversal particulièrement unificateur et qu'il faut sans doute repenser en termes de Bien public : un redoutable défi.

La question qui divise aujourd'hui est la suivante : à terme, les sociétés sont-elles « condamnées » à vivre sur une base de ressources exclusivement renouvelables ? Ce nouveau défi est énorme et soulève des interrogations sur la capacité des options exclusives en termes d'énergies renouvelables à offrir un autre choix que la sobriété volontaire comme mode de vie (Aries, 2011).

Cette synthèse sur les processus de transition remet donc en question l'accès inégal aux moyens d'existence et une certaine idée de la liberté de choix consumériste, en échange d'une promesse de qualité de vie à imaginer (ou à découvrir) et de « vivabilité » pour tous. La co-construction de la transition, dans le sens de volonté politique et consensus social, apparaît comme la seule démarche et la seule pédagogie de l'acceptation sociale du changement. La plate-forme participative proposée ici a été imaginée dans ce but précis : élaborer dans des territoires-test, avec des acteurs locaux et en temps réel, les trajectoires de leur transition.

Références

ADAMS W.M. *et al*, 2003, "Managing Tragedies: Understanding Conflict over Common Pool Resources", *Science* 302, 1915-1917.

ARIÈS P., *La simplicité volontaire contre le mythe de l'abondance*, La Découverte, 2010, 301 p.

BAUDRILLARD J., *La société de consommation,* Gallimard, 1970, 318 p.

BELLIARD D., 2013, « *Big data*, le nouvel eldorado d'Internet », *Alternatives Economiques*, 327.

BOYES E., Stanisstreet M., 2012, "Environmental Education for Behaviour Change: Which actions should be targeted?" *Int. J. Sci. Educ.* 34, 1591–1614.

BROWN L., When Population Growth and Resource Availability Collide, from *Plan B 3.0: Mobilizing to Save Civilization,* Earth Policy, New York, 2008.

BROWN L., 2014 update, Full Planet, Empty Plates: The New Geopolitics of Food Scarcity, New York: W.W. Norton & Co (www.earth-policy.org/books/fpep/fpepch6).

BRAUDEL F., Civilisation matérielle, économie et capitalisme, XVè – XVIIIè siècle. Tome 3. Le temps du monde, Armand Collin, 1979.

BRUGÈRE F., 2010, Quelle société voulons-nous ? Le soin et le *care* ; http://www.laviedesidees.fr/IMG/pdf/20101004_care.pdf

CALLENBACH E., 2011, "Sustainable Shrinkage: Envisioning a Smaller, Stronger Economy", *Solutions* 2/4: 10-15; http://www.thesolutionsjournal.com

CLERC D., 2013, « Les objecteurs de croissance » (pp. 62-63) et « Une brève histoire de la croissance » (pp. 14-17), *Alternatives Economiques* Hors-série 97 (l'ensemble des articles de ce numéro *Faut-il dire adieu à la croissance ?*, est ciblé sur la problématique de la croissance / décroissance).

CLIP 21, 2012, Mode de vie et empreinte carbone. Prospective des modes de vie en France à l'horizon 2050 et empreinte carbone - rapport 2012, IDDRI.

COUTROT T. *et al*, 2012, Rapport de la Fondation Copernic, en finir avec la compétitivité, octobre 2012 ; http://www.fondation-copernic.org/spip.php?article789

COSTANZA R. *et al*, 2007, "Quality of life: An approach integrating opportunities, human needs, and subjective well-being", *Ecological Economics* 61, 267-276.

DASGUPTA P., 2010, "The Place of Nature in Economic Development" In: Rodrik, D & Rosenzweig, M (eds.) Handbook of Development Economics 5, 4039-5061.

DEMARTHON F., 2012, « Des masses de données à donner le vertige », *CNRS Le Journal* 269.

DE RAVIGNAN A., 2013, « Du charbon dans le nuage », *Alternatives économiques*, 328.

DESCOLA Ph., Leçon inaugurale au Collège de France pour la Chaire d'anthropologie de la nature, Paris, Collège de France, 29 mars 2001.

ELLIS E. C. *et al*, 2011, "Anthropogenic transformation of the terrestrial biosphere". *Philosophical Transactions of the Royal Society A* 369, 1010-1035.

« Et si on changeait tout... 60 initiatives et propositions pour changer le monde », *Alternatives Economiques poche*, Hors-série n° 49, Avril 2011.

Feuille de Route, 2012, http://www.developpementdurable.gouv.fr/IMG/pdf/Feuille_de_Route_pour_la_Transition_Ecologique.pdf

FOXON T.J., 2011, "A co-evolutionary Framework for analysing a transition to a sustainable low carbon economy". *Ecological Economics* 70, 2258-2267.

FRÉMEAUX Ph., La nouvelle alternative ? Enquête sur l'économie sociale et solidaire, Les Petits Matins, 2013 ; http://www.alternatives-economiques.fr/la-nouvelle-alternative-_fr_pub_1090_liv.html

FRÉMEAUX Ph., Lalucq A., 2013, « Bienvenue dans l'Anthropocène », *Alternatives Economiques* 323: 74-86.

GADREY J., 2013, « Il faut mettre fin à la course à la productivité », *Alternatives Economiques*, Hors-séries 97, 74-75.

GOMEZ P. Y., *Le travail invisible. Enquête sur une disparition*, François Bourin, 2013, 253 p.

GRANGE J., Pour une philosophie de l'écologie, Agora, 2012, 151 p.

GUICHARDAZ O., 2013, « Economie circulaire : il y a encore du chemin à faire », *Alternatives Economiques* 329.

GUILLAUD H, 2013, « D'autres outils et règles pour mieux contrôler les données » ; http://www.internetactu.net/2013/07/03/dautres-outils-et-regles-pour-mieux-controler-les-donnees/

LARRÈRE C., « Ethique et philosophie de l'environnement » in *Le développement durable à découvert,* sous la direction de Euzen *et al*, Les Editions du CNRS, 48-49, 2013.

LIBÉRATION, 28 juin 2013, *Energie Lost in Translation*, p. 34-35.

LIBÉRATION, 14-15 septembre 2013, *La crise est une arnaque, un récit inventé par une oligarchie mondiale*, interview de Patrick Viveret, p. 8.

MAGANDA C., Petit O., *Strategic Natural Resource Governance. Contemporary Environmental Perspectives*, Bruxelles, PIE Peter Lang, Coll Regional Integration and Social Cohesion, 2012, 241 p.

MAGNEN J.P., 2011, « Comment penser la transformation écologique ? » Rubrique *La transformation écologique et sociale*, http://www.jeanphilippemagnen.fr/la-transformation-ecologique-et-sociale/comment-penser-la-transformation-ecologique.html

Manifeste convivialiste, 2013, éditions Le Bord de l'eau, http://lesconvivialistes.fr/?page_id=8

MASLOW A., 2006, *Etre humain : la nature humaine et sa plénitude*, Eyrolles, 432 p.

NEF 2009, The Great Transition: A tale of how it turned out right | New Economic Foundation (NEF); http://www.neweconomics.org/publications/entry/the-great-transition

NEUMAYER E., 2000, "Scarce or abundant? The economy of natural resources availability". *J Economic Surveys* 14, 307-329.

NOÉ A., « Jeremy Rifkin, La troisième révolution industrielle. Comment le pouvoir latéral va transformer l'énergie, l'économie et le monde, Paris, Les Liens qui Libèrent, 2012, 414p. », *Développement durable et territoires* [En ligne], Vol. 4, n° 1 | Avril 2013.

ORGANISATION INTERNATIONALE DU TRAVAIL, 2012, La transition vers l'économie verte pourrait générer jusqu'à 60 millions d'emplois ; http://www.ilo.org/global/about-the-ilo/newsroom/news/WCMS_181803/lang--fr/index.htm

PÔLE RHÔNE-ALPES DE L'ORIENTATION, 2013, L'impact de l'économie verte sur les métiers et formations ; http://www.rhonealpes-orientation.org/les-metiers-de-l-economie-verte-en-rhone-alpes-63056.kjsp

POPULATION MATTERS, *Overshoot Index 2011*; https://www.populationmatters.org/documents/overshoot_index_2011.pdf

RAVALLION M., 2007, "Urban Poverty", *Finance & Development* 44/3, 15-17; http://www.imf.org/external/pubs/ft/fandd/2007/09/ravalli.htm

REICH R., *Supercapitalisme. The Transformation of Business, Democracy, and Everyday Life*, A.A. Knopf Ed, 2007, 288 p.

RENNER M. *et al*, 2008, UNEP report: Towards Decent Work in a Sustainable, Low-Carbon World; http://www.unep.org/publications/search/pub_details_s.asp?ID=4002

RICKINSON M., 2001, Learners and Learning in Environmental Education: A critical review of the evidence. *Environ. Educ. Res.* 7, 207–320.

ROCKSTRÖM J. *et al*, 2009, A safe operating space for humanity, *Nature* 461, 472-475.

SCHMID L., 2013, Transition écologique et modification du travail, *Le Huffigton Post Environnement*, 21/11/13 ; http://www.huffingtonpost.fr/lucile-schmid/transition-ecologique-et-_b_4314622.html

Scientists'Consensus on Maintaining Humanity's Life Support Systems in the 21st Century, 2013; http://mahb.stanford.edu/wp-content/uploads/2013/05/Consensus-Statement.pdf

SCHUMPETER J., *Business cycles. A theorical, historical, and statistical analysis of the capitalist process*, vol. I, Mc Graw-Hill Book Company, New York and London, 1939, 1122 p.

SEITZINGER S.P. *et al*, 2012, "Planetary stewardship in an urbanizing world: beyond city limits". *AMBIO*, DOI 10.1007/s13280-012-0353-7.

SETO K.C. *et al*, 2011, "A Meta-Analysis of Global Urban Land Expansion". *PloS One 6*, e23777. Doi:10.1371/journal.pone.0023777.

SHAH A., 2013, "*Poverty facts and stats. Global Issues*", http://www.globalissues.org/article/26/poverty-facts-and-stats

SPEIDEL J.J. *et al*, 2009, "Population policies, programmes and the environment", *Philos. Trans. R. Soc. B Biol. Sci.*, 364, 3049-3065.

STEFFEN W. *et al*, 2011, "The Anthropocene: From global change to planetary stewardship", *AMBIO: A Journal of the Human Environment* 40, 739-761.

Stern *Review Report, 2007, H. M. Treasury*, http://webarchive.nationalarchives.gov.uk/+/http:/www.hm-treasury.gov.uk/independent_reviews/stern_review_economics_climate_change/stern_review_report.cfm.

STIGLITZ J., *Le rapport Stiglitz. Pour une vrai réforme du système monétaire et financier international*, Les liens qui libèrent, 2010, 304 p.

Stockholm Memorandum, 2011, *AMBIO: A Journal of the Human Environment* 40, 781–785.

TISDELL C., *Competition, diversity and economic performance*, E. Elgar Ed., Cheltenham, UK, Chapter 7, pp. 132-159.

TOURAINE A., *La fin des sociétés*, Seuil, 2013, pp. 341-345.

WESTLEY F. *et al*, 2011, "Tipping Toward Sustainability: Emerging Pathways of

Transformation". *AMBIO : A Journal of the Human Environment* 40, 762–780

TUBIANA L., 2013, « Qu'est-ce qu'une croissance durable ? » In : *Le développement durable à découvert*, sous la direction de Euzen *et al*, Les Editions du CNRS, pp. 318-319.

VIVERO Pol J.-L., 2013, "*Food as a Commons: Reframing the Narrative of the Food System*", http://papers.ssrn.com/sol3/papers.cfm?abstract_id=2255447

Les sols, l'eau et la production agricole : des ressources de base face à l'étalement urbain et aux changements climatiques

Fabienne TROLARD * & Marie-Lorraine DANGEARD **

L'indéfini médiatique a tendance à affirmer que les progrès scientifiques permettront de répondre aux besoins de la population en 2050 par l'amélioration des rendements et la conquête de nouvelles terres agricoles dans des zones encore sous-exploitées (e.g. l'Afrique). Mais dernièrement, les experts et économistes des organisations internationales qui avaient souvent assez directement contribué à propager ce type d'idées reçues, s'en distancient de façon croissante. De fait, les travaux de recherche prospectifs (AGRIMONDE[1] et certains META programmes[2] de l'INRA et européens sur le sujet) et les épisodes de crise apparus sur certains grands marchés ont confirmé ces dernières années, que ces prévisions optimistes, reflets d'une vision mécaniciste de la nature, ne cadraient tout simplement pas avec les faits.

Bien que de nombreux aspects des cycles de la nature et de la vie restent encore mystérieux, certaines des lois physico-chimiques qui les caractérisent sont incontournables. Ainsi, aucun organisme vivant (végétal, animal ou humain) ne peut fonctionner sans :

* Directeur de Recherches à l'INRA dans l'UMR Environnement Méditerranéen et Modélisation des Agro-Hydrosystèmes à Avignon, responsable scientifique du programme ASTUCE & TIC et lead du projet européen PRECOS.

** Juriste et project manager du projet européen PRECOS, Ingénieur d'Etudes à l'INRA dans l'UMR Environnement Méditerranéen et Modélisation des Agro-Hydrosystèmes à Avignon.

[1] Agrimonde : scénarios et défis pour nourrir le monde en 2050 (2011) S. PAILLARD, S. TREYER, B.DORIN coord., Edition QUAE., 296 pp.

[2] Les métaprogrammes de l'INRA au nombre de huit ont pour objectifs de regrouper et/ou d'initier des travaux de recherche élargis, à la confluence de plusieurs disciplines, pour mieux répondre aux défis sociétaux. Par rapport à notre propos, trois d'entre eux sont plus directement impliqués ; il s'agit de ACCAF (Adaptation de l'agriculture de la forêt au changement climatique) et en gestation GLoFoods (Etude des transitions pour la sécurité alimentaire mondiale) et ECOSERV (pratiques et services des écosystèmes anthropisés).

- un espace définissant un milieu aux propriétés physiques et chimiques suffisamment stationnaires dans le temps pour permettre aux mécanismes biologiques de s'organiser ;
- des éléments chimiques différents et nombreux qui combinés entre eux détermineront leurs structures, leurs fonctions métaboliques et de reproduction ;
- des ressources pour ces êtres vivants, lesquelles sont le produit de dynamiques et transformations intra-ou extra milieu de matière ou d'énergie entre compartiments hétérogènes.

Les systèmes agricoles sont régis par certaines règles intangibles dont le marché ne peut s'abstraire. Ils forment une synthèse entre les caractéristiques spécifiques des ressources locales, les conditions climatiques et le mode d'exploitation pratiqué sur ces territoires.

Pour un espace donné, les caractéristiques du sol (pH, épaisseur, constituants minéraux, teneur en matière organique...) et du climat (température, précipitation, fréquence des évènements extrêmes) définissent le potentiel de production primaire de l'écosystème et la performance des chaînes alimentaires qui peuvent s'y développer. Ces conditions dites « pédoclimatiques » sont dynamiques dans le temps. Elles dépendent d'abord du climat et de son évolution et de la géologie en particulier, de la durée d'altération et de la formation des sols sur les surfaces continentales.

Ainsi, dans les zones tempérées de la Terre ayant connu la dernière période glaciaire, les sols sont jeunes et contiennent une importante fraction argilo-limoneuse capable de fournir les principaux éléments nécessaires à la croissance des plantes (éléments dits organophiles comme e.g. calcium, magnésium, sodium, fer, silice...). L'apport d'engrais (N, P et K)[3] par l'Homme, quant à lui, vient compenser les déficits chroniques des sols en ces éléments.

Dans la zone intertropicale, les sols sont très différents. Les couches de surface sont très pauvres en éléments organophiles du fait d'une altération et d'une pédogénèse de plusieurs millions d'années. La biomasse s'auto-entretient mais l'enrichissement minéral de ces sols n'est assuré que

[3] N, P et K représentent la principale trilogie des fertilisants utilisée en agriculture. Ce sont respectivement des composés à base d'azote (N), de phosphore (P) et de potassium (K).

par des apports éoliens (e.g. vent de sable saharien sur la forêt amazonienne, ou les dépôts de cendres volcaniques sur les rizières en Indonésie qui permet d'assurer trois récoltes par an). En d'autres termes, chaque espèce de plantes, qui sont les producteurs primaires de la chaîne alimentaire, ne peut pas se développer sur n'importe quels sols et/ou hémisphères.

L'action de l'Homme d'une part, les pressions climatiques de l'autre vont impacter le fonctionnement des écosystèmes de manière plus ou moins radicale et redéfinir en un lieu donné de nouveaux états stationnaires. Ces pressions annoncent des évolutions inéluctables des fondamentaux naturels, mais aussi socio-économiques des territoires qu'il convient d'anticiper et de gérer aux mieux de l'intérêt collectif.

Les pressions accrues qui pèseront sur les milieux en liaison avec l'accroissement des événements extrêmes et des modifications du climat, permettent d'ores et déjà de prévoir l'apparition, la disparition, la prolifération ou la migration des espèces animales et végétales et un accroissement sensible des risques liés au manque d'adaptation des infrastructures. Une telle évolution aura aussi probablement pour conséquence une requalification de certains espaces, y compris d'espaces protégés (Natura 2000[4], Convention de Ramsar[5], ZNIEFF[6]...), et leur réappréciation et réaffectation dans une perspective dynamique. L'hypothèse de telles modifications de la vocation initiale de l'usage des terres semble d'autant plus probable que, face au risque anticipé de pertes économiques significatives dues à un amoindrissement des services de production et de régulation des écosystèmes, la préservation d'espaces naturels est identifiée comme une action

---

[4] Natura 2000 est un réseau européen regroupant l'ensemble des sites naturels, terrestres et marins, dits d'intérêt communautaire. Ils sont identifiés pour la rareté ou la fragilité des espèces sauvages, animales ou végétales, et de leurs habitats et couverts par les directives « habitats » (93/43/CE) et/ou « oiseaux » (2009/147/CE). En France le réseau Natura 2000 comprend 1753 sites.

[5] La Convention de Ramsar est un traité intergouvernemental qui sert de cadre à l'action nationale et à la coopération internationale pour la conservation et l'utilisation rationnelle des zones humides d'importance internationale et de leurs ressources. Elle a été signée le 2 février 1971 à Ramsar en Iran.

[6] ZNIEFF = Zone Naturelle d'Intérêt Ecologique, Faunistique et Floristique. Les ZNIEFF constituent une base pour la constitution de zone conservation de la biodiversité.

d'adaptation au changement climatique pour les espèces comme pour les milieux [1].

Toutefois, et bien que la modélisation globale du climat connaisse des progrès manifestes grâce à la convergence d'études conduites par des spécialistes inscrits chacun dans leur champ disciplinaire et malgré d'importants efforts de synthèse [2], l'aperçu de ce que ces processus vont impliquer pour les sociétés demeure encore un des aspects fragiles et relativement discutables de ces travaux, tant les schémas proposés pêchent par leur caractère à la fois spéculatif et prospectif. Assises sur un déterminisme immédiat dans l'interprétation donnée des relations sociétés – environnement, ces lectures conduisent le plus souvent à des projections catastrophistes dont beaucoup relèvent de l'improbable. Elles gagneront en réalisme même pour un futur aux contours imprécis, lorsque des approches holistiques deviendront la règle d'analyse de la réactivité des sociétés face à un cadre climatique et environnemental changeant dans un contexte de ressources rares.

Les interventions de l'Homme sur son environnement elles aussi, ont tendance à entraîner volontairement ou non, la dégradation des milieux. Celle-ci se traduit par des pertes de qualité et/ou de quantité de la production agricole, l'érosion des sols arables, et l'émergence de situations conflictuelles pour l'accès à l'eau et aux terres. L'eau, la terre et la production agricole représentent les ressources de base essentielles pour le fonctionnement de la vie collective et sont des actifs stratégiques pour l'activité économique.

Aujourd'hui plus d'un Homme sur deux vit en ville. Une des dérives les plus inquiétantes pour la sécurité alimentaire est l'artificialisation des terres pour les besoins de l'expansion urbaine. Cette dernière est très imparfaitement comptabilisée (cf. Astuce et tic[7]) et d'autant plus difficile à maîtriser qu'outre les besoins liés à la croissance démographique et à ceux nécessaires au rattrapage des populations vivant actuellement dans

[7] Anticipation de l'Aménagement Sécurisé des Territoires Urbanisés, des Campagnes et de leur Environnement par les Technologies de l'Information et de la Communication. Programme Fonds Unique Interministériel dans le cadre du pôle de compétitivité « Gestion des risques et vulnérabilité des territoires » qui a mobilisé dans un partenariat public/privé une trentaine de chercheurs et ingénieurs entre 2008 et 2011.

l'habitat informel (World Urban Forum[8]), nombre de secteurs de l'économie restent fortement consommateur d'espaces (e.g. activité de logistique).

De plus, l'urbanisation se fait aux dépens des meilleures terres. Historiquement, la majorité de nos villes s'est implantée sur des lieux où la fourniture en denrées alimentaires et en eau était facilitée par les capacités intrinsèques des milieux à porter des activités agricoles et/ou à l'intersection de voies de communication et de transport [3]. Ainsi, en 2009, 10 % du territoire européen est devenu urbain ; cette urbanisation s'étant opérée le long des axes de transport et autour des grandes villes aux dépens des terres les plus arables. Il en va de même dans les autres régions du monde.

Combinés à ceux du climat, ces effets génèreront de nouvelles dynamiques de transformations aboutissant à l'émergence de « nouveaux états » stationnaires plus ou moins de bonne qualité et/ou conduiront les milieux jusqu'à un point de bascule, seuil critique au-delà duquel la résilience du territoire deviendra difficile à envisager. Le risque de dépassement de ces seuils compromet la sécurité alimentaire et économique des populations et des territoires et plaide en faveur d'une veille continue et intégrée des indicateurs de basculement des grands équilibres des territoires.

Pour anticiper et prévenir les risques, encore faut-il avoir conscience de leur existence et se donner les moyens pour les définir. Les systèmes agraires conditionnent notre alimentation et sa qualité, permettent la gestion de la ressource en eau et fournissent, via les fibres et la biomasse, une partie de notre énergie [4]. Pourtant, l'Homme n'est plus aujourd'hui conscient de sa dépendance à l'égard de la terre nourricière. Le fossé entre l'urbain et le cycle de la nature se creuse de plus en plus et, nombre d'enfants ne font plus le lien entre leur carré pané servi à la cantine et le poisson vivant dans la mer ou la rivière ou entre leur fromage en portion et la vache qui broute dans les prés.

---

[8] Forum international organisé par UN – Habitat, organisme des Nation Unies, tous les deux ans. Le thème du Forum en 2012 était « The Urban Future » et s'est tenu à Naples (Italie).

Depuis la fin de la Seconde Guerre mondiale, les performances de l'agriculture contemporaine et la domestication des écosystèmes qu'elle a entrainé ont permis aux producteurs de prendre quelques distances avec les règles de culture normalement imposées par les conditions pédoclimatiques. Un nouveau modèle de production alimentaire s'est imposé. Cette « révolution agricole », fondée sur la mécanisation des tâches, l'amélioration et la sélection génétique de certaines des espèces animales et végétales les plus productives ainsi que le recours massif aux engrais et xénobiotiques (herbicides et pesticides) et à l'énergie, a conduit nos sociétés urbaines à oublier leur dépendance à l'égard des fondamentaux de la vie.

Ces progrès ont apporté des améliorations incontestables mais ont conduit également à des aberrations tant au plan social (monoculture intensive pour l'exportation) que du point de vue de ses conséquences pour la préservation du potentiel de production des sols sur le long terme. Ainsi des zones entières du grenier à blé de l'Inde, le Pendjab ont perdu une grande partie de ce potentiel du fait de l'épuisement des nappes phréatiques lié à la pratique excessive de l'irrigation [5]. Par ailleurs, aujourd'hui et en dépit de l'innovation technique, les rendements stagnent dans le monde [6].

Est-ce que la conquête de nouvelles terres pour l'agriculture pourra compenser cette stagnation des rendements et surmonter les obstacles que représentent à la fois, la lutte pour l'usage des terres face à l'urbanisation galopante et la perspective de tensions accrues sur la disponibilité des autres ressources essentielles à la croissance des plantes ? Il est certes devenu possible de faire pousser du maïs dans le désert ou du mil en Beauce, mais cela se fait nécessairement au prix d'un usage intensif de la ressource en eau et/ou en énergie et d'importants autres surcoûts. L'économie réelle a pu ne pas en tenir compte ces dernières décennies. Mais il sera de plus en plus difficile de faire fi de cette donne avec la montée des pressions et des surcoûts associés à la rareté des ressources et à la perspective de l'épuisement de certaines d'entre elles (*e.g.* engrais essentiels d'origine minière comme le phosphore et le potassium).

Dans une économie de marché, un bouleversement radical des critères d'appréciation du capital et des actifs environnementaux non délocalisables comme les sols et l'eau, va sans doute devoir s'imposer.

L'Agence Européenne de l'Environnement (AEE) [7] a, par exemple, (mais le constat est pertinent pour le reste du monde) commencé d'alerter sur le coût des impacts négatifs de l'artificialisation sur la croissance européenne dans ses rapports sur l'extension urbaine. Dans le même sens les Fédérations d'Assurance et de Réassurance [8] commencent à s'inquiéter de l'augmentation des coûts des dommages matériels et humains en rapport avec l'intensité et la récurrence de risques naturels et d'évènements extrêmes climatiques.

A ce jour, l'efficacité des mécanismes permettant d'intégrer les ressources et les services des écosystèmes dans l'économie réelle (écotaxes, mesures compensatoires, fiscalité environnementale et réglementation urbaine type PLU, SCOT etc.) peinent à être considérés. Des efforts de régulation et de mise en cohérence institutionnelle entre les différents niveaux territoriaux ont bien été engagés par l'Union européenne et les Etats membres mais, fragmentées et sectorielles, elles n'ont pas permis que la somme des initiatives locales, régionales, nationales, voire communautaires permette d'espérer la coexistence durable d'usage des sols et de la ressource. Au contraire sur des territoires contraints et généralement en crise, elles auraient plutôt tendance à favoriser des situations de distorsions de concurrence et/ou des pratiques d'évitement. La succession de projets d'infrastructure et la pression urbaine continuent de faire progresser la fragmentation des territoires qui multiplie les ruptures de continuité écologique et, avec elle, l'érosion des espaces agricoles et de la biodiversité. Force est de constater que ce millefeuille législatif relativement illisible se lit aussi comme l'aveu de l'impuissance du régulateur à maîtriser l'occupation des sols. Ainsi, c'est encore et toujours le marché foncier qui reste le principal indicateur de la valeur attachée aux sols et aux ressources. En l'état actuel du droit positif, les conditions de rémunération d'une gestion durable des sols ne suffisent pas à compenser l'absence de reconnaissance de la valeur économique des ressources contenues par le foncier, fût-il protégé. Aucune des mesures existantes en ce domaine ne peut soutenir la comparaison avec les bénéfices susceptibles d'être attendus par les propriétaires d'autres modes d'exploitation et/ou d'usage du foncier [9].

Dans l'intervalle, l'érosion des actifs naturels se poursuit. C'est bien ce que confirme le dernier bilan de la Commission européenne sur la biodiversité [10], et le rapport sur l'état de conservation des espèces et des habitats d'intérêt communautaire en France [11] indique que les objectifs assignés pour 2010 ne seraient pas atteints, car les synergies et les compatibilités avec les autres politiques (développement régional, changement climatique…) sont très insuffisantes.

Se préparer à fonctionner dans une économie de la ressource rare passera nécessairement, par une réévaluation du poids des actifs naturels pour permettre aux acteurs locaux de fédérer leurs intérêts autour de stratégies de développement susceptible de surmonter collectivement les conflits d'usage des milieux et des ressources.

Face à ce qui s'apparente à un aveu d'impuissance des régulateurs et aussi, aux contraintes pesant sur les perspectives de développement dans les territoires, l'idée qu'il pourrait être de l'intérêt des acteurs locaux de reprendre en main la maîtrise de leur sort, par la co-construction d'une sorte de « filet de sécurité » fait son chemin. De fait, dans la mesure où aucun des cinq grands schémas prospectifs de développement[9] actuellement proposés ne paraît durable [12] (*e.g.* développement ouvert et mondialisée, repli régional etc.) et/ou réaliste (*e.g.* sobriété énergétique), les acteurs locaux auront tout intérêt à miser sur leur propres atouts pour essayer de se construire collectivement un horizon.

L'idée de développer des approches concertées et intégrées pour maîtriser la gestion d'une ou plusieurs ressources sur les territoires n'est pas neuve. On retrouve dans l'histoire, surtout dans le domaine de la ressource en eau, de nombreux dispositifs inventifs permettant une gestion des ressources raisonnée au quotidien et/ou de surmonter les crises (associations d'irrigants, contrats de Canaux, SDAGE[10] etc.). Ce type de processus de concertation et les accords qui en découlent sont assis sur la reconnaissance et l'identification des intérêts communs des acteurs. Leurs avan-

---

[9] Cinq familles de scénarios types décrivent un monde (1) donnant la priorité au développement durable (scénario SSP1); (2) caractérisé par la poursuite des tendances actuelles (SSP2) ; (3) fragmenté, affecté par la compétition entre pays avec une croissance économique lente et peu soucieuse de l'environnement (SSP3) ; (4) marqué par de grandes inégalités au service d'une petite minorité (SSP4) ; qui se concentre sur un développement traditionnel et rapide des pays émergeants fondé sur l'usage d'énergie fossile (SSP5).

[10] SDAGE = Schéma Directeur d'Aménagement et de Gestion des Eaux.

cées sont souvent bien plus tangibles que nombre de dispositifs législatifs (le processus de négociation du « contrat de nappe » en cours avec le SYMCRAU[11], dans les Bouches-du-Rhône en est une illustration). Souvent c'est une situation de crise liée à la tension sur un ou plusieurs actifs naturels et les difficiles conséquences qu'elles ont entrainées qui convainquent les acteurs locaux de la nécessité de recourir à ce type de dispositif. Le dispositif de concertation proposé par ECOLOC[12] dans diverses collectivités locales d'Afrique de l'Ouest [13] suite au Sommet de Rio de 1992 en est un autre exemple. L'Union européenne avec la directive cadre sur l'eau[13], reconnaît – pour ce qui est de la ressource en eau – le caractère indispensable de ces pratiques concertées au niveau des bassins versants et c'est déjà un grand progrès. Les avancées récentes de la science, en matière de technologie de l'information, de la communication et de modélisation ont permis la mise au points d'outils d'accompagnement particulièrement intégrés et accessibles pour les usagers. La démarche Astuce & Tic [14] (maintenant en cours de dimensionnement pour l'échelle européenne sous le nom de PRECOS[14]) en est un exemple qui pourra considérablement aider à la mise en évidence des risques de points de bascule susceptibles de bloquer irrémédiablement la croissance des territoires. A différentes échelles d'un géo-territoire, il permet à la fois un suivi de l'évolution et des interactions entre actifs (eau, sol, climat, potentiel de production) et des conséquences sur eux des projets de développement en cours ou projetés (urbanisation, commerces et industrie) et ce, en temps réel et sur base de scénarios à horizon de 20/30 ans.

L'ambition de convaincre les acteurs locaux de préserver les actifs naturels pour les services éco-systémiques qu'ils rendent dans un marché

[11] SYMCRAU = Syndicat Mixte en charge de la gestion de la nappe de la Crau.

[12] ECOLOC est une méthode de concertation développée par le CGLUA (Conseils et Gouvernements Locaux Unis d'Afrique) en Afrique de l'Ouest. Elle combine des phases d'étude, de consultations de partenaires publics et privés, de débats publics et d'organisation d'actions de développement.

[13] Directive cadre EAU = directive 2006/11/CE du 15 février 2006 (version codifiée de la directive 76/464/CEE du 4 mai 1976) fixe plusieurs objectifs : (1) atteindre un bon état des eaux en 2015 ; (2) réduire progressivement les rejets, émissions ou pertes pour les substances prioritaires ; (3) supprimer les rejets d'ici à 2021 des substances prioritaires dangereuses.

[14] www.inra.fr/precos

ouvert se heurte à de nombreuses résistances aux changements. L'adoption de stratégies de développement en co-construction, permettra demain d'accroître la valeur ajoutée et la résilience et donc, la sécurité du territoire face aux risques. Ces stratégies doivent aussi pouvoir proposer des avantages hic et nunc comme celui, via l'optimisation, de maîtriser autant que faire se peut la montée des coûts liés à la raréfaction des ressources sur un territoire. Ainsi la conception collective de stratégies locales de développement peut ne pas être synonyme de décroissance et de repli sur soi mortifère. Elle peut aussi constituer la base de réflexion à partir de laquelle les acteurs locaux trouveront les moyens d'innover pour rebondir et affronter les défis formidables de production auxquels l'humanité sera confrontée à l'avenir en anticipant lucidement les contraintes sur la ressource.

Références

[1] Grenelle II (2009) *Evaluation du coût des impacts du changement climatique en France.* Groupe II, Rapport Interministériel.

[2] IPCC (2013) *Climate Change 2013 – The physical Science Basis*, Summary for policymakers, 5ième Rapport du GIEC. Work Group 1 : Stocker T.F. & Qin D. co-chairs, 33 pp.

[3] TROLARD F. et le consortium Astuce & Tic (2010) Etalement urbain et changements globaux : l'urgence de considérer les sols et l'eau dans un modèle intégratif. *Liaison Energie – Francophonie*, 86, 135-140.

[4] MAZOYER M. et ROUDART L. (1997) *Histoire des agricultures du monde. Du néolithique à la crise contemporaine*. Ed. Seuil, Paris, 533 pp.

[5] PRIHAR, S.S., KHEPAR, S.D., SINGH, R., GREWAL, S.S., SONDHI, S.K. (1990) *Water resources of Punjab – A critical concern for the future of its agriculture.* Punjab Agricultural University ed., 60 pp.

[6] SPIETZ, J.H.J., EWERT, F. (2009) Crop production and resource use to meet the growing demand for food, feed and fuel: opportunities and constraints. *NJAS, Wageningen Journal of Life Science*, 56, 4, 281-300.

[7] EEA (2006) *Urban sprawl: the ignored challenge*, Report n°10/2006.

[8] FFSA (2009) *Synthèse de l'étude relative à l'impact du changement climatique et de l'aménagment du territoire sur la survenance d'évènements naturels en France.* Colloque Impacts du changement climatique, Paris, 29 avril 2009, 13 pp. http://www.ffsa.fr/sites/upload/docs/application/pdf/2010-05/synthese_etude_changement_climatique.pdf

[9] BIELSA, S., CHEVASSUS-AU-LOUIS, B., MARTIN, G., PUJOL, J.L., RICHARD, D., SALLES, J.M. (2009) *Approche économique de la biodiversité et des services liés aux écosystèmes – Contribution à la décision publique*, Rapport CAS (Centre d'Analyse Stratégique), La Documentation Française éd., 399 pp.

[10] EUROPEAN COMMISSION (2008) *« Progress towards halting the loss of biodiversity by 2010: a first assessment of implementing the EC biodiversity action plan »*.

[11] MEDAD DNP (2008) *Etat de conservation des espèces et des habitats d'intérêt communautaire : première évaluation*. Article 17, Report: National summary, France.

[12] MEDDE (2013) *Découvrir les nouveaux scénarios RCP et SSP utilisés par le GIEC – Synthèse*, Paris, 12 pp.

[13] ECOLOC handbook (2001) *Managing the economy locally in Africa. Assessing local economics and their prospects*, vol 1, Summary. Programme de développement municipal, Club du Sahel/OCDE, SAH/D, 511, Paris.

[14] TROLARD, F., REYNDERS, S., DANGERAD, M.L., BOURRIE, G., DESCAMPS, B., KELLER, C., DE MORDANT DE MASSIAC, J.C. (2013) *Territoires, villes et campagnes face à l'étalement urbain et aux changements climatiques. Une démarche intégrative pour préserver les sols, l'eau et la production agricole*, Ed. Johanet, Paris, 156 pp.

Les ressources – le grand enjeu de la transition sociétale et écologique

I. NEGRUTIU [*1], D. COUVET [*2], I. DOUSSAN [*3], W. KALINOWSKI [*4], C. MALWE [*5], L. ROUDART [*6], J.-M. SALLES [*7], J.-L. WEBER [*8]

Résumé

A travers la problématique des ressources, ce travail questionne la finalité des activités économiques et des modes de production. Il propose une démarche socio-environnementale intégrée et pluri-disciplinaire pour, à travers les droits et les devoirs de l'homme, (1) préserver les fonctions et les services écosystémiques, (2) satisfaire aux besoins vitaux des humains et (3) construire un projet culturel et politique cohérent reliant, pour l'ensemble des secteurs d'activité et pour l'ensemble de la société, l'alimentation, la santé, l'environnement, l'éducation/la culture. Ces conditions étant posées, deux aspects sont approfondies : identifier des concepts et des outils nécessaires pour répondre à ces trois contraintes et, sur cette base, définir comment construire des programmes de recherche multi-acteurs pour analyser et quantifier les changements attendus au niveau territorial.

[*1] Biologiste, Directeur de l'Institut Michel Serres, ENS de Lyon.

[*2] Professeur au Muséum National d'Histoire Naturelles et à l'Ecole Polytechnique, Directeur du Centre d'Ecologie et de Sciences de la Conservation (CESO - UMR 7204), Directeur du Centre de Recherches sur la Biologie des populations d'Oiseaux (CRBPO).

[*3] Directrice de recherche INRA, CREDECO (GREDEG) UMR 7321.

[*4] Sociologue et historien, Co-directeur de l'Institut Veblen pour les réformes économiques (Paris).

[*5] Chercheur invité au Collegium de Lyon. Maître de conférences à l'Université de Rennes 1, Institut du Droit Public et de la Science Politique (EA 4640).

[*6] Professeur de Développement agricole, Université Libre de Bruxelles.

[*7] Directeur de recherche CNRS, LAMETA, SupAgro Montpellier.

[*8] Economiste et Statisticien. Conseiller spécial pour la comptabilité économique-environnementale au sein de l'Agence Européenne de l'Environnement, Copenhague.

I. NEGRUTIU, D. COUVET, I. DOUSSAN, W. KALINOWSKI,
C. MALWE, L. ROUDART, J.-M. SALLES, J.-L. WEBER

Avant-propos

Lors de la table ronde ***Les enjeux écologiques, alimentaires et démographiques de l'exploitation des ressources naturelles***[1], pilotée par l'**Institut Michel Serres**, **Lyon** (http://institutmichelserres.ens-lyon.fr), nous avons révélé que « la guerre des ressources » (« *la guerre que les hommes font au Monde* », dit Michel Serres dans *Temps des Crises*, 2009) court toujours, sans avoir été ouvertement déclarée. Nous l'avons fait à cette occasion. Cela permet enfin de poser les conditions de la « paix des ressources », de la transition sociétale et écologique, dans laquelle les questions de sécurité et de démocratie alimentaires doivent jouer un rôle prépondérant.

> « *Cela conduit à entretenir le monde et à le cultiver, et non pas à l'exploiter* » (Michel Serres, *De l'inventaire des ressources au souci des choses*, 2011).

1. Introduction

L'Occident a choisi un certain axe de développement depuis le Moyen Age qui porte la marque d'une forte empreinte culturelle (Thuilllier, 1996). Celle de la dette, par exemple (Graeber, 2013 la dette aux origines de l'économie ?), cumulant dumping social et environnemental. Dans les deux cas, c'est par des mécanismes de forçage (Barnowski *et al*, 2012) sur l'ensemble des ressources (donc y compris humaines) que ce développement a été assuré. La Grande Accélération entamée dans les années 1950 (Steffen *et al*, 2007) nous met devant la double réalité des limites physiques de la biosphère et celles des inéquités devant des besoins fondamentaux de chaque personne humaine. Sans oublier que les jeux de pouvoirs qui sous-tendent l'essentiel des activités humaines passent systématiquement par la case « ressources » (Negrutiu, 2011). Dasgupta (2010) souligne : *"Individuals and communities over-exploit natural capital (i.e. a mesh of*

---

[1] Table ronde organisée par l'Institut Michel Serres à l'occasion des Rencontres internationales du programme Lascaux « Penser une démocratie alimentaire », les 25 – 27 novembre 2013 à Nantes. Nos remerciements vont au Programme Lascaux qui nous a généreusement donné l'occasion d'exprimer nos idées à l'occasion de son prestigieux bilan. Nous remercions également Jean-Pascal Bassino, Marie-Claude Maurel, Gérard Escher, Philippe Frémeaux et Doru Pamfil pour avoir stimulés ces échanges d'idées. *Last but not least*, Ioan Negrutiu remercie l'IUF pour l'avoir soutenu dans cette démarche.

resources), meaning that *the ecological services are subsidized. Social norms and legal rules are at the root of the system".*

Nous questionnons donc les finalités des activités économiques et des modes de production, de création de valeurs et richesses et de consommation de nos sociétés. Un préalable pour repenser le changement culturel et démocratique à engager par rapport à l'accès, la gestion et le réajustement des ressources.

Alors, comment faire la transition du *business as usual* à une autre culture de développement (Figure1) ? Et même si la substance du projet transition sera adaptative, expérimentale, avec des possibles trajectoires car informées différemment par l'histoire des lieux et des gens, ces trajectoires et les mécanismes mêmes de la transition vont devoir être imaginés pour que des enjeux socio-environnementaux fondamentaux (pauvreté humaine et appauvrissement des ressources) rentrent en même temps dans le champ des droits et des devoirs de l'homme :

(1) Préserver les fonctions et les services écosystémiques (i.e. faire rentrer l'économie et autres activités dans la biosphère). En effet, le fait d'inclure *« le capital naturel dans le raisonnement économique modifie non seulement notre évaluation de l'expérience actuelle du développement, mais aussi notre compréhension du processus de développement » (Dasgupta, 2010).*

(2) Satisfaire aux besoins vitaux des humains (i.e. vaincre les inégalités et la pauvreté, ce qui demande un nouveau contrat et ordre social avec d'importants investissements socialement nécessaires et des règles de gouvernance adaptées) ;

(3) Construire un projet culturel et politique cohérent pour l'ensemble des secteurs d'activité et pour l'ensemble de la société.

Satisfaire simultanément aux 3 conditions :

- implique une approche-système de la problématique ressources dans le sens de la « résilience socio-écosystémique », en liant systématiquement ***Alimentation, Santé, Environnement, Education/Culture***.
- nécessite de sortir de la culture de la dette, du déficit, comme de la culture de la pauvreté ;

- pose la question des biens communs dans cet ensemble précis de contraintes en tant que « garantie des droits fondamentaux, qui peut exiger que ceux-ci soient placés à l'abri de toute forme de commodification » (De Schutter, http://cridho.uclouvain.be/fr/).

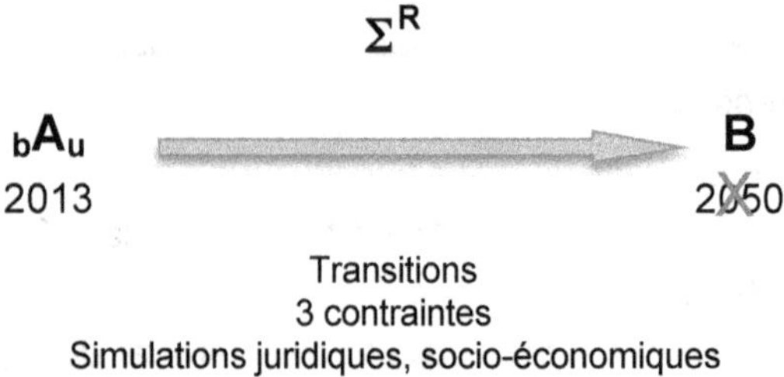

Figure 1. Les enjeux de la transition sont esquissés pour comprendre le passage de la situation actuelle (*business as usual*, bAu) à une « société » (B) guidée par un nouveau contrat stipulant des contraintes précises pour gérer les ressources naturelles accessibles (ΣR) : la sécurité socio-environnementale comme fonction des spécificités et du potentiel de l'ensemble des ressources d'un territoire donné. Nous pensons que l'échéance temporelle est 2024-2025, compte tenu des projections démographiques (8 milliards de terriens) et de la consommation de ressources associées (capacité de charge, production et productivité des systèmes biologiques en situation de forçage).

Le concept « ressources naturelles » se révèle un outil pédagogique surprenant, avec l'agriculture en tant que maillon premier de la réflexion sur la transition : 1er employeur et utilisateur d'espace-facteur de production (des socio-agro-écosystèmes), multifonctionnalité et « exception agricole » au service d'une économie circulaire et des divers besoins fondamentaux, facteur géo-politique en ressources naturelles, liens directs entre alimentation / santé / environnement, diverses formes collectives et solidaires dans le travail et la valorisation des ressources.

Ces conditions étant posées, deux aspects nécessitent approfondissement : de quels concepts et outils avons-nous besoins pour concevoir la transition ? Et, sur cette base, comment construire des programmes de recherche multi-acteurs pour analyser et quantifier le changement attendu au niveau territorial ?

2. Avons-nous les outils conceptuels et opérationnels de la transition ou faut-il les imaginer ?

Commençons par définir grossièrement d'où nous partons.

Le premier constat est que dans la pensée dominante, « les études des liens entre pauvreté, croissance démographique et la nature et l'efficacité des institutions et du capital naturel ne sont pas intégrées dans les modèles de croissance actuels » (les services écosystémiques sont sous-évalués par le marché et, de plus, des transactions s'effectuent également via un large spectre d'institutions autre que le marché) ; sans oublier que les « droits de propriété sur le capital naturel sont soit vaguement définis, soit témoignent de la faiblesse des engagements contractuels » (Dasgupta, 2010).

Le deuxième constat est que les deux principaux verrous sont liés à l'articulation entre dimension sociale et environnementale et entre analyse environnementale et analyse économique.

Pour la première articulation, une forte asymétrie existe entre :

(1) les avancées sur les politiques sociales définies par le Sommet du Millénaire 2010 (*the social protection floor*) comportant la sécurité des revenus de base et l'accès universel à des services essentiels (santé, eau et assainissement, éducation, sécurité alimentaire et logement) et

(2) la démarche de l'écologie économique (soutenabilité faible ou forte ; Rotillon, 2010), qui peine à monter en puissance. C'est dans ce double contexte qu'il est important de reconsidérer les notions et les situations de concurrence / compétitivité débridées et du *reporting* non-financier (état et dynamique des ressources naturelles et leur liens avec les systèmes d'assurances, placements financiers, ...) dans un territoire politiquement organisé.

Pour la seconde articulation, il faut produire une analyse considérée à la fois comme de la bonne science environnementale et de la bonne science économique. Les aspects les plus problématiques sont :

- l'estimation de la valeur économique de certaines composantes du capital naturel telles que la biodiversité ;

- l'évolution dans le temps de la valeur du stock de capital naturel, suite au progrès technique et à la croissance démographique.

3. Des enjeux de l'écologie et de l'agriculture aux enjeux du droit, de l'économie et de la sociologie.

Pour développer le cadrage ci-dessus, sont présentés ici les analyses et arguments des intervenants à la table ronde.

Denis Couvet : ***L'écologie scientifique s'efforce à identifier les enjeux écologiques majeurs***. Ils concernent la préservation des services écosystémiques de régulation et de support et de la biodiversité ordinaire associée.

La préservation des services écosystémiques de régulation et de support nécessite d'évaluer les conséquences écologiques des politiques et des outils de gestion proposés. Ces conséquences déterminent la pertinence des outils socio-économiques et juridiques, de leur combinaison, mais aussi des outils sociaux, notamment les modes d'organisation des systèmes d'exploitation des ressources naturelles comme l'agriculture, la pêche... Dans ce domaine, une difficulté est de quantifier les impacts des différentes activités humaines sur les écosystèmes et la biodiversité.

Jusqu'à récemment, on a utilisé la relation surface-espèce, qui permet d'évaluer le nombre d'espèces qui resteront présentes, selon la quantité de terres non perturbées. L'inconvénient de cette estimation est de ne pas tenir compte de l'intensité de l'utilisation (terres agricoles notamment). Aussi utilise-t-on de manière croissante l'Appropriation Humaine de la Production primaire nette (HANPP), ou proportion de la PPN prélevée par les humains, comprenant consommation et dégradation. Moyenne de 30 %, avec de grandes variations, souvent plus de 50 % en Asie, de 40 à 50 % en Europe. Cette HANPP a un impact sur les services écosystémiques présents, notamment de régulation et support. En conséquence, des calculs économiques simples suggèrent qu'il est souvent économiquement intéressant de diminuer notre emprise sur les écosystèmes. Parmi des exemples, la gestion des bassins-versants des villes de New York et de Pékin (pour lesquels sont organisés des Paiements pour Services Ecosystémiques) ou l'inventaire des services à l'échelle de l'ensemble de la Grande-Bretagne, ou encore des coûts/bénéfices des nitrates, à l'échelle de l'Europe.

Il s'agit ensuite d'examiner les effets à moyen terme de ces outils. En effet, ces derniers suscitent parfois des réactions fortes, que ce soit la notion de service écosystémique et la notion associée de paiement pour service écosystémique, ou encore les écotaxes. En décrivant les conséquences biophysiques et sociales, selon les réactions des acteurs, des différents outils proposés, l'analyse scientifique doit éclairer le débat. Les conséquences sociales d'outils techniques simples pourraient être profondes. Ainsi, dans le domaine de la pêche, les quotas individuels transférables auraient stimulé la création de coopératives de pêcheurs aux USA.

Il s'agit enfin d'évaluer les conséquences écologiques, sociales des différentes politiques proposées, de scénariser. Il importe de ne pas oublier la possibilité d'effets rebonds de la consommation lorsque les coûts de production diminuent. Cet effet montre que les intérêts des producteurs, consommateurs, citoyens, peuvent diverger.

Laurence Roudart - ***L'agriculture au cœur de la transition écologique et sociétale***. La transition écologique et sociétale ne pourra pas advenir sans les agriculteurs, car l'agriculture se trouve au cœur de plusieurs enjeux majeurs de développement et d'environnement. Avec leurs familles, ces agriculteurs représentent 40 % de la population mondiale. Ils cultivent à peu près 10 % des terres émergées et en exploitent 20 % en pâturages naturels. Ainsi, un tiers environ des terres de la planète sont consacrées à l'agriculture, soit une superficie équivalente à celle des terres recouvertes de forêts. Par ailleurs, quelque 70 % de l'eau utilisée par la population humaine sert à des fins agricoles. L'agriculture occupe ainsi une place très importante dans l'utilisation des ressources naturelles de la planète.

Or l'agriculture se trouve au cœur de trois grands défis de développement. Celui de la *sécurité alimentaire* d'abord : d'après les dernières estimations de la FAO, près de 840 millions de personnes dans le monde – soit 1 personne sur 8 – sont sous-alimentées, c'est-à-dire ont faim pratiquement tous les jours. Or, parmi elles, autour de 70 % exercent une activité agricole. Cette profession est donc la première touchée par la faim. De manière liée, elle est très affectée par la *pauvreté* aussi, puisque 70 % des pauvres du monde vivent en milieu rural et plus leurs revenus dépendent de l'agriculture, plus ils sont pauvres. Enfin, l'agriculture est au cœur du défi des *inégalités*, en particulier des inégalités d'accès aux ressources productives que sont la terre, l'eau d'irrigation et le crédit. Cette question des inégalités est quasiment absente des grands débats actuels sur le développement, tout concentrés qu'ils sont sur la problématique de la pauvreté. Pourtant, si l'on s'intéresse à la pauvreté liée à l'accès à des ressources qui sont finies, la question des inégalités d'accès à ces ressources s'impose très vite. Pour s'en convaincre, on peut citer quelques chiffres relatifs à l'accès à la terre, émanant du *Recensement général de l'agriculture* conduit par la FAO : ces chiffres concernent 81 pays qui représentent les deux tiers de la population du monde : 73 % des exploitations agricoles font moins de 1 hectare ; 85 % moins de 2 hectares ; 95 % moins de 5 hectares.

Mais l'agriculture se trouve aussi au cœur de trois grands défis environnementaux : les pollutions par les nitrates, les phosphates et les pesticides ; les émissions de gaz à effet de serre ; et la gestion de la biodiversité. Bien sûr, toutes les agricultures du monde actuel ne sont pas également concernées par ces défis : des centaines de millions d'agriculteurs pauvres n'utilisent aucun engrais d'origine industrielle, aucun pesticide, ou presque, et ont une empreinte écologique extrêmement faible.

Alors, une question essentielle, qui anime beaucoup d'équipes de recherche de par le monde, est de savoir si les agriculteurs, dans leurs interactions avec les ressources naturelles de la planète, pourront relever ces défis, sachant que la population humaine continue d'augmenter rapidement. La démographie est souvent liée au concept de capacité de charge humaine, concept très controversé, notamment parce qu'il fut par le passé instrumentalisé par divers mouvements racistes. Néanmoins, ce concept figure explicitement dans l'Agenda 21 issu de la Conférence de Rio en 1992. La capacité de charge humaine n'est pas une notion absolue, mais bien une notion relative, qui dépend des caractéristiques écologiques des milieux, bien sûr, mais qui dépend aussi de la manière dont les sociétés s'organisent pour répartir l'accès aux ressources naturelles, pour utiliser ces ressources et pour ensuite répartir les produits obtenus.

Si l'on prend l'exemple du territoire français dans ses limites actuelles, une bonne partie de ses 10 millions d'habitants criaient famine aux alentours de l'an mil. Ce monde paraissait alors « plein ». Pourtant, trois cents ans plus tard, le même espace nourrissait environ 20 millions d'habitants, après d'énormes transformations dans les modes de mise en valeur des territoires. De nouveau, le monde paraissait alors « plein ». Pourtant, vers 1900, ce même espace nourrissait environ 40 millions d'habitants, après d'autres transformations sociales et agro-écologiques, mais sans pratiquement aucun engrais d'origine industrielle ni pesticide.

Pour conclure, la capacité de charge humaine d'un territoire dépend bien de la Nature et de ses ressources, mais elle dépend aussi et elle varie même grandement selon la manière dont les sociétés s'organisent pour utiliser ces ressources. Il s'agit donc d'une question éminemment politique.

Isabelle Doussan : ***Le droit comme frein ou levier des changements.*** Prenons l'exemple de la production agricole avec le mode de production dit « conventionnel » (i.e. caractérisé par une dépendance aux intrants - pesticides, engrais, semences standardisées) et le droit.

Le droit français et la PAC ont été construits, des années 1960 à 90 à peu près, autour d'un modèle technico-économique de production, dit conventionnel, dans lequel l'environnement est perçu comme un facteur soit absent soit extérieur et contraignant/limitant. Exemples : la PAC (avec ses aides à la production, politique des structures), le Droit rural français (avec la possibilité pour le locataire du fonds d'arracher les haies, araser les talus, etc, sans l'accord du propriétaire ; ou l'appréciation par le juge français de l'exploitation du fonds en « bon père de famille » selon quantité d'intrants utilisés), le Droit des semences (et les critères d'inscription au catalogue).

En ce sens, le droit peut contribuer à verrouiller un système en interdisant ou en freinant la mise sur le marché et le développement de produits et pratiques innovants, rendant ainsi la transition écologique plus difficile. En outre, lorsque le droit de l'environnement se préoccupe de l'agriculture (début années 90), il agit comme pour n'importe quelle activité industrielle en considérant aussi l'environnement comme un facteur externe et contraignant qu'il s'agit de faire « internaliser » de force (réglementation) ou de gré (aides publiques) par les entreprises.

Or, dans le domaine agricole, l'environnement est un facteur de production ; les caractéristiques agronomiques du sol, l'eau (en quantité et qualité), la biodiversité (domestique et sauvage) participent à l'acte de production agricole. Dès lors, l'application d'un droit de l'environnement « industriel » soit ne fonctionne pas (ex. de la pollution par les nitrates), soit participe au mouvement d'industrialisation et d'artificialisation de l'agriculture (avec toutes ses impasses et ses risques y compris éthiques). En conséquence, le chemin vers une transition écologique nécessite une modification même de l'approche juridique de l'environnement dans le domaine de la production agricole. Cette modification est actuellement émergente (mais assez timidement). Exemples du droit des produits phytopharmaceutiques qui s'ouvre aux pratiques alternatives à l'usage de ces produits et aux principes de la lutte intégrée des cultures ; du dispositif français Haute Valeur Environnementale (HVE) qui appréhende l'exploitation agricole comme un agro-écosystème ; du bail rural « environnemental ». Ce mouvement peut bénéficier de l'introduction en droit d'une approche plus dynamique et fonctionnelle des écosystèmes avec les concepts de services écologiques (qui n'est toutefois pas lui-même exempt de critiques) et d'agro-écologie.

Claire Malwe – *explorer et améliorer les outils juridiques existants.* Pour illustrer l'importance de l'institution judiciaire dans des processus de négociations permettant de définir des droits d'accès à des ressources, mais aussi d'obtenir la légitimité nécessaire pour qu'ils soient acceptés par les utilisateurs, le « Resource Management Act » (RMA – 1991), de la Nouvelle Zélande est appelé en exemple (une analyse plus détaillée est présentée dans Weber *et al*, p. 143 et ss. du présent ouvrage).

Cette législation est le résultat d'une politique de réforme à part entière ayant permis la création d'un système intégré de prise de décision sur les ressources naturelles du pays. Ce système remplace entièrement les assemblages précédents opérant par secteurs et qui consistaient en des régimes d'utilisation des ressources fragmentés.

Ainsi, le RMA devient le sommet d'une hiérarchie législative affichant sans ambiguïté son but : poser le « management durable » des ressources naturelles au centre du dispositif législatif de tel sorte qu'il puisse explicitement orienter la prise de décision dans toutes les autres politiques, plans et projets de développement. C'est la rencontre entre la comptabilité environnementale et ce droit-là qui permettra au mieux d'utiliser les comptes comme instrument de preuve en droit des affaires, droit commercial, droit fiscal, droit civil, ou droit social.

Jean-Michel Salles - ***L'idée de partager les ressources « démocratiquement » ou « équitablement »*** pose, en parallèle avec les débats théoriques sur la définition retenue de l'équité et ses « fondements axiomatiques » (le débat est, me semble-t-il, très actifs et ses enjeux ne sont pas seulement académiques), la question de sa mise en œuvre ; c'est-à-dire des mécanismes qui permettront non seulement d'aller vers une situation préférable, mais de s'y maintenir.

Depuis bien longtemps, la pensée dominante en économie a considéré que la propriété individuelle d'agents conscients de leurs intérêts était le mécanisme le plus prometteur, une fois que les questions d'allocation initiale et de redistribution, laissées à la sphère politique, étaient résolues. Ce faisant, on sépare les enjeux d'efficacité (chaque agent a intérêt à tirer le maximum des ressources dont il dispose pour que le gâteau soit le plus avantageux possible), des enjeux de justice (des formes d'expression de l'intérêt général, l'Etat et autre, permettent d'allouer les ressources nouvelles « sans maître » ou de compenser des inégalités socialement mal acceptées). Dans ce cadre, le concept d'« externalité », c'est-à-dire d'un transfert de valeur qui n'est pas régulé et, en particulier, ne fait pas l'objet d'une compensation, est devenu le cœur des justifications d'interventions publiques, comme lorsque des effets « technologiques » se transmettent via l'environnement et les écosystèmes.

Evidemment, un ensemble d'approches, parfois regroupées comme « néo-institutionnalistes », ont étudié la réalité des institutions supposées permettre le fonctionnement de ces mécanismes et en ont mis en évidence de multiples carences ; alors que d'autres (la plus connue étant évidemment Elinor Ostrom) montraient que les sociétés s'organisent de multiples manières pour gérer l'articulation des droits privés (et lesquels) et les choix collectifs.

Ceci étant rappelé, il me semble que parmi les questions auxquelles une attention doit être portée, il y a d'abord celle de l'importance de favoriser une production qui intègre les enjeux de long terme et de viabilité écologique (via des instruments réglementaires et financiers), pour avancer vers l'idée que le travail restant une forme d'intégration et de reconnaissance sociale essentielle, la réalité de la « transition écologique » pourrait être avant tout d'orienter le travail vers ces formes de production. Derrière ces mots sibyllins, je veux dire une exploitation raisonnée et différenciée des écosystèmes (mais sans doute pas tous, de façon, même en gardant une perspective anthropocentrée, à laisser des espaces d'évolution et d'adaptation aux problèmes imprévus) qui reconstruise le lien entre production et distribution des richesses.

J'espère que la version courte de ces quelques phrases n'est pas que je souhaite revenir au bon vieux temps d'une économie basée sur l'agriculture et la petite production marchande, car ce n'est pas ce à quoi je crois, certains grandes organisations ayant à l'évidence un rôle majeur à jouer dans le développement et la diffusion de nouvelles technologies.

Jean-Louis Weber - *Comment prendre en compte la nature ?* Deux approches économiques contrastées sont considérées pour prendre en compte la Nature / capital naturel[2]:

1. Le capital naturel est intégré et valorisé selon le modèle standard de la théorie économique dominante. Le choix politique devient une question d'optimisation économique. Tout se résout dans le champ de l'économie et des valeurs de marché.

L'extension du champ de la production et du marché permet de mieux valoriser la nature et ses services. Ainsi, le capital naturel est valorisé en tant que somme des bénéfices futurs actualisés, tandis que dans le cas des services écosystémiques non-marchands, l'estimation de prix fictifs se fait soit sur la base du prix de remplacement par des procédés artificiels ou sur la base de préférences individuelles exprimées (enquêtes…) ou révélées indirectement.

Les méthodes dérivées des études coûts-bénéfices s'appliquent bien quand des marchés peuvent être organisés pour comparer des options, des projets et pour calculer la valeur de services écosystémiques particuliers. Par contre, la valorisation générale en monnaie pose des problèmes comptables d'agrégation (incohérence des prix, double-comptes fréquents) et philosophiques (en particulier, la substituabilité générale entre économie et nature).

[2] V. sur cette question la note de J.-L. WEBER (Supplemental File N°1) sur le site Internet de l'Institut Michel Serres (http://institutmichelserres.ens-lyon.fr/spip.php?article169)

2. Approche basée sur la reconnaissance de la multiplicité de systèmes interagissants, en coévolution : économique, social, naturel (géologique, écosystémique...).

L'Agence Européenne pour l'Environnement a réalisé sa mise en œuvre sous le nom de « comptes du capital-écosystème ». Les comptes du capital naturel sont relativement neutres. Ils sont capables de fournir des données utilisables par toutes sortes de théories et modèles, y compris des approches non-conventionnelles comme le calcul des dettes écologiques (Weber *et al*, p. 143 et ss. du présent ouvrage; http://projects.eionet.europa.eu/leac/library/case_study_mauritius/enca-mu_draft-final-report_jlw 2013/enca-mu_draft-final report_part1_jlw2013 et)

Cette comptabilité écosystémique a été imaginée pour :

- mesurer la capabilité des écosystèmes en tant que capacité durable à fournir des services privatifs, marchands et services collectifs, publics ;
- mesurer la dégradation ou l'amélioration du point de vue de la productivité, robustesse, résilience, santé... la capacité à produire l'ensemble des services possibles (pas seulement les produits marchands...).

Concernant la dégradation du capital et l'amortissement, son amortissement n'est pas financé, c'est une consommation non payée, c'est une dette vis-à-vis des générations futures (et des générations actuelles d'autres pays quand la dégradation est incorporée dans les importations). La dégradation doit s'estimer par rapport à des normes sociales (par ex., la logique de la Directive sur la Responsabilité Environnementale de 2004).

Cette comptabilité nécessite une unité de compte équivalente à la monnaie bilan écologique, en unité de valeur écologique. Ce retour à l'économie se fait, par exemple, en intégrant le bilan écologique en unités de valeur écologique dans les procédures d'audit, de notation, d'évaluation. Le résultat, en cas d'accumulation des dettes signale une accumulation des risques et peut avoir des effets immédiats sur les taux d'intérêt ou les primes d'assurance.

Wojtek Kalinowski - *La valorisation des ressources.* La transition écologique passe par une profonde revalorisation des ressources, mais les ressorts de cette revalorisation sont d'ordre social et politique, voire culturel autant qu'économique ; sans une nouvelle conception de la richesse, sans un certain découplage du bien-être et de la consommation de ressources matérielles, les technologies « vertes » et les modélisations sophistiquées des économistes ne nous sauveront pas, elles peuvent même empirer notre situation. Poser la question de cette façon revient à « remettre l'économie à sa place », sans rien enlever à la valeur des outils économiques lorsqu'ils sont utilisés dans un cadre approprié.

Face à l'enjeu des ressources, la réponse économique standard est insuffisante. Elle consiste à dire qu'il faut modifier les prix des biens et des services, en augmentant ceux des biens dont la production et la consommation augmentent la pression sur les ressources précieuses. Comment les modifier ? Pour les ressources épuisables, nombre d'économistes parient sur la rareté elle-même pour envoyer un signal-prix aux acteurs du marché. Certains d'entre eux vont jusqu'à nous rassurer que nous n'allons jamais épuiser les matières premières, car à mesure que telle ou telle d'entre elles se raréfie, son prix relatif va augmenter et l'intérêt propre des acteurs va les pousser à chercher des alternatives : la rareté peut être relative mais jamais absolue. De même, plus les « biens environnementaux » comme l'air pur deviennent rares, plus les consommateurs seront prêts à payer davantage pour en avoir, et les marchés ne tarderont pas à satisfaire la demande, trouvant un point d'équilibre entre les « coûts » et les « bénéfices ». Dans les deux cas, ces promesses d'un marché autorégulateur (signaux-prix envoyés aux agents économiques) s'avèrent bien souvent trompeuses. Les marchés sont particulièrement mal placés pour prévoir l'avenir. Or, c'est bien là tout l'enjeu.

Même la théorie économique standard admet cependant de nombreuses défaillances de marché sous forme d' « externalités négatives », lorsque les dégâts sociaux et/ou environnementaux liés à une décision sont reportés sur un tiers (le coût social), tandis que les bénéfices restent individuels. Elle en conclut qu'une action publique est nécessaire pour internaliser ces externalités ; nous disposons pour cela de toute une batterie d'outils de régulation (taxes, quotas...). Ces outils sont indispensables mais là encore, tout dépend du cadre dans lesquels ils sont utilisés. L'intégration des externalités négatives ne sera jamais autre chose qu'une solution très partielle : pour intégrer toutes les externalités dans tous les prix, il faudrait introduire l'hypothèse parfaitement irréaliste d'un planificateur omniscient. Cette voie comporte aussi le risque d'homogénéiser l'hétérogène (devenu « capital naturel ») alors qu'il s'agit au contraire de reconnaître la pluralité des systèmes de valeurs (valeur intrinsèque de la nature). Il faut donc autre chose, une planification écologique couplée à une lente mutation des modes de vie.

Ces quelques remarques trop rapides débouchent sur les enjeux suivants ; la liste est non exhaustive mais ces points me paraissent fondamentaux :

(1) Passer de la substituabilité faible à la substituabilité forte dans la valorisation. Ce combat concerne les indicateurs, les normes comptables, les référentiels techniques à utiliser dans la valorisation. Par exemple, des analyses multicritères sont à préférer aux valeurs monétaires qui « résument » les différentes dimensions.

(2) Renforcer la cohérence et la qualité démocratique des régulations. Aussi bien du côté des régulations publiques que du côté des normes privées (labels, standards, chartes), il faut réduire l'écart entre théorie et pratique (« greenwashing », lois jamais appliquées, administrations incompétentes, agences indépendantes captées par les lobbies, etc.)

(3) Augmenter la participation citoyenne, car participation et acceptation du changement vont souvent de pair. On sait par exemple que l'installation des éoliennes ou des stations de pompage-turbinage se heurte bien souvent à la résistance locale ; ces projets n'auraient-ils pas plus de chances d'aboutir si les habitants étaient eux-mêmes en charge du processus ?

(4) Réduire les inégalités au nom de la transition écologique. Par exemple, il est techniquement facile de soutenir l'essor des énergies renouvelables en faisant payer les consommateurs, mais alors il faut prendre en compte les effets distributifs, sous peine de voir les réformes bloquées ou rejetées par la population.

(5) Soutenir l'innovation sociale et l'émergence des nouveaux modes de vie. Une revalorisation sociale de la richesse ne se décrète pas, mais elle peut être soutenue par les autorités publiques à l'échelle locale, où de nombreuses « niches » tentent déjà, à leur niveau, de

redéfinir la richesse. Il peut s'agir par exemple des outils de résilience territoriale (gestion en bien communs, systèmes d'échange locaux...).

4. Discussion – mettre les nouveaux outils au banc d'essai de la recherche

Explorer ces idées et outils devrait permettre d'esquisser l'ampleur des changements à venir en évaluant concrètement les effets des contraintes du *package* socio-écosystémique (Figure 1) sur les prises de décisions. Il est donc question d'internaliser les coûts socio-environnementaux réels, de les maîtriser et de procéder à l'ajustement des ressources aux besoins fondamentaux, le tout au nom d'une gestion adaptative, intégrée et durable des ressources accessibles. Cela revient à établir des bilans en quasi-temps réel permettant de concevoir des systèmes de boucle de rétrocontrôle nulle ou positive (tendre vers des externalités nulles) dans le cadre d'une économie plus locale et circulaire et qui intègre l'ensemble des échanges commerciaux. Cet aspect est déterminant car, *in fine*, on souhaite comprendre quels sont les seuils relatifs des capacités de régénération des ressources d'un territoire en rapport avec son niveau théorique d'autosuffisance, ainsi que ses atouts en s'engageant dans une démarche choisie de sobriété volontaire. Sur ces bases, il devient possible de modéliser et donc d'anticiper les trajectoires qui transforment les modes de vie actuels dans des options de développement compatibles avec les équilibres socio-écosystémiques évoquées ici.

Le débat que cette démarche alimente est celui, difficile, de la distinction responsable entre des *needs* et des *wants*, encore une fois à considérer en fonction des spécificités et du potentiel ressources d'un territoire donné, capacités de gouvernance comprises (bonnes pratiques, politiques de taxes, subventions etc). C'est par là que passe la sortie de la culture de la dette, permettant de donner du sens à nos productions-consommations, à nos modes et qualité de vie.

La démarche abordée dans ce travail ouvre-t-elle la voie à une transition sociétale et écologique s'appuyant sur une transformation culturelle ? Voici deux arguments, sans vouloir être exhaustif :

(1) L'approche-système des ressources, par son interdisciplinarité très élaborée et par sa dimension pédagogique, peut changer les représen-

tations. Par exemple, celles des agricultures et leur multifonctionnalité, en intégrant les problématiques sols / foncier, eau, biomasse, *etc.* avec un ensemble de considérations concernant les acteurs, les circuits courts, l'économie circulaire. Mais aussi, en questionnant la théorie standard du capital quand cela concerne les ressources naturelles. Si, aujourd'hui, l'objectif est de maximiser la valeur économique telle que vue par les marchés et élargie à la nature à l'aide de prix fictifs, demain, l'objectif sera de maximiser la résilience des systèmes (du potentiel financier, économique), par l'usage non-destructif des ressources renouvelables (une soutenabilité écologique des systèmes de production)[3]. Car il est frappant de voir que des réflexions se développent (dans la suite du rapport Stiglitz, www.stiglitz-sen-fitoussi.fr/fr/ ou les travaux du collectif FAIR en France : http://www.idies.org/index.php?category/FAIR) sur l'observation de la résilience de tous les systèmes, naturels, financiers, économiques, sociaux. Dans les deux exemples, la part du droit dans cette transition culturelle sera déterminante.

(2) En se donnant comme objectif de réaliser la gestion en temps réel des ressources sur un ensemble de territoires (Weber *et al*, p. 143 et ss. du présent ouvrage), se dessine probablement une première transgression de la tenace culture de la dette. Une priorité immédiate concerne la production, l'accès aux, la transparence, la libre circulation des données. En même temps, cette synchronicité des représentations intégrées du « réel – ressources » devrait permettre de penser et d'imaginer des rapprochements avec le fonctionnement des écosystèmes.

Par exemple, les écosystèmes font de la croissance et de la compétition calibrées, adaptatives, avec des efficacités énergétiques redoutables et des niveaux de productivités robustes. On observera que les taux de retour en vigueur dans les secteurs de l'économie sont supérieurs aux taux de renouvellement / reproduction des populations ou de la photosynthèse (1 - 4 % ; Rotillon, 2010). Mais, ces taux-là intègrent déjà toutes les « externalités » des réseaux trophiques en faisant de l'économie parfaitement circulaire. Certes, en se plaçant plutôt dans l'autosuffisance, mais sans que la

[3] V. sur cette question la note de J.-L. WEBER (Supplemental File N°2) sur le site Internet de l'Institut Michel Serres (http://institutmichelserres.ens-lyon.fr/spip.php?article169)

décroissance soit un « comportement » recherché par le système, qui génère, sauf accident, une « réserve » écologique, un surplus (Running, 2012).

C'est, par exemple, le calibrage socio-environnemental d'une ruche. A nous de faire mieux socio-culturellement : *« entretenir le monde et le cultiver »*.

Références

Alternatives Internationales, Hors-série 11, *Les guerres des matières premières*. 2012.

BARNOSKY A. et *al* (2012), "Approaching a state shift in Earth's biosphere", *Nature* 486: 52-58

COUVET D., « Interactions entre biodiversité et sécurité alimentaire », In: Collart Dutilleul F., Bréger Th. (Eds.), *Penser une démocratie alimentaire*, Vol. 2, pp. 375-383.

DASGUPTA P. (2010), "The Place of Nature in Economic Development" In: Rodrik, D. & Rosenzweig, M. (eds.), *Handbook of Development Economics 5*, 4039-5061

GRAEBER D., *Dette, 5000 ans d'histoire*, Les liens qui libèrent Edition, 2013, 624 p.

Les ressources, Les colloques de l'Institut universitaire de France. Negrutiu I., Del Fatti N., Bravard J.-P., Vieira C. (Eds). PUSE St. Etienne, 2011 (Collart Dutilleul F., pp. 63-80 ; Negrutiu I., pp. 327-337).

RIST G., *Le développement, l'histoire d'une croyance occidentale*. Presses des Sciences-Po. Paris, 2007, 483 p.

ROTILLON G., *Economie des ressources naturelles*, La découverte, 2010, 125 p.

STEFFEN W., Crutzen P.-J., McNeill J.-R., 2007, "The Anthropocene: are humans now overwhelming the great forces of nature", *Ambio* 36: 614-621

THUILLIER P., interview 1996 (http://sergecar.perso.neuf.fr/textes_1/thuillier6.htm)

WEBER J.-L. et *al*, A Natural Resource-Systems approach: Targeting the Ecological Transition at the Regional Scale. In: Collart Dutilleul F., Bréger Th. (eds.), *Penser une démocratie alimentaire*, Vol. 2, pp. 143-167.

A Natural Resource-Systems approach: Targeting the Ecological Transition at the Regional Scale[1]

J.-L. WEBER [*1], E. FERNANDEZ [*2], C. MALWE [*3], J.-M. SALLES [*4], F. COLLART DUTILLEUL [*5], I. NEGRUTIU [*6]

1. Introduction

Human history can be mirrored in a geo-history of natural resources (Dasgupta, 1982 and 2010). Humans, by over-exploiting resources ("forcing"), have produced extensive land use changes and have altered complex food webs, ecosystems, and habitats with as a consequence systematic natural biocapacity erosion, biodiversity loss, energy crises, pollution, climate deregulation (Pauly *et al*, 1998, Griffon, 2006, Ellis *et al*, 2010; Foley *et al*, 2005 and 2011; Lotze *et al*, 2011; Dittrich *et al*, 2012). In other terms, a global resources "rush" has led to chronic socio-ecosystemic deficits, thus creating the conditions for local and global state shifts within the biosphere and / or society (Ravillon *et al*, 2007; Ferone, 2008; Barnosky *et al*, 2012; Running, 2012).

[1] The present work is part of the Michel Serres Institute research program (http://institutmichelserres.ens-lyon.fr) on natural resources and public goods supported by the Research Fund of the ENS de Lyon and hosted at IXXI Institute for complex systems. CM and EF are fellows of the Collegium de Lyon. Their contribution has been coordinated through the ERC Lascaux program (http://www.droit-aliments-terre.eu/). The authors are much indebted to many colleagues and students for stimulating discussions during seminars, courses, and conferences organized during the last two years while teaching the Masters degree course "Bioresources and biodiversity".

[*1] Economiste et Statisticien. Conseiller spécial pour la comptabilité économique-environnementale au sein de l'Agence Européenne de l'Environnement, Copenhague.

[*2] Chercheur invité au Collegium de Lyon. Chercheur associé à l'Institut Ouest : Droit et Europe de l'Université de Rennes 1.

[*3] Chercheur invité au Collegium de Lyon. Maître de conférences à l'Université de Rennes 1, Institut du Droit Public et de la Science Politique (EA 4640)..

[*4] Directeur de recherche CNRS, LAMETA, SupAgro Montpellier ;

[*5] Professeur à l'Université de Nantes. Directeur du Programme Lascaux (ERC).

[*6] Biologiste, Directeur de l'Institut Michel Serres, ENS de Lyon.

Therefore, research must serve to increase human understanding of those resources and how best to use them for the public good.

The question is how to approach the problem in order to integrate the economy into the cycles and functions of the biosphere, while providing society-wide access to vital resources and services (Costanza 2004 and 2010; Brown, 2006). According to the SCAR 3rd foresight (Freibauer *et al*, 2011) "*the increasing scarcity of natural resources and destabilization of environmental systems represent a real threat not only to future food supplies, but also to global stability and prosperity, as it can aggravate poverty, disturb international trade, finance and investment, and destabilise governments*". In addition, Dasgupta (2010) considers that "*individuals and communities over-exploit natural capital, meaning that the ecological services are subsidized. Social norms and legal rules are at the root of the system*".

We therefore argue that natural resources as a whole (human resources included) represent the central issue in sustainable development and the ecological transition. An integrated resource-driven approach and the reframing of the geopolitics of natural resources appear as prerequisites in addressing more coherently and in a context-specific manner most, if not all, of the present time challenges: greenhouse gas emissions, climate change, biodiversity, food security, as well as energy and other poorly interconnected resources (water-soil-air, food-health-education-environment etc) (Negrutiu, 2011; also see Scheffer *et al*, 2009; Deffuant *et al*, 2012; Dittrich *et al*, 2012).

Developing a natural resource-systems approach is expected to provide a proper conceptual frame and integrative tools and methods from diverse disciplines (such as natural sciences, economy-finance, social and legal studies) for (1) the maintaining of a strong life-supporting capacity of the natural capital and (2) the sustainable/equitable production, access, use, distribution, and circulation of natural resources according to territorial natural resources capacities / specificities and governance skills. This implies analysing the socio-economic / financial / normative-legal contexts, policy instruments, and institutions characterizing the considered territorial entity (a region, a country, the EU), while jointly addressing the issues of (and measuring very precisely) the present ecological deficits (Thara Srinivasan *et al*, 2008), the internalization of socio-environmental costs, as well as controversial questions such as carrying capacity and economic competition.

Before exploring these aspects, a broad-brush analysis of the resource problematic is presented.

2. Current Understanding of the Natural Resources Problematic

The natural capital can be defined as a mesh of resources (Dasgupta, 2010). Resources are a socio-cultural construction: the culture, the law, and the technology define what is (or could be) a resource. Their perception through life-styles and technological change is constantly evolving. Today, the political statement that current economies can grow indefinitely in a world with finite resources is a gamble.

Resources remain elusive as both identified and measured, but also undiscovered and inferred resources feed systematic controversies. Reserves, by contrast, are identified resources that meet extraction and production criteria in terms of investment and profitability (US Geological Survey glossary). Considerations such as exploration versus production, prices versus costs, and the accuracy and veracity of reporting by companies and countries all have impacts on resources information (Aschzet *et al*, 2011). They also affect the science devoted to them, with technological advances continuously modifying the resource to reserve balance.

An increasing number of compounds from biotic and non-biotic, renewable and non- renewable resources are being transformed according to inferred needs into a diverse range of functional materials. Not surprisingly, the resource issue is largely restricted to its economic and market logic, natural resources being merely considered as fluxes of values and exploited with no consideration of environmental or social costs (EEA report, 5/2011). Of note, the exploitation of non-renewable resources is dealt with in terms of potential substitutable materials, while renewable resources are managed as available stocks. The demographic and market pressures, and the global natural resources "rush" have led to chronic socio-ecosystemic deficits / debts (Weber, 2011; E-risk report 2012), mirrored by food-health-environment-poverty/culture disequilibria (Meadows *et al*, 2005; Brown, 2006). Taken together, such considerations have prompted research on the Common-Pool Resources concept (Dasgupta, 1982; Ostrom *et al*, 2002;

Baron *et al*, 2011). They may further stimulate work revisiting the renewable resources concept in regard to questions such as: how pertinent the term "renewable" is today for resources which are expected to maintain their regeneration potential (biocapacity) and which in reality undergo extensive degradation / deterioration, and fast or frequent devaluation.

2.1 Non-renewable Resources: Differential Scarcity and Material Intensity

Given the volumes physically available in the Earth crust and oceans, and the potential to recycle, there is no theoretical constraint for any of the chemicals / minerals under consideration. The Earth crust is approx 30 km thick, but most explorations rarely go deeper than 1-2,000 meters deep (Aschzet *et al*, 2011).

During 1980 – 2005 the resource extraction intensity has been increased by 160% with material intensity being reduced by 25%. Since the population growth averaged 45% during the same time period, the decoupling of economic growth from natural resources use has not been achieved yet (UNEP report 2011, http://www.unep.org/greeneconomy).

Furthermore, there is the tightly linked soil fertility and water shortages problem (Griffon, 2006; Foley *et al* 2005; Hoekstra and Mekonen, 2011). While land pressure for bio-based products (biofuels and a variety of biomaterials) is growing in competition with food production needs, severe water shortfalls are predicted for two-thirds of countries (http://water.worldbank.org/node/84122; http://www.weforum.org/issues/water/index.html).

"*Energy is the one and only real limiting factor in the long run, because given enough energy there will always be enough natural non-energy resources extractable from the crust of the Earth*" (Neumayer, 2000). Energy consumption is increasing steadily, with electricity as the dominant form. Today, over 60 metallic elements are involved in energy pathways, so their availability, functionality, substitutability and recyclability are of concern in decision-making (Aschzet *et al*, 2011). The environmental and human health performance of such materials and the generated waste are crucial societal issues in terms of dissipation and dispersion, recycling capacity etc and significantly can impact supply and demand.

2.2 Renewable but Exhaustible Biological Resources

The environmental considerations and the expected relative scarcity of non-renewable reserve stocks set the scene for alternative solutions based on renewable natural resources (Barbault and Weber, 2009; Alternatives Internationales, 2012, Griffon, 2013). The challenge is huge as the weight ratio of non-renewable to renewable resource intake is 50 :1, raising concerns about the capacity of the "*exclusive renewable energies options to offer but simple material-based life style societies with high level of self-sufficiency*" (Neumayer, 2011 and refs therein; Smith *et al*, 2012). The main question so far is not decarbonating the economy, but how to manage the transition from a fossil carbon to a green carbon economy.

Let's have a closer look. The green carbon economy is totally dependent on biomass generated as Net Primary Production (NPP), which subtends the Carbon cycle of the biosphere. The state and dynamics of NPP (Running, 2012) support most of the basic functions and services of ecosystems and habitats, the various food webs (i.e species diversity / biodiversity) and humans' ecological footprint (Pauly *et al*, 1998; Living Planet report 2012).

The contribution of biomass as a multi-use resource for human needs is rapidly increasing: from a global NPP of 536 billion tons, 7 billion humans co-opt 38%, with a theoretical 10% available for additional human use with respect to non-harvestable parts required for biosphere equilibria (Running, 2012). Further forcing on NPP through today´s food production systems compromise the capacity of Earth to produce food in the future (Godfray *et al*, 2010; Foley *et al*, 2011; Beddington, 2011).

2.3 The Human Resource

Humans are a paradoxical resource as both diversified consumers of exhaustible resources and creators of unlimited ones: knowledge and personal data are continuously and fast growing raw materials.

The projected increase in human population to 8 billion in the next decade and improving living standards are expected to increase the demand for food, water, and energy by approx. 35, 40, and 50% respectively by 2030 (Global Trends 2030, www.dni.gov/nic/globaltrends). The controversial demographic and related carrying capacity issues (Agenda 21,

1992; Turchin, 2009; Engelman, 2011) require therefore an increased involvement of the scientific community. For example, agricultural expansion beyond 50% of available land / ecosystems is considered as a critical threshold (Barnoski *et al*, 2012; also see Good and Beatty, 2011).

2.4 Unequal Distribution of and Access to Resources: the "Boomerang Effect"

The unequal (quantity and quality) distribution of resources has generated an annuity system, on which, in turn, an ambiguous relationship with economic development has been created and constitutes a permanent source of geo-political conflicts. A contrasting picture prevails.

(1) Financial, but also non-financial accounting systems are presently considered worldwide in sovereign credit assessments. The "E-RISC report" describes methods and metrics for quantifying natural resources, renewable resources in particular, and the corresponding environmental risks. The assessment is particularly critical for countries that "*depend, in net terms, on levels of renewable resources and services beyond what their own ecosystems can provide*". Obviously, this is the situation for most countries today. The E-RISC approach is a major step forward in putting upfront the concept of ecological debts as a risk factor. There is a need for a real systemic and global accounting for the natural capital (as much as economic accounts are systemic), including natural resources production, supply, use, consumption, accumulation, and trade, with corresponding remunerations, profits, taxes and subsidies, financial flows and assets, and debts originating from the entire process (i.e., a robust statistical base to support ecosystemic debts calculation).

(2) Most States are not capable of adapting their resources to the basic needs of their populations (FAO, 2009; Mazoyer *et al*, 2008) for reasons that are strongly linked with the international laws pertaining to international investments and trade, and with the regulations of the World Trade Organisation (Collart Dutilleul, 2012 a and b; Honet & Negrutiu, 2012). Other States develop strategies for the more sustainable management of their natural capital. A useful study case is the Management Resources Act, 1991 of the New Zealand that restates and reforms the law relating to the use of land, air, and water (see *Section 5.2*).

3. Why the Regional Scale Matters?

Natural resources at the regional level have economic, financial, environmental, and socio-cultural meaning at the same time. Therefore they are likely to "speak" more directly to society and individuals in terms of stock, flux, and footprint, but also in terms of responsible attitudes and actions through social networks and links. The temporal and spatial representations of the state and dynamics of regional resources, such as ecological deficit and debt (not erasable, contrary to financial debts by contractual agreement or government bailout), carrying capacity, internalization of socio-environmental costs, socio-economic competition, etc are likely to become politically and society-wise more readily meaningful than equivalent global figures. The socio-ecosystemic virtues of circular economy systems make sense at local-to-regional territorial scales. Therefore, the coordinated and integrated management of natural resources at the regional scale is likely to become an important political issue in the short run. To that end, enabling regional monitoring and accounting will allow devising optimized solutions adapted to local specifics (Seitzinger *et al*, 2012; Griffon 2013) by engaging various stakeholders, economic actors, and policy-makers . This should contribute to enhancing the responsibility levels in decision-making and in society at large, therefore facilitating the ecological transition process.

Converging elements indicate that the decision / action power is emerging at the regional scale. For example, the EU has operationally defined a regional grid of policies across the continent for a variety of developmental strategies, objectives, and projects (European Regional Development Fund). Furthermore, at the national level, the French law dealing with the modernization of agriculture and fisheries (2010) and, more generally, the emerging territorial sustainable development policies, have created in each region overlapping bodies and /or programs:

(1) A "Plan Régional de l'Agriculture Durable" (PRAD – regional sustainable agriculture plan) for a seven-year period. The PRAD includes the implementation of indicators and assessment criteria (http://draaf.rhône-alpes.agriculture.gouv.fr/Plan-regional-de-l-agriculture);

(2) A "Plan régional pour l'agriculture et le développement rural" (PRADR – regional plan for agriculture and rural development) was voted in 2010 and includes, for example, the territorialization of action by the Region through strategic rural development projects (PSAD-ER);

(3) The CESER (the economic, social and environmental regional council) produces periodic assessments at the cross-road of economic, social, and environmental questions;

(4) The PSDR approach ("Pour et Sur le Développement Rural"), an INRA-IRSTEA research program on regional rural development has been operational for a dozen or so years (http://www6.versailles-grignon.inra.fr/sadapt/Equipe-Proximites/Les-programmes-PSDR). Among the PSDR3 key-recommendations, the preservation and valorisation of territorial resources and regional specificities stands out as a program on its own.

Last but not least, information technology is fostering big data systems. Data storage and processing power, together with extensive networking, is providing global access and pervasive services (Global Trends 2030), making regional capacities in decision-making feasible and necessary. The EU has established an in-house expertise on big data production within a network of institutes coordinated by the Joint Research Centre and the European Environment Agency (http://ec.europa.eu/dgs/jrc/index.cfm), with clear-cut objectives on a series of environmental and ecosystem indicators.

4. The Resource-Systems Approach

Specific natural resources (water, soil / land use, food-biomass-agriculture, bio-energy, etc) have recently been thoroughly analyzed at planetary scale (Foley *et al*, 2005 and 2011; Ramankuty *et al*, 2008; Ellis *et al*, 2010; Hookstra and Mekonen, 2011; Smith *et al*, 2012). This patchy knowledge gives an idea of the immensity of the task at global level. Three components are considered in building the systems approach, namely the conceptual level (identified as the "missing link"), the methodological and governance levels to be calibrated at the regional scale to start with (identified as the "missing tools)". The overall expected result is a continuously upgraded natural resources monitoring, accounting, and diagnosis as an aid to decision-making allowing the discrimination of facts and trends from ideological considerations. These are basic prerequisites for a coherent and effective ecological transition process.

4.1 The Conceptual Level – Reframing the Natural Resources

The conceptual level considers the necessity to entirely reframe the field of natural resources and public goods, starting with clarifying the terminology relative to natural resources and related terms. At the same time, it is important to proceed towards an interdisciplinary academic appropriation of the natural resources problematic as a whole (Negrutiu, 2011; *Figure 1*) through questions such as "How to coherently define, address, and manage human fundamental needs and rights (food-health-environment-education/culture), the common / public goods issues and the competition / innovation syndromes?", or "Why are humans primarily resource-minded and wrongly resource-framed?". Setting up a renewed experimental framework should encompass, among others:

(1) Surveys, questioning the perception and relationship between humans (individually and collectively) and resources (natural, human, economic, institutional or cognitive);

(2) Inventories and critical analysis of institutions, programs, and corporate bodies that have recognized expertise on natural resources, allowing the identification of the main gaps and overlaps in the field. For example, the World Resources Forum (WRF) is the science-based platform for sharing knowledge about the "*economic, political, social and environmental implications of global resource use*; (http://www.worldresourcesforum.org/).

(3) Studies on the geo-history and geo-politics of functional and cultural materials, including work on questions such as functional materials for agriculture, industry, services, e-economy, but also innovation / technology and resources typology and topology across time (politics, conflicts, diplomacy, and governance; Gabriel-Oyhamburu, 2010; Goetschel and Péclard, 2006) and the Great Acceleration (Steffen, *et al,* 2007).

(4) Translate the resources problematic as a whole by systematically and globally linking food-health-education/culture-environment, a fundamental equity problem of present-time generations. Such an "equation" has largely been neglected so far, despite ongoing efforts through the Millenium Development Goals (goals 1-3 and 5-8; http://en.wikipedia.org/wiki/Millennium_Development_Goals).

Figure 1. The resource-systems matrix of development and ecological transition. Reframing the conceptual and operational field of natural resources makes it possible to establish more coherent and effective links between vital needs and otherwise unrelated or poorly related factors/components and the corresponding risks: food-health-education/culture, environment, energy, climate change, biodiversity, future generations and so on. This requires deep interdisciplinarity across fields encompassing legal and socio-economic studies, and life-sciences.

4.2 The Methodological Approach – Integrating the Big Data Revolution

The methodological approach aims at adapting and/or developing (real-time) monitoring tools and methods at the regional scale in order to establish, understand, and model the state, dynamics, and accounting of physical natural resources as a whole according to territorial natural resources capacities / specificities and governance skills. Modelling of natural resources requires the production, access, and circulation of data sources and coordinated interdisciplinary work (also see Purves *et al,* 2013 on climate change and "all life" modelling and ecological transition timing at http://www.neweconomics.org/publications/greattransition). In parallel, the financial, socio-economic, legal, normative, and political contexts, instruments, institutions, and skills need to be analysed and articulated according to trade-offs between environmental, legal, economic, social, and cultural outcomes.

These aspects are presented and discussed below and address the renewable resources in the first place.

5. Cross-talk between Natural Sciences and Social Studies

The systems approach to the natural capital and ecological transition *(Figure 1)* requires coherent and concerted thinking and action across disciplines, in particular in economic, legal, social, and life-sciences. We identify below several key questions that require a consistent cross-talk between these disciplines in the first place.

5.1 Resources Economy and Environmental Economy Studies

The economy is not yet accountable for Nature's degradation (Dasgupta, 2010; Weber, 2007 and 2011; Dittrich *et al,* 2012). National, regional or local governments or companies do not keep ecological balance sheets. Consuming ecosystem capital (i.e. loss of ecosystem capability) without accounting for it is equivalent to creating ecological debts that are transmitted to others, to our present and future generations or to countries from which imported products are produced under unsustainable conditions (Dittrich *et al*, 2012).

The "E-Risk" approach has been described in *Section 2.4*, but the ecological footprint indicator has recently been questioned (Blomqvist *et al*, 2013). Among the alternatives, we analyze here the "ecosystem capital simplified accounts" that are currently being implemented in Europe by the European Environment Agency (Weber, 2011). Their objective is to measure the ecosystem resources that are accessible without degradation, their intensity of use, and the change in the capability of ecosystems to deliver their services over time.

The state of the ecosystem can be assessed without going into the detail of the services provided. Valuation is limited to critical flows of services on the one hand, and to ecosystem change (no need to value the ecosystems themselves) on the other hand, for which estimations can be based on the observable costs of management and restoration/rehabilitation actions of land and soil, forestry, water, rivers, and catchments or even biodiversity.

To territorial debt, should be added the consumption of non-paid ecosystem capital that is embedded in international transactions. The ecological debts (and symmetrically credits when improvements occur) can be subsequently incorporated into portfolios of financial instruments organized in ecological balance sheets.

Presently such accounts increasingly benefit from big data systems allowing the continuous monitoring of state change and variation through Earth monitoring by satellite programs, *in situ* monitoring systems, and fast processing of socio-economic statistics. In other words, (near) real-time monitoring and accounting tools are becoming accessible at various territorial scales.

The "ecosystem capacity of production and servicing" in a given territory is measured with the aid of an ecosystem capability accounting tool. This is based on a composite index measuring changes in available resources, the intensity of their use for private and public benefits, and direct and indirect qualitative impacts (pollution, landscape integrity and biodiversity).

The first step consists in establishing the land-cover stocks and flows (i.e. the territorial land repertoire as gross and net changes, Weber, 2007). On that land matrix, the productivity capacity of biological resources (with biomass as a major concern; de Bossoreille de Ribou *et al,* 2013), but also water and soil productivity and footprints, are critical and can now be monitored (Ellis *et al,* 2010, Hoekstra and Mekonen, 2011; Benwart, 2011, Smith *et al*, 2012). In our hands, such indicators inform the Landscape Ecosystem Potential and integrate qualitative variables reflecting (agro)ecosystem health (Weber, 2011). The geographic data management is required firstly to analyse short-term degradation of the socio-ecosystems. This is important because the extent to which we manage the productive potential of natural resources will determine the range of options and solutions we can count on in the (near) future.

A complete grid of these factors and their equivalence with economic units is given in Figure 2. The calculations in ecosystem potential (or capability) unit-equivalent (EPUE or ECU) are described in the Technical Report 13/2011 of the European Environment Agency and in a spreadsheet with mock-up numbers (downloaded from http://projects.eionet.europa.eu/leac/library/e_c_a_fast_track_provisional_repository/background_documents/seca_ecu_model-annex_tables_to_simplifed_framework). It includes detailed tables as well as charts and a small tutorial showing how to calculate ECU values for a given ecosystem.

This approach has manifold implications because it:

1. Reveals the dual aspect of the natural capital, based on the fact that the ecosystem assets are both suppliers of goods used for final consumption and a capital that reproduces such goods and can be degraded in case of excessive exploitation;
2. Allows translation of debt and risk concepts into versatile metrics allowing in turn to operate with the aid of restoration / compensation equivalent values;
3. Identifies the causes of natural capital degradation (stress factors) and the corresponding liabilities of economic sectors and agents or of the community itself (e.g. in case of land planning impacts);
4. Demonstrates the need for high quality of and access to various public data sources in order to foster scientifically sound and verifiable measurements prone in turn to support effective policy measures;
5. Identifies improvements needed in public and private accounting standards for measuring the management behaviour of and liability to the natural capital.

The results can be compared to other available tools that measure the human impact on the natural capital, namely:

1. Ecological Footprint and regional biocapacity / bioproductivity as described in the "E-risk" protocol (E-Risk report 2012) and protocols and indicators according to Sutton and Costanza, (2002);
2. HANPP (Human Appropriation of Net Primary Productivity) measuring the primary production appropriated by humans (Haberl *et al*, 2007);

3. Resource-use indicators integrating materials, water, land area, and GHG emissions (Dittrich *et al*, 2012).

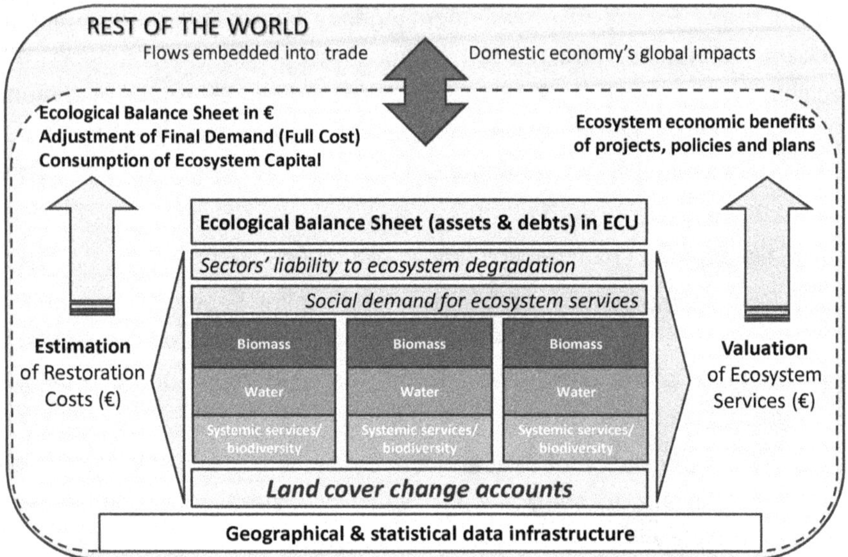

Figure 2. The overall framework of ecosystem capital accounts and applications by ecosystems, sectors, or regions. The Ecosystem Capital Account (ECA) framework is based on the measurement of ecosystems performance, enhancement or degradation of their capacity of delivering services in a perpetual way. Each ecosystem is recorded considering firstly three quantitative balances of biomass, water, and system-based functional services. These quantitative accounts pay attention to the measurement of an effectively accessible resource (instead of the theoretically available one) considering quality, timeliness, and randomness issues. In addition to quantitative measurements, the ECA framework includes qualitative indexes in order to reflect intrinsic ecosystem values, such as the stability of carbon pools (linked to the age of the systems), their intoxication, and dependency on artificial inputs (labour, energy, chemical, irrigation water…), their integrity and biodiversity. A composite index integrates these quantitative and qualitative indexes into a measurement of the ecosystem capital capability – so-called Ecosystem Capability Unit (ECU). This unit-equivalent can be used for any ecosystem, at any scale by central, regional or local governments as well as by companies. It can measure stores of ecological values and their change resulting from modification of any of the three basis components. It can be used in the context of mitigation systems and support compensations and to measure ecosystem capital consumption embedded into international trade. These are the characteristics of a currency: universal equivalent, usable for storage of value and in exchanges. Accounts in ECU are finally integrated into a balance sheet, as are the economic accounts. The second dimension of ECA is valuation, which is made easier by the existence of well structured accounts in physical units. This approach is in line with the TEEB stepwise approach to

valuation (http://www.cbd.int/doc/meetings/im/rwim-wafr-01/other/rwim-wafr-01-teeb-en.pdf).

5.2 Legal Studies and Natural Resources Management

Such studies are particularly necessary for both paving the road of the ecological transition process and identifying the corresponding limits, obstacles or breaks (such as transparency of data and information, dissemination of results and choice of solutions, security / sovereignty issues, human and property rights, legislation incompatibilities, etc). Legal and social considerations on the accelerated erosion of physical natural resources can reveal risk factors of induced social shrinkage. For instance, a transition process should jointly address the issues of vital needs and public goods by linking food, health, education, and environmental factors in both time (present and future generations) and space (local versus global). Their regional security, according to the territorial potential and an optimized resources efficiency, requires adaptive governance and persistent good practices (see for ex. the 2004 Environmental Liability Directive 2004/35/CE).

Legal studies are also conducted to evaluate the conditions of an equilibrium of local versus global-level legal systems as a sort of limit to globalization, i.e. to what extent a region can develop its own policies relative to natural resources security and public goods without infringing upon the international rules (intellectual property rights, WTO laws, international investment law, etc). A relevant example is the marine resource (food, energy, minerals, etc) and the contrasting to controversial legal status of sea zones, protected areas, etc (Jarmache, 2013).

We analyse below the 1991 Resource Management Act of New Zealand that restates and reforms the law relating to the use of land, air, and water (also see Ostrom *et al*, 2002; Thoyer, 2006, Baron *et al*, 2011, Levebvre *et al*, 2012).

5.2.1 The Resource Management Act (RMA) - a significant reform in New Zealand's environmental law

The RMA constitutes a major effort in order to bring together more than 50 disparate and punctual environmental laws (mainly dedicated to sector-based subjects) under one single and transversal text. According to the Parliamentary Commissioner for the Environment, RMA's "*passage into law was preceded by a well funded, intensive and extensive process, called the Resource Management Law Reform (RMLR), that was tasked to explore new approaches to resource management, influenced by concepts of sustainability as well as by ideas of efficiency and accountability*" (Parliamentary Commissioner for the Environment, 2002, p. 138.).

The RMA's purpose "*is to promote the sustainable management of natural and physical resources*" (Section 5). This act addresses jointly several environmental matters (Sections 6 and 7). It promotes a model of development that takes into account a range of aspects, such as the recognition of the intrinsic values of ecosystems, life dependence on natural resources and the maintenance and enhancement of the quality of the environment, the necessity to preserve them for the protection of historic heritage and customary rights, but also for future generations. An additional main objective is the evaluation of the impacts of human activities on the environment, in order to avoid, remediate, or mitigate any adverse effects of activities on the environment.

5.2.2 The RMA: reframing the environmental decision process

The general structure of the environmental decisions process is built on a hierarchy of documents that must be considered when deciding to grant or not a resource consent (Section 104): at the top, "national environmental standards", "national policy statements", and the "New Zealand coastal policy statements" (Sections 43, 45 and 56); in the middle, "regional policy statements" and "regional plans" (Sections 59 and 63); and finally, at the bottom, "district plans" (Section 72). The documents at the middle should be consistent with those at the top, and documents at the bottom must be consistent both with documents at the top and documents in the middle.

From an institutional point of view, the RMA involves various sectors of society. For example, the granting of resource consents requires the consultation of various governmental, regional, and local agencies. This situation resulted in a break-up of participants in the decision process and in the increase of administrative departments concerned. Consequently, the decision process planned in the RMA has affected the uniformity of local decisions. This was particularly blatant in cases in which it was necessary to integrate economic and social factors taking into consideration the regional or local context, since every agency could have a different approach on common subjects.

The RMA is considered as an "information intensive" statute (Parliamentary Commissioner for the Environment, 2002, p. 156.), i.e. it requires data about natural resources and, more widely the environment. To this end, Section 35 asks local authorities to gather information in relation to the state of the environment, effectiveness of policy statements, and plans and resource consents.

According to New Zealand's Ministry for the environment (Ministry for the Environment, 2011, p. 6), a "*credible state of the environment monitoring and reporting is critical to good decision-making. In order to build a reliable and accurate national picture of New Zealand's natural capital, we need a regular and independent state of the environment reporting system which is underpinned by high quality, consistent statistics that conform to standards for official statistics*".

5.2.3 Limitations and gaps of the RMA - a narrower concept of sustainable development

If this conception of "sustainable management" and the sustainability discourse of the 90's have been, in some way, a success story, today's doctrine and politics underline that "*New Zealand has not followed an overall strategic approach, but taken a variety of steps related to sustainable development*" (Bosselmann, 2007, p. 1). These steps include various legal reforms (see the Environment Court Act 1996 and the Local Government Act 2002) and policy documents such as the "Environment Strategy 2010" (1995) or the "Government's approach to sustainable development" in 2002. But "*there is no coherent approach behind these initiatives as they vary in purpose, content and scope. Moreover, they do not include any of the features typical of a National Sustainable Development Strategy, such as an analysis of existing practices, public debate, capacity-building, monitoring and an independent advisory body*" (K. Bosselmann, 2007, p. 2). For this reason, doctrine and politicians wonder which concept of "sustainable development" is being pursued, what it clearly means, and how it relates to current practices (see Paper to the Cabinet Policy Committee, 2001; the report The Government's Approach to Sustainable Development, 2002; the report of the Parliamentary Commissioner for the Environment, 2002).

The exact contribution of the RMA to sustainable management of natural resources in New Zealand is difficult to evaluate because of the absence of dedicated assessment tools ever since the RMA was enacted. Many years after the enactment of the RMA, the major efforts of advised commentators have pointed to the interpretation of the Act's provisions. Few efforts have been made to evaluate the effectiveness of these provisions and their outcomes, as well as to establish an advisory body responsible for overseeing and coordinating the decision process meant to achieve local as well as national goals.

Furthermore, considering difficulties of the local authorities in assuming environmental reporting functions, the national government proposed a series of environmental performance indicators for air, marine, climate change, land, waste, transport, pest and diseases, energy, biodiversity, etc. However, not all of them have been completed or used. Moreover, the costs of obtaining information and the availability of environmental information (there are disparities of criteria and indices because there is no requirement in the RMA for local authorities to supply standardised data to the Ministry's environmental statistics programme (2011, p.15) constitute two key problems in the implementation of the RMA provisions.

Another difficulty is that local reports tend to exclude social and economic dimensions and some do not reflect the RMA's emphasis on natural resources management. Moreover, some issues (e.g. resource use efficiency) are not addressed by the RMA. Finally, reactions to the effectiveness of RMA over the last ten years point to the lack of additional tools, and in particular, of economic instruments (such as incentives, funds, and green taxes). As a consequence, admitting a narrow interpretation of the RMA scope, "*many local authorities deliberately operated a separation between social/economic planning and environmental planning. Doctrine and politics are still debating over the meaning of sustainable management*".

5.2.4 Green indicators and the effectiveness of the RMA legislation

In the report "Creating our future: sustainable development for New Zealand", the Parliamentary Commissioner for Environment paints a broad-brush picture of sustainable indicators as part of an upcoming national strategy: "*The 'green' GDP and a proposed 'composite index of sustainable development" were considered the ones that most adequately reflected all aspects of sustainable development. The Ecological Footprint and the Human Development Index were rated the highest in terms of practicalities (data availability, cost, long-term data available), but had a number of weaknesses*" (p. 106). How can a country develop useful indicators that, reflecting the state of natural resources, will influence decision-making? The Ministry for the Environment of New Zealand has been working for some time on a set of Environmental Performance Indicators to measure changes caused by various pressures on environment and guide decisions on environmental problems. However, this set of indicators remains incomplete (Patterson, 2002).

5.3 Reframing the Legal System(s) of Natural Resources

The rather unique case of New Zealand illustrates the fact that from the legal point of view it is difficult today to devise coherent, long-term policies on the global management of natural resources. Thinking about France, for example, we are witnessing a segmentation of powers (also see *Section 3*) when actually coordination is necessary to ensure such management:

- the state is in charge of the territorial administration; it adopts rules of international law relative to economic activities, protection of the environment, etc;
- the Region is in charge of developing economic activities;
- the Department puts in practice agricultural policies and covers the field of agriculture and farmers;
- the Commune manages land administration and establishes its own land use plans over its entire territory;

- private owners have full power to manage the natural resources they own; this gives them property rights, which is a human right protected by the Constitution.

From the point of view of Law, it is therefore necessary to rethink the legal and political organisation of powers in order to define where and how to place the "centre of gravity" in managing natural resources. Our working hypothesis is that the regional level could be an ideal centre (also see *Section 3*). However, the regional political level across the world is characterized by a diversity of statutes. This diversity, associated with a variety of resource management systems, deserves further studies on how particular types of regional political organization should best be adapted for a more efficient management of natural resources.

An additional concern is the situation of the States in regard to the rules of international trade and international investment. International law favours the freedom of choice of productions, the free flow of investments, and the free movement of goods by empowering private operators. These rules deprive governments of the ability to adjust local, regional or national production (what is produced from natural resources) to meet the population needs, but are also preventing States from opposing those rules in a binding and significant way.

To address these problems, we must imagine new legal tools for natural resource management upstream of the production stage. Overcoming the limits posed by international trade laws implies conceiving reasonable modifications of the latter, in order to give States the capacity to develop (sovereign) public policies addressing the basic needs of the population.

6. Conclusions

The above considerations can be summarized as follows:

1. The increasing overexploitation of natural resources, the 8 billion demographic challenge in terms of unsustainable life styles versus persistent poverty within the next decade, and the fast contraction of ecosystems' resilience are expected to produce undesired state shifts in the biosphere and society;

2. Such shifts are setting limits to growth and will determine the range of future options and solutions for developmental policies. It is therefore extremely urgent to address the resources problematic via a systems approach mobilizing deep-interdisciplinary expertise;
3. Natural capital monitoring and accounting, and non-financial reporting will become the norm in the very near future and require continuous development and refinement of dedicated tools by the scientific community;
4. Natural resources management as a whole is a main driver of sustainable developmental policies and calibrated territorial ecological transitions;
5. The objective is to globally achieve optimized resources efficiency according to the territorial potential and to ensure their regional security through adaptive and responsible governance and persistent good practices;
6. Regions and countries with diverse and resilient socio-ecosystemic conditions and policies are going to be at a strong competitive advantage over the medium- to long-term;
7. In spite of the difficulties noted, the Resources Management Act of the New Zealand constitutes a major advance in environmental law that clearly revolutionised the approach to natural resources, as well as the process that guides environmental decisions. The approach deserves a more general consideration and developments in the international community as a whole.
8. Our analysis sets the stage for a systems approach to natural resources through (real-time) big data exploitation in combination with socio-economic and legal instruments. Such tools and instruments will generate more coherent legal, social, economic and ecosystemic frameworks that can secure a system of sustainable food, health, education, and environment for the society at large. A must if we want to tackle the 8 billion challenge through local development.

References

Agenda 21, the Rio Conference in 1992, Chapter 5: "Demographic dynamics and sustainability".

Alternatives Internationales, 2012, Hors-série 11, *Les guerres des matières premières.*

ASCHZET B., RELLER A., Zeft V., RENNIE C., ASHFIELD M., SIMMONS J., 2011, *Materials critical to the energy industry. An introduction,* http://www.bp.com/liveassets/bp_internet/globalbp/STAGING/global_assets/e_s_assets/e_s_assets_2010/downloads_pdfs/Materials_March2012.pdf

BANWART S., 2011, "Save our soils", *Nature* 474: 151-152.

BARBAULT R., WEBER J., 2009, *La vie, quelle entreprise !* Seuil, coll. *Science ouverte*, 2010, 195 p.

BARNOSKY A.D., HADLY E.A., BASCOMPTE J., BERLOW E.L., BROWN J.H., *et al*, 2012, "Approaching a state shift in Earth's biosphere", *Nature* 486: 52-58.

BARON C., PETIT O., ROMAGNY B., 2011, « Le courant des "Common-Pool Resources" : un bilan critique », in : Dahou T., Elloumi M., Molle F., Gassab M. et Romagny B. (dir.), *Pouvoirs, Sociétés et Nature au Sud de la Méditerranée*, Paris/Tunis, Editions INRAT/IRD/Karthala, 29-51.

BEDDINGTON J., 2011, *The Future of Food and Farming: Challenges and choices for global sustainability*. London: Government Office for Science Report 2011. (www.bis.gov.uk/Forsight)

BLOMQVIST L., BROOK B.W., Ellis E.C., KAREIVA P.M., NORDHAUS T., *et al*, 2013. "Does the Shoe Fit? Real versus Imagined Ecological Footprints". PLoS Biol 11(11): e1001700. doi:10.1371/journal.pbio.1001700

BOSSELMANN K., 2007, "Why New Zealand needs a National Sustainable Development Strategy", in Parliamentary Commissioner for the Environment, *Sustainability Review* 2007: New Zealand's Progress Towards Sustainable Development, Background Paper, Wellington. http://www.pce.govt.nz/projects/susstrategy.pdf

DE BOSSEOREILLE DE RIBOU S., DOUAM F., HAMANT O., FROHLICH M., NEGRUTIU I., 2013, "Plant science and agricultural productivity: why are we hitting the yield ceiling?" *Plant Science* 210: 159– 176.

BROWN L. R., 2006, Plan *B 2.0: Rescuing a Planet Under Stress and a Civilization in Trouble* Earth Policy Institute, Washington DC (* - and the series 3.0 and 4.0 in 2008 and 2009 respectively).

COLLART DUTILLEUL F., 2012a, « La problématique juridique des investissements dans les terres agricoles des pays en développement », In : *La promotion de l'investissement pour la production agricole : aspects de droit privé* (colloque Unidroit, Rome, 8-10 nov. 2011), *Uniform Law Review/ Revue de droit uniforme,* 1-2.

COLLART DUTILLEUL F., 2012b, « Le végétal et la sécurité alimentaire: approche juridique internationale ». In: *Le végétal saisi par le droit*, Ed. Bruylant, pp 47-64 (http://fr.bruylant.be/titres/128378/).

COSTANZA R., 2004, "Changing visions of humans' place in the world and the need for an ecological economics". pp. 237-246 in: E. Fullbrook (ed). *A guide to what's wrong with economics*. Anthem Press, London.

COSTANZA R., 2010, "Toward a new sustainable economy", in: *Macroeconomic Theory and its Failings: Alternative Perspectives on the Global Financial Crisis,* S. Kates (ed), pp 237-246, E. Elgar, http://www.eelgar.co.uk/

DASGUPTA P., 1982, *The Control of Resources.* Harvard University Press, 240 p.

DASGUPTA P., 2010, "The Place of Nature in Economic Development" In: Rodrik, D & Rosenzweig, M (eds.) *Handbook of Development Economics 5*, 4039-5061.

DEFFUANT G., ALVAREZ I., BARRETEAU O., DE VRIES B., EDMONDS B., GILBERT N., GOTTS N., JABOT F., JANSSEN S., HILDEN M., KOLDITZ O., MURRAY-RUST D., ROUG C., SMITS P., 2012, "FuturICT Exploratory for Sustainability of Human Well-being in Global Environmental Change", *European Physics Journal Special Topics* (http://moseph.com/node/550).

Directive 2004/35/CE du Parlement européen et du Conseil, 21 avril 2004, sur la responsabilité environnementale en ce qui concerne la prévention et la réparation des dommages environnementaux.

DITTRICH M., GILJUM S., LUTTER S., POLZIN C., 2012, "Implications of resource use for development and the environment", Vienna. SERI report: Green economies around the world?

EEA report 5/2011, *Resources efficiency in Europe*, www.eea.europa.eu/publications/earnings.../file ; www.eea.europa.eu/publications/resource-efficiency-in-europe/at.../fi

ELLIS E.C., K.K. GOLDEWIJK, S. SIEBERT, D. LIGHTMAN, N. RAMANKUTTY, 2010, "Anthropogenic transformation of the biomass, 1700 to 2000, *Global Ecol Biogeogr* 19 : 589-606.

ENGELMAN R., 2011, "An End to Population Growth: Why Family Planning Is Key to aSustainable Future", *Solutions* 2(3), http://www.thesolutionsjournal.com/node/919E-RISC report 2012 - http://www.footprintnetwork.org/en/index.php/GFN/page/upcoming_events/

FERONE, G., 2008, *2030, le krach écologique*, Grasset, Paris, 286 p.

FOLEY J.A., DEFRIES R., ASNER G.P., BARFORD C., BONAN G., CARPENTER S.R., CHAPIN F.S., COE M.T., DAILY G.C., GIBBS H.K., 2005, "Global consequences of land use", *Science* 309: 570–574.

FOLEY J.A., RAMANKUTTY N., BRAUMAN K.A., CASSIDY E.S., GERBER J.S., JOHNSTON M., MUELLER N.D., O'CONNELL C., RAY D.K., WEST P.C., BALZER C., BENNETT E.M., CARPENTER S.R., HILL J., MONFREDA C., POLASKY S., ROCKSTRO J., SHEEHAN J., SIEBERT S., TILMAN D., ZAKS D.P.M., 2011, "Solutions for a cultivated planet", *Nature* 478: 337-342.

FREIBAUER A., MATHIJS E., BRUNORI G., 2011, "Sustainable food consumption and production in a resource-constrained world", SCAR 3rd foresight exercise, Publications Office of the European Union, www.scp-knowledge.eu

GABRIEL-OYHAMBURU K, 2010, « Le retour d'une géopolitique des ressources? », *L'espace politique* 12, http:// espacepolitique.revues.org/1796 *Global trends 2030: alternative worlds* (2012) A publication of the National Intelligence Council, NIC 2012-001. At: www.dni.gov/nic/globaltrends

GODFRAY H.C.J., BEDDINGTON J.R., CRUTE I.R., HADDAD L., LAWRENCE D., MUIR J.F., PRETTY J., ROBINSON S., THOMAS S.M., TOULMIN C., 2010, "Food security: the challenge of feeding 9 billion people", *Science* 327: 812-818.

GOETSCHEL L, PÉCLARD D., 2006, « Les conflits liés aux ressources naturelles. Résultats de recherches et perspectives », *Annuaire suisse de politique de développement*, vol. 25, n° 2, URL : http://aspd.revues.org/255

GOOD A.G., BEATTY P.H., 2011, "Fertilizing nature: a tragedy of excess in the commons", *PLoS biology* 9, 1-8.

Government's Approach to Sustainable Development, August 2002, New Zealand, Wellington (report).

GRIFFON M., 2006, *Nourrir La Planète - Pour Une Révolution Doublement Verte*, Ed. O. Jacob, 456 p.

GRIFFON M., 2013, *Qu'est-ce l'agriculture écologiquement intensive?* Quae, Versailles, 219 p.

HABERL H., HENNZ ERB K., KRAUSMANN F., GAUBE V., BONDEAU A., *et al*, 2007, "Quantifying and Mapping the Human Appropriation of Net Primary Production, *PNAS* 104 : 12942-47.

HONET C., NEGRUTIU I., 2012, « De l'agriculture comme problème à l'agriculture comme solution: des plantes et des homes » In: *Le végétal saisi par le droit* (Coordination Dross W), Ed. Bruylant, Bruxelles.

HOOKSTRA A.Y., MEKONEN M.M., 2011, "The water footprint of humanity", *PNAS* 109: 3233-3237.

JARMACHE E., 2013, « La zone: un concept érvolutionnaire, ou un rêve irréaliste? » In: *La mer et les resources maritimes, Responsbilité et Environnement* 70: 71-76 (* - this special issue covers an entire set of questions relevant to marine resources).

LEFEBVRE M., GANGADHARAN L., THOYER S., 2012, "Do security-differentiated water rights improve the performance of water markets?" *Am. J. Agr. Econ*, http://www.lameta.univ-montp1.fr/Documents/DR2011-14.pdf.

Living Planet report 2012, http://wwf.panda.org/about_our_earth/all_publications/living_planet_report/

LOTZE H.K., COLL M., DUNNE J.A., 2011, "Historical changes in marine resources, food-web structure and ecosystem functioning in the Adriatic Sea", *Mediterranean Ecosystems* 14:198-222.

MAZOYER M., ROUDARD L., MAYAKI I.A., 2008, "World development report", *Mondes en Développement* 36: 1-20.

MEADOWS D., MEADOWS D., RANDERS J., 2005, *The Limits to Growth: The 30-Year Update*, Earthscan, Bath Press London.

Ministry for the Environment, 2011, *Measuring Up: Environmental Reporting – A Discussion Document*, Wellington, Ministry for the Environment.

NEGRUTIU I., 2011, "Interdisciplinarity for the long-term: targetting resources", In: *Les ressources*, Les colloques de l'Institut universitaire de France. Negrutiu I, Del Fatti N, Bravard J.P., Vieira C. (Eds). PUSE St. Etienne, pp. 327-337.

NEUMAYER E., 2000, "Scarce or abundant? The economy of natural resources availability", *J Economic Surveys* 14: 307-329.

OSTROM E., DIETZ T., DOLŠAK N., STERN P.C., STONICH S., WEBER E.U. (eds.), 2002, *The Drama of the Commons*, Washington DC, National Academy Press.

Paper to the Cabinet Policy Committee, *Proposal – New Zealand Sustainable Development Strategy*, 2001.

PARLIAMENTARY COMMISSIONER FOR THE ENVIRONMENT, 2002, *Creating our Future: Sustainable Development for New Zealand*, Wellington (report).

PATTERSON M., 2002, "Headline indicators for tracking progress to sustainability in New

Zealand", *Technical paper No. 71 Sustainability*, prepared for the Environmental Reporting Programme of the Ministry for the Environment, Wellington, MFE.

PAULY D., CHRISTENSEN V., DALSGAARD J., FROESE R., TORRES F., 1998, "Fishing down marine food webs", *Science*, 279:860.

PURVES D., SCHARLEMAN J., HARFOOT M., NEWBOLD T., TITTENSOR D.P., *et al*, 2013, "Time to model all life on Earth", *Nature* 493: 295-297.

RAMANKUTTY N, EVANS A.T., MONFREDA C., FOLEY J.A., 2008, "Farming the planet: 1. Geographic distribution of global agricultural lands in the year 2000". *Global Geochem. Cycles* 22, 1-19.

RAVILLON M., CHEN S., SANGRAULA P., "New Evidence on the Urbanization of Global Poverty", 2007, *Population and Development Review* 33: 667-702.

RUNNING S.W., 2012, "A measurable planetary boundary for the biosphere", *Science* 337, 1458-59.

The Resource Management Act 1991, New Zealand, an Act (RMA) (http://en.wikipedia.org/wiki/Resource_Management_Act_1991).

SCHEFFER M., SUGIHARA G., BASCOMPTE J., BROCK W.A., BROVKIN V., *et al*, 2009, "Early-warning signals for critical transitions", *Nature* 416, 53-56.

SEITZINGER S.P., SVEDIN, U., CRUMLEY, C., STEFFEN, W., ABDULLAH, S.A., *et al*, 2012, "Planetary stewardship in an urbanizing world: beyond city limits", *AMBIO*, 41: 787-94, DOI 10.1007/s13280-012-0353-7.

SMITH W.K., M. ZHAO M., RUNNING S.W., 2012, "Global bioenergy capacity as constrained by observed biospheric productivity rates", *Bioscience* 62, 911-922.

SRINIVASAN T. U., CAREY S.P., HALLSTEIN E., HIGGINS P.A.T., KERR A.C., *et al*, 2008, "The debt of nations and the distribution of ecological impacts from human activities", *PNAS* 105:1768-1773.

STEFFEN W., CRUTZEN P.J., MCNEILL J.R., 2007, "The Anthropocene: are humans now overwhelming the great forces of nature", *Ambio 36:* 614-621.

THOYER S., 2006, "How to reallocate water rights when environmental goals conflict with existing entitlements", *International Journal of Sustainable Development* 9/2, 122-136.

TURCHIN P., 2009, "Long-Term Population Cycles in Human Societies", Ann. N.Y. Acad. Sci. 1162: 1–17.

UNEP report 2011, http://www.unep.org/greeneconomy - http://water.worldbank.org/node/84122

WEBER J.L., 2007, "Implementation of land and ecosystem accounts at the European Environment Agency", *Ecological Economics* 61(4): 695–707 http://www.sciencedirect.com/science/article/pii/S0921800906004629

WEBER J.L., 2011, "An experimental framework for ecosystem capital accounting in Europe", *EEA Technical report* No 13/2011, ISSN 1725-2237 http://www.eea.europa.eu/publications/an-experimental-framework-for-ecosystem

La patrimonialisation des sols affectés à la production de denrées alimentaires

Maylis DESROUSSEAUX *

1. La qualification des éléments naturels au titre de patrimoine commun : objet de controverses

Les éléments de l'environnement, l'eau, le sol, la biodiversité et leurs interactions ont très tôt été reconnus, au cas par cas, comme formant un patrimoine commun naturel[1]. Le professeur Kiss relevait « qu'il est curieux de noter que ce concept a fait son apparition dans les relations internationales en même temps que s'est manifestée la prise de conscience mondiale des dangers que court notre biosphère »[2]. A cet égard il convient de distinguer selon que la reconnaissance s'effectue au niveau national ou international. Ainsi en droit français, l'eau, peu importe son usage ou son état, fait partie du patrimoine commun de la nation[3]. Une telle reconnaissance au niveau international se heurte toutefois aux velléités souverainistes des Etats, qui tiennent à conserver un contrôle sur leurs ressources naturelles et il est vrai que « ce qui a été déclaré jusqu'à présent patrimoine commun de l'humanité n'avait jamais été soumis à une souveraineté quelconque, qu'il s'agisse de l'Antarctique, des grands fonds marins ou de la Lune »[4].

Les discussions tendant à la reconnaissance des forêts et des ressources génétiques en tant que patrimoine commun de l'humanité cristalli-

---

* Doctorante à l'Institut de droit de l'environnement, Université Jean Moulin Lyon 3

[1] « La notion de patrimoine commun est utilisée pour soustraire certains espaces ou ressources naturelles à l'accaparement ou à la revendication de souveraineté de la part des Etats et à toute appropriation privée. », A. VAN LANG, *Droit de l'environnement*, PUF, 3ème éd., 2011, p. 180.

[2] A. KISS « La forêt et le patrimoine commun de l'humanité », *in* M. PRIEUR (dir.), *Forêts et environnement*, PU de Limoges, 1984, p. 282.

[3] « L'eau fait partie du patrimoine commun de la nation. Sa protection, sa mise en valeur et le développement de la ressource utilisable, dans le respect des équilibres naturels, sont d'intérêt général. », Art. L. 210-1 du Code de l'environnement.

[4] A. KISS, « La forêt et le patrimoine commun de l'humanité », *op. cit.,* p. 285.

sent l'essentiel des résistances[5]. Ce sont de véritables stratégies qui s'échafaudent, à l'instar de celle menée par les pays du Sud à l'occasion de l'adoption de la Convention de Rio sur la diversité biologique et qui a abouti à la rédaction du Principe 3 dans les termes suivants : « les Etats ont le droit souverain d'exploiter leurs propres ressources selon leur politique d'environnement et ils ont le devoir de faire en sorte que les activités exercées dans les limites de leur juridiction ou sous leur contrôle ne causent pas de dommage à 1'environnement dans d'autres Etats ou dans des régions ne relevant d'aucune juridiction nationale »[6]. Ce rejet du concept de patrimoine commun appliqué aux ressources naturelles s'explique notamment par la volonté des pays en développement, au « fort poids écologique », de conserver la maîtrise de leurs ressources afin de mieux se protéger contre les immixtions des Etats industrialisés[7]. L'édification des sols au titre du patrimoine commun se heurte à des obstacles similaires mais renforcés par les dimensions symbolique et juridique inhérentes aux sols ; le territoire étant un constitutif de l'Etat[8]. Une telle conception contribue à la dégradation des sols dans la mesure où, tenues à l'écart, les instances internationales n'ont aucune possibilité d'agir sur des compétences telles que le régime d'affectation des sols des Etats. Cette conception ignore également les préconisations du Conseil de l'Europe. Dès 1972, celui-ci affirmait ainsi que la puissance des Etats devrait s'effacer face aux impératifs de protection des sols considérés comme « un des biens les plus précieux de l'humanité » qui permet « la vie des végétaux, des animaux et de l'homme à la surface de la terre »[9].

L'intégration d'un élément naturel ou culturel au titre de patrimoine commun résulte d'une démarche de l'Etat ou de la communauté internatio-

---

[5] J.-P. BEURIER, A. KISS †, *Droit international de l'environnement*, 4ème éd., Pedone, 2010, p. 170.

[6] Convention sur la diversité biologique du 5 juin 1992, Rio de Janeiro, Nations Unies, Recueil des Traités 1993 vol. 1760 I- 30619, p. 170.

[7] V. MARIS, *La protection de la biodiversité : entre science, éthique et politique*, thèse de philosophie, Université de Montréal, 2006, p. 250.

[8] A. ZABALZA, *La terre et le droit, du droit civil à la philosophie du droit*, éd. Bière, 2007, p.168 et s.

[9] Article 1er de la Charte européenne des sols, Résolution (72)19 du Conseil de l'Europe du 30 mai 1972.

nale de préserver ledit élément. Le concept de patrimoine commun contribue à la sauvegarde d'un intérêt général, qui peut revêtir une dimension nationale ou mondiale. Il confère à l'élément visé une protection qui réside avant tout dans la mise en lumière des qualités qu'il présente. La dimension qualitative du concept est prégnante, tout autant qu'elle est variable. Il n'existe pas *a priori* de limite matérielle qui exclurait cette qualification, mais on ne peut cependant nier qu'elle demande une certaine distinction qualitative. C'est en effet le cas de la qualification des biens culturels ou naturels au titre du patrimoine mondial de l'Unesco qui doivent présenter un « intérêt exceptionnel » pour « l'humanité toute entière »[10]. Or cet intérêt se mesure aussi à l'aune de la menace qui pèse sur leur intégrité, de telle sorte que leur dégradation doit causer « un appauvrissement néfaste du patrimoine de tous les peuples du monde ». La distinction appuie ici la rareté ou le caractère remarquable de l'élément, tout comme elle peut résulter de sa vulnérabilité proportionnellement au besoin qu'en a la population humaine pour conserver un état de bien-être tel que défini par les conventions. Par conséquent, il n'existe pas non plus d'ordre de grandeur qui puisse limiter la qualification d'un bien au titre de patrimoine commun : à différentes échelles, une œuvre architecturale[11] y est éligible, tout autant que le territoire d'une nation[12].

2. La mise en exergue des spécificités des sols pour surmonter les obstacles à leur patrimonialisation

Il s'avère que certains types de sols ont pénétré la sphère de la patrimonialisation au regard des qualités qu'ils présentent. En réponse à l'appropriation individuelle qui caractérise une part conséquente des sols du monde, l'Unesco, par la préservation du patrimoine mondial naturel, a contribué à la reconnaissance des qualités des sols et des multiples intérêts qui résident dans leur protection. Ainsi parmi les 193 éléments du patri-

---

[10] Convention concernant la protection du patrimoine mondial, culturel et naturel du 16 novembre 1972, 17ème session de la Conférence générale de l'Organisation des Nations Unies pour l'éducation, la science et la culture.

[11] La cathédrale de Gaudi à Barcelone, pour ne citer qu'un seul exemple ; UNESCO, 1984.

[12] Art. L. 110 du Code de l'urbanisme.

moine naturel identifiés par le comité du patrimoine mondial[13], on observe que les caractéristiques des sols importent. Les trésors dont ils recèlent sont les témoins de l'histoire de l'humanité et les sites fossilisés méritent à ce titre d'être protégés[14]. D'un point de vue plus environnemental, certains sites constitués de sols hydromorphes communément appelés « zones humides » sont considérés comme présentant un intérêt général mondial. Il s'agit notamment de la mer des Wadden constituée de chenaux à marée, de bancs de sable, de prairies d'herbes marines, de moulières, de vasières, de marais salés, d'estuaires, plages et dunes[15]. Enfin les sols justifient la protection de sites pour les paysages dont ils sont l'élément principal. Sur ce point il est important de noter que les différents usages agricoles font partie intégrante de ce patrimoine et que leur préservation garantit la protection du site. Elle opère comme une patrimonialisation de l'usage qui répond à l'objectif commun de la préservation des ressources naturelles et à la production alimentaire, comme c'est le cas des époustouflantes rizières en terrasse des Hani de Honghe en Chine ou de celles situées dans les cordillères des Philippines[16]. Mais une telle protection, aussi efficace soit-elle, demeure insuffisante au regard de l'aspect sélectif très poussé qu'elle présente. Vu le modèle agricole productiviste dans lequel s'est engagé un grand nombre d'Etats, les sols affectés à la production des denrées alimentaires ne correspondent plus aux critères de classification au titre du patrimoine mondial proposés par l'Union internationale pour la conservation de la nature (UICN)[17]. Il ne faut pourtant pas conclure à une exclusion de fait

---

[13] Le Comité est responsable de la mise en œuvre de la Convention du patrimoine mondial, détermine l'utilisation du Fonds du patrimoine mondial et alloue l'assistance financière suite aux demandes des Etats parties ; cf. art. 8 de Convention concernant la protection du patrimoine mondial, culturel et naturel.

[14] Cf. par exemple le site fossilifère de Messel en Allemagne et qui contient des fossiles compris entre -57 et -36 millions d'années et les falaises fossilifères de Joggins au Canada.

[15] UNESCO 2009, classée vingt ans après la première proposition en 1989, la mer des Wadden est un bien transnational du patrimoine mondial des Pays-Bas et de l'Allemagne mais qui s'étend au Danemark.

[16] Dès 1995, ce site a suscité l'intérêt de l'UNESCO qui l'inscrira au titre de patrimoine mondial comme bien culturel. Ce site fut classé un temps « bien en péril ».

des sols du patrimoine commun. Le service écosystémique de production de sols est en effet un facteur crucial du bien-être de l'humanité pouvant ainsi justifier leur préservation en tant que patrimoine commun de l'humanité.

3. La reconnaissance du service écosystémique de production des sols, moteur de leur intégration au titre de patrimoine commun de l'humanité

« Ce qui est commun n'est d'aucun usage[18] ». Locke se prononçait en faveur d'une appropriation de la terre afin de pouvoir mieux l'exploiter. Il excluait ainsi l'idée qu'un bien commun puisse avoir une quelconque utilité. Mais au-delà de la parcelle de terre appropriée, les fruits de *l'usus* participent à la satisfaction d'un intérêt commun résidant dans la production de denrées alimentaires. De ce fait, la ressource en sol crée un pont entre la distinction qui oppose les *res extra patrimonium* et les *res in patrimonio*. Or si le principe de patrimoine commun est susceptible d'agir sur le droit de propriété, il n'a pas vocation à exclure les sols de leur vocation productive, d'autant plus si c'est cette dernière qui a justifié l'édification de ce statut. Il en est ainsi pour l'eau en droit français. Déclarée patrimoine commun de la nation par la loi du 3 janvier 1992[19], s'en sont suivi des règles de gestion qui répondent aux exigences de l'équilibre et du développement durable[20]. Une logique d'exploitation n'apparaît donc pas fondamentalement antinomique du statut de patrimoine commun, à la condition délicate qu'elle se conforme à une sorte de « désintéressement »[21] en ce qu'elle impose « une

[17] *Orientations devant guider la mise en œuvre de la Convention du patrimoine mondial*, Organisation des Nations Unies pour l'éducation, la science et la culture, Comité intergouvernemental pour la protection du patrimoine mondial, culturel et naturel, WHC.13/01, Juillet 2013, 181p.

[18] J. LOCKE, *Second traité du gouvernement*, PUF 1994, p. 155.

[19] Loi n° 92-3, JO du 4 janvier 1992 p. 187.

[20] Art. L. 211-1 c. env ; Ph. BILLET « L'usage de l'eau mis en règle : entre droit des équilibres et équilibre des droits », *rev. env.* n° 7, juillet 2005, étude 17.

[21] J.-L. GAZZANIGA, « Le droit de l'eau dans une perspective historique », *in* A. FARINETTI *La protection juridique des cours d'eau. Contribution à une réflexion sur l'appréhension des objets complexes*, Johanet 2012, p. 603.

certaine forme de retenue dans l'exploitation [des] composantes [du patrimoine commun] »[22].

Les caractéristiques pédologiques des sols affectés à une activité de production alimentaire sont multiples et variables mais l'universalité de l'usage agricole qui supplante la diversité des pratiques agit comme un élément fédérateur conduisant à la définition d'un patrimoine commun de l'humanité. La gestion du service écosystémique de production présente le double avantage de contourner d'une part l'obstacle principal à leur qualification patrimoniale et d'autre part, de mettre l'accent sur la nécessaire préservation des sols exploités. C'est en tout cas un levier puissant qui serait en mesure de remettre en cause la souveraineté des Etats tout comme les prérogatives des propriétaires, l'idée sous-jacente étant de garantir le droit « de chaque être humain d'avoir accès à des aliments sains et nutritifs en quantité suffisante, conformément au droit à une alimentation adéquate et au droit fondamental de chacun d'être à l'abri de la faim »[23]. Cette formulation, sans force juridique, rappelle les aspirations plus concrètes de l'article 14 de la Convention relative aux peuples indigènes et tribaux de 1989[24] : « Les droits de propriété et de possession sur les terres qu'ils occupent traditionnellement doivent être reconnus aux peuples intéressés. En outre, des mesures doivent être prises dans les cas appropriés pour sauvegarder le droit des peuples intéressés d'utiliser les terres non exclusivement occupées par eux, mais auxquelles ils ont traditionnellement accès pour leurs activités traditionnelles et de subsistance. Une attention particulière doit être portée à cet égard à la situation des peuples nomades et des agriculteurs itinérants ». Le service de production alimentaire n'appartiendrait plus aux possesseurs mais aux consommateurs, c'est-à-dire à l'humanité toute entière. Les sols agricoles bénéficieraient alors d'un statut proche de celui

---

[22] G. MEUBLAT, « Sciences économiques, gestion de l'eau, gestion du fleuve », *in Le fleuve et ses métamorphoses*, Didier Erudition, 1993 p. 19 ; *in* A. FARINETTI, *ibid.*, p. 603

[23] §108 de la déclaration de la Conférence Rio +20, L'avenir que nous voulons, 19 juin 2012, A/CONF.216/L.1.

[24] Convention n° 169 de l'Organisation internationale du travail, 1989 ; cf. Ph. BILLET, « Droit d'accès aux ressources naturelles et nomadisme : identité, propriété et écologie », *env.* n° 6, juin 2011, alerte 51.

accordé par la Convention sur la désertification[25], mais dans un cadre plus large que les zones touchées ou menacées par un tel processus de dégradation.

A ce jour, parmi l'identification des services écosystémiques dans les zones sèches, élaborée par le *Millenium Ecosystem assessment*[26], la seule valeur patrimoniale reconnue figure au titre des « Services culturels » ; bénéfices « immatériels » tirés des écosystèmes[27]. La reconnaissance patrimoniale du service de production contribuerait dès lors à la valorisation d'une agriculture fondée sur des pratiques traditionnelles et paysannes, les plus à même de réaliser une sécurité alimentaire pérenne et équitable.

---

[25] Les parties à la présente Convention reconnaissent « l'importance et la nécessité d'une coopération internationale et d'un partenariat dans la lutte contre la désertification et pour l'atténuation des effets de la sécheresse », Convention internationale sur la lutte contre la désertification dans les pays gravement touchés par la sècheresse et/ou la désertification, en particulier en Afrique, adoptée à Paris le 14 octobre 1994 [Entrée en vigueur le 26 décembre 1996], Recueil des Traités des Nations Unies (1996) vol. 1954 I Nos 33480-33482, p. 3.

[26] *Le Millenium Ecosystem Assesment* est un groupe de travail international réuni sous l'égide de l'ONU et chargé d'évaluer les écosystèmes pour le millénaire afin d'évaluer les conséquences des changements écosystémiques sur le bien-être humain et d'établir la base scientifique pour mettre en œuvre les actions nécessaires à l'amélioration de la conservation et de l'utilisation durable de ces systèmes,

[27] « L'Évaluation des Écosystèmes pour le Millénaire », 2005, *Ecosystèmes et bien-être humain: Synthèse*, Island Press, Washington, DC, p. 5.

The commons-based international Food Treaty: A legal architecture to sustain a fair and sustainable food transition

Jose Luis VIVERO POL *

> *"Between the strong and the weak, between the rich and the poor, between the lord and the slave, it is freedom which oppresses and the law which sets free"*
>
> Henri-Dominique Lacordaire (1802-1861)

Summary

Food as a purely private good prevents millions to get such a basic resource, since the purchasing power determines access and the price of food does not reflect its multiple dimensions and the value to society. With the dominant no money-no food rationality, hunger still prevails in a world of abundance. Hunger is needlessly killing millions of our fellow humans, including 3.1 million young children every year, condemning many others to life-long exposure to illness and social exclusion. This paper argues this narrative has to be re-conceived and a binding Food Treaty, based on a commons approach to food, will create a more appropriate framework to work together towards a fairer and more sustainable world. The eradication of hunger no later than 2025 would be the main objective within a broader framework whereby food and nutrition security shall be understood as a Global Public Good. Within the treaty framework, those governments that are genuinely determined to end hunger (a coalition of the willing) could commit themselves to mutually-agreed binding goals, strategies and predictable funding. The paper presents the rationale to substantiate the treaty, as well as objectives, provisions and a possible route map for the process.

Introduction

Widespread malnutrition and the role of the state in fighting food insecurity, namely hunger and obesity, are issues at the forefront of contemporary debates. Record levels of world hunger prevail despite bountiful

---

* PhD research fellow, Centre of Philosophy of Law, Université Catholique de Louvain, Belgium. Email: Jose-luis.viveropol@uclouvain.be

harvests and soaring profits for the transnational corporations that dominate the global food supply (De Schutter, 2010). With millions of people needlessly dying each year because of hunger in a world of ample food supplies[1], nobody can dispute the need for institutional mechanisms that raise the level of attention given to food security and nutrition-related issues and lead to better coordinated action among the many actors that are concerned with the multiple dimensions of the problem. The world is not doing well with hunger reduction, the closing of the inequality gap and the growing obesity pandemic and thus unconventional and radical perspectives need to be brought to the debate (Krasner, 1999).

One of those radical perspectives would be to consider food as a common or a public good that should be governed in a commons-based manner, and not just produced and distributed as any other commodity. At present, food is largely regarded as a pure private good, as it is excludable and rival, although wild foodstuff could perfectly be considered a commons. The value of food is no longer based on its many dimensions that bring us security and health, values that are related to our cultural foundations (food as culture), to human rights considerations (the right to food), to the way food is produce (food as a sustainable natural resource) or to its essential nature as fuel for human body. Those multiple dimensions are superseded by the tradable features, being value and price thus mixed up. This article defends that a fairer and more sustainable food system shall revalue the non-monetary dimensions of food, and hence the global and local food production and distribution systems shall not be exclusively governed by supply-demand market rules[2]. Food can and must be shared, given for free, guaranteed by the State, cultivated by many and also traded in the market. The purchasing power cannot exclusively determine our access to such

[1] Today, 7100 children under five have died of malnutrition, what means 300 every hour and 5 every minute. More than double also died of causes directly associated to malnutrition such as diarrhea or pneumonia.

[2] Moreover, following the philosopher Michael SANDEL, market rules not only put prices to goods but in doing so markets corrupt their original nature (SANDEL, 2012). The commodification of food crowds out non-market values worth caring about, such as recipes associated to some types of food, the conviviality of cropping, cooking or eating together, the local names of forgotten varieties and dishes or the traditional moral economy of food production and distribution, materialised in the ancient and now proscribed practices of gleaning or famine thefts.

essential. Food is a *de facto* impure public good, governed by public institutions in many aspects (food safety regulations, seed markets, fertilizer subsidies[3], the EU CAP[4] or US Farm Bill[5]), provided by collective actions in thousands of customary and post-industrial collective arrangements (cooking recipes, farmers' seed exchanges, consumer-producers associations) but largely distributed by market rules: you eat as long as you have money to purchase either food or food-producing inputs. We have to change that narrative.

Another daring proposal to combat the growing inequalities the free-trade globalisation is exacerbating would be to share higher areas of state sovereignty and transfer them to international semi-sovereign institutions (Brauer and Haywood, 2010), such as those already functioning in internet (ICANN, the Internet Corporation for Assigned Names and Numbers), the industrial sector (ISO, the International Organization for Standardization), the humanitarian affairs (ICRC, the International Committee of the Red Cross) or sports (IOC, the International Olympic Committee or FIFA, Federation International of Football Associations).

In a world whose food production is threatened by climate change, global stagnant yields, diminishing water, soil and agro-biodiversity resources and the current energy and economic crises, sharing sovereignty seems to be, at least, a debatable option to safeguard our existence (Cor-

---

[3] Fertilizer subsidies are widely used all over the world, either explicitly or in more subtle ways, as government recognizes that the agricultural sector is a strategic one. http://www.voanews.com/content/fertilizer-subsidy-costs-could-outweigh-benefits/1693403.html [Accessed January 7 2014].

[4] The Common Agricultural Policy (CAP) of the European Union is a multi-state supported programme to help food producers to earn a better living, increase price competitiveness in the international market and incentivize the rural inhabitants to remain in rural areas so as to become custodians of the landscapes and the environment. In 2011, total CAP budget for 27 EU countries was 58 billion euro http://ec.europa.eu/agriculture/statistics/factsheets/pdf/eu_en.pdf Comparative data on state support to agriculture can be found in EU (2012). [Accessed January 7 2014].

[5] The US Farm Bill incorporates not only schemes to support agriculture but also nutrition programs such as food stamps and school lunches. In 2012, only the food stamps amounted 100 billion $ and the US Senate schedules nearly 1 trillion $ for the next 10 years of the Farm Bill. http://capreform.eu/the-us-farm-bill-lessons-for-cap-reform/ [Accessed January 7 2014].

ner, 2008). The objective of sharing any given nation´s sovereignty and submitting to an international treaty would be to address global problems with worldwide implications that cannot be solved with the current nation-state set up, implications that can be considered Public Bads (Stiglitz, 1999). Each nation-state, during international talks, tends to maximize its own benefit (for its citizens, economy or environment) and this plays against the maximum benefit for all, as the tragedy of the commons theory has already proven (Hardin, 1968). Sharing of sovereignty should come in exchange of sustainable food production, fair food trade and social stability for the entire world.

If food security is to be achieved, a binding international convention with redress and sanctioning mechanisms and the partial sharing of sovereignty to supranational institutions are two of the previously-considered anathemas[6] that need to be re-examined with a sight into the post-2015 talks to be concluded in 2015. Those two political options (food as a commons and a binding food treaty), amply discarded in the past decades, should be reconsidered in light of the current failures of the global food system to provide food for all.

I.- Reasons that can justify a negotiation process towards a binding food treaty

More and more, it seems evident the dominant fuel-based industrial food system must be reinvented as it has failed to fulfill its goal. The four major driving forces to justify that rationale are a hungry world, the depletion of current energy sources, the increasingly evident negative consequences of climate change to human societies and the over-reliance on market-driven mechanisms to attain global food security.

A Hungry World: The failure of the global food system to feed the world.

The industrial technology-dominated food system has achieved remarkable outputs during the second half of the 20th century by increasing

[6] The definition of anathema stands for a thing detested, loathed, accursed or consigned to damnation or destruction. In the political arena, it refers to ideas that are non-treated, discarded or attacked by being naïve, out-fashioned or impossible. The *Real Politik* does not count on them at national and international talks. However, any potential option should be explored to improve the weak global governance of food and its nemesis, hunger.

food production and facilitating food access to millions of urban and rural consumers. As a matter of fact, between 1960 and 1990, the share of undernourished people in the world fell significantly since improved availability and decreased staple food prices dramatically improved energy and protein consumption of the poor (Hazell, 2010; FAO, 2013a). FAO reports a reduction of 173 million hungry people from 1015 million (19%) in 1990 to 848 (12%) in 2013, representing 7.5 million less per year (FAO, 2013b). And the UN also confirms that 700 million fewer people lived in conditions of extreme poverty in 2010 than in 1990 (UN, 2013a). This linear increase in food production has outpaced the population growth benefiting virtually most consumers in the world and the poor relatively more because they spend a greater share of their income on food[7].

Productivity gains, however, have been uneven across crops and regions (Evenson and Gollin, 2003) and global increases in production have been confined to a limited range of cereal crops (rice, maize, and wheat) with smaller increases in crops such as potato and soybean (Godfray *et al.*, 2010). Increased cereal production has supported the increase in chicken and pig production, but also led to concerns that human diets are becoming less diverse and more meat-based, with the subsequent increase in the ecological footprint. We produce 4600 kcal per person of edible food harvest, enough to feed a global population of 12-14 billion (UNCTAD, 2013), but after waste, animal feed and biofuels, we end up with no more than 2000 Kcal per person (Lundqvist *et al.*, 2008). And it seems that yield improvements are already reaching a plateau in the most productive areas of the world (Cassman *et al.*, 2010; Lobell *et al.*, 2009), rendering almost impossible to double food production by 2050 with the current trends (Ray *et al.*, 2013). That explains why many scientists and agri-food corporations are calling for a Greener Revolution or Green Revolution 2.0 (Pingali, 2012).

However, this mechanisation and commodification of the industrial food system did not come for free and many undesirable externalities and consequences are evident nowadays. Globally speaking, we have a troublesome relationship with food, as more than half the world eats in ways

---

[7] Although consumers generally benefited from declines in food prices, farmers benefited only where cost reductions exceeded price reductions (Evenson and Gollin, 2003).

that damage their health. Eating is not a source of pleasure for billions but a compulsory habit and certainly a cause of concern. Obesity and undernutrition affect an estimated 2.3 billion people globally, about one third of the world's population (GAIN, 2013), and food and nutrition security is at the forefront of contemporary political debates. Hunger is the largest single contributor to maternal and child mortality worldwide, with 3.1 million children dying every year of hunger-related causes (Black *et al.*, 2013). Additionally, overweight and obesity cause 2.8 million deaths (WHO, 2012). Despite years of international anti-hunger efforts, rising gross national incomes and per capita food availability, the number of hungry people has been reduced at a very slow pace since 2000 and we have 848 million undernourished people in the world (FAO, 2013a). Obesity is rapidly mounting and 1120 million obese people are expected by 2030 (Kelly *et al.*, 2008). The ironic paradoxes of the globalised industrial food system are that half of those who grow 70% of the world's food are hungry (ETC Group, 2013), food kills people, food is increasingly not for humans (a great share is diverted to biofuel production and livestock feeding) and 1/3 of global food production ends up in the garbage every year, enough to feed 600 million hungry people (FAO, 2011).

The side-effects of the industrial food system can be illustrated by the fact that 70% of hungry people are themselves small farmers or agricultural labourers (UNCTAD, 2013), agriculture is highly demanding of water and it makes a poorly use of that scarce public good, the industrial system diminishes the nutritious properties of some foods, by storing in cold rooms, peeling, boiling and the transformation processes (Sablani *et al.*, 2006; Toor and Savage, 2005), an overemphasis on production of empty and cheap calories renders obesity a growing global pandemic, food production is highly energy inefficient as we need 10 kcal to produce 1 kcal of food (Pimental and Pimental, 2008), soil degradation and biodiversity loss amongst others. With the current levels of food production and consumption, if we all were a standard US citizen, we would need 5.2 planets to cover our needs (WWF, 2012). And nevertheless the 1.2 billion poorest people account for only 1 per cent of world consumption while the billion richest consume 72 per cent (UN, 2013b). And the future looks gloomier as hunger will likely increase in the future (UK Government, 2011).

Moreover, in the last decade it seems to have gone too far in the radical consideration of food as a pure commodity that can be speculated with, diverted from human consumption to biofuel production and used as a justification for unethical land grabbing in the poorest but land-rich countries by the richest but land-poor ones. And this excessive commodification has not even rendered more efficient or cost-benefit than the more sustainable food systems (either modern organic or customary) as the industrial food system is heavily subsidized and amply favoured by tax exemptions[8]. The great bulk of national agricultural subsidies in OECD countries are mostly geared towards supporting this large-scale industrial agriculture[9] that makes intensive use of chemical inputs and energy (Nemes, 2013), and that helps corporations lower the price of processed food compared to fresh fruits and vegetables. The alternative organic systems are more productive, both agronomically and economically, more energy efficient and they have a lower year-to-year variability (Smolik *et al.*, 1995) and they depend less on government payments for their profitability (Diebel *et al.*, 1995).

The Depletion Dilemma: The decadence of fossil fuels

The world is approaching the sunset of the oil era in the first half of the 21st century (Rifkin, 2002). The oil peak will arguably be reached before 2020 (Sorrell *et al.*, 2010), unless oil reserves not yet accessible can be open up for commercial purposes, and it is forecasted that before 2050 oil will no longer be a commercial source of energy for the world. Most oil-exporting countries will reach the plateau of production between 2010 and 2020, starting the decline from 2020 (Mitchell and Stevens, 2008). This declining of oil and gas stocks while the growing population does not cease to demand more energy is a huge challenge. On top of that, the global food system is living outside its means, consuming resources faster than are

---

[8] The Global Subsidies Initiative http://www.iisd.org/gsi/ [Accessed January 7 2014].

[9] The average support to agricultural farmers in OECD countries in 2005 reached 30% of total agricultural production, equalling to 1 billion $ per day (UNCTAD, 2013). In OECD countries, agricultural subsidies amount $400 billion per year. Moreover, the world is spending half a trillion dollars on fossil fuel subsidies every year. In 2011 the US government gave $1billion in fuel tax exemptions to farmers. The overall estimate for EU biofuels subsidies in 2011 was €5.5–€6.8 billion (IISD, 2013; WWF, 2011).

naturally replenished (IAASTD, 2009). Substantial changes will be required throughout the food system and related areas, such as water use, energy use and addressing climate change, if food security is to be provided for a predicted nine billion or more people out to 2050. By improving the knowledge of agro-ecological practices, we can delink the production of food from its current dependency on fossil energy, which has nowadays become unsustainable

The threats of Climate change: an external problem that requires global solutions

Climate change is already modifying weather and rainfall patterns. In many vulnerable areas of the Global South, the gradual rise of temperatures, the diminishing rainfall and the impact of extreme weather events are already having impacts in food production and food security. Climate change will contribute to food and water scarcity and it will increase the spread of disease, and may spur or exacerbate mass migration and the further weakening of fragile states (US Department of Defense, 2010) which in turn may increase the likelihood of global instability and risk to national security (World Economic Forum, 2011). Human civilization and ecosystems will surely change to adapt to the rapidly changing global climate, and that transition will not be easy or fast. Climate change and its consequences for food and nutrition security, health and economic development will likely be the external agent that may trigger a re-conceptualization of our nation-state approach to global problems as well as to global public goods, opening up the debate on the leading role of the states vis a vis the transnational agri-food corporations and the unregulated markets. In such scenario, could it be possible to broker an international food security treaty to end world hunger through the rule of law?

The over-reliance on market forces

One of the dominant economic doctrines of recent decades has been that market forces by themselves could regulate the national and international food systems to pull hungry people out of the plight of starvation and destitution. It was praised that market-led food production and allocation would finally achieve a better-nourished population, as long as the world's average wealth increased. However, reality has proven otherwise as unregulated markets may still not provide a socially efficient quantity of food even if enough income was distributed to low-income groups. Moreover, despite the reliance on industry self-regulation and public–private partnerships to improve public health and nutrition, there is no evidence to support their effectiveness against hunger, obesity and safety considerations (Hawkes and Buse, 2011; Moore-Lappe *et al.,* 1998). Transnational corporations are major drivers of obesity epidemics by maximising profit from increased consumption of ultra-processed food and drink (Ludwig *et al.*, 2001; Monteiro *et al.,* 2011). Marion Nestle has recently uncovered how Coca Cola is supporting scientific research to influence in the public opinion towards their industrial fatty and high-sugar products[10]. These conflicts of interest between economic profit and scientific knowledge have proven to exert a reporting bias in industry-financed academic research so as to mask or discard the direct relationship between ultra-processed sweetened drinks and obesity (Bes-Rastrollo *et al.,* 2013). The consumption of unhealthy food and drinks is occurring faster in food systems that are highly penetrated by foreign multinationals in poor countries (Stuckler *et al.*, 2012), where government regulations and public opinion are usually not capable of controlling corporate leverage. That explains why the only evidence-based mechanisms that can prevent harm caused by unhealthy commodity industries are public regulation and market intervention[11]. This means, more state not less.

A food system anchored in the consideration of food as a commodity to be distributed according to the demand-supply market rules will never achieve food security for all (Rocha, 2007). It is evident that the private sector is not interested in people who do not have the money to pay for their services or goods, whether be healthy food or staple grains. Moreover, markets, governed by private, individual self-interest, will not provide an adequate quantity of public goods, such as public health, good nutrition or hunger eradication, with enormous although non-monetised benefits to human beings, as the positive externalities cannot be captured by private

---

[10] http://www.foodpolitics.com/2013/10/annals-of-nutrition-science-coca-cola-1-nhanes-0/ [Accessed January 7 2014].

[11] Strong laws consistently had a biggest impact in curbing school sales of junk food and sweetened drinks and thus in slowing childhood obesity (Moodie *et al.,* 2013; Taber *et al.,* 2012; WHO, 2013).

actors. Those public goods have to be sought and maintained by the public sector and the collective actions of citizens.

II.- A legally-anchored food transition that guarantees sustainability: practical implications

With millions of people needlessly dying prematurely each year from hunger and obesity in a world of ample food supplies, nobody can dispute the need for a change. The mass industrial food model, which is becoming highly dominant, is increasingly failing to fulfil its basic goals: producing food in a sustainable manner, feeding people adequately and avoiding hunger. There is a need to bring unconventional and radical perspectives into the debate on possible solutions for a transition towards a fairer and sustainable food system. Following Wrights' real utopias, there is an urgent need to develop alternative visions to the industrial food system, no matter how little support that may get, since the mere fact of proposing alternatives outside the dominant mainstream may contribute to creating the conditions in which such support can be built (Wright, 2010). And the power of food to generate a substantial critique to the neoliberal corporate and industrialized food system and to harness multiple and different alternative collective actions for food shall not be underestimated (McMichael, 2000). Food is a powerful weapon for social transformation.

At present, the globalised world is at the crossroad of two food transition streams: the well advanced nutritional transition from vegetable- to meat-dominated diets and the incipient food transition from oil-dependent industrial agriculture to more sustainable and local food systems. The path selected by the majority of the population and the new food paradigm that will emerge from these transitions will greatly affect our survival within the Earth's carrying capacity. Nevertheless, all previous transitions shared a common denominator: food was always viewed as a private good produced by private means and traded in the market. Almost none of the most relevant analyses produced in the last decades on the fault lines of the global food system and the very existence of hunger has ever questioned the nature of food as a private good (FAO, 2012; UK Government, 2011; World Bank, 2008; World Economic Forum, 2013), although some authors already suggested the idea (Anderson, 2004; Ausin, 2010; Wittman *et al.*, 2010). And therefore the common understanding affirms the main problem nowadays is the lack of food access, reaffirming the private nature of food and its absolute excludability[12]. But problems cannot be solved with the same mind-set that created them, as Einstein wrote.

If food is considered a commons, the legal, economic and political implications would be paramount. Food would be kept out of trade agreements dealing with pure private goods (Rosset, 2006) and there would thus be a need to establish a commons-based governing system for production, distribution and access to food, such as those agreements proposed for climate change and universal health coverage. That would definitely pave the way for more binding legal frameworks to fight hunger (MacMillan and Vivero, 2011). In the same line, a Universal Food Coverage[13] could also be a sound scheme to materialise this new narrative. This social scheme would guarantee a daily minimum amount of food for all citizens (HLPE, 2012) (i.e. one loaf of bread or ten *tortillas*). This universal entitlement would protect the only human right declared as fundamental in the ICESCR: freedom from hunger, and it would recognize that eating is a fundamental human need. The food coverage could also be implemented as a Basic Food Entitlement (Van Parijs, 2005) or a Food Security Floor (Deacon, 2012). During the transition period, and as an immediate mechanism, the state should guarantee the minimum salary equals the food basket. Moreover, there would be a legal and ethical ground to ban futures trading in agricultural commodities, as the speculation on food influences considerably the international and domestic prices and benefits none but the speculators. Considering food as a commons would prioritize the use of food for human

---

[12] All researchers and policy makers implicitly agree that food is purely a private good, that you gain access to when you purchase it in the market or produce it yourself with other privately-owned inputs. Along those lines, there is a common understanding that the main problem nowadays is the lack of food access, although food production concerns are also gaining momentum. This approach is evident in the following global food security policy documents: MDG and WFS Plans of Action, the CFS Global Strategic Framework for Food Security and Nutrition 2012, the G-8 New Alliance for Food Security and Nutrition 2012, the G-20 L'Aquila Food Security Initiative, The G-20 Action Plan on food price volatility and agriculture 2012 and the World Economic Forum New Vision for Agriculture. Additional references can also be found in Vivero (2013).

[13] An idea called for by Nobel Prize Amartya Sen http://www.governancenow.com/news/regular-story/amartya-sen-bats-universal-food-coverage [Accessed January 7 2014].

consumption, limiting the non-consumption uses. Today, by applying the economic rationale, the best use of any commodity is where it can get the best price (i.e. feed for livestock, pharmaceutical by-products or biofuel).

Food as a commons would provide the adequate rationale to support the non-economic arguments favouring a more sustainable and fairer food system, arguments more related to valuing the multiple dimensions of food to human beings other than its artificially-low price in the market. For instance, dimensions related to fair production and nutritional and enjoyable consumption, compared to the mono-dimensional approach to food as a commodity, where the major driver for agri-businesses is to maximize profit by producing and delivering cheap food with low nutritional value and high-energy demanding. Those dimensions should be legally-anchored in an international Food Treaty, downsizing the trade and commodity dimensions of food and emphasizing its importance for human bodies and human cultures.

III.- Finding a more adequate framework to negotiate food production and trade

The three self-contained legal regimes that currently regulate food and agriculture, namely international human rights law, international environmental law and international trade law, are still working separately, with international trade law taking precedence over the other two to the detriment of small farmers and the environment. The absence of coordination among these regimes and the fact that trade and investment rules are often enforced by sanctions, while human rights obligations are not, gives trade and investment rules the de facto advantage. We urgently need a better coherence regarding the three major sets of international law related to food and agriculture (CEHAP, 2009).

Many critics have long argued that removing agriculture from the WTO would be the necessary first step (Rosset, 2006). The converging food, climate and agrobiodiversity crises, combined with the difficulties encountered during the Doha Round at the World Trade Organization (WTO), have made imperative a new debate on global food politics and our food production and trade model. WTO law does not really consider the full range of human, social and environmental rights and the factors that define agricultural specificity. Therefore, the WTO and the international trade legal framework do not seem to be the appropriate scenario where the world´s food security should be debated. No government should be forced to choose between honouring its commitments made under free trade treaties or at the WTO, and honouring its obligations regarding the right to food (De Schutter, 2011). Even if the current gridlock could be overcome, it is unlikely that the WTO Agreement of Agriculture, with its single-minded emphasis on export production, will encourage farming practices that respect ecological limits and contribute to food security (Gonzalez, 2012). In addition to that, the international regulation is necessary to address the domination of agricultural markets by a handful of transnational corporations (Gonzalez, 2010; Clapp and Fuchs, 2009).

The more challenging step now is to devise a system of global governance that overcomes the fragmentation of international law, invites the participation of civil society, and promotes sustainable approaches to food production, distribution and consumption. But, what type of governance? Still a Westphalian sovereign state-based architecture? Recent history suggests that even if the level of government representation is more elevated than at present[14] existing inter-governmental bodies are unlikely to be successful in ensuring the level of commitment required to trigger action on the scale needed to bring about a massive reduction in hunger and malnutrition. There are three main reasons for this:

a) Firstly, in spite of the commitments repeatedly made, only a few governments are strongly motivated to address food security and nutrition issues. Most prefer to assume that the problems will disappear as a consequence of economic growth (Sumner *et al.*, 2007).

b) Secondly, unscrupulous governments use hunger as a political weapon to appease the demanding citizens or to attract international attention to the humanitarian crisis.

c) Thirdly, the general pattern in existing multilateral institutions dealing with food security and agriculture is for national delegates to assume positions that respond to the short-term interests of their domestic constituencies rather than ones which ensure the greatest good to

[14] Recent efforts to raise the level of government representation at the CFS have failed, as few ministers and no head of state have so far shown up in those meetings. A highly-reputed Canadian think tank has proposed a re-arrange of the existing UN agencies dealing with food and agriculture (ETC Group, 2009).

mankind as a whole. The need to arrive at consensual agreements acceptable to all nations makes it virtually impossible to engage themselves in binding commitments.

In the case of food and hunger, the declarations of successive World Food Summits do not commit individual countries to any specific goals or actions for reducing hunger at a national level or for providing funds towards the costs of hunger eradication in other countries. To a certain extent the same is true of the International Covenant on Economic, Social and Cultural Rights (ICESCR). This has been ratified by 160 countries that recognise "the fundamental right of everyone to be free from hunger" amongst many other rights, but the time-scale within which these rights are to be assured is not defined. In spite of this progress, however, the ICESCR remains a "soft instrument" that is unlikely, alone, to bring about a rapid drop in deaths caused by hunger and malnutrition, though it provides an extremely important element in the arsenal of weapons with which to address the problem. Therefore, in parallel to adjustments to the existing institutions, priority should also be given to creating a new binding framework within which they can operate with greater effectiveness[15], as a result of sharpened time-bound goals, an agreed plan of action and more predictable funding.

IV.- A Food Treaty for better coherence between food, environment, human rights and trade

A food treaty, to be useful, shall give hierarchical priority to human rights and environmental norms over obligations contained in trade and investment agreements, with good examples being the right to food or the right to a healthy environment. A convention or treaty to end deaths related to hunger and malnutrition would strengthen the hand of existing intergovernmental institutions to fulfil their mandates in addressing the various dimensions of food security, defining their obligations with greater clarity and encouraging a fuller integration of their programmes, especially at national

[15] There would seem to be obvious advantages in combining expertise of FAO (expansion of small-scale farm production), WFP (social protection), WHO (nutrition/health), UNICEF (children), UNEP (environment) and IFAD (finance) on assisting countries in implementing national programs to eradicate hunger and malnutrition.

levels within developing countries. By putting the rule of law behind the aim of eradicating hunger, the Food Treaty would lend legal support to ongoing global food security and nutrition initiatives, such as the Scaling Up Nutrition (SUN), the UN Inter-Agency Renewed Efforts to End Child Hunger (UN REACH), Ending Child Hunger and Undernutrition Initiative (ECHUI) or Hunger-Free Latin America and the Caribbean (ALCSH), and it would complement the Universal Declaration of Human Rights and the ICESCR.

The application of a convention-based approach to the issue of hunger and malnutrition could be successful not only in translating "soft" into "hard" (i.e. accountable) commitments by individual governments, but also in raising the level and predictability of commitments, and hence lead to a marked acceleration in relevant actions and achievement of results. The road towards this treaty will not be easy, being the main obstacles the big and powerful agri-business transnational companies, which already control the complete food chain in most developed countries, and some states where those same companies have the headquarters and, worryingly, strong political ties.

The intermediate target of halving the proportion of hungry people by 2015 has distracted attention from the ultimate goal of eradicating hunger, to the extent that this tends to be forgotten. It is vital to do everything possible to achieve the 2015 target on the road to eradication by 2025, but the 2015 target has all the weaknesses of any half-measure: it fails to inspire a sense of urgency and unity and, even if achieved, it effectively condemns the "other half" to continued hunger and premature death. Nothing short of an absolute goal of eradicating hunger and malnutrition throughout the world (and reflecting this in national goals) within a relatively short period will galvanize the necessary public support, political commitment, creativity and action[16]. The strongest argument is that is now technically possible and

[16] It is relevant to mention that President Lula mobilized Brazil by adopting a "zero hunger" goal for his national food security programme, and thereby imbued it with a sense of urgency that caught popular imagination and led to the rapid creation of institutions and laws for its implementation.

financially affordable[17]. The Food Treaty must retain this goal of hunger eradication as its political compass.

Why should Governments support a Food Treaty?

1.- The food price crisis has made governments increasingly conscious of the huge perils of inaction about food issues, namely food riots, mounting budgets for food imports, high dependence of staple food produced in other countries, land grabbing and loss of food sovereignty among others.

2.- A second political rationale for the treaty would also include to discourage migration towards developed countries, as food secure households tend to stay in their countries (Wainer, 2011); to abate poverty-fuelled terrorism linked to economic exclusion and food deprivation (Pinstrup-Andersen and Shimokawa, 2008) and to mitigate national civil unrest (Holt-Giménez and Patel, 2009).

3.- The growing realisation of the huge economic and social benefits to be gained from reducing hunger and malnutrition should also play a major argument in a market-dominated world. Cohabiting with hungry people is more expensive than putting a remedy to their situation. The World Bank estimates that chronic malnutrition reduces the GDP of developing countries by between 2 and 3 per cent (World Bank, 2006). Children with stunted growth can have an IQ 15 points lower than a well-fed child's. Adults who were malnourished as children earn at least 20% less on average than those who were not (Grantham-McGregor *et al.*, 2007).

4.- The evident failure of business-as-usual approaches to hunger reduction (Fan, 2010): the world produces more food than required to feed appropriately everyone, but there 848 million hungry people in 2011, and that figure is expected to keep on rising due to the economic crisis.

5.- Increasing evidence that well designed national programmes anchored in appropriate legal and institutional frameworks can work (i.e. Brasil, Thailand, Ghana, Peru, Europe and Japan after the Second World War).

6.- Recognition of benefits of shifting from "soft" to "hard" legally binding reciprocal commitments for the achievement of major global objectives,

---

[17] About 40 developing countries are on course to meet the World Food Summit goal of halving the number of hungry by 2015, demonstrating that this is possible.

as it has been the case during the recent climate conference in Durban, where the Durban Platform for Enhanced Action has been established. This platform, including all the Kyoto Protocol signatories plus the United States, aims to bring both developed and developing countries together in a legally binding treaty between 2015 and 2020. This political endeavour is a proof that previous non-binding agreements have been toothless in moving climate change issues in the positive direction.

7.- Growing public consciousness of human rights and especially of the fundamental right to be free from hunger, strongly associated to the right to life.

V.- Lessons learned from other legally-binding international agreements

In fields other than food security, international conventions have been used as instruments within which genuinely interested nations can come together to commit themselves in an explicit and binding manner to work jointly towards the attainment of agreed global goals. Amongst the best known are the Geneva Convention on the Treatment of Prisoners of War, the Ottawa Convention on the prohibition of the use, stockpiling, production and transfer of anti-personnel mines and the Rio Convention on Biological Diversity and the additional protocols, such as the Montreal Protocol on Substances that Deplete the Ozone Layer and the Cartagena Protocol on Biosafety. These agreements, later on, are translated into national legislation designed to enable each signatory nation to fulfil its commitments. In the food and agriculture domain, as well as in other areas of environmental protection, there are binding treaties that can enlighten us on how to fix the goals, steer the processes to reach the agreements and their success and level of fulfilment.

a.- *The International Treaty on Plant Genetic Resources for Food and Agriculture* (ITPGRFA) is a convention that was approved in 2001 and entered into force on 29 June 2004, being signed so far by 125 member states and ratified by 56 (Esquinas-Alcazar *et al.*, 2011).

b.- *The Cartagena Protocol on Biosafety to the Convention on Biological Diversity* is an international treaty governing the movements of living modified organisms that provides international rules and procedure on liability and redress for damage to biodiversity resulting from living modified organisms.

c.- *The Montreal Protocol on Substances that Deplete the Ozone Layer* has recently been proven as a successful binding tool to reduce methane emissions to the atmosphere and thus lowering the rate of global warming (Estrada *et al.*, 2013).

d.- *The Ottawa Convention on the prohibition of the use, stockpiling, production and transfer of anti-personnel mines* is a milestone in the history of multilateralism, as by first time hundreds of NGOs, UN agencies and Red Cross movement, in a coordinated manner, introduced a legally-binding topic in the international agenda (Cameron, 1999).

e.- Another specific agreement is the already expired *Food Aid Convention*, a post-II World War agreement between food aid supplying countries to guarantee an agreed minimum amount of food assistance each year[18]. A major flaw is that recipient countries were not included in this Convention.

f.- *The International Covenant on Economic, Social and Cultural Rights* (ICESCR) is a binding treaty that does include recognition of the right to food but it does not, however, include time-bound goals or any provision for funding commitments that can be monitored. The recent approval of an Operational Protocol, creating a mechanism for handling complaints of violations, will greatly strengthen the effectiveness of the ICESCR (Villan-Duran, 2009).

Some lessons learned that can be drawn from the history of these processes shows that: a) the process itself raises the level of public knowledge of the issues being addressed; b) a relatively small number of governments may sign up to a convention at early stage, but once ratified by the required number, more nations progressively become signatories (i.e. the ITPGRFA), and c) the fact that the governance of each convention is provided only by signatories means that the types of actions for which

[18] A number of NGOs are pressing for a revision of the FAC and the transfer of its secretariat from the London-based International Grains Council to a UN agency. The FAC could easily be covered by a Protocol to the proposed Food Treaty.

commitments are made are on a higher plane than if they were defined through negotiations involving all governments in a decision-making role.

VI.- Elements and main bodies of a Food Treaty

Those governments and institutions that are willing to enter into long-term commitments to end hunger shall elaborate, negotiate and sign an international Treaty that would provide a legally binding framework for inter-country cooperation and for real mutual accountability for agreed actions at national and international levels, involving defined roles and responsibilities for governments, UN agencies and civil society.

The Food Treaty would aim to establish enforceable international law guaranteeing the right to be free from hunger and it should trigger the issuance of anti-hunger laws, also called food security and nutrition laws, as the seven laws already issued and the 10 draft laws being developed in Latin America (Vivero, 2010). A preliminary draft of a possible Treaty has already being proposed by the author and a colleague in 2011 (MacMillan and Vivero, 2011). This draft, however, should be considered essentially as an academic exercise so as to help countries launch the necessary debate. Judging from the experience of recent conventions, the above process could take as long as 10 years. The process itself, however, will from the outset generate awareness, commitment and institutional support.

Some features of the Treaty are presented as follows:

a.- The focus of any convention should be on "eradication" rather than "halving" hunger.

b.- The goal should be achieved no later than 2025, because we have already the means and knowledge to do it, and the treaty needs to set up a feasible timeframe that does not delay the goal beyond a reasonable political time.

c.- The Food Treaty should cover both hunger as well as other manifestations of malnutrition that are contributing to premature death[19].

[19] One issue is whether, in addressing malnutrition, the Convention should cover both under-nutrition and the food consumption and life-style habits that are leading to a rapidly growing incidence of obesity and related life-threatening diseases in

d.- The provisions of the Food Treaty should be set up in such a way that they act in the long-term global interest.

e.- They must also involve the self-imposition by all governments that are motivated to participate of binding and monitorable long-term commitments.

f.- Link the commitments of developing country parties to embark on defined comprehensive long-term programmes to end hunger no later than 2025 with commitments by donor countries to assist in funding their programmes and in providing technical cooperation services in a predictable manner[20]. In any case, the donor and the recipient country should deposit the pledge at the International Register of Commitments against Hunger, a unit established in the Secretariat of the Treaty[21].

g.- The agreements included in the Food Treaty should incorporate provisions whereby countries abide by decisions taken by the Conference of the Parties so as to improve governance and accountability during the lifespan of the treaty.

h.- Whereas the signatories of the Treaty would be nations, the governance arrangements should be broadened to engage the UN system, civil society organizations, the private sector, philanthropic foundations, academia and churches. Small-scale and large-scale food producers and consumers shall be given an appropriate decision-making space.

i.- The secretariat of the Treaty could be hosted by an existing UN agency or, better still, by the Committee of Food Security (CFS). However, other possibilities could also considered, such as a consortium of UN agencies or any other suitable institution that may

---

both developed and developing countries. This consideration should be raised during early discussions of the Food Treaty amongst interested parties.

[20] Funds could be channelled directly to requesting countries or through a multilateral fund operated by an existing multilateral financing institution.

[21] A register-like process has been launched within the G-8, under the L'Aquila Food Security Initiative (AFSI), to monitor the delivery of public and private financial investments by donors, in partnership with OECD and to monitor the implementation of food security programmes and the extent to which funds are contributing to these programmes.

emerged from current debates at CFS, G-8, G-20, G-77, Rio+20 or the UN General Assembly.

j.- The Food Treaty shall have a double accountability system, being operating at national and international level. The international mechanism could be based on a peer-review process similar to those undertaken by the Human Rights Council's Universal Periodic Review, the OCDE or the New Partnership for Africa´s Development. On the other side, the national accountability system could be led by the National Ombdusman Office or any other independent Human Rights institution.

k.- Support the creation and implementation at national and global levels of real-time systems for monitoring delivery on commitments and progress towards the goal adopted by the Treaty.

l.- Offer a forum where ratifying countries could agree on strategies to be adopted in international negotiations that may have a significant effect on hunger and malnutrition, especially those related to food trading, regulation of market speculation and food monopolies, land grabbing, safe global food stock levels and agricultural research for small-scale farming.

m.- Bring the failure by any state party to honour its commitments to the attention of the Conference of the Parties (or the Claim and Redress Committee), and put in place procedures requiring them to remedy the situation.

The Food Treaty could form the legal backbone to vertebrate the global food system, a revamped institutional architecture compounded by the following institutions:

1) ***The Committee of Food Security***, as the inter-governmental forum for political decisions (the Conference of the Parties of the Food Treaty), where civil society organisations, famers´ associations and the private sector would also be represented. Systems of representation and voting weights should be discussed along the process.

2) ***A Treaty Secretariat*** that would be ideally formed by a merge of the four Rome-based UN agencies plus the CGIAR steering Committee,

taking stock from the ad-hoc UN High Level Task Force on the Global Food Security Crisis (the Technical Subsidiary Body of the Treaty).

3) ***An annual report of the State of Food Insecurity***, with data provided annually by the countries, according standard formats. This annual report is already done by FAO, WFP and IFAD.

4) ***The Global Food Information system*** that has been proposed by the L´Aquila Food Security Initiative.

5) ***The Global Food Security and Agricultural Fund***, currently hosted by the World Bank, would be the funding mechanism to support the implementation of the treaty agreements.

6) ***A mechanism of claims, sanctions and redress of violations to the Treaty***, whose rulings would be compulsory. The mechanism to enforce the Treaty shall take shape in different forms, such as a Specific Treaty Court; or the current UN Human Rights Council, should specific judicial powers be given to that Council under the Treaty umbrella; or a Peer-to-Peer Assessment whose decisions would be compulsory to fulfil.

7) ***An external monitoring panel***, consultative but not binding, that supervises and provides recommendations on the implementation of the Treaty by the member states. This panel could be either a peer-to-peer regular assessment process or a high-level panel of experts selected by personal and professional capacities.

VII.- A possible path to kick start the process: the "coalition of willing" and an accompanying civil society campaign

During the initial stages of the ITPGRFA, a US think-tank (the Keystone Center) hosted and funded several meetings with specific people who were leaders and well-reputed specialists in agriculture, environment and rural development, so as to propose and discuss main guidelines, intermediate goals and the initial draft that later on would be approved as the IT-PGR[22]. A similar approach could be proposed in this case: a series of meetings with a highly-respected and strongly-committed group of people could

[22] This series of meetings were known as the "Keystone Process" and the visionary group that gave shape the idea of a binding treaty to share benefits from plant genetic resources was known as the "Keystone Group".

be arranged so as to analyse the idea, draft the structure, goals and provisions that could be part of a Treaty, and liaise with a broader network of key players so as to pulse the idea and have preliminary outcomes peer-reviewed. After that process, or in parallel if so considered, preliminary talks would be initiated by a "coalition of the willing" formed by countries, international institutions, private entities and CSOs that are really committed to end hunger and are willing to abide themselves to an international convention that establishes goals and objectives.

Finally, the process leading to the creation of an international Treaty should ideally be accompanied by a well-orchestrated national and international campaign, led by NGOs/CSOs, aimed at reinforcing citizen support for urgent large-scale action against hunger and malnutrition. The immediate objective of the campaign[23] would be to call on governments to negotiate and later on sign up to the Food Treaty, as well as to ensure that their governments deliver on their World Food Summit and Millennium Summit commitments to halve the number of hungry people between 1990 and 2015. Moreover, the campaign would raise public awareness and understanding of the hunger problem and of solutions and it should be based on already existing movements/campaigns, networks and initiatives, fostering partnerships, based on a common commitment to eradication, while respecting their autonomy and special interests at national level. As a suggestion, the anti-hunger campaigners and institutions should draw ideas from the successful multi-agency campaigns that are so frequent in the biodiversity domain, achieving concrete results in preserving animals and plants[24]. Why not a similar campaign to preserve stunted and wasted human beings?

VIII.- Ethical epilogue: Preventing hunger-related deaths is a moral imperative

The existing flaws in global governance of the world's food production are well-acknowledged. From energy, forests to food security, water

---

[23] The term "campaign" means in this case a sustained, time-framed and coordinated effort by a group of stakeholders to raise public awareness of specific goals and to make a change happen.

[24] The Alliance for Zero Extinction (http://www.zeroextinction.org) is a good example.

and desertification, global governance has repeatedly fallen short when it comes to proactive and swift responses to risk, even in the face of worst case scenarios (Oosterveer, 2007). In that sense, exploring the international human rights framework so as to pulse the timing for a binding international Food Treaty to regulate specific considerations on food security and hunger in a changing climate may sound foolish today although rather necessary in the near future. Moreover, re-conceiving the nature of food as a purely private good to start seeing it as a commons is a rather necessary narrative and a moral imperative. Preventing death from hunger and malnutrition through enabling all human beings to eat adequately would be a huge moral victory for those who believe in a more just and equitable global society. It would add credibility to the processes of globalization. And it would also release a huge amount of latent human energy and creativity for the benefit of mankind.

The de-commodification of food will imply to delink commodities and well-being and sharing sovereignty in the food domain to international regulating bodies for the sake of the global common good. A globalised world demands a truly global food system geared towards feeding everybody adequately, producing food sustainably and valuing the non-commercial dimensions of such essential element. Using McMichael's food regimes conceptual framework (McMichael, 2009), the re-commonification of food and its practical implications would certainly open up the transition towards a new food regime, different from the corporate one we have at present. We need to develop a food system that provides meaning, and not just utility, to food production, trading and consumption (Anderson, 2004). To achieve this sustainable food system we need to reconsider how food is regarded by our society, not merely as a privatized commodity but as common good to be enjoyed by all at any time. A binding Food Treaty would provide a legal architecture to that vision, giving primacy to sustainable production and fair distribution of food, spurring the development of Universal Food Coverage in all signatory states.

Last but not least, the fight against hunger must also recall the fraternity between human beings, a concept that stemmed from the French Revolution triad but it was quickly surpassed by their companions, liberty and equality (Rawls, 1999; Gonthier, 2000), both of them considered as the political, philosophical and ethical foundations of the neoliberal economy and democratic societies. Fraternity, understood as solidarity between states, societies and human beings, implies a sense of civic friendship, cosmopolitanism (Held, 2009), reciprocity and social solidarity that are so much needed in those times of growing self-interest, isolationism and private rights.

Bibliography

ANDERSON, M. 2004. Grace at the table. *Earthlight*, 14 (1), Spring.

AUSIN, T. 2010. El derecho a comer: Los alimentos como bien público global. *Arbor, Ciencia, Pensamiento y Cultura* 745, 847-858.

BES-RASTROLLO M., M.B. SCHULZE, M. RUIZ-CANELA and M.A. MARTINEZ-GONZALEZ. 2013. Financial Conflicts of Interest and Reporting Bias Regarding the Association between Sugar-Sweetened Beverages and Weight Gain: A Systematic Review of Systematic Reviews. *PLoS Med* 10 (12): e1001578. doi:10.1371/journal.pmed.1001578

BLACK, R.E., C.G. VICTORA, S.P. WALKER, Z.A. BHUTTA, P. CHRISTIAN, M. de ONIS, M. EZZATI, S. GRANTHAM-MCGREGOR, J. KATZ, R. MARTORELL, R. UAUY and THE MATERNAL AND CHILD NUTRITION STUDY GROUP. 2013. Maternal and child undernutrition and overweight in low-income and middle-income countries. *The Lancet* 382 (9890), 427-451.

BRAUER, J. and R. HAYWOOD. 2010. *Non-state Sovereign Entrepreneurs and Non-territorial Sovereign Organizations*. Working paper 2010/09, United Nations University WIDER, Helsinki. http://www.wider.unu.edu/publications/working-papers/2010/en_GB/wp2010-09/ [Accessed January 7 2014]

CAMERON, M.A. 1999. Global civil society and the Ottawa process: Lessons from the movement to ban anti-personnel mines. *Canadian Foreign Policy Journal*, 7(1), 85-102

CASSMAN, K.G., P. GRASSINI and J. VAN WART. 2010. Crop yield potential, yield trends, and global food security in a changing climate. In: C. Rosenzweig and D. Hillel, eds. *Handbook of Climate Change and Agroecosystems*, Imperial College Press: 37–51

CORNER, M. 2008. *Towards a Global Sharing of Sovereignty*. European Essay 44. The Federal Trust. London, UK.

CEHAP. 2009. *A call from the Cordoba Group for coherence and action on food security and climate change*. October 2009, Chair on Hunger and Poverty Studies, University of Cordoba. http://www.etcgroup.org/content/call-cordoba-group-coherence-and-action-food-security-and-climate-change [Accessed January 7 2014]

CLAPP, J. and D. FUCHS, eds. 2009. *Corporate power in global agrifood governance*. MIT press, Cambridge.

DE SCHUTTER, O. 2010. *Addressing Concentration in Food Supply Chains: The Role of Competition Law in Tackling the Abuse of Buyer Power*. Briefing note 3. UN Special Rapporteur on the right to food, December 2010

DE SCHUTTER, O. 2011. *The World Trade Organization and the post-global food crisis agenda: putting food security first in the international trade system*. Briefing note 4.

UN Special Rapporteur on the Right to Food, November 2011.

DEACON, B. 2012. The social protection floor. *CROP Poverty Brief.* http://www.crop.org/viewfile.aspx?id=415 [Accessed January 7 2014]

DIEBEL, P.L., J.R. WILLIAMS and R.V. LLEWELYN. 1995. An economic comparison of conventional and alternative cropping systems for a representative northeast Kansas farm. *Review of Agricultural Economics* 17 (3), 323-335

ESQUINAS-ALCÁZAR, J.T., C. FRISON and F. LÓPEZ. 2011. A treaty to fight hunger: past negotiations, present situation and future challenges. In: Frison, C. *et al.* (eds.). *Plant genetic resources and food security. Stakeholder perspectives on the International Treaty on Plant Genetic Resources for Food and Agriculture.* Earthscan, London.

ESTRADA, F. P. PERRON and B. MARTÍNEZ-LÓPEZ. 2013. Statistically derived contributions of diverse human influences to twentieth-century temperature changes. *Nature Geoscience*, 6, 1050–1055.

ETC GROUP (2009). *Who Will Govern? Rome's Food Summit may determine who decides who will eat.* ETC Group, Ottawa. http://www.etcgroup.org/es/node/4922 [Accessed January 7 2014]

ETC GROUP. 2013. *With climate change…Who will feed us? The industrial food chain or the peasant food webs?* http://www.etcgroup.org/sites/www.etcgroup.org/files/Food%20Poster_Design-Sept042013.pdf [Accessed January 7 2014]

EVENSON, R.E. and D. GOLLIN. 2003. Assessing the Impact of the Green Revolution, 1960 to 2000. *Science* 300 (5620), 758-762.

EU. 2012. *Comparative analysis of agricultural support within the major agricultural trading nations.* Directorate General for Internal Policies, European Union, Brussels.

FAN, S. 2010. *Halving hunger: meeting the first Millennium Development Goal through business as unusual.* International Food Policy Research Institute, Washington D.C. http://www.ifpri.org/sites/default/files/publications/pr22.pdf [Accessed January 7 2014]

FAO. 2011. *Global food losses and food waste. Extent, causes and prevention.* FAO, Rome and Swedish Institute of Food and Biotechnology, Gothenburg.

FAO. 2012. *The future we want. End hunger and make the transition to sustainable agricultural and food systems.* FAO, Rome.

FAO. 2013a. *FAO statistical yearbook 2013.* FAO, Rome.

FAO. 2013b. *The State of food insecurity in the world 2013.* FAO, WFP & IFAD, Rome.

GAIN. 2013. *Access to nutrition index. Global Index 2013.* Global Alliance for Improved Nutrition.

GODFRAY H.C.J., J.R. BEDDINGTON, I.R. CRUTE, L. HADDAD, D. LAWRENCE, J.F. MUIR, J. PRETTY, S. ROBINSON, S.M. THOMAS and C. TOULMIN. 2010. Food security: the challenge of feeding 9 billion people. *Science* 327, 812-818.

GONTHIER, C.D. 2000. Liberty, Equality, Fraternity: The Forgotten Leg of the Trilogy. *McGill Law Journal* 45, 567-589.

GONZALEZ, C.G. 2010. The Global Food Crisis: Law, Policy, and the Elusive Quest for Justice. *Yale Human Rights and Development Law Journal* 13, 462-468.

GONZALEZ, C.G. 2012. The global food system, environmental protection, and human rights. *Natural Resources & Environment,* 26, 3.

GRANTHAM-MCGREGOR, S., Y.B. CHEUNG, S. CUETO, P. GLEWWE, L. RICHTER, B. STRUPP and THE INTERNATIONAL CHILD DEVELOPMENT STEERING GROUP. 2007. Development potential in the first 5 years for children in developing countries. *The Lancet*, 369, 60–70.

HARDIN, G. 1968. The Tragedy of the Commons. *Science* 162 (3859), 1243-1248

HAWKES, C. and K. BUSE. 2011. Public health sector and food industry interaction: it's time to clarify the term 'partnership' and be honest about underlying interests. *Eur. J. Public Health* 21 (4), 400-401.

HAZELL P. 2010. The Asian Green Revolution In: Spielman D. and R. Pandya-Lorch, eds. *Proven Successes in Agricultural Development*, International Food Policy Research Institute Washington, DC. Pp. 67–97.

HELD, D. 2009. Restructuring global governance: cosmopolitanism, democracy and the Global Order. *Millenium: Journal of International Studies*, 37 (3), 535-547.

HLPE. 2012. *Social protection for food security*. A report by the High Level Panel of Experts on Food Security and Nutrition of the Committee on World Food Security, Rome 2012. 58-59.

HOLT-GIMENEZ, E. and R. PATEL. 2009. *Food Rebellions: Crisis and the Hunger for Justice*. Fahumu Books, UK.

IAASTD. 2009. *Agriculture at a crossroads: the global report*. International Assessment of Agricultural Knowledge, Science and Technology for Development. Island Press.

IISD. 2013. *Biofuels–At What Cost? A review of costs and benefits of EU biofuel policies. Addendum*. August 2013. International Institute of Sustainable Development, Geneva.

KRASNER, S.D. 1999. Globalization and sovereignty. In: D.A.Smith, D.J. Solinger and S C. Topik, eds. *States and sovereignty in the global economy*. Routledge. Pp. 34-53.

KELLY, T., W. YANG, C.S. CHEN, K. REYNOLDS and J. HE. 2008. Global burden of obesity in 2005 and projections for 2030. *Int. J. Obesity* 32, 1431-37.

LOBELL, D.B., K.G. CASSMAN and C.B. FIELD. 2009. Crop yield gaps: their importance, magnitudes, and causes. *Annual Review of Environmental Resources*, 34, 179–204.

LUDWIG, D.S., K.E. PETERSON and S.L. GORTMAKER (2001). Relation between consumption of sugar-sweetened drinks and childhood obesity: a prospective, observational analysis. *The Lancet*, 357 (9255), 505-508.

LUNDQVIST, J., C. DE FRAITURE and D. MOLDEN. 2008. *Saving Water: From Field to Fork – Curbing Losses and Wastage in the Food Chain*. SIWI Policy Brief. Stockholm International Water Institute.

MACMILLAN, A. and J.L. VIVERO. 2011. The governance of hunger. Innovative proposals to make the right to be free from hunger a reality. In: Martín-Lopez, M.A. and J.L. Vivero, eds. *New challenges to the Right to Food*. CEHAP, Cordoba and Editorial Huygens, Barcelona.

MCMICHAEL, P. 2000. The power of food. *Agriculture and Human Values* 17, 21–33

MCMICHAEL, P. 2009. A food regime genealogy. *Journal of Peasant Studies* 36(1), 139-169.

MITCHELL, J.V. and P. STEVENS. 2008. *Ending Dependence. Hard Choices for Oil-Exporting*

States. Chatham House, London.

MONTEIRO C.A., R.B. LEVY, R.M. CLARO, I.R. DE CASTRO and G. CANNON. 2011. Increasing consumption of ultra-processed foods and likely impact on human health: evidence from Brazil. *Public Health Nutr.* 14(1), 5-13.

MOODIE, R., D. STUCKLER, C. MONTEIRO, N. SHERON, B. NEAL, T. THAMARANGSI, P. LINCOLN, S. CASSWELL on behalf of The Lancet NCD Action Group. 2013. Profits and pandemics: prevention of harmful effects of tobacco, alcohol, and ultra-processed food and drink industries. *The Lancet*, 381 (9867), 670 – 679.

MOORE LAPPE, F., J. COLLINS, P. ROSSET and L. ESPARZA. 1998. *World Hunger: Twelve Myths*. The Institute for Food and Development Policy, California.

NEMES, N. (2013). Commentary IX (UNCTAD TER 2013): Comparative analysis of organic and non-organic farming systems: a critical assessment of on-farm profitability. In: *UNCTAD. Trade and Environment report 2013*. UNCTAD. Geneva.

OOSTERVEER, P. 2007. *Global governance of food production and consumption: issues and challenges*. Edward Elgar, Oxford.

PIMENTAL, D. and M.H. PIMENTAL. 2008. *Food, energy and society*. CRC Press, Boca Raton.

PINGALI, P.L. 2012. Green Revolution: Impacts, limits, and the path ahead. *Proc. Natl. Acad. Sci. USA* 109 (31), 12302-8.

PINSTRUP-ANDERSEN, P. and S. SHIMOKAWA. 2008. Do poverty and poor health and nutrition increase the risk of armed conflict onset? *Food Policy* 33 (6), 513–520

RAWLS, J. 1999. *A theory of justice*. Revised edition. Harvard University Press.

RAY D.K., N.D. MUELLER, P.C. WEST and J.A. FOLEY. 2013. Yield trends are insufficient to double global crop production by 2050. *PLoS ONE* 8(6): e66428. doi:10.1371/journal.pone.0066428

RIFKIN, J. 2002. *The hydrogen economy*. Tarcher/Putnam.

ROCHA, C. 2007. Food Insecurity as Market Failure: A Contribution from Economics. *J. Hunger & Environmental Nutrition* 1 (4), 5-22.

ROSSET, P.M. 2006. *Food is Different: Why the WTO Should Get out of Agriculture*. Zed Books, London, UK.

SABLANI, S.S., L.U. OPARA and K. AL–BALUSHI. 2006. Influence of bruising and storage temperature on vitamin C content of tomato fruit. *Journal of Food, Agriculture & Environment* 4, 54–56.

SANDEL, M.J. 2012. What isn't for sale? *The Atlantic*, Feb. 2012. http://www.theatlantic.com/magazine/archive/2012/04/what-isnt-for-sale/308902/ [Accessed January 7 2014].

SMOLIK, J.D., T.L. DOBBS and D.H. RICKERL. 1995. The relative sustainability of alternative, conventional, and reduced-till farming systems. *American Journal of Alternative Agriculture* 10 (1), 25-35.

SORRELL, S., J. SPEIRS, R. BENTLEY, A. BRANDT and R. MILLER. 2010. Global oil depletion: A review of evidence. *Energy Policy,* 38(9), 5290-5295.

STIGLITZ, J. E. 1999. *Knowledge as a Global Public Good*. In: I. Kaul, I. Grunberg and M. Stern, eds. *Global Public Goods: International Cooperation in the 21st Century*. Oxford University Press. Pp. 308-325.

STUCKLER D., M. MCKEE, S. EBRAHIM and S. BASU. 2012. Manufacturing Epidemics: The Role of Global Producers in Increased Consumption of Unhealthy Commodities

Including Processed Foods, Alcohol, and Tobacco. *PLoS Med* 9(6): e1001235.

SUMNER, A., J. LINDSTROM and L. HADDAD. 2007. *Greater DFID & EC Leadership on Chronic Malnutrition: Opportunities and Constraints.* Institute of Development Studies, University of Sussex.

TABER, D.R., J.F. CHRIQUI, F.M. PERNA, L.M. POWELL and F.J. CHALOUPKA. 2012. Weight status among adolescents in states that govern competitive food nutrition content. *Pedriatrics*, doi: 10.1542/peds.2011-3353.

TOOR, R. and G. SAVAGE. 2005. Antioxidant activity in different fractions of tomatoes. *Food Res. Int.* 38, 487-494.

UK Government. 2011. *The future of food and farming: challenges and choices for global sustainability.* Final project report. Foresight, Department for Business Innovation and Skills. The Government Office for Science, London.

UN. 2013a. *The Millennium Development Goals Report 2013.* New York.

UN. 2013b. *A new global partnership: Eradicate poverty and transform Economies through sustainable Development.* The Report of the High-Level Panel of Eminent Persons on the Post-2015 Development Agenda. United Nations, New York.

UNCTAD. 2013. *Trade and Environment report 2013. Wake up before it is too late: Make agriculture truly sustainable now for food security in a changing climate.* UNCTAD, Geneva.

US Department of Defense. 2010. *Quadrennial review report.* www.defense.gov/QDR/images/QDR_as_of_12Feb10_1000.pdf. [Accessed January 7 2014]

VAN PARIJS, P. 2005. Basic income. A simple and powerful idea for the twenty-first century. In: B. Ackerman, A. Alstott and P. van Parijs. *Redesigning Distribution: basic income and stakeholder grants as cornerstones of a more egalitarian capitalism.* The Real Utopias Project Volume V. Verso, London. Pp. 4-39.

VILLAN-DURAN, C. 2009. El nuevo Protocolo Facultativo del Pacto Internacional de Derechos Económicos, Sociales y Culturales. In: Vivero, J.L. and X. Erazo, eds. 2009. *Derecho a la Alimentación, Políticas Públicas e Instituciones contra el Hambre.* Serie Ciencias Humanas, LOM Editores, Santiago.

VIVERO, J.L. 2010. El enfoque legal contra el hambre: el derecho a la alimentación y las leyes de seguridad alimentaria. In: X. Erazo, L. Pautassi and A. Santos, eds. *Exigibilidad y realización de derechos sociales. Impacto en la política pública.* Editorial LOM, Santiago, Chile. Pp 163-188.

VIVERO, J.L. 2013. *Food as a commons: reframing the narrative of the food system.* SSRN Working paper series http://papers.ssrn.com/sol3/papers.cfm?abstract_id=2255447 [Accessed January 7 2014].

WAINER, A. 2011. *Development and migration in rural Mexico.* Working paper 11, Bread for the World Institute.

WHO. 2012. *Obesity and overweight factsheet # 311.* http://www.who.int/mediacentre/factsheets/fs311/en/ [Accessed January 7 2014]

WHO. 2013. *Marketing of foods high in fat, salt and sugar to children: update 2012–2013.* WHO Regional Office for Europe. Copenhagen.

WITTMAN, H., A.A. DESMARAIS and N. WIEBE. 2010. The origins and potential of food sovereignty. In: H. Wittman, A.A. Desmarais and N. Wiebe, eds. *Food sovereignty.*

Reconnecting food, nature and community. Fernwood Publishing. Pp. 1-14.

World Bank. 2006. *Repositioning nutrition as central to development. A strategy for large-scale action*. Washington, DC.

World Bank. 2008. *World development report 2008: Agriculture for development*. Washington, DC.

World Economic Forum (2011). *Global Risks 2011*. Davos, Switzerland. http://reports.weforum.org/wp-content/blogs.dir/1/mp/uploads/pages/files/global-risks-2011.pdf [Accessed January 7 2014]

World Economic Forum. 2013. *Achieving the new vision for agriculture. New models for action*. The World Economic Forum, Davos, Switzerland.

WRIGHT, E.O. (2010). *Envisioning real utopias*. Verso, London.

WWF. 2011. *Livewell: a balance of healthy and sustainable food choices*. WWF and the Rowett Institute of Nutrition and Health.

WWF. 2012. *Living Planet Report 2012. Biodiversity, biocapacity and better choices*. WWF, Global Footprint Network and National Zoological Society.

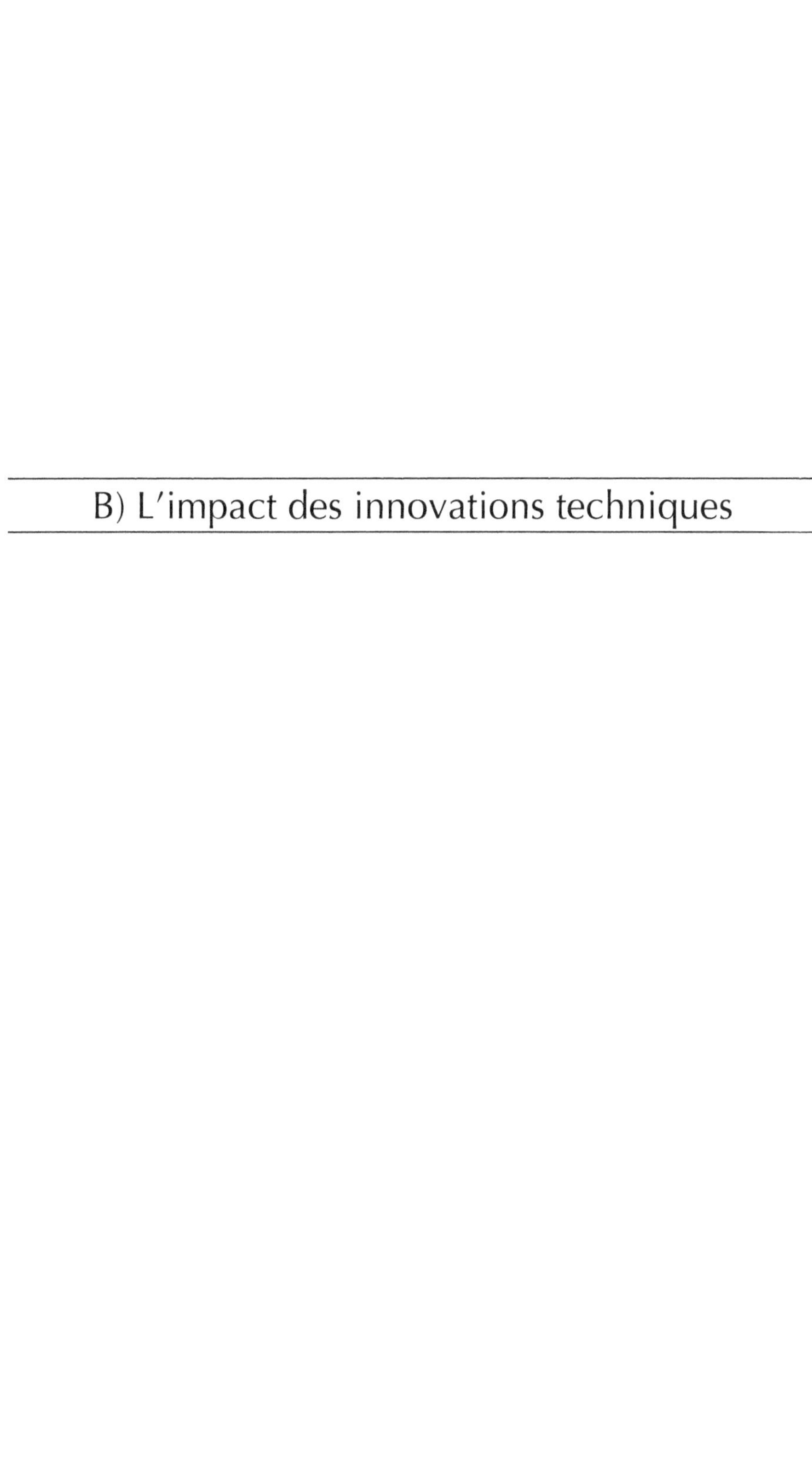

B) L'impact des innovations techniques

Accès aux variétés végétales et propriété intellectuelle internationale : les chercheurs à l'écoute des analyses des ONG

Programme Lascaux [*]

Lors des Rencontres internationales organisées par le programme Lascaux à Nantes en novembre 2012, les chercheurs se sont mis à l'écoute des ONG et des associations ou organisations de la société civile. Le texte qui suit est une synthèse, faite par des membres du programme Lascaux, des analyses présentées par un ensemble d'organisations à partir du rapport introductif émanant de Robert Brac de la Perrière, coordinateur de l'organisation Biodiversité : Echanges et Diffusion d'Expériences (BEDE) et l'un des administrateurs du Réseau Semences Paysannes (RSP), avec les contributions du CETRI, du CFSI, de la Coalition pour la souveraineté alimentaire, de la Confédération paysanne, du Conseil citoyen d'union Hidalgo, de FIAN, de l'Observatoire du droit à l'alimentation et à la nutrition, de GRAIN, de l'OAPI et du Réseau Semences Paysannes[1].

Introduction

Les semences et plus largement les variétés végétales constituent les premiers intrants agricoles. Elles sont à la base de l'agriculture, et donc de l'alimentation. Elles constituent de plus en plus à la fois un objet et un enjeu de propriété intellectuelle.

Pour de nombreux observateurs, paysans et ONG, l'influence des entreprises semencières sur l'écriture du droit de la propriété industrielle

* Ce texte est la synthèse des échanges tenus lors des Rencontres du programme Lascaux « Nourrir le monde : la parole aux citoyens » (12-13 novembre 2012), à Nantes. La rédaction de cette synthèse a été coordonnée par François COLLART DUTILLEUL (Directeur du programme Lascaux) et Sarah TURBEAUX (Ingénieur d'étude du programme Lascaux).

[1] Les sites internet des organisations : Oakland Institute (www.oaklandinstitute.org), BEDE (www.bede-asso.org), CETRI (www.cetri.be), CFSI (www.cfsi.asso.fr), Coalition pour la souveraineté alimentaire (www.nourrirnotremonde.org), Confédération paysanne (www.confederationpaysanne.fr), FIAN (www.fian.org), Observatoire du droit à l'alimentation et à la nutrition (www.rtfn-watch.org), Réseau Semences Paysannes (www.semencespaysannes.org), GRAIN (www.grain.org/fr), OAPI (www.oapi.int).

sur les semences et les variétés suscite d'autant plus d'inquiétudes que le droit international de la propriété intellectuelle qui en est issu tend à se renforcer et à se généraliser.

Quelques définitions[2] :

Variétés population : ensemble de plantes qui se reproduisent librement entre elles au cours de leur culture dans un même milieu biologique, auquel elles sont adaptées. D'un côté, leur pollinisation libre entraîne des individus tous différents dans des proportions non définies et variables d'une année sur l'autre, de l'autre leur culture répétée dans un même milieu biologique et avec des objectifs de production et de sélection issus d'une même communauté humaine détermine les caractères communs qui les réunissent en une même entité distincte des autres[3].

Semences paysannes : semences issues de la sélection et de la multiplication réalisées par les agriculteurs dans leurs champs.

Semences de ferme : semences issues de la sélection de l'industrie semencière, multipliées et ressemées par l'agriculteur.

Certificat d'Obtention Végétale : pour l'industriel, l'intérêt est de mettre en valeur des variétés particulières et distinctes de ses concurrents. Cet intérêt a conduit à la création du Certificat d'Obtention Végétale (COV) dans le cadre de la Convention de l'Union pour la Protection des Obtentions Végétales (UPOV) signée en 1961 et modifiée plusieurs fois depuis. Un COV peut porter sur des variétés nouvelles, distinctes, homogènes et stables (critères DHS). Il donne à son obtenteur des droits exclusifs. Quiconque commercialise la variété protégée doit lui acquitter une redevance. La ressource est cependant libre d'accès à des fins de recherche. Au 5 décembre 2012, 71 États ont déjà adhéré à la Convention de l'UPOV.

En France, le COV est délivré par le Comité de la protection des obtentions végétales (CPOV), instance nationale placée auprès du ministère de l'Agriculture. Il donne à son détenteur le droit d'exploiter exclusivement la variété protégée pendant 25 ou 30 ans selon l'espèce. L'obtenteur peut également, en fonction de ses objectifs, opter pour une protection européenne. Celle-ci s'étend sur 25 ou 30 ans.

[2] Plus généralement, voir : http://www.gnis-pedagogie.org

[3] Définition du Réseau Semences Paysannes (site Semences Paysannes : http://www.semencespaysannes.org).

Dans ce cas, il doit s'adresser à l'Office communautaire des variétés végétales (OCVV), installé à Angers.

Brevet : Le brevet est un titre de propriété industrielle destiné à assurer la protection d'une invention. Pour ce faire trois conditions doivent être remplies à savoir, la nouveauté, l'activité inventive et l'application industrielle. Le brevet peut être national, régional (communautaire) ou international. Il donne à son titulaire le droit exclusif d'exploiter l'invention pendant une durée de 20 ans. Le maintien de ces droits est subordonné au paiement des annuités auprès de l'office auquel le brevet est enregistré. En France, ce titre est délivré par l'Institut National de la Propriété Intellectuelle (INPI) alors que, au plan communautaire, l'Office européen des brevets est l'institution compétente.

Le droit de la propriété intellectuelle a été intégré à l'OMC en 1994 à la suite des accords de Marrakech, notamment à travers l'Accord sur les aspects des droits de propriété intellectuelle qui touchent au commerce (ADPIC). A la suite de l'article 27 alinéa 3 b de cet Accord, tous les États sont obligés de protéger les micro-organismes soit par brevet, soit par un système *sui generis*. Cet accord qui renforce les droits des titulaires de brevets, a pour conséquence l'extension des monopoles des entreprises semencières sur les intrants agricoles.

Catalogue : Le catalogue des variétés et espèces a été créé en France par décret en 1932. Par la suite, l'Union Européenne a émis trois directives en vue d'une harmonisation du catalogue au niveau européen (2002/53, 2002/55 et 98/95). Ces directives, transposées en droit national, fixent les principes d'éligibilité des variétés au catalogue. Les variétés éligibles sont celles qui répondent aux critères DHS. Pour pouvoir être commercialisée, une variété doit être inscrite au catalogue.

I.- Un système de propriété industrielle qui suscite des inquiétudes

A. Une évolution du système de propriété industrielle qui a peu à peu privé les agriculteurs de leur accès aux semences et de leurs droits quant à l'utilisation de ces semences [4]

Depuis 1961, par un jeu de dominos entre les niveaux de législation internationale, européenne et nationale (française), le système de propriété industrielle a peu à peu écarté les agriculteurs de l'accès aux semences et du droit à produire, échanger, reproduire dans leurs champs, sélectionner et vendre à petite échelle leurs variétés. Pour le *Réseau Semences Paysannes*, les lobbies de l'industrie semencière et les législateurs nationaux, européens, mondiaux, en sont les principaux responsables.

Les effets associés du certificat d'obtention végétale, qui protège la variété et les produits issus de cette variété, et du brevet, qui protège l'invention (procédé de création d'une variété, gène transformé...), ont peu à peu privé les agriculteurs de leur qualité d'obtenteurs, au profit des semenciers.

Le tableau ci-après résume les étapes juridiques ayant conduit à l'élimination des droits des agriculteurs.[5]

---

[4] Ce titre s'inspire de l'intervention introductive de Robert BRAC DE LA PERRIERE lors du séminaire « Et si la faim justifiait les moyens...du Droit » (12 et 13 novembre 2013 à Nantes) et du rapport de la Confédération Paysanne « Droits de propriété industrielle et droits des agriculteurs » (accessible à l'adresse suivante : http://www.confederationpaysanne.fr/sites/1/mots_cles/documents/COV_brevets_et_droits_des_agriculteurs.pdf?PHPSESSID=gbkl9k0gmbcnnafv9bfv20vrh6)

[5] Sources du tableau : *idem*.

Année	Niveau de législation	Texte	Points importants	Conséquences pour l'agriculteur
1961	International	Convention UPOV	Création du COV qui ne peut porter que sur des variétés distinctes, homogènes et stables (DHS)	Les variétés paysannes ne peuvent être protégées par un COV
1970	National	Loi française	Réduit la définition de la « stabilité ». Interdit de faire des semences de ferme sur des variétés protégées par un COV Possibilité de protéger une variété créée ou « découverte ».	Toutes les variétés paysannes sont exclues de la protection par une obtention végétale. L'agriculteur a l'interdiction de replanter une semence achetée si elle est protégée par COV. Risque de bio-piraterie puisque l'on peut difficilement découvrir une variété ailleurs que dans le champ d'un paysan.
1978	International	Convention UPOV	Entérine la loi française puisque l'on peut désormais obtenir un COV sur une variété notoire en dehors des variétés du catalogue. Ce catalogue indique quelles variétés ont le droit d'être commercialisées sur la base des critères DHS.	Entérine la possibilité de bio-piraterie. Les variétés paysannes ne peuvent pas être commercialisées puisqu'elles ne répondent pas aux critères DHS.
1991	International	Convention UPOV	Introduit un changement dans la définition de « variété ». Celle-ci se faisait jusqu'à présent sur les caractéristiques phénotypiques visibles de la plante. Elle se base désormais sur le génotype ou une combinaison de génotype. Le COV peut porter désormais sur le produit de la récolte et dans certains États sur le produit transformé. Autorisation du brevet sur les gènes des variétés et création de la variété essentiellement dérivée (VED).	Le critère de distinction échappe à l'agriculteur qui n'a pas les moyens d'identifier un génotype. Les multinationales de la chimie absorbent la plupart du secteur semencier traditionnel. Les agriculteurs ne peuvent pas avoir accès à la technologie permettant le brevet, très coûteuse. La double protection, par brevet et COV, devient possible.

Année	Niveau de législation	Texte	Points importants	Conséquences pour l'agriculteur
1994	Européen	Règlement	Interdit la multiplication de semences de ferme à l'exception de 21 espèces à condition de payer des royalties.	Les agriculteurs n'ont plus le droit de multiplier leurs semences.
1998	Européen	Directive	Confirme que le brevet peut s'étendre au produit de la récolte et de la transformation agroalimentaire. Fait disparaître l'exception du sélectionneur.	
2004	National	Loi française	Exclut les agriculteurs de l'exception de sélection.	Non reconnaissance du rôle des agriculteurs dans l'adaptation des variétés depuis des centaines d'années
2011	National	Loi française	Donne à l'État la possibilité de récupérer les royalties des obtenteurs qui jusque-là n'étaient pas en mesure de les récupérer pour les semences de ferme. Etend la règlementation aux semences à utilisation non commerciale.	Les agriculteurs se voient contraints de reverser des royalties. Suppression du dernier espace sur lequel les agriculteurs pouvaient jouer pour cultiver des semences de ferme et échanger leurs semences.

B. Un système destructeur de la biodiversité

Le deuxième principal reproche fait au système de propriété industrielle relatif aux semences est qu'il tend, par les restrictions qu'il impose, à réduire la biodiversité. D'autre part, il ne reconnait pas le rôle que les agriculteurs ont joué depuis des années dans la préservation de la biodiversité.

Pour le *Réseau Semences Paysannes*, les variétés paysannes permettent une plus grande biodiversité.

Les variétés paysannes constituent une opportunité pour accroître la biodiversité cultivée (agrobiodiversité)

Chaque terroir, chaque système agraire, chaque besoin alimentaire ou culturel nécessite sa variété contrairement au système « engrais-pesticides » qui impose partout un nombre restreint de variétés. De plus, les modes de cultures qui sont liés à ces variétés paysannes sont facteurs de préservation des ressources naturelles au sens large, car les plantes tendent vers une utilisation optimale des possibilités du milieu environnant, avec un impact positif sur plusieurs composantes de l'environnement, par exemple en matière de stabilisation des sols ou de biodiversité sauvage ou cultivée.

http://www.semencespaysannes.org – *Pourquoi ce réseau ?*

La biodiversité des semences apparaît fondamentale, et nécessaire, afin que les cultures puissent s'adapter aux changements climatiques à venir. Or, les agriculteurs ont détenu pendant longtemps un savoir-faire en matière de semences, et les fréquents échanges de semences faisaient d'eux les garants de la biodiversité. Dans les villages d'Afrique sahélienne notamment, il existe encore actuellement une grande biodiversité. Celle-ci permet l'adaptation aux aléas climatiques fréquents. Les variétés paysannes sont dominantes dans les centres de recherche publics de plusieurs pays africains, et libres d'accès. La tradition veut que les paysans échangent leurs semences pour tisser des solidarités et accroître la biodiversité.

Aujourd'hui, la réglementation du système semencier industriel, parce qu'elle exclut les variétés paysannes et réduit considérablement le nombre de variétés autorisées à la commercialisation via le catalogue commun des variétés[6], va à l'encontre de la biodiversité. En effet, les tests imposés pour l'inscription au catalogue, ainsi que le coût élevé d'inscription constituent un frein à l'inscription de semences paysannes.

Pour être inscrites au catalogue officiel des espèces et variétés, les semences doivent répondre aux critères DHS (Distinction, Homogénéité, Stabilité) et VAT (Valeur Agricole et Technologique), et le demandeur doit payer des frais d'inscription

<u>Critères DHS / VAT</u>

Pour échanger ou commercialiser des semences et plants destinés à une exploitation commerciale, il faut que les variétés soient inscrites au catalogue officiel des espèces et variétés. Pour cette inscription, la variété doit actuellement subir une série de tests afin de :

- vérifier son adéquation aux normes de Distinction, d'Homogénéité et de Stabilité (tests DHS) ;

- évaluer l'amélioration par rapport aux variétés existantes (test VAT : Valeur Agronomique et Technologique), lorsqu'il s'agit de plantes de grandes cultures.

Cependant, pour les variétés paysannes et de terroir, l'expression des plantes en fonction du milieu et l'évolution des lignées et populations sur les fermes rendent quasi impossible la description suivant ces critères officiels DHS et VAT, ces variétés étant souvent peu homogènes et peu stables pour préserver leurs possibilités d'adaptation et d'évolution. Leur inscription devient alors impossible, ce qui les empêche d'accéder au marché pour être commercialisées puis cultivées, seul moyen de ne pas disparaître.

<u>Coût d'inscription</u>

D'autre part, le coût de l'inscription (pour une variété de céréales, plus de 6.000 € auxquels il faut ajouter le maintien au catalogue, soit plus de 2.000 € pour les 10 premières années) empêche l'inscription des variétés issues de sélections paysannes : celles-ci sont trop nombreuses et concernent des volumes limités. Dans le cas des variétés potagères, un catalogue annexe de « Variétés anciennes pour jardiniers amateurs » a aussi été créé et dont les frais d'inscription sont moins importants.

[6] Définition dans l'encadré p. 210.

Source : « Réglementation sur la commercialisation des semences et plants », Site internet du Réseau Semences Paysannes.

Si la biodiversité a été reconnue comme essentielle au développement économique et social de l'humanité lors de plusieurs sommets et conventions internationales au cours des dernières années, le processus de négociation de ces conventions ne permettra sans doute pas d'atteindre l'objectif affiché de protection de la biodiversité. L'une des raisons à cela est qu'une fois encore, les agriculteurs praticiens qui renouvellent la biodiversité cultivée en sont exclus.

C. La Convention sur la diversité biologique, le Traité sur les semences et le Protocole de Nagoya : vers un partage des avantages et la protection de la biodiversité ?

Trois textes importants sur la biodiversité et le partage des avantages

La Convention sur la diversité biologique (CDB) est un traité international adopté lors du sommet de la Terre à Rio de Janeiro en 1992, ayant pour buts la conservation de la biodiversité, l'utilisation durable des espèces et des milieux naturels et le partage juste et équitable des avantages découlant de l'exploitation des ressources génétiques.

Le Traité international sur les ressources phyto-génétiques pour l'alimentation et l'agriculture, autrement appelé Traité sur les semences a été adopté en 2001 par la 31ème Conférence de l'Organisation des Nations Unies pour l'alimentation et l'agriculture (FAO), et est entré en vigueur le 29 juin 2004. Il a pour objectif « la conservation et l'utilisation durable des ressources phytogénétiques pour l'alimentation et l'agriculture, et le partage juste et équitable des avantages découlant de leur utilisation en harmonie avec la Convention sur la diversité biologique, pour une agriculture durable et pour la sécurité alimentaire »[7].

Le Protocole de Nagoya est un traité international adopté par la Conférence des Nations Unies sur la diversité biologique à Nagoya en 2010. Il fait suite à la CDB qu'il renforce, en particulier l'un de ses trois objectifs : le partage juste et équitable des avantages découlant de l'utilisation des ressources génétiques. Il fixe les

[7] *Traité international sur les ressources phytogénétiques pour l'alimentation et l'agriculture*, FAO, 2009.

règles selon lesquelles les pays peuvent collaborer pour partager et tirer profit des ressources génétiques.

Il est reproché à la CDB d'avoir favorisé, par le biais des contrats bilatéraux négociés par les États, une commercialisation massive des ressources génétiques comme matières premières alors que ces dernières étaient auparavant partagées avec des droits collectifs par les communautés à l'intérieur du territoire. Il lui est aussi reproché de réaliser une privatisation de ces ressources par le biais de la propriété intellectuelle[8].

Le Traité international sur les ressources phyto-génétiques pour l'alimentation et l'agriculture, censé mettre en application les réglementations de la CDB sur le partage des avantages sur la plupart des principales espèces cultivées, suscite lui aussi la polémique. Pour le *Réseau Semences Paysannes,* il s'agit d'un traité « fait par les industriels, pour les industriels » puisqu'il vise à mettre en place un mécanisme multilatéral d'accès aux ressources génétiques d'une part, et puisque les agriculteurs ont été exclus des négociations de ce traité d'autre part ; la mise en œuvre de leur droit étant à la discrétion des gouvernements.

Les ONG craignent que ce traité « donne aux entreprises privées un accès libre à la majeure partie des collections publiques de matériel génétique du monde sans aucune obligation de partager leurs propres ressources en contrepartie »[9], sachant que les ressources génétiques collectées actuellement dans les banques de gènes sont essentiellement des semences paysannes. Les entreprises peuvent ensuite protéger les variétés développées à partir de ces semences, la plupart du temps sans avoir à en partager les avantages et bénéfices avec les pays ou régions d'où elles sont issues.

En effet, la notion de « partage des avantages » pose question, puisque les industries semencières ne sont pas contraintes d'expliquer comment la variété homogénéisée ou transformée a été sélectionnée. Il est donc malaisé de prouver qu'une variété protégée est issue d'une variété

---

[8] *Le Traité sur les semences de la FAO: des droits des agriculteurs aux privilèges des obtenteurs*, GRAIN, 15 octobre 2005, (Site de GRAIN : http://www.grain.org).

[9] Idem

paysanne. Dès lors, il apparaît difficile de réaliser effectivement le partage des avantages.

Pour autant, les articles 5, 6 et 9 du Protocole de Nagoya offrent des dispositions intéressantes pour les agriculteurs. L'article 5, sur « Le partage juste et équitable des avantages » dispose que les parties doivent « s'assurer que les avantages découlant de l'utilisation des ressources génétiques qui sont détenues par les communautés autochtones et locales, conformément au droit interne relatif aux droits établis de ces communautés autochtones et locales sur ces ressources génétiques, sont partagées de manière juste et équitable avec les communautés concernées conformément à des conditions convenues d'un commun accord ». L'article 6 précise que « l'accès aux ressources génétiques pour leur utilisation est subordonné au consentement préalable donné en connaissance de cause par la Partie qui fournit lesdites ressources ». L'article 9 enfin, indique que « les avantages découlant de l'utilisation des ressources génétiques » doivent être orientés « vers la conservation de la diversité biologique et l'utilisation durable de ses éléments constitutifs ».

II.- Un système de propriété intellectuelle qui tend à s'exporter

A. L'exemple de l'Organisation Africaine de Propriété Intellectuelle

L'Organisation Africaine de Propriété Intellectuelle (OAPI), basée à Yaoundé, est constituée de seize États membres. Cette organisation a été créée en 1977 sur les cendres de l'Office Africain et Malgache de la Propriété Intellectuelle (OAMPI)[10]. Depuis 1962, elle a pour mission la délivrance des titres de propriété industrielle. Elle est régie par l'Accord de Bangui de 1977, texte supranational en matière de propriété intellectuelle au sein des États membres de l'OAPI. L'Accord de Bangui a été révisé pour la dernière fois en 1999. Cette révision est la conséquence de l'Accord sur les ADPIC qui oblige les États membres de l'OMC à prévoir des critères minimums de protection sur les standards prévus par les ADPIC. Elle a consisté à intégrer une Annexe X relative à la protection des obtentions végétales dans l'Accord de Bangui Révisé (ABR).

[10] L'OAMPI a été créée en 1962.

Le système de l'OAPI est pour l'essentiel inspiré des conventions UPOV successives. Une variété doit également être distincte, homogène et stable pour pouvoir être protégée. Le titulaire de la variété possède un droit exclusif sur cette variété, qui lui donne l'autorisation de poursuivre un tiers qui contrefait son droit[11].

Demeurent toutefois quelques différences entre le système occidental et le système de l'OAPI :

- Les variétés ne peuvent pas être protégées par brevet à l'OAPI. Elles ne peuvent l'être que par un certificat d'obtention végétale (COV) qui confère un droit exclusif sur la variété protégée.
- En cas d'urgence nationale, l'autorité compétente peut décider de manière unilatérale de s'octroyer ou d'octroyer à un tiers une licence d'exploitation sans l'autorisation du titulaire du COV. Il est tenu toutefois de reconnaitre le droit du titulaire.

L'OAPI reprend ainsi, avec certaines variantes, l'essentiel du système de propriété intellectuelle européen et américain.

La principale raison invoquée à cela est l'obligation qu'ont les États membres de l'OMC (soit la totalité des États membres de l'OAPI) de mettre en place un dispositif pour protéger les variétés végétales. Cette obligation est mentionnée par l'article 27-3 b) de l'Accord sur les ADPIC. Il en résulte que l'Annexe X de l'Accord de Bangui Révisé, qui est une transposition fidèle de la Convention UPOV de 1991, n'est pas orientée vers la sécurité alimentaire en Afrique. En effet, le contrôle des critères DHS aboutit à la promotion des variétés industrielles de rente au détriment des variétés paysannes. L'étendue des droits des titulaires de COV leur permet de revendiquer le matériel de reproduction et les récoltes qui en sont issues.

L'autre raison invoquée est le manque de moyens dont disposent les États pour financer la recherche, souvent très coûteuse.

Pourtant, l'article 27-3 b) indique que « les Membres prévoiront la protection des variétés végétales par des brevets, par un système *sui gene-*

[11] Cette présentation s'inspire de l'intervention de Régine GAZARO, Directrice du département de la protection de la propriété industrielle de l'Organisation Africaine de la Propriété Intellectuelle.

ris[12] efficace, ou par une combinaison de ces deux moyens ». Il aurait donc été possible pour les États membres de l'OAPI d'élaborer un système de propriété industrielle différent du système existant et plus adapté à leurs cultures, leurs traditions et leurs spécificités.

L'élaboration d'un tel système *sui generis* a été tentée avec le projet de « Loi-modèle pour la protection des droits des communautés locales, des agriculteurs et des sélectionneurs et la réglementation de l'accès aux ressources biologiques ». Ce projet est issu de l'Organisation de l'Unité Africaine - actuellement Union Africaine -. Il aurait pu constituer une alternative au modèle occidental de protection industrielle des semences. Cette « loi-modèle » est en effet une tentative d'équilibre entre les droits des obtenteurs et ceux des agriculteurs.

Cette loi singulière prend en compte la sécurité alimentaire, la souveraineté des États sur leurs ressources biologiques, « l'importance des connaissances, technologies, innovations et pratiques communautaires pour les systèmes entretenant la vie de l'humanité ». Par ailleurs, elle s'oppose au brevet sur le vivant[13].

Elle a été approuvée par les chefs d'États de l'OUA en 1998, qui ont recommandé qu'elle devienne la base des lois nationales sur l'accès et la protection des ressources biologiques en Afrique. Depuis, des discussions ont été engagées pour adapter la Loi-modèle aux cadres nationaux. Toutefois, cet instrument reste peu utilisé, et actuellement seuls quelques pays africains s'en sont inspirés (Namibie, Zimbabwe, Ouganda, Nigéria)[14].

---

[12] « De son propre genre », qualifie une situation juridique dont la singularité prévient tout classement dans une catégorie déjà répertoriée et nécessite de créer des textes spécifiques.

[13] Loi-Modèle de l'OUA pour la protection des droits des communautés locales, des agriculteurs et des sélectionneurs et la réglementation de l'accès aux ressources biologiques, J.A. Ekpere, ICTSD.

[14] S Yamthieu « Loi Modèle Africaine », *in Dictionnaire juridique de la sécurité alimentaire dans le monde*, F. Collart Dutilleul, J-P. Bugnicourt (dir.), Larcier, 2013, pp. 414-416.

B. Un système qui s'exporte sous la pression de l'Occident

Il n'existe peu, voire pas d'entreprises semencières en Afrique, et la création de nouvelles variétés, homogènes, distinctes et stables, est très couteuse et donc souvent hors de portée des centres de recherche publics africains. Dès lors, l'adoption d'un système de protection industrielle sur le modèle européen et américain pose question.

On peut considérer que l'adoption de ce système conduira au développement d'industries semencières africaines, et que le développement de variétés à meilleur rendement pourra être une opportunité de développement économique. Pour l'instant cependant, ce système de propriété industrielle, qui protège les droits des obtenteurs, s'adresse avant tout aux entreprises semencières étrangères et les effets positifs ne se font pas sentir en Afrique.

Les États africains sont en outre contraints de se conformer à une norme internationale à la négociation de laquelle ils n'ont pas toujours été en mesure de participer. Alors que les grandes puissances envoient plusieurs experts pour négocier dans les instances internationales, les États ayant peu de moyens sont souvent représentés par les mêmes personnes dans les différentes institutions. Leurs représentants sont donc moins préparés et moins armés pour les négociations.

En outre, les délégations des États-Unis et d'Europe comportent des cadres des grandes multinationales des semences qui vont défendre leurs propres intérêts, quand les agriculteurs sont absents de la table des négociations.

Conclusion

- Le système de propriété industrielle tel qu'il existe aujourd'hui en Europe et aux États-Unis a conduit à l'appropriation des premiers intrants nécessaires à la sécurité alimentaire par des entreprises semencières qui défendent leurs propres intérêts.

- Par la même occasion, la protection des ressources biologiques et des semences a échappé aux États garants de l'intérêt général et aux agriculteurs garants de la biodiversité.

- Ce système tend aujourd'hui à s'exporter vers les pays en développement via leurs engagements internationaux. Or les textes internationaux ont été négociés majoritairement entre pays développés et par des représentants des entreprises semencières. Afin d'inciter les pays en développement à ratifier les textes internationaux, la possibilité leur a été donnée d'instaurer des systèmes *sui generis*, mais qui sont dans les faits pratiquement inexistants.

- Pourtant des alternatives existent, comme la loi-modèle africaine, qui nécessiterait d'être davantage diffusée et utilisée en Afrique.

- Un appui juridique de délégations peu dotées en ressources humaines et techniques pourrait également contribuer à rétablir davantage d'équilibre dans les négociations internationales.

Les ressources génétiques dans l'alimentation : Les droits de propriété intellectuelle face aux droits des communautés locales en Afrique francophone

J. ZOUNDJIHEKPON [*], M. YOLOU [*], S. I. ANIZEHOU [*] & J.D. ZONGO [**]

Contexte général

Les ressources génétiques africaines exploitées par l'agriculture et la médecine traditionnelle ont toujours été gérées par les communautés locales avec des règles sociales propres à chaque groupe ethnique ou à chaque zone agroécologique. Jusqu'aujourd'hui, l'agriculture africaine est basée sur des échanges de semences entre agriculteurs, et les guérisseurs traditionnels qui utilisent les plantes médicinales sont généralement au service de leurs communautés. De ce fait, les ressources génétiques locales sont exploitées par la médecine traditionnelle et l'agriculture pour l'alimentation, sur la base du droit collectif communautaire. Ainsi, les droits des communautés locales ont presque toujours fait l'objet de consensus et de respect au sein de la même ethnie, et entre les différents groupes ethniques. C'est ainsi que les sociétés traditionnelles africaines ont évolué depuis des millénaires jusqu'à ce jour.

Mais, si les droits collectifs africains ne faisaient aucune différence entre les semences agricoles et les plantes médicinales, l'introduction des droits de propriété intellectuelle internationale a entrainé une différence fondamentale entre les droits de propriété intellectuelle relatifs aux semences utilisées dans l'agriculture, avec les Certificats sur les Obtentions Végétales (Accord de Bangui révisé – OAPI, 1999) et les brevets sur des extraits de plantes médicinales africaines (www.grain.org). Ainsi, l'introduction des droits de propriété intellectuelle internationale dans l'agriculture africaine n'est pas en adéquation avec les réalités sociales locales, et les droits des communautés locales qui y sont associés. Sans

---

* Unité de Génétique Ecologique – Faculté des Sciences et Techniques – Université d'Abomey – Calavi – 06 BP 2026 - Cotonou - BENIN – agboyinou@gmail.com

** Laboratoire de Génétique et des Biotechnologies Végétales – Université de Ouagadougou – BURKINA FASO.

nul doute, cette situation entrainera des difficultés pour l'alimentation sur le continent.

Etat des lieux des droits de propriété intellectuelle (DPI) en Afrique francophone

En Afrique, les plantes alimentaires font partie des ressources génétiques exploitées, tant par les producteurs que par les chercheurs. Bien que la conservation des ressources génétiques africaines ait été l'œuvre des communautés locales pendant des millénaires, aujourd'hui leur exploitation est réglementée par des textes internationaux (Organisation Mondiale de Propriété Intellectuelle, Organisation Mondiale du Commerce, UPOV, Convention sur la diversité biologique...) et / ou régionaux (Accord de Bangui révisé, Loi Modèle de l'Union africaine, etc....). Les pays se retrouvent alors pris en otage entre les intérêts des communautés locales et les conventions, traités et protocoles internationaux qu'ils ont signés, sans aucune réflexion préalable, et sans concertation avec les principaux acteurs concernés sur le sol national. Ainsi, si certains pays ont pris des positions responsables comme l'Algérie qui n'a toujours pas adhéré à l'Organisation Mondiale du Commerce (OMC), d'autres par contre, ont commencé la culture de semences génétiquement modifiées, sans consultation de leurs citoyens et sans règlementation préalable de la biosécurité ; c'est le cas du Burkina Faso (COPAGEN – Burkina Faso, 2008).

Semences agricoles

Après l'adhésion de plusieurs pays africains, dont les pays membres de l'OAPI (pour la plupart francophones) à l'OMC, ces derniers ont été contraints, conformément aux prescriptions de l'Accord sur les aspects des droits de propriété intellectuelle qui touchent au commerce (ADPIC) d'adhérer à l'UPOV (Union pour la Protection des Obtentions Végétales), en révisant l'Accord de Bangui en 1999. Interpellée sur la question à Cotonou en 2001, la Directrice du Centre National de Propriété Intellectuelle (CENAPI devenu aujourd'hui, Agence Nationale de la Propriété Industrielle – ANaPI), a déclaré avoir travaillé avec le ministère de l'Agriculture de son pays, le Bénin, avant de signer la version révisée de l'Accord de Bangui. Mais, les organisations paysannes de la Fédération des Unions de Producteurs du Bénin (FUPRO) n'ont jamais été consultées, alors que les paysans sont les premiers concernés par les questions relatives aux semences.

C'est alors que la société civile active au Bénin a demandé à l'Assemblée Nationale de ne pas ratifier l'Accord de Bangui révisé.

Quand en 2008, au temps fort de la crise alimentaire dans le monde, et des émeutes au Burkina Faso, au Sénégal et au Cameroun, le réseau JINUKUN (Bénin) a réalisé une enquête nationale et parcouru tout le territoire béninois, les semences observées sur le terrain ou indiquées par les services nationaux chargés de l'agriculture, sont pour la plupart des semences améliorées ou introduites par la recherche agronomique ; c'est le cas des variétés de riz « *gambiaca* » rencontrées à Dassa – Zoumé (Centre du Bénin) et « *Nerica* » rencontrée à Bariénou (Nord du Bénin). Ceci montre comment le ministère de l'Agriculture fait la promotion des variétés améliorées dans le pays, au détriment des variétés locales traditionnelles qui ont pourtant fait leurs preuves.

Plantes médicinales

En Afrique, la limite entre les plantes alimentaires et les plantes médicinales n'est pas toujours claire. En effet, nombreuses sont les plantes qui sont consommées comme aliments, et qui, dans le même temps servent de médicaments. L'on peut citer le cas de l'igname jaune *Dioscorea dumetorum,* consommée presque quotidiennement dans certaines régions du Sud – Bénin, et qui est indiqué par plusieurs autres pays africains comme étant une plante médicinale servant à soigner le diabète (GRAIN, 2002). C'est également le cas de la feuille amère (*Vernonia amygdalina*) qui sert à préparer le plat national camerounais, le « *Ndolé* », et qui est également consommée au Bénin sous le nom de « *Amanvivè* », alors qu'elle est une plante médicinale au Burkina Faso, au Mali et au Rwanda ; dans ce dernier pays, cette plante sert à soigner les maladies hépatiques (Mukazayire, 2011). De ce fait, même si les pays membres de l'OAPI ont préféré adopter le Certificat sur les Obtentions Végétales (COV) en révisant l'Accord de Bangui, le brevet (Art.27.3.b de l'ADPIC) qui concerne les produits extraits des plantes médicinales s'imposent à eux. Ainsi, dans l'esprit comme dans la lettre, les droits de propriété intellectuelle internationale sont en conflit permanent avec les droits collectifs des communautés locales. C'est d'ailleurs ce que la société civile active en Afrique a vu venir avec la révision de l'Accord de Bangui, et au Burkina Faso, les associations de lutte contre le SIDA ont lutté contre cette révision, avec deux pétitions qui ont recueilli en son temps plusieurs centaines de signatures ; l'une, adressée au Président de la République du Faso, avec pour titre : « *Sauvez nous des Accords de Bangui* », et l'autre, adressée au Chef du gouvernement du Burkina Faso avec pour titre « *Sauvez nous du piège de Bangui* ».

A titre de rappel, en 1999, au sommet de l'OMC à Seattle, l'Afrique a rejeté le brevet sur le vivant, par respect aux us et coutumes de la majorité des pays de ce continent. La décision des pays membres de l'OAPI d'adopter le COV est donc conforme à cette position africaine. Mais paradoxalement, comme le montre le tableau 1, des brevets continuent d'être déposés (après 1999) sur des extraits de plantes médicinales (et alimentaires) africaines.

Espèces	N° de brevet	Nom du détenteur	Origine	Utilisation
Dioscorea dumetorum (Igname jaune)	US 5 019 580	Sharma Pharmaceuticals M. Iwu	Afrique de l'Ouest	Traitement du diabète en Afrique de l'Ouest. Le brevet s'applique à l'utilisation de la dioscorétine pour le traitement du diabète.
Dioscoreophyllum cumminisii	US 3 998 798 JP 5 070 494	Université de Pennsylvanie (USA) et Kirin Brewery Ltd (Japon)	Afrique de l'Ouest	Sert à sucrer des aliments et des boissons depuis des siècles
Vigna subterranea (Voandzou)	-	Europe et Etats Unis	Afrique Subsaharienne	Produits cosmétiques, shampoing, crème, mousse
Tamarindus indica (Tamarin)	US 6 251 878 (26 Juin 2001)	Dr James C. Arie, Université de Texas aux Etats Unis	Toute l'Afrique	Prévention et traitement des brûlures solaires de la peau
Vernonia amygdalina (Feuille amère)	US 6 849 604 (1er février	Dr Ernest Izevbigie, Jackson State	Afrique Subsaharienne	Lutte contre le cancer

	2005)	University – Etats Unis		
Adansonia digitata (Baobab)	France (1997)	Cognis (France)	Afrique Sub-saharienne	Produits cosmétiques pour la peau, les cheveux, les cils et les ongles.

Tableau 1 : Quelques brevets sur des plantes alimentaires servant de plantes médicinales en Afrique (www.grain.org)

L'accès aux ressources génétiques et le partage des Avantages (APA)

Après plus d'une décennie de mise en œuvre de la Convention sur la diversité biologique (CBD)[1], le troisième objectif de cette convention « *le partage juste et équitable des bénéfices tirés de l'utilisation des ressources génétiques* » n'a toujours pas été mis en œuvre. C'est alors que la communauté internationale a décidé d'y consacrer quatre ans de réflexion et de négociations à partir de 2006, pour aboutir au Protocole de Nagoya au Japon en 2010.

Mais, les pays africains tardant comme à l'accoutumée à prendre leur responsabilité, la coopération allemande (GTZ devenue GIZ) a alors décidé de soutenir l'Afrique dans cette initiative planétaire, en organisant différentes rencontres de renforcement des capacités entre 2007 et 2010 au Maroc, au Sénégal, en Tunisie et au Bénin. A l'issue du sommet de Nagoya, le Protocole sur l'Accès aux ressources génétiques et le Partage juste et équitable des Avantages découlant de leur utilisation relatif à la Convention sur la diversité biologique (APA) a été adopté. Mais tout porte à croire que ce Protocole est plus au service des multinationales que des communautés locales ; le problème de la mise en œuvre de ce Protocole pour la défense des intérêts des communautés sur leurs semences locales traditionnelles et leurs plantes médicinales reste posé.

Quelles solutions pour l'Afrique ?

En ce troisième Millénaire bien entamé, sans aucun doute la « démocratie alimentaire » exige l'évolution du DPI en Afrique. Cette démocratie

---

[1] *Convention sur la diversité biologique*, 5 juin 1992 (1993) 1760 R.T.N.U. 79 (no 30619).

alimentaire nécessite également l'évolution des concepts et normes existant en faveur de la souveraineté alimentaire, mais également la révision des programmes d'enseignement supérieur, surtout dans les universités africaines. En effet, comment enseigner aujourd'hui dans ces universités, des disciplines comme la biologie ou physiologie végétale, la biologie cellulaire, la chimie ou biochimie, la génétique, l'agronomie et autres sciences connexes, sans évoquer les problèmes sociaux ou juridiques posés par l'exploitation des ressources génétiques ? Aujourd'hui, les ressources génétiques africaines sont littéralement pillées par les multinationales, sans aucun respect des réglementations nationales. C'est alors que le Rapporteur Spécial sur le droit à l'alimentation, Olivier De Schutter, parle de « *risques de détournement des ressources génétiques* » (Nations Unies, 2009). « L'accès aux ressources génétiques et le partage des avantages (APA) » n'est sans doute pas la solution aux problèmes relatifs à l'alimentation en Afrique. Même si le *Traité International sur les ressources phytogénétiques pour l'alimentation et l'agriculture*[2] constitue une certaine avancée pour les *droits des agriculteurs* en Afrique, il doit intégrer les réserves de *Via Campesina* publiées dans un communiqué de presse le 30 septembre dernier[3].

Avec la coexistence dans la plupart des pays africains du droit coutumier et du droit moderne en matière de gestion des ressources génétiques alimentaires, l'Afrique ne devrait-elle pas innover ? Malheureusement, l'héritage du droit européen en Afrique a conduit l'OAPI à réviser l'Accord de Bangui, en faisant peu de place à l'innovation dans le domaine de l'adaptation du droit coutumier des pays africains. De plus, l'évolution des DPI en Afrique nécessite un travail interdisciplinaire entre des chercheurs de différents horizons (biologie, droit, anthropologie, etc...) dans chaque pays, pour proposer une autre façon d'aborder le droit, surtout dans le domaine de la gestion des ressources génétiques alimentaires.

---

[2] FAO, *Traité international sur les ressources phytogénétiques pour l'alimentation et l'agriculture*, Résolution 3/2001, 3 novembre 2001 (2004) 2400 RTNU (no 43345) (entré en vigueur le 29 juin 2004).

[3] Via Campesina, « Traité sur les semences : une résolution en faveur du droit des agriculteurs », communiqué de presse, Oman le 30 septembre 2013. Disponible à l'adresse suivante : http://viacampesina.org/fr/index.php/les-grands-ths-mainmenu-27/biodiversitt-resources-gtiques-mainmenu-37/853-traite-sur-les-semences-une-resolution-en-faveur-du-droit-des-agriculteurs

Conclusion

En Afrique, chaque peuple, chaque groupe ethnique fonctionne suivant les règles sociales qui lui sont propres. Ces règles respectées de tous les membres de la communauté ont assuré depuis des millénaires, une utilisation durable des ressources génétiques des différents terroirs. Tout dispositif qui n'est pas fondé sur cette réalité sociale africaine sera toujours au bénéfice des multinationales qui ne cherchent que le profit. Aujourd'hui, l'Afrique a besoin de textes juridiques qui soutiennent les intérêts des agriculteurs et des guérisseurs traditionnels, dans un processus de travail interdisciplinaire qui prend comme option d'écouter les communautés locales, de travailler avec elles, et non pas de les utiliser comme faire valoir dans des accords internationaux.

Références

COPAGEN – Burkina Faso, 2008. *Semences de la biodiversité*, N° 76. http://www.grain.org/fr

MUKAZAYIRE, M.J. ; MINANI, V. ; RUFFO, C.K. ; BIZURU, E. ; STEVIGNY, C. et DUEZ, P. 2011. *Journal of Ethnopharmacology.*, doi:10.1016/j.jep.2011.09.025.

Nations Unies, 2009. Assemblée Générale des Nations Unies, Soixante – quatrième Session (Point 71b). A/64/170. 23 Juillet 2009 : 25 p.

www.oapi.org

Accès aux aliments et droit de la propriété industrielle dans les pays en développement

Sylvestre YAMTHIEU *

Dans son rapport 2012 sur l'état de l'insécurité alimentaire dans le monde, l'Organisation des Nations Unies pour l'alimentation et l'agriculture (FAO) souligne que, entre 2010 et 2012, 850 des 870 millions de personnes sous-alimentées recensées dans le monde vivent dans les pays en développement (PED)[1]. Alors que ce nombre tend à diminuer sur le plan mondial, l'Afrique, malgré l'abondance des ressources naturelles dont elle dispose, est le seul continent où la sous-alimentation chronique a progressé ces vingt dernières années. Si le Rapport de la FAO souligne que « *la croissance économique est nécessaire (sans être suffisante) pour accélérer la réduction de la faim dans le monde* », cela signifie que les causes naturelles et les conflits armés ne justifient pas à eux seuls la faim dans le monde[2]. Celle-ci s'explique par des causes conjoncturelles et structurelles, notamment par des choix politiques et juridiques inadaptés[3]. Il y a alors lieu de se demander si le droit de la propriété industrielle est l'une des causes ou la solution de l'insécurité alimentaire des PED.

Selon la FAO, la sécurité alimentaire existe lorsque tous les êtres humains ont un accès permanent aux aliments en quantité et en qualité

---

* Docteur en droit privé de l'Université de Nantes – IRDP- (France) et de l'Université de Ngaoundéré (Cameroun). Membre du programme Lascaux. Cet article aborde les points saillants de la thèse de doctorat présentée par l'auteur en avril 2013 à Nantes et publiée aux éditions Larcier en janvier 2014. S. YAMTHIEU, « Accès aux aliments et droit de la propriété industrielle », Préface : J.-P. CLAVIER, Avant-propos : F. COLLART DUTILLEUL et Postface : O. DE SCHUTTER, Larcier, coll. *Droit / Economie international*, Bruxelles, 394 p.

[1] FAO, *L'état de l'insécurité alimentaire dans le monde 2012, La croissance économique est nécessaire, mais elle n'est pas suffisante pour accélérer la réduction de la faim et de la malnutrition*, Rome, octobre 2012.

[2] S. PARMENTIER, « Et soudain ressurgit la faim », *Le Monde diplomatique*, n° 24, novembre 2009, p. 24.

[3] O. DE SCHUTTER, *Politiques semencières et droit à l'alimentation : accroître l'agro biodiversité et encourager l'innovation*, Rapport du Rapporteur spécial des Nations Unies sur le droit à l'alimentation, Genève, 23 juillet 2009, A/64/170.

suffisante selon leurs préférences[4]. Or, la production des aliments est subordonnée au modèle agricole, ce d'autant que « l'agriculture est dans l'alimentation ce que représenterait le sang pour le corps humain »[5]. Les semences qui constituent le premier intrant agricole sont ainsi au cœur des rapports entre la sécurité alimentaire et le droit de la propriété industrielle.

La propriété industrielle est une branche de la propriété intellectuelle[6]. Elle comprend le droit des créations industrielles (droit des brevets, droit des obtentions végétales[7]) et celui des signes distinctifs. Elle favorise notamment l'innovation par la reconnaissance de droits exclusifs aux inventeurs en contrepartie de leurs apports à la société. Toutefois, elle comporte ses propres garde-fous[8] contre les abus, auxquels s'ajoutent ceux tirés du droit de la concurrence. Cet instrument, longtemps considéré comme un outil d'équilibre entre intérêt individuel et intérêt collectif est en crise de légitimité[9], car on lui oppose de nouveaux impératifs. Il s'agit notamment des considérations éthiques et environnementales, de l'accès aux médicaments[10] ou plus largement, de la protection des ressources génétiques dans ses rapports avec l'alimentation et la santé.

---

[4] FAO, *Sommet mondial de l'alimentation*, Rome 13-17 novembre 1996. Pour un compte rendu de ce sommet, v. A REVEL, « Sommet mondial de l'alimentation », *Économie rurale*, n° 238, 1997, pp. 44-46.

[5] J.- P. SIKELI, *Les biotechnologies modernes à l'épreuve des droits de l'homme* : *les OGM face à la question de la sécurité alimentaire* : controverse et dilemme, Mémoire DESS en Droit de l'homme, Université de Cocody, 2005, [en ligne], [www.memoireonline.com] (consulté le 7 janvier 2013).

[6] La propriété intellectuelle désigne un ensemble de droits qui portent sur un objet immatériel. Elle est constituée de deux principales branches : la propriété littéraire et artistique (ou droit d'auteur) et la propriété industrielle (v. C. BERNAULT, J.-P. CLAVIER, *Dictionnaire de droit de la propriété intellectuelle*, Ellipses, Paris, 2008, p. 348).

[7] Dans le contexte OAPI, on y ajoute les modèles d'utilité et les schémas de configuration.

[8] De manière classique, le système de propriété industrielle prévoit des mécanismes pour faire prévaloir les impératifs d'intérêt général. Parmi ceux-ci on peut citer l'obligation d'exploiter le titre de protection et les licences obligatoires.

[9] v. M. HIANCE, « La propriété industrielle, un outil de développement économique », *La Propriété intellectuelle en question (s)-Regards croisés européens, IRPI*, Litec, Paris 2006, p. 9 -14.

[10] Au sujet de l'accès aux médicaments, v. Th. BREGER, *L'accès aux médicaments des pays en développement, - Enjeu d'une rénovation des politiques de développement,* L'Harmattan, Paris, 2011; J.-P. CLAVIER, « L'accès au médicament breve-

La mondialisation du droit de la propriété intellectuelle contribue à entretenir cette crise de légitimité. Dans le secteur agricole, cette mondialisation s'est faite, d'un côté, dans le cadre de la convention de l'Union pour la Protection des obtentions Végétales (UPOV) et de l'autre sous l'impulsion de l'Organisation Mondiale du Commerce (OMC), notamment à travers l'accord sur les Aspects des Droits de Propriété Intellectuelle qui touchent au Commerce (ADPIC). Ces modèles, conçus dans les pays industrialisés en considération de leurs niveaux de développement socio-économiques et culturels d'une part, et en fonction de leur climat et de leur environnement d'autre part, sont imposés aux PED. Or, ils ne correspondent pas toujours aux réalités de ces pays.

Toutefois, l'objet de cette étude n'est pas de contester le principe de la protection des innovations agricoles dans les PED. Il ne s'agit pas de soutenir que les droits intellectuels sont néfastes pour les PED et de conclure, par conséquent, que moins il y en aura, mieux cela vaudra. Il s'agit au contraire de rechercher de nouveaux points d'équilibre entre les intérêts (privés) de ceux qui investissent dans l'innovation et l'amélioration des semences et l'intérêt général de l'accès aux aliments. Dans cette perspective, à partir de quelques exemples, l'étude examine les conséquences du système de la propriété industrielle globalisé sur la sécurité alimentaire (pris du point de vue quantitatif) dans les PED. Cette approche, qui est doublée d'un recours au droit comparé, se justifie par l'absence de système de propriété intellectuelle unifié en Afrique[11] ou dans les PED, alors que les diffi-

---

té », *Open science et marchandisation des connaissances, Cahiers Droit, Sciences et Technologies,* CNRS éditions, n° 3, juin 2010, pp. 179-190 ; M. D. VARELLA, « L'organisation mondiale du commerce, les brevets, les médicaments et le rapport nord-sud : un point de vue du sud », *RIDE*, n° 1, 2004 pp. 79-117 ; E. COMBE, É. PFISTER, « Brevet et prix des médicaments dans les pays en développement », *Propr. int.*, n° 8, juillet 2003, pp. 269-277 ; Rapport de la Commission britannique des droits de propriété intellectuelle, *Intégrer les droits de propriété intellectuelle et la politique de développement,* 2002, [en ligne], [www.iprcommission.org] (consulté le 6 novembre 2012).

[11] La protection de la propriété industrielle en Afrique, présente plusieurs visages dans la mesure où, sur le continent, il existe plusieurs offices de propriété intellectuelle qui, au fond, ont été construits sous les cendres de la colonisation. Ainsi, l'Organisation Africaine de la Propriété Intellectuelle (OAPI) a été mise en place par les anciennes colonies françaises et les pays qui ont été sous la tutelle de la France. En revanche, certains pays qui ont été sous l'influence britannique sont

cultés et les conséquences de la transposition des conventions internationales relatives à la propriété intellectuelle sont les mêmes.

Pour s'en convaincre, il convient d'examiner les critères de protection (1) et les règles relatives à l'exercice du monopole conféré par le brevet (issu de l'accord sur les ADPIC) et le certificat d'obtention végétale (COV) (issu de la convention UPOV) (2).

1.- La remise en cause de l'accès aux aliments par l'octroi des monopoles sur les semences

L'article 27§3 (b) de l'accord sur les ADPIC donne la possibilité aux États de prévoir la protection des variétés végétales par le brevet, par un système *sui generis* ou par la combinaison de ces deux moyens. Seulement, l'OMC et l'Organisation Mondiale de la Propriété Intellectuelle (OMPI) présente le système UPOV comme la seule alternative « efficace » au brevet ; même si une telle démarche est discutée[12]. En effet, qu'il s'agisse du brevet issu de l'accord sur les ADPIC (a) ou du certificat d'obtention végétale promu par l'UPOV (b), les critères de protection retenus sont tantôt insuffisants, tantôt inadaptés aux réalités locales.

a- L'insuffisance du contrôle des critères de brevetabilité

De manière classique, la brevetabilité d'une invention est soumise à trois conditions, à savoir : la nouveauté, l'activité inventive (inventivité) et l'application industrielle. Ces critères qui constituent les conditions positives de brevetabilité[13], se superposent aux conditions négatives : la non-appropriation préalable, la non-conformité à l'ordre public et aux bonnes mœurs et la non-appartenance à une catégorie exclue par le législateur.

---

réunis au sein de l'*African Regional Industrial Property Organization* (ARIPO). Contrairement au système OAPI dont les Annexes de l'Accord de Bangui Révisé (ABR) constituent le droit supranational pour les États-Membres, le système de l'ARIPO complète les systèmes nationaux de propriété intellectuelle de ses membres. Dans ce contexte, les titres de protection peuvent être nationaux ou régionaux. Á côté de ces deux offices sous-régionaux, certains États ont mis en place des offices nationaux de propriété intellectuelle. C'est le cas des pays de l'Afrique du Nord (Maroc, Algérie, Tunisie, etc.), du Nigeria et de l'Afrique du Sud entre autres.

[12] v. S. YAMTHIEU, *La protection des obtentions végétales dans l'espace OAPI,* Mémoire de DEA, Université de Ngaoundéré (Cameroun), 2008.

[13] J. M. MOUSSERON, *Traité des brevets*, Litec, Paris, 1984, p. 168 et s.

Dans le principe, l'objectif de ces critères, initialement conçus pour les matières inertes, est d'éviter la délivrance de brevets triviaux. Or, on observe la violation de ces critères par les offices de brevets, notamment lorsque l'objet de la demande de brevet porte sur une matière vivante. Cela aboutit à la biopiraterie des ressources naturelles comme le montrent les exemples de brevets sur le gène sucré de la *thaumatine* et sur celui de la *brazzéine*. Ces brevets ont été délivrés sans que les critères de nouveauté et de l'activité inventive n'aient été remplis. Cela remet sur le devant de la scène, la nécessité de renforcer les conditions et la procédure de délivrance des brevets.

Á cet effet, deux pistes peuvent être explorées. La première consiste à prévoir des critères supplémentaires de brevetabilité tels que la divulgation de l'origine géographique de la ressource génétique et le consentement préalable de l'État à son exploitation. La seconde piste consiste à prévoir la participation du public à l'examen de la demande de brevet. Dans cette hypothèse, le système *peer patent* expérimenté aux États-Unis pourrait être un exemple à suivre. Ce système vise à créer une communauté publique d'examinateurs de brevets afin de faire participer le public (*third party*) à la procédure d'examen des brevets. Plus concrètement, il s'agit, lors de l'examen d'une demande de brevet[14], de permettre au public de formuler des observations et de fournir des informations aux examinateurs de manière à les renseigner sur l'état antérieur de la technique.

b- L'inadaptation des critères UPOV[15] de protection des variétés végétales

Le système UPOV prévoit quatre critères de protection des obtentions végétales : la nouveauté, la distinction, l'homogénéité et la stabilité[16] auxquelles s'ajoute la dénomination variétale. Les PED qui ont transposé ce modèle dans leur ordre interne ont repris ces critères de protection. C'est le cas des États de l'Afrique de l'ouest et du centre à travers l'Organisation Africaine de la Propriété Intellectuelle (OAPI)[17]. L'exigence

---

[14] C. SAEZ, « "*Peer to patent*" pourrait servir de modèle pour les offices de brevets », [en ligne], [www.ip-watch.org] (consulté le 14 avril 2012).

[15] Convention de l'Union pour la Protection des Obtentions Végétales.

[16] v. Chapitre III de la Convention UPOV de 1991.

[17] v. Art. 4 de l'Annexe X de l'ABR.

de l'homogénéité et de la stabilité permettrait de mesurer le travail d'amélioration des plantes. Toutefois, la stabilité et l'homogénéité exigées au Nord ne sauraient être les mêmes au Sud où la nature des sols, le climat et les méthodes de sélection sont différents. Par exemple, les variétés paysannes[18] qui représentent encore l'essentiel de la production agricole des denrées alimentaires dans PED ne répondent pas aux exigences du système UPOV. Cela s'explique par le fait que ce système n'est pas orienté vers la sécurité alimentaire.

Pour s'en convaincre, l'étude présente un bilan du système UPOV transposé (entre autres) dans les États membres de l'OAPI[19] ainsi qu'au Kenya. Dans le cas de l'OAPI, au 1er janvier 2013[20], soit six années après la mise en application de l'Annexe X de l'Accord de Bangui Révisé (ABR) relative à la protection des obtentions végétales, cet office a délivré 16 COV. Parmi ces titres, 9 portent sur des variétés de coton ; 2 sur le sorgho ; 1 sur le gombo ; un sur la tomate ; 1 sur le navet ; 1 sur la pastèque et 1 autre sur le *Mexican bamboo.* En réalité, sauf à démontrer que les populations de l'Afrique centrale et occidentale ont adopté le coton comme un aliment de consommation de base, aucune disposition de l'Annexe X de l'Accord de Bangui révisé (ABR), n'oriente la sélection des plantes vers la promotion des cultures de consommation courante.

Pour ce qui concerne le Kenya, en 2002, afin de se conformer au système UPOV de 1991, le législateur kenyan a modifié sa loi de 1972 relative à la protection des variétés végétales[21]. Avant cette modification, sous la version 1978 de l'UPOV, aucune demande de protection des variétés végétales ne portait sur une culture de consommation de base jusqu'en

---

[18] Les variétés paysannes encore appelées variétés traditionnelles sont celles qui sont sélectionnées par un paysan ou par une communauté de paysans. Elles sont souvent qualifiées de « variété-population » pour marquer l'importance de la diversité intra-variétale que le mode de sélection implique. Dans la plupart elles résultent des échanges informels réguliers entre agriculteurs.

[19] L'OAPI est composée de 15 États membres : le Bénin, le Burkina Faso, le Cameroun, la Centrafricaine, le Congo (Brazzaville), la Côte d'Ivoire, le Gabon, la Guinée, la Guinée Bissau, le Mali, la Mauritanie, le Niger, le Sénégal, le Tchad, le Togo.

[20] À cette même date (janvier 2013), 102 demandes de certificats d'obtention végétale sont en cours d'examen à l'OAPI.

[21] v. Kenya, *The Seeds and Plant Varieties Act*, 1972, (as Amended in 2002), PVP Gazette, n° 94, décembre 2002.

mai 1999[22]. En réalité, « presque toutes (les demandes) ont visé des cultures commerciales : plantes ornementales, canne à sucre, café et orge pour les brasseries industrielles. Un certificat d'obtention végétale a été délivré pour une variété de haricot vert - que le Kenya cultive pour le marché européen »[23]. En effet, le système kenyan de protection des obtentions végétales est reconnu pour les belles fleurs qu'il produit et non pour avoir favorisé la sécurité alimentaire des populations kenyanes. Plus de la moitié (52 %) des variétés protégées au Kenya sont des plantes ornementales[24]. Or, la culture de ces plantes, favorisée par les critères de protection retenus par le système UPOV, occupe des espaces de terres et requiert des quantités d'eau qui sont pourtant indispensables à la production agricole des denrées alimentaires. On pourrait alors y voir une nouvelle forme d'accaparement des terres dans les PED.

Finalement, loin de déboucher sur la production des aliments de base qui correspond à la culture alimentaire des différentes populations dans les PED, la transposition du système UPOV conduit ces communautés à « produire ce qu'elles ne consomment pas et à consommer ce qu'elles ne produisent pas »[25]. L'étendue des droits conférés contribue à entretenir cette situation.

---

[22] Le Bureau des obtentions végétales fut établi en mars 1997. À compter de cette date et jusqu'en mai 1999, 136 variétés ont subi des examens pour l'octroi du droit. Sur ce nombre, 123 concernaient des plantes ornementales, 6 la canne à sucre, 5 l'orge (le sélectionneur étant brassier), 1 portait sur le café et 1 autre sur un type de haricot vert (Kephis Public Notice, Nairobi, 3 mai 1999).

[23] GRAIN, « La protection des obtentions végétales pour nourrir l'Afrique ? Rhétorique contre réalité », décembre 1999 [en ligne], [www.grain.org] (consulté le 3 septembre 2011).

[24] R. Jödens, « Les avantages de la protection des variétés végétales », OMPI, juin 2010 [en ligne] [www.wipo.int] (consulté le 11 juillet 2011). Au moment de la rédaction de ce document, l'auteur est Directeur Général adjoint de l'UPOV. L'incidence du système UPOV sur le secteur horticole au Kenya est confirmée dans une étude réalisée par l'UPOV sur l'impact de l'application de ce système ; v. UPOV, « The Report on the impact of plant variety protection », 2005 [en ligne], [www.upov.int] (consulté le 5 août 2011).

[25] O. Bain mis en ligne par J. M. Liotier, « L'agriculture à l'aube des indépendances », [en ligne], [http://afriquepluriel.ruwenzori.net/agriculture.htm] (consulté le 27 novembre 2012).

2.- La remise en cause de l'accès aux aliments par l'étendue des droits sur les semences

Le brevet et le COV donnent au titulaire du monopole le droit de revendiquer respectivement le gène et la variété végétale protégés lorsqu'ils sont utilisés comme semences (a). Á certains égards, ce droit s'étend aux produits obtenus à partir du gène ou de la variété végétale protégée (b).

a- La revendication des semences obtenues à partir du matériel de reproduction

Dans le cas du brevet, l'étendue des droits sur la semence résulte de l'article 34 de l'accord sur les ADPIC. Cet article assimile l'invention de procédé à l'invention de produit. Ainsi, sous le prétexte de protéger le procédé de transformation ou d'extraction d'un gène, les titulaires de droits en viennent à s'approprier une plante entière. Or, de manière classique, le droit des brevets établit une distinction entre les inventions de procédés et ceux qui portent sur les produits. Dans le premier cas, l'exclusivité porte sur le processus de fabrication, alors que dans le second, elle concerne le résultat lui-même. En effet, lorsque le brevet porte sur l'invention de produit, le breveté a le monopole d'exploitation de ce produit, quel que soit le procédé utilisé pour l'obtenir. En revanche, s'il s'agit d'une invention de procédé, le brevet ne couvre que ce procédé et non les autres moyens qui permettent d'obtenir le même produit ou le même résultat[26]. Or, l'accord sur les ADPIC oblige tous les États membres de l'OMC d'accorder des brevets sur les procédés de modification génétique des plantes et sur les gènes eux-mêmes. Le brevet étant un monopole d'exploitation de l'invention, il affecte directement l'accessibilité aux produits et donc aux semences[27]. Cela conduit à s'interroger sur la frontière entre le gène breveté et la plante non brevetable.

Dans le cas du COV, il convient de souligner l'évolution de la convention UPOV. Sous la version de 1978 de cette convention, seule la reproduction ou la multiplication de la variété végétale à des fins commer-

---

[26] F. POLLAUD-DULIAN, *La propriété industrielle*, Economica, Paris, 2011, n° 225, p. 160.

[27] OMS, « Mondialisation et accès aux médicaments », *Économie de la santé et médicaments*, n° 007, 1999, p. 32, [en ligne], [www.who.int] (consulté le 17 septembre 2012).

ciales étaient soumises à l'autorisation préalable de l'obtenteur. L'accomplissement de ces actes à titre non commerciaux échappait ainsi au contrôle de l'obtenteur. Cependant, cette possibilité est amoindrie dans la version UPOV de 1991 qui étend, à certains égards, les droits de l'obtenteur sur les variétés essentiellement dérivées (de la variété principale).

Dans certaines hypothèses, les droits conférés au titulaire du monopole s'étendent à la revendication des produits obtenus à partir du matériel de reproduction protégé.

b- La revendication des produits obtenus à partir du matériel de reproduction

Le brevet et le COV confèrent à leurs titulaires la possibilité de s'opposer à l'utilisation du gène ou de la variété végétale sur lesquels portent leurs droits respectifs. Ceux-ci sont fondés à réclamer la semence ou le gène protégé. Une question se pose alors, celle de savoir si en plus de cette réclamation, le détenteur des droits sur le gène d'une semence ou sur une variété végétale peut être fondé à revendiquer les récoltes ou les produits qui en sont issus. La réponse à cette question dépend du titre de propriété industrielle concerné. Lorsque le matériel de reproduction est protégé par un brevet, son titulaire est fondé à réclamer des droits sur les produits obtenus directement à partir du procédé breveté.

En revanche, lorsqu'il s'agit du COV, l'évolution de la convention UPOV en 1991 a rendu possible la revendication des droits sur les produits obtenus à partir de la variété protégée. En effet, l'alinéa 3 de l'article 14 de cette convention consacre une exception facultative qui permet à un État de prévoir la possibilité pour un obtenteur de réclamer les produits fabriqués directement à partir d'un produit de récolte de la variété protégée. Il faut donc que l'utilisation n'ait pas été autorisée par l'obtenteur, à moins qu'il ait pu exercer son droit en relation avec le produit de la récolte. Ainsi, la réclamation des aliments directement obtenus à partir de la variété végétale protégée reste une exception soumise à une condition : l'épuisement des droits[28] de l'obtenteur. En effet, aussi longtemps que ses droits sur la varié-

---

[28] La règle de l'épuisement des droits de propriété intellectuelle signifie que la première vente du produit épuise le monopole du titulaire du titre de protection sur le

té végétale ne seront pas épuisés, celui-ci pourra être fondé à réclamer cette variété et les récoltes qui pourront en être issues.

En conclusion, la transposition du système international de propriété industrielle dans les PED montre les conséquences d'un système inadapté aux besoins locaux. Qu'il s'agisse du contrôle DHS (Distinction – Homogénéité - Stabilité) ou des critères de brevetabilité (à savoir, la nouveauté, l'activité inventive et l'application industrielle), ils font partie d'un système qui aboutit à la monoculture et au détournement des ressources génétiques et des savoirs traditionnels qui y sont associés. Il est donc impératif de repenser le système actuel afin de le diversifier. Á cet effet, des alternatives à la convention UPOV et à l'accord sur les ADPIC doivent être envisagées. Parmi celles-ci, on relève l'originalité de la loi modèle africaine et celle de la loi indienne de protection des obtentions végétales[29]. Cependant, le modèle le plus abouti est sans doute celui du système thaïlandais de protection des obtentions végétales[30]. Celui-ci retient particulièrement l'attention pour la prise en compte de la diversité des situations à considérer et pour son orientation vers la sécurité alimentaire. Ces trois modèles pourraient (devraient) inspirer les législateurs nationaux et constituer des modèles de références à l'UPOV et à l'OMC.

bien objet de la vente. Cette vente doit se faire par le titulaire des droits ou avec son consentement.

[29] v. *The protection of plant varieties and farmers's rights Act*, 2001, disponible sur le site de l'OMPI, collection des lois accessible en ligne, [www.wipo.int] (consulté le 12 janvier 2013).

[30] v. *The Plant varieties protection Act*, BE 2542 1999), disponible sur le site de l'OMPI, collection des lois accessible en ligne, [www.wipo.int] (consulté le 12 janvier 2013).

Les OGM, illustration des obstacles et des potentialités offertes par le droit pour une meilleure démocratie alimentaire

Mai-Anh NGO *

Pour tenter de construire une démocratie alimentaire, il faut s'interroger sur ce que cela signifie. La démocratie étant définie comme « un régime politique dans lequel le pouvoir suprême est attribué au peuple qu'il exerce pour lui-même ou par l'intermédiaire des représentants qu'il élit »[1]. Transposée dans le domaine alimentaire, une telle définition implique selon nous que le peuple ou ses représentants choisissent l'alimentation qu'il décide de consommer. Cette proposition de définition rejoint celle d'un droit plus affirmé, ces dernières années : le droit à l'alimentation adéquat. Celui-ci est défini comme « le droit à un accès régulier, permanent et non restrictif, soit directement soit en l'achetant, à une quantité de nourriture suffisante et d'une qualité adéquate, correspondant aux traditions culturelles du peuple auquel le consommateur appartient, qui lui permet de profiter sans crainte d'une vie physique et mentale, individuelle et collective, épanouissante et digne »[2].

Cette étude a choisi d'aborder le thème de la démocratie alimentaire sous l'angle des organismes génétiquement modifiés (OGM). Ce choix s'explique par le fait que les OGM mettent en exergue l'importance cruciale du choix en matière d'alimentation et les difficultés à maintenir une diversité indispensable à la démocratie alimentaire. L'étude de la réglementation des OGM et de son évolution démontre d'une part les problématiques liées aux obstacles que rencontrent la démocratie alimentaire (I), mais illustre d'autre part les potentialités contenues dans le droit pour favoriser l'émergence d'une véritable démocratie alimentaire (II).

---

* Ingénieur de recherche - Docteur et HDR en droit GREDEG (UMR 7321 Université de Nice Sophia / CNRS) [ngo@gredeg.cnrs.fr].

[1] G. CORNU, *Vocabulaire juridique*, Presses Universitaires de France, 1997.

[2] Olivier DE SCHUTTER, Rapporteur spécial des Nations Unies, 2002 (http://www.srfood.org/fr/droit-a-l-alimentation).

I. Les obstacles à l'expression d'une véritable démocratie alimentaire en matière d'OGM

L'idée d'une démocratie alimentaire dans laquelle il existe un véritable choix de l'alimentation appliquée à la thématique OGM conduit à s'interroger sur la possibilité ou non d'en consommer. Concrètement cela pose le problème d'une part du maintien d'une diversité entre produits conventionnels, produits OGM, produits non OGM, produits biologiques (A) et d'autre part d'un choix éclairé de la part du consommateur (B).

A. Une règlementation limitant l'agriculture vivrière et la souveraineté alimentaire

Le fort développement des OGM[3] rend la question du maintien des autres agricultures tout à fait sensible, et par conséquent fragilise la démocratie alimentaire. L'expansion des OGM soulève avec acuité la question de la disponibilité et de l'acceptabilité des produits, qui sont deux éléments clés du droit à l'alimentation.

L'importance des cultures OGM pose également des problèmes juridiques majeurs, liés en particulier aux risques de dérives que peut provoquer la propriété intellectuelle. Le droit des brevets peut conduire à une appropriation privative d'une partie de l'agriculture par quelques firmes biotechnologiques, grâce aux brevets qui confèrent de véritables monopoles à leurs détenteurs. Une telle conjoncture constitue sans conteste un obstacle à la démocratie alimentaire. La puissance des entreprises biotechnologiques est telle qu'elles arrivent à imposer le paiement des royalties, même lorsque le pays en question a choisi une protection par le certificat d'obtention végétale et non par le brevet. De façon plus générale, le droit actuel de protection des variétés végétales, extrêmement favorable aux obtenteurs, fait craindre à certains pays en voie de développement une insécurité alimentaire et une dépendance par rapport aux obtenteurs commerciaux

[3] L'accroissement annuel de la culture OGM entre 2011 et 2012 est de 6 %. Au total, 160 millions d'hectares d'OGM sont cultivés dans le monde. Pour certaines variétés, comme le soja, 81 % des produits sont constitués d'OGM. Voir J. CLIVE, Rapport ISAAA 2012.

étrangers en ce qui concerne les semences[4]. Cet exemple est édifiant concernant la remise en cause la souveraineté alimentaire d'un pays[5].

Au-delà du fait de favoriser les OGM, le droit actuel limite le maintien d'une agriculture vivrière, en particulier avec la restriction de l'usage et/ou de l'échange des semences de ferme[6].

Cette pratique ancestrale en matière agricole pose d'importants problèmes en droit. En effet, elle se heurte de plein fouet à la propriété intellectuelle. Différents textes ont tenté de limiter son champ d'application, à l'image de l'évolution de l'UPOV[7]. L'interprétation de ce privilège reste l'objet d'importants débats au sein du Conseil des ADPIC et la tendance dominante est de privilégier l'interprétation la plus restrictive possible[8]. Ainsi au sein du Conseil des ADPIC certains pays développés considèrent que ce privilège de l'agriculteur a pour effet d'autoriser les paysans à réensemencer leurs terres avec les variétés protégées qu'ils ont récoltées <u>sur ces mêmes terres</u>[9]. L'avis contraire est qu'il ne faut pas limiter la mise en réserve de la variété protégée et son réensemencement aux propres terres de l'agriculteur concerné[10] mais l'élargir aux communautés locales.

---

[4] Voir sur ce sujet, G. DOWNES, "TRIPs and food security: Implications of the WTO's TRIPs Agreement for food security in the developing world", *British Food Journal* no. 5, 2004 p 366s; G. TANSEY et T RAJOTTE, *The future control of food a guide to international negotiations and rules on intellectual property, biodiversity and food security*. Sterling, VA: Earthscan, 2008 et Kenya, IP/C/M/40, paragraphe 108.

[5] M.-D. VARELLA « Point de vue propriété intellectuelle et semences : les moyens du contrôle des exportations agricoles par les entreprises multinationales », *Revue internationale de droit économique* 2/2006 (t. XX, 2), p. 211-228.

[6] Voir S. YAMTHIEU, « Semences » in *Dictionnaire juridique de la sécurité alimentaire dans le monde*, F. COLLART DUTILLEUL et J.-Ph. BUGNICOURT (dir.), Larcier, 2013, pp. 625-627.

[7] L. BOY, « L'évolution de la réglementation internationale : vers une remise en cause des semences paysannes ou du privilège de l'agriculteur », *Revue internationale de droit économique* 3/2008 (t. XXII, 3), p. 293-313.

[8] M-A NGO et P. REIS « La protection des variétés végétales dans le commerce international : le droit un outil stratégique », *Propriété industrielle,* n° 10, octobre 2008, p 33s.

[9] Souligné par nous, voir la position des Etats membres suivants : Communautés européennes, IP/C/M/25, paragraphe 74 ; Suisse, IP/C/M/29, paragraphe 179 ; Etats-Unis, IP/C/M/25, paragraphe 71, IP/C/W/162.

[10] Kenya, IP/C/M/28, paragraphe 145 ; Groupe africain, IP/C/W/404, page 3.

Ces quelques éléments rapidement esquissés montrent que la réglementation actuelle est favorable aux entreprises biotechnologiques, bénéficiant de monopole. De fait, la liberté de production est mise à mal. La liberté de consommation l'est également dans la mesure où il est extrêmement difficile d'identifier les produits non OGM.

B. La règlementation complexe de l'étiquetage OGM et non OGM rendant un choix éclairé délicat

La démocratie alimentaire implique de pouvoir choisir les produits que l'on consomme. Or en matière de produits agroalimentaires, il faut rappeler premièrement que, l'on est en présence, d'un bien de confiance. De sorte que le consommateur ne peut pas distinguer de lui-même s'il s'agit d'un produit OGM ou non OGM. Dans un tel contexte, l'importance de l'étiquetage n'est plus à démontrer pour permettre l'effectivité de la démocratie alimentaire. Or, cette règlementation est relativement complexe.

En Europe, l'étiquetage obligatoire est imposé au-delà du seuil de 0,9 % d'OGM[11].

Il faut souligner qu'au niveau européen rien n'a été précisé en ce qui concerne un étiquetage « sans OGM ». Le règlement 1830/2003 n'évoque pas ce sujet et la communication de la Commission au Conseil et au Parlement européen sur la mise en œuvre des mesures nationales relatives à la coexistence des cultures génétiquement modifiées et de l'agriculture conventionnelle et biologique affirme qu'en la matière c'est le principe de subsidiarité qui s'applique[12]. De sorte, qu'à l'heure actuelle les Etats sont libres de légiférer sur la définition du « sans OGM ». Or, tous les Etats de l'Union n'ont pas adopté de règlementation uniforme. La disparité est encore plus forte à l'échelle mondiale. Beaucoup de pays ne prévoit aucun

---

[11] Règlement (CE) n° 1830/2003 du Parlement européen et du Conseil du 22 septembre 2003 concernant la traçabilité et l'étiquetage des organismes génétiquement modifiés et la traçabilité des produits destinés à l'alimentation humaine ou animale produits à partir d'organismes génétiquement modifiés, et modifiant la directive 2001/18/CE, *JOCE L 268 du 18.10.2003.*

[12] Communication de la Commission au Conseil et au Parlement européen « Rapport sur la mise en œuvre des mesures nationales relatives à la coexistence des cultures génétiquement modifiées et de l'agriculture conventionnelle et biologique », COM(2009) 153 final, le 2.4.2009.

étiquetage des OGM par conséquent le consommateur ne dispose d'aucun moyen pour savoir ce qu'il consomme.

II. Les évolutions de la réglementation des OGM, une démonstration d'une potentielle amélioration de la démocratie alimentaire

L'émergence d'une véritable démocratie alimentaire est perceptible dans la réglementation des OGM à travers deux axes. Il existe d'une part une véritable volonté de maintenir une alternative aux OGM et une diversité des cultures (A) et d'autre part, les initiatives se multiplient pour instaurer un étiquetage permettant un choix éclairé (B).

A. Le maintien d'une diversité des cultures

La volonté de préserver la diversité des cultures s'illustre de trois manières différentes et concerne une multitude d'acteurs sur l'ensemble de la planète. La question de la démocratie alimentaire se pose bien à l'échelle mondiale.

Premièrement, en ce qui concerne essentiellement les pays en développement, il y a une véritable volonté d'instaurer une réglementation *sui generis* concernant les obtentions végétales garantissant le maintien de l'agriculture vivrière. Ainsi l'Union Africaine a rédigé une loi sur « la protection des droits des communautés locales, des agriculteurs et des obtenteurs et sur les règles d'accès aux ressources biologiques »[13] qui reconnaît le privilège de l'agriculteur. Dans le même sens, il est possible de citer la décision n° 391 du Pacte andin sur le régime commun d'accès aux ressources génétiques de juillet 1996 et l'initiative de l'association sud asiatique de coopération régionale de mars 1999 sur le transfert des ressources phytogénétiques aux pays non membres. Ces initiatives s'appuient sur l'article 27§3-b de l'Accord ADPIC permettant d'adopter une réglementation *sui generis* en matière de protection des végétaux, offrant de la sorte une alternative aux brevets et à la Convention UPOV. Les pays défendant cette option insistent sur le fait qu'il existe un risque de conflit entre l'Accord sur les ADPIC et la Convention sur la diversité biologique de Rio de 1992. Le

---

[13] S. MALJEAN-DUBOIS, « Biodiversité, biotechnologies, biosécurité : le droit international désarticulé », *JDI, 2000, p. 949, et spéc. 968.*

premier Accord cité permet effectivement la délivrance de brevets ou d'autres outils de protection sans garantir le respect des dispositions de la Convention de Rio relatives au consentement préalable donné en connaissance de cause et le partage des avantages[14].

La deuxième illustration de cette volonté de garantir la diversité des cultures se retrouve au sein de l'Union européenne par l'instauration par certains Etats membres (Autriche, France, Hongrie...) de différents moratoires concernant les cultures OGM sur les fondements de l'article 23 de la directive 2001/18 et de l'article 114§5 (ex 95§5) du Traité de Lisbonne[15].

Une troisième illustration concerne l'apparition des consommateurs comme source de droit en matière d'OGM. Ce dernier phénomène est véritablement symbolique de l'émergence de la démocratie alimentaire. La volonté de consommer sans OGM, dans certains pays d'Europe et maintenant d'Amérique latine, est telle que le réseau « région sans OGM » s'est imposé comme un interlocuteur incontournable en matière de réglementation. Ainsi la question de la coexistence OGM / non OGM / produits conventionnels qui apparaissait uniquement en filigrane dans la première recommandation de la Commission européenne de 2003, est expressément envisagée dans la recommandation de 2010. Cette législation a ainsi été modifiée sous l'impulsion d' « illégalités créatrices » de droit[16]. Or, l'objectif premier de la coexistence est de permettre aux consommateurs et aux producteurs d'avoir le choix entre une production utilisant des OGM, une production biologique et une production conventionnelle[17].

---

[14] M-A NGO et P. Reis, *op.cit.*

[15] M-A NGO et Ch. CHARLIER « Le choix du non OGM dans un contexte de coexistence », *RJE 4/2013*, à paraitre.

[16] M-A HERMITTE, « La nature juridique du projet de coexistence entre filières OGM et non OGM : pluralisme technologique et liberté du commerce et de l'industrie », *cahier de droit sciences et techniques* 2008/1. Sur la démocratisation d'un enjeu technique, voir aussi N. SCHIFFINO, « comment démocratiser la régulation des enjeux techniques. Le cas des OGM belge » *In* S. MAHIEU et P. NIHOUL (eds), *La sécurité alimentaire et la réglementation des objets, perspective nationale, européenne et internationale*, Larcier 2005, p 301s.

[17] Communication de la Commission au Conseil et au Parlement européen, « Rapport sur la mise en œuvre des mesures nationales relatives à la coexistence des cultures génétiquement modifiées et de l'agriculture conventionnelle et biologique », COM(2006)104 final, 9 mars 2006.

C'est également sous la pression des consommateurs qu'apparaissent les étiquetages « sans OGM ».

B. Un étiquetage garantissant un choix éclairé

S'agissant des OGM la question de l'acceptabilité est incontournable. Or, l'évolution actuelle démontre une réticence à la consommation d'OGM en Europe en particulier et la revendication d'une possibilité de choisir son alimentation. Pour ce faire il a fallu imposer l'intérêt d'un étiquetage sans OGM. Cette option ne va pas de soi, en dépit du fait qu'il s'agisse d'un bien de confiance. Pour preuve, dans l'avis rendu par les États Unis rendu à l'occasion du différend commercial porté devant l'OMC, l'étiquetage des OGM est même présenté comme une information non pertinente pour le consommateur, qui cherche plutôt la composition, la valeur ou les effets nutritionnels[18]. Or, même aux États-Unis cette position évolue. Le Connecticut envisage un étiquetage sans OGM[19].

Les étiquetages « sans OGM » se multiplient, même s'ils ne sont pas uniformes et pas toujours très lisibles[20], ils permettent de disposer d'éléments de choix. En France, le dispositif est assez complexe et distingue plusieurs cas de figure[21]. Premièrement, les ingrédients d'origine végétale pourront porter la mention « *sans OGM* » s'ils sont issus de matières premières contenant au maximum 0,1 % d'OGM. Deuxièmement, l'étiquetage des ingrédients d'origine animale précisera « *nourri sans OGM* (< 0,1%) » ou « *nourri sans OGM* (< 0,9%) ». Troisièmement, les ingrédients d'origine apicole pourront être étiquetés « *sans OGM dans un rayon de 3 km* (autour des ruchers) ».

---

[18] OMC, Comité des obstacles techniques au commerce, communication des États-Unis, règlement n° 1139/98 du Conseil européen concernant la mention obligatoire sur l'étiquetage de certaines denrées alimentaires produites à partir d'organismes génétiquement modifiés, 16 octobre 98, OMC, doc G/TBT/W/94 point 6.

[19] Voir C. NOISETTE, « Bientôt un étiquetage obligatoire des OGM dans le Connecticut ? », inf'omg juin 2013. Disponible à l'adresse suivante : http://www.infogm.org/spip.php?article5432

[20] Voir *supra*

[21] Voir le décret n° 2012-128 du 30 janvier 2012 relatif à l'étiquetage des denrées alimentaires issues de filières qualifiées « sans organismes génétiquement modifiés », *JORF* n° 0026 du 31 janvier 2012 page 1770, texte n° 27.

En conclusion, cette étude démontre bien les potentialités contenues par le droit pour permettre l'émergence d'une démocratie alimentaire à l'échelle de la planète avec plus généralement un droit mondial de l'alimentation en construction.

Les nanotechnologies dans l'assiette. Les règles sur les nanofoods *

Alessandra DI LAURO **

1. Introduction

Les nanotechnologies sont dans nos assiettes. Les inventaires de produits, toujours plus nombreux, contenant des nanomatériaux, le confirment[1]. L'usage des nanosciences et des nanotechniques[2] dans le champ alimentaire est toujours plus vaste et les connaissances en la matière ouvrent la voie à la réalisation de substances capables, entre autre, de décomposer les matières grasses pour créer des aliments qui donnent une sensation de satiété ou qui ralentissent la digestion, d'améliorer la capacité d'agglomération des ingrédients, ou destinées à venir au contact avec les aliments (films plastiques, bouteilles, etc.).

Les nanotechnologies sont donc dans nos assiettes. Elles nous arrivent en raison de leur utilisation intentionnelle lors de l'élaboration des aliments et elles nous arrivent en tant que résidus de matériaux nanotechnologiques fabriqués, utilisés, abandonnés par d'autres secteurs (chimie, physique, électronique, médecine...). Il faut bien avoir conscience que la présence de « nanorésidus » dans les aliments, résidus « capturés » par les animaux ou les plantes, en provenance du sol, de l'eau, de l'air, par contact, migration et absorption, n'a pas encore été l'objet d'analyses approfondies. Par exemple, les recherches qui visent à vérifier comment et si les nanomatériaux interagissent avec les plantes, par « diffusion » des racines aux feuilles des matériaux absorbés, ou quelles sont les interactions entre

---

* Le présent texte a été traduit par L. BODIGUEL

** Professeur de Développement agricole, Université Libre de Bruxelles. Professore Ordinario, Università di PISA

[1] Voir l'inventaire récent du Woodrom Wilson Institute sur The Project Emerging Nanotecnhologies in *www.nanotechproject.org*.

[2] Les termes sont souvent utilisés ensemble pour indiquer les liens forts et les confusions caractéristiques de ce secteur entre le champ de la recherche scientifique et celui de l'application technologique ; ils sont aussi utilisés au pluriel pour mettre en évidence les nombreux champs de recherche et de techniques impliqués.

nanomatériaux présents dans l'eau et les poissons, n'en sont qu'à leurs premiers pas[3].

Si la question de la « contamination » indirecte par les nanomatériaux reste quasi inexplorée et échappe aux inventaires susmentionnés, on peut en revanche se demander quelles sont les règles qui encadrent la production d'aliments lorsqu'elle use intentionnellement des nanotechnologies.

A mon avis, la recherche de ces règles conduit à une inquiétante constatation : nous sommes en présence d'un domaine marqué par de forts et nombreux déséquilibres. Nonobstant la clameur avec laquelle ont été accueillies les nanotechnologies, clameur qui a provoqué la multiplication de commissions, groupes de travail, comités[4], le phénomène reste pour le moment parmi les plus méconnus du grand public. En outre, l'importante

---

[3] Pour un premier cadrage général sur l'un des secteurs les plus étudiés, voir M. CARRIERE, S. LANONE, Que savons-nous des risques toxicologiques et écotoxicologiques liès aux nanotubes de carbone?, in *De l'innovation à l'utilisation des nanomatériaux. Le cadre normatif des nanotubes de carbone*, S. LACOUR, S. DESMOULIN-CANSELIER, N. HERVE FOURNEREAU (dir.), Bruxelles, 2012, p. 17.

[4] Pour un premier et incomplet inventaire des communications et avis émis par plusieurs institutions, organismes ou comités de compositions diverses, voir : Communication de la Commission, *Vers une stratégie européenne en faveur des nanotechnologies*, COM(2004) 338, 12 mai 2004 ; Communication de la Commission au Conseil, au Parlement et au Comité économique et social, *Nanosciences et nanotechnologies : un plan d'action pour l'Europe 2005-2009*, COM(2005) 243 du 7 juin 2005 ; Recommandation de la Commission, *Code de conduite pour une recherche responsable en nanosciences et en nanotechnologies, février 2008*, COM (2008) 424 final du 7 février 2008 ; Communication de la Commission au Conseil, au Parlement et au Comité économique et social, *Aspects réglementaires des nanomatériaux*, COM (2008) 366, du 17 juin 2008 ; Communication de la Commission au Conseil, au Parlement et au Comité économique et social, *Nanosciences et nanotechnologies : un plan d'action pour l'Europe 2005-2009. Second rapport de mise en œuvre 2007-2009*, COM(2009) 607 du 20 octobre 2009. Entre les avis des comités éthiques de niveau national ou international, voir : *Nanoscienze e nanotecnologie*, Comitato nazionale per la bioetica italiano, 9 juin 2006 ; Comité Consultatif National d'Ethique pour les Sciences de la Vie et de la Santé (France) *Questions éthiques posées par les nanosciences, les nanotechnologies et la santé,* avis n 96 du 7 mars 2007 ; UNESCO, Commission mondiale d'éthique des connaissances scientifiques et des technologies (COMEST), *Les nanotechnologies et l'éthique. Politiques et stratégies*, 2008; House of Lords, *Nanotechnologies and Food*, octobre 2009 ; Communication de la Commission au Conseil, au Parlement et au Comité économique et social européen, Deuxième examen réglementaire relatif aux nanomatériaux, COM(2012) 572 final, http://ec.europa.eu/nanotechnology/policies_en.html.

présence des nanotechnologies sur les marchés et les discussions scientifiques, nombreuses et animées, qui se sont déjà déroulées, n'ont pas débouché sur un ensemble adéquat de règles. Les dispositions qui ont été élaborées et aussi celles issues de la *soft law*, se présentent souvent de manière incohérente, lacunaire et sont, dans tous les cas, inadaptées à la gestion des incertitudes liées aux risques dérivant de l'usage de nanomatériaux. Enfin, pour conclure cet examen sommaire et assurément non exhaustif de la complexité des déséquilibres dominant le monde nanotechnologique, il faut souligner que même les alertes lancées autour du thème de la « nanopauvreté »[5], autrement dit de la crainte d'un accès inégal aux nanotechnologies dans les diverses zones du monde, ne semblent pas être suffisamment prises en compte par les gouvernements.

Le silence qui a caractérisé le recours aux nanotechnologies dans le secteur alimentaire jusqu'à aujourd'hui, doit prendre fin. La seule diffusion des listes de produits contenant des nanomatériaux ne suffira pas pour déchirer le voile qui a, jusqu'à maintenant, enveloppé le phénomène ; ni, encore moins, les préoccupations liées aux différences de connaissances entre les divers pays et aux conséquences en termes de démocratie et de souveraineté alimentaires[6].

Deux autres événements, dans le cadre européen, contribueront à faire connaitre le monde des nanotechnologies au grand public. Je me réfère à l'introduction de l'obligation d'indication sur les produits cosmétiques et alimentaires[7] de la présence de nanomatériaux. Les deux secteurs, sur la base de deux réglementations évidemment distinctes et suivant des voies diverses, ont bénéficié d'une obligation similaire visant à permettre aux consommateurs un choix conscient ou « en connaissance de cause ».

Comment sommes nous arrivés à introduire une telle obligation ? S'agit-il d'une exigence qu'il faut saluer ou nuancer en raison de l'adage

---

[5] Cet argument est surtout traité par les comités qui ont examiné les questions d'éthique liées au développement des nanosciences et des nanotechnologies.

[6] Sur ce point, voir la littérature du programme Lascaux : http://www.droit-aliments-terre.eu/pages/menu3/bibliotheque_lascaux.html.

[7] Règlement (CE) 1223/2009 du Parlement européen et du Conseil du 30 novembre 2009 relatif aux produits cosmétiques, JO L 342 ; Règlement (UE) 1169/2011 du Parlement européen et du Conseil du 25 octobre 2011 concernant l'information des consommateurs sur les denrées alimentaires, JO L 304.

selon lequel « tout ce qui brille n'est pas d'or » ? Quelles sont les règles qui accompagnent cette obligation et quel est le contexte juridique dans lequel elles vont devoir s'insérer ?

2. Une définition complexe pour une obligation aux contours incertains

Le règlement concernant l'information des consommateurs a l'ambition d'intervenir sur le phénomène nanotechnologique dans le but déclaré de vouloir faire émerger « le monde de l'infiniment petit ».

Une des premières données qui devrait attirer l'attention est celle liée à la présence d'une définition légale des « nanomatériaux » (art. 2.2 t, Règlement 1169/2011).

Le recours à une définition n'est pas, en fait, aussi évident que cela peut sembler. Le législateur européen nous a désormais habitué à la présence de glossaires insérés dans le texte, une sorte de dictionnaire portable adossé au texte juridique et destiné à éclairer les utilisateurs, à établir un vocabulaire commun aux pays membres et à délimiter le champ d'application des dispositions. De même, nous devrions être habitués à la présence de définitions relevant d'autres champs scientifiques, ce qui pourrait bien être le cas des nanotechnologies.

Cependant, justement dans ce secteur, l'adoption d'une définition n'était pas et n'est pas acquise à l'avance. Celle présente dans le règlement sur l'information des consommateurs sur les denrées alimentaires, est bien loin d'être satisfaisante, mais elle met en évidence un effort de détermination que bien peu d'autres secteurs, qui recourent aussi aux nanotechnologies de façon importante, ont tenté ou accompli.

Il suffit de penser, par exemple, à la grande confusion en matière de définition qui règne dans le secteur de la production de nanotubes de carbone, où on est encore à la recherche de classifications véritablement partagées[8]. Il faut en outre rappeler, en général, la difficulté de délimiter les contours de la nanoscience et de la nanotechnologie, même dans les secteurs de la chimie et de la physique.

---

[8] A.-J. ATTIAS, B. BARTENLIAN, S. DESMOULIN-CANSELIER, Réflexion interdisciplinaire sur les définitions scientifiques et juridiques : application aux nanosciences, nanomatériaux et nanotubes de carbone, *in De l'innovation à l'utilisation des nanomatériaux*, *op. cit.*, p. 41.

Dans les différents domaines, on peut généralement noter une concordance sur la taille, c'est-à-dire sur la référence à l'échelle nanométrique. Cependant, non seulement cette définition, que l'on peut qualifier de « plus petit dénominateur commun », est peu explicite, mais elle n'est pas partagée par tous et n'est certainement pas suffisante pour constituer un élément valide de gestion du risque. Bien autres devraient être les critères pris en considération, comme les modalités de production, la forme, l'effet... etc. En somme, parler seulement de l'échelle « nano » s'avère bien limité, ce qui est confirmé par toutes les recherches conduites en matière de risques liés aux nanotechnologies.

Le secteur alimentaire n'échappe pas à cette lacune en établissant une définition « à larges mailles »[9]. Certainement toutefois, cette définition a l'avantage d'offrir une délimitation du champ d'action des nanotechnologies même si cette vertu pourrait aussi être considérée comme un défaut, vu qu'elle laisse au dehors de la sphère d'application du règlement sur l'information des consommateurs, les matériaux qui en sont exclus.

Le récent document de l'EFSA sur les risques dans le secteur alimentaire, précisément dans le paragraphe dédié au terme « nanomatériaux manufacturés » (ENM), finit par déclarer « *It is not intention of this ENM Guidance to provide any definitions* »[10]. En outre, dans le document dédié à la gestion des risques, coexistent, de façon préoccupante pour le moins, une distinction des nanomatériaux en six catégories diverses correspon-

---

[9] Est considéré comme « nanomatériau manufacturé » : « tout matériau produit intentionnellement présentant une ou plusieurs dimensions de l'ordre de 100 nm ou moins, ou composé de parties fonctionnelles distinctes, soit internes, soit à la surface, dont beaucoup ont une ou plusieurs dimensions de l'ordre de 100 nm ou moins, y compris des structures, des agglomérats ou des agrégats qui peuvent avoir une taille supérieure à 100 nm mais qui conservent des propriétés typiques de la nanoéchelle » (art. 2 Règlement UE 1169/2011).

[10] *Guidance on the risk assessment of the application of nanoscience and nanotechnologies in the food and feed chain*, EFSA Scientific Committee, 2011, qui a fait suite à *The Potential Risks Arising from Nanoscience and Nanotechnologies on Food and Feed Safety*, EFSA, 2009. Il faut en outre considérer que dans la Recommandation de la Commission du 18 octobre 2011 relative à la définition des nanomatériaux, 2011/696, L 275, il a été précisé qu'il « convient que la définition établie dans la présente recommandation évite de préjuger ou de s'inspirer du champ d'application de tout acte législatif de l'Union ou de toute disposition susceptible de fixer des exigences supplémentaires applicables auxdits matériaux, notamment en matière de gestion des risques ».

dant à différentes procédures d'analyse des risques[11] et l'abandon de la recherche d'une définition des nanomatériaux.

A fortiori, il faut souligner que, avec imprécisions et imperfections, le règlement sur l'information aux consommateurs, a tenté une intervention en matière de définition. Puis, avec un saut en avant surprenant, il a établi qu'il faudra indiquer sur l'étiquette la présence de nanomatériaux, par la parole « nano » après la dénomination des ingrédients (art. 18.3).

Cette intervention législative a été considérée comme propre à garantir la transparence et le « choix en connaissance de cause » des consommateurs et, en quelque sorte, semble tendre vers cette direction[12].

C'est le moment maintenant de se demander dans quel contexte cette disposition s'intègre.

3. Les *Novel Foods*

Nombreux sont ceux qui se seraient attendus à voir émerger le phénomène des nanotechnologies utilisées dans le secteur alimentaire dans le règlement sur les *Novel Foods*[13]. Ce règlement prévoit une procédure d'autorisation préalable pour la mise sur le marché de nouveaux aliments et nouveaux ingrédients alimentaires parmi lesquels on trouve ceux à qui a été appliqué un procédé de production qui n'est pas couramment utilisé, qui comporte des modifications significatives de leur valeur nutritive, de leur métabolisme ou de leur teneur en substances indésirables et ceux dont la structure moléculaire primaire est nouvelle ou a été délibérément modifiée.

Cependant, la formulation actuelle du règlement *Novel Foods* n'est pas suffisante pour encadrer adéquatement les nanoproduits alimentaires,

---

[11] Dans le document, six situations sont distinguées: « *No persistence of ENM in preparations/formulations as marketed ; No migration from food contact materials (i.e. no exposure) ; Complete ENM transformation in the food/feed matrix before ingestion ; Transformation during digestion; Information on non-nanoform available ; No information on non-nanoform available.* »

[12] E. STOKES, *You are what you eat: market citizens and the right to know about nano foods*, in *Journal of Human Rights and the Environment*, Vol. 2 No. 2, September 2011, pp. 178.

[13] Règlement (CE) n° 258/97 du Parlement européen et du Conseil du 27 janvier 1997 relatif aux nouveaux aliments et aux nouveaux ingrédients alimentaires. S. RIZZIOLI, Novel foods, in *European Food Law*, (a cura di) L. COSTATO, F. ALBISINNI, Padova, 2012, p. 393.

du moins en ce qu'elle laisse au seul producteur la possibilité de choisir si le produit en cause est nouveau ou non, selon qu'il le juge différent du produit conventionnel ou semblable à ce dernier.

Suivant les travaux en cours sur la modification du règlement, la Commission avait prévu d'introduire une définition spécifique pour « les aliments qui contiennent ou sont constitués de nanomatériaux manufacturés ». En première lecture, le Parlement avait opté pour une meilleure protection, réclamant la soumission des nanomatériaux utilisés dans le secteur alimentaire à de nouveaux tests, l'application du principe de précaution, la création d'une liste de nanomatériaux utilisables au contact d'autres aliments et une obligation générale d'étiquetage pour les ingrédients de forme « nano ». Le Conseil, généralement favorable à la position du Parlement, n'a cependant pas partagé l'exigence d'étiquetage. Après une phase de conciliation, la proposition a été abandonnée.

Dans le même temps, le secteur des substances chimiques semble avoir les mêmes difficultés que ce qui ressort du texte *Novel Foods*, qui paraissait pourtant à première vue le plus adapté pour encadrer juridiquement les rapports entre les nanotechnologies et les aliments. En effet, le règlement REACH risque de ne pas prendre en considération spécifiquement les technologies « nano », puisqu'il laisserait aux producteurs le choix de considérer, par exemple, les nanotubes de carbone comme des « substances chimiques comme les autres » déjà connues[14].

4. Les additifs alimentaires

Dans le secteur alimentaire, l'une des références aux nanotechnologies se trouve dans la matière relative aux additifs alimentaires[15]. Il s'agit d'une référence qui, par certains côtés, pourrait être jugée satisfaisante en

[14] Il s'agit du Règlement (CE) 1907/2006 du Parlement européen et du Conseil du 18 décembre 2006 concernant l'enregistrement, l'évaluation et l'autorisation des substances chimiques, ainsi que les restrictions applicables à ces substances (REACH), JO L. 396. Pour débattre, voir E. JUET, S. LACOUR et N. LECA, Les nanotubes de carbone dans REACH. Les NTC sont-ils des substances chimiques comme les autres ?, in *De l'innovation à l'utilisation des nanomatériaux,* cit, p. 229.

[15] Règlement (CE) 1333/2008 du Parlement européen et du Conseil, du 16 décembre 2008 sur les additifs alimentaires, JO L. 354.

ce que l'additif alimentaire qui a subi un « changement significatif » dans la méthode de production, par exemple « par l'emploi des nanotechnologies », sera considéré comme un aliment différent, soumis à une procédure nouvelle visant à l'insérer dans la liste communautaire avant d'être mis sur le marché (art. 12). Cette disposition est plus incisive et claire que ne le laissait suggérer le considérant 13 du même règlement dans lequel le recours maladroit au conditionnel pouvait laisser planer quelques doutes. En effet, dans la version italienne et anglaise (et pas dans la version française qui est plus affirmative), on peut lire « devrait » être effectuée une nouvelle évaluation des risques pour l'additif alimentaire qui utilise « des matières premières diverses » ou recourt à des « méthodes significativement diverses » de celles utilisées pour d'autres additifs, qui ont déjà fait l'objet d'une évaluation des risques de la part de l'Autorité pour la sécurité alimentaire.

La formulation de l'article 12 ne laisse en revanche aucun doute. A la différence de ce qui se passe trop fréquemment dans d'autres contextes disciplinaires - je pense aux règles sur les substances chimiques et à celles relatives aux matériaux destinés à entrer en contact avec les aliments -, dans la réglementation sur les additifs alimentaires, est opérée une distinction entre nanomatériaux et matériaux équivalents et est requise explicitement la soumission de la nanosubstance à une nouvelle procédure d'autorisation, même en présence d'une autorisation de la substance conventionnelle parentale.

A ce jour, le domaine des additifs est donc celui qui laisse émerger de la manière la plus large le phénomène du recours aux nanotechnologies. En la matière, le cadre réglementaire est de plus en plus rigoureux : les prescriptions générales prévues dans les règlements 1334 et 1332 de 2008 ont été complétées par un récent règlement 234 de 2011 qui institue une procédure uniforme d'autorisation pour les additifs, enzymes et arômes alimentaires. Avec l'entrée en vigueur de ce dernier règlement, il ne sera pas facile pour le requérant de démontrer la sécurité de ses produits et de fournir les éléments nécessaires pour l'évaluation du risque, vu la grande incertitude scientifique qui règne dans le champ des nanotechnologies et de leurs risques.

Cependant, si l'ensemble des règles sur les additifs montre une grande attention pour le « nanomonde », il reste encore des ouvertures grâce auxquelles le recours aux nanotechnologies n'est pas détectable. On pense ainsi aux additifs déjà autorisés pour lesquels s'applique une procédure particulière (Règlement 257 de 2010) et aussi aux difficultés de distinguer entre additifs, enzymes, arômes et auxiliaires technologiques.

5. Conclusions

L'encadrement règlementaire des nanotechnologies est donc largement imparfait. Nombreuses sont les lacunes et les brèches qui ont déjà été mises en évidence au cours de ce bref écrit et auxquelles il faudrait ajouter toutes celles qui découlent du domaine des matériaux au contact avec les aliments (FCM[16]).

Vu le grand nombre de difficultés ainsi repérables dans ce secteur, en premier celle liée à la définition, on peut être surpris qu'on ait pu arriver à obtenir une indication obligatoire sur l'étiquette de la présence des nanomatériaux.

Le consommateur semble en apparence pouvoir bénéficier de cette évolution. Malheureusement, le domaine de la protection du consommateur continue à être lié à la quantité d'informations fournies aux consommateurs, comme si la localisation sur l'étiquette d'une donnée rendait possible la compréhension. Le recours aux OGM dans le domaine alimentaire aurait pourtant déjà dû fournir au législateur des indications précises sur les limites de ce mode opérationnel[17].

Dans un champ comme celui des nanotechnologies caractérisé par une forte incertitude liée aux risques pour la santé et l'environnement, ce mode de procéder est encore plus grave. Cette pratique pourrait conduire à abandonner d'autres voies qui devraient peut-être être suivies quand les doutes sont consistants. Dans tous les cas, elle implique de s'interroger sur le fait que de plus en plus, et pas toujours de façon opportune, la responsabilité de choix est transférée de la collectivité à l'individu.

---

[16] Voir A. Di Lauro, *Le nanotecnologie e gli alimenti*, à paraître.

[17] A. Di Lauro, *Nuove regole per le informazioni sui prodotti alimentari e nuovi analfabetismi. Verso la costruzione di una responsabilità del consumatore*, in www.rivistadirittoalimentare.it, n. 2, 2012, p. 4; Ead, *Nanotecnologie e nanoscienze negli alimenti: informazioni ed incertezze*, in Legal aspects of sustainable agriculture, The Slovak University of Agriculture in Nitra , 2013, p. 149-154.

II.- L'ajustement de l'exploitation des ressources naturelles avec les besoins alimentaires

A) L'accès aux ressources naturelles

Souveraineté sur les ressources naturelles et investissements internationaux : les chercheurs à l'écoute des analyses des ONG

Programme Lascaux [*]

Lors des Rencontres internationales organisées par le programme Lascaux à Nantes en novembre 2012, les chercheurs se sont mis à l'écoute des ONG et des associations ou organisations de la société civile. Le texte qui suit est une synthèse, faite par des membres du programme Lascaux, des analyses présentées par un ensemble d'organisations à partir du rapport introductif émanant de Frédéric Mousseau, *Policy Director* du *Oakland Institute*, avec les contributions de BEDE, du CETRI, du CFSI, de la Coalition pour la souveraineté alimentaire, de la Confédération paysanne, du Conseil citoyen d'union Hidalgo, de FIAN, de l'Observatoire du droit à l'alimentation et à la nutrition, de GRAIN, et du Réseau Semences Paysannes[1].

Introduction

« L'accès à la terre et à la sécurité d'exploitation sont indispensables pour pouvoir jouir du droit à l'alimentation »[2]. Ainsi commence le rapport sur le droit à l'alimentation d'Olivier de Schutter, Rapporteur spécial des Nations Unies sur le droit à l'alimentation. En effet, la terre, tout comme l'eau,

---

* Ce texte est la synthèse des échanges tenus lors des Rencontres du programme Lascaux « Nourrir le monde : la parole aux citoyens » (12-13 novembre 2012), à Nantes. La rédaction de cette synthèse a été coordonnée par François COLLART DUTILLEUL (Directeur du programme Lascaux) et Sarah TURBEAUX (Ingénieur d'étude du programme Lascaux).

[1] Les sites internet des organisations : Oakland Institute (www.oaklandinstitute.org), BEDE (www.bede-asso.org), CETRI (www.cetri.be), CFSI (www.cfsi.asso.fr), Coalition pour la souveraineté alimentaire (www.nourrirnotremonde.org), Confédération paysanne (www.confederationpaysanne.fr), FIAN (www.fian.org), Observatoire du droit à l'alimentation et à la nutrition (www.rtfn-watch.org), Réseau Semences Paysannes (www.semencespaysannes.org), GRAIN (www.grain.org/fr).

[2] "Accès à la terre et droit à l'alimentation", Rapport du Rapporteur spécial sur le droit à l'alimentation présenté à la 65ième session de l'Assemblée générale des Nations Unies [A/65/281], 21 octobre 2010.

est le premier moyen de production à portée des petits agriculteurs qui nourrissent aujourd'hui la majeure partie de la population mondiale.

Depuis des années les ONG dénoncent le phénomène d'accaparement des terres qui s'est accéléré ces dernières années et qui contribue à l'expulsion et à l'expropriation de populations et de paysans ainsi qu'à la concentration de la terre agricole aux mains de quelques-uns. Ce faisant, l'accaparement des terres est jugé comme allant à l'encontre de la sécurité alimentaire.

L'expression d' « accaparement des terres » vient de l'anglais « *land grabbing* » (« *to grab* » : saisir). Elle fait référence à la prise de contrôle et à l'exploitation de grandes étendues de terres, souvent acquises ou louées par des investisseurs étrangers. Cette expression est issue du rapport de l'ONG GRAIN « Main basse sur les terres agricoles »[3] en octobre 2008.

Le phénomène d'accaparement des terres par des gouvernements ou des sociétés étrangers est un phénomène massif, même s'il est difficile d'en évaluer précisément l'importance. La difficulté d'évaluation vient de ce que nombre d'opérations sont non transparentes ou masquées derrière des prises de participation dans des sociétés. Le site *Land matrix* (http://www.landmatrix.org/) a au moins identifié des opérations pour un total de plus de 34 millions d'hectares depuis 2000, essentiellement dans les pays en développement. Le *Oakland Institute* estime le phénomène à 56 millions d'hectares depuis 2008 (http://www.oaklandinstitute.org/land-rights-issue).

Pour ce dernier, cette ruée vers les terres s'explique par la combinaison de trois crises[4] :

- Une **crise financière** : les fonds d'investissement et les banques d'affaires ont dû trouver de nouveaux placements après l'explosion de la bulle immobilière en 2007.
- Une **crise pétrolière** : compte tenu des prix élevés et volatils et des incertitudes sur les marchés pétroliers, de nombreux gouvernements

---

[3] *Main basse sur les terres agricoles en pleine crise alimentaire et financière*, GRAIN, Octobre 2008.

[4] Source : Rapport introductif de Frédéric MOUSSEAU, *Policy Director* du *Oakland Institute*, à l'occasion des séminaires Lascaux « Et si la faim justifiait les moyens... du Droit » des 12 et 13 novembre 2012.

et entreprises ont fait la promotion des agro-carburants, qui nécessitent des terres.

- Une **crise alimentaire** : les pays importateurs de denrées alimentaires ont compris l'importance de sécuriser leur approvisionnement. Les investisseurs quant à eux, ont vite perçu la future rentabilité des investissements dans les terres agricoles, puisque, selon les experts, il faudra nourrir 9 milliards d'individus en 2050.

Le phénomène d'accaparement des terres pose de nombreuses questions, notamment sur la nécessité des investissements dans la terre agricole que les institutions internationales considèrent comme une condition du développement économique. D'autres questions portent sur le principe même et sur les modalités de la marchandisation et de la commercialisation de la terre sur les marchés internationaux. Il interroge aussi la souveraineté des Etats d'accueil et/ou des populations sur les ressources naturelles de leur territoire.

Pourquoi le phénomène d'investissement dans les terres, désigné comme un accaparement des terres par les ONG, est-il dénoncé aujourd'hui ? Quelles sont ses caractéristiques et les moyens de l'encadrer, ou du moins d'obtenir des contreparties équitables ? A l'énoncé de ces questions, il est clair que le croisement des regards des ONG et des chercheurs, en particulier juristes, peut être utile et fécond.

I. L'analyse du *Oakland Institute*[5] sur le phénomène d'accaparement des terres

Selon le *Oakland Institute*, qui travaille sur l'accaparement des terres notamment en Afrique, trois éléments majeurs sont à retenir :

- Un discours généralement positif autour des investissements.
- Le manque d'information et de transparence sur ce qui se passe dans les pays touchés.
- Le fait que l'Afrique soit considérée comme le continent où les terres sont inutilisées et disponibles.

[5] Le *Oakland Institute* est un think tank indépendant basé aux Etats-Unis, créé en 2004. Sa démarche est d'associer à la recherche les populations locales et les organisations de la société civile des pays du Sud, et de faire écho à leur voix. Il combine recherche et action de plaidoyer.

A. Le Oakland Institute tire trois enseignements de ses recherches

1) Investissement ou accaparement ?

- Les investissements dans la terre aboutissent presque systématiquement à des accaparements.
- Le plus souvent, les droits des populations rurales sur les terres et les ressources naturelles sont méconnus ou violés.
- Dans les pires cas, les populations sont déplacées de force, regroupées dans de nouveaux villages. Ce phénomène concerne 1,5 millions de personnes en Ethiopie.
- Il n'existe encore aucune application satisfaisante du principe internationalement reconnu de Consentement Libre et Informé Préalable (CLIP)[6]. Selon ce principe, en effet, les populations locales touchées par un investissement étranger dans la terre doivent être consultées et associées à l'opération en donnant à celle-ci leur consentement libre et éclairé. Or les informations fournies aux populations sur les projets sont le plus souvent sinon toujours insuffisantes ou incomplètes.
- Même lorsque les responsables publics insistent sur le fait qu'il s'agit non de vente de terres mais de location, la durée des contrats, allant fréquemment de 50 à 99 ans renouvelable, leur fait produire des effets qui s'apparentent à ceux d'une cession.

2) Le mythe des terres disponibles

- L'affirmation des responsables gouvernementaux et des organismes internationaux, selon laquelle une grande partie des terres serait inutilisée, se révèle souvent sans fondement. En effet, l'utilisation importante de la jachère en Afrique peut donner l'impression que les terres sont inutilisées alors que ce n'est pas le cas.

---

[6] Le « consentement libre, préalable et éclairé » est le principe selon lequel une communauté a le droit de donner ou de refuser de donner son consentement à des projets proposés susceptibles d'avoir une incidence sur les terres qu'elle possède, occupe ou utilise traditionnellement.

- Les terres ciblées en priorité sont en réalité souvent des biens communs (*Commons*) tels que les forêts et les prairies, sur lesquelles les droits des populations ne sont pas reconnus par des titres officiels. Souvent ces terres ont un usage non pas individuel mais collectif ou communautaire, qui revêt une importance majeure au niveau social, culturel et économique. Les populations touchées sont le plus souvent des populations indigènes, des populations pastorales ou agropastorales, des femmes, des réfugiés.
- Les investisseurs ne recherchent des terres marginales que pour autant qu'ils puissent y avoir un large accès aux ressources en eau. D'ailleurs, l'accès à l'eau est dans la plupart des cas offert gracieusement dans les contrats sur la terre, comme un accessoire « naturel » du foncier.

3) Des acteurs multiples et inattendus

- L'accaparement des terres implique de nombreux acteurs. Les pays émergents comme l'Inde ou des pays ayant des terres peu fertiles comme les pays du Golfe ne sont pas les seuls impliqués. De nombreux investisseurs européens et Nord-américains sont aussi très actifs.
- Les investisseurs privés sont notamment des entreprises agroalimentaires, des entreprises du secteur de l'énergie, des grandes universités américaines, des fonds d'investissement ou des fonds de pension.

B. Pour le Oakland Institute, l'accaparement des terres n'est pas inéluctable

Plusieurs cas ont été identifiés où les gouvernements ont, le plus souvent sous la pression, privilégié les intérêts des populations locales actuelles ou futures sur ceux des investisseurs.

- En Tanzanie, des projets ont été rejetés par le gouvernement ou n'ont pu obtenir les surfaces demandées.
- La Tanzanie et le Mozambique ont adopté des lois censées protéger les droits et la sécurité alimentaire de leurs citoyens. Malheureuse-

ment les mesures prises sont parfois temporaires et s'avèrent souvent inefficaces (exemple du Mozambique).

Le rôle du *Oakland Institute* :

- Exposer au grand jour les pratiques des investisseurs, les projets et leur impact permet dans certains cas que ceux-ci soient arrêtés ou du moins sérieusement freinés ou révisés.
- Soutenir les communautés affectées via la publication et la diffusion d'informations et d'analyses sur la réalité des acquisitions foncières dans certains pays. L'écho donné aux combats des paysans au niveau international renforce leur position et leur capacité de négociation. Cela passe également par la publication de contrats qui ne sont souvent pas du domaine public.
- Mobiliser les étudiants des universités américaines autour de ce phénomène, en utilisant la force de l'information du côté des investisseurs.

Cet état des lieux nous donne une idée de l'ampleur et des principaux enjeux liés au phénomène d'accaparement des terres.

Ce phénomène est en réalité juridiquement complexe. Il suppose la coordination de nombreuses branches du droit (national, international, coutumier, occidental, foncier…) ce qui complique la possibilité d'un encadrement.

II. Les éléments juridiques constitutifs de l'accaparement des terres

A. L'orientation du droit national

Les Etats sont souverains sur leurs ressources naturelles[7]. Dès lors, c'est avant tout le droit national du pays d'accueil qui va servir de cadre juridique aux investissements dans la terre. Le concept d'accaparement des terres fait appel à de nombreuses branches du droit associant des règles spéciales et le droit général ou commun à l'ensemble des activités économiques. Cela concerne le droit des investissements, le droit foncier, le droit de l'agriculture, le droit de l'environnement, le droit forestier, le droit

[7] Résolution 1803 de l'Assemblée Générale des Nations Unies du 14 décembre 1962 ; Charte des droits et devoirs économiques des Etats (Résolution 3281 de l'AG du 12 décembre 1974).

minier, le droit fiscal, le droit des contrats, le droit des sociétés, le droit du commerce... Mais, au plan du droit national, la base juridique des opérations est fournie par le droit foncier et le droit des investissements.

Or l'accaparement des terres pose avant tout des questions foncières. Dans de nombreux pays en développement, on constate la faiblesse du droit foncier coutumier face au droit foncier « moderne ». Le droit coutumier est non écrit, communautaire et les paysans ne disposent pas d'un titre officiel reconnaissant leur « propriété » de la terre qu'ils exploitent. Ils ont une ancienneté d'usage, le plus souvent sur une longue durée couvrant plusieurs générations. En revanche, le droit foncier « moderne » est un « droit à l'occidentale », fondé sur des titres de propriété officiels.

La question du droit coutumier est très importante. Sa valorisation pourrait contribuer à freiner les investissements à grande échelle lorsqu'ils sont réalisés contre l'accord des paysans locaux, à condition bien sûr que ce droit coutumier soit effectif. Souvent les institutions et formations professionnelles ne reconnaissent pas le droit coutumier. Ainsi, avec l'aide de l'Agence Française de Développement et à l'incitation de la Banque Mondiale, la « Fondation pour la promotion du droit continental et le notariat latin » se met au service de pays en développement pour réaliser des cadastres et titrer les occupants à la manière du droit dit « moderne »[8]. Mais, comme le montre l'exemple de Madagascar qui a conduit à une révolution populaire en 2008-2009, la distribution de titres de propriété privée se fait souvent au détriment des paysans pauvres et des communautés qui occupent pourtant la terre depuis des générations.

La plupart des pays d'Afrique ont un régime de domanialité publique, c'est-à-dire que la terre appartient à l'Etat qui en concède, transfère ou reconnait l'usage aux communautés ou aux personnes privées selon ses propres règles. Il en résulte que l'Etat, en cadastrant et en privatisant la terre avec des titres de propriété conformes au droit moderne, méconnait les droits coutumiers de populations qui ne disposent ni des moyens de prouver l'antériorité de leur occupation, ni de l'aptitude à accéder aux formalités pour se faire titrer, ni des moyens financiers pour acquérir un titre.

---

[8] http://www.notaires.fr/notaires/titrement

Dès lors, l'Etat considère que les communautés et populations concernées n'ont aucun droit sur les terres et peut les en déposséder.

Peu de pays donnent à la propriété coutumière la même valeur qu'à la propriété fondée sur des titres cadastraux « modernes »[9]. Même dans ces cas de figure, la pression commerciale sur les terres est telle que les lois sont parfois suffisamment ambiguës pour être interprétées contre la coutume, mal appliquées ou même contournées. C'est ainsi par exemple qu'au Mozambique, la législation foncière (1997) réalise un certain équilibre entre le droit des communautés locales et la nécessité d'investissements. Mais cela n'empêche pas des opérations lourdes d'investissements étrangers dans la terre agricole[10].

Certains pays en développement commencent à être sensibilisés à la situation des communautés et des populations locales. Par ailleurs, des ONG accompagnent ces communautés et populations afin de faire valoir leur droit coutumier. Des procédures simplifiées sont parfois mises en place pour transformer un droit coutumier en un titre du droit moderne. Mais cette sensibilisation demeure insuffisante.

Les textes prévoient parfois une immatriculation collective, ce qui peut assurer une meilleure garantie pour faire reconnaître un droit ancestral d'occuper une terre. Mais les titres collectifs demeurent exceptionnels.

Le droit coutumier reste un droit par nature fragile. Il l'est d'abord parfois du fait des populations locales elles-mêmes. C'est ainsi qu'au Vanuatu, bien que le droit coutumier soit reconnu par la Constitution, les populations refusent souvent d'immatriculer leurs terres. En effet, l'enregistrement des droits de propriété sur les terres modifie ce droit de propriété qui devient cessible, le transformant en droit « moderne ». Dès lors, et même si le droit

[9] V. par ex. Le Rapport préparé par Liz ALDEN WILY pour "International Land Coalition" et le CIRAD, qui, en Afrique, a trouvé 6 pays sur 30 étudiés reconnaissant la valeur de la propriété coutumière : "*The tragedy of public lands: The fate of the commons under global commercial pressure*", Janvier 2011 : http://www.landcoalition.org/sites/default/files/publication/901/WILY_Commons_web_11.03.11.pdf

[10] V. not. Les contrats évalués sur le site Land matrix (http://www.landmatrix.org/get-the-idea/web-transnational-deals/), ainsi que le projet de développement agricole sur plus de 14 millions d'hectares par le Brésil et le Japon (http://www.autresbresils.net/entretiens/article/les-interets-multiples-et).

de propriété est collectif, la terre peut être vendue, alors qu'elle était inaliénable et ne pouvait qu'être louée dans le droit traditionnel.

Sa fragilité vient aussi de ce que le droit coutumier est souvent variable, peu connu et mal délimité. Dans certains pays, comme le Mali, le contenu des règles coutumières est mal connu. Elles dépendent d'un chef de village ou d'une communauté qui se prononce selon l'opportunité. Une autre difficulté est qu'au Mali certains groupes ethniques ne reconnaissent pas le droit coutumier. Il est d'ailleurs important de souligner qu'en Afrique diverses ethnies et réalités sociales coexistent dans un même pays. Au Bénin, dans une ethnie du Nord, les femmes peuvent hériter de la terre, mais elles ne le peuvent pas dans certaines ethnies du Sud. La reconnaissance du droit des femmes à la terre est d'ailleurs un problème récurrent dans nombre de pays. Cette grande variabilité du droit coutumier, au sein d'un même pays ou d'un même territoire, affaiblit la situation juridique des populations locales parce que l'insécurité juridique s'ajoute à la fragilité de l'occupation sans titre.

Le Mexique fournit un autre exemple de fragilité du droit coutumier. Jusqu'à la réforme constitutionnelle de 1991, la propriété de la terre avait un caractère inaliénable, imprescriptible et insaisissable garanti par la Constitution (art. 27). Elle l'a perdu lors de cette réforme. La terre est ainsi devenue une marchandise, ouverte à la concurrence et au marché. Il en est résulté le développement de transferts fonciers qui, certes, ont un impact économique fort, mais qui, dans le même temps, dépossèdent les paysans locaux de leur outil de travail et du moyen de nourrir leurs familles. C'est ainsi que des projets comme celui du parc éolien de l'Isthme de Tehuantepec ont pu voir le jour.

De telles manipulations de la loi risquent d'ouvrir plus grande la porte de la corruption.

Par exemple, en Sierra Leone aujourd'hui, toutes les terres de l'intérieur, en dehors de la péninsule autour de Freetown, relèvent du droit coutumier et appartiennent aux communautés locales. Cependant beaucoup de chefs se laissent manipuler et acceptent de voir partir les terres et les forêts au profit d'étrangers.

La réforme foncière de 2013 au Bénin

Le nouveau code foncier adopté au Bénin en 2013 (Loi n° 2013-01) réalise des avancées en faveur des paysans qui exploitent en vertu de la coutume, mais dans un contexte plutôt favorable aux grands exploitants et aux investisseurs[11]. En effet, cette loi nouvelle permet de faire reconnaître officiellement l'occupation coutumière de la terre (art. 4), selon une procédure écrite tout en restant relativement accessible aux paysans qui l'exploitent. Cette procédure est assise sur l'obtention préalable d'un certificat de détention dont l'obtention dépend de la commune. Il reste qu'il faut suivre une procédure écrite, ce qui ne va pas de soi pour des paysans pauvres et sans une instruction suffisante. A défaut, ceux qui exploitent la terre de manière coutumière mais sans titre officiel de propriété n'ont sur elle qu'un droit d'usage fragile car non protégé (art. 359). En réalité, dans ce pays, l'accaparement se fait surtout au détriment de paysans sans terre et qui aspirent à en trouver pour vivre, puisqu'on permet à toute personne même étrangère d'acquérir jusqu'à 1000 hectares (art. 361) alors que le pays compte environ 7 millions d'hectares agricoles et 60% de ruraux. Le problème vient en particulier de ce que nombre de propriétaires de terres agricoles ne sont pas des paysans et n'exploitent pas la terre qu'ils ont acquise. Sans doute, ceux qui ont un titre de propriété sur la terre doivent obligatoirement la « mettre en valeur » (art. 367). Mais les conditions pour contester ne sont pas à la portée d'un paysan pauvre.

Au regard du droit national, les difficultés ne viennent pas seulement du droit foncier. Elles viennent aussi du droit des investissements et plus particulièrement dans l'articulation du droit national avec les traités bilatéraux sur les investissements étrangers.

B. L'articulation du droit national avec le droit international

Une autre source de difficulté vient de l'articulation du droit national et du droit international des investissements étrangers dans l'agriculture.

Dans les années 90, un projet d'Accord multilatéral sur les investissements a été négocié dans le cadre de l'OCDE. Lorsqu'il a été rendu public, ce projet a été rejeté, notamment par la France et par de nombreuses organisations civiles, puis abandonné. Il a été rejeté parce qu'il accordait trop de droits aux grandes sociétés susceptibles d'investir et parce qu'il remettait en cause des législations nationales de protection de l'environnement, d'aide à l'emploi et d'aide aux pays en développement. Il comportait aussi un système de règlement des différends qui permettait aux sociétés étrangères de mettre directement en cause la responsabilité des Etats.

---

[11] Voir les analyses du syndicat national des paysans du Bénin - Synergie paysanne - et de son secrétaire général Simon Bodea : http://synergiepaysanne.org/

Suite à l'échec de ce projet d'Accord, les Etats ont multiplié les traités bilatéraux, qui constituent aujourd'hui les véritables sources des droits des investisseurs. Plus de 3000 traités bilatéraux, répertoriés auprès de l'ONU, servent ainsi de cadre aux « investissements directs étrangers » (IDE) et par conséquent aux investissements dans la terre agricole.

Dans l'ensemble, ces traités visent essentiellement à protéger les investisseurs étrangers et leurs biens. Ils ne comportent généralement pas d'engagements ni d'obligations susceptibles de limiter la liberté d'entreprendre des investisseurs. Ces derniers ont le droit de rapatrier leurs bénéfices, et ne peuvent être expropriés si ce n'est pour cause d'utilité publique et moyennant une indemnisation que le pays hôte, lorsqu'il s'agit d'un pays en développement, est rarement en mesure de verser.

Les droits des investisseurs sont encore renforcés par l'Accord OMC sur les mesures concernant les investissements liés au commerce (MIC). Sous réserve de dérogations possibles pour les pays en développement, l'accord sur les MIC interdit à un Etat de prendre toute mesure visant à favoriser l'achat de produits nationaux ou à limiter l'exportation de la production.

Les litiges relatifs aux investissements étrangers dans la terre sont généralement tranchés par le Centre international pour le règlement des différends relatifs aux investissements (CIRDI)[12]. Pour prendre ses décisions, le CIRDI va se fonder sur le contrat. Or, à la différence des contrats miniers, les contrats dans la terre agricole sont souvent très brefs, peu explicites, assez flous. S'ils ne comportent pas d'obligations sociales et environnementales explicites, il sera difficile de faire valoir une argumentation à caractère social ou environnemental devant le CIRDI. Par ailleurs, l'investisseur invoque généralement son droit de propriété auquel l'Etat d'accueil porte atteinte par une expropriation, une résiliation du contrat ou par une limitation de ses droits. Dans ces cas, le litige se porte sur la fixation d'une indemnisation correspondant à cette atteinte. Or le CIRDI l'estime en fonction de l'ensemble des investissements réalisés, valeur de la terre comprise, indépendamment de ce que son acquisition a réellement coûté, de l'amortissement des investissements et des profits d'ores et déjà

[12] Lien vers le site en anglais : https://icsid.worldbank.org/ICSID/Index.jsp

réalisés. Ce mode d'évaluation a souvent un effet dissuasif sur les Etats d'accueil.

III. Le rôle des différents acteurs impliqués : Etats, entreprises, institutions internationales.

A. L'influence des institutions internationales et des pays occidentaux sur les investissements dans la terre agricole.

« *L'idée que les pays en développement devraient se nourrir eux-mêmes est un anachronisme d'un autre âge. Ils pourraient nettement mieux assurer leur sécurité alimentaire en comptant sur des produits US disponibles à moindre coût* ». Cette phrase, prononcée en substance par John Block, alors ministre de l'Agriculture de Ronald Reagan, apparait comme une justification des politiques qui ont commencé à être menées au cours des années 1980. Ces politiques ont promu l'investissement dans les terres, perçu comme la condition sine qua non du développement économique dans les pays du Sud. Ces politiques, qui ont conduit à l'accaparement des terres, ont été faites, et c'est tout le paradoxe, au nom de la sécurité alimentaire, du développement économique et de la lutte contre la faim.

En Afrique notamment, il existe actuellement dans la plupart des Etats une agence nationale de l'investissement, mise en place sur le modèle prôné par les experts de la Banque Mondiale depuis une vingtaine d'années, pour la promotion des investissements fonciers étrangers. Ces agences prennent parfois le pas sur les ministères nationaux pour négocier avec les investisseurs et abattre les obstacles qui pourraient leur être opposés. Il existe ainsi une tension ente le système poussé par la Banque Mondiale et le rôle des ministères tel qu'il était dans le passé. Toutefois dans plusieurs pays africains, les ministères ont pu jouer leur rôle et faire respecter les différents codes et les droits tels qu'ils étaient établis.

En réalité, la question du marché est au cœur de la problématique de l'accaparement des terres. On constate un conflit entre le droit des investissements, le droit du commerce, et les autres types de droit qui n'ont pas connu un tel développement au cours des trente dernières années. Les discours font majoritairement état de l'appétit de profits des investisseurs, mais il est peu question des Etats qui se livrent une bataille sans merci pour attirer des investissements, présentés comme la clé du développement.

Les institutions internationales participent de cette rhétorique. Même les directives de la FAO, présentées comme une avancée majeure, sont à double tranchant. En donnant l'impression que les investisseurs et les populations victimes de l'accaparement de leurs terres ont développé grâce à ces directives un rapport de force égal, alors que ce n'est pas le cas dans la réalité, elles permettent au rapport de force inégal de perdurer.

En Tanzanie par exemple, la société civile s'est fortement opposée au développement des agro-carburants. Cette opposition a conduit le Gouvernement à adopter un moratoire et un code de bonne conduite sur les agro-carburants. Les travaux sur ce code ont été menés par la FAO avec le soutien de la coopération allemande. Après la rédaction du code, les investissements ont pu reprendre avec une opposition aplanie dans le pays. Il existe donc un vrai risque de manquer les enjeux majeurs malgré les codes de bonne conduite, qui ne freinent pas, ou pas suffisamment du moins, les mauvaises conduites.

B. La collusion entre secteur public et secteur privé

Les liens entre sphère publique et sphère privée donnent lieu à des conflits entre l'intérêt général, que se doivent de défendre les institutions publiques, et les intérêts particuliers, privés.

La question de la contrepartie dans les contrats d'investissement en est une démonstration. On observe parfois des situations où les fonctionnaires négocient des contrats d'investissement dans la terre au nom du gouvernement, tout en espérant obtenir une place auprès de l'entreprise concernée en contrepartie, et s'assurer ainsi une carrière lucrative.

Il arrive également que des entreprises proches des Etats, ou des Etats qui soutiennent leurs entreprises agro-alimentaires et énergétiques, soient impliqués dans des investissements associés à de l'accaparement de terres. En Ethiopie par exemple, la banque d'import-export indienne, une institution publique, soutient les opérations commerciales des entreprises indiennes présentes dans le pays africain par les biais d'un financement direct au gouvernement éthiopien, de la consultance, du financement d'entreprises d'Etat éthiopiennes dans la mise en place de plantations et de raffineries de canne à sucre... Il en va de même pour les Etats-Unis, le Canada et l'Europe.

Selon le dernier rapport de l'Observatoire du droit à l'alimentation et à la nutrition[13], le secteur privé est fortement impliqué dans la prise de décision concernant les investissements étrangers dans la terre agricole. Arguant que les entreprises ne sont pas absolument nécessaires pour combattre la faim, l'Observatoire prône plutôt la mise en place de politiques agricoles en accord avec la population.

C. L'implication d'acteurs nationaux

Si les acteurs internationaux, au premier rang desquels les entreprises multinationales, sont le plus souvent pointés du doigt, des acteurs nationaux, et en particulier les élites, sont également accusés par les populations locales d'accaparer et de concentrer la terre. C'est le cas de l'Ethiopie, où 95 % des investisseurs sont des nationaux, avec de vrais enjeux de pouvoirs et une partie de la population qui souffre des investissements menés par les élites en place.

Dans certains pays, l'accaparement peut aussi venir de communautés religieuses, comme c'est le cas au Sénégal par exemple. Ces cas d'accaparement sont peu documentés.

Au Bénin, ce sont aussi les élites locales qui achètent en majorité la terre, et qui parfois semblent jouer le rôle d'intermédiaires pour des investisseurs étrangers qui désirent investir principalement dans la production de biocarburants. Certains achètent la terre sans pour autant l'exploiter, attendant que les prix augmentent pour la revendre[14].

D. La question de l'environnement et des ressources

Il existe un lien entre le droit à l'alimentation et la question de l'environnement, car dans les pays en développement, le dommage environnemental fragilise encore plus la production agricole et débouche souvent sur un problème de sécurité alimentaire.

---

[13] Rapport 2012 de l'Observatoire du droit à l'alimentation et à la nutrition « Qui décide des questions d'alimentation et de nutrition à l'échelle mondiale ? Les stratégies pour reprendre le contrôle » : http://www.rtfn-watch.org/fileadmin/media/rtf-watch.org/ENGLISH/pdf/Watch_2013/Watch_2013_PDFs/Watch_2013_fr_WEB_final.pdf. L'Observatoire est un consortium d'ONG internationales.

[14] V. plus haut.

Or dans le cas des accaparements de terres, la société civile dénonce très souvent des projets agricoles destructeurs de l'environnement. Le cas des biocarburants en est un bon exemple. Au Brésil notamment, la production intensive et industrielle de canne à sucre a conduit à une forte dégradation de la biodiversité doublée d'une importante pollution.

Au Mexique, un projet de parc éolien dans l'isthme de Tehuantepec menace actuellement un écosystème lagunaire qui pendant des milliers d'années a nourri 5000 familles indigènes. Cet isthme est en outre l'un des couloirs de migration d'oiseaux les plus importants du monde. Selon Carlos Manzo, du Conseil citoyen d'union Hidalgo qui s'oppose au projet, les études d'impact environnemental recommandaient de ne pas réaliser ce projet, mais les investisseurs sont passés outre.

La question environnementale est à double tranchant, puisque c'est parfois au nom de l'environnement que des biens sont « marchandisés ». C'est notamment le cas de l'eau, un bien de plus en plus rare, devant être préservé, utilisé au mieux. La « dissociation de la ressource » est également un problème, puisque l'on décrète parfois que l'eau étant vitale, une petite partie sera préservée, une petite partie sera destinée à la population, et la part principale sera considérée comme un bien marchand.

IV. Les voies d'un encadrement juridique

Plusieurs textes internationaux prônent un équilibre environnemental et social des investissements dans la terre agricole. Ainsi le Rapporteur spécial des Nations Unies sur le droit à l'alimentation, Olivier de Schutter, a proposé en 2009 un code de bonne conduite. Parmi les principes évoqués, ce rapport prône la transparence des négociations avec participation des populations concernées, le consentement des communautés locales, une législation nationale protectrice des droits et intérêts des populations locales, la priorité donnée aux productions créatrices d'emplois, l'affectation d'une partie de la production à l'approvisionnement des populations locales, la protection des droits des travailleurs agricoles salariés[15].

[15] Rapport du Rapporteur spécial des Nations Unies sur le droit à l'alimentation, Olivier De Schutter, 2009 « *Acquisitions et locations de terres à grande échelle:*

L'un des plus récents textes internationaux relatifs aux régimes fonciers et aux investissements dans la terre sont « les directives pour une gouvernance responsable des régimes fonciers applicables aux terres, aux pêches et aux forêts », autrement appelées « Directives de la FAO »[16].

Les « Directives de la FAO »

Elles ont été approuvées le 11 mai 2012 par le Comité de la Sécurité Alimentaire mondiale (CSA), au terme d'un processus de trois ans, auquel la société civile a été associée.
Les organisations de la société civile (OSC) avaient auparavant émis des propositions pour les Directives de la FAO en 2011, qui résument le projet et les aspirations de la société civile concernant les modalités de gestion de la terre et des ressources naturelles.
Bien que plusieurs propositions des OSC aient été appuyées par les gouvernements et ainsi intégrées aux directives, les OSC se sont retrouvées isolées sur un certain nombre de questions, et en opposition avec le consensus atteint par les Etats membres du CSA.
Les Directives de la FAO, bien que porteuses d'un certain nombre d'avancées – reconnaissance du droit fondamental à la terre, des droits coutumiers et informels – n'en ont pas moins des limites. En effet, afin de « parvenir à un consensus, le texte final a été formulé de manière générale et ambigüe »[17], la question de l'eau n'y est pas traitée, le « transfert à grande échelle de droits fonciers » est admis dans son principe, bien que limité par des mesures préventives, les droits des peuples autochtones n'y sont pas consolidés.
Enfin, comme l'indique leur intitulé, ces directives sont volontaires et donc non contraignantes pour les Etats.

En Afrique, la Charte africaine des droits de l'homme et des peuples garantit le droit de propriété. Elle dispose également qu'en cas de spoliation, le peuple spolié a le droit à la légitime récupération et à une compensation adéquate. Pourtant aucune de ces dispositions n'a jamais été appliquée.

Il existe également des principes généraux ayant pour vocation d'encadrer les investissements internationaux. Ainsi, les **principes Equateur** ont été créés en 2003 à l'initiative de banques internationales et de la

ensemble de principes minimaux et de mesures pour relever le défi au regard des droits de l'homme. »

[16] Ces directives sont disponibles sur le site de la FAO : http://www.fao.org/fileadmin/user_upload/newsroom/docs/VG_FR_March_2012_final.pdf

[17] S. Monsalve Suarez, « Les directives pour une gouvernance responsable des régimes fonciers applicables aux terres, aux pêches et aux forêts : un tournant décisif dans la gouvernance mondiale des ressources naturelles ? », in le Rapport 2012 de l'Observatoire du droit à l'alimentation et à la nutrition (voir plus haut).

Banque Mondiale. Ces principes conduisent notamment à catégoriser les projets (principe 1). Les projets sont ainsi notés de A à C par les banques qui les financent selon l'importance de leurs effets sociaux et environnementaux. Lorsqu'ils sont classés A ou B (projets ayant des impacts significatifs), les investissements envisagés doivent donner lieu à une évaluation de leurs conséquences et l'investisseur dont le projet est financé doit proposer des mesures adaptées pour atténuer ou gérer ces conséquences (principe 2)[18].

Les principes pour des Investissements Agricoles Responsables (RAI) ont été élaborés par la FAO, la FIDA, la CNUCED et la Banque Mondiale. Ces principes visent la reconnaissance et le respect des droits fonciers et des droits aux ressources, l'obligation de renforcer la sécurité alimentaire, la nécessité d'opérations d'investissement transparentes, la consultation et la participation des populations directement touchées, la viabilité économique, la durabilité sociale et environnementale. Mais ces principes sont globalement rejetés par les organisations de la société civile dans la mesure où, indirectement, ils conduisent à légitimer le principe de l'accaparement des terres[19].

Le **programme Lascaux** a acquis la certitude que la sécurisation foncière des populations fragiles passe par une évolution juridique au niveau des droits nationaux et au niveau des contrats. Il a ainsi identifié deux voies permettant d'aller dans le sens d'un rééquilibrage des investissements internationaux dans la terre agricole des pays en développement. La première est la promotion de la **propriété collective**, qui présente l'avantage d'éviter la discrimination hommes-femmes au regard de l'appropriation des terres, et de sécuriser la propriété foncière d'une communauté sur un territoire dont elle tire ses moyens de subsistance. Le programme Lascaux a par ailleurs conçu un « **clausier** » des obligations et engagements de l'investisseur. La présence de ces clauses dans un con-

---

[18] F. COLLART DUTILLEUL, « La problématique juridique des investissements dans les terres agricoles des pays en développement », *in La promotion de l'investissement pour la production agricole : aspects de droit privé* (colloque UNIDROIT - Rome, 8-10 novembre 2011), Revue de droit uniforme, n° 2012/1-2.

[19] *Idem.*

trat, et leur respect effectif pourraient conduire à une certification internationale « d'investissement responsable durable », sous l'égide de la FAO[20].

Conclusion

L'accaparement des terres est un phénomène complexe qui concerne de multiples types de droits. Le niveau de droit le plus concerné, et sur lequel il serait le plus opportun d'agir est le droit national des pays investisseurs et des pays investis. Une multitude d'acteurs sont également impliqués. La collusion entre les secteurs publics et privés, la corruption, sont de nature à favoriser l'accaparement des terres.

Pour les organisations de la société civile, ce phénomène est le résultat de plusieurs années de pression internationale en faveur des investissements, présentés comme la seule voie possible de développement. Si les investissements peuvent s'avérer nécessaires, il est toutefois indispensable que ces derniers soient très encadrés, que les populations concernées soient consultées et écoutées au préalable et que les contrats soient équilibrés.

Le renforcement des organisations, paysannes, villageoises, intermédiaires, s'avère très important pour lutter contre les aspects négatifs de ce phénomène. En Amérique Latine, la progression anarchique des mines a pu être stoppée par des organisations agricoles renforcées par le commerce équitable.

De même, une communauté ayant l'usage d'une terre collective est souvent plus forte pour négocier contre d'éventuels accapareurs dont la stratégie est de diviser.

Si les multiples codes fonciers, codes d'investissements, codes forestiers, sont suffisamment bien construits, ils peuvent être autant de possibilités de s'opposer à des investissements abusifs. Ainsi au Cameroun, le ministère des forêts a pu stopper un projet de palmiers à huile allant à l'encontre des droits prescrits par le code forestier. Dans ce pays, des actions en justice sont également menées au niveau local. C'est pourquoi le

---

[20] F. COLLART DUTILLEUL « Proposition Lascaux – Investissements internationaux et accaparement des terres : la recherche d'un équilibre », in *Penser une démocratie alimentaire*, vol.1, F. COLLART DUTILLEUL, Th. BREGER (dir.), Edición INIDA, 2013, pp. 84-102.

droit et les juristes ont un rôle crucial d'expertise, d'alerte et d'accompagnement des populations et des communautés locales.

Je suis un paysan

Simon BODEA *

Je suis un paysan. Pour nous, le paysan est celui qui pratique une agriculture responsable, dans le but de préserver l'environnement, de préserver la terre. Je suis un paysan installé au centre du Bénin. J'y possède une exploitation de six hectares, sur laquelle je fais de l'élevage et de la production végétale. Je suis dans le même temps le secrétaire général du Syndicat National des Paysans du Bénin (Synergie Paysanne) qui lutte depuis plus de dix ans pour l'accès des paysans du Bénin à la terre, à l'eau et aux ressources de la biodiversité agricole[1].

Le Bénin compte environ 7 300 000 hectares de terres cultivables. Or il existe actuellement une ruée sur ces terres. Cette ruée est d'abord le fait d'hommes d'affaire béninois et d'hommes politiques, qui ne sont pas des agriculteurs, mais qui achètent des centaines, des milliers d'hectares et se voient remettre un titre foncier. Elle est ensuite le fait d'étrangers. Ces terres acquises ne sont pas mises en valeur, et sont mêmes interdites d'accès aux paysans. Or au Bénin aujourd'hui, de nombreux paysans sont à la recherche de terres cultivables. C'est là tout le paradoxe : des paysans recherchent des terres alors que des non paysans possèdent des milliers d'hectares qu'ils thésaurisent.

C'est dans ce contexte que l'État béninois a reçu un financement du « Millenium Challenge Corporation », une organisation américaine, en vue de la réalisation d'une réforme foncière. Cette réforme a consisté à élaborer

* Intervention de Simon Bodéa à l'occasion des Rencontres internationales du programme Lascaux « Penser une démocratie alimentaire », 25-17 novembre 2013 à Nantes. Simon Bodéa est Secrétaire général du Syndicat national des paysans du Bénin (SYNPA / Synergie Paysanne), coordonnateur de l'Alliance pour un code foncier et domanial consensuel et socialement juste, président de la Fédération agro-écologique (Bénin).

[1] Synergie Paysanne fédère toutes les solidarités paysannes au plan national pour représenter et défendre les intérêts des paysans béninois devant les instances nationales et internationales en développant des actions de stratégie d'influence des politiques [http://synergiepaysanne.org/]

un code foncier et domanial[2] afin de regrouper dans un seul document toutes les lois de gestion foncière jusque-là existantes au Bénin.

Au départ, aucune organisation de producteurs agricoles ou de la société civile n'était associée à cette réforme foncière. En tant que syndicalistes nous avons réussi à obtenir la première version de ce code foncier. Plusieurs articles de cette version nous ont inquiétés.

L'article 5 disposait que la terre appartient à l'État en République du Bénin. Ayant à l'esprit des exemples tels que l'Éthiopie, ou encore la Papouasie Nouvelle Guinée, où les terres sont vendues aux investisseurs nationaux et étrangers par le gouvernement, nous avons pris conscience qu'il serait très dangereux que la terre appartienne à l'État dans notre pays. Nous nous sommes engagés dans un plaidoyer afin que l'article 5 ne soit pas voté en l'état, et ce plaidoyer a porté ses fruits.

L'article 14 quant à lui, permettait à toute personne, et notamment aux non béninois, d'acquérir des terres agricoles. Ainsi quelqu'un venant de l'étranger et possédant un niveau de vie plus élevé que le niveau de vie au Bénin aurait pu concurrencer fortement les béninois dans l'achat de ces terres. Nous avons fait un plaidoyer pour que l'achat des terres agricoles soit limité aux personnes de nationalité béninoise, et là encore nous avons obtenu gain de cause.

L'article 361 est l'article pivot de l'actuel code foncier et domanial. Il dispose que quiconque est porteur d'un projet agricole peut acheter jusqu'à 1000 hectares de terres. Nous considérons que cette superficie de terre que la loi autorise une personne à acheter est exagérée. En effet, compte tenu du nombre d'hectares de terres au Bénin, 7 300 personnes pourraient posséder toutes les terres agricoles du pays, alors que le Bénin compte 10 millions d'habitants dont près de 75 % de paysans. Ce type de développement ne profitera pas aux paysans.

Nous avons fait des propositions pour modifier l'article 361, qui n'ont pas été prises en compte. Toutefois, ce même article dispose qu'en préalable de l'acquisition de toute terre, le maire de la commune concernée doit

---

[2] Adoptée à l'unanimité par les députés béninois le 14 janvier 2013, la loi n° 2013-01 portant code foncier et domanial en République du Bénin comporte 543 articles répartis en 10 titres.

donner son aval, avant même le passage devant le Conseil des ministres. Le maire possède ainsi un pouvoir important.

Comment sont perçus les paysans au Bénin ? La plupart d'entre eux sont analphabètes et possèdent des moyens de production agricoles faibles. Les outils agricoles ne sont pas très perfectionnés, les paysans n'ont pas accès au financement agricole. Leur niveau de vie est faible, qu'il s'agisse de leur revenu, de l'accès aux soins, de la scolarisation des enfants, bien que des efforts aient été faits sur ce dernier point. Vu sous cet angle, le paysan béninois est brimé dans tous ses droits parce qu'il ne les connaît pas, parce qu'il ne les défend pas.

Dans certains cas, la terre des paysans, sur laquelle leurs ancêtres ont travaillé depuis plus de 100 ans, a été vendue sans leur consentement, sans même qu'ils en aient été informés. Dans un cas, l'acquéreur était un commandant de gendarmerie. A chaque fois que les paysans protestaient, ils étaient emprisonnés. Ces paysans ont entendu parler de la Synergie Paysanne, et ont fait appel à nous. Nous leur avons expliqué quels étaient leurs droits, leurs devoirs et quelles sont les lois qui régissent la gestion foncière. Nous les avons accompagnés à la gendarmerie afin de régler ce conflit foncier. Le gendarme chef de brigade a compris que ces paysans n'étaient plus seuls, mais accompagnés par un syndicat. Depuis ils ne sont plus enfermés dès qu'ils ont des revendications. Aujourd'hui cette affaire est pendante devant la juridiction d'Abomey. C'est la première fois que des paysans portent plainte contre un « intellectuel ». Il existe beaucoup de cas similaires, qui montrent à quel point ces problèmes fonciers sont complexes au Bénin.

Face à ces problèmes fonciers, la Synergie Paysanne, lorsque qu'elle a commencé à faire du plaidoyer pour influencer le code foncier et domanial, s'est rendu compte que le lobbying serait plus efficace s'il n'était pas fait que par les paysans. Nous nous sommes donc associés à d'autres organisations de la société civile, dont JINUKUN, PASIB, la PNOPPA, WILDAF Bénin, CAO, RAPDA, ALCRER, SOCIAL WACTH, ASOPIL bénin etc. et nous avons formé l'Alliance pour un code foncier et domanial consensuel et socialement juste[3]. C'est justement cette alliance qui nous a

[3] http://www.hubrural.org/L-Alliance-pour-un-code-foncier.html?lang=fr&id=28

permis de porter très loin le plaidoyer et le lobbying, de rencontrer le Président de l'Assemblée nationale du Bénin et un certain nombre de députés afin de leur expliquer ce que nous cherchions à travers notre plaidoyer : l'accès des petits paysans à la terre. C'est en nous rassemblant que nous avons pu avoir une influence.

Face à tous les problèmes des paysans, les solutions que nous avons privilégiées sont juridiques. Par rapport au 1er point qui est de les protéger contre l'accaparement des terres et la thésaurisation, nous ne sommes pas entièrement satisfaits du code foncier actuel, mais nous pouvons exploiter un certain nombre d'articles de ce code foncier pour atteindre notre objectif. Nous avons eu déjà des échanges avec le programme Lascaux en ce sens.

Au départ nous n'acceptions pas que l'immatriculation des terres concerne aussi les terres agricoles. Dans notre plaidoyer, nous avons demandé que l'immatriculation s'arrête au niveau des villes et qu'une autre forme de sécurisation des terres soit faite sur les terres agricoles, afin qu'elles ne puissent pas être mises sur le marché et considérées comme de simples marchandises. C'était l'objectif de départ de la réforme foncière au Bénin, à savoir que la terre soit un actif monnayable comme toute marchandise sur le marché. Mais nous n'avons pas eu gain de cause.

Suite à nos échanges avec le programme Lascaux, nous nous sommes dit que pour contrer l'accaparement des terres, il serait intéressant que l'on arrive à accompagner les paysans à obtenir un titre de propriété foncière collectif. Un titre qui mette en commun les terres individuelles des paysans serait intéressant car face à un acquéreur potentiel, un seul paysan ne pourra pas représenter tous les autres, mais il faudra nécessairement que la majorité des paysans propriétaires donnent leur aval avant que la transaction ne se fasse. La réflexion continue sur ce point-là.[4]

Au niveau de l'article 361, nous sommes en train de faire un travail de fond par rapport aux maires. Nous cherchons à leur faire prendre cons-

[4] Pour un exposé détaillé de la proposition Lascaux relative aux investissements internationaux et l'accès des paysans à la terre, V. F. COLLART DUTILLEUL, « Investissements internationaux et accaparement des terres : la recherche d'un équilibre » in *Penser une démocratie alimentaire - Vol. I*, F. COLLART DUTILLEUL et Th. BREGER (dir), *Edición* INIDA, San José, novembre 2013, pp. 83-102.

cience de leurs responsabilités, et nous insistons sur le fait qu'avec l'article 361 du code foncier et domanial, s'il y a encore des cas d'accaparement des terres dans une commune, c'est parce que le maire y consent. Il est donc important d'informer les maires et les paysans afin qu'ils prennent conscience du pouvoir qui est le leur pour empêcher l'accaparement des terres. Si un maire ne donne pas son accord à une transaction foncière, même le Président de la République ne peut l'autoriser selon le nouveau code foncier et domanial. Les paysans doivent aussi s'organiser afin qu'aucune autorisation de transaction d'une grande superficie de terre ne se fasse sans qu'ils soient consultés.

S'agissant de l'article 367, bien que le code actuel ne limite pas la superficie de terres qu'une personne peut acquérir comme nous le souhaitions, il dispose que quiconque est propriétaire d'un fond de terre a l'obligation de le mettre en valeur. Nous avons commencé à faire du plaidoyer pour dire qu'il est important que cet article soit correctement mis en application dans notre pays. Et nous obtenons déjà des résultats. Un homme d'affaire béninois qui a acquis 1 350 hectares de terres a ainsi fait passer un communiqué sur une radio locale pour dire qu'il met ces 1 350 hectares de terres à la disposition de tous les jeunes agriculteurs qui veulent s'installer.

Le Titre 2, Sections 1 à 10 du code donne un certain nombre de droits d'accès à la terre : droit d'usage, droit à plantation, droit à construction, etc. Donc nous sommes en train d'expliquer ces articles aux maires afin qu'ils sachent comment les utiliser pour faciliter l'accès des paysans à la terre.

Toujours par rapport à l'accès des paysans à la terre, à l'eau et aux ressources de la biodiversité agricole, nous avons opté pour le renforcement des connaissances des élus, des cadres municipaux, des leaders paysans et des paysans quant aux articles juridiques qui traitent de la gestion des ressources naturelles. Nous y travaillons actuellement en partenariat avec nos partenaires HELVETAS[5] et la SNV[6].

---

5 HELVETAS [http://www.helvetas.ch/fr/nos_activites/pays_d_engagement/benin.cfm] est aujourd'hui la plus grande organisation suisse de coopération au développement. Helvetas est active au Bénin depuis 1995, avec des projets orientés en priorité sur l'eau potable et les infrastructures sanitaires. En outre, Helvetas

Le Bénin est doté d'un Plan Stratégique de Relance du Secteur Agricole que nous avons pu influencer avec la Plateforme Nationale des Organisations Paysannes et de Producteurs Agricoles ; au départ, ce programme était orienté vers l'agrobusiness et pas du tout vers les petits paysans. Aujourd'hui l'agriculture paysanne occupe 75 % de ce plan et l'agrobusiness 25 %. Le Gouvernement, qui n'a pas vraiment accepté cette nouvelle orientation du Plan, tarde à le mettre en œuvre, mais nous faisons le plaidoyer nécessaire afin que le financement agricole se fasse au profit des paysans, car ce sont eux qui ont nourri le peuple béninois jusqu'à aujourd'hui, et cela sans aucune aide. Ils ne doivent pas être oubliés maintenant que des aides sont susceptibles de leur être attribuées.

Nous plaidons également en faveur de l'adoption par le Parlement béninois d'une loi d'orientation agricole. Nous avons observé jusqu'à présent des changements fréquents de politiques agricoles en fonction des personnes au pouvoir. Aujourd'hui, au sein de la plate-forme de producteurs agricoles, qui regroupe toutes les organisations de producteurs, nous pensons que ce sont les paysans qui doivent donner le cap, dire vers quelle agriculture nous devons aller. Nous sommes donc en train de préparer une loi d'orientation agricole que nous souhaitons faire adopter par les députés pour qu'elle s'impose à tous les hommes politiques.

En conclusion, Synergie Paysanne est convaincue que les problèmes du monde paysan trouveront leurs solutions par la voie juridique. Il est donc important que les paysans le sachent et s'engagent sur le terrain juridique avec leurs leaders pour contraindre les gouvernants à ne plus faire comme bon leur semble, mais d'agir selon les lois en vigueur.

---

appuie les familles de petits paysans pour produire des fruits biologiques et défendre leurs terres traditionnelles. La formation fait également l'objet de projets spécifiques.

[6] Organisation néerlandaise de développement, la SNV Bénin [http://www.snvworld.org/en/countries/benin] travaille en collaboration avec d'autres partenaires pour réduire la pauvreté à travers le renforcement des capacités des acteurs locaux.

Accès à la terre et à l'eau dans la zone de l'Office du Niger au Mali : les propositions de réforme du Syndicat des exploitants agricoles familiaux

Laurence ROUDART * & Benoît DAVE **

En 2006, le gouvernement du Mali promulgua une Loi d'orientation agricole qui reconnaît l'existence et le savoir-faire des exploitations agricoles familiales, mais qui ouvre aussi la voie à des attributions de terres à de nouveaux acteurs. En effet, l'article 82 de cette loi dispose que « Dans le cadre de la promotion de l'investissement, de la capitalisation et de l'accroissement de la production agricole, des dispositions sont prises pour alléger le coût et simplifier les procédures d'établissement des titres fonciers et de concessions rurales et la conclusion de baux de longue durée pour les exploitants agricoles ». Depuis lors, de très nombreuses attributions de terres ont eu lieu dans la zone de l'Office du Niger, qui est située dans le delta intérieur du fleuve Niger, à plus de 200 km au nord-est de Bamako. L'aménagement de cette zone pour l'irrigation a commencé dans les années 1930. Aujourd'hui, près de 100 000 hectares (ha) irrigués sont mis en valeur par des exploitants familiaux, qui y cultivent du riz principalement et des légumes. La canne à sucre est cultivée dans une grande entreprise de 6 400 ha, employant des ouvriers salariés. Une superficie totale plus étendue pourrait être irriguée mais son estimation varie selon les hypothèses adoptées et les auteurs.

A l'Office du Niger, l'attribution des terres est en principe réglée par le Décret N° 96-188/P-RM, dit Décret de gérance publié en 1996, et par l'Arrêté N° 96-1695/MDRE-SG porteur du cahier des charges correspondant. Ce Décret confère à l'Administration de l'Office du Niger le plein pouvoir de gérer les terres, que celles-ci soient irriguées ou non. Pendant longtemps, cette administration fut sous la tutelle du ministère de l'Agriculture mais, en 2009, elle fut rattachée à un secrétariat d'Etat auprès du Premier ministre, secrétariat qui devint un ministère à part entière en 2011. Mais, les pratiques réelles de tenure de la terre sont parfois très éloignées des dis-

---

* Professeur de Développement agricole, Université Libre de Bruxelles.

** Assistant d'enseignement et de recherche, Université Libre de Bruxelles.

positions du Décret, qui est considéré comme obsolète par la plupart des acteurs et dont la révision est en cours depuis plusieurs années.

Dans cet article, nous présenterons les modalités actuelles d'accès à la terre pour les exploitants agricoles familiaux et pour les nouveaux acteurs. Nous exposerons ensuite les propositions de réforme formulées par le Syndicat des exploitants agricoles de l'Office du Niger (SEXAGON), ainsi que les résultats des analyses de faisabilité économique et juridique de celles-ci.

1. Des conditions d'accès à la terre très inégales

1.1 Exploitants agricoles familiaux

Conformément au Décret de gérance, la très grande majorité des exploitants agricoles familiaux ont accès à la terre via un *contrat annuel d'exploitation*, renouvelable par tacite reconduction. Le titulaire du contrat doit cultiver et entretenir les parcelles, maintenir en bon état les canaux d'irrigation les desservant, et payer à l'Office du Niger une redevance hydraulique annuelle. Faute de quoi le contrat est résilié et les biens de l'exploitant peuvent être saisis. Certains exploitants sont titulaires d'un *permis d'exploitation agricole*, à durée indéterminée et transmissible aux héritiers ayant participé à la mise en valeur des terres concernées. Les motifs de résiliation de ce permis sont néanmoins les mêmes que pour le contrat annuel, ce qui les rend l'un et l'autre très *précaires* (Keita, 2012). Dans les faits, même si cela est formellement interdit par le Décret de gérance, certains titulaires de contrats ou de permis cèdent leurs droits sur la terre, à titre temporaire contre une somme d'argent annuelle ou bien à titre définitif contre une somme d'argent libératoire. Une sorte de marché informel s'est ainsi développé.

D'après l'enquête que nous avons réalisée en 2011 auprès de 380 agriculteurs, la superficie moyenne des exploitations familiales de la zone est de 3,8 ha et la superficie médiane de 2,6 ha. Il s'agit donc de superficies très faibles, d'autant plus faibles qu'une famille paysanne comporte en moyenne 16 personnes, d'où une superficie moyenne par personne de 0,22 ha (Roudart *et al.*, 2013). Selon Bélières *et al.* (2011), la superficie irriguée par famille baisse de manière très importante depuis la fin des années 1970, au point que l'accès à la terre irriguée est devenu « le principal enjeu pour le devenir de l'agriculture familiale dans cette zone ». Cette analyse est très convergente avec celle du SEXAGON (2009), qui estime que la faiblesse des superficies allouées aux exploitations familiales est la cause principale de leur pauvreté.

1.2 Autres acteurs

Le Décret de gérance prévoit pour les acteurs de l'agro-industrie des modes d'accès à la terre bien différents des précédents. En effet, il prévoit un bail emphytéotique d'une durée de 50 ans, renouvelable par accord exprès, pour des terres non aménagées. Le preneur doit donc assurer les aménagements hydrauliques et autres, et payer une redevance annuelle. Le Décret prévoit également un bail ordinaire, très semblable au précédent mais d'une durée de 30 ans. Ces baux peuvent être résiliés en cas de non-paiement de la redevance et de non-entretien du réseau hydraulique (Keita, 2012).

Avec la promulgation de la Loi d'orientation agricole en 2006, le Gouvernement a fortement incité les étrangers et les Maliens eux-mêmes à investir dans la zone de l'Office. Ainsi, à la fin de 2010, environ 400 000 ha avaient été attribués à près de 500 investisseurs nationaux : la plupart d'entre eux détenaient des superficies inférieures à 50 ha mais une poignée de compagnies privées avaient acquis des droits sur près de 300 000 ha. De plus, quelque 470 000 ha avaient été alloués à des projets d'investisseurs étrangers, qui détenaient ainsi des superficies allant de 2 500 à 100 000 ha, assorties de quantités d'eau d'irrigation le cas échéant (Hertzog *et al.*, 2012). Le plus emblématique de ces projets est certainement Malibya, qui attribue 100 000 ha et des quantités illimitées d'eau d'irrigation à des conditions très avantageuses pour la partie lybienne (Collart Dutilleul, 2013).

La plupart de ces attributions furent décidées par le secrétariat d'Etat puis par le ministère en charge du développement de l'Office du Niger, sans consultation des populations locales concernées, sans qu'aucune compensation des dommages ne paraisse prévue, et dans l'opacité la plus totale, les contrats demeurant secrets en général (Oakland Institute, 2011). Sous la pression des médias, d'organisations paysannes et d'autres organisations de la société civile, l'Office du Niger et son ministère de tutelle décidèrent en 2011 d'annuler des contrats portant sur 280 000 ha. Mais, il reste que 600 000 ha ont été attribués, soit plus de 6 fois la superficie irriguée actuelle (Hertzog *et al.*, 2012). Or, d'après de nombreux analystes, une telle superficie ne peut être irriguée compte tenu du débit du fleuve et de l'état du système d'irrigation. Bien sûr, les troubles politiques récents et la guerre au Mali ont imposé un coup d'arrêt à presque tous ces projets, mais pour une durée inconnue. Ces attributions risquent donc toujours de faire surgir de graves conflits pour l'accès à l'eau. D'un autre côté, il s'avère que même avant le début des troubles politiques au Mali, la plupart de ces terres n'avaient pas, ou que très peu, été aménagées, comme si l'objectif des acquéreurs consistait plus à réserver des terres qu'à faire des investissements productifs (Adamczewski *et al.*, 2013).

C'est dans ce contexte incertain et menaçant que le SEXAGON, s'appuyant sur la volonté du Gouvernement d'élaborer une nouvelle politique foncière, a fait des propositions de réforme de l'accès à la terre à l'Office du Niger.

2. Les réformes de l'accès à la terre proposées par le SEXAGON

2.1 Contenu

Le SEXAGON part du constat que les superficies des exploitations agricoles familiales de l'Office du Niger sont en général trop petites pour subvenir aux besoins essentiels des familles paysannes, que leur accès à la terre est précaire, que les nouveaux aménagements réalisés sur fonds publics ou avec l'appui des bailleurs de fonds internationaux sont très faibles, et que le Gouvernement privilégie les attributions de terres à des acteurs affirmant qu'ils vont investir. Dès lors, le SEXAGON propose que les exploitants familiaux, jusqu'à présent bénéficiaires à titre gratuit de leurs parcelles, versent dorénavant, pour l'attribution de nouvelles parcelles, une contribution financière annuelle significative à un fonds d'investissement permettant de financer de nouveaux aménagements destinés aux exploitants familiaux. C'est pourquoi la proposition du SEXAGON a reçu le nom de « Paysans investisseurs » (Dave *et al.*, 2012). En contrepartie de ce versement, limité dans le temps, les exploitants auraient accès aux nouvelles parcelles via un bail emphytéotique sécurisé, transmissible aux héritiers. Le SEXAGON a opté pour ce type de bail plutôt que pour le titre de propriété privée afin d'éviter le développement d'un marché foncier spéculatif et l'éviction de familles paysannes. Pour autant, il souhaite que le bail emphytéotique puisse être hypothéqué en vue d'obtenir du crédit, tout en étant assorti de clauses visant à préserver les intérêts des exploitants familiaux.

2.2 Faisabilité économique

Pour instruire la question de la faisabilité économique de la proposition du SEXAGON, nous avons réalisé une étude mobilisant le concept de *système de production agricole*, défini comme la combinaison des facteurs de production et des activités productives dans une exploitation agricole (Chombart de Lauwe *et al.*, 1957 ; Mazoyer, 1963). Ce concept fut décliné dans une enquête détaillée auprès de 380 chefs d'exploitations familiales, tirés au hasard dans 19 villages répartis dans 5 secteurs de l'Office du Niger, à raison de 20 exploitants par village. L'enquête a ainsi produit des données quantitatives et des données qualitatives sur le foncier, la main d'œuvre, l'outillage, les bâtiments, les produits et les coûts de chaque culture et de chaque élevage, qui ont permis de calculer le revenu agricole familial de chaque exploitation et d'élaborer des modèles représentant l'évolution de ce revenu en fonction de la superficie cultivée par famille, pour différentes catégories de systèmes de production et de familles.

Cette étude montre que les superficies attribuées aux familles paysannes sont en général très inférieures à celles qu'elles pourraient cultiver. Et que ces familles sont parfaitement capables d'atteindre des revenus suffisants pour tout à la fois couvrir leurs besoins essentiels, investir dans le développement de leur activité agricole et participer à l'investissement foncier. Mais, pour cela, elles doivent disposer pour le moins d'un matériel de culture attelée et d'une superficie irriguée proche de la superficie maximale qu'elles peuvent cultiver, leur permettant ainsi de maximiser leur revenu. La superficie maximale cultivable par une famille dépend de sa taille et de sa composition : il faut compter 5 ha pour une famille comportant une seule cellule maternelle (c'est-à-dire une mère et ses enfants)[1], 8,5 ha pour une famille à deux cellules maternelles, et ensuite 2,5 ha en plus par cellule maternelle supplémentaire. Une autre condition essentielle est que leurs

[1] Le raisonnement est conduit en fonction du nombre de cellules maternelles car un homme peut avoir jusqu'à 4 épouses.

parcelles soient convenablement irriguées et drainées durant la saison des pluies pour y cultiver le riz avec succès, et convenablement irriguées sur un tiers au moins de leur superficie durant la saison sèche afin d'y cultiver du riz et des légumes. L'accès à l'eau et l'accès à la terre sont donc cruciaux.

2.3 Faisabilité juridique

Selon A. Keita, qui a analysé les textes officiels maliens relatifs aux modes de tenure dans le pays et spécifiquement dans la zone de l'Office du Niger, le Code domanial et foncier prévoit bien un bail emphytéotique et un bail avec promesse de vente. Mais, aucune loi, aucun règlement n'encadre le bail rural. De plus, l'Office du Niger est une zone spéciale où c'est le Décret de gérance qui règle l'accès à la terre. Or, ce Décret prévoit un bail emphytéotique pour les acteurs agro-industriels seulement, et il ne prévoit pas l'inscription de ce type de bail dans le Livre foncier du Service des domaines, ce qui le rend non hypothécable.

Dès lors que le Décret de gérance est en cours de révision, et que la Loi d'orientation agricole appelle à l'élaboration d'une loi foncière, le contexte se prête à l'avancée de nouvelles propositions. Celles-ci pourraient inclure un bail emphytéotique de longue durée, renouvelable, transmissible aux héritiers ayant participé à la mise en valeur des terres, passable entre l'Office du Niger et un exploitant agricole familial et devant être enregistré au Service des domaines afin d'être hypothécable. Mais, un tel bail devrait être assorti de clauses s'inspirant de l'expérience de nombreux pays qui ont cherché à préserver les intérêts des exploitants agricoles familiaux et à éviter le développement d'un marché foncier spéculatif, notamment de clauses restrictives quant à la cessibilité du bail, à la sous-location des terres et à leur usage agricole (Keita, 2012).

Conclusion

À l'Office du Niger au Mali, dans un contexte de très nombreuses attributions de terres et d'eau d'irrigation à de nouveaux acteurs, maliens ou étrangers, le SEXAGON demande que les exploitants agricoles familiaux aient accès, par des baux emphytéotiques, à des parcelles irriguées supplémentaires, tout en participant au financement de l'aménagement de nouvelles parcelles. L'analyse de ces propositions montre qu'elles sont parfaitement réalisables du point de vue économique et du point de vue juridique. L'analyse économique montre même que l'attribution de terres, d'eau d'irrigation et de crédits supplémentaires aux exploitations agricoles familiales existantes pourrait conduire le Mali près de l'autosuffisance céréalière. D'un autre côté, la plupart des nouveaux receveurs de terres n'y ont pas, ou que très peu, investi. Pour renforcer la sécurité alimentaire au Mali, la voie des exploitations agricoles familiales est donc la plus crédible.

Références

ADAMCZEWSKI, A., JAMIN J.-Y., BURNOD P., BOUTOUT LY E.H., et TONNEAU J.-P. (2013), « Terre, eau et capitaux : investissements ou accaparements fonciers à l'Office du Niger ? » *Cahiers Agricultures* 22 (1): 22-32.

ASSEMBLEE NATIONALE DE LA REPUBLIQUE DU MALI. 2006. « Loi N° 06-40/AN-RM portant loi d'orientation agricole ». Bamako (Mali): Assemblée nationale de la République du Mali.

BELIERES, J.-F., HILHORST T., KEBE D., KEÏTA M. S., KEÏTA S., et SANOGO O. (2011), « Irrigation et pauvreté: le cas de l'Office du Niger au Mali ». *Cahiers Agricultures* 20 (1): 144–149.

CHOMBART DE LAUWE, J., et POITEVIN J. (1957), *La gestion des exploitations agricoles*. Paris: Dunod, 222 p.

COLLART DUTILLEUL, F (2013), « Investissements internationaux et accaparement des terres : la recherche d'un équilibre ». In F. Collart Dutilleul, Th. Bréger (dir), *Penser une démocratie alimentaire*, vol. 1, Edición INIDA, San José (Costa Rica), pp. 83-102.

DAVE, B., MAZOYER M., et ROUDART L. (2012), « Paysans investisseurs. La faisabilité économique de la proposition du SEXAGON ». Bamako (Mali): SEXAGON.

HERTZOG, T., ADAMCZEWSKI A., MOLLE F., POUSSIN J.-C., et JAMIN J.-Y. (2012), « Ostrich-Like Strategies in Sahelian Sands? Land and Water Grabbing in the Office du Niger, Mali ». *Water Alternatives* 5 (2): 304–321.

KEITA, A. (2012), « Paysans investisseurs. La faisabilité juridique de la proposition du SEXAGON ». Bamako (Mali): SEXAGON.

MAZOYER, M. (1963), « Les modalités d'application de la recherche opérationnelle en agriculture ». *Revue française de recherche opérationnelle* (27): 107-129.

OAKLAND INSTITUTE. « Comprendre les investissements fonciers en Afrique. Rapport : Mali ». Oakland (Etats-Unis): Oakland Institute.

ROUDART, L., et DAVE B. (2013), « Superficies agricoles minimales assurant la viabilité économique des exploitations rizicoles familiales de l'Office du Niger (Mali) ». *Cahiers Agricultures* 22 (5): 411–417.

SEXAGON (Syndicat des exploitants agricoles de l'Office du Niger) (2009), « La position du SEXAGON concernant la question foncière en zone Office du Niger ». Niono, Mali: SEXAGON.

L'affaire Aguas Argentinas et al. v./ República Argentina : l'apport processuel [*]

Tarak BACCOUCHE [**]

Présentation générale. La décision arbitrale (03/19) rendue le 30 juillet 2010 par le Centre International pour le Règlement des Différends relatifs aux Investissements (CIRDI - ICSID) entre un consortium européen et l'Etat Argentin[1] a fait couler beaucoup d'encre[2]. La sentence statue sur un différend survenu à propos d'une concession octroyée en 1993 pour une période de 30 ans, relative à l'approvisionnement et la distribution de l'eau et le traitement des eaux usées de l'agglomération de Buenos Aires (10 millions de consommateurs).

Faits de l'espèce. L'espèce apprend qu'en avril 2003, donc dix ans après la conclusion de l'accord, les investisseurs ont saisi le CIRDI. L'Etat argentin a pris, sous l'effet de la crise financière -qui a violemment secoué le pays et qui a culminé fin 2001 début 2002- bon nombre des mesures

---

* Commentaire de l'*Order in Response to a Petition for Transparency and Participation As* Amicus Curiæ, 19 Mai 2005, ICSID Case No . ARB /03/19

** Faculté de droit de Sousse (université de Sousse) Tunisie/ IMC for Shari'a and Law, Dubai, EAU.

[1] ICSID, Case No ARB/03/19 et AWG Group v./ Repúbilca Argentina (CNUDCI), Decision on Liabilty, 30 July 2010, (Doc. ALS. 98). Aguas Argentinas S. A. (AASA) est une filiale de droit argentin fondée pour les besoins de la concession entre Suez, Vivendi, AWG, SCP, Meller SA, AGBAR, Banco Galicia et ESOP. En 2006, Aguas Argentinas s'est retirée de la procédure (Order No 1 concerning the Discontinuance of Proceedings with respect to Aguas Argentinas SA). L'affaire s'est poursuivie entre les autres membres du consortium (Suez et *al.*). AWG Group Limited s'est jointe à la procédure et le Tribunal a estimé bon de statuer sur les deux affaires par un seul jugement (ICSID Case No ARB/03/19, Décision préc., §. 25 : "*... the tribunal has determined that it is appropriate to issue a single statement of its conclusions, as it did in deciding on jurisdiction...*"), à la suite de quoi l'*aff.* sera connue sous le nom de Suez *et al.*

[2] Parmi les commentaires les plus récents : François COLLART DUTILLEUL, V° Aguas argentinas, in *Dictionnaire juridique de la sécurité alimentaire dans le monde*, François COLLART DUTILLEUL et J.-Ph. BUGNICOURT (dir.), *éd.* Larcier 2013, p. 60-61 ; Marie CUQ, « Le droit des investissements étrangers et l'accès à une alimentation adéquate », in *Penser une démocratie alimentaire*, Vol. 1, François COLLART DUTILLEUL (dir.) et Th. BREGER (coord.), *éd.* Inida, 2013, p. 128 et bibilogr. citée à la p. 129.

réglementaires en violation des traités bilatéraux d'investissement (TBI) conclus avec la France (1993) et l'Espagne (1991). Pour les investisseurs, les mesures ainsi prises ont sensiblement dévalorisé leur investissement et ont rendu la concession coûteuse et peu rentable. Il s'agit notamment de l'abandon de la parité du peso avec le dollar USA (qui s'échangeait 1 contre 1) et le gel des prix des prestations et des tarifs de l'eau. L'abandon du régime d'indexation, de la convertibilité du peso a entrainé la chute de la monnaie locale. Désormais, un dollar USA vaut 3,6 voire 4 pesos. Une hausse vertigineuse des prix de production calculés en fonction des Indices des Prix à la Production (IPP) s'en est suivie. Au résultat, le montant de la facture d'eau a plus que triplé. Le Gouvernement argentin était, sous l'effet conjugué de la crise et de la pression de la rue, incapable de répercuter la hausse des prix due à la dévaluation sur les prix des services sociaux dont ceux de la desserte de l'eau. Il a été, toujours sous l'effet d'énormes contestations populaires, contraint de maintenir les tarifs de l'eau, de résilier la concession et de la transférer à une entreprise étatique (AySA).

Moyens des parties. D'après les investisseurs, l'Etat argentin aurait (1) manqué à son obligation de s'abstenir de prendre des mesures d'expropriation illégales directes ou indirectes sans garantie, (2) violé son devoir d'offrir aux investisseurs une protection et une sécurité absolue et (3) failli à son obligation d'offrir un traitement juste et équitable (*Fair and Equitable Treatment: FET*). Les demandeurs reprochaient à l'Etat hôte différentes omissions et mesures réglementaires prises par les autorités de régulation aux fins de forcer les investisseurs à renégocier les termes de la concession, ainsi que le refus injustifié de l'administration de ce pays d'augmenter les tarifs de l'eau et de son assainissement.

En réponse, l'Etat argentin met fin à la concession en 2006 et charge une entité étatique des services de distribution de l'eau et de son traitement. Pour ce dernier, l'eau fournie contenait un taux élevé de nitrate (Décision *on liability* préc, §. 52 et 244) ; les investisseurs ont donc failli à leur obligation de fournir une eau propre à la consommation. Pour exclure sa responsabilité, l'Etat argentin développe, quant au fond, le moyen tiré de l'exception « d'état de nécessité » (*estado de necesidad*). La crise financière qui a foudroyé le pays constitue un état de nécessité qui a commandé, et partant justifié, les mesures critiquées. Il faut dire, ici, qu'en droit international coutumier (CIL), il est bien acquis, et les parties en conviennent parfaitement, que l'état de nécessité, lorsqu'il est avéré, constitue un fait justificatif qui absout l'Etat de ses responsabilités (art. 25 du projet d'articles de la Commission du droit international sur la responsabilité de l'Etat pour fait internationalement illicite). Entre temps, le 28 janvier 2005, un ensemble d'ONG a présenté une requête au Tribunal arbitral pour se voir autoriser à assister aux différentes audiences (*access to the arbitral hearing*), à accéder librement à tous les documents soumis au Tribunal et à formuler, ès qualité d'*amicus curiæ,* des arguments légaux (*to present legal arguments as amicus curiæ*)[3].

Enjeux. On l'aurait deviné : les enjeux de la question sont nombreux et fort importants. Tout d'abord, comment résoudre le conflit entre le droit de l'Homme à l'eau et le droit de l'investisseur sur son investissement, et selon quels critères ? Par ailleurs, faut-il traiter les contrats conclus par une puissance publique de la même façon que les autres contrats du commerce international ?

La troisième question concerne la responsabilité des Etats et l'exception de nécessité : comment et selon quel critère doit-on apprécier cette responsabilité ? La dernière question est d'ordre procédural. Elle est la suite logique des trois premières. Si l'on admet que la question posée au Tribunal touche une collectivité de personnes, faut-il par là même reconnaitre le « droit de saisir » le CIRDI aux membres de la société civile ? Et, dans l'affirmative, quel est le contenu exact de ce droit et sous quelles conditions s'exerce t-il ?

Le Tribunal arbitral a répondu avec un bonheur variable, il est vrai, à toutes ces questions.

---

[3] V. ICSID Case No. ARB/03/19, *Order in Response to a Petition for Transparency and Participation As Amicus Curiæ*, May 19, 2005, *ICSID Review-Foreign Investment Law Journal*, p. 342-350 (2006); V. L'*introductory note* du Secrétaire du Tribunal, Mr Gonzalo FLORES, ICSID Case No. ARB/03/19, *ICSID Review-Foreign Investment Law Journal*, p. 339-341. Le 12 février 2007, le Tribunal a prononcé un deuxième *Order in Response to Petition by five Non-Governmental Organizations for Permission to make an amicus Curiæ submission*. Pour d'évidentes raisons de clarté, cet ordre sera noté Order II, (tous accessibles en ligne).

Nous nous limitons dans cette note à l'aspect processuel de la question[4]. Seule donc la dernière question sera en l'occurrence traitée.

Décision *on Juridiction*. Le Tribunal a unanimement refusé dans l'*Order in Response* du 19 mai 2005 précité aux ONG requérantes[5] le droit d'assister aux audiences, d'y participer et de présenter des demandes orales (*Order in Response* préc., §.7). Il a, par contre, admis le bien fondé d'intervenir en *amicus curæ* et en a posé les conditions. S'agissant enfin du droit d'accès illimité aux documents soumis, le Tribunal a jugé inopportun, à ce stade spécifique de la procédure, de se décider. Il a ajourné sa décision à la soumission et à la sélection des parties agissant en *amicus curiæ* (§.31 et 32).

Appréciation critique. Sur le plan processuel, on ne peut que se féliciter de la décision du CIRDI d'autoriser l'intervention des ONG en *amicus curiæ*.

Mérites. La décision est doublement courageuse.

D'une part, et en l'absence d'accord des parties, l'article 32 (2) du Règlement arbitral limite l'accès au Tribunal aux parties, leurs représentants, témoins, experts et officiers du tribunal. Or, l'investisseur a fait savoir son refus relatif à l'intervention *d'amicus curiæ* (*Order in Response* préc, § 3 et 6 *in fine*). Les requérants produisent au soutien de leur pétition une sentence (Methanex *v.* United States of America, sentence rendue sous les règles d'UNICITRAL / NAFTA)[6] qui avait autorisé l'intervention d'*amicus curiæ*. Le Tribunal a fait justement remarqué que les différentes parties concernées avaient acquiescé à la demande, ce qui fait défaut en

[4] V. Sur l'ensemble de la question: Andrew DE LOTHINIERE MC DOUGALL et Ank SANTENS, ICSID Tribunals apply new rules on amicus Curiæ, *Mealey's International arbitration Report*, Vol. 22.

[5] V. *Petition for Transpaency and Participation As* Amici Curiæ in Case No ARB/03/19 before ICSID, Arguas Argentinas et *al.* v./ Repúlica Argentina, January 27, 2005 (accessible en ligne).

[6] Dans leur pétition précitée, les ONG évoquaient dans leurs conclusions aux pages 5 et 7 l'*aff. Methanex v. USA* (*Decision of the Tribunal on Petitions for Intervention and Participation as* "Amici Curiæ", January 15, 2001).

l'occurrence (*Order in Response* préc, §. 6 *in fine*)[7]. Et le Tribunal de rejeter unanimement la demande sur le fondement de l'article 32 (2). Il ne restait au Tribunal que de puiser dans son pouvoir d'appréciation pour considérer la constitution d'*amicus curiæ* comme question de procédure. Et il décide, sous le visa de l'article 44 de la Convention CIRDI, d'autoriser unanimement le principe d'intervention d'*amicus curiæ* (*Order in Response* préc, §.16, *cf.* Case ARB/03/17, *Order in response*, 17 mars 2006, §.11, 12 et 16). Il faut aussitôt remarquer que pour les arbitres les conclusions d'*amicus curiæ* ne lient aucunement le Tribunal qui demeure libre (*Order in Response* préc, §.13) ; que cette intervention ne doit nullement affecter les droits substantiels et processuels des parties en litige (*Order in Response* préc, §. 14, 21 et 29)[8] ; ces droits devant demeurer inchangés avant et après l'intervention d'*amicus curiæ* (*Order in Response* préc., §. 14 « ... *the Tribunal in the present case finds that the acceptance of amicus submissions is a procedural question that does not affect a disputing party's substantive rights since the parties' rights remain the same both before and after the submission...* »).

D'autre part, et c'est là le deuxième mérite de la décision, le Tribunal justifie sa décision[9] par « *the appropriateness of the subject matter of the case amicus curiæ submission* » (qu'on peut traduire approximativement

---

[7] *Cf* Aguas Provinciales de santa Fe et al. *v.* Repúlica Argentina (ICSID Case ARB/03/17), *Order in Response to a Petition for Participation as* Amicus Curiæ, March 17, 2006 (§. 7 et 8).

[8] La même solution fut adoptée dans l'affaire l'aff. *Biwater Gauf (Tanzania) limited v. United Republic of Tanzania* (ICSID Case No ARB/05/22) dans le *Procedural Order No5 Concerning a petition for* Amicus curiæ, February 2, 2007.

[9] L'autre justification tient à la volonté d'ouverture et de transparence du tribunal pour les matières qui traitent des questions d'intérêt public. La démarche vise à réduire le déficit démocratique du recours à l'arbitrage international et à renforcer la légitimité du processus arbitral en l'ouvrant aux ONG (§. 22 : « *The acceptance* of amicus *submissions would have the additional desirable consequence of increasing the transparency of investor-state arbitration. Public acceptance of the legitimacy of international arbitral process, particularly when they involve states and matters of public interest, is strengthened by increased openness and increased knowledge as to how these process function ... Through the participation of appropriate representatives of civil society in appropriate cases, the public will gain increased understanding of ICSID processes.*"), *cf.* avec *Procedural Order* No5 *Concerning a petition for* Amicus curiæ, February 2, 2007, préc; Methanex Corporation v. USA, préc. (§. 49).

par la pertinence de l'affaire s'apprêtant à une intervention en *amicus curiæ*). Il est clair pour les arbitres qu'il ne s'agit pas d'une simple affaire ordinaire opposant des parties privées[10]. Toujours pour les arbitres, il est certain que « ... *the Tribunal finds that the present case potentially involves matters of public interest ... The international responsibility of state, the Argentine Republic, is also at stake, as opposed to the liability of a corporation arising out of private law. While these factors are certainly matters of public interest, they are present in virtually all case of investment treaty arbitration under ICSID jurisdiction. The factor that gives this case particular public interest is that the investment dispute centers around the water distribution and sewage systems of a large metropolitan area, the city of Buenos Aires and surrounding municipalities. Those systems provide basic public services to millions of people and as a result may raise a variety of complex public and international law questions, including human rights considerations. Any decision rendered in this case, whether in favor of the Claimants or the Respondent, has the potential to affect the operation of those systems and thereby the public they serve* » (*Order in Response* préc., §.19; *adde* Order II, §. 3). La nature de l'affaire, ses enjeux, et les éventuels effets de la décision à prendre sur les usagers ont lourdement pesé sur la décision du Tribunal et constituent son *ratio decidendi*[11]. On peut surtout le vérifier à propos des critères retenus par le Tribunal pour

---

[10] *Order in Response* préc., §. 20: "*These factors lead the tribunal to conclude that this case does involve matters of public interest of such a nature that have traditionally led courts and other tribunals to receive amicus submissions from suitable non-parties. This case is not simply a contract dispute between private parties non-parties attempting to intervene as friends of the court might be seen as officious intermeddles.*"

[11] Le consortium a critiqué la pertinence du recours à l'amicus curiæ après le retrait d'Aguas argentinas. Pour ce dernier: "... *the termination of AASA's concession and the discontinuance of the proceedings with respect to AASA, the former operator of that water and sewage system, changes the nature of this case since any decision in this arbitration can no longer have an impact on the operation of AASA or the water and sewage system it formerly operated. The Claimants contend that the only effect of any decision in this case is to determine the monetary liability, if any, in respect of alleged treaty breaches.*" (Order II, §. 17). Le Tribunal rejette le moyen: "... *this case continues to present sufficient aspects of public interest to justify an amicus submission even after the discontinuance of the proceeding with respect to AASA.*" (Order II, §. 18 *in fine*).

autoriser l'intervention d'*amicus curiæ*[12]. Pour le Tribunal, l'affaire s'apprête et commande, eu égard à l'intérêt public (*public interest*) qu'elle présente, le recours à l'*amicus curiæ* (*Order in Response* préc., §. 21).

Limites. Mais cette ouverture du Tribunal aux représentants de la société civile n'est pas totale ; le droit de développer un argumentaire juridique ne fait pas de l'*amicus curiæ* une partie au litige (ce qui est d'ailleurs conforme à l'esprit de l'institution). Ce droit de soumettre des écritures (soumissions dit l'*Order in Response*) n'est donc pas synonyme de droit d'agir. Certes, les observations écrites des *amici* n'est pas tributaire de l'apparition des « nouveaux faits » (Order II, §. 20) ; ils peuvent toujours argumenter en fait et en droit et émettre un avis d'expert. « *The role of the petitioners in this arbitration is not to serve as a litigant as would be the case in a domestic case, but to assist the Tribunal, the traditional role of an* amicus curiæ », pose fermement le Tribunal (Order II, §. 19). Il ne comporte pas le droit d'assister et de participer aux débats, d'accéder aux documents confidentiels par exemple (Order II, §. 25). Il n'autorise pas à discuter les moyens des parties ou à en contester la preuve : «... *it must be emphasized that the role of* amicus curiæ *is not to challenge arguments or evidence put forward by the Parties* » (Order II, §. 25). L'admission de l'*amicus curiæ* ne permet pas, en outre, d'exercer des voies de recours, ou de suppléer l'une des parties en cas de carence par exemple. Il reste, par ailleurs, fort limité par les droits processuels des différentes parties en cause (Order II, §. 21). Il s'agit d'une intervention d' « ami » *stricto sensu* et nullement de constitution de partie.

Evolutions. Pourtant, il faut saluer la décision comme un précédent en matière d'arbitrage CIRDI. Elle a permis, en avril 2006, l'amendement de l'article 37 (2) du Règlement d'arbitrage. Le deuxième paragraphe de l'article 37 permet désormais au Tribunal « *après la consultation des parties* », d'autoriser toute *« personne ou entité qui n'est pas partie au différend (appelée dans le présent article la « partie non contestante ») de dé-*

---

[12] Trois critères ont été retenus: (i) la nature de l'affaire soumise (*appropriateness of the subject matter fo the case*), (ii) les conditions relatives à l'aptitude des soumissionnaires (*suitability of specific nonparties a*s amicus curæ) qui renvoient à la compétence, l'expérience et l'indépendance, et (iii) la procédure à suivre pour postuler. Le Tribunal a pu constater la réunion des critères dans les ONG soumissionnaires dans le deuxième Order de 2007 (Order II, §. 16).

poser une soumission écrite auprès du Tribunal relative à une question qui s'inscrit dans le cadre du différend ». Cette intervention, faut-il toujours le rappeler, ne doit pas constituer « *une charge excessive à l'une des parties* » ou lui causer « *injustement un préjudice* ». Il faut en outre que les deux parties aient « *la faculté de présenter leurs observations sur la soumission de la partie non contestante* » (art. 37 (2) *in fine*). Cette décision a constituée, et ce n'est pas son moindre mérite, un précédent qui a été suivi par les arbitres dans d'autres affaires[13] ; ces derniers sont allés jusqu'à demander à certains Etats tiers d'intervenir ès *amicus curiæ*[14].

Les solutions retenues dans la décision commentée ont inauguré une nouvelle ère dans le combat pour les droits de l'homme. Désormais, le milieu associatif a voix au chapitre. Le mouvement est amorcé et rien ne semble pouvoir l'arrêter.

---

[13] Citons entre autres : Aguas Provinciales de santa Fe et al. *v.* Repúlica Argentina (ICSID Case No. ARB/03/17), *Order in Response to a Petition For Participation as* Amicus Curiæ, March 17, 2006 (Dans le§. 10 de *l'Order in Response* du 17 mars 2006 préc., le Tribunal fait expressément référence à l'affaire commentée); V. aussi : Biwater Gauff (Tanzania) limited *v.* United Republic of Tanzania (ICSID Case No ARB/05/22, *Procedural Order N°5 Concerning a Petition for* Amicus curiæ, February 2, 2007, (accessible en ligne). *Adde* la note de synthèse de Mme Martina POLASEK, ICSID *ICSID Review-Foreign Investment Law Journal* (2007), p. 149-154, spec. 152 et suiv. La chose ne coule pas de source ; rien en matière d'arbitrage n'oblige un arbitre ou un panel à se plier à un précédent. En droit d'arbitrage international, Il n'y a pas *stricto sensu* de jurisprudence.

[14] V. par ex. Aguas del Tunari SA *v.* The Republic of Bolivia (ICSID Case No. ARB/03/2). Dans cette affaire le Tribunal a admis l'interprétation du TBI par un *non-disputing State Party* qui est une « *entity that not a party to the dispute* » au sens du nouvel art. 37 (2) du Règlement d'arbitrage CIRDI. V. sur l'ensemble de la question la note de synthèse (*Introductory Note* sous l'aff. *Aguas del Tunari SA v. The Republic of Bolivia (ICSID Case No ARB/03/2),* de Mr Ucheora ONWUAMAEGBU, *ICSID Review-Foreign Investment Law Journal* , Cases, p. 445-449, spéc. pp. 448 et 449.

Finances solidaires et accès des paysans à la terre au Nord

Pascal GLEMAIN *

Les finances solidaires sont envisagées comme des activités financières, portées par la promotion de l'épargne solidaire en vue du financement et de l'accompagnement d'un accès non seulement aux services de logement, à l'emploi, à la culture ; mais aussi, d'un accès à la terre dans les pays dits « développés », et à des activités génératrices de revenus dans les pays en développement (PED), dits : « du Sud ». Dans ce contexte, bien que l'on puisse se féliciter d'une réduction de la faim dans le monde selon l'Organisation des Nations Unies pour l'alimentation et l'agriculture (FAO), il n'en demeure pas moins que plus d'un Homme sur 8 est encore en situation de faim chronique.

Face à cet état de fait, le CCFD-SIDI[1] a créé en 1983 le premier Fonds Commun de Placement (FCP) « faim et développement » avec le soutien du Crédit Coopératif, pour aiguiller l'épargne solidaire vers les financements des investissements et des activités agricoles dans les pays du Sud. Ce sont ainsi 4,7 millions d'euros de prêts qui ont été octroyés par la SIDI en 2011, pour soutenir les organisations paysannes tant dans leur organisation technique, que dans la valorisation des terres. Mais, depuis lors, l'accès à la terre pour exploiter et élever ne concerne plus seulement les PED. En quoi les finances solidaires constituent-elles une solution pour l'accès au foncier agricole, et pour le soutien à une agriculture paysanne dans les pays du Nord ?

---

* Economiste et Gestionnaire. Maître de conférences-HDR, CIAPHS EA 2241, Université de Rennes 2-Ueb.

[1] Le CCFD-Terre Solidaire est la première ONG de développement en France, reconnue d'utilité publique en 1984. Elle regroupe des mouvements laïcs et des Services de l'Eglise catholique. La SIDI (Solidarité Internationale pour le Développement et l'Investissement) est un investisseur social labellisé « entreprise solidaire » crée en 1983 par le CCFD. Elle propose un appui financier et technique à ses partenaires du Sud, des structures de proximité qui offrent des services financiers adaptés aux populations exclues des circuits bancaires traditionnels.

Après avoir dévoilé quelques éléments de constats du passage de l'économie agricole à l'économie rurale (I), nous discuterons les solutions que semblent apporter les finances solidaires, ainsi que leurs limites (II).

Nous réservons notre analyse à l'accès des paysans à la terre dans les pays du Nord, tout en ouvrant en fin de chapitre notre réflexion aux pays du Sud.

I.- De l'économie agricole à l'économie rurale.

Il est deux phénomènes conjoints qui rendent difficile l'accès à la terre des paysans dans les pays du Nord : d'une part la fin de l'économie agricole, et d'autre part la mutation socioprofessionnelle du secteur agricole du modèle de l'exploitant à celui de salarié.

Ainsi que le soulignent Abdelhakim et Pellissier (2008), rejoignant un grand nombre de conclusions en la matière : « en termes d'emplois et de revenus, l'agriculture perd partout de son importance tandis que les aides se réduisent au profit de mécanismes d'accompagnement souvent plus complexes et moins directement liés à la production. Cette évolution est particulièrement marquée au Nord. Les agriculteurs n'y représentent plus en moyenne plus que 10 % de la population rurale et une économie nouvelle, fondée sur le tourisme et les activités de services aux nouveaux résidents, se développe ». Il en résulte une forte augmentation du prix des terres agricoles sous la pression de la demande foncière, que celle-ci vienne des particuliers pour y construire leur habitation principale, ou bien des collectivités locales pour doter leurs nouveaux habitants des équipements sportifs et culturels dont ils ont besoin.

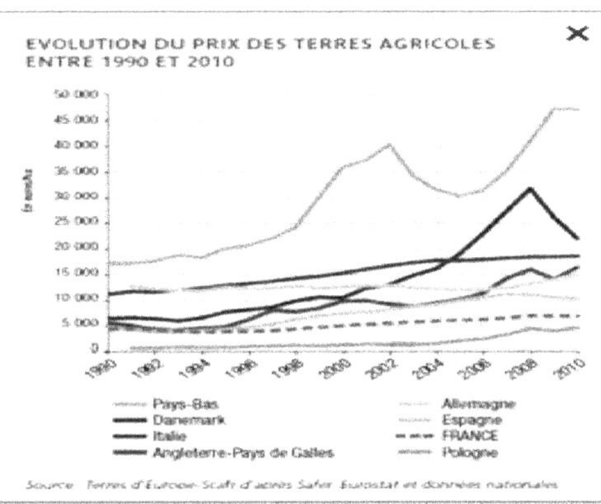

Si, selon la Fédération nationale des sociétés d'aménagement foncier et d'établissement rural (FNSAFER) (2012), le prix moyen des terres agricoles libres en France est passé de 5 230 euros l'hectare en 2010 à 5 430 euros en 2011 (soit une hausse de 6 % l'an), le plus inquiétant concerne la montée du prix des terres louées. Celui-ci atteint 3 830 euros/ha sur un marché plus tendu que celui des terres agricoles libres. La région Bretagne – première région agricole – a perdu près du tiers de ses fermes sur la période 2003-2010 (Terres de Liens, 2013).

Ce sont ainsi 6 400 ha par an qui sont sacrifiés, aux dépens de l'économie agricole, et en faveur de l'économie rurale.

Mais, toujours selon la FNSAFER (2012), le plus inquiétant, c'est que : « *les terres louées sont potentiellement acquises davantage par des acteurs non agriculteurs que par les fermiers en place.* Or, la diminution du marché des terres libres au profit de celui des terres louées « *pénalise l'installation des jeunes mais aussi l'agrandissement d'exploitation, au profit de restructurations d'exploitations* ». En Bretagne, ce sont près de 1 600 porteurs de projets en agriculture qui se retrouvent en privation d'accès à la terre.

Ce phénomène devrait continuer à progresser car, on assiste en France depuis les années 1970 à une réduction de la main-d'œuvre familiale au profit du salariat. Cela se traduit par une montée significative de l'emploi de salariés permanents à temps partiels dans les exploitations (Elyakime et Loisel, 2008) (travailleurs occasionnels, travailleurs saisonniers, travailleurs qualifiés à temps partiel). Parallèlement, on assiste avec le développement des Associations pour le Maintien d'une Economie Paysanne (AMAP), et la consommation de produits agricoles en circuit court, à une volonté de s'installer et à ce titre, de trouver du foncier agricole disponible. Les finances solidaires tentent de répondre à ce défi.

II.- L'accès des paysans à la terre : la réponse des finances solidaires.

Parmi les acteurs de la finance solidaire en France, c'est la société coopérative financière La Nef[2] qui apparaît comme l'un des acteurs clés de l'accès à la terre, en partenariat avec l'association Terre de Liens. Il s'agit pour la Nef – dans le cadre d'une stratégie proxémique – de permettre de développer une agriculture soucieuse de l'environnement et de ses salariés. A ce titre, elle appuie le modèle de finance solidaire de Terre de Liens

Les outils financiers de Terre de liens

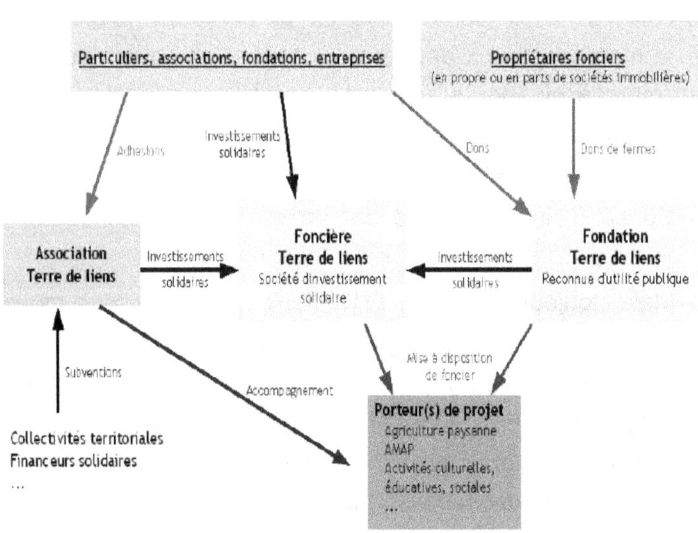

Source : Terre de Liens.

Il s'agit de financer l'agriculture de transmission, c'est-à-dire celle qui concerne de nouveaux agriculteurs non-issus du monde agricole, et l'agriculture traditionnelle. Mais surtout de relayer les groupes bancaires coopératifs pour lesquels les projets agricoles sont soit peu rentables, soit

[2] www.lanef.com

trop risqués. Ainsi Philippe Leconte, Président du conseil de surveillance de la NEF considère que : « *le Crédit Agricole a de l'argent qu'il pourrait investir dans des projets agricoles ou dans l'achat de terres pour des familles, des jeunes, mais ils ne le font pas, car les agricultures paysanne et biologique, dans leur optique, ne sont pas viables* » (Calmé, 2012, p. 131). C'est pour combler ce creux bancaire que la Nef et Terre de Liens ont fondé en 2006, la société en commandite d'actions : « la Foncière Terre de Liens ». En 2010, ce sont 25 millions d'euros qui ont été réunis pour acheter une centaine de fermes.

La proxémie spatiale, sur laquelle repose le modèle économique de La Nef, participe à la mise en coopération d'acteurs spatialement proches. D'un côté, il s'agit bien de consolider une proximité relationnelle entre les acteurs de la finance solidaire locale, l'association Terre de Liens et les porteurs de projet pour une agriculture paysanne. D'un autre côté, il s'agit aussi de faire le lien entre l'épargne de proximité et les investissements de proximité qui vont être réalisés au niveau local, au profit de sociétaires-clients en attente de produits issus de l'agriculture paysanne.

Dans les pays du Sud, la coopération d'épargne et de crédit est une « *base du développement* ». C'est au sein de villages, voire de quartiers d'habitation, que se développent les relations bancaires d'épargne et de crédit. Il en va de même désormais dans les pays du Nord. Ainsi, sur la période 2002-2012, l'association Terres de Liens aura acquis quatre-vingt fermes, représentant 2000 hectares soustraits à l'exploitation extensive. Cela représente le maintien ou l'installation de 200 paysans et paysannes, soit 0,1 agriculteur par hectare contre 0,05 en moyenne nationale. En 2012, la Foncière a acquis 21 nouvelles fermes et procédé à 2 compléments d'acquisition. Ces 23 biens représentant 290 ha (248 ha en 2011 et 740 ha en 2010), 7 logements et 31 bâtiments à vocation agricole ou d'accueil. Ces acquisitions représentent un montant immobilisé[3], ou en cours d'immobilisation, total de : 3 444 463 €.

Dans ce système, l'argent devient un bien commun local qu'il faut s'approprier au service d'un projet de développement local socialement soutenable, en ce sens qu'il cherche le « plus grand bonheur non pas pour le plus grand nombre » (vision utilitariste), mais bien « pour chacun et pour

[3] (Prix du bien + frais d'acquisition + travaux).

tous ». Il s'agit là au sens de Di Méo (2001, p. 35) d'un « *espace de bien-être soi et bien-être ensemble* », mais aussi d'un enracinement de l'agriculture paysanne grâce au soutien de la finance solidaire au service d'un projet de développement soutenable des territoires.

Bibliographie indicative :

ABDELHAKIM T., PELLISSIER J-P., 2008, « Elaborer des stratégies de développement pour les territoires ruraux », p. 281-308, dans Hervieu B. (dir.), *Méditerra. Les futurs agricoles et alimentaires en méditerranée.* Condé-sur-Noireau, CIHEAM, Les Presses de SciencesPo, 368 p.

CALME N., 2012, *Economie fraternelle et finance éthique. L'expérience de La NEF.* Paris, éditions Yves Michel, 304 p.

DI MEO G., 2001, *Géographie sociale et territoires.* Paris, Nathan Université, 317 p.

ELYAKIME B., P.LOISEL P., 2008, « Incitation salariale et Groupement d'Employeurs », *Revue Economique,* n°1-Vol.59, janvier, p. 33-50.

TERRE DE LIENS, 2007, *L'accès collectif et solidaire au foncier et au bâti. Guide méthodologique, juridique et financier.* Paris, Terre de Liens. Disponible à l'adresse suivante : http://www.terredeliens.org/IMG/pdf/guide_foncier_tdl_version 2007.pdf

TERRE DE LIENS, 2013, *Note de présentation.* Assises de l'Installation - 4ème réunion du COPIL du 29 janvier 2013. Disponible à l'adresse suivante : http://agriculture.gouv.fr/IMG/pdf/Note_de_presentation_de_Terre_de_Liens_cle85 89a7.pdf

WAMPFLER B., DOLIGEZ F., LAPENU C., 2010, *Organisations professionnelles agricoles et institutions financières rurales : Construire une nouvelle alliance au service de l'agriculture familiale.* Les Cahiers de l'IRC, Supa-Agro Montpellier, IRAM et CERISE. Disponible à l'adresse suivante : https://www.lamicrofinance.org/ files/24546_file_financementagriculture.pdf

B) L'encadrement du commerce agroalimentaire

La sécurité alimentaire à l'épreuve du commerce international *

Frédéric PARE **

Les acheteurs et les vendeurs qui transigent des aliments sont consentants. On ne les oblige pas à acheter ou vendre. Mais ces transactions alimentaires profitent-elles plus aux uns qu'aux autres ? Certains opérateurs seraient-t-ils plus libres que d'autres dans ce processus commercial ? La mise en concurrence des agricultures du monde fait-elle des perdants ? Entre les 2,6 milliards de paysans et les 100 entreprises qui achètent 74 % de leurs récoltes, lesquels sont avantagés ? Quel est le prix de la libre concurrence appliquée à la production d'aliments ? Y a-t-il un « bien commun » en alimentation ? De quoi est-il constitué ? Qui l'assure ? Autant de questions situées au cœur du travail de nombreuses ONG comme la Coalition pour la souveraineté alimentaire.

On dit que les questions agricoles et alimentaires sont complexes, que seuls les spécialistes peuvent réalistement en débattre. Il faut se méfier de tels propos. Ils nourrissent le statut quo et dressent des barrières suspectes à la participation citoyenne. Ce sont des questions cruciales où des enjeux nettement perceptibles se jouent, où des paradigmes clairs opèrent.

On ne demande pas à un menuisier de soigner des personnes. Que demande-t-on à un État et pas à une entreprise ? Qu'est-ce qu'une entreprise, sinon que des moyens de production, y compris de la main d'œuvre, détenus ou utilisés par des individus pour produire des biens ou des services dans le but d'accroître leur richesse personnelle ? Qu'est-ce qu'un État, sinon que la somme d'institutions capables de mettre en œuvre un contrat social liant les citoyens d'un même territoire géopolitique, dans le but d'assurer leur bien commun ? Jean-Jacques Rousseau, né il y a 300 ans, dit dans « ***Du contrat social ou Principes du droit politique*** » :

---

* Rapport introductif sur l'interface entre sécurité alimentaire et commerce international exposé lors des séminaires scientifiques du programme Lascaux - « Nourrir le monde : la parole aux citoyens » - à Nantes, les 12 et 13 novembre 2012.

** Agronome, Coordonnateur de la Coalition pour la souveraineté alimentaire (CSA).

« ... La volonté générale peut seule diriger les forces de l'État selon la fin de son institution (création), qui est le bien commun; car, si l'opposition des intérêts particuliers a rendu nécessaire l'établissement des sociétés, c'est l'accord de ces mêmes intérêts qui l'a rendu possible. C'est ce qu'il y a de commun dans ces différents intérêts qui forme le lien social; et s'il n'y avait pas quelque point dans lequel tous les intérêts s'accordent, nulle société ne saurait exister. Or, c'est uniquement sur cet intérêt commun que la société doit être gouvernée[1] ».

Les aliments sont essentiellement produits, transformés, emballés, transportés et commercialisés par des entreprises mises en concurrence entre elles de plus en plus à l'échelle planétaire. On ne contestera pourtant pas qu'ils répondent à un besoin fondamental. N'y a-t-il pas dans l'accès économique et physique pour tous et en tout temps, à des aliments sains provenant de ceux qui les produisent et qui font partie du même contrat social, un élément légitime de ce contrat ?

Des États ou juridictions ont érigé l'eau en tant que bien collectif. Ce statut leur procure une franche marge de manœuvre pour en contrôler fortement l'exploitation et le commerce. Au Québec, un pays du Nord, l'énergie hydroélectrique a été nationalisée dans les années 60. Il apparaissait à l'État que l'exploitation de cette ressource essentielle au bien être collectif ne devait pas être laissée entre les mains des entreprises en tant que moyen d'enrichissement d'actionnaires et que l'électrification de tout le Québec ne surviendrait qu'à ce prix. Dans les mêmes années (1965-1970), le Québec s'est également doté de systèmes publics et universels d'éducation et de santé, au nom du bien commun. Pourquoi, dans le cas des aliments, les États semblent préférer le marché pour assurer le droit à l'alimentation et la sécurité alimentaire ?

On confond souvent la sécurité, l'autonomie et la souveraineté alimentaire. La Coalition a donc rapidement ressenti le besoin d'arrimer ces concepts, question d'être comprise.

L'autonomie alimentaire, au sens de la déclaration de Montréal « *pour un contrat social renouvelé sur la base de la souveraineté alimen-*

---

[1] Jean-Jacques ROUSSEAU (1762), *Du contrat social ou Principes du droit politique*, document produit en version numérique par Jean-Marie TREMBLAY, professeur de sociologie, dans le cadre de la collection : Les classiques des sciences sociales, février 2002, p. 20.

taire »[2], sorte d'acte de naissance de notre Coalition, apparaît comme la proportion des aliments consommés sur un territoire, généralement un État, qui en provient. Il ne faut pas confondre ce concept avec celui de la balance commerciale agroalimentaire d'un État ou d'une région. La balance commerciale exprime plutôt le rapport entre la production d'aliments sur un territoire, sans égard à leur lieu de vente et les achats d'aliments fait par les citoyens sur ce même territoire, sans égard de leur provenance. C'est au tournant de l'an 2000 que le Québec a atteint une balance commerciale agroalimentaire positive, c'est-à-dire que les ventes alimentaires faites par les entrepreneurs de l'agriculture et de l'agroalimentaire ont excédé les achats d'aliments réalisés par les citoyens ou institutions sur ce même territoire québécois. Considérant les chiffres-mêmes du gouvernement du Québec pour l'année 2008, l'autonomie alimentaire du Québec était alors de 33 %, ce pourcentage ayant déjà été de l'ordre de 75 %, il y a 25 ans.

Pour peu que l'on conçoive que la sécurité alimentaire d'un peuple relève du bien commun et donc d'une responsabilité publique et non d'une responsabilité individuelle d'entrepreneur ou de consommateur, la Coalition croit qu'un État normal ne peut se contenter de mesurer et surveiller l'état de sa balance commerciale, mais qu'il doit **aussi** surveiller son degré d'autonomie alimentaire. Qu'il doit mieux encore fixer et mettre en œuvre un niveau ambitieux d'autonomie alimentaire au nom d'un meilleur contrôle de sa sécurité alimentaire.

Cela suppose toutefois que l'État puisse pleinement et librement adopter ses politiques publiques en la matière, notamment des mesures de protection aux frontières, de manière à préserver ce rapport légitime entre ceux, sur son territoire, qui produisent les aliments et ceux qui les consomment. C'est là qu'entre en scène la souveraineté alimentaire, soit le droit des peuples à leur politique agricole et alimentaire, à l'encadrement des marchés. La souveraineté alimentaire restaure ainsi la responsabilité et la

---

[2] Adopté le 7 septembre 2007 par 42 organisations de la société civile du Québec et du Canada, ce texte est en quelque sorte la déclaration de principe ayant conduit à la création de la Coalition pour la souveraineté alimentaire un peu plus d'une année plus tard. La déclaration de Montréal est consultable à l'adresse suivante : http://www.nourrirnotremonde.org/SiteWeb_Coalition/documents/Declaration_de_Montreal_(finale).pdf

capacité du pouvoir public à réguler les activités des « opérateurs alimentaires », aux fins de cette sécurité alimentaire et du droit au travail décent.

Ces liens établis, il importe d'exposer quelques faits avérés à propos de la conduite de nos systèmes alimentaires, des faits qui rappellent l'importance de la restauration de l'espace politique abandonné à l'autel du libre échange, de la « loi de l'offre et de la demande », du droit au commerce...

Une étude réalisée par 3 chercheurs de l'École polytechnique de Zurich en septembre 2011 démontre que 40 % de l'économie mondiale serait dirigée par 147 compagnies de la finance ou des assurances. Ces 147 compagnies sont en lien étroit, par des participations croisées ou des participations au sein de conseils d'administration, avec un très vaste réseau d'autres entreprises.

En octobre 2011, le *Conference board of Canada* rendait publique une étude sur la répartition des richesses. Elle conclue que les riches continuent de s'enrichir tandis que les pauvres sont de plus en plus pauvres. Que l'écart des revenus s'accroît plus vite au Canada qu'aux USA, depuis 1995 et que les 20 % les plus favorisés récoltent 40 % des revenus totaux. Que partout sur la planète, l'écart entre les riches et les pauvres s'agrandit. En fait, 72 % de la population mondiale vit dans un pays où l'écart a cru durant la période étudiée.

Un autre rapport rendu public en décembre dernier par l'OCDE sur le même sujet, décrit le même problème à l'échelle des pays les plus riches. Pour le décrire, le secrétaire général de l'organisation, M. Angel Gurría, dit :

> « Le contrat social commence à se lézarder dans de nombreux pays. Cette étude balaie l'hypothèse qui voudrait que les bienfaits de la croissance économique se répercutent automatiquement sur les catégories défavorisées et qu'un surcroît d'inégalité stimule la mobilité sociale. Sans stratégie exhaustive de croissance solidaire, le creusement des inégalités se poursuivra ».

Depuis quelques décennies, les politiques agricoles et commerciales nationales, au Nord comme au Sud, invitent les agriculteurs du monde à la COMPÉTITIVITÉ. Le message s'incarne dans des mesures diverses, adoptées au cours des années par les gouvernements des pays occidentaux capables de soutenir financièrement leur agriculture nationale, le plus souvent par des programmes de subvention comblant le manque à gagner entre les prix du marché et les coûts de production. Dans les pays en développement, c'est par la mise en œuvre des mesures d'ajustement structurel déployées par le *Fonds monétaire international* et de la *Banque Mondiale* que les agricultures ont été intégrées au marché global.

Ces politiques sont cohérentes avec la présence de ces pays au sein d'instances multilatérales de libre échange comme l'OMC ou l'ALENA. Peu à peu, des pays et régions comme l'Australie, la Nouvelle-Zélande et l'Europe, ont ainsi mis fin au contingentement de leur production laitière domestique, par exemple. En Australie, 8 ans après la déréglementation totale de l'industrie laitière, le nombre de fermes laitières a diminué de 40 %. Suivant cette réforme, la baisse significative du prix du lait au détail a été complètement annulée, puis renversée dans les années suivantes, malgré la diminution du prix payé aux éleveurs. En somme, la position commerciale dominante des intermédiaires (transformateurs et distributeurs) dans le marché, a empêché la diminution durable du prix au détail et accaparé en leurs mains les gains d'efficacité des fermiers[3]. Après le démantèlement de l'Accord international sur le café en 1989, le prix mondial moyen à la consommation a doublé et celui aux producteurs a diminué de moitié.

Après l'introduction de l'agriculture à l'OMC en 1994, les États-Unis et l'Europe ont adopté des programmes de subvention dits « découplés » des prix et des volumes de production. Ces subventions, versées en fonction de la superficie des fermes, sont réputées conformes à l'OMC car elles ne distorsionneraient pas les échanges commerciaux. Qu'elle soit enregistrée à l'enseigne de la « boite verte » de l'OMC ou ailleurs, on conviendra que toute subvention contribue par définition à cette distorsion, à moins d'être versée également partout sur la planète. Les gouvernements proposent aussi de nombreux programmes visant à soutenir les producteurs dans leurs efforts de « saine gestion » ou d' « innovation technologique », deux autres façons de concourir à leur compétitivité.

Devant un tel rapport des États à l'agriculture, comment reprocher aux agriculteurs d'adopter les pratiques agricoles les plus susceptibles de

---

[3] Groupe AGÉCO, *La gestion de l'offre dans le secteur laitier, un mode de régulation toujours pertinent – Mise à jour de l'analyse du cas australien.* Mars 2008, Canada.

réduire le risque d' « expulsion » des marchés ? La FAO estime ainsi qu'en à peine 100 ans, 75 % des espèces nourricières de la planète seraient disparues[4], trop improductives ou difficilement commercialisables. Des régions du monde sont favorisées par leur climat, pour produire par exemple des céréales, des légumes ou des fruits, d'autres pour les élevages. On pense au maïs du Brésil, au blé de l'Ukraine, aux fruits et légumes de la Floride et aux vaches laitières ou aux agneaux de la Nouvelle-Zélande. La théorie des avantages comparatifs, développée par l'économiste anglais David Ricardo[5], propose de laisser ces avantages agir et de ne pas intervenir dans les marchés pour permettre aux consommateurs d'en profiter. Elle est encore aujourd'hui défendue par les ministres du commerce et le Directeur général de l'OMC. À quoi bon se battre contre de tels avantages ? S'il coûte moins cher de produire des tomates en Andalousie, parce que l'ensoleillement y est inégalé en Europe et que les salaires aussi y sont les plus bas du continent, alors que l'Andalousie produise nos tomates, disent les libre-échangistes.

En 2050, la terre hébergera 9 milliards de personnes. Conséquemment, toutes les agricultures seront requises, les moins productives comme les plus productives. Mais que restera-t-il des premières lorsque les secondes auront fini de les remplacer, et les paysans qui en vivent de devenir de nouveaux urbains pauvres, à la faveur de cette théorie des avantages comparatifs, amplifiée par des subventions agricoles drapées de vertus écologiques (découplées - boite verte de l'OMC) ? Entre le paysan pauvre d'Afrique, qui cultive la terre à l'aide de quelques outils (pratiquée par les 3/4 des agriculteurs), sans traction animale, et celui du Brésil qui pratique l'agriculture mécanisée (pratiquée par 2 % des agriculteurs) qui embauche du personnel de ferme et commerce ses récoltes à la bourse de Chicago, un écart de rendement de 1 pour 2000[6] les sépare.

---

[4] Solange LEVESQUES, « Pour la sauvegarde du patrimoine végétal », Le Devoir, 21 mars 2003, p. B8, *in* Laure WARIDEL, (2003), *L'envers de l'assiette et quelques idées pour la remettre à l'endroit,* Éditions Écosociété et Environnement Jeunesse. 173 p.

[5] http://www.alternatives-economiques.fr/david-ricardo--1772-1823-_fr_art_222_27852.html

[6] Conférence de Marcel MAZOYER, 25 mars 2011 à Longueuil, tirée *de La fracture agricole et alimentaire mondiale Nourrir l'humanité aujourd'hui et demain*, Marcel MAZOYER et Laurence ROUDART (dir.), Universalis, 2005, 193 p.

Selon le *World Watch Institute*, les aliments voyagent d'ailleurs de plus en plus entre le lieu où ils sont produits et celui où ils sont consommés. Ils franchissent en moyenne 2 600 km[7]. La spécialisation des territoires productifs et ce transport alimentaire accru, sont un corolaire de la théorie des avantages comparatifs. En 2009, le Québec a importé des pommes du Chili, des poivrons des Pays-Bas, du céleri de la Californie, des tomates de la Floride, des framboises du Mexique, etc. Tous ces aliments sont pourtant produits aussi au Québec. Selon une analyse du Conseil québécois de l'horticulture, l'importation de 11 produits parmi tous ceux qui sont importés, a généré 139 000 tonnes de CO_2, soit l'équivalant à 43 523 automobiles[8]. Le tiers des camions qui sillonnent nos routes transportent des aliments.

Les OGM, les pesticides, les engrais minéraux et l'augmentation de la dimension des fermes répondent de la même logique marchande. Si on appliquait la moyenne des troupeaux laitiers de l'Ouest américain au Canada, il en resterait 900, et au Québec 350, au lieu des 6 400 qu'il compte aujourd'hui. Ce sont des stratégies de compétitivité et d'adaptation au libéralisme alimentaire qui ne sont pas sans conséquence sur le dynamisme et l'occupation des régions rurales. Même de grands philanthropes comme Bill Gates soutiennent des projets de productivité pour l'Afrique agricole, fondée notamment sur l'accès à des semences OGM et à des engrais, sans questionner la spirale compétitrice dans laquelle ils poussent ses paysans. Où sont les mécènes prêts à soutenir un changement de paradigme, une voie plus politique que technique ?

Il vient souvent à nos oreilles que cette idée de mettre les agricultures en concurrence profiteraient aux consommateurs, logiquement. C'est ignorer la structure de l'industrie qui a d'ailleurs grandement changé depuis 30 ans à la faveur du libre marché. Devant les 2,6 milliards de paysans et agriculteurs de la terre, 100 entreprises accaparent 74 % des achats de denrées de base rappelle l'agronome Marcel Mazoyer. À moins d'être franchement bien organisés, en coopératives par exemple, et qu'un cadre législatif n'oblige ces acheteurs à s'approvisionner de tels regroupements domestiques, les paysans n'arrivent pas à tirer un revenu décent de la de-

---

[7] Brian HALWEIL. *in* Laure WARIDEL (2003), *L'envers de l'assiette et quelques idées pour la remettre à l'endroit*, *op.cit.*

[8] http://www.cqh.ca/upload/pdf/Bulletin_2_7_kilometre_alimentaire.pdf

mande alimentaire solvable. Les vendeurs au détail d'aliments sont également en contrôle face à cette demande solvable de sorte que les gains d'efficacité réalisés à la production agricole sont capturés par eux et remis à leurs actionnaires plutôt qu'aux consommateurs. Au Québec, les 4 plus grandes entreprises de transformation contrôlent 66 % des achats de denrées de base[9]. Heureusement, deux d'entres elles sont des coopératives agricoles. 85 % des aliments consommés au Québec sont vendus par 3 grandes chaînes d'alimentation[10]. À l'échelle planétaire, 10 entreprises de vente au détail, où figurent de grandes multinationales comme Carrefour ou Walmart, réalisent 25 % des ventes alimentaires au détail[11]. Ces ventes s'élèvent à plus de 350 milliards de $. Cette concentration s'opère aussi à la transformation. Aux États-Unis, les marques de commerce alimentaires détenues par le tabatier Philip Morris, accaparent 10 cents pour chaque dollar de vente alimentaire[12]. Pourtant, 11 % des ménages et 18 % des enfants américains fréquentent les banques alimentaires alors que les opérateurs alimentaires américains arrivent à produire deux fois la valeur de tous les aliments consommés aux USA[13]. Un *avis et rapports du Conseil économique et social*[14] de la République française déposé au gouvernement français en 2008 sur l'enjeu des liens entre la faim et les politiques agricoles et alimentaires, présenté par l'économiste Jocelyne Hacquemand, rappelle d'ailleurs que la faim gagne de plus en plus les pays riches où les filets sociaux s'effritent et où les écarts de richesse se creusent sans cesse. Selon le Bilan Faim[15], 851 000 canadiens ont régulièrement fréquenté une banque alimentaire en 2011. La récente mission d'Olivier De Schutter au

---

[9] Union des producteurs agricoles. *Établissement d'une politique québécoise de la transformation alimentaire*. Mémoire présenté au ministre du MAPAQ, septembre 2001. Page 5

[10] Gouvernement du Québec, Ministère de l'agriculture, des pêcheries et de l'alimentation, Bio Clips, Vol. 4, numéro 4, oct. 2001

[11] *Op. cit.*

[12] NORBERG-HODGE *et al. in* Laure WARIDEL (2003), *op.cit.*

[13] Sophia MURPHY, *Securing Enough to Eat*, International Institute for Sustainable Developpement (IISD), janvier 2005

[14] http://www.ladocumentationfrancaise.fr/var/storage/rapports-publics/084000210/0000.pdf

[15] http://www.banquesalimentaires.org/flextop/upload/pdf/b05022725f0ca77f39799ced4326a6d1.pdf

Canada (mai 2012) lui a aussi permis de constater la pauvreté dont plus de 3 millions de Canadiens souffrent. C'est sans compter les 56 % de Canadiens en situation de surcharge pondérale qui accaparent une très large part du coût de notre système de santé[16]. Selon la Direction de la santé publique du Québec, ce phénomène vise d'ailleurs l'offre alimentaire. On la qualifie à juste titre d'obésogène[17].

Comment en sommes-nous arrivés là ? Pour quelles raisons historique, économique, sociologique ou politique les États en sont-ils arrivés à ce rapport marchand aux aliments ?

La question se pose d'autant que la vaste majorité des pays du monde, le Canada compris, a convenu de plusieurs principes et conventions internationales, érigeant l'alimentation, la santé ou le travail décent au rang de droits universels. On peut lire dans la Déclaration universelle des Droits de l'homme, aux articles 23 et 25, que chacun a droit au travail, à une rémunération équitable et satisfaisante qui assure aux travailleurs et à sa famille une existence conforme à la dignité humaine. Le Pacte international relatif aux droits économiques, sociaux et culturels (PIDESC), engage aussi les États au droit des peuples de disposer d'eux-mêmes. En vertu de ce droit, ils déterminent librement leur statut politique et assurent librement leur développement économique, social et culturel. Pour atteindre leurs fins, tous les peuples peuvent disposer librement de leurs richesses et de leurs ressources naturelles, sans préjudice des obligations qui découlent de la coopération économique internationale, fondée sur le principe de l'intérêt mutuel, et du droit international. En aucun cas, un peuple ne pourra être privé de ses propres moyens de subsistance. Les États parties au Pacte reconnaissent aussi le droit de toute personne à un niveau de vie suffisant pour elle-même et sa famille, y compris une nourriture, un vêtement et un logement suffisants, ainsi qu'à une amélioration constante de ses conditions d'existence.

Nous ne manquerions donc pas de droits individuels. Les mécanismes qui permettraient de les mettre en œuvre, voir de les judiciariser, ne sont pas à la hauteur des sanctions économiques qu'encourent **pour vrai**

---

[16] Panorama de la santé 2009, OCDE

[17] http://publications.msss.gouv.qc.ca/acrobat/f/documentation/2012/12-289-08W.pdf

les pays qui ne se soumettent pas aux décisions finales de l'Organe de règlement des différends de l'OMC, par exemple. Plusieurs analystes et juristes arrivent à cette conclusion. Dans son rapport de mission à l'OMC, le Rapporteur spécial des Nations Unies pour le droit à l'alimentation soumet que les pays favoriseraient apparemment le droit au commerce en cas de doute, car la sanction économique sera certaine. Il y aurait effectivement un déséquilibre entre la force en droit du droit économique et celle des droits de l'homme. Le défi ne serait donc pas d'imaginer et mettre en œuvre de nouveaux droits individuels, comme le droit des paysans, par exemple, mais de restaurer les capacités nationales, systémiques, le droit des peuples et de leurs États, le droit collectif, aux fins de la réalisation des droits de l'homme, justement.

Plusieurs ONG militent toutefois pour les droits de l'homme et leur application, ou pour l'accès libre à la terre, aux semences, à l'eau, ou pour le droit de fixer leur prix, ou pour le droit aux circuits courts. D'autres militent contre les OGM ou promeuvent les solutions marchandes qu'elles ont imaginées et développées, comme les AMAP en France, ou l'Agriculture soutenue par la communauté ou les marchés de solidarité au Québec. Ces alternatives sont des plus valables, mais elles ne questionnent pas le rôle de l'État, sauf s'il s'agit de les soutenir davantage. Les ONG, comme notre Coalition, qui militent pour que le commerce, y compris le leur, soit contraint, encadré, sont rares. Elles doivent non seulement convaincre les États de prendre leur responsabilité mais aussi leurs pairs pour les convaincre de ne pas limiter leur travail à la promotion de solutions qui n'interpellent pas le politique.

Certains objectent que des États ont utilisé leur souveraineté contre le mieux-être de leurs commettants, sous l'emprise de dictateurs corrompus ou de dirigeants néolibéraux, par exemple. C'est là un problème politique et non juridique. Il faut éviter de poursuivre l'érosion des souverainetés nationales sous ce mauvais prétexte. Il vaut mieux restaurer ces souverainetés nationales, dans l'espoir que les États s'en servent à bon escient, pour le bien-commun, le mieux-être collectif. Car ils en sont les seuls vrais gardiens. Poursuivre l'érosion des souverainetés nationales revient aussi à obliger les gouvernements à se mettre au service des entreprises transnationales qui savent bien faire le jeu de ce droit au commerce sans frontière. Les missions économiques à l'occasion desquelles les élus du peuple prennent l'avion avec des gens d'affaire pour la conquête de nouveaux marchés, démontrent bien l'asservissement du politique par l'économique. Lorsque les biens essentiels comme la terre, l'eau, les aliments ou les semences auront été complètement consacrés en tant que marchandise, à force de droit économique, à quoi serviront les États, sinon qu'à soutenir les entreprises devenues transnationales, pour la sauvegarde d'emplois que l'on sait d'autre part en sursis ? Cette question n'évoque-t-elle pas une réalité ? Cette mécanique n'est-elle pas une fuite en avant qui conduit au chaos ? Un chaos d'où proviendront inévitablement de nouveaux contrats sociaux, à terme. Sommes-nous collectivement assez matures pour éviter ce genre de cycle entre le tout JE et le tout NOUS, en 2014 ?

Amender le libre-échange en matière alimentaire ? *

Alain BERNARD ** & Fabrice RIEM ***

L'accord de Bali, arraché en décembre 2013 entre les 160 représentants des pays membres de l'OMC, marque-t-il un nouveau départ du *Projet de paix perpétuelle* d'Emmanuel Kant ? Ce premier accord, depuis la naissance de l'OMC en janvier 1995, ne concrétise qu'une toute petite partie de l'agenda du « cycle de développement » initié à Doha en 2001. Il comprend trois volets. Le premier, celui du développement des pays les moins avancés, ne contient que des déclarations de principe, alors même que le cycle de Doha était placé sous le signe du « développement ». Le deuxième volet, consacré à la « facilitation du commerce », s'inscrit dans une perspective d'accroissement des échanges commerciaux. Tous les pays, même les plus démunis, s'engagent à simplifier les procédures douanières et à « mettre à niveau » leur administration pour réduire les coûts de transaction. Selon les estimations de l'OMC, passablement farfelues, cet aspect devrait dégager 21 millions d'emplois et permettrait de réaliser 1000 milliards de dollars d'économies. S'agissant du troisième volet, l'agriculture et la sécurité alimentaire, l'accord prévoit une « clause de paix » qui, sous des conditions restrictives, couvre des exceptions aux règles du GATT, l'Accord sur l'agriculture signé à l'occasion des négociations de Marrakech. Alors qu'un groupe de 46 pays « en développement », réunis au sein du G 33, proposait de permettre aux pays les plus pauvres de soutenir leur agriculture afin de réduire les risques de famine, les pays industrialisés, les États-Unis en tête, n'ont concédé à l'Inde qu'une bien modeste « clause de paix » ne couvrant que les dispositifs existants. Ils ne pourront pas faire l'objet

* Ce texte prolonge les communications présentées par les auteurs lors des Rencontres internationales du programme Lascaux des 25 - 27 novembre 2013, ainsi que l'article « Sécurité alimentaire et commerce international : nourrir la planète par le marché ou sauver le "pacte colonial" ? », publié dans le volume 1 de *Penser une démocratie alimentaire* (dir. F. COLLART DUTILLEUL, Th. BREGER), *Edición* INIDA, San José, 2013, p. 69 et s.

** Agrégé des Facultés de droit, Professeur à la Faculté pluridisciplinaire de Bayonne (CDRE). Professeur à la Faculté de Bayonne (CDRE).

*** Maître de conférences HDR à la Faculté de Bayonne (CDRE).

d'une plainte devant l'ORD (Organe de règlement des différends) de l'OMC pendant le temps de la négociation d'une solution de fond.

Un bilan lucide du résultat des négociations conduit à constater que les misérables des pays les plus pauvres n'en tirent aucun avantage alors que les multinationales du commerce international vont profiter à plein des mesures de « facilitation du commerce ». En effet, ces mesures vont peser lourdement sur les pays en voie de développement démunis, le plus souvent, d'une administration douanière suffisante et formée aux subtilités du droit douanier[1]. L'essentiel du profit ira donc entre les mains des quelques acteurs qui concentrent l'essentiel de l'activité[2].

Le multilatéralisme ne change rien à l'affaire : les relations internationales obéissent à la loi du plus fort et non au principe de la coopération. Autant dire que l'adoption par le concert des nations d'une exception alimentaire[3] - sur le modèle de l'exception culturelle[4], telle que prévue par la Charte de La Havane instituant une Organisation Internationale du Commerce adoptée par la Conférence des Nations Unies sur le commerce et l'emploi en 1948, Charte n'ayant jamais été ratifiée - risque fort de se heurter à un veto. Elle supposerait de passer de la logique de la puissance à celle de la coopération.

---

[1] Sur le coût en investissement économique, humain et intellectuel de l'adhésion à l'OMC, on consultera avec intérêt, HUA CAI, « La Chine, un éléphant tranquille sur la scène des échanges internationaux », *in* M. ABELES, *Des anthropologues à l'OMC. Scènes de la gouvernance mondiale*, Paris, CNRS Éditions, 2011, p.201.

[2] Le Rapport sur le commerce mondial 2013 de l'OMC indique, par exemple que 1 % des exportateurs contribue pour plus de 80 % aux exportations totales aux États-Unis. Cette très forte concentration s'observe également en Europe mais aussi dans les pays en développement, 81 % des exportations sont concentrés entre les cinq plus grandes entreprises exportatrices, Rapport précité, page 88.

[3] Sur cette proposition Lascaux, cf. F. COLLART DUTILLEUL, « Propositions pour la reconnaissance internationale d'une "exception alimentaire" » sur le modèle de "l'exception culturelle" », *in* F. COLLART DUTILLEUL, *Penser une démocratie alimentaire*, *op. cit.*, p. 13. Sur la question on consultera avec intérêt l'ouvrage novateur de Jean Christophe GRAZ, *Aux sources de l'OMC. La Charte de La Havane. 1941-1950*, Librairie Droz, Genève, 1999.

[4] On peut d'ailleurs s'étonner que l'alimentation ne soit pas déjà comprise dans cette exception culturelle tant la cuisine peut apparaître comme la matrice de la culture. Cf. C. LEVI-STRAUSS, *Mythologiques. Le cru et le cuit*, Paris, Plon, 1964.

Or parmi les nombreux « trous noirs »[5] de la science économique classique, celle de l'équilibre général, il existe une question qui reste largement inexplorée jusqu'à aujourd'hui, celle du pouvoir et de la domination[6]. L'ambition scientifique des fondateurs de la doctrine explique, en partie, cette cécité. François Quesnay, un médecin, cherche à établir des « lois souveraines » qui, comme les lois physiques, s'imposent à tous, sujets comme souverains[7]. Le recours à la mathématique par Walras ou Pareto pour formaliser l'équilibre de l'interdépendance générale et tenter de donner une coloration scientifique à la discipline, conduit à ignorer le pouvoir qui présente le grave défaut de ne pas autoriser la mise en équation. Par ailleurs, toute doctrine, même à prétention scientifique, s'insère dans une histoire sociale. Ainsi le libéralisme du XVIIIe siècle s'élabore aussi contre le mercantilisme, c'est-à-dire contre une espèce de pouvoir politique et de hiérarchie des pouvoirs sociaux. Aussi, les premiers économistes libéraux, Adam Smith par exemple, contribuent à la construction d'une représentation devenue banale, celle de la coupure entre l'État et le marché. En conséquence, écrit François Perroux, « si le pouvoir est confondu avec le pouvoir public et si l'économie est, *en principe*, privée, on ne montrera pas trop de curiosité pour les pouvoirs que cette dernière contient. D'autant moins que les détenteurs du pouvoir ne cherchent ordinairement pas en livrer les secrets »[8].

---

[5] Pour reprendre l'expression de Jacques SAPIR, *Les trous noirs de la science économique. Essai sur l'impossibilité de penser le temps et l'argent*, Paris, Seuil, 2003 pour l'édition de poche. Pour une appréciation scientifique, V° Protectionnisme et libre-échange (L. DESPRES), *in Dictionnaire juridique de la sécurité alimentaire dans le monde* (dir. F. COLLART DUTILLEUL, J.-Ph. BUGNICOURT), Bruxelles, Larcier, 2013, p. 551.

[6] L. DESPRES (préc., p. 553) écrit dans ce sens que la « théorie économique néoclassique dans son ensemble, néglige l'importance des rapports de forces ». Comme exception notable dans la littérature économique française, voir F. PERROUX, *Pouvoir et économie généralisée*, la première édition date de 1973. Nous utilisons ici la réédition dans les *Œuvres complètes*, tome V, éditées par les Presses Universitaires de Grenoble, 1994, p. 137 et s.

[7] Voir les références citées par A. BERNARD, « La guerre des farines », *in* F. COLLART DUTILLEUL et F. RIEM, *Droits fondamentaux, ordre public et libertés économiques*, Paris, Institut Universitaire Varenne, 2013, p. 153 et s.

[8] Précité, page 150.

Au plan des idées, le procès de l'application à l'alimentation de l'idéologie économique néolibérale et de ses conséquences désastreuses sur les politiques menées, notamment par l'Union européenne, n'est plus à faire[9]. Mais le phénomène de dépendance au sentier (*path dependance*) conduit à constater que les présupposés de la théologie libérale s'inscrivent aujourd'hui dans le marbre des institutions internationales - FMI, Banque mondiale ou même FAO et tout particulièrement à l'OMC - car la puissance sociale dévastatrice de cette théologie résulte du fait que le « Consensus de Washington » constitue le référentiel unique et partagé de toutes les institutions de gouvernance mondiale. Des lambeaux de théories douteuses jouent comme justificatifs indiscutés des actions publiques entreprises. Ainsi la vieille théorie des « avantages comparatifs » continue de légitimer les politiques les plus injustes à l'égard des plus pauvres en leur faisant miroiter un avenir radieux[10]. Alors que cette théorie ne signifie plus rien lorsque les économies nationales n'échangent pas des biens, mais qu'elles constituent des étapes dans la production d'une même marchandise par des acteurs privés déterritorialisés.

L'hypothèse - il ne s'agit que d'une simple hypothèse ne prétendant pas au statut de vérité universelle - qui servira de fil conducteur à notre contribution est qu'il conviendrait d'abandonner les dichotomies qui structurent la réflexion notamment celle qui oppose l'État et le marché ou la société civile, qui distingue marché et capital ou celle qui sépare le national de l'international. La réforme du monde, si c'est de cela qu'il s'agit, suppose d'abord de changer les outils pour le penser. Il faudrait tout considérer en-

---

[9] Voir L. DESPRES, « Comment le fonctionnement actuel du système économique mondialisé influence-t-il la sécurité alimentaire ? », *in* F. COLLART DUTILLEUL, *Penser une démocratie alimentaire*, précité, p. 57. Pour une archéologie des idées et des politiques, on consultera avec intérêt J.C. KROLL et T. POUCH, « Régulation *versus* dérégulation des marchés agricoles : la construction sociale d'un clivage économique », *L'homme et la société*, n° 183-184, janvier-juin 2012,181. Pour une analyse rigoureuse des contradictions de la PAC en mode libéral, J.-C. KROLL, « Le découplage des aides : une chimère théorique, un frein à l'innovation agronomique », *Agronomie Environnement & Sociétés*, vol. 3, n° 1, juin 2013, p. 51.

[10] Tous les articles réunis par Marc ABELES, précité, constatent que l'argument revient de façon récurrente dans les discours des acteurs de l'OMC.

semble sous l'égide de la puissance ou la souveraineté, comme on voudra[11].

Dans cette voie, on observera que l'État moderne, en France tout du moins, ne se construit pas selon le modèle du contrat social mais sur celui de la concurrence et de la rivalité[12]. Déjà sous la monarchie, le discours historique, maîtrisé par le pouvoir, servait de justification à l'existence du souverain. À la fin du XVIIe siècle, l'opposition nobiliaire à la monarchie allait réinvestir le discours historique pour revendiquer ses droits perdus. Henri de Boulainvilliers, le représentant type selon Michel Foucault de cette contestation nobiliaire, déchire le voile d'un accord spontané et immémorial entre le roi et ses sujets, et démontre que la monarchie est née dans la fureur et le sang des batailles. Sous les lois et les institutions dont l'origine se perdrait dans la nuit des temps, la lutte et la guerre se trouvent toujours à leur fondement. Si l'espace international résulte de l'interaction des États, il n'est pas moins vrai que cet espace produit les États. Voilà un paradoxe, le marché international, la « facilitation du commerce » dans le langage de l'OMC, suppose l'existence d'États organisés.

De même, l'économie internationale ne constitue pas un simple reliquat des économies nationales. Il ne s'agit pas non plus, comme chez Ricardo, d'une harmonie naturelle entre les nations. Il conviendrait plutôt, comme le suggérait Fernand Braudel[13], de l'analyser comme un réseau composé de multiples chaînes de subordination fondées sur l'échange inégal. Dans cette perspective, l'État et le capital ne peuvent pas se dissocier : « ce n'est pas l'État qui a créé le capitalisme, ni le capitalisme l'État : ces deux figures mythiques sont deux aspects de notre image de la puissance sociale »[14].

---

[11] Le livre de François FOURQUET, *Richesse et puissance. Une généalogie de la valeur*, Paris, Éditions La Découverte, 1989, nous servira de guide.

[12] N. ELIAS, *La dynamique de l'Occident*, Paris, Pocket, 2003 [1939] et notamment toute la première partie. Cf. également M. FOUCAULT, *Il faut défendre la société*, Cours au Collège de France, 1976, Paris, Gallimard, Seuil, Hautes Études, 1997.

[13] *Civilisation matérielle, économie et capitalisme, XVe-XVIIIe siècle*. Tome 3. *Le temps du monde*, Paris, Armand Colin, 1979, spécialement p. 13 et s.

[14] F. FOURQUET, préc., p. 32.

Dans l'espace international tout au moins, il conviendrait d'appeler « politique » la synthèse des trois fonctions indo-européennes analysées par Georges Dumézil, la fonction religieuse ou justicière, la fonction guerrière et la fonction d'abondance ou économique. La souveraineté ou la puissance, résulterait de la conjonction de ces trois fonctions[15]. Dans cette perspective, ainsi que l'écrit Michel Beaud, « dès sa formation même le capitalisme est national et mondial, privée et étatique, concurrentiel et monopolistique ». L'auteur ajoute « pour le capitalisme dominant, pour la bourgeoisie triomphante, le cadre géographique et d'activité est le monde : c'est à l'échelle internationale qu'elle se procure la main-d'œuvre et les matières de base, qu'elle vend, qu'elle trafique et qu'elle pille ». Il conclut « en Europe même, la principale force transformatrice est l'État : c'est par lui et autour de lui que se crée l'unité nationale, l'unification monétaire, la cohérence juridique, la force militaire et l'ébauche d'une économie nationale »[16].

Or la théorie libérale, économique comme politique, se construit sur la séparation, voire l'antinomie, entre la sphère politique et celle de l'économie dans une dimension uniquement interne. Elle prend pour référence l'État-nation, oubliant au passage que la France ou l'Angleterre, par exemple, sont jusqu'au début des années 1960 des empires coloniaux[17]. Depuis les origines au XVIIIe siècle, elle développe une vision irénique du commerce international, celle de l'échange égal de Quesnay, Smith ou Ricardo : « à valeur égale, tout le monde prospère et tout le monde est content »[18]. Le libre-échange, dans cette perspective, constitue un bienfait pour l'humanité. Il pourrait même servir de ressort au développement.

---

[15] *Idem*, p. 21.

[16] *Histoire du capitalisme*, Paris, collection Points, 2010, 6e éd., p. 65.

[17] Cf. J.-F. BAYART, *Les études postcoloniales. Un carnaval académique*, Paris, Karthala, 2010, p. 68. L'auteur écrit : « l'État-nation est né de l'empire, non de la nation, et la plupart du temps ce bâtard n'a pas été désiré, sinon par quelques pervers ».

[18] F. FOURQUET, préc., p. 110. Le titre même de l'ouvrage d'Adam SMITH, *Recherches sur la nature et les causes de la richesse des nations*, montre bien que l'auteur, regardé par beaucoup comme le père fondateur de l'économie libérale, évacue la question de la puissance pour enquêter que sur la « richesse » des nations.

Les mercantilistes adoptent un tout autre point de vue, beaucoup plus scientifique car beaucoup plus réaliste. Leur horizon est celui de la compétition internationale, la recherche du meilleur moyen pour gagner la course à l'hégémonie mondiale. Dans cette course, disposer de l'économie intérieure la plus productive ne suffit pas. Au Moyen Âge, ce sont des villes, Venise ou Amsterdam, qui conduisent le commerce international. Dans la compétition pour le contrôle du commerce mondial que l'Angleterre livre à la Hollande et à la France à la fin du XVIIe siècle, ce n'est pas le plus étendu ou le plus peuplé qui l'emportera, mais le mieux organisé. William Petty, par exemple, dans son œuvre majeure, *Arithmétique politique*, démontre qu'il a une claire vision des enjeux. Le sommaire du chapitre premier se lit de la façon suivante : « qu'un petit pays et une population peu nombreuse, par leur situation, leur commerce et leurs politiques, peuvent égaler en richesse et en puissance un peuple et un territoire beaucoup plus grand ». Alors qu'il écrit en 1671 et que l'Angleterre se trouve dans une situation désastreuse - guerres civiles, révolte irlandaise, peste, menace militaire et que le pays se remet à peine du grand incendie de Londres de 1666 - il affirme « que les sujets du roi d'Angleterre ont un capital convenable et suffisamment commode pour mener le commerce du monde commercial tout entier »[19]. Pour parvenir à cette conclusion, Petty constate que la seule comparaison des richesses des nations ne suffit pas, mais qu'il faut prendre en considération les emplois du capital qui permettent de s'emparer du « monde commercial ». Dans cette perspective, l'investissement maritime est l'usage le plus productif. En France, le roi ignorera les conseils de Richelieu ou de Colbert. Alors que l'Angleterre s'ouvre au grand large, la France reste un État territorial, englué dans le continent. Les physiocrates proposent même de faire de la terre la source de toutes les richesses. Comme l'Union européenne d'aujourd'hui, puissance commerciale mais nain politique, les gouvernements de la France se méprennent sur le jeu qui se joue sur la scène internationale : celui de la puissance. Or la leçon de l'histoire c'est que le capital sans la puissance ne sert à rien.

[19] Cité par G. Caire, « Un précurseur négligé : William Petty, où l'approche systématique du développement économique », *Revue économique*, Volume 16, n° 5, 1965, p. 738.

Il ne faut pas se tromper de registre. Le libre-échange est le régime de la force[20]. Il permet à ceux qui contrôlent la puissance de tirer la substance d'échanges inégaux par nature. Ceux qui pensent pouvoir passer de façon unilatérale d'une logique de concurrence à une logique de coopération, se désarment de façon inconsidérée. La politique agricole comparée entre les États-Unis d'Amérique et l'Union européenne le démontre de façon éclairante. Alors que l'Union est en voie de démanteler de façon unilatérale les subventions à l'exportation, les États-Unis, après avoir emprunté la voie libérale en 1996, sont revenus à une politique protectrice de leur agriculture. Aujourd'hui, il faut constater « un isolement croissant du marché américain »[21], alors que les États-Unis s'opposent victorieusement à l'OMC, au nom du libre marché, au développement des politiques de survie alimentaire des populations les plus pauvres de la planète.

L'hypothèse du programme Lascaux, celle de la révolution par le droit, consiste, ni plus ni moins, à changer totalement de logique, à passer de celle de la concurrence à celle de la coopération qui se trouvait au fondement même des accords de La Havane. Or l'histoire montre que de telles révolutions symboliques - car il s'agit avant tout de changer de point de vue, installé depuis des lustres dans les esprits et dans les institutions - ne sont possibles que dans les moments tragiques de l'histoire. La France invente la sécurité sociale à la Libération car la guerre a réveillé la conscience de l'unité de destin de tous ses citoyens. De même le projet de La Havane s'explique par la Seconde Guerre mondiale et ses ravages. Mais ces périodes de prise de conscience de la communauté de destin de l'humanité sont rares et relativement courtes. Dès la fin de la Seconde Guerre mondiale, le monde bascule à nouveau dans une logique de concurrence avec la guerre froide. De même, la récente crise financière mon-

---

[20] M. WEBER, *La Bourse*, Paris, Editions Allia, 2010 [1894-1896]. Il écrit : « tant que les nations poursuivront la lutte économique inexorable et inéluctable pour leur existence nationale ... il est impossible de procéder à un désarmement *unilatéral* ». Il ajoute qu'une politique économique nationale « a le *devoir* de veiller *avant tout* à ce que des fanatiques défendant leurs intérêts ou à ce que des apôtres ingénus de la paix économique n'aillent pas désarmer leur propre nation » (souligné par l'auteur).

[21] J.-C. BUREAU et S. JEAN, « Les transformations des échanges agricoles bousculent l'agenda multilatéral », *La Lettre du CEPII*, n° 336, 31 octobre 2013, p. 3 ; cf. également l'article précité de J.-C. KROLL.

diale a ouvert une brève fenêtre à l'action des États pour reprendre le contrôle de la finance. Si certains ont pu, à cette occasion, parler du retour de l'État, ce constat doit être largement nuancé. L'État intervient plutôt comme gérant du marché financier qui conserve son hégémonie, même sur les finances publiques. On constate « suivant le point de vue, la transformation du marché en institution étatique ou de l'État en institution du marché »[22].

Le libre-échange par le multilatéralisme ne conduit pas à la création d'un marché mondial, mais à la production d'une arène propre à l'expression des rivalités de puissance. Or, force est de constater, et les accords de Bali le confirment, la domination des États-Unis qui se dirigent pourtant vers une « hégémonie discrète »[23]. Tirant les leçons des dernières aventures militaires de l'hyper puissance, l'Amérique se propose de « gouverner par derrière » (*Leading from behind*)[24]. Dans cette stratégie, le droit occupe, à n'en pas douter, une place centrale. Car une hégémonie durable suppose, chez les gouvernés, une croyance minimum en la légitimité de la domination. Dans cette voie, le droit fournit un outil irremplaçable[25]. De ce

[22] B. BERNARDI, « Octobre 2008 : le retour de l'État ? Perspective politique sur la crise financière », *La vie des idées*, disponible sur Internet. Pour l'analyse de ce mouvement qui peut être vu comme la mainmise des intérêts économiques les plus puissants sur l'État, voire J. K. GALBRAITH, *L'État prédateur. Comment la droite à renoncer au marché de libre et pourquoi la gauche devrait en faire autant*, Paris, seuil, 2009 [2008]. Il écrit par exemple qu'une coalition « cherche à prendre le contrôle de l'État, pour empêcher l'intérêt public de s'affirmer mais aussi pour braconner dans les flux économiques créés par l'intérêt public passé ». La raison d'être de ces coalitions est de « tirer de l'argent de l'État tant qu'elles le contrôlent » (p. 192). L'observation conforte, cela va sans dire, l'hypothèse de cette contribution, l'État et le capital c'est la même chose, un phénomène de pouvoir.

[23] Le dernier numéro de la revue *Questions internationales*, n° 64, novembre-décembre 2013, contient un dossier spécial très instructif consacré à ce thème.

[24] Philip S. GOLUB, « Puissance et « leadership » américains dans un monde en mutation », *in* B. BADIE et D. VIDAL, *Puissances d'hier et de demain. L'état du monde 2014*, Paris, La Découverte, 2013, p. 25.

[25] Voir Max WEBER, *Économie et société*, tome 1. Paris, Plon, 1995, spécialement p. 64 et s. À propos du « concept de l'ordre légitime », il écrit : « l'activité, et tout particulièrement l'activité sociale, et plus spécialement encore une relation sociale, peut s'orienter, du côté de ceux qui y participent, d'après la *représentation* de l'existence d'un *ordre légitime* ». Dans cette perspective, Marc ABELES écrit « dans nos sociétés, c'est la représentation de la règle, le devant-être qui flotte dans nos têtes, qui fait fonctionner la relation politique » (*Anthropologie de l'État*, Paris, Payot pour l'édition de poche, 2005 [1990], p. 112. Le droit international s'adresse classiquement à l'État qui sert de relais à cet « ordre légitime ». Pour s'exercer, le

point de vue aussi la puissance américaine dispose d'une position hégémonique sur les savoirs d'Etat et particulièrement sur le droit. Yves Dezalay constate que « la position dominante des États-Unis repose en grande partie sur des investissements importants dans le champ des savoirs d'État, qui leur ont permis d'imposer et de diffuser à l'ensemble du monde un modèle de gouvernement, qui est le produit de son histoire spécifique. La mondialisation servirait ainsi d'alibi à cette entreprise d'impérialisme symbolique qui vise à restructurer les champs nationaux du pouvoir d'État »[26]. Deux exemples permettre d'illustrer les conditions et les modalités de ce « soft power ».

Dans la course à la puissance, la maîtrise de l'information et du savoir constitue un atout déterminant. Faire du savoir un domaine exclusif, monopolistique, permet de s'assurer de conserver l'hégémonie de la connaissance. En transformant des résultats scientifiques en propriété privée exclusive, protégée par toute la force répressive du pouvoir d'État[27], la puissance dominante fait coup double en nationalisant le savoir scientifique et en offrant à ses entreprises des sources de profit exclusives. L'Accord du 15 avril 1994 sur les aspects des droits de propriété intellectuelle qui touchent au commerce marque le triomphe d'une campagne de lobbying commencé dans les années 1980 par une douzaine de compagnies américaines menées, entre autres, par la société Pfizer et appuyées par la puissance publique nationale. Ces quelques acteurs, mais extrêmement puissants, ont su mener une négociation internationale impliquant plus d'une centaine d'États. « Cet accord apparaît comme la résultante d'une forme sophistiquée de gouvernance par réseaux du secteur privé »[28]. Il montre la

---

pouvoir des États dominants suppose le relais d'États efficacement organisés chez les dominés.

[26] « Les courtiers de l'international. Héritiers cosmopolites, mercenaires de l'impérialisme et missionnaires de l'universel », *Actes de la recherche en sciences sociales*, n° 151-152, p. 12.

[27] L'Amérique fait du droit américain, ou du moins de certaines de ses branches, au mépris du principe de la territorialité de la loi, un mode de contrôle redoutable du marché global. Voir, très instructif, A. GARAPON et P. SERVAN-SCHREIBER, *Deals de justice. Le marché américain de l'obéissance mondialisée*, Paris, PUF, 2013.

[28] Voir l'article très instructif de Peter DRAHOS et John BRAITHWAITE (« Une hégémonie de la connaissance. Les enjeux des débats sur la propriété intellectuelle », *Actes de la recherche en sciences sociales*, n° 151-152, 69) qui détaille de façon

capacité de ces réseaux à s'attacher la complicité de l'administration fédérale et à élaborer un discours à prétention universelle qui fait de la propriété privée des résultats de la recherche la condition même du progrès.

La collaboration, voire la symbiose entre les intérêts économiques les plus puissants et l'administration étatique est facilitée par l'omniprésence des « experts » dans l'espace des relations économiques internationales. L'OMC constitue de ce point de vue un excellent champ d'observation de la production d'une « bureaucratie globale »[29]. Il conduit à constater que l'élaboration et la mise en œuvre des dispositions juridiques de l'Organisation relèvent d'un champ complexe qui réunit des professionnels du droit et du développement appartenant à des administrations étatiques, à des cabinets de conseil privé ou à des ONG. Alors que le système international repose sur la fiction de la souveraineté, la réalité de la gouvernance démontre l'omniprésence d'un personnel - extrêmement mobile entre les différentes structures, privées ou publiques - qui ne fait allégeance qu'à ce groupe d'appartenance très limité d'experts qui partagent une culture commune acquise dans les grandes universités américaines. La composition de l'Organe d'appel de l'OMC[30] révèle bien le monopole de formation des élites acquis par les universités anglo-saxonnes puisque cinq des juges, dont même le juge chinois, ont été formés ou enseignent dans une université américaine, les deux autres dans une université anglaise. Dans ces circonstances il n'y a rien d'étonnant à constater la « juridisation des relations commerciales internationales »[31]. La puissance impériale, qui est la première utilisatrice de l'Organe de règlement des différends (sur 470 procédures recensées en décembre 2013, les États-Unis sont présents dans 334 d'entre elles), se trouve dans cette enceinte sur un terrain connu qu'elle maîtrise mieux que personne. La thèse du complot devient inutile à

---

précise les modalités de cette mobilisation des réseaux d'influence et leur collaboration étroite avec l'administration fédérale.

[29] M. BADARO, « Le régime d'invisibilité des experts », *in* M. ABELES, *Des anthropologues à l'OMC*, préc.,p. 83.

[30] Sur le fonctionnement de la « juridiction » de l'OMC, voir par exemple E. CANAL-FORGUES, *Le règlement des différends à l'OMC*, 3e éd., Bruxelles, Bruylant, 2008, spéc. p. 88 et suivantes pour l'Organe d'appel.

[31] C.-E. COTE, La participation des personnes privées au règlement des différends internationaux économiques : l'élargissement du droit de porter plainte à l'OMC, Bruxelles, Bruylant et Édition Yvon Blais, 2007, spéc. p. 15 et s.

l'explication de l'hégémonie. Il suffit d'éduquer les esprits dans la bonne direction.

Devrait-on pour autant renoncer au projet de faire de l'exception alimentaire un régime spécial des échanges internationaux ? Sans doute pas. Mais il faut légiférer avec modération. Liora Israël observe ainsi que « l'existence de droits activables supplémentaires ne constitue pas automatiquement une ressource pour les acteurs : au contraire, la technicité et la superposition des dispositifs législatifs et réglementaires sont souvent l'obstacle le plus efficace à une véritable démocratisation de la société passant par le droit »[32]. De façon plus immédiatement accessible, les opposants au libre-échange pourraient contribuer, comme le fait le groupe Lascaux, à l'élaboration d'un nouveau référentiel[33]. Enfin, il faudrait, pourquoi pas, imaginer de nouveaux modes d'action. Les « faucheurs volontaires » montrent la voie, celle du braconnage sur le terrain d'autrui. Dans cette voie, pourquoi ne pas prendre l'initiative, sur le modèle du Tribunal Russel, d'un Tribunal Lascaux pour l'alimentation ? Il faudrait montrer qu'un autre droit et qu'une autre justice sont possibles, à partir d'une pyramide des normes reconstruite, avec à son sommet le droit à l'existence, et avec pour juge suprême le tribunal de l'opinion publique au sens de la philosophie du XVIIIème siècle.

Revenons, pour conclure, à la question posée par le titre de notre texte : faut-il *amender* le « libre-échange » en matière alimentaire ? Ne serait-il pas plus pertinent de s'attacher à rendre l'échange libre ?

De nombreux travaux ont décrit la manière dont les grandes entreprises organisent et contrôlent la production alimentaire et sa distribution, processus conduisant trop souvent à la destruction des systèmes alimentaires locaux. Les pratiques « libre-échangistes » se réduisent dans la plupart des cas à des rapports de domination. Le jeu combiné des politiques

---

[32] *L'arme du droit*, Paris, Presses de Sciences Po, 2009, p. 132.

[33] Dans cette voie, le Pape François est un allié de choix. L'exhortation apostolique, *Evangelii Gaudium*, du 24 novembre 2013 affirme que nous avons développé « une mondialisation de l'indifférence ». Il démonte en quelques phrases la thèse de la « rechute favorable » (« *trickle domn* » ou ruissèlement) qui justifie l'enrichissement des riches en pariant que la prospérité finit par irriguer toute la société. Magnifique théorie, mais depuis toujours « les exclus continuent à attendre » que les effets bénéfiques se produisent.

d'ajustement structurel, des accords bilatéraux de libre-échange et du droit de l'OMC aboutit à de puissants processus d'éviction. Ces politiques donnent au commerce mondial un cadre juridique fondamentalement favorable aux grandes entreprises : loin d'instaurer le libre marché, elles créent une économie dominée par une poignée d'intérêts privés[34]. La théorie des avantages comparatifs reste la principale justification de la doctrine libre-échangiste. Même revisitée par le théorème « Hecksher, Ohlin, Samuelson », celle-ci apparaît pourtant « totalement dépassée, ne serait-ce que parce qu'elle présente le libre-échange comme la stratégie optimale des Etats et ne rend pas compte du rôle des firmes dans les évolutions du commerce international »[35]. Dit autrement, la théorie néglige les rapports de forces qui façonnent pourtant le commerce mondial.

Dès le XIXème siècle, F. List avait montré que le libre-échange pouvait empêcher « les industries dans l'enfance » de se développer et proposé un « protectionnisme éducateur »[36] dont ont largement usé tous les pays industrialisés, notamment les Etats-Unis et l'Allemagne pour se protéger contre la concurrence des industries britanniques. On ne peut qu'être frappé par le « paradoxe du monde économique actuel qui est tout à la fois un monde de protectionnisme lourd (monopoles de propriété industrielle, subventions) et un monde de libre-échange (investissements, OMC) »[37]. Comme l'observe O. de Schutter, la promotion du modèle libéral de développement agricole dans les pays du Sud « a noyé les paysans locaux dans un système de concurrence illimitée et maîtrisé par les firmes multinationales agroalimentaires occidentales en anéantissant l'agriculture vivrière »[38]. La plupart des Etats qui ont récemment libéralisé leurs rapports

---

[34] Cf. les nombreux exemples fournis par W. BELLO, *La fabrique de la famine*, Carnets nord, Paris, 2012, not. le cas de l'agriculture mexicaine, p. 41 et s. L'auteur montre que depuis la mise en place des politiques d'ajustement structurel, 47 % du PNB mexicain est contrôlé par 25 holdings.

[35] V° Protectionnisme et libre-échange (L. DESPRES), précité.

[36] *Ibid.*

[37] F. COLLART DUTILLEUL et V. PIRONON, « Droit économique et sécurité alimentaire », *RIDE* 2012/4, p. 5. Les auteurs ajoutent que « c'est d'ailleurs là le vrai paradoxe de la doctrine des pays développés : militer pour le libre-échange dans les rapports avec les PED tout en étendant et en renforçant les monopoles à leur profit ».

[38] V° « Souveraineté alimentaire » (Th. BREGER et F. PARE), in *Dictionnaire juridique de la sécurité alimentaire dans le monde*, précité.

avec l'extérieur ne disposent pas d'une législation effective permettant de lutter contre les pratiques de monopolisation des entreprises étrangères. Les pères de la construction européenne avaient été plus prudents en décidant d'accompagner la promotion de la liberté de circulation des marchandises d'un droit de la concurrence destiné à prévenir ces effets délétères, effets d'autant plus traumatisants pour les pays du Sud où la production paysanne n'est pas seulement une activité économique, mais une dimension du lien social.

C'est, sans doute, que « l'indifférence aux valeurs » constitue le « corollaire de la transformation progressive du "droit des gens" en un droit international régissant les rapports entre "Etats souverains" »[39]. L'argument inusable selon lequel la normativité coutumière serait une entrave à la modernité et au développement est contredit par les faits. C'est surtout que, pour contrôler l'économie, il faut aussi « contrôler les formes d'organisations sociales qui interfèrent avec l'économie »[40]. Les droits coutumiers, mais aussi les modèles de sécurité sanitaire, spécifiques à chaque culture locale, sont présupposés constituer des obstacles à l'unification du marché mondial. Alors qu'on aurait pu s'attendre à ce qu'un droit international soit pluriculturel, le droit du commerce international éradique la diversité juridique. Chaque pays ayant une histoire, un niveau de développement et des structures sociales différents, il n'y a sans doute pas de loi-modèle unique à laquelle faire référence. L'exemple rapporté par François Collart Dutilleul du traité signé entre la province de Colombie britannique, l'Etat du Canada et la nation Nisga'a fournit cependant une bonne illustration de la manière par laquelle le commerce international pourrait se marier harmonieusement avec la reconnaissance des droits collectifs des peuples sur leurs terres ancestrales[41].

Organiser les relations entre le droit coutumier, le droit de l'Etat et le droit international suppose un droit pluriculturel, un dialogue des cultures.

---

[39] M. CHEMILLIER-GENDREAU, *Humanité et souverainetés. Essai sur la fonction du droit international*, La Découverte, Paris, 1995, p. 102.

[40] P. ROSANVALLON, *Le libéralisme économique. Histoire de l'idée de marché*, Seuil, 1989, p. 211.

[41] Cf. F. COLLART DUTILLEUL, « Investissements internationaux et accaparement des terres : la recherche d'un équilibre », in *Penser une démocratie alimentaire*, *op. cit.*, p. 89-90.

Encourager la libre circulation des ressources agricoles et alimentaires « n'en déplaise » aux instruments du libéralisme économique : une question de sécurité alimentaire mondiale

Sonya MORALES [*]

Depuis la fin du régime communaliste[1], le statut juridique du vivant végétal oscille entre l'appropriation privative par l'application des droits de propriété industrielle (DPI) et la contractualisation soutenue notamment par la *Convention sur la diversité biologique* (CDB)[2]. Le contrat et la propriété deviennent les nouvelles figures de régulation juridique de la nature[3] et s'imposent comme des instruments du libéralisme économique appuyant la rentabilité de la biodiversité.

Ce court texte présente quelques effets de ces instruments de droit économique sur la sécurité alimentaire et particulièrement sur la circulation et l'échange des semences agricoles (I) et insiste sur l'importance d'un système juridique différencié à l'égard des ressources agricoles et alimentaires (II).

I.- Un aperçu des effets restrictifs des instruments du libéralisme économique sur l'usage et l'échange des ressources.

La montée en puissance de la propriété industrielle et des brevets accordés sur la matière vivante végétale a fragilisé le concept de patri-

---

* Chargée de cours et doctorante à la Faculté de droit de l'Université Laval à Québec.

[1] L'*Engagement international sur les ressources phytogénétiques* fut le premier instrument juridique dédié aux ressources alimentaires et agricoles. Adopté sous l'égide de l'Organisation des Nations Unies pour l'alimentation et l'agriculture (FAO) en 1983, l'Engagement maintenait dans le patrimoine commun les ressources alimentaires et par conséquent valorisait la libre circulation de celles-ci, voir : *Engagement international sur les ressources phytogénétiques*, Résolution 8/83 de la Conférence de la FAO. En 1991, la FAO annexa à l'Engagement une résolution rectificatrice accordant aux États des droits souverains sur leurs ressources phytogénétiques (*Résolution 3/91,* 26e session de la Conférence de la FAO, 27 nov. 1991).

[2] *Convention sur la diversité biologique*, 5 juin 1992 (1993) 1760 R.T.N.U. 79 (n° 30619).

[3] François OST, *La nature hors la loi*, Paris, Éditions La Découverte, 1995, p.89.

moine commun, autrefois attribué aux ressources génétiques végétales (phytogénétiques) le substituant au principe de la souveraineté des États sur leurs ressources, plus conforme au droit international public[4].

Incidemment, l'absence de réglementation nationale concernant l'accès aux ressources génétiques et au partage des avantages découlant de leur utilisation a donné aux bioprospecteurs une liberté de prélèvements et d'usage des ressources à des fins commerciales sans obligation envers les pays hôtes souvent identifiés comme les centres d'origine de la biodiversité. Au bénéfice des relations internationales, il était impératif d'élaborer un système de droit qui ambitionne la conservation des ressources, modère l'accès et compense les pays du Sud pour l'évolution et l'entretien de la biosphère, incluant dans cette économie marchande, les communautés locales autochtones et paysannes.

Issue de la Conférence de Rio de 1992, la CDB a permis aux États hôtes de contrôler l'accès à leurs ressources, de réglementer les opérations de collecte et de conserver un droit de regard sur les opérations *in situ*, en plus de prévoir le partage des avantages monétaires et non monétaires résultant de la commercialisation des ressources ainsi prospectées[5]. Un changement majeur dans les relations Nord-Sud s'amorce par une ère de négociation autour de l'exploitation des ressources biologiques, incluant les ressources génétiques et les savoirs associés. Les possibilités législatives et contractuelles sont désormais très vastes et la capacité de négociation, influencée par les capacités techniques et surtout juridiques des pays four-

---

[4] Résolution 1803 (XVII) de l'Assemblée générale en date du 14 décembre 1962, « *Souveraineté permanente sur les ressources naturelles* », Doc. off. A.G., 17 e sess., suppl. n° 17, A/5217 (1962).

[5] *Convention sur la diversité biologique*, préc., note 2, art. 3 et 15.1. La Convention prévoit deux dispositifs contractuels essentiels permettant de légitimer l'accès de la partie utilisatrice, à savoir : le *consentement préalable donné en connaissance de cause* qui est une autorisation donnée par les autorités nationales du pays fournisseur à un utilisateur avant d'accéder aux ressources génétiques conformément à un cadre juridique et institutionnel établi (art. 15.5, CDB) ; et l'imposition de *conditions convenues d'un commun accord* entre le pays fournisseur des ressources et l'utilisateur qui fixent les conditions d'accès et d'utilisation des ressources, ainsi que le partage des avantages entre les deux parties (art. 15.4, CDB).

nisseurs, déteindra sur la qualité de l'entente contractuelle[6]. La CDB apparait donc comme une convention *à la carte* malléable au gré des ententes publiques, mais surtout privées[7] garantissant l'accès aux ressources, le partage des avantages et le développement des biotechnologies au cas par cas. Elle s'impose également comme un outil économique qualifié de « donnant-donnant entre le Nord et le Sud[8] » dont la portée se trouve réduite aux seuls contractants, excluant le plus souvent, les communautés locales autochtones admises comme les gardiennes des ressources biologiques, mais sans droit de propriété matériel sur celles-ci. Le commerce mondial de la biodiversité devient un privilège octroyé aux sociétés semencières. Dès lors, une valeur quasi exclusivement économique fut attribuée aux ressources génétiques d'origine végétale. Ce point de vue strictement mercantile n'est pas une solution pour la sécurité alimentaire.

Figer le sort des ressources génétiques dans une démarche contractuelle, pose également le problème de l'identification du propriétaire et du partage des bénéfices. Toutes ces dispositions issues du droit moderne détonnent avec la réalité des peuples traditionnels. Le concept de propriété n'est pas universel et n'est pas adapté « pour décrire les relations que les sociétés traditionnelles entretiennent avec les biens »[9]. Leurs valeurs ainsi que leurs convictions mettent l'accent sur la gérance, le partage et la conservation des ressources détachés de l'exclusivisme et de toute domination envers la nature. Ces peuples privilégient la mise en commun des éléments de la nature incluant le savoir-faire qui est collectif par nature[10].

---

[6] Jean-Frédéric MORIN, « Les accords de bioprospection favorisent-ils la conservation des ressources génétiques? » (2003) 34 :1 *Revue de droit de l'Université de Sherbrooke* 22.

[7] Hélène ILBERT et Sélim LOUAFI, « Biodiversité et ressources génétiques: La difficulté de la constitution d'un régime international hybride » (2004) 1 :177 *Revue Tiers Monde*, p.110, 113 et 115.

[8] Jean-Maurice ARBOUR et Sophie LAVALLEE, *Droit international de l'environnement*, Cowansville, Éditions Yvon Blais/Bruylant, 1re éd., 2006, p. 449.

[9] Sylvio NORMAND, *Introduction au droit des biens*, Montréal, Wilson & Lafleur Ltée, 2000, 1re éd., p.81.

[10] Les savoirs traditionnels des communautés locales autochtones comme l'inventaire des ressources et des espèces, leur usage, la dynamique des écosystèmes, les connaissances pédoclimatiques, *etc.*, sont souvent transmis oralement

Or, avec l'adoption de la CBD, la ressource et les savoir-faire traditionnels ne sont plus d'usage commun et deviennent monnayables. La CDB a contribué à faire admettre l'idée, désormais largement acceptée tant par les pays du Nord que ceux du Sud, que les ressources sont des marchandises comme les autres[11]. Cette représentation des ressources génétiques ne correspond pas aux conditions de la sécurité alimentaire qui réfèrent à la disponibilité des produits alimentaires, à la stabilité de l'approvisionnement, ainsi qu'à la consommation de denrées saines et suffisantes, nutritives et culturellement acceptables[12]. L'agriculture combine la matière vivante afin d'élaborer des variétés mieux adaptées aux conditions climatiques, plus résistantes aux prédateurs et appropriées aux exigences des sols. Il s'agit d'un processus cumulatif de croisement souvent aléatoire, non uniforme et peu stable et, par conséquent difficilement brevetable. La disponibilité (accès physique ou économique et circulation) des ressources phytogénétiques pour l'alimentation et l'agriculture est un enjeu majeur pour le développement agricole et la sécurité alimentaire des pays. Basé sur l'échange (le plus souvent informel) entre paysans et agriculteurs qui tend à faire évoluer le plus largement possible les nouvelles variétés de semences —, l'essentiel de notre alimentation est donc créé et transmis à partir des savoirs locaux sans contrat de valorisation monétaire sur ces connaissances. Les exemples illustrant la brevetabilité des éléments d'ores et déjà présents dans la nature et utilisés couramment chez les peuples autochtones pour des usages alimentaires sont nombreux. Citons le cas du *Thaumatococcus danielli*, une plante découverte en Afrique de l'Ouest au début du 19e siècle, utilisée afin de sucrer les aliments[13]. La propriété édulcorante de la plante

---

entre les générations. Donna CRAIG et Michael DAVIS, « Ethical relationship for biodiversity research and benefit-sharing with indigenous people » (2005) 2 *MqJICEL* 31, 36-37.

[11] Jean-Maurice ARBOUR, Sophie LAVALLEE et Hélène TRUDEAU, *Droit international de l'environnement,* 2e éd., Cowansville, Éditions Yvon Blais, 2012, p. 667.

[12] Geneviève PARENT et Sonya MORALES, « Sécurité alimentaire » *in* F. COLLART DUTILLEUL et J.-P. BUGNICOURT (dir.), *Dictionnaire juridique de la sécurité alimentaire dans le monde*, Bruxelles, Larcier, 2013, p. 618; voir aussi : FAO, *Déclaration de Rome sur la sécurité alimentaire mondiale,* Rome, FAO, 13-17 novembre 1996 [en ligne] [http://www.fao.org/DOCREP/003/W3613F/W3613F00.HTM] (consulté le 14 décembre 2013).

[13] Wojciech S. WALISZEWSKI, Seth OPPONG, John B. HALL et Fergus L. SINCLAIR, « Implications of local knowledge of the ecology of a wild super sweetener for its

fut récemment brevetée par la société pharmaceutique *Lucky Biotech Corporation* en collaboration avec l'Université de Californie[14]. Les retombées pour les usages alimentaires et particulièrement en faveur de la multinationale *Unilever* se chiffrent en multi-milliards de dollars américains minant dans cette foulée, la production conventionnelle des États ouest-africains ainsi que toute tentative d'exporter ce produit. Les paysans africains craignent désormais d'être dénoncés pour contrefaçon. Dans ce cas, la connaissance indigène est supplantée par des procédés biotechnologiques commercialisables mettant en péril la capacité des peuples et notamment des populations autochtones, de relever le défi de la sécurité alimentaire.

La CDB semble également avoir échoué dans son ambition de créer un accord multilatéral sur la biodiversité, puisqu'au final, le système mis en place se résume en une gestion des ressources naturelles sous l'égide du droit des contrats, le plus souvent bilatéraux, ce qui n'est pas pour déplaire aux multinationales. Il semble que l'orientation contractuelle et souveraine de la CDB ne soit pas adaptée à la nature collective des ressources alimentaires et agricoles dont l'érosion demeure une problématique d'envergure commune.

Au-delà de la CDB, plusieurs systèmes juridiques issus de la propriété industrielle[15] ont été créés afin de gérer la diversité du vivant végétal en termes de rentabilité de la ressource, créant au final une « [...] homogénéisation sans précédent des modes de vie. On retrouve dans le monde les mêmes semences industrielles, les mêmes chaînes d'alimentation rapide, les mêmes produits d'une culture de masse »[16]. L'exploitation planétaire des semences dont les performances agricoles et économiques sont garan-

domestication and commercialization in west and central Africa » (2005) 59:3 *Economic Botany* 231.

[14] Jean-Marie PELT, « Plantes médicinales et biotechnologies. Moteur de la nouvelle économie? », *in* J. FLEURENTIN, J.-M. PELT et G. MAZARS (dir.), *Des sources du savoir aux médicaments du futur*, Éd. IRD, 2002, à la p. 277.

[15] Nous référons notamment aux conventions successives de l'*Union pour la protection des obtentions végétales* (UPOV, de 1961 à 1991) ainsi qu'à l'*Accord sur les aspects des droits de propriété intellectuelle qui touchent au commerce* (ADPIC) adopté par l'Organisation mondiale du commerce (OMC) en 1994.

[16] Virginie MARIS, *Philosophie de la biodiversité. Petite éthique pour une nature en péril*, Paris, Buchet/Chastel, 2010, p.102.

ties a accéléré l'érosion de la diversité génétique des plantes, appauvri la culture alimentaire et contrecarré l'atteinte de la sécurité alimentaire.

Le manque de reconnaissance par ces différents instruments juridiques internationaux de la spécificité agricole et alimentaire de certaines ressources a conduit la FAO à se saisir de la problématique pour revendiquer, au bénéfice des ressources alimentaires et agricoles, un système juridique différencié.

II.- Vers un système de droit différencié à l'avantage de la sécurité alimentaire mondiale et durable.

La privatisation croissante du vivant végétal, l'érosion de la diversité agricole ainsi que le besoin de reconnaître certains droits aux agriculteurs ont contribué à l'avancement des travaux entrepris par la FAO vers l'adoption du *Traité international sur les ressources phytogénétiques pour l'alimentation et l'agriculture*[17]. Ce Traité occupe une place importante dans la lutte contre la faim et la pauvreté puisque tous les pays sont tributaires de la diversité génétique des plantes cultivées originaires des autres pays[18]. L'interdépendance entre les générations est également soulignée, la biodiversité agricole étant un héritage précieux.

Les ressources phytogénétiques sont importantes comme ressources directes dans l'alimentation et l'agriculture, mais aussi comme base de développement de nouvelles variétés mieux adaptées aux particularités des zones rurales plus marginales ou pour intégrer une plus grande diversité des espèces végétales ainsi qu'une plus grande variété *intraspécifique*[19]. L'agrobiodiversité est le résultat des efforts des paysans et des agriculteurs

---

[17] FAO, *Traité international sur les ressources phytogénétiques pour l'alimentation et l'agriculture,* Résolution 3/2001, 3 novembre 2001 (2004) 2400 RTNU (n° 43345) (entré en vigueur le 29 juin 2004), (ci-après « Traité sur les ressources phytogénétiques »).

[18] L'interdépendance des pays au regard des semences les plus importantes se situe entre 50 à 100 % selon les régions: Ximena FLORES PALACIOS, *Contribution à l'estimation de l'interdépendance des pays en matière de ressources phytogénétiques.* Étude de fond, N° 7, Rev.1, W/W5246/f-F, Rome, 1997, 28p. [en ligne] [ftp://ftp.fao.org/docrep/fao/meeting/015/j0747e.pdf] (consulté le 14 décembre 2013).

[19] Gerald MOORE et Witold TYMOWSKI, *Guide explicatif du traité international sur les ressources phytogénétiques pour l'alimentation et l'agriculture*, Bonn, UICN, N° 57, 2008, p. 3.

depuis l'invention de l'agriculture ; le renouvellement de celle-ci se doit d'être pérenne. Le Traité sur les ressources phytogénétiques ambitionne le renouvellement de l'agrobiodiversité, protège les ressources alimentaires et facilite l'accès ainsi que la circulation de ces ressources pour une meilleure sécurité alimentaire mondiale durable. La conservation et l'utilisation durables des ressources de l'agrobiodiversité deviennent des obligations à la charge de toutes les Parties contractantes dans une approche différenciée du Nord au Sud, en fonction de leurs capacités techniques et financières, conformément au droit international[20]. Ces exigences constituent la première des obligations prescrites par le Traité sur les ressources phytogénétiques, mais elle ne saurait être complète sans un accès facilité aux ressources ainsi conservées. Il est en effet essentiel que tous aient accès au plus large éventail possible de ressources qu'elles soient rustiques ou améliorées. Les sélectionneurs utilisent parfois des variétés locales provenant de 20 à 30 pays dans la création d'une nouvelle variété végétale[21]. Aussi la coopération internationale et la libre circulation des ressources génétiques végétales contribuent à la richesse héréditaire utile à l'atteinte de la sécurité alimentaire de tous les pays. L'érosion des ressources biologiques pose un problème de taille au sein d'une société qui demeure dépendante des services écosystémiques rendus par la nature. Outre les services esthétiques (beauté des paysages naturels) et culturels[22], les services d'approvisionnement, notamment alimentaire, s'étiolent au même rythme que disparait la diversité génétique des plantes comestibles. Aujourd'hui, le riz, le blé, le maïs et les plantes sucrières représentent à elles seules 65 % de l'apport énergétique d'origine végétale[23].

Si l'on considère l'atteinte de la sécurité alimentaire, le respect du droit à l'alimentation, la réduction de la pauvreté et l'utilisation durable des éléments de biodiversité agricole comme prééminents dans l'échelle des

---

[20] Le principe de la *responsabilité commune et différenciée* est issu du Principe 7 de la *Déclaration de Rio sur l'environnement et le développement*, Rio de Janeiro, Brésil, 3-14 juin 1992, A/CONF.151/26.

[21] G. MOORE et W. TYMOWSKI, préc., note 19, p. 3.

[22] « […] attachement des peuples à leurs territoires, aux paysages ou aux espèces qui les caractérisent », V. MARIS, préc., note 16, p.102.

[23] G. MOORE et W. TYMOWSKI, préc., note 19, p. 5.

valeurs humaines, nous soutenons que le retour au libre accès des ressources alimentaires et agricoles est un objectif stratégique à l'avantage des agriculteurs et des paysans. Nous croyons que le *Système multilatéral d'accès et de partage des avantages* conçu par le Traité sur les ressources phytogénétiques possède une longueur d'avance sur les autres systèmes de droit au regard de l'accès et du partage « juste et équitable » des avantages des ressources améliorées, puis commercialisées. Le Système multilatéral s'applique aux ressources phytogénétiques pour l'alimentation et l'agriculture énumérées à l'Annexe I du Traité, sélectionnées et négociées par les parties contractantes sur la base des critères de sécurité alimentaire et d'interdépendance[24]. Le Système multilatéral constitue un *pool* commun de ressources phytogénétiques gérées et administrées par les Parties contractantes[25]. Elles deviennent accessibles aux fins de conservation et d'utilisation pour la recherche, la sélection et la formation pour l'alimentation et l'agriculture sur la base d'un simple accord de transfert de matériel[26]. En contrepartie, les bénéficiaires du Système ne peuvent revendiquer des droits de propriété intellectuelle sous la « forme reçue du Système multilatéral »[27]. L'objectif étant d'éliminer, autant que faire se peut, les restrictions à l'accès par opposition aux systèmes de DPI.

Le Traité de la FAO a mis en place un mécanisme de partage des avantages découlant de l'utilisation des ressources génétiques où l'équité vient rectifier une situation d'inégalité[28] créée par l'utilisation des ressources conservées par d'autres, pour un usage commun. L'accès facilité aux ressources phytogénétiques compte pour un avantage ; l'échange d'informations, l'accès aux technologies et le transfert de celles-ci, le renforcement des capacités ainsi que le partage des bénéfices découlant de la commercialisation des ressources constituent les autres avantages prévus par le

---

[24] FAO, Traité sur les ressources phytogénétiques, préc., note 17, art. 11.1. L'Annexe I contient 64 espèces cultivées vivrières et fourragères.

[25] *Ibid.*, art. 11. 2.

[26] FAO, Traité sur les ressources phytogénétiques, préc., note 17, art. 12.4. Par l'intermédiaire de cet accord, les utilisateurs s'engagent à redistribuer les bénéfices reçus de la commercialisation.

[27] Les dérivés du matériel génétique devront se distinguer de son parent sur plus d'un caractère, *ibid.*, art. 12.3(d).

[28] ARISTOTE, *Éthique à Nicomaque*, Paris, Librairie générale française, 1992, p. 229-230.

Traité[29]. Les profits de la commercialisation d'une variété améliorée sont versés dans un fonds fiduciaire géré par l'Organe directeur du Traité[30] au bénéfice de tous les usagers.

Si la terminologie empruntée par la FAO pour qualifier les ressources phytogénétiques parait s'éloigner du concept de patrimoine commun, force est de constater que plusieurs attributs demeurent identifiables. Par exemple, la motivation première pour la conservation, l'exploitation et le partage des ressources de l'agrobiodiversité demeure l'humanité en général, elle transcende autant que possible, les intérêts privés. La perte de l'agrobiodiversité - problème agronomique planétaire – et l'interdépendance des pays au regard des semences et des variétés végétales fournissent des arguments supplémentaires pour pousser les protagonistes à privilégier une gestion collective des ressources basée sur une *justice commutative* où l'équivalence des obligations et des charges sont librement consentis[31]. En outre l'absence d'exclusivisme ou de domination sur la ressource, la gestion pérenne et l'exploitation soutenable de celle-ci ainsi que le partage des résultats de la recherche et des bénéfices monétaires entre tous forment un ensemble de caractéristiques véhiculées et proposées par le Traité qui n'ont de cesse de nous ramener vers cet ancien statut juridique dont la congruence semblait incertaine[32].

Le traitement unique accordé aux ressources phytogénétiques par le Traité de la FAO confirme leur particularité. Elles sont essentielles au développement et au commerce agricoles et revêtent une importance capitale pour garantir la sécurité alimentaire mondiale durable et le respect du droit à l'alimentation.

---

[29] FAO, Traité sur les ressources phytogénétiques, préc., note 17, art. 13.2.

[30] L'Organe directeur est composé de toutes les Parties contractantes, *ibid.*, art. 19.1 et 19.3 f).

[31] ARISTOTE, préc., note 28, p.199-200.

[32] Christopher C. JOYNER, « Legal implications of the concept of the common heritage of mankind » (1986) 35 *International and Comparative Quartely*, 191-192; Kemal BASLAR, *The concept of the Common heritage of mankind in international law*, The Hague/Boston/London, Martinus Nijhoff Publishers, 1998, p.85 à 111.

Réflexions sur la volatilité des prix et la spéculation sur le marché des matières premières agricoles

Brice HUGOU *

La définition de la sécurité alimentaire établie par la FAO en 1996 précise que celle-ci « *est assurée quand toutes les personnes, en tout temps, ont économiquement, socialement et physiquement accès à une alimentation suffisante, sûre et nutritive qui satisfait leurs besoins nutritionnels et leurs préférences alimentaires pour leur permettre de mener une vie active et saine* »[1]. Bien qu'elles soient aussi indispensables à l'homme que l'air, les denrées alimentaires n'en demeurent pas moins des marchandises pouvant faire l'objet d'échanges commerciaux. Dès lors, toute personne qui souhaite se nourrir doit pouvoir être capable de produire – ou à défaut d'acheter – de quoi assurer sa subsistance. L'accès économique des personnes aux denrées alimentaires suppose donc que celles-ci soient mises sur le marché à un prix raisonnable pour l'acheteur et le vendeur. Il convient donc de s'interroger sur le processus de formation de ce prix.

La nature de l'activité agricole rend ce prix très difficile à fixer à un niveau idéal, celle-ci prenant place dans un temps long et devant composer avec divers aléas qui vont affecter les capacités de production des vendeurs, les besoins des acheteurs[2], soit l'offre et la demande. En effet, entre le moment où l'agriculteur va prendre la décision de semer ses semences et le moment où il procèdera à la récolte de sa production puis à sa vente, de nombreuses semaines ou mois vont s'écouler. Or, la survenance d'évènements climatiques, économiques, politiques ou encore sociaux peuvent bouleverser l'équilibre qui existait entre l'offre et la demande au moment où le producteur a pris la décision de semer, ce qui peut provoquer une forte volatilité des prix que beaucoup ont cherché à maîtriser.

* Doctorant de la Faculté de droit et des sciences politiques de Nantes, IRDP (E.A. 1166). Membre du programme Lascaux.

[1] ftp ://ftp.fao.org/es/ESA/policybriefs/pb–02–fr.pdf

[2] J. CORDIER, « Assurance, marchés financiers et puissance publique », *Économie Rurale*, 2001, n° 266, p. 111 ; F. DECLERCK et M. PORTIER, *Comment utiliser les marchés à termes agricoles et alimentaires*, France Agricole, 2007, pp. 19-21.

Certes, les pouvoirs publics ont, en différentes époques et en différents lieux, tenté d'encadrer le prix des denrées pour assurer la sécurité alimentaire en soustrayant sa détermination à la seule confrontation de l'offre et de la demande. En Égypte ancienne par exemple, certaines lois ont fixé des prix maximum dont il était impossible de s'écarter sous peine de sanctions[3]. Même constat en Grèce[4] ou en France avec certains capitulaires de Charlemagne. Mais la plupart de ces mesures ont été mal reçues, jugées inadaptées aux besoins du commerce, et finalement supprimées afin de laisser au marché le soin de réguler les prix.

Dans la pratique, la gestion de la volatilité du prix des denrées alimentaires s'est finalement surtout faite directement au moment des échanges entre les acheteurs et les vendeurs. En modifiant les modalités du contrat de vente, ceux-ci ont en effet créé des contrats à leur mesure qui leur permettaient à la fois de faire du commerce et de maîtriser la volatilité des prix. À l'origine, les modifications ont simplement consisté à adapter le contrat au temps qui s'écoule entre la production et la vente des biens en y ajoutant ce que l'on pourrait qualifier rétroactivement de terme suspensif. Celui-ci va avoir pour effet de différer l'exigibilité de l'obligation et permettre ainsi de s'accorder sur le prix à payer et les marchandises à livrer au moment de la formation du contrat, mais de ne procéder au paiement du prix et à la livraison de la marchandise que plus tard. C'est donc en dissociant les phases de formation et d'exécution du contrat que les conventions ont été adaptées afin de neutraliser les effets du passage du temps sur la valeur marchande de la marchandise. Le contrat a ainsi été modifié en vue de le doter d'une nouvelle finalité. Certes, il opère toujours le transfert de propriété de la marchandise, mais protège également en même temps les cocontractants contre la variation de son prix en créant entre l'acheteur et le vendeur « *un monde fermé, protégé, imperméable aux influences extérieures ou intérieures [...] qui traverse le temps sans être affecté par les*

---

[3] A. Berg, "The rise of commodity speculation: from villainous to venerable", in *Safeguarding food security in volatile global markets*, edited by Adam Prakash, FAO, 2011, p. 242, citant en partie J.-P. Lévy, *The Economic Life of the Ancient World*. University of Chicago Press, 1967.

[4] W.H. Waddington, *Édit de Dioclétien établissant le maximum dans l'Empire romain*, 1864, p. 5.

changements »[5]. Une fois le contrat conclu, peu importe que le prix de marché du bien ne soit plus le même au moment de l'exécution du contrat : les parties qui se sont engagées à livrer une marchandise et à payer un prix déterminés demeurent définitivement tenues par le contrat. Elles sont donc assurées de ne pas subir l'influence des variations des prix du marché et de recevoir ce qu'elles s'étaient promis lorsqu'elles se sont engagées.

Mais si les contrats se sont révélés être des outils très efficaces, le fait de laisser au secteur privé le soin de maîtriser les variations de prix a toutefois eu certaines conséquences dès lors que, là où les pouvoirs publics peuvent établir des normes afin d'assurer la sécurité alimentaire, les personnes privées pensent avant tout à assurer leurs propres intérêts. Or, les contrats demeurent des outils dont l'usage dépend de la volonté des parties, et ceux qui permettent de maîtriser la volatilité des prix peuvent être utilisés dans des optiques opposées de protection contre le risque (la « couverture ») et de son exploitation (la « spéculation »).

Assez logiquement, puisque ce fut le but de leur création, les contrats furent d'abord utilisés pour des opérations de couverture. L'acheteur qui craignait une hausse contractait avec le vendeur qui craignait une baisse, et ils se protégeaient ainsi réciproquement de toute variation de prix qui pourrait pénaliser leurs marges. Néanmoins, il ne peut y avoir en permanence une adéquation parfaite entre ceux qui souhaitent se couvrir contre la hausse et la baisse des prix. Or, cette absence d'équilibre aboutirait à ce que certains ne puissent pas se couvrir faute de cocontractant disponible, ce qui a rendu l'intervention de tiers nécessaires. Ces tiers sont historiquement les premiers spéculateurs : ils acceptent de prendre la place d'un acheteur ou d'un vendeur au sein d'un rapport contractuel afin de lui permettre de se couvrir contre un risque. Se faisant, ils s'exposent au risque de perdre de l'argent, mais espèrent bien en gagner. Si les prix montent, le spéculateur-acheteur pourra en effet revendre plus cher le blé qu'il vient d'acheter. De son côté, le vendeur aura perdu l'occasion de faire une bonne affaire mais il n'aura pas perdu d'argent. Inversement, si les prix baissent, le spéculateur aura perdu de l'argent tandis que le vendeur ne subira pas les effets de la baisse des prix.

---

[5] C.Thibierge-Guelfucci, « Libres propos sur la transformation du droit des contrats », *RTD civ.*, 1997, p. 357.

Le problème, c'est que ces contrats ont connu un tel succès qu'ils ont été intégrés au sein des marchés et sont progressivement devenus de purs outils de gestion du risque de prix, abandonnant leur finalité première de soutenir des opérations commerciales. Et dès lors que les marchés permettent à un grand nombre d'acheteurs et de vendeurs de s'échanger un type de marchandise, ils jouent un rôle d'indicateurs des prix de cette marchandise et vont impacter tous les contrats conclus même en dehors de son enceinte. Or si la capacité à maitriser un risque de prix n'était au départ qu'un effet secondaire du contrat, dont l'objet principal restait de procéder à la vente des denrées alimentaires, elle est progressivement devenue le but principal du contrat. En effet, les règles des marchés ont modifié les dispositions des contrats et introduit des dispositifs juridiques destinés à faire en sorte que le transfert de propriété des marchandises ne soit plus obligatoire mais seulement facultatif. En pratique, cela engendra une déconnexion quasi absolue entre le commerce et les opérations de gestion du risque de prix[6]. Au sein des règles des marchés, les denrées alimentaires sont ainsi considérées comme des actifs financiers comme les autres et plus aucune considération n'est accordée à la spécificité qu'elles tirent de leur caractère vital.

Économiquement, cette transition fut un véritable succès puisque ces marchés ont connu une croissance exponentielle. Mais si au départ il y avait dix commerçants qui cherchaient à se couvrir pour un seul spéculateur, le rapport s'est depuis inversé et ces derniers sont aujourd'hui beaucoup plus nombreux. Il apparaît donc que les prix des denrées alimentaires sont fortement influencés par les prix des marchés financiers, lesquels sont déterminés par des opérations qui sont pour la plupart de nature spéculative et non commerciale. Certes, le système est tout à fait efficace pour ceux qui y sont initiés. Sans intervention extérieure, il s'agit néanmoins d'un système dont l'efficacité n'est mesurée qu'à l'aune de ses performances intrinsèques et occulte toute préoccupation relative à la sécurité alimentaire.

---

[6] Sur les marchés financiers, 97 % des contrats ne s'exécutent pas par une livraison de la marchandise et constituent donc de pures opérations de gestion du risque de prix.

De là à dire qu'il n'y a dans la spéculation que des aspects négatifs, il n'y a qu'un pas que nous ne franchirons pas. D'abord parce que nous avons déjà souligné son utilité pour ceux qui cherchent à se couvrir contre le risque de variation des prix. Ensuite parce que même si la spéculation est admise, elle ne l'est qu'en respectant certaines règles qui visent à s'assurer qu'elle ne porte pas atteinte à la libre formation du prix. Néanmoins, cela ne doit pas masquer le fait que la croissance de la spéculation a poussé les marchés à adopter un fonctionnement parfois trop artificiel, ce qui inquiète lorsqu'on sait qu'ils participent à la détermination du prix des aliments que l'on consomme. En effet, les volumes de denrées alimentaires concernés par les contrats conclus sur les marchés financiers sont tels que si chacun demandait par exemple à prendre livraison du blé, il n'y aurait sûrement pas assez de blé sur terre pour que tous les contrats soient honorés.

Or, si les marchés ne sont finalement que des lieux au sein desquels « *des personnes vendent ce qu'elles ne possèdent pas à ceux qui n'en veulent pas* »[7], peut-on encore considérer qu'il s'agit bien d'offre et de demande de denrées alimentaires ?

Il est vrai que si l'on se contente de lire la lettre des contrats, ceux-ci prennent la forme de ventes assorties d'un terme, et prévoient que lors de la survenance de celui-ci, l'acheteur devra prendre livraison de la marchandise et en payer le prix au vendeur. Mais les mécanismes introduits par les marchés viennent court-circuiter le système en permettant de s'affranchir du transfert de propriété au profit du règlement d'une somme d'argent. Le prix du marché est donc formé par une somme de contrats qui sont annoncés comme pouvant donner lieu à une opération commerciale mais qui ne le feront pas pour la plupart.

C'est pourquoi sans aller jusqu'à interdire la spéculation sur les denrées alimentaires, ce qui a déjà été tenté plusieurs fois sans succès, il nous semble important de remettre un peu « d'ordre juridique » et de valeurs non marchandes dans le fonctionnement économique des marchés afin de ré-

---

[7] M. ROTHSTEIN, « Frank Norris and Popular Perceptions of the Market », *Agricultural History*, vol. 56, n° 1, janvier 1982, p. 58.

duire les effets négatifs qu'ils peuvent produire sur les prix des denrées, tout en conservant leur efficacité économique.

Le droit des contrats : outil de sécurité alimentaire dans le commerce et les investissements internationaux ?

Pierre-Etienne BOUILLOT *, Alhousseini DIABATE ** &
Fanny GARCIA ***

La sécurité alimentaire des pays du Nord n'est pas celle des pays du Sud. Aux objectifs de diversité, de qualité des produits, d'information et de santé des consommateurs des premiers, répondent des préoccupations vitales d'autosuffisance alimentaire des seconds, traversant la propriété des terres, leurs cultures, l'approvisionnement en produits agroalimentaires et en intrants.

Dès lors, les échanges commerciaux et les investissements internationaux dont les objets sont ces biens particuliers que sont la terre agricole et l'aliment, répondent à des objectifs inéluctablement différents, dont on sait qu'ils ne permettent pas pour l'essentiel, d'assurer l'effectivité du droit à l'alimentation, droit subjectif pourtant fondamental. Par ailleurs, au-delà de cette préoccupation essentielle, il peut s'avérer intéressant de s'interroger sur les outils contractuels qui régissent ces rapports économiques. S'il est bien un domaine dans lequel le sacro-saint principe de sécurité juridique n'est pas ébranlé, c'est celui des échanges agroalimentaires internationaux. Cependant, c'est paradoxalement à cet endroit qu'il est utile d'engager quelques réflexions.

D'une part parce que le prix à payer de la sécurité juridique ne peut être celui du surendettement et dans ce prolongement, de la famine de certaines populations du Sud, c'est-à-dire de l'insécurité alimentaire (I).

* Doctorant et attaché d'enseignement à l'Université de Nantes (France), Membre du Programme européen Lascaux.

** Doctorant à l'Université de Nantes (France), Membre du programme européen Lascaux et du Groupe de recherche (GRAAL) de la Faculté de droit privé de l'USJP de Bamako (Mali).

*** Maître de conférences en droit privé, Faculté de Droit de Vannes, Université de Bretagne-sud (France), Membre du Programme européen Lascaux, I.R.D.P., I.R.E.A., C.R.D.I.

D'autre part, parce que concevoir des outils permettant, si ce n'est de réviser, à tout le moins renégocier un contrat, ne constitue pas véritablement une entrave à la sécurité juridique, seulement aux objectifs économiques originels, ce qui est bien différent. Qu'est-ce qui pourrait justifier qu'un contrat soit renégocié ? La réponse la plus évidente est celle d'une clause spécifique. Toutefois, l'on sait les déséquilibres économiques qui gouvernent la formation de ces contrats internationaux, cela relève alors d'une déclaration d'intention utopique. En revanche, rechercher, parmi les outils contractuels internationaux, des principes permettant de renégocier un contrat, en situation de catastrophes naturelles (grande sécheresse), économico-sociales (famine), nous semble tant utile qu'impérieux (II).

I.- Le contrat, source potentielle d'insécurité alimentaire dans le commerce et les investissements internationaux

Ces dernières années les marchés internationaux des terres arables et des produits agroalimentaires ont connu un regain d'attractivité.

Guidés par des intérêts stratégiques pour assurer la sécurité de leurs approvisionnements alimentaires, certains États ont montré une appétence particulière pour les terres arables, et particulièrement en Afrique. Guidées par des intérêts essentiellement économiques, diverses entreprises sont également de la partie. L'investissement dans des terres arables est devenu rentable pour approvisionner des filières alimentaires de plus en plus consommatrices de protéines de soja ou pour remplir les réservoirs des voitures avec des agrocarburants. Derrière ces investissements se cachent des contrats de location - parfois à très long terme - ou d'achat, qui viennent bousculer les environnements locaux. Ici, des paysans sont expulsés de leurs terres ancestrales, là-bas ce sont des forêts primaires qui sont abattues au profit d'une culture de rente, chassant par la même occasion une communauté autochtone[1].

Le marché international des produits agroalimentaires s'est trouvé investi par les nouvelles technologies et partant la propriété industrielle,

[1] Sur ce point voir par exemple : L. DELCOURT, « L'avenir des agricultures paysannes face aux nouvelles pressions sur la terre », *In De la terre aux aliments, Des valeurs au droit,* F. COLLART DUTILLEUL (dir.), éd. Inida, San José, Costa Rica, 2012, pp. 94-124.

plus particulièrement par celle assortissant le commerce des organismes génétiquement modifiés. Nouvelle manne des industriels du Nord, le développement de ce marché singulier n'a pas épargné de sa conquête les pays du Sud. Or, l'économie agricole déjà fragilisée dans certains États africains par des catastrophes climatiques de sècheresse se trouve aujourd'hui terrassée suite aux initiatives d'exploitants autochtones dans les cultures de coton et de maïs génétiquement modifiés. Les OGM n'ont pas tenu leurs promesses scientifiques et ont plié sous les lois de la nature. Or, ces exploitants agricoles du continent africain, engagés dans des ensembles contractuels indivisibles divers (contrats de ventes, contrats de crédits) à exécution successive se trouvent dépourvus de tout espoir de récolte et en outre inéluctablement condamnés au surendettement. Certains États africains ont également apporté des aides au soutien de ces contrats, qui représentent alors un effort d'investissement dont les effets sont simultanément anéantis au seul profit des industriels des pays du Nord.

Ce constat impose alors de s'interroger sur les règles internationales qui entourent la formation et l'exécution de ces contrats, en ce qu'ils touchent à des biens particuliers et ont des conséquences économiques autant irréversibles que dramatiques pour les exploitants agricoles mais au-delà, pour les populations voire les États.

S'agissant de la formation de ces contrats, capacité juridique des parties mise à part, les premiers réflexes de recherche s'orientent autour du consentement des exploitants et de l'existence de la cause de l'obligation des industriels, mais cette dernière se révèle une exception juridico-culturelle française[2] à l'échelle du commerce international. C'est donc sur ce dernier point qu'il va convenir de s'arrêter spécifiquement. S'agissant de l'exécution des contrats, un certain nombre d'outils présentent de l'intérêt.

---

[2] La cause devrait toutefois être amenée à disparaître des conditions de formation du contrat, pour faire place à l'exigence d'un « *contenu licite et certain* », V. : *Avant-projet de réforme du droit des obligations*, ministère de la Justice, document de travail, 23 octobre 2013, spéc. art. 35 (préparant le *Projet de loi relatif à la modernisation et à la simplification du droit et des procédures dans les domaines de la justice et des affaires intérieures*, enregistré à la Présidence du Sénat le 27 novembre 2013, Projet n° 175).

II.- Les outils contractuels internationaux au service de la sécurité alimentaire

À l'heure où le Gouvernement français s'apprête à intégrer par voie d'ordonnance, au vu des Projets des Professeurs CATALA (2005) et TERRE (2013), une obligation de renégociation des contrats en cas d'imprévision[3], la recherche dans les outils contractuels internationaux de mécanismes similaires est fondée car ces divers Projets ont été élaborés, entre autres, à la lumière des droits européen et international des contrats.

La difficulté, concernant les règles générales gouvernant les contrats dans le domaine du commerce et des investissements internationaux, est qu'elles relèvent de différentes sources, relatives aux contrats dans le domaine du droit international en général, d'une part, dans le domaine du droit agroalimentaire international en particulier. L'on recense, dans ce qui s'apparente à une sorte de droit commun international des échanges internationaux, un ensemble normatif très vaste, lui-même issu de diverses sources : la *lex mercatoria*, les Accords de l'OMC – Accords ADPIC, de Marrakech, MIC ... -, les textes de la CNUDCI – dont le CVIM -, les principes UNIDROIT[4], la reconnaissance d'une *lex publica*[5], ainsi que de multiples conventions bi- et multilatérales. Appliquées plus spécifiquement au commerce des produits agroalimentaires, il convient d'y ajouter les règles issues du *Codex Alimentarius,* la Convention UPOV.

C'est en leur sein qu'il convient de rechercher des outils contractuels permettant de renégocier les contrats internationaux, en cas d'imprévision, qu'il s'agisse d'ailleurs de contrats relatifs au commerce comme aux inves-

---

[3] « *La théorie de l'imprévision sera en outre consacrée, offrant aux parties la possibilité d'adapter le contrat en cas de changement imprévisible de circonstances rendant l'exécution excessivement onéreuse pour celle qui n'aurait pas accepté d'en assumer le risque* », Exposé des motifs, extraits, *Projet de loi relatif à la modernisation et à la simplification du droit et des procédures dans les domaines de la justice et des affaires intérieures*, enregistré à la Présidence du Sénat le 27 novembre 2013, Projet n° 175. Et V. spéc. art. 3, 6° : le Gouvernement devra « *préciser les règles relatives aux effets du contrat entre les parties et à l'égard des tiers, en consacrant la possibilité pour celles-ci d'adapter leur contrat en cas de changement imprévisible de circonstances* ». V. art. 104 (« changement de circonstances »), *Avant-projet de réforme du droit des obligations*, ministère de la Justice, document de travail, 23 octobre 2013.

[4] Principes d'UNIDROIT relatifs aux contrats du commerce international, 2010.

[5] X. BOUCOBZA, « La méthode de promotion de la sécurité alimentaire. Une application de la *lex publica* ? », *RIDE* 2012/4, pp. 71-85.

tissements[6]. Naturellement, le caractère d'ordre public de ces mécanismes contractuels internationaux permettra d'imposer aux différents acteurs une renégociation du contrat, alors que cela est plus limité voire impossible s'agissant des règles d'ordre public interne. Il s'agirait à cet endroit, de renforcer l'ordre public international visant à protéger des intérêts particuliers que sont les intérêts humains et sociaux, c'est-à-dire non marchands[7], inhérents à l'ambivalence de l'objet de ces contrats, touchant au droit économique et aux droits de l'homme. C'est dans la conjugaison de ces intérêts, en se départissant de leur opposition naturelle[8] et sans renoncer à l'un ou aux autres, que doit être reconnu l'ordre public international contractuel, dans sa double dimension : marchande et non marchande. En effet, d'une part les biens agroalimentaires sont régis comme tout contrat portant sur des biens par des intérêts marchands, cela relève de l'évidence ; d'autre part, et c'est la spécificité de ces produits, en ce qu'ils assoient le droit fondamental à l'alimentation, il convient de renforcer l'ordre public non marchand encore à l'état de prémices, mais qui existe en germe, il ne faudrait donc pas le créer mais plus simplement le reconnaître – à cet endroit il reste indéniable que l'outil juridique ne sera efficace que par un levier politique, une volonté politique commune, afin de défendre un droit fondamental vital. Pour les convaincre, il est possible de rappeler que le droit à l'alimentation s'inscrit dans un cercle vertueux, qui emporte avec lui,

---

[6] Pour une étude détaillée : F. COLLART DUTILLEUL, A. DIABATE, « La sécurité alimentaire et le droit à l'alimentation à l'épreuve des investissements internationaux en Afrique de l'Ouest : les risques d'une désillusion », HAL 2013 (accessible en ligne) ; F. COLLART DUTILLEUL, « La problématique juridique des investissements dans les terres agricoles des pays en développement », *Rev. dr. unif.* 2012-1/2, pp. 73-88.

[7] Plus largement sur ce point : F. COLLART DUTILLEUL, V. PIRONON, « Droit économique et sécurité alimentaire », *RIDE* 2012/4, spéc. pp. 11-13 ; Cl. JOURDAIN-FORTIER, E. LOQUIN, « Droit du commerce international et sécurité alimentaire », *RIDE* 2012/4, spéc. pp. 45-46 ; H. ULLRICH, « La mondialisation du droit économique : vers un nouvel ordre public économique. Rapport introductif », *RIDE* 2003/3, spéc. pp. 308-309.

Plus spécifiquement, appliqué aux brevets : J.-P. CLAVIER, « Les dérogations au monopole en droit des brevets », *in Aspects juridiques de la valorisation des denrées alimentaires, Actes du colloque international, San José, Costa Rica*, 29-30 novembre 2010, Siedin, 2011, spéc. pp. 109-113.

[8] En ce sens : G. PARENT, « Droit économique et sécurité alimentaire : un couple mal assorti ? », *RIDE* 2012/4, pp. 15-19.

l'effectivité de différents droits subjectifs fondamentaux – le droit à la santé, le droit à la vie, le droit à l'emploi - et partant, la relance de l'économie généralisée à l'ensemble d'un pays, les efforts ponctuels ne sont donc rien de moins que des investissements pour l'avenir en réalité.

Tout en gardant comme fil rouge celui de la sécurité juridique, il est possible d'envisager différents mécanismes invocables par les opérateurs contraints à l'inexécution malgré eux. Les causes de la mise en œuvre de ces outils, les « faits justificatifs »[9] d'une renégociation des contrats pourraient être divers et s'apparenter à un événement de force majeure, c'est-à-dire revêtant les caractères d'imprévisibilité et d'irrésistibilité : sécheresse, famine, crise économique grave. En fonction de la gravité des faits justificatifs (personnels au cocontractant ou généralisés à une sous-région ou un État), ils pourraient s'étendre de la suspension de l'exécution, à l'aménagement voire la renégociation de la contrepartie pécuniaire. L'on pourrait envisager, dans ce prolongement, que les compagnies d'assurance trouvent utilement à s'investir, à l'instar des polices offertes aux propriétaires bailleurs afin de se protéger d'éventuels loyers impayés. De façon ponctuelle, mais cette mesure est plus politique que juridique, la suspension des importations, lorsque les terres sont exploitées par des investisseurs étrangers, devrait relever de l'ordre public international non marchand, lorsqu'il en va de la survie de populations locales. Par ailleurs, cette voie reste, malgré les enjeux vitaux qui en dépendent, encore contrainte par le principe de la libre concurrence, du jeu – naturellement reconnu par l'OMC - du marché.

Concrètement, un certain nombre de textes peuvent déjà être mis à profit, dans le sens d'une renégociation de contrats commerciaux internationaux, sous réserve de leur intégration dans l'ordre public international.

À titre de premier exemple, nous pouvons citer l'Accord international de la FAO de 2012 relatif à la Gouvernance responsable des régimes foncier, qui prévoit à titre préventif comme à titre de sanction, de réguler les

[9] En ce sens : F. COLLART DUTILLEUL, V. PIRONON, « Droit économique et sécurité alimentaire », *RIDE* 2012/4, spéc. p. 10.

manquements aux droits fondamentaux[10], voire de procéder éventuellement à des restitutions[11].

Par ailleurs, au sein des Principes UNIDROIT, nombre de règles appuient une obligation de renégociation, ou plus largement, offrent des sanctions : en cas « d'avantage excessif », la sanction par la nullité du contrat ou de la clause litigieuse, fondée sur le manquement à la bonne foi et/ou à la loyauté[12] ; en cas de circonstances entraînant une altération fondamen-

---

[10] FAO, Directives volontaires pour une gouvernance responsable des régimes fonciers, applicables aux terres, aux pêches et aux forêts dans le contexte de la sécurité alimentaire nationale, Rome, 11 mai 2012, spéc. point 3.2 : « *Les acteurs non étatiques, y compris les entreprises, sont tenus de respecter les droits de l'homme et les droits fonciers légitimes. Les entreprises devraient agir avec la diligence nécessaire afin d'éviter d'empiéter sur les droits fondamentaux et les droits fonciers légitimes d'autrui. Elles devraient prévoir des systèmes adaptés de gestion des risques afin de prévenir les violations des droits de l'homme et des droits fonciers légitimes et de remédier à leurs effets. Les entreprises devraient prévoir des mécanismes non judiciaires, ou coopérer avec de tels mécanismes, afin d'offrir des voies de recours, y compris, s'il y a lieu, des mécanismes efficaces de règlement des différends au niveau opérationnel, pour les cas où elles auront porté atteinte à des droits de l'homme ou à des droits fonciers légitimes ou joué un rôle à cet égard. Les entreprises devraient identifier et évaluer toute violation potentielle ou avérée des droits de l'homme ou de droits fonciers légitimes dans laquelle elles auraient pu jouer un rôle. Les États devraient, conformément aux obligations internationales qui leur incombent, assurer l'accès à des voies de recours efficaces en cas d'atteinte aux droits de l'homme ou à des droits fonciers légitimes par des entreprises. Dans le cas des sociétés transnationales, les États d'origine doivent fournir une assistance tant à ces sociétés qu'aux États d'accueil afin de garantir que les sociétés en question ne contribuent pas à des atteintes aux droits de l'homme ou à des droits fonciers légitimes. Les États devraient prendre des mesures supplémentaires pour prévenir les violations des droits de l'homme et des droits fonciers légitimes par des entreprises appartenant à l'État ou contrôlées par celui-ci, ou bénéficiant d'un appui ou de services importants de la part d'organismes publics* ».

[11] FAO, Directives volontaires pour une gouvernance responsable des régimes fonciers, applicables aux terres, aux pêches et aux forêts dans le contexte de la sécurité alimentaire nationale, op.cit., spéc. point 14. Plus largement à cet égard : F. COLLART DUTILLEUL, A. DIABATE, « La sécurité alimentaire et le droit à l'alimentation à l'épreuve des investissements internationaux en Afrique de l'Ouest : les risques d'une désillusion », HAL 2013 (accessible en ligne) ; F. COLLART DUTILLEUL, « La problématique juridique des investissements dans les terres agricoles des pays en développement », *Rev. dr. unif.* 2012-1/2, pp. 73-88.

[12] Notamment lorsque l'une des parties a « *profité d'une manière déloyale de l'état de dépendance, de la détresse économique, de l'urgence des besoins, de l'imprévoyance, de l'ignorance, de l'inexpérience ou de l'inaptitude à la négociation* » de l'autre partie, art. 3.2.7, Principes d'UNIDROIT, préc. Dans le prolonge-

tale de l'équilibre des prestations (l'imprévision de la culture juridique française, le principe de *hardship* de la culture du commerce international), l'ouverture de renégociations du contrat est envisageable[13] ; à l'inverse la force majeure (l'*empêchement,* ou *frustration* dans la culture du commerce international) permettra davantage de sortir du contrat, en étant exonéré de sa responsabilité[14].

En conclusion, le droit des contrats offre des outils pouvant utilement servir à l'objectif de sécurité alimentaire dans le cadre du commerce et des investissements internationaux. Pour s'en convaincre il suffit d'observer, les outils contractuels internationaux, permettant au cocontractant, qu'il s'agisse d'ailleurs d'un exploitant-particulier ou d'un Etat, de renégocier le contrat en cas de déséquilibre économique excessif, de ne pas exécuter son obligation contractuelle en invoquant un fait justificatif, ou, en cas de force majeure d'envisager purement et simplement la rupture du lien contractuel. Toutefois, pour faire de ces outils des mécanismes permettant de concourir efficacement à la sécurité alimentaire, il est nécessaire, sans occulter les valeurs marchandes, de renforcer l'ordre public non marchand dans le commerce et les investissements internationaux.

ment de cette sanction, des restitutions sont dues, V. art. 3.2.15 et 7.3.2, Principes d'UNIDROIT, *préc.*

[13] Art. 6.2.3, Principes d'UNIDROIT, *préc.*

[14] Art. 7.1.7 et 6.2.2 (6.), Principes d'UNIDROIT, *préc.*

Les circuits courts et de proximité face à la libre circulation des marchandises : une reconnaissance parcellaire

Pierre-Etienne BOUILLOT *

La démocratie est un régime politique dans lequel le pouvoir est exercé pour le peuple, par le peuple ou ses représentants élus. La démocratie alimentaire s'exprimerait-elle par un vote spécifique pour nos « représentants alimentaires » ? À notre connaissance, aucun peuple ne décide directement de son alimentation, ni n'élit un représentant spécial à l'alimentation. Rares sont les partis politiques à s'attarder sur cette question dans leurs programmes de campagne, c'est pourtant un sujet qui concerne quotidiennement les citoyens. Certes, nos représentants agissent en la matière, mais sans mandat spécifique à ce propos. D'une certaine manière, nous votons chaque jour, à chaque repas, un vote qui s'opère par nos choix de consommation[1] : végétarien par conviction, consommateur de produits biologiques et équitables, de produits de marques, ou de produits locaux ; dans la rue, au fast-food, à la cantine, au restaurant...

Si l'on imagine cette « démocratie alimentaire » dans laquelle le consommateur-citoyen s'exprimerait par un suffrage direct sur ce qu'il souhaite manger, que choisirait-il ? Voterait-il en pensant directement au contenu de son assiette ou prêterait-il attention à la provenance de ses produits, aux circuits qu'ils intègrent et en particulier, voterait-il pour le raccourcissement des filières agroalimentaires ? Si c'est le cas, il serait bien inspiré si l'on en croit le Rapporteur spécial des Nations Unies sur le droit à l'alimentation, O. De Schutter, qui démontre que la mondialisation de la chaîne alimentaire est source d'insécurité alimentaire. En effet, outre ses effets néfastes sur les systèmes alimentaires locaux et sur l'environnement, eu égard notam-

---

* Doctorant Lascaux et Attaché temporaire d'enseignement et de recherche à la Faculté de droit de l'Université de Nantes.

[1] V. not. : Rencontres internationales « Penser une démocratie alimentaire », 25-26 et 27 novembre 2013 à Nantes, Table ronde « penser un nouveau contrat social pour préserver les ressources naturelles et nourrir l'humanité », [en ligne], http://webtv.univ-nantes.fr/fiche/4106/table-ronde-penser-un-nouveau-contrat-social-pour-preserver-les-ressources-naturelles-et-nourrir-l-humanite

ment à l'empreinte carbone des produits, la mondialisation du commerce des aliments est également responsable de déséquilibres sanitaires[2].

Le raccourcissement des chaînes d'approvisionnement implique le développement des circuits courts et de proximité par rapport aux circuits dits longs. Les circuits courts[3] se caractérisent par un nombre restreint d'intermédiaires (inférieur ou égal à un) entre le producteur et le consommateur ; au-delà, il s'agit d'un circuit long[4]. Les circuits de proximité s'inscrivent dans une approche spatiale des circuits de distribution et renvoient à la proximité géographique entre le lieu de production et le lieu de consommation de l'aliment.

Ces circuits sont reconnus comme favorisant une alimentation plus saine[5] et à des prix abordables pour le consommateur. Cela repose sur le fait qu'ils ne sont pas contrôlés « *par de grands distributeurs ou entreprises agroindustrielles et ne dépendent pas de politiques nationales qui obéissent à des intérêts économiques plus larges* »[6]. Ils permettent ainsi une autre distribution de la valeur ajoutée. De plus, les circuits courts favorisent l'accès au marché des agriculteurs locaux et donc les circuits de proximité, tant dans les pays du Nord que dans les pays du Sud[7]. Sur ce point, le développement des circuits de proximité favorise la biodiversité agricole en privilégiant les variétés locales à celles uniformisées qui sont destinées aux marchés mondiaux[8]. En outre, selon O. De Schutter, les circuits courts

---

[2] Rapport soumis par le Rapporteur spécial sur le droit à l'alimentation, O. DE SCHUTTER, 2011, A/HRC/19/59, § 35 et s.

[3] À ce propos : P.-E. BOUILLOT, « Circuits courts », *Dictionnaire de la sécurité alimentaire dans le monde*, F. COLLART DUTILLEUL (dir.), Larcier, 2013, p. 156.

[4] V. en ce sens : N. DISSAUX, « Distribution-Généralités », *JCl. Concurrence consommation*, fasc. 600, n° 6.

[5] OMS, « Prévention et maîtrise des maladies non transmissibles », Rapport du Secrétaire général, A/66/83, 19 mai 2011, n° 60.

[6] O. DE SCHUTTER, *op. cit.*, A/HRC/19/59, § 44 ; FAO, "Food, Agriculture and Cities: Challenges of food and nutrition security, agriculture and ecosystem management in an urbanizing world", FAO Food for the Cities multi-disciplinary initiative position paper, 2011, p. 29.

[7] Rapport, *op. cit.*, A/HRC/19/59, § 44.

[8] Les bénéfices en termes de protection de l'environnement sont également appréciables par rapport aux pratiques agricoles. En effet, les agriculteurs engagés dans ces circuits cultivent souvent en agriculture biologique. *Cf.* : G. MARECHALA, A. SPANU, « Les circuits courts favorisent-ils l'adoption de pratiques agricoles plus

comme les circuits de proximité participent à la réduction des dépenses énergétiques en limitant l'emballage et le transport des aliments[9].

À plus d'un titre, le raccourcissement des circuits des filières agroalimentaires, tant sur le plan relationnel (circuit court) que sur le plan géographique (circuit de proximité), est vecteur de potentialités positives, particulièrement pour la sécurité alimentaire.

Dès lors, pour « penser une démocratie alimentaire » il convient de s'attarder sur la place que donne le droit à la réduction des intermédiaires et des distances entre « la fourche et la fourchette ». Le sujet est vaste et peu abordé par la doctrine sous cet angle[10]. Il y aurait sans doute beaucoup à dire sur l'influence du droit du commerce international sur les circuits de distribution et par exemple sur leur responsabilité dans la déstabilisation des circuits locaux[11]. En effet, il est difficile de privilégier des producteurs nationaux ou de prévoir un système dérogatoire pour les produits locaux, sans que ces mesures ne soient qualifiées de mesures d'effet équivalent à une barrière tarifaire ou d'aide d'État portant atteinte à la libre circulation des marchandises. En France, l'évolution législative récente relative aux circuits courts et de proximité atteste de ces difficultés.

---

respectueuses de l'environnement ? », *Courrier de l'environnement de l'INRA*, n° 59, octobre 2010, p. 33 et s.

[9] Sur ce dernier point, un rapport remet en cause l'idée reçue selon laquelle ces circuits sont moins émetteurs de gaz à effets de serre (GES) que les circuits classiques. En effet, on pouvait penser que la réduction des distances de transport des produits alimentaires entraînait une réduction des émissions de ces gaz. Cependant, le rapport montre d'une part, que la phase de transport compte pour une partie mineure du bilan carbone des denrées alimentaires (17 %), et d'autre part, que le commerce local implique souvent l'utilisation de moyens de transports (camionnette) dont le ratio émissions de GES à la tonne/kilomètre est largement plus élevé que celui des moyens de transports utilisés par les circuits plus longs (bateau, camion, train...) *Cf.* : Commissariat général au développement durable, « Consommer local, les avantages ne sont pas toujours ceux que l'on croit », *Le point sur...*, n° 158, mars 2013, 4 p.

[10] V. spéc.: G. THEVENOT, « Politique agricole de promotion des circuits courts : quelle place pour la protection de l'environnement ? », *Droit de l'environnement*, n° 204, sept 2012, p. 263-272.

[11] V. l'exemple du marché de l'oignon au Sénégal : C. JOURDAIN-FORTIER, V. PIRONON, « La sécurité alimentaire dans le droit de l'OMC ; analyse critique et prospective », *in Penser une démocratie alimentaire*, F. COLLART DUTILLEUL (dir.) vol. 1, Inida, 2013, p. 256.

Depuis la loi de modernisation de l'agriculture de 2010 (LMA), le développement des circuits courts et de proximité est un objectif de la politique publique de l'alimentation. Cette politique, développée par le Gouvernement, vise à assurer la sécurité alimentaire ; elle est définie dans le programme national de l'alimentation, qui vise notamment à « *développer des circuits courts, [encourager] la proximité géographique entre producteurs et transformateurs et l'approvisionnement en produits agricoles locaux dans la restauration collective publique comme privée* », selon l'article L. 230-1 du Code rural. Ces objectifs étant posés, ils ont été intégrés différemment selon que les opérateurs se situent sur un marché public (1) ou un marché privé (2).

1. Les marchés publics : une reconnaissance partielle

Dans le cadre des marchés publics, le législateur français a traduit cet intérêt des circuits courts pour la sécurité alimentaire, mais les critères liés à l'implantation géographique n'ont pas été retenus.

Depuis 2011, la législation a intégré les objectifs que s'est fixé l'État français dans la loi de modernisation de l'agriculture de 2010 concernant les circuits courts. Le législateur a admis une exception pour les produits agroalimentaires en ajoutant un critère d'attribution aux dispositions de l'article 53 du Code des marchés publics. Le pouvoir adjudicateur peut ainsi se fonder sur les « *performances en matière de développement des approvisionnements directs de produits de l'agriculture* » pour attribuer un marché. Cette disposition offre la possibilité aux personnes publiques de fonder l'attribution d'un marché au candidat qui a présenté l'offre économiquement la plus avantageuse au regard notamment de la longueur du circuit de distribution. Elle permet ainsi de favoriser le circuit le plus court. Toutefois, techniquement, le critère de l'approvisionnement direct pourrait également bénéficier à un producteur non français, puisqu'ici c'est le critère relationnel qui est mis en avant. Dès lors, si les circuits courts ont tendance à favoriser la proximité géographique entre le producteur et le consommateur, cela n'est pas une conséquence directe des effets de ce régime.

À ce propos, la proximité géographique ne peut servir de critère d'attribution d'un marché. Les clauses de préférences régionales sont condamnées par la haute juridiction de l'Union européenne[12] et par les juridictions administratives françaises. La proximité géographique de l'agriculteur ne peut servir de critère à l'attribution d'un marché, quand bien même cela favoriserait l'activité économique et sociale locale[13] ou limiterait les émissions de CO_2[14]. En arrière-plan, c'est à la protection de la libre-circulation des marchandises que se heurte ici la promotion des circuits de proximité. La protection de cette liberté économique influence également les marchés privés.

2. Les marchés privés : l'absence de reconnaissance

Sur les marchés privés, ces circuits bénéficient de quelques exonérations[15] qui existaient antérieurement à la reconnaissance de leur importance dans les textes. Leur caractère anecdotique et leur cohérence ne permettent pas d'identifier un régime spécifique et les objectifs énoncés par la LMA n'ont pas pris pied dans les marchés privés. Le régime juridique appliqué aux circuits courts et de proximité est celui de tout circuit de distribution agroalimentaire. Il n'est pas fait de distinction entre les circuits longs, les circuits courts et les circuits de proximité. Ceux-ci sont soumis au même régime libéral et notamment à la libre circulation des marchandises et à la liberté contractuelle. Ainsi, les produits agroalimentaires doivent circuler librement ; les opérateurs ne doivent pas, par exemple, entraver ce fonctionnement. Ainsi, les opérateurs de la filière sont libres dans la manière de céder ou d'acheter les produits, et donc dans leur façon de fonctionner, ou non, en circuits courts et de proximité.

Dans ce contexte libéral, il est possible de s'attarder sur deux points. Concernant les circuits courts, nous évoquerons les faiblesses de la voie

---

[12] Dans un arrêt du 11 juillet 1991, la Cour de justice a interprété les dispositions du traité comme s'opposant à ce qu'une réglementation nationale réserve aux entreprises établies dans certaines régions un pourcentage des marchés publics. CJCE, 11 juill. 1991, aff. C-351/88, Rec. CJCE 1991, I, p. 3641.

[13] V. en ce sens. : CE, 29 juill. 1994, n° 131562, cne Ventenac-en-Minervois; Rec. CE 1994, p. 1035.

[14] Rép. min. n° 10874, JO Sénat Q 21 janv. 2010, p. 130.

[15] Par exemple, le « paquet hygiène » ne s'applique pas totalement aux agriculteurs vendant directement au consommateur final (v. not. : Règlement (CE) n° 853/2004 fixant des règles spécifiques d'hygiène applicables aux denrées alimentaires d'origine animale, n° 12).

contractuelle telle qu'elle est proposée depuis la LMA (a). Concernant les circuits de proximité, nous verrons que l'information du consommateur pourrait être un levier pour leur promotion (b).

a) Circuits courts : les faiblesses de la voie contractuelle.

Si les objectifs énoncés dans la LMA à propos des circuits courts n'ont pas été traduits dans l'organisation des marchés privés, d'autres ont fait l'objet d'une attention particulière de la part du législateur. Les objectifs affichés étaient également d'introduire de la transparence dans la relation commerciale et d'offrir une sécurité juridique et économique à la partie faible du contrat, le producteur, et de développer la compétitivité de l'agriculture française. À cet effet, le législateur a introduit des dispositions spécifiques à la contractualisation des relations commerciales agricoles[16]. Si cette innovation était attendue dans certains secteurs, la mise en œuvre de la contractualisation n'a pas le même effet sur les différents types de circuits de distribution.

L'incitation à la conclusion de contrats de vente écrits entre les producteurs et les acheteurs apparaît contraire au développement des circuits courts. Les contrats-types négociés au sein des interprofessions prévoient des clauses relatives à la durée du contrat afin de stabiliser les relations commerciales dans le temps. Cette stabilité est profitable au producteur, car elle lui offre une meilleure prévisibilité des besoins et donc de ce qu'il doit produire. Toutefois, en fixant une durée minimale d'engagement, l'Autorité de la concurrence signale que cela pourrait nuire aux circuits courts[17]. Cette durée minimale fixe la périodicité de la revalorisation du prix fixé par le contrat, période sur laquelle les cocontractants partagent les risques. Or, plus le contrat est long, plus ce risque devient élevé et plus il est difficile pour les parties de s'accorder sur une formule d'indexation. Cette périodicité doit être étudiée avec attention, et l'Autorité de la concurrence a estimé que celle-ci était trop longue pour deux des accords inter-

[16] Plus largement sur la contractualisation des relations commerciales agricoles : C. DEL CONT, « Filières agroalimentaires et contrat : l'expérience française de contractualisation des relations commerciales agricoles », *Rivista di diritto alimentare*, Anno VI, n° 4 - Ottobre-Dicembre 2012, pp. 23-35.

[17] L'article L. 632-4 du Code rural et de la pêche maritime a rendu obligatoire la consultation de l'Autorité de la concurrence sur tout projet d'accord conclu dans le cadre d'une organisation interprofessionnelle définissant des clauses-types.

professionnels qu'elle a eu à viser[18]. Son instruction fait notamment ressortir l'exemple des détaillants de fruits et légumes dont la valeur ajoutée réside dans la proposition chaque semaine d'un choix varié et de qualité à leurs clients, qui serait remise en cause par un contrat direct à long terme avec un producteur.

L'Autorité de la concurrence soulève à juste titre qu'il y a « *dès lors un arbitrage à faire entre un gain de court terme pour le consommateur et un choix de plus long terme consistant à préserver la production française* ». De ce point de vue, il n'est pas sûr qu'un marché libre soit le plus apte à opérer cet arbitrage.

b) Circuits de proximité : les vertus de l'information.

Concernant les circuits de proximité, c'est le consommateur même qui peut être placé comme arbitre, si on lui donne les informations nécessaires à ce rôle[19]. Certes, indiquer, ne serait-ce que le pays d'origine, devient très compliqué lorsqu'il s'agit d'un produit transformé et intégrant de multiples ingrédients.

Mises à part quelques pratiques volontaires aux moyens de marques[20] et d'associations[21] et certains produits bruts (fruits, légumes, viandes), le consommateur n'a pas les moyens d'opérer ce choix. L'exercice d'un libre choix, c'est-à-dire d'un choix véritablement éclairé se révèle alors difficile et partant, constitue une entrave à l'exercice d'une démocratie alimentaire.

---

[18] Avis n° 10-A-28 du 13 décembre 2010 relatif à deux projets de décret imposant la contractualisation dans des secteurs agricoles, 10-A-28, n° 21 à 26.

[19] V. : M. FRIANT-PERROT, « Information et qualité des aliments : de l'étiquette à l'assiette, comment garantir au consommateur européen le choix de son alimentation ? », *in Penser une démocratie alimentaire*, F. COLLART DUTILLEUL (dir.) vol. 1, Inida, 2013, p. 437.

[20] V. par ex. : la marque simple qui allie circuits courts et circuits de proximité « *produits de chez nous partenariat direct avec les producteurs locaux* » (titulaire : SODIRETZ).

[21] V. par ex. : les AMAP (associations pour le maintien d'une agriculture paysanne) qui ont pour objectif de favoriser le maintien d'une agriculture locale. Elles réunissent des producteurs agricoles et des consommateurs. Ces derniers sont donc informés de la provenance des produits qu'ils consomment.

À ce titre, sans intervenir directement sur les marchés privés, le législateur a la possibilité de rendre obligatoire l'indication de l'origine du produit et ainsi de permettre au consommateur de choisir le produit offrant le meilleur rapport qualité/prix au regard de la distance qu'aura parcourue le produit. La LMA a modifié le Code de la consommation en ce sens. L'article L. 112-11 dispose que *« l'indication du pays d'origine peut être rendue obligatoire pour les produits agricoles et alimentaires et les produits de la mer, à l'état brut ou transformé »*. C'est au Conseil d'État qu'il revient de fixer une liste des produits concernés et les modalités d'application. Mais nos recherches ne nous ont pas permis de trouver cette liste... Au regard des prochaines évolutions législatives, il semble que le législateur se mette en cohérence avec ce qu'il avait annoncé en 2010. Dans la dernière version du projet de loi relatif à la consommation, l'indication du pays d'origine serait « *rendue obligatoire* ». Toutefois, cette avancée sera toujours conditionnée par la liste et les modalités fixées par le Conseil d'État, mais aussi « *après que la Commission européenne a déclaré compatible avec le droit de l'Union européenne l'obligation prévue au présent article* ». Si dans son dernier rapport sur l'indication de l'origine des viandes, celle-ci souligne d'ailleurs qu'un tel scénario encourage la consommation *via* des circuits de proximité[22], il n'est pas sûr qu'elle valide le renforcement de l'information du consommateur sur ce point. En effet, pour l'instant, et ce malgré les scandales de la viande de cheval, elle n'a écarté aucun scénario, pas même celui de maintenir l'indication de l'origine sur une base volontaire...

---

[22] Rapport de la Commission au Parlement européen et au Conseil concernant l'indication obligatoire du pays d'origine ou du lieu de provenance pour la viande utilisée comme ingrédient, 17 décembre 2013, COM(2013) 755 final, p. 13.

C) Le rôle des politiques publiques

Interactions entre biodiversité et sécurité alimentaire

Denis COUVET *

La biodiversité désigne la diversité biologique du vivant (faune, flore, micro-organismes) à différents niveaux d'organisation écologique. Déclinée en diversité spécifique, génétique et écosystémique, elle englobe sa composition, sa structure et ses fonctions. Un enjeu est de maintenir ces propriétés, les capacités évolutives du vivant, d'adaptation face aux changements globaux.

L'agriculture dépend de la biodiversité, du bon fonctionnement des écosystèmes, à travers la diversité biologique nécessaire à la domestication, la fertilité des sols ou la pollinisation.

En conséquence, le devenir de la biodiversité et de l'agriculture sont liés. Nous envisagerons dans cet article les concepts majeurs permettant de formaliser et comprendre leurs interactions, donc leurs dynamiques, présentes et futures.

I.- Interactions biophysiques entre biodiversité et agriculture

Ces relations s'envisagent de deux manières.

A - Impacts de l'agriculture sur la biodiversité

L'agriculture est la première menace pesant sur les espèces (Greene *et al.* 2005), par son occupation des sols - près de 40 % des terres émergées de la planète occupées par l'agriculture -, et l'intensité de l'usage de ces sols. Cette occupation des écosystèmes peut être évaluée à travers l'Appropriation Humaine de la Production Primaire Nette (HANPP), qui évalue la quantité de biomasse produite par les écosystèmes qui est consommée directement, ou détournée par les humains, et qui n'est donc plus disponible pour la biodiversité.

* Professeur au Muséum National d'Histoire Naturelle, UMR CESCO, MNHN-CNRS-UPMC

Cette HANPP est de l'ordre de 30 % à l'échelle de la planète, variant selon les continents, pouvant atteindre plus de 70 % dans certaines parties de l'Asie, étant de l'ordre de 50 % en Europe de l'Ouest (Häberl *et al.* 2007).

Les autres impacts de l'agriculture sur la biodiversité résultent de l'utilisation d'intrants toxiques et/ou de polluants, entrainant directement le déclin de certaines espèces, ou indirectement, à travers l'eutrophisation des milieux, ou le réchauffement climatique.

Ces impacts peuvent avoir un effet différé, résultant en une dette d'extinction : certaines espèces n'ont pas encore disparu, mais leur maintien n'est que transitoire. En d'autres termes, l'espace et les ressources encore disponibles ne sont plus suffisants pour maintenir l'ensemble de la biodiversité présente.

B - Importance de la biodiversité pour la sécurité alimentaire

A travers les services écosystémiques, de régulation et de support, la biodiversité joue un rôle majeur dans le bon fonctionnement des agro-écosystèmes.

Les services de régulation d'importance la plus directe pour l'agriculture sont la fertilité des sols, le contrôle biologique (des ravageurs des cultures), et la pollinisation. Les deux premiers sont cruciaux notamment pour les agriculteurs les plus pauvres, lorsqu'ils ne peuvent substituer à ces fonctions des intrants coûteux (fertilisants, pesticides).

D'autres services ont une importance significative pour l'agriculture. Ainsi la régulation locale et globale du climat, assurée par les arbres, les haies, les forêts. Cette régulation, est particulièrement importante en zones tropicales, où la disparition de ces formations arborées pourrait conduire à un basculement vers un climat aride. Ces formations arborées permettent aussi d'atténuer les contrastes thermiques dans les régions de latitude élevée, ou encore d'atténuer les vents et l'évapotranspiration associée.

Enfin, la diversité génétique des espèces cultivées, leurs apparentées, où peuvent être cherchées des sources de diversité génétique, est une autre fonctionnalité majeure de la biodiversité. Ainsi 10 % des gènes de la tomate proviennent de croisements avec des espèces apparentées. Cette diversité est donc un élément crucial de la sécurité alimentaire, à venir, permettant l'adaptation nécessaire des cultures au changement global.

II.- Interactions sociales entre agriculture et biodiversité

Une analyse économique faite à l'échelle de la Grande-Bretagne suggère qu'une plus grande préservation des services écosystémiques non marchands, stockage du carbone, préservation des espaces verts et des espaces protégés, aux dépens de l'agriculture, conduirait à un gain économique collectif significatif (Batemann *et al.* 2013). En d'autres termes, la dégradation des services de régulation a des effets sociaux négatifs, non compensées par les activités humaines générées par cette dégradation.

En conséquence, un effort des politiques publiques en faveur des services de régulation se ferait au bénéfice du bien être humain et de la biodiversité (Figure 1), les deux pouvant être agrégés avec la notion de capabilité, que l'on pourrait définir comme le pouvoir de réaliser, en toute indépendance, ce à quoi nous accordons de la valeur. Les capabilités incluent les moyens d'existence et la liberté de choix (Sen, 2009).

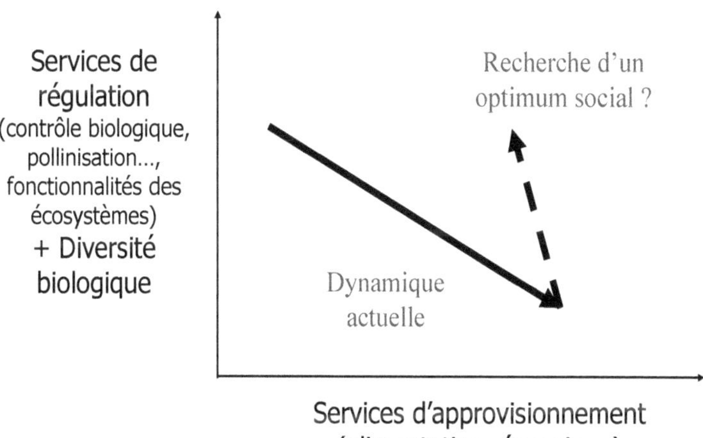

Figure 1. Dialectique entre services écosystémiques : différences entre dynamique actuelle et optimum social

Au moins deux raisons majeures peuvent expliquer que la biodiversité soit peu prise en compte dans les politiques publiques, à la hauteur de son importance sociale, face à l'agriculture.

- La marchandisation d'une seule de ces deux entités. Alors que l'agriculture est organisée à travers les activités marchandes permettant de coordonner production et consommation, la biodiversité, les services écosystémiques de régulation et de support, ne sont pas l'objet de marchés. Il existe par ailleurs peu de normes suppléant à ce manque d'incitations économiques, d'activités rémunératrices en faveur des acteurs préservant la biodiversité et les services de régulation, où à l'inverse de pénalisation des acteurs qui les dégradent.
- Les modalités du choix public. La biodiversité, les services écosystémiques de régulation, sont un bien commun, non marchand. De tels intérêts sont généralement moins bien représentés que les intérêts privés, marchands, dans les instances d'arbitrage (Olson, 1965).

III.- Relations systémiques entre biodiversité et agriculture

La construction de politiques publiques permettant de mieux atteindre l'optimum social demande à bien comprendre la mécanique des relations entre agriculture et biodiversité, de construire une vision systémique de leurs relations, prenant en compte les rétroactions majeures, biophysiques et sociales. Il s'agit de comprendre le fonctionnement du système afin de pouvoir intervenir.

Au-delà du choix des échelles, spatiale et temporelle (unités administratives, régions, états...) envisagées dans la formalisation du système biodiversité-agriculture, un point délicat et d'importance majeure est de définir les entités biophysiques et sociales impliquées, acteurs humains, espèces biologiques, écosystèmes. Il s'agit d'avoir le niveau de complexité qui soit le plus simple possible, tout en n'omettant pas les processus les plus importants.

Nous illustrerons l'importance du système envisagé, du cadre d'analyse, à propos d'un débat majeur portant sur la relation entre intensification agronomique, sécurité alimentaire et biodiversité.

A - Système Production alimentaire - Biodiversité

Le système le plus simple envisage deux entités, biodiversité et production alimentaire, entre lesquelles il s'agit d'arbitrer, de minimiser leur antagonisme, en tenant compte des possibilités respectives de maintien de la biodiversité au sein des espaces agricoles et à l'extérieur des espaces agricoles.

Si la possibilité de maintien de la biodiversité dans les espaces agricoles est importante, alors une agriculture extensive est intéressante, et inversement (Green *et al.* 2005). Les données empiriques suggérant que la biodiversité se maintient beaucoup mieux à l'extérieur des espaces agricoles, ce serait l'intensification de l'agriculture qui permettrait au mieux de combiner les deux objectifs, production alimentaire et maintien de la biodiversité, en minimisant les espaces occupés par l'agriculture.

B - Système Producteurs – Consommateurs – Biodiversité

Le système précédent ne tient pas compte des interactions pouvant exister entre production et consommation. La demande en produits agricoles est considérée constante, alors que les mécanismes économiques suggèrent qu'elle dépend du mode de production, notamment des coûts marchands. En d'autres termes, à travers les consommateurs, la production a une rétroaction sur elle-même, par l'intermédiaire des coûts de production.

On constate alors que la demande et la consommation augmentent lorsque les coûts de production diminuent, donc généralement avec l'intensification de l'agriculture, effet défavorable à la biodiversité (Desquilbet *et al.* 2013). L'effet de l'intensification est donc inverse du cas précédent, illustrant l'effet rebond bien connu des économistes (Alcott, 2008). Une manière d'expliquer cet effet divergent est de l'associer à la liberté d'accès aux écosystèmes : l'intensification a un effet favorable pour la biodiversité en cas de limitation de l'accès -modèle théorique de Green et al. 2005-, défavorable lorsque ce sont les marchés qui régulent le développement des activités agricoles (Figure 2).

Un autre enseignement de cette modélisation est que le choix social devrait dépendre des acteurs convoqués. Ainsi des consommateurs sensibles uniquement au prix des denrées alimentaires arbitreront en faveur de l'intensification de l'agriculture, offrant des denrées agricoles moins coûteuses. Les citoyens arbitreront en faveur de la dés-intensification, afin de maintenir la biodiversité, s'ils accordent peu d'importance au prix des denrées agricoles. L'effet sur les producteurs dépend de la valeur de plusieurs paramètres (Desquilbet et al. 2013). Une restriction de l'offre agricole, afin de limiter l'impact climatique de l'agriculture, aurait un impact économique favorable pour les producteurs, les augmentations de prix compensant largement la diminution de production (Golub et al. 2013), suggérant que la restriction de l'offre est généralement favorable aux producteurs.

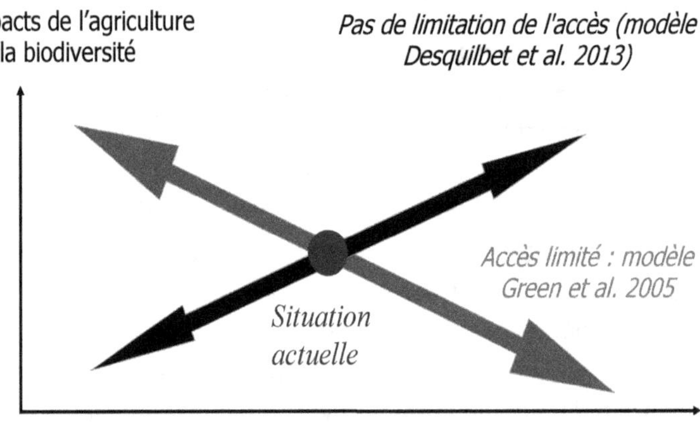

Figure 2. Relation entre rendements et biodiversité, selon la régulation de l'accès de l'agriculture aux écosystèmes

L'effet d'une dés-intensification sur les consommateurs les plus pauvres, souffrant d'insécurité alimentaire, restent difficiles à évaluer. Ce sont sans doute les populations les plus exposées aux désordres climatiques et écosystémiques, qui devraient donc le plus bénéficier d'une meilleure protection de la biodiversité, des écosystèmes. Par ailleurs, des programmes spécifiques d'aide alimentaire à ces populations sont sans doute largement à la portée des Etats.

C - Sécurité alimentaire : interactions entre les filières biocarburants, protéines animales et végétales

Surtout, pour examiner les effets d'une dés-intensification de l'agriculture sur la sécurité alimentaire, il importe d'examiner l'interaction entre les différentes filières. Ces dernières contribuent diversement à la sécurité alimentaire, bien que toutes en compétition avec la biodiversité. Le passage à une alimentation moins carnée permettrait de nourrir beaucoup plus d'humains, de l'ordre de 40 %. Ainsi, près de 75 % de la production de maïs est destinée à l'alimentation animale ou aux biocarburants (Cassidy *et al.* 2013).

Ces filières ont par ailleurs des relations différentes avec la demande. La demande de protéines animales ayant sans doute une forte élasticité –forte dépendance aux coûts de production– alors que la production de biocarburants est plutôt fixée par des normes sociales, moins sensible aux coûts de production. L'avantage pour la biodiversité de l'agriculture extensive reste présent, et surtout la sécurité alimentaire dépend avant tout de l'arbitrage entre les trois filières (Desquilbet *et al.* 2013).

En résumé, et par comparaison avec le modèle A, notons que si la dés-intensification est avantageuse, c'est parce qu'il n'y a pas de régulation de l'accès aux écosystèmes par l'agriculture, offrant la possibilité d'un effet rebond de la consommation. A l'inverse, en présence d'une telle régulation, la conclusion redeviendrait intuitive, réconciliant l'intérêt des consommateurs et des citoyens : l'intensification de l'agriculture n'est alors plus désavantageuse pour la biodiversité, car elle permet alors de réduire les impacts de l'agriculture, au lieu de conduire à l'extension des marchés.

D - Interactions entre les acteurs des filières agricoles

Quelle que soit la relation entre intensification agronomique et biodiversité, l'état de cette dernière devrait être amélioré par un rôle plus important de l'agro-écologie, ou approche agronomique accordant un rôle accru à la biodiversité, aux services écosystémiques dans la production agricole remplaçant un certain nombre d'intrants. Le succès écologique de cette agro-écologie dépend évidemment des stratégies des différents acteurs de la filière agricole, au-delà des agriculteurs.

En effet, au sein des filières agricoles interviennent d'autres acteurs économiques que les agriculteurs, semenciers et autres fournisseurs d'intrants, collecteurs et distributeurs. Le choix des pratiques peut se faire en amont ou en aval des agriculteurs, notamment selon des critères uniquement industriels : type de production plus facilement standardisable, plus forte utilisation de tel type d'intrant, donc de rémunération des acteurs de la filière... La coopération des différents acteurs est cruciale, car l'introduction de nouvelles pratiques demande à ce que les intrants nécessaires soient disponibles et que les débouchés marchands soient assurés (Meynard *et al.* 2013).

IV.- Conclusions

Le choix social, notamment entre agriculture intensive et extensive, est crucial pour le devenir de la biodiversité. Ses effets dépendent des relations entre production et consommation, des différentes filières en présence, des modalités d'accès aux écosystèmes de l'agriculture.

Une régulation de l'accès à la biodiversité et aux services écosystémiques, traitant notamment les externalités agricoles, semble une voie prometteuse permettant de mieux concilier biodiversité et agriculture, s'inspirant des travaux menés sur la gouvernance des biens communs (Ostrom, 1990). Cette régulation de l'accès aux écosystèmes est donc un sujet majeur pour les politiques publiques.

Vis-à-vis de cette régulation, les acteurs peuvent avoir des intérêts conflictuels, variant dans l'espace et dans le temps, selon la sécurité alimentaire régionale et locale. Il importerait donc de tenir compte de la diversité des contextes locaux, distinguant pays importateurs et exportateurs, riches et pauvres, selon l'état de la sécurité alimentaire. La théorie des jeux doit aider à comprendre la mécanique des choix publics, les mécanismes de l'inertie institutionnelle, les moyens de la contourner. Donc de déterminer les institutions nécessaires, qu'il s'agit de bâtir, afin de parvenir à des relations agriculture-biodiversité plus équilibrées, et plus proches des capabilités humaines. Il s'agirait ainsi d'examiner les possibilités de négociations entre les différents acteurs de la filière, mais aussi avec la puissance publique, selon leurs préférences, pouvant conduire les acteurs à mieux se coordonner, développer des coalitions (circuits courts...) et ainsi optimiser le bien commun.

Enfin, la construction de politiques publiques de régulation de l'accès nécessite des indicateurs pertinents, aussi bien dans le domaine de l'agriculture et de la biodiversité. On peut classiquement distinguer trois types d'indicateurs, des indicateurs d'impact, d'état du système et d'efficience (Kuemmerle *et al.* 2013). Ces trois types d'indicateurs ont des rôles sociaux complémentaires. Les indicateurs d'impact permettent la fixation d'objectifs collectifs, la définition et la construction des politiques publiques, la régulation. Ils permettent aussi de vérifier que l'amélioration de l'efficience agronomique n'entraîne pas d'effets rebonds (voir Figure 2). Les indicateurs d'état sont nécessaires au diagnostic écologique, alors que les indicateurs d'efficience permettent la négociation sociale, la contractualisation entre acteurs, l'arbitrage des consommateurs.

Références

ALCOTT B. 2008. "The sufficiency strategy: Would rich-world frugality lower environmental impact ?", *Ecological Economics*, 64, 770-786.

BATEMAN, I., et al. 2013. Bringing Ecosystem Services into Economic Decision-Making: Land Use in the United Kingdom. *Science* 341, 45-50.

DESQUILBET M., DORIN B., COUVET D. 2013. Land sharing ou land sparing pour la biodiversité : Comment les marchés agricoles font la différence. *Innovations agronomiques* 32, 377-389.

GOLUB A. et al. 2013. Global Climate Policy Impacts on Livestock, Land Use, Livelihoods, and Food Security. *PNAS* 110, 20894–20899.

GREEN R.E., CORNELL S.J., SCHARLEMANN J.P.W., BALMFORD A., 2005. Farming and the fate of wild nature. *Science* 307, 550-555.

HÄBERL H. et al. 2007. Quantifying and mapping the human appropriation of net primary production in earth's terrestrial ecosystems, *PNAS*, 104, 12942-12947.

KUEMMERLE, T. et al. 2013. *Challenges and opportunities in mapping land use intensity globally. Current Opinion in Environmental Sustainability* 5, 1–10.

MEYNARD J.M. et al. 2013. *Freins et leviers à la diversification des systèmes de culture.* Etude INRA prospective.

OLSON, M. 1965. *The Logic of Collective Action: Public Goods and the Theory of Groups.* Harvard University Press

OSTROM, E. 1990. *Gouvernance des biens communs*. De Boeck, Bruxelles.

SEN, A. 2009. *The idea of Justice*. Penguin books.

Que proposent les économistes pour gérer les ressources naturelles en fonction des besoins socio-économiques fondamentaux des populations ?

Laure DESPRES [*] & Thomas VALLEE [**]

Les ressources naturelles (terres arables, pétrole, poissons...) sont inégalement réparties et peuvent être utilisées à différents usages, qui sont parfois complémentaires, ou parfois se font concurrence entre eux. En effet, la croissance démographique, la pression des modes de consommation facilités par les mécanismes d'échange par le marché, ou encore les changements environnementaux, accroissent cette concurrence qui n'est cependant pas uniquement intragénérationnelle mais aussi intergénérationnelle. Autrement dit, la rareté est plus que jamais de retour et devient polymorphe. Aux ressources traditionnellement rares (énergie fossile par exemple) se sont rajoutés de nouvelles raretés, comme l'air ou l'eau considérés naguère comme des biens libres (Orsenna, 2007). Cela pose inévitablement à la fois la question de la bonne gestion de ces ressources au regard d'une finalité précise (profit, gestion durable, richesse, bonheur, etc.), et celle du niveau de gouvernance susceptible d'assurer cette bonne gestion.

On pourrait penser intuitivement qu'une finalité raisonnable serait d'organiser cette gestion de façon à satisfaire les besoins fondamentaux d'une population. Or, ou hélas, la notion de besoins, et plus encore de besoins fondamentaux, est étrangère à l'analyse économique dominante. Cette dernière ne connaît que la demande solvable, donc suppose que chacun possède un revenu monétaire suffisant pour couvrir ses besoins fondamentaux, ce qui est loin d'être le cas, même dans les pays riches (Bouget, 2013).

Pour décider quel usage faire d'une ressource naturelle, comme de n'importe quelle ressource d'ailleurs, les économistes sont très divisés.

---

* Professeur émérite en sciences économiques, Laboratoire d'Economie et de Management de Nantes-Atlantique (LEMNA), Université de Nantes.

** Professeur en sciences économiques, Directeur du LEMNA, Université de Nantes.

Ceux du courant dominant d'inspiration néoclassique préconisent de mener une analyse coût-bénéfice, et de choisir le projet qui maximise le profit et qui répond donc de façon satisfaisante aux demandes solvables qui s'expriment sur les marchés. Les partisans de la croissance verte constatent que les prix de marché ne reflètent pas la totalité des coûts nécessaires pour produire les différents biens du fait d'externalités qui, par essence, ne sont pas intégrées dans le prix de marché. La puissance publique doit donc intervenir pour internaliser ces coûts externes, assurer la production et la gestion de biens publics (routes...), la redistribution des revenus (revenu minimum, retraites, assurance maladie...) et la régulation de l'économie (budget, change, monnaie...). A cette condition, les marchés et les progrès techniques doivent pouvoir répondre à tous les défis que nous posent la croissance démographique et les excès de pollution. Enfin, un troisième courant, celui de l'économie écologique, soutient que l'empreinte écologique des humains dépassant désormais la biocapacité de la planète, l'accès de plus en plus coûteux aux ressources naturelles va entraver puissamment la tendance du système économique mondial à la croissance permanente. Ceci nous conduit, si nous ne changeons pas de critère de choix pour l'utilisation de ces ressources, à un effondrement catastrophique, et à la non-couverture généralisée des besoins fondamentaux des populations.

La présente contribution se propose d'effectuer un tour d'horizon des trois courants précédemment nommés, afin d'illustrer leurs difficultés de mises en œuvre, voire leur aporie.

I.- La règle d'affectation des ressources naturelles dans une économie de marché

Depuis Adam Smith et en opposition avec la conception mercantiliste, la notion de richesse est étroitement liée à celle de croissance : il s'agit de produire toujours plus pour accumuler plus. Dans cette logique, l'indicateur de performance est l'évolution du PIB.

Rapidement, des économistes classiques comme Matlhus, Ricardo ou encore Jevons, se sont préoccupés de la difficulté implicite de cette vision de la richesse qui présuppose de devoir gérer une rareté de fait (quantité donnée de terres disponibles) ou de conséquences (surexploitation des ressources naturelles). Cette difficulté doit trouver sa solution dans une allocation efficace des ressources disponibles grâce au mécanisme de marché concurrentiel : la confrontation entre l'offre et de demande engendre un prix, qui reflète à la fois l'utilité et la rareté du bien. Ce qui est rare est cher et ce qui est cher ne sera que peu utilisé. Un calcul économique doit alors être mis en œuvre qui permet de savoir dans quelle mesure il est plus rentable ou non de laisser telle ou telle quantité de ressources *in situ* pour demain ou *ad vitam eternam*.

Ce calcul rationnel, soulève immédiatement une première difficulté. En effet, il faut calculer les coûts et les bénéfices sur plusieurs années (le temps d'utilisation de cette ressource). Or pour les économistes, un euro aujourd'hui est plus utile qu'un euro demain, qui lui-même est plus utile qu'un euro après-demain, etc. Le taux permettant de transformer un euro de demain en un certain nombre de centimes aujourd'hui est appelé taux d'actualisation. Un taux élevé, par exemple 20 %, n'accorde que peu de valeur à un euro demain (80 cts), et encore moins à un euro après-demain (64 cts). Au contraire, un taux nul nous dit que demain compte autant qu'aujourd'hui. L'évaluation de projets concurrents visant à l'exploitation ou la transformation d'une ressource par le biais d'un taux d'actualisation strictement positif amène implicitement à rejeter des projets dont les bénéfices sont à long terme. Si une ressource n'a que peu de valeur aujourd'hui, mettons 50 euros, mais vaudrait un million dans 100 ans, alors la destruction de cette ressource est recommandée par le calcul économique si la valeur actualisée d'un million dans 100 ans est inférieure à 50 euros. On comprend aisément que ce principe d'actualisation est contraire à l'équité intergénérationnelle. Par ailleurs, il se fonde sur l'idée d'une croissance infinie : c'est parce qu'on suppose que la richesse augmentera demain que la valeur relative d'un euro demain est moindre que celle d'aujourd'hui. Qui peut faire aujourd'hui le pari que la société sera plus riche dans 100 ans qu'aujourd'hui !

L'absurdité de ce principe concernant des enjeux à très long terme, comme le réchauffement climatique, est bien connue. Ainsi, supposons que les conséquences économiques de ce changement puissent être évaluées à 100 milliards d'euros dans 100 ans. Alors, si l'on adopte un taux d'actualisation de 4 %, il ne faudrait pas dépenser plus de 20 millions d'euros aujourd'hui pour s'éviter cette dépense future. Il est bien clair que le seul taux d'actualisation utilisable pour le long terme compatible avec un développement durable est un taux zéro. L'actualisation implique au contraire une « tyrannie du présent » (Cline, 1999).

Pour conclure sur le principe d'actualisation, pour un économiste, une population affamée qui ira pêcher les derniers poissons réduisant à zéro la biomasse ne fait que répondre à un besoin impératif de se nourrir aujourd'hui, attitude compatible avec un problème de maximisation avec un taux d'actualisation infini. Seul compte le temps présent. Poussé à l'extrême, le calcul économique commande de convertir en monnaie sonnante et trébuchante toutes les ressources halieutiques dont la faculté à se reproduire est jugée trop lente, afin de placer cet argent au taux de rendement des capitaux, qui est bien plus élevé !

Ce paradoxe est au fondement même d'une règle d'allocation optimale des ressources dans une économie de marché, à savoir la règle d'Hotelling. Celle-ci est née d'un questionnement sur la gestion optimale d'un gisement minier (Hotelling, 1931). C'est une règle inter-temporelle qui nous dit sous quelle condition il est préférable d'exploiter une unité de plus de ressource naturelle, ou bien de la laisser *in situ*, par exemple en terre pour une ressource extractive. Le calcul est financier. Supposons que si vous exploitez la ressource, vous gagnez 10 euros en la vendant. Or vous savez que vous pouvez placer ces 10 euros à 10 % par exemple, et que vous aurez ainsi 11 euros l'année prochaine. Il faut donc laisser la ressource sous terre cette année si vous anticipez que son prix futur est susceptible de dépasser 11 euros. De la même façon cela peut s'appliquer aux ressources renouvelables comme une biomasse de poisson. Si vous laissez du poisson, alors le supplément de poisson pêchable demain doit augmenter à un rythme équivalent à celui des intérêts si le prix de vente est inchangé.

On comprend que cette règle amène à regarder le capital naturel comme n'importe quel actif financier. Seule compte sa rémunération. Il n'existe pas de valeur en soi pour un quelconque service non directement marchand que pourrait rendre la nature[1].

Cette règle nous dit aussi que le mécanisme de prix (hausse régulière par exemple) peut suffire à signaler la rareté et éviter l'épuisement en

[1] Ce qui renvoie au problème de la valeur à attribuer aux services environnementaux, qui sera discuté dans la deuxième partie.

entrainant une baisse de la demande. Cela signifie que le prix est censé refléter la totalité des coûts, y compris les effets externes, et qu'il est directement observable. A l'évidence c'est problématique. Les marchés des ressources naturelles notamment extractives sont souvent des marchés imparfaits, non concurrentiels, les prix y reflètent alors tout autant le pouvoir de marché des producteurs ou des intermédiaires ou les distorsions (taxes, subvention, ...) que la rareté de la ressource. Enfin cela présuppose qu'il existe des substituts, au moins imparfaits, à la ressource, par exemple des sources d'énergies renouvelables pour les énergies fossiles.

La règle d'Hotelling n'empêche donc pas l'épuisement d'une ressource au profit d'une production de biens marchands basée sur l'accumulation de capital productif. Il y a donc une substitution de capital productif à du capital naturel. La question est de savoir si cette substitution est ou non problématique. En effet, si on considère le capital naturel comme un actif financier, cela implique d'arbitrer en faveur de l'utilisation la plus rémunératrice (i.e. l'actif au meilleur rendement) dans une logique de rentabilité à court terme si le taux d'actualisation est élevé. On est poussé alors à remplacer « rationnellement » du capital naturel sauvage (forêt) par un capital naturel « produit » (agriculture). Ou encore on transformera une exploitation agricole à visée alimentaire en exploitation agricole à visée énergétique (bio carburant), et ceci d'autant plus que le prix sur le marché de la ressource naturelle extractive énergie est lui-même à la hausse. Le capital devient également exposé, par cette transformation, à la spéculation des traders : devenue « *commodity* », cette ressource peut voir son prix entraîné dans une bulle spéculative dans laquelle la demande ne répond plus de la même manière au signal de prix (Parachkevova, Teller, Després, 2013).

Autre conséquence, cette transformation implicite du capital naturel sauvage en capital naturel produit ou en autre forme de capital ne peut se faire sans l'existence de droits de propriétés privés associés à ce capital naturel, quelle que soit sa forme, afin que l'arbitrage sous forme d'actifs à valoriser puisse pleinement jouer. Mais alors, il peut apparaître un conflit d'usage entre les agents utilisant la ressource mais ne la valorisant pas comme actif (populations vivant dans une économie traditionnelle) et ceux qui, dans une logique purement économique, sont prêts à l'exploiter directement comme un actif ou encore à la transformer en un actif différent plus rémunérateur.

Enfin, le calcul économique doit intégrer l'ensemble des coûts associés à l'exploitation de la ressource naturelle. Or, il n'est pas rare que des conséquences négatives indirectes apparaissent (pollution des sols, disparition d'un bien commun, etc.), que les économistes nomment des effets externes négatifs. Mais alors, il faut aussi clairement évaluer l'ensemble des conséquences financières, et pas seulement celles qui impactent uniquement et directement l'exploitant de la ressource[2].

Comme nous allons le voir dans la partie suivante, l'économie « verte » essaie d'apporter des éléments de réponse à ces dernières interrogations sans pour autant quitter la cadre dominant de l'économie de marché. Quelle substitution ? Quels droits de propriété ? Quelles valorisations exactes ? C'est en quelque sorte une vision optimiste de l'économie classique.

II.- Vers une meilleure affectation des ressources naturelles en voie de raréfaction : la croissance verte

Si on comprend aisément qu'il puisse exister un lien entre exploitation des ressources naturelles et perspective de croissance économique, le signe du lien donne lieu à deux courants de pensée que l'on peut appeler les « optimistes » et les « pessimistes ». L'approche optimiste perçoit les ressources naturelles comme un possible facteur de développement durable. Pour les optimistes, les enjeux environnementaux actuels ne constituent pas une limite à l'action humaine. La rareté des ressources va s'inverser grâce à la révolution verte qui s'opère elle-même grâce à la croissance économique[3].

---

[2] Voir OCDE (2009) : « Tarifer les ressources au juste prix. Des droits d'accès clairement définis peuvent limiter la surexploitation et la dégradation de ressources naturelles renouvelables, les ressources étant ainsi mieux employées. Les taxes et les droits d'utilisation sont aussi à envisager pour améliorer la gestion des ressources, mais il faut souvent recourir à d'autres instruments comme le zonage, les permis et les systèmes d'étiquetage [...] »

[3] OCDE (2009) : « Moyennant une gestion rationnelle, les ressources naturelles peuvent étayer durablement la croissance pro-pauvres ».

Directement ancrée dans cette vision optimiste, une deuxième grande règle de gestion des ressources naturelles, la règle d'Hartwick, est fondée sur la logique suivante : l'épuisement ou la destruction d'une ressource naturelle n'est pas en soi préjudiciable dès lors qu'elle peut être remplacée par du capital construit. Par exemple, une zone humide peut être remplacée par une station d'épuration, les stocks de poissons sauvages épuisés peuvent être remplacés par des poissons d'élevage. Cette règle est censée réguler le transfert de capital entre les générations de manière à ce que la soutenabilité soit assurée, par un critère d'équité. La consommation par tête doit être constante à travers le temps de façon à ce qu'aucune génération ne soit favorisée par rapport à une autre. Il suffit donc de compenser en permanence la destruction du capital naturel par un investissement en capital reproductible. Autrement dit, il n'existe pas de capital naturel essentiel, ni d'effet de seuil au-delà duquel la consommation progressive de capital naturel entrainerait sa destruction soudaine. Cette règle admet que la substitution est possible sans conséquences à long terme, que l'on peut mesurer le stock de capital et surtout que l'on peut attribuer une valeur à ce stock. Cela présuppose aussi des droits de propriété privés sur le capital naturel[4].

Pour savoir si on a maintenu la valeur du capital global, en remplaçant des ressources naturelles par du capital construit, encore faut-il être capable de mesurer la valeur de ces ressources naturelles. Or on en est très loin. A vrai dire, même le capital construit et le capital humain sont loin d'être correctement évalués, *a fortiori* le capital naturel.

Toutes les méthodes d'évaluation économique du capital naturel reposent sur l'idée que sa valeur est déterminée par l'ensemble des services, marchands et non marchands, rendus par cet écosystème. Quels sont ces services ? Il s'agit des services de production (nourriture, eau douce, bois et fibres, combustible), des services de régulation (du climat, des inonda-

[4] OCDE (2009) : « il est souvent possible de transformer une forme de capital en une autre. La conversion du capital naturel en capital humain et en capital artificiel peut être un moyen d'accroître la production totale si cette conversion vise des formes de capital plus productives. Au capital naturel « sauvage » peut se substituer du capital naturel « produit » par l'activité humaine, par exemple lorsqu'une forêt est convertie en plantation arboricole, en pâturage ou en terre agricole, ou qu'une mangrove laisse place à une pisciculture ».

tions, de la santé, de purification de l'eau), des services culturels (esthétiques, spirituels, éducatifs, récréatifs). Enfin, les derniers, les moins visibles mais non les moindres, des services de maintien de la vie qui permettent le bon fonctionnement de ces écosystèmes (cycles des nutriments, formation des sols, production primaire végétale et animale).

Quelles sont ces méthodes ? Lorsque ces services sont marchands, comme c'est le cas par exemple pour le droit d'entrée dans un parc naturel en Amérique du Nord, le problème ne se pose pas, la valeur sera mesurée par le prix. On peut y ajouter le coût du transport que les visiteurs ont payé pour arriver jusque-là, en leur demandant d'où ils viennent. Ajouté au droit d'entrée, il constituera la valeur minimale qu'ils y accordent. La moyenne de ces valeurs servira de base à l'estimation minimale de la valeur globale de cet espace de nature. On pourra y ajouter éventuellement la valeur du bois vendu grâce à l'exploitation raisonnée de la forêt. Cependant, cette valeur ne reflète que deux des nombreux services rendus, les services récréatifs et la production de bois. Ni les services de régulation, ni surtout ceux de maintien de la vie ne sont en général pris en compte, alors que leur valeur est en réalité énorme.

Une autre méthode adaptée à l'évaluation de la valeur des aménités paysagères ou des services récréatifs d'un espace naturel est la méthode hédonique. Il s'agit de déduire des prix de biens marchands influencés par la proximité de ce type d'espace, comme un bien immobilier par exemple, la valeur que les agents économiques y accordent. Là encore, ce n'est pas la totalité des services rendus qui va être prise en compte.

Pour pallier cet inconvénient, on peut avoir recours à la méthode de l'évaluation contingente. Il s'agit de mener une enquête auprès d'un échantillon représentatif de la population. Après avoir expliqué à chacun les fonctions de l'écosystème en question (forêt, espaces humides, bocage, etc.), on leur demandera combien ils sont prêts à payer pour éviter sa destruction. Malheureusement, cette méthode, elle aussi, sous-évalue largement la « vraie » valeur des écosystèmes, dans la mesure même où les enquêteurs ne couvrent jamais l'ensemble des fonctions réelles. De plus, les évaluations obtenues pour un même type d'écosystème varient très largement, ce qui peut être dû à la mauvaise connaissance des enquêteurs ou des personnes interrogées, mais aussi à la variabilité intrinsèque de la valeur des services rendus : une forêt située à proximité d'une grande ville européenne sera normalement plus valorisée qu'une autre située dans des espaces beaucoup moins densément peuplés. En outre, la valeur est également variable dans le temps puisque de nombreux espaces de nature sont en voie de raréfaction, en particulier les espaces humides et les forêts tropicales, et prennent donc de ce fait une valeur plus grande (Choblet, Maslianskaia-Pautrel, 2009a).

Ce qui nous amène à une première critique fondamentale de cette approche : le calcul de la valeur des services rendus par un écosystème doit être mené pour chaque cas particulier pour que le calcul coût-bénéfice ait du sens. Cela demande un travail considérable, long et coûteux, qui peut ne pas déboucher faute des données statistiques indispensables[5].

La deuxième critique fondamentale tient à la nature même des services de maintien de la vie (cycle de l'eau, reconstitution des terres arables, production primaire). La vie dans un milieu entièrement artificialisé (comme dans un vaisseau spatial par exemple) coûte très cher en argent, mais aussi en énergie et en ressources de toutes sortes. Elle est impossible à généraliser à l'ensemble de l'humanité. On peut ainsi soutenir que la valeur des services de soutien de vie est pratiquement infinie !

Enfin, à ces difficultés de mesure de la valeur du capital naturel s'ajoutent celles liés à l'évaluation des effets externes tels que la pollution, dont il va falloir tenir compte pour rendre le calcul économique plus « vert ». En effet, la croissance verte repose sur l'idée que cet échec de marché, à savoir la non prise en compte dans le calcul économique des producteurs de possibles effets externes, peut être corrigé par l'intervention de l'Etat via un processus d'internalisation des effets externes. Deux méthodes peuvent être principalement utilisées pour ce faire : la puissance publique peut établir des éco-taxes ou elle peut créer de nouveaux marchés de droits à polluer.

Pour calculer les éco-taxes, si l'on veut réellement couvrir l'ensemble des effets externes négatifs des pollutions par exemple en matière de santé publique, ou des coûts de production supplémentaires subis par d'autres producteurs, il faut une administration pléthorique et permanente compte

[5] Voir l'exemple de la fonction d'habitat pour les poissons des vasières de l'estuaire de la Loire *in* CHOBLET, MASLIANSKAIA-PAUTREL, 2009b.

tenu du changement très rapide des techniques de production et de l'apparition constante de nouveaux produits. On risque de réinventer le *Gosplan*[6], mais avec le problème dual. Au lieu de calculer les quantités, on calculera les prix.

La création de marchés de droits à polluer peut *a priori* paraître plus satisfaisante puisque la puissance publique n'a plus qu'à fixer des quotas de pollution imposés à chaque entreprise, prévus pour diminuer progressivement à chaque période. Ces quotas sont échangeables afin de minimiser le coût de réduction de la pollution. Le prix de la pollution va résulter alors de la confrontation des offres et des demandes des entreprises, et non pas du calcul d'agents publics éloignés des réalités économiques. Or, jusqu'à présent, ces marchés ont été organisés comme des marchés financiers où la spéculation joue un rôle prépondérant dans la détermination du prix. C'est le cas en particulier du marché européen des quotas d'émission de gaz à effet de serre[7]. En outre, les très grandes entreprises concernées ont joué de leur pouvoir d'influence sur les autorités publiques pour obtenir des quotas très peu contraignants. Enfin, on a largement sous-estimé le coût de création et de fonctionnement de ces nouvelles institutions, ce qui a entraîné des fraudes et des dysfonctionnements graves. Au total, le bilan de ce marché de droits à polluer est aujourd'hui pour le moins mitigé, au point que certains en réclament la suppression[8].

Quoiqu'il en soit des difficultés pratiques, un prix élevé du droit de polluer doit inciter à la substitution, c'est-à-dire à une production plus efficace basée notamment sur le recours aux technologies vertes. Il doit donc se produire à terme une restructuration radicale des appareils productifs vers une meilleure qualité « environnementale » de production. De nouveaux indicateurs macroéconomiques ont été proposés pour mesurer les progrès dans cette direction : c'est par exemple l'épargne véritable qui

---

[6] Le Gosplan était en URSS l'administration d'état pléthorique chargée d'élaborer les plans quinquennaux de production, obligatoires pour les entreprises.

[7] Sur le fonctionnement des marchés de droits à polluer, voir L. DESPRES (2013), p.61 à 63.

[8] Entretien avec Maxime COMBES, économiste et membre du conseil scientifique d'Attac et Pierre-André JOUVET, Directeur scientifique de la Chaire économie du climat à l'Université Paris Dauphine. Propos recueillis par Hervé KEMPF, *Alternatives Internationales Hors-série* n° 014 - janvier 2014.

prend en compte non seulement la dépréciation du capital construit, l'amélioration du capital humain, mais aussi la destruction du capital naturel (Bolt et alii, 2002).

Depuis quelques années, les entreprises ont mené un grand nombre d'expériences diverses, qui constituent l'amorce de ce bouleversement radical. Il s'agit d'une part d'économiser l'énergie en accroissant l'efficacité énergétique du système et de remplacer progressivement les sources d'énergies carbonées par des énergies renouvelables (soleil, vent, force motrice de l'eau), à la fois pour diminuer les émissions de gaz à effet de serre et pour éviter une hausse trop forte du coût de l'énergie. Il s'agit ensuite de pallier la difficulté et le coût croissants d'obtention des autres ressources non renouvelables, et de la gestion des déchets et des pollutions. Par exemple, l'éco-conception permet dès le tout début du cycle de vie d'un produit de prévoir que sa production soit la plus économe possible en matières premières, qu'il soit facilement réparable et recyclable en fin de vie. Le recyclage permet de passer d'une économie linéaire à une économie circulaire, qui à la limite n'a plus besoin de prélever de ressources non renouvelables dans la nature, et ne produit qu'un minimum de déchets et de pollution. L'écologie industrielle cherche à développer les synergies entre entreprises situées sur un même territoire, afin de favoriser la circulation des flux d'énergie et de matières, les déchets des uns pouvant servir de matières premières aux autres.

Une économie totalement circulaire reste cependant une utopie, car il existe des limites au recyclage liées par exemple au fait que de nombreux produits utilisent un très grand nombre de matériaux, en quantités très faibles, et qu'il est donc pratiquement impossible de les récupérer. En outre, une part très importante des métaux (de 10 à 30 % selon les cas) est utilisée en usage dispersif (pigments, additifs...) et est donc de ce fait irrécupérable. Enfin, beaucoup de matières recyclées ne peuvent être utilisées que sous des formes dégradées. Par exemple, les bouteilles en plastique deviennent du tissu polaire ou des chaises de jardin et l'acier high-tech finit en acier bas de gamme.

Développer l'économie de fonctionnalité constitue une autre méthode pour économiser les matières premières. Il s'agit de lutter contre l'obsolescence programmée et d'inciter les entreprises productrices, par des mesures soigneusement calibrées, à allonger la vie des produits durables tels que l'équipement électroménager, les automobiles, etc. La règlementation peut leur imposer par exemple de donner aux acheteurs une garantie de 5 ou 10 ans. Elle peut aussi favoriser la vente des services rendus par ce bien plutôt que l'achat du bien lui-même ce qui est déjà le cas de Decaux qui loue ses vélos ou de Michelin qui facture les kilomètres parcourus par ses pneus de camion[9].

Les partisans de la croissance verte placent beaucoup d'espoirs dans la haute technologie pour augmenter l'efficacité énergétique de notre appareil productif et plus généralement l'efficacité de notre utilisation des ressources naturelles en voie de raréfaction. Malheureusement les technologies vertes sont à l'heure actuelle du moins, grosses utilisatrices de métaux rares et aggravent la complexité des produits, freinant ainsi la possibilité de recyclage, voire la rendant impossible comme dans le cas de l'utilisation de nanomatériaux. Pour résumer le dilemme, pour économiser l'énergie, il faut avoir recours à plus de métaux rares. Pour extraire les métaux en voie de raréfaction de minerais moins riches et plus inaccessibles, il faut plus d'énergie (et d'eau, autre ressource en voie de raréfaction !) (Bihouix, 2013).

III.- L'affectation des ressources naturelles en fonction des besoins fondamentaux : l'économie écologique

Malgré l'importance des modifications dans l'appareil productif et dans la vie quotidienne des citoyens qu'implique le passage à une croissance verte, de nombreux scientifiques, spécialistes de l'analyse des systèmes ou économistes, doutent que ces réformes suffisent à réduire suffisamment la pression qu'exerce l'homme sur la nature. En effet, l'humanité surexploite tellement les ressources naturelles et pollue tellement les écosystèmes au-delà de leur capacité de régénérescence, qu'il paraît impossible de continuer à augmenter longtemps la production économique telle qu'elle est mesurée par le PIB.

[9] Sur l'économie circulaire, l'écologie industrielle et l'économie de fonctionnalité, voir *Toward the Circular Economy* (2012 et 2013) et *L'écologie industrielle et territoriale, un outil de développement économique durable* (2013).

L'empreinte écologique est un indicateur qui évalue la surface productive nécessaire à une population pour répondre à sa consommation de ressources et à ses besoins d'absorption de déchets. Elle se mesure en hectares « globaux » et peut se comparer au nombre d'hectares (normalisés) disponibles, la biocapacité. En 1970, l'empreinte écologique mondiale correspondait à peu près à la biocapacité de la planète. Elle n'a cessé d'augmenter depuis, sous l'influence de la croissance de la population et de la croissance économique. Elle dépasse désormais de 50 % la biocapacité, ce qui se traduit concrètement par l'épuisement des ressources renouvelables (poissons, forêts, terres arables...) et par le réchauffement climatique. Si l'humanité continue sur cette lancée, elle aurait besoin de plus de deux planètes pour répondre à ses besoins en 2030.

En outre toutes les dimensions de la pression anthropique sur la nature ne sont pas prises en compte dans cet indicateur. Ainsi, il ne nous renseigne pas sur la surexploitation de la ressource en eau douce dans de nombreux bassins hydrographiques. C'est l'empreinte eau qui mesure le volume d'eau douce utilisé, directement ou indirectement, pour produire des biens et services. Il existe aussi une cartographie des zones en stress hydrique. L'indice Planète Vivante nous renseigne lui, sur l'effondrement actuel de la biodiversité. A l'échelle de la planète, il a diminué de près de 30 % depuis 1970, mais beaucoup plus dans les régions tropicales : moins 60 % pour l'indice global et jusqu'à moins 70 % pour l'indice eau douce tropical[10].

Dès les années 70, Nicholas Georgescu-Roegen et les auteurs du fameux Rapport Meadows rédigé à la demande du Club de Rome, soutiennent que la recherche effrénée de la croissance exerce une pression insoutenable sur les ressources naturelles et donc sur l'environnement (Georgescu-Roegen, 1971, Meadows *et alii*, 1972). Cette relation inverse entre croissance et durabilité est mise en évidence par le modèle systémique utilisé par l'équipe Meadows qui affirme que si les tendances démographiques, économiques et environnementales courantes se perpétuent, les ressources naturelles disponibles seront de plus en plus coûteuses à obtenir, ce qui risque d'empêcher toute croissance future voire de conduire

---

[10] Sur tous ces indicateurs de surexploitation de la nature, voir le *Rapport Planète Vivante* (2012).

à un effondrement économique et démographique dans l'avenir. Quarante ans plus tard, pour Dennis Meadows, mais avec lui pour les économistes se réclamant de l'économie écologique, la décroissance n'est plus une option, mais une certitude : il est désormais trop tard pour le développement durable (Meadows, 2013). Il s'agit bien là d'une vision pessimiste, en opposition avec l'optimisme des partisans de la croissance verte.

En réalité, les limites à la croissance ne portent pas sur la valeur du PIB, mais sur l'utilisation des ressources naturelles. Parce que nous vivons sur notre capital naturel, et non sur le « revenu » tiré de ce capital, c'est-à-dire la quantité de ressources naturelles renouvelables que nous pouvons utiliser sans toucher au stock, inévitablement notre capacité à produire des biens physiques va devenir de plus en plus limitée. Ceci est dû au fait que, contrairement à ce que postulent les partisans de la croissance verte, d'une part, la capacité du capital produit à remplacer le capital naturel détruit est limitée, d'autre part, il existe des effets de seuils dans le fonctionnement des écosystèmes. Malheureusement, nos connaissances limitées rendent ces limites imprévisibles.

Compte tenu de ces contraintes, les économistes écologiques proposent les trois règles de Daly pour la gestion des ressources naturelles afin de remplacer les règles d'Hotelling et de Hartwick (Daly, 1990)[11].

La première concerne les ressources renouvelables, sols, eau, forêts, poissons... « Leur utilisation durable ne doit pas dépasser le rythme auquel ces ressources se régénèrent ». Il s'agit d'une règle biologique, qui repose sur l'idée que la substituabilité entre capital naturel et capital construit est limitée. Par exemple, l'élevage de poissons ne remplace pas de façon satisfaisante la pêche du poisson sauvage, ne serait-ce que parce que, actuellement, pour produire 1 kilo de truite d'élevage, il faut pêcher 2,4 kg de poisson sauvage !

La seconde règle s'applique aux ressources non renouvelables, combustibles fossiles, minerais, eaux souterraines fossiles... « Leur utilisation durable ne doit pas dépasser le rythme auquel une ressource renouvelable, utilisée de façon soutenable, peut les remplacer ». Par exemple, on ne doit utiliser les eaux souterraines fossiles que le temps de restaurer un

[11] C'est la version de MEADOWS (2013), p. 99, qui est citée ici.

cycle de l'eau renouvelable durable sur un territoire et de rendre la consommation d'eau compatible avec ce niveau de ressource renouvelable. En un sens, il s'agit d'une règle analogue à celle d'Hartwik, mais modifiée. On ne substitue plus du capital construit au capital naturel que l'on détruit, mais un autre capital naturel qui, lui, est renouvelable.

La troisième règle concerne les polluants : « Le taux d'émission soutenable ne doit pas dépasser le rythme auquel ces polluants peuvent être recyclés, absorbés ou rendus inoffensifs dans l'exutoire ». Il s'agit de préserver la capacité de régénérescence de ces ressources naturelles que constituent les écosystèmes (eau, air et sols). Il s'agit d'une règle de nature écologique.

Comment mettre en œuvre ces règles, dans un monde où les ressources renouvelables sont déjà très menacées, où 60 % des écosystèmes sont en mauvais état[12] et où les ressources non renouvelables ont vu leur prix augmenter très fortement ces dernières années en raison de leur raréfaction et de leur accès plus difficile ? Le choix n'est pas entre croissance et décroissance, mais entre stratégie consciente et organisée de décroissance de notre consommation de ressources naturelles ou risque d'un effondrement économique brutal si on continue la stratégie au fil de l'eau que nous avons suivie jusqu'à maintenant, jusqu'à atteindre un seuil critique.

Le but est donc de penser un système politique et économique qui permette d'internaliser les effets externes positifs (services rendus par les écosystèmes) et négatifs (pollution, surconsommation de ressources naturelles...) dans la prise de décision, sans dépendre d'un système de calcul des coûts externes et de prélèvement d'éco-taxes effroyablement complexe, coûteux, mal accepté par la population et pratiquement impossible à mettre sur pied. De plus, pour rendre socialement supportable la décroissance dans l'utilisation des ressources naturelles, il est nécessaire de les consacrer prioritairement à la satisfaction des besoins fondamentaux des populations.

Pour ces deux raisons, l'instauration d'une forme de démocratie délibérative et décentralisée à laquelle les citoyens de base participeront acti-

---

[12] Voir le site L'Évaluation des écosystèmes pour le millénaire, http://www.maweb.org/fr/About.aspx

vement, est absolument indispensable. C'est à ce niveau seulement qu'on peut à la fois connaître finement le fonctionnement des écosystèmes et permettre aux citoyens de décider eux-mêmes ce que sont leurs besoins fondamentaux. Pour faciliter une prise de décision collective qui internalise effectivement tous les impacts non monétaires, il sera certainement nécessaire d'étendre la propriété commune des ressources et des espaces naturels ainsi que des terres agricoles. Pour couvrir les besoins fondamentaux, il faudra amplifier la production de biens publics gratuits ou à prix très faibles (santé, éducation, logement). En même temps, une forme de planification globale à l'échelle nationale et internationale s'avère indispensable. Par exemple, la stratégie de limitation des émissions de gaz à effet de serre et de reconstitution de la couche d'ozone, ou celle de protection des stocks de poissons ne peut se concevoir qu'à l'échelle internationale. Les politiques fiscales, de lutte contre les inégalités et la pauvreté doivent être coordonnées par les Etats, afin d'organiser la solidarité entre régions riches et régions pauvres (Costanza et alii, 2013).

A tous les niveaux, dans tous les pays, on peut observer une multitude d'expérimentations qui vont dans ce sens.

Ainsi en France, les autorités locales ont la possibilité d'utiliser leur plan d'occupation des sols et les autres documents d'urbanisme (SCOT par exemple) pour limiter la surexploitation de leurs ressources naturelles. C'est le cas du moins dans les communes littorales, par exemple, où elles peuvent invoquer la notion de capacité d'accueil de leur territoire, comme le leur permet la Loi littoral[13]. Un projet de recherche, financé par le Plan Urbanisme Construction Architecture et la DREAL Pays de la Loire, a permis à une équipe pluridisciplinaire d'économistes, géographes et juristes de l'Université de Nantes de proposer aux élus une méthode d'évaluation de la capacité d'accueil. Cette méthode confronte le projet de territoire avec l'objectif général de préserver ou de renforcer les ressources naturelles, mais aussi économiques et sociales de celui-ci, à charge au politique d'arbitrer entre les différents projets d'utilisation de ces ressources[14].

[13] Dans son article 146-2 de la Loi n° 86-2 du 3 janvier 1986.

[14] Ce projet a fait l'objet de nombreuses publications, accessibles sur le site de la DREAL Pays de la Loire.

L'instauration d'une planification destinée à encadrer et coordonner les prises de décisions locales, ne peut évidemment pas s'inspirer directement des expériences du passé, que ce soit les économies de guerre (allemande de la Première Guerre mondiale, anglaise, états-unienne et allemande encore de la Seconde Guerre mondiale), la planification soviétique ni même la planification indicative à la française des années 60. Les conditions sont trop différentes, les contraintes également, même si dans les deux premiers cas au moins, l'objectif était bien de consacrer les ressources naturelles rares (terres agricoles, charbon, métaux...) à la satisfaction des besoins fondamentaux ... de l'effort de guerre. En particulier, les critères de performance doivent être profondément repensés.

C'est à cet effort de réflexion que se consacre par exemple le Forum pour d'Autres Indicateurs de Richesse[15]. De nombreuses tentatives locales se sont aussi développées dans les régions françaises (Laure Després et alii, 2009). Mais l'exemple le plus intéressant pour ce qui concerne l'utilisation des ressources naturelles pour couvrir les besoins fondamentaux des populations, concerne le Vanuatu, un petit pays insulaire où 70 à 80 % de la population vit en autosubsistance. Trois domaines du bien être sont explorés : l'accès libre et gratuit aux ressources (terre, droit de pêche, ressources forestières...), les pratiques culturelles (connaissance des danses, chants ou jeux traditionnels, maîtrise des compétences de production traditionnelles...), et la vitalité communautaire (participation aux réunions de la communauté, participation aux activités bénévoles communautaires, indicateur de confiance envers les voisins, qualité de la gouvernance ...). A noter que de nombreux indicateurs sont des quantités objectives, mais que de nombreux autres résultent de l'évaluation personnelle des personnes interrogées. L'objectif final est que toute politique publique soit évaluée à l'aune de son impact attendu ou observé sur ces indicateurs (Tanguay, 2012).

La question de savoir si ces changements sont compatibles avec le fonctionnement d'un capitalisme même profondément réformé, reste posée. A la lecture du manifeste des économistes écologiques paru très récem-

[15] Ce Forum a été créé en 2008, en parallèle avec la création de la Commission STIGLITZ-SEN, chargée par le Gouvernement français de réfléchir sur un indicateur alternatif au PIB.

ment (Costanza *et alii*, 2013), on peut en douter. Mais ceci est une autre histoire, qui dépasse largement le cadre de cette contribution.

Références

Alternatives Internationales Hors-série n° 014 - janvier 2014, Entretien avec Maxime Combes, économiste et membre du conseil scientifique d'Attac, association signataire de l'appel "Il est temps de mettre fin au marché carbone européen" et Pierre-André Jouvet, directeur scientifique de la chaire économie du climat à l'Université Paris Dauphine. Propos recueillis par Hervé Kempf.

BIHOUIX Philippe (2013), « Matérialité du productivisme », in SINAÏ Agnès (dir), *Penser la décroissance, Politiques de l'Anthropocène,* Nouveaux Débats, SciencesPo Les Presses.

BOLT Katarine, MATETE Mampite, CLEMENS Michael (2002), *Manual for Calculating Adjusted Net Savings*, Environmental Department, World Bank, September.

BOUGET Denis (2013), « Besoins fondamentaux » in COLLART-DUTILLEUL François et BUGNICOURT Jean-Philippe (dir.), *Dictionnaire juridique de la sécurité alimentaire dans le monde,* Editions Larcier en français et en anglais, *Edición* Inida en espagnol.

CHADENAS Céline, POUILLAUDE Agnès, POTTIER Patrick, STRUILLOU Jean-François (2010), *Evaluer la capacité d'accueil et de développement des territoires littoraux,* Guide pratique, DREAL Pays de la Loire, 2e édition, 103 pages, http://www.pays-de-la-loire.developpement-durable.gouv.fr/

CHOBLET Claire, MASLIANSKAIA-PAUTREL Masha (2009a), « Les zones humides dans l'estuaire de la Loire : état des principales fonctions environnementales et des méthodes d'évaluation économique associées » in DESPRES Laure (coord.) *L'estuaire de la Loire, un territoire en développement durable ?* PUR.

CHOBLET Claire, MASLIANSKAIA-PAUTREL Masha (2009b), « Comment mesurer la fonction d'habitat pour les poissons ? Pistes pour une évaluation économique des vasières estuariennes » in DESPRES Laure (coord.) *L'estuaire de la Loire, un territoire en développement durable?* PUR.

CLINE William R. (1999), "Discounting for the very long term", in PORTNEY Paul R. and WEYANT John P. (dir), *Discounting and Intergenerational Equity*, Resources for the Future, p.131-140.

COSTANZA Robert et alii (2013), *Vivement 2050 ! Programme pour une économie soutenable et désirable*, Institut Veblen, Les Petits matins, paru en anglais en 2012.

DESPRES Laure (2013), « Comment le fonctionnement actuel du système économique mondialisé influence-t-il la sécurité alimentaire? » in COLLART-DUTILLEUL François. et BREGER Thomas (dir.), *Penser une démocratie alimentaire* Vol.1, *Edición* Inida, San José, pp. 57-67.

DESPRES Laure et alii (2009), « Les indicateurs de développement durable : leçon de quelques expériences locales », in DESPRES Laure (coord.) *L'estuaire de la Loire, un territoire en développement durable?* PUR.

DALY Herman (1990), "Toward Some Operational Principles of Sustainable Development", *Ecological Economics*, 2.

Forum pour d'Autres Indicateurs de Richesses, http://www.idies.org/index.php?category

/FAIR

GEORGESCU-ROEGEN Nicholas (1971), *The Entropy Law and the Economic Process*, Harvard University Press, traduit en français *La décroissance - Entropie - Écologie - Économie*, Edition Pierre-Marcel Favre, Lausanne, 1979.

HOTELLING Harold (1931) "The economics of exhaustible resources", *The Journal of Political Economy*, 39(2), 137-175.

L'écologie industrielle et territoriale, un outil de développement économique durable (2013), Orée, http://www.oree.org/presentation/objectifs.html

L'Évaluation des écosystèmes pour le millénaire, Organisation des Nations Unies, http://www.maweb.org/fr/About.aspx

MEADOWS Donella, MEADOWS Dennis, RANDERS Jorgen, BEHRENS William III (1972), *Halte à la croissance ?* Fayard, paru en anglais en 1972.

MEADOWS Donella, MEADOWS Dennis, RANDERS Jorgen (2012), *Les limites à la croissance dans un monde fini*, Rue de l'échiquier, paru en anglais en 2004.

MEADOWS Dennis (2013), « Il est trop tard pour le développement durable », in Sinaï Agnès (dir), *Penser la décroissance, Politiques de l'Anthropocène,* Nouveaux Débats, SciencesPo Les Presses.

OCDE (2009), *Ressources naturelles et croissance pro-pauvres, Enjeux économiques et politiques,* Lignes directrices et ouvrage de référence du CAD. Document sur les bonnes pratiques.

ORSENNA Erik et le Cercle des économistes (2007), *Un monde de ressources rares*, Librairie Académique Perrin, 207 p.

PARACHKEVOVA Irina, TELLER Marina, DESPRES Laure, « Spéculation » in COLLART-DUTILLEUL François et BUGNICOURT Jean-Philippe (dir.), *Dictionnaire juridique de la sécurité alimentaire dans le monde,* Editions Larcier en français et en anglais, *Edición* Inida en espagnol.

TANGUAY Jamie (coord.) (2012), *Alternative Indicators of Well-Being for Melanesia. Vanuatu Pilot Study Report,* Vanuatu National Statistics Office, Malvatumauri National Council of Chiefs.

Rapport Planète vivante 2012, Biodiversité, biocapacité: faisons les bons choix (2012), WWF, Zoological Society of London, Global Footprint Network, Agence Spatiale Européenne.

STIGLITZ Joseph E., SEN Amartya, FITOUSSI Jean-Paul (2008), *Report by the Commission on the Measurement of Economic Performance and Social Progress,* http://www.stiglitz-sen-fitoussi.fr/documents/rapport_anglais.pdf#page=1&zoom=auto,0,842

Toward the Circular Economy (2012 et 2013), Report, Fondation Ellen MacArthur, Vol 1 et Vol 2.

Peut-on assurer le droit à l'alimentation sans la souveraineté alimentaire ?

Michel BUISSON * & Priscilla CLAEYS **

Le droit de tou(te)s à l'alimentation est un droit humain reconnu et codifié en droit international des droits de l'Homme. Il met l'accent sur la nécessaire prise en compte des populations vulnérables et sur l'importance d'une alimentation durable et équilibrée. Il implique l'obligation, pour les Etats et institutions internationales, de mettre en place un ordre économique mondial favorisant la réalisation universelle de ce droit[1]. Le droit à l'alimentation a connu récemment des avancées notables grâce aux efforts combinés de certains Etats s'étant engagés à le mettre en œuvre, de la FAO et d'organisations de la société civile, ainsi que du Rapporteur spécial des Nations Unies pour le droit à l'alimentation : élaboration de son contenu normatif, reconnaissance de sa justiciabilité[2] et mise en évidence des facteurs structurels contribuant à sa réalisation[3]. Néanmoins, ces avancées ont eu une portée avant tout nationale et n'ont que marginalement contribué à la mise en place du nouvel ordre mondial qui serait nécessaire à sa mise en œuvre.

Cette contribution défend l'idée que le droit à l'alimentation ne peut être réalisé sans une profonde modification des règles et politiques régissant le système alimentaire mondial, actuellement dominé par les Etats agro-exportateurs et les entreprises agroalimentaires transnationales. Elle explore les avancées que pourrait apporter l'élaboration de nouvelles règles fondées sur la souveraineté alimentaire, ainsi que les obstacles auxquels

* Agroéconomiste

** Chercheuse en sciences sociales à l'Université de Louvain (UCL), Belgique, et conseillère auprès du Rapporteur spécial sur le droit à l'alimentation depuis 2008.

[1] De Schutter O., *Rapport sur la mission auprès de l'OMC présenté devant le Conseil des Droits de l'Homme*, Rapporteur spécial sur le droit à l'alimentation, février 2009 ((A/HRC/10/5/Add.2).

[2] Golay C., *Droit à l'alimentation et accès à la justice*, Bruylant, 2011, 356 p.

[3] De Schutter O., *Rapport intérimaire du Rapporteur spécial sur le droit à l'alimentation devant l'Assemblée générale du 7 août 2013* (A/68/288).

sont confrontés, à l'heure actuelle, les mouvements paysans et organisations de la société civile revendiquant le « droit à la souveraineté alimentaire »[4].

Les politiques actuelles, qu'elles soient commerciales, financières, d'investissement ou ayant trait à l'environnement et au développement rural, ne répondent pas aux besoins de l'humanité et de la planète. Elles n'assurent pas la sécurité alimentaire de nombreuses sections des populations du Nord et du Sud et sont responsables d'une catastrophe écologique sans précédent : dérèglement climatique particulièrement lourd de conséquences pour l'agriculture des zones tropicales et équatoriales, perte de fertilité et de biodiversité, pollutions, déforestation. Les crises récentes ont démontré l'incapacité de la communauté internationale à réguler les échanges des produits agricoles et alimentaires, tout en aggravant les conséquences de la mise en concurrence de systèmes agricoles fort différents. Les accords de l'Organisation mondiale du commerce (OMC) signés dans un contexte de croissance productiviste et de baisse tendancielle des prix agricoles[5] déjà fort contestables en 1994, le sont de plus en plus. Ainsi, l'objectif d'assurer la sécurité alimentaire par des marchés libéralisés, qui a provoqué l'émergence de la revendication de la souveraineté alimentaire en 1996 lors du Sommet mondial de l'alimentation (SMA), est de plus en plus remis en cause[6].

Le paradigme néolibéral, fondement de ces accords, est de plus en plus contesté par des mouvements sociaux, paysans et autres, et par certains gouvernements, alors que celui de souveraineté alimentaire a connu un succès considérable depuis sa formulation initiale en 1996 par la Via

---

[4] Pour une analyse de la trajectoire institutionnelle de ce droit nouveau, voir CLAEYS P., « The Creation of New Rights by the Food Sovereignty Movement: The Challenge of Institutionalizing Subversion », *Sociology*, 46(5), 2012, p. 844-860.

[5] A la fin des années 1980, lors de la préparation des accords de l'OMC, l'indice FAO des prix des produits alimentaires en termes réels (indice de la valeur nominale, assez stable, corrigée par l'évolution des prix des produits manufacturés), terminait une longue période de baisse engagée en 1973. Cette baisse a été suivie d'une stabilité des deux indices jusqu'en 2004, puis d'une croissance rapide ensuite ; ainsi en 2013, par rapport à la base 100 en 2002-2004, l'indice en valeur nominale est de 210 et celui en valeur réelle est de 160. Source FAO, Perspectives alimentaires, novembre 2013, 11 pages.

[6] BUISSON M., « La crise alimentaire dans l'entrelacs des crises ». *Ecologie & politique*, 2009, n°38.

Campesina. Le paradigme de la souveraineté alimentaire met en avant un ensemble de changements structurels radicaux qui seraient rendus possibles et efficaces par de nouveaux instruments de gouvernance au niveau international[7]. Ce paradigme insiste par ailleurs sur l'accès des paysans aux ressources naturelles (terre, eau, semences) avec des niveaux d'emploi et des revenus satisfaisants (prix, marchés), l'autonomie dans leurs choix productifs, la nécessaire intervention de l'état pour protéger et développer les marchés alimentaires locaux, nationaux et régionaux et la définition démocratique des politiques agricoles[8].

Malgré la vitalité des mouvements paysans revendiquant, depuis 20 ans, la nécessaire transition vers cet autre paradigme, il nous semble qu'un important travail reste à réaliser pour imaginer et construire ensemble les nouvelles règles qui permettraient l'articulation de systèmes agricoles locaux, nationaux et régionaux, répondant aux critères d'équité, de durabilité et aux besoins alimentaires de tous. Deux champs du droit international et deux voies parallèles mais se renforçant mutuellement, dans le cadre du « pluralisme ordonné » défini par Mireille Delmas-Marty[9], pourraient être explorés pour obtenir de nouvelles règles fondées sur la souveraineté alimentaire : le champ des droits humains et le champ du droit international commercial.

Dans le champ des « droits humains », la reconnaissance du « droit des peuples à la souveraineté alimentaire », comme droit humain collectif, représenterait une avancée considérable. Ce droit nouveau pourrait être défini, dans sa dimension externe, comme le droit des Etats de choisir son

---

[7] Pour une présentation complète des instruments qui permettraient l'avènement de ce paradigme, voir BUISSON M., *Construire la souveraineté alimentaire*, L'Harmattan, 2013, 226 p.

[8] Le paradigme de souveraineté alimentaire est en évolution constante mais la Déclaration de Nyeleni de 2007 qui le présente sous forme de 7 piliers est généralement considérée comme représentative.

[9] « Pour tenter d'échapper à la fois au désordre du monde (séparation radicale et relativisme absolu) et à l'ordre qui serait imposé par le plus fort au nom d'un universalisme de surplomb (fusion totale de type hégémonique) il faut donc chercher une issue par delà le relatif et l'universel. Autrement dit, explorer les voies et moyens d'un droit qui réussirait à ordonner la complexité sans la supprimer, apprenant à la transformer en un "pluralisme ordonné" », in DELMAS-MARTY M., *Le pluralisme ordonné*, p. 28, T II des Forces imaginantes du droit (4 tomes), Seuil, Paris, 2006, 301 p.

propre système agricole et alimentaire (contre l'imposition extérieure par des Etats plus puissants, des organismes internationaux ou des firmes). Dans sa dimension interne, ce droit pourrait être traduit par l'obligation, pour un Etat, d'impliquer toutes les sections de la population dans l'élaboration des politiques agricoles et alimentaires. La reconnaissance du droit à la souveraineté alimentaire pourrait relever d'une déclaration ou convention adoptée par les Nations Unies[10]. Dans un second temps, la mise en œuvre de ce droit nouveau nécessiterait la déconstruction des règles commerciales actuelles et la mise en place de nouvelles règles[11].

Dans le champ du droit international commercial, trois types d'avancées devraient être articulées pour permettre la transition vers un système alimentaire mondial fondé sur la souveraineté alimentaire. Un tout autre « accord sur l'agriculture » devrait être négocié, complété par des règles contraignantes pour les firmes multinationales de l'agrobusiness, une forte restriction dans l'application de la règle du « traitement national », et la mise en place d'instruments permettant l'organisation des marchés internationaux (régulation de l'offre, suppression de toute possibilité de dumping ou d'introduction des produits agricoles dans les produits dérivés, ...).

Au plan juridique, le droit à la souveraineté alimentaire « accorderait » aux Etats une autonomie supérieure à l'actuelle en matière de politique agricole et alimentaire mais n'imposerait aucun contenu particulier à ces politiques, au-delà du respect des autres règles internationales, notamment en matière de droits humains et de protection de l'environnement. L'autonomie des pouvoirs nationaux et locaux serait donc particulièrement nette en matière de choix agricoles et alimentaires. Dans la même ligne, les nouvelles règles commerciales doivent permettre, mais n'imposeraient pas, des techniques particulières et un modèle de production particulier dont le

---

[10] Si une telle convention a longtemps constitué une demande des organisations paysannes réunies au sein de La Via Campesina, ainsi que d'un certain nombre d'alliés, elle semble aujourd'hui reléguée au second plan.

[11] Cette exigence ne serait pas satisfaite par la proposition visant à l'adoption d'une reconnaissance internationale d'une "exception alimentaire" telle qu'avancée par F. Collard Dutilleul. Voir: COLLART DUTILLEUL F., « Proposition pour la reconnaissance internationale d'une "exception alimentaire" sur le modèle de "l'exception culturelle" » in COLLART DUTILLEUL F., BREGER Th. (dir.) *Penser une démocratie alimentaire* Vol. 1, pp. 13-46, San José, *Edición* INIDA, 2013, 482 p.

choix dépendrait des choix sociétaux et politiques, et des décisions des producteurs agricoles.

La traduction du paradigme de la souveraineté alimentaire en instruments, droit(s) et politiques, nécessiterait l'articulation de trois niveaux : le local, le national/régional et l'international. En effet, l'obtention de nouvelles règles internationales est nécessaire pour permettre à chaque Etat d'exercer sa souveraineté alimentaire. Dans le même temps, la modification fondamentale des règles, y compris au plan international, ne sera possible que si, aux niveaux local et national, des forces sociales et politiques construisent, par leurs actions et propositions, de nouvelles pratiques et de nouveaux cadres légaux justifiant et imposant, lors des négociations internationales, des règles relevant du paradigme de la souveraineté alimentaire. La traduction de la souveraineté alimentaire en règles internationales alternatives est donc à la fois déterminant et insuffisant à lui seul. Aux niveaux local et national/régional, il s'agira de valoriser au mieux le nouveau cadre international. Cette valorisation va dépendre des rapports de force aux plans politique et social et entre ces deux champs, rapports de force qu'il revient aux mouvements sociaux d'établir.

Le processus de construction d'un système alimentaire mondial fondé sur la souveraineté alimentaire (SA) impliquerait donc un double mouvement simultané et articulé entre les trois niveaux, ainsi que des mouvements dans les deux sens, au sein des niveaux national et local comme schématisé dans ce tableau :

Niveau	Mouvement des règles	Mouvement des propositions
International	Elaboration à l'ONU ou au CSA… de nouvelles règles fondées sur la SA Reconnaissance internationale du droit à la SA	Mouvements sociaux, pays, institutions, proposant d'autres règles à l'ONU…
National/régional	Elaboration et mise en œuvre de politiques nationales alternatives compatibles avec le paradigme de la SA	Elaboration de propositions pour d'autres règles internationales et d'autres politiques nationales
Infra-national/local	Elaboration et mise en œuvre de politiques locales alternatives compatibles avec le paradigme de la SA	Luttes et pratiques mettant en œuvre le paradigme de la SA (obtention d'autonomie pour les producteurs et pour les consommateurs)

Les avancées au niveau international seront les plus difficiles à obtenir, compte tenu de la diversité des enjeux selon les pays et des fondements néolibéraux de l'OMC. Néanmoins, il nous semble que la crise du paradigme néolibéral et les échecs des marchés à assurer la sécurité alimentaire, ainsi que le blocage de l'OMC non résolu par l'accord de Bali de décembre 2013[12] devraient permettre, graduellement, la mise en place d'une réflexion sur la nécessité de nouveaux fondements. Par ailleurs, l'inscription par plusieurs pays du droit à la souveraineté alimentaire dans leur constitution (Bolivie, Equateur, Népal)[13], la récente réforme du Comité de la Sécurité Alimentaire et le rôle accru qu'y joue la société civile, ainsi que la négociation d'une Déclaration sur les droits des paysans et autres personnes vivant dans les zones rurales au Conseil des Droits de l'Homme à l'ONU, constituent autant d'avancées qui peuvent renforcer les multiples initiatives et alternatives locales. Enfin, partout dans le monde, des luttes pour la défense des droits des peuples indigènes, pour l'accès à la terre, pour la mise en place de réseaux alimentaires alternatifs, s'inscrivent au sein de revendications pour l'autonomie des peuples et pour la démocratie, donc pour de nouvelles formes de souveraineté.

Conclusion

Pour permettre à ces initiatives et alternatives locales de perdurer et se développer, il est urgent que le mouvement transnational pour la souveraineté alimentaire (au sens large) mette en place une stratégie coordon-

---

[12] L'accord obtenu lors de la Conférence ministérielle de début décembre 2013 constitue un accord à minima: la « facilitation des échanges » (premier volet) favorise les pays riches et exportateurs, tout en imposant des nouvelles normes aux autres ; le second volet obtenu sous la pression de l'Inde permet seulement la prolongation, à titre provisoire, des dispositifs de stockage existants (Inde et quelques autres pays) au nom de la « clause de paix ». La mise en place d'un groupe de travail au sein du comité de l'agriculture de l'OMC peut permettre d'engager un débat sur les questions des politiques nationales de sécurité alimentaire et, peut-être, au delà (voir Jacques Berthelot, www.solidarite.asso.fr). Pour l'instant, les impératifs, notamment des pays africains, ne sont toujours pas pris en compte (voir la déclaration du réseau Afrique sur le commerce, http:/twnafrica.org).

[13] Il serait souhaitable que des groupes de pays construisent leur souveraineté alimentaire en dérogation aux règles actuelles, déconstruisant ainsi le système actuel et construisant, avec d'autres, le système alternatif fondé sur la souveraineté alimentaire. Force est de reconnaître que les expériences en cours dans les pays cités ne sont pas satisfaisantes de ce point de vue.

née pour élaborer et demander de nouvelles règles commerciales internationales. Ces dernières années, et pour une série de raisons, la construction de la souveraineté alimentaire au niveau international n'a pas constitué la priorité du mouvement, d'abord centré sur l'objectif stratégique de délégitimation de l'OMC, ensuite accaparé par d'autres luttes telles que le changement climatique, les accaparements des terres, les OGM et la privatisation des semences, aujourd'hui focalisé sur la mise en place d'alternatives concrètes, fondées sur l'agroécologie, l'accès à la terre et la défense du territoire et les alliances avec d'autres groupes sociaux.

Il nous semble néanmoins nécessaire d'entamer une réflexion sur les outils permettant la traduction en termes de droit(s) de l'objectif de souveraineté alimentaire, si celui doit un jour être atteint. Cette traduction implique un nouveau droit humain collectif, le droit à la souveraineté alimentaire, base de nouvelles règles commerciales internationales. Ces nouvelles règles permettront l'élaboration et la mise en œuvre, en cohérence avec le paradigme de souveraineté alimentaire, de nouvelles politiques régionales et nationales du type de celles proposées à Nyéléni, et de nouvelles pratiques de production et d'échange aux différents niveaux. En lien avec ces alternatives, le travail sur les changements nécessaires aux niveaux national et international implique que, ensemble, le mouvement social élargi et des institutions (recherche, juristes,...) fassent, avec des gouvernements, progresser la conquête de ces nouveaux droits au sein de l'ONU puis sur le plan commercial.

La Convention de 2012 relative à l'assistance alimentaire : une avancée pour l'aide et le développement en faveur d'un accès à une alimentation adéquate ?

Marie CUQ [*]

Dès 1966, l'Assemblée générale des Nations Unies (NU) souligne que « l'aide alimentaire internationale devrait être l'objet de mesures concertées et planifiées afin d'assurer aux pays un flux régulier de produits alimentaires »[1]. Dans cette perspective, un mécanisme multilatéral pour l'aide alimentaire fut créé à destination des populations dans le besoin - le Programme alimentaire mondial (PAM). En pratique, le PAM envoie des équipes auprès des populations pour « identifier la quantité de vivres nécessaires, le nombre de bénéficiaires et la durée de l'urgence », puis il « élabore une opération d'urgence [...] » et « lance un appel à la communauté internationale pour récolter des fonds et de l'aide alimentaire »[2]. Principalement financé par les Etats, le PAM fournit près d'un quart de l'aide alimentaire et constitue actuellement, dans un contexte généralisé de baisse de l'aide, le « plus grand pourvoyeur » mondial[3]. Dans son fonctionnement, il est toutefois confronté à des défis tenant au fondement volontaire des contributions des Etats dont la fourniture s'est souvent réalisée « à contretemps » des besoins des populations[4]. En effet, les Etats octroient

---

* Doctorante au Centre de droit international de l'Université Paris Ouest Nanterre La Défense. Ancienne assistante de recherche auprès du Rapporteur spécial des Nations Unies pour le droit à l'alimentation.

[1] Rés. 2155 (XXX) de l'Assemblée générale des NU, 22 novembre 1966, 4ème considérant, [http://www.un.org/].

[2] J.-M. THOUVENIN et C. PHILIPPE, « Le droit à l'alimentation», in *Droit international social* (J.-M. THOUVENIN et A. TREBILCOCK dir.), Bruylant, 2013, p. 1708, par. 39.

[3] A. MAHIOU, « Sécurité alimentaire », Introduction *in La sécurité alimentaire* (A. MAHIOU et F. SNYDER dir.), Académie du Droit international de La Haye, 2006, pp. 25 et 26.

[4] Rapport d'O. DE SCHUTTER, Rapporteur spécial des NU pour le droit à l'alimentation, *Le rôle de la coopération en faveur du développement et de l'aide alimentaire dans la réalisation du droit à une alimentation suffisante : de la charité à l'obligation*, A/HRC/10/5, 11 février 2009, par. 14.

volontiers leur aide par le biais d'un écoulement des excédents alimentaires qu'ils produisent, profitant de cette opportunité pour éviter de faire chuter les prix de ces denrées par une offre surabondante sur le marché mondial. Cette pratique rend la fourniture d'aide irrégulière et parfois inadéquate puisque non définie par les besoins des populations et des Etats bénéficiaires.

Pour faciliter son adéquation et sa prévisibilité mondiale, plusieurs Etats ont, dès 1967, adopté une Convention relative à l'aide alimentaire par laquelle ils s'engageaient à fournir une quantité annuelle minimum d'aide en faveur de pays dans l'incapacité de financer suffisamment d'importations pour satisfaire les besoins de leurs populations[5]. Cette première Convention fut prorogée et modifiée à plusieurs reprises, jusqu'à sa dernière version en 1999[6]. Sa mise en œuvre fut cependant régulièrement axée sur la recherche de nouveaux débouchés pour l'écoulement des stocks alimentaires des Etats fournisseurs d'aide et ne prenait pas assez en compte les besoins des populations bénéficiaires. Elle peinait également à minimiser les effets pernicieux de l'aide sur les politiques agricoles des Etats bénéficiaires. En proposant des denrées à titre gratuit ou à un prix inférieur au marché, l'aide alimentaire peut en effet désorganiser les marchés régionaux de consommation et décourager les producteurs locaux d'aliments[7].

Du fait de la succession de crises alimentaires dans les années 2000, il devenait urgent d'améliorer les modalités de l'aide et de porter une attention plus grande aux besoins en développement des Etats bénéficiaires[8]. En 2012, après huit années de négociations, les Etats adoptèrent la Convention relative à l'assistance alimentaire dont l'objectif se définit à la fois comme celui de « sauver des vies » en améliorant les modalités de l'aide alimentaire mais également « de réduire la faim ainsi que d'améliorer

---

[5] *Convention relative à l'aide alimentaire du 15 octobre 1967*, RTNU, vol. 727, p. 199.

[6] Elle fut elle-même prorogée jusqu'au 30 juin 2012 : Convention relative à l'aide alimentaire du 13 avril 1999, Londres, *RTNU*, vol. 2073, p. 135. (Parties : Argentine, Australie, Canada, Commission européenne et ses Etats membres, Japon, Norvège, Suisse, Etats-Unis).

[7] O. De Schutter, *op.cit.,* par. 30.

[8] Par ex. en ce sens : O. De Schutter, *op.cit.,* pars. 30 à 35 ; A. Mahiou, *op.cit.*, pp. 26 et 27.

la sécurité alimentaire et l'état nutritionnel des populations les plus vulnérables »[9] par des mesures qui contribuent à plus long terme au développement des Etats. Son objectif ambitieux et particulièrement adapté aux besoins actuels de nombreux pays contraste toutefois avec l'analyse de son contenu. Les modalités de l'assistance alimentaire ne connaissent qu'une amélioration à géométrie variable (I) tandis que la Convention limite elle-même la portée de ses dispositions en exigeant leur compatibilité avec le droit de l'Organisation Mondiale du Commerce (OMC), en particulier avec les futurs aboutissements des négociations commerciales agricoles (II).

I.- L'amélioration contrastée des modalités de l'assistance alimentaire

L'aide en nature est le moyen classiquement utilisé par les Etats donateurs. Au fur et à mesure de sa mise en œuvre, il a été souligné l'importance d'une meilleure adéquation de celle-ci avec les besoins alimentaires des bénéficiaires. À l'origine, la Convention de 1967 fixait un montant d'aide attribué exclusivement sous forme de blé[10]. Avec l'adoption de la Convention de 1999, l'aide ne concernait plus uniquement le blé, mais également d'autres céréales, le riz, les légumineuses, les huiles comestibles, la poudre de lait, le sucre et les tubercules comestibles (manioc, pommes de terre, etc.)[11]. Dans un sens favorable, la Convention de 2012 marque une nouvelle extension des produits admissibles puisque l'aide concerne désormais tous les « produits destinées à la consommation humaine » conformes aux législations de l'Etat bénéficiaire, aux normes internationales relatives à la salubrité et à la qualité alimentaires et aux besoins nutritionnels dans les situations d'urgence[12]. Une attention accrue est donc portée à la qualité de l'aide en nature, que ce soit en termes d'innocuité,

---

[9] Art. 1 de la Convention relative à l'assistance alimentaire, Londres, 25 avril 2012, [http://treaties.un.org]. (Parties : Autriche, Canada, Danemark, Etats-Unis, Finlande, Japon, Suisse et UE). Les Etats bénéficiaires sont ceux inscrits sur la liste de l'aide publique au développement de l'OCDE : art. 4 de la Convention de 2012, *précit.*

[10] Art. II par. 1 de la *Convention relative à l'aide alimentaire de 1967*, *précit.*

[11] Art. IV a) de la Convention de 1999, *précit.*

[12] Art. 4 par. 3 de la Convention de 2012, *précit.*

d'apports nutritionnels et d'adéquation culturelle. Cependant, la Convention de 2012 ne va pas jusqu'à fournir une liste précise des aliments admis et prévoit seulement qu'une liste sera adoptée ultérieurement par les Etats[13]. De même, elle ne fixe plus directement de montants chiffrés des engagements étatiques qui feront également l'objet d'une décision annuelle des Etats[14]. Ces dispositions rendent moins prévisibles le contenu et le montant de cette aide au détriment des intérêts des bénéficiaires[15]. Au surplus, la Convention ne définit pas les engagements étatiques en fonction des besoins identifiés des bénéficiaires. Cette proposition avait pourtant été soutenue par plusieurs auteurs et instances internationales comme un outil intéressant pour améliorer l'efficacité de l'aide[16]. La Convention de 2012 ne diffère pas de la Convention de 1999 sur ce point puisque les engagements des Etats peuvent toujours, selon leur propre intérêt, être exprimés en valeur et/ou en quantité (en tonnes de blé ou son équivalent en d'autres aliments)[17]. Enfin, la Convention de 2012 ne semble pas suffisamment tirer les conséquences de la fluctuation des prix des produits agricoles sur la quantité d'aide alimentaire fournie. Déjà la Convention de 1999 autorisait les Etats à fournir jusqu'à 5 % du total de leurs engagements annuels en aide lorsque les prix des aliments étaient bas sur le marché mondial[18]. Cet étalement de leur obligation annuelle leur permettait, lorsque les cours mondiaux remontaient, d'être dispensés de la fourniture d'aide et d'orienter les produits vers un écoulement commercial. Seulement, c'est au moment où les prix sont au plus haut qu'une aide est particulièrement importante pour des Etats dans l'incapacité de financer suffisamment d'importations

---

[13] *Ibid.*

[14] Art. 5 pars. 4, 5 et 6 de la Convention de 2012, *précit.* Les Etats ont fixé le montant de leur engagement annuel le 15 février 2013, v. Summary Record of the 1st Session of the Food Assistance Committee, doc. SR(FAC1).

[15] J. CLAPP and C. STUART CLARK, "The 2012 Food Assistance Convention: Is a Promise Still a Promise?", May 2012, [http://triplecrisis.com].

[16] V. O. DE SCHUTTER, *op.cit.,* pars. 16 et 17.

[17] Art. III b) de la Convention de 1999, *précit.* ; Art. 5 par. 2 de la Convention de 2012, *précit.*

[18] Art. VI c) de la Convention de 1999, *précit.*

alimentaires pour satisfaire les besoins nationaux[19]. Sur cette question, la Convention de 2012 ne prévoit pas non plus de dispositions pour inciter les Etats à fournir cette aide à contretemps.

A côté de l'aide en nature, la Convention de 2012 est surtout présentée comme novatrice car elle permet aux Etats donateurs de recourir à d'autres actions au titre de l'assistance alimentaire. Les Etats peuvent, par exemple, effectuer des achats d'aliments sur les marchés locaux et régionaux des Etats bénéficiaires[20]. Cela permet de minimiser les effets négatifs d'une aide extérieure en maintenant, par le rachat des surplus régionaux, la viabilité d'une offre locale en aliments. Le développement agricole et rural des Etats bénéficiaires est ainsi mieux considéré. Les Etats donateurs peuvent également « monétiser » leur aide c'est-à-dire proposer à l'achat des denrées à des prix subventionnés en vue de leur vente à moindre coût dans le pays bénéficiaire pour financer des projets de développement[21]. Cette assistance peut également, par le biais de projets d'aide à la production locale d'aliments, contribuer à atténuer la trop grande dépendance des Etats bénéficiaires aux importations internationales. Mais, en réalité, la Convention de 1999 prévoyait déjà cette diversité d'actions puisque les Etats pouvaient choisir parmi des « dons de produits alimentaires ou dons en espèces devant servir à l'achat de produits alimentaires pour ou par le pays bénéficiaire », des « ventes de produits alimentaires contre monnaie du pays bénéficiaire [...] » ou des « ventes de produits alimentaires à crédit »[22]. Du fait de cette simple reprise, certains auteurs ont considéré que la Convention de 2012 se contentait d'entériner, sous l'intitulé « assistance alimentaire », ce qui existait déjà sous la Convention de 1999[23]. D'autres

---

[19] En 2007-2008, il a cependant été constaté une chute brutale des volumes d'aide au moment où les prix des produits agricoles étaient au plus haut sur les marchés : O. De Schutter, *op.cit.,* par. 14.

[20] Art. 2 b) iii) de la Convention de 2012, *précit.*

[21] *Ibid.*, art. 2 b v).

[22] Art. IX a) et e) i) de la Convention de 1999, *précit.*

[23] J. L. VIVERO POL, "Analysis of the new Food Assistance Convention 2012: Do we need it?" July 2012, [http://hungerpolitics.wordpress.com]; E. CLAY, "What's the use of the 2012 Food Assistance Convention?" June 2012, [http://www.odi.org.uk/].

ont minimisé son caractère innovant en soulignant que « [l]e fort accent mis sur les mesures de secours à court terme, combiné avec un soutien limité à l'agriculture locale, est non seulement moins efficace pour surmonter les causes structurelles de l'insécurité alimentaire, mais il pourrait même décourager les investissements dans l'agriculture et la production alimentaire nationale »[24]. Le contenu de cette Convention ne serait donc pas à la hauteur des attentes exprimées en faveur du développement des Etats bénéficiaires. Plusieurs auteurs s'interrogent même sur la pertinence de l'adoption de cette Convention qui, selon eux, laisse une trop grande liberté aux Etats dans le choix des modalités de l'assistance et atténue fortement le contenu des obligations étatiques[25]. Les critiques portent enfin sur une disposition du texte de 2012 précisant que la Convention « n'a pas pour effet de déroger aux obligations existantes ou futures qui s'appliquent entre les Parties dans le cadre de l'OMC. En cas de conflit entre de telles obligations et la présente Convention, les premières l'emportent »[26]. Cette exigence de respect du droit de l'OMC influe pourtant directement sur la portée de la Convention du fait d'un encadrement particulièrement strict de l'assistance alimentaire au sein de l'OMC.

II.- Une portée conditionnée par l'exigence de respect du droit l'OMC

La Convention de 2012 permet aux Etats de recourir à une diversité d'actions pouvant être confondues avec un contournement des obligations des Etats membres de l'OMC. Par exemple, la « monétisation » de l'aide alimentaire peut être assimilée à une subvention aux exportations commerciales d'un Etat, soumis par principe à une obligation progressive de réduction à l'OMC[27]. Les Etats peuvent également octroyer des prêts conces-

---

[24] M. METOU BRUSIL, « Ouverture à la signature de la Convention de Londres du 25 avril 2012 relative à l'assistance alimentaire », *Sentinelle SFDI*, Bull. 306, 27 mai 2012, [www.sentinelle-droit-international.fr].

[25] Par le biais de nombreuses références telles que « lorsqu'il s'agit du moyen le plus efficace et le mieux adapté » : art. 2 a) de la Convention de 2012, *précit.* Pour d'autres ex. v. J. L. VIVERO POL, *op.cit.* V. aussi en ce sens : E. CLAY, *op.cit.* ; J. CLAPP and C. STUART CLARK, *op.cit.*

[26] Art. 3 de la Convention de 2012, *précit.*

[27] Art. 8 et 9.de l'Accord sur l'Agriculture (AA), Accord instituant l'OMC du 15 avril 1994, *1869 RTNU,* 426.

sionnels dont la distinction avec un crédit à l'exportation pour le commerce agricole est délicate[28]. Pourtant, la Convention de 2012 ne prévoit pas de critères pour opérer ces distinctions, laissant le traitement de cette question aux instances de l'OMC. L'Accord sur l'Agriculture (AA) de l'OMC prévoit des dispositions en ce sens. Sur son fondement, l'aide alimentaire n'entre pas dans le champ de l'obligation de réduction des subventions à l'exportation si sa fourniture n'est pas liée « aux exportations commerciales de produits agricoles à destination des pays bénéficiaires », que son versement se réalise, dans la mesure du possible, sous forme de dons et dans le respect des principes de l'Organisation des Nations Unies pour l'alimentation et l'agriculture (*Food and Agriculture Organization* - FAO) en matière d'écoulement des excédents[29]. Ces derniers principes tendent en particulier à assurer que les aides alimentaires « ne remplacent pas des importations commerciales normales »[30]. Pour cela, l'Etat bénéficiaire doit offrir des garanties contre la revente ou la réexpédition des produits, prouver que l'aide dont il bénéficie répond à des besoins de consommation nouveaux qui n'auraient pas pu être satisfaits par d'autres moyens que cette aide et doit maintenir, par principe, un niveau normal d'importations du produit dont il bénéficie au titre de l'aide[31]. L'ensemble de ces conditions encadre donc déjà strictement le bénéfice d'une aide alimentaire dans le but de maintenir les flux commerciaux internationaux.

Les exigences d'une nouvelle libéralisation du commerce mondial entraînent, en outre, un nouvel encadrement, plus restrictif, de l'assistance alimentaire. La dernière version du projet de révision de l'AA rappelle ainsi que l'aide alimentaire doit être fournie afin « d'empêcher le détournement

---

[28] Sur cette question, v. FAO, *Etudes de la FAO sur les aspects sélectionnées des négociations de l'OMC sur l'agriculture*, FAO, Rome, 2002, pp. 75 et s.

[29] Art. 10 : 4 a), b) et c) de l'AA, *précit. ;* Principes de la FAO en matière d'écoulement des excédents et obligations consultatives des États membres de 1954, tels que révisés en 2000, FAO, Rome, 2001, p. 39.

[30] FAO, *Etudes de la FAO sur les aspects sélectionnées des négociations de l'OMC* (...), op.cit., p. 73.

[31] Art. 4 et art. 7 des Principes de la FAO en matière d'écoulement des excédents, *précit.*

commercial »[32]. Les Etats doivent fournir l'aide sans qu'elle soit liée aux exportations commerciales[33]. Elle ne doit pas servir « aux objectifs de développement des marchés des Membres donateurs » et sera, dans la mesure du possible, achetée auprès « de sources locales ou régionales »[34]. L'aide devra aussi être fournie sans pouvoir raisonnablement prévoir « que cela causerait, un effet défavorable sur la production locale ou régionale » et devra se baser sur une évaluation des besoins de l'Etat bénéficiaire[35]. En cela, ce projet intègre les dernières orientations concernant l'efficacité de l'assistance alimentaire en portant une attention aux besoins nutritionnels des populations et aux exigences de développement des Etats. Mais le projet précise surtout que seule l'aide d'urgence peut être exclue de l'obligation de réduction des subventions à l'exportation et cela, seulement si elle est fournie sous forme de vivres et répond à un appel d'une institution internationale ou d'un Etat[36]. Selon l'OMC, ces critères permettent de vérifier « s'il existe un besoin authentique d'aide alimentaire » et, par là, de distinguer cette aide des détournements commerciaux[37]. Les actions d'assistance alimentaire, y compris les aides en nature, qui ne relèvent pas de situations d'urgences seront donc assimilées à des subventions à l'exportation soumises, à l'OMC, à des obligations de réduction substantielle[38]. A cela s'ajoute que la « monétisation » de cette assistance alimentaire sera, par principe, prohibée sauf à l'intention des pays les moins avancées et des pays importateurs nets de produits alimentaires pour « financer le transport intérieur et la livraison de l'aide » ou « l'achat d'intrants agricoles destinés à des producteurs ayant de faibles revenus ou dotés de ressources limitées »[39]. Tout cela restreint donc largement la possibilité,

---

[32] Art. 1, annexe L du Projet révisé de modalités concernant l'agriculture, 6 décembre 2008, TN/AG/W/4/Rev.4.

[33] *Ibid.*, art. 2 c).

[34] *Ibid.*, art. 2 b) et d).

[35] *Ibid.*, art. 3 et art. 6 a) et b).

[36] *Ibid.*, art. 6 a) et b).

[37] V. le site de l'OMC, *Le premier projet révisé de "modalités" sur l'aide alimentaire*, [http://www.wto.org].

[38] Art. 11, annexe L du Projet révisé de modalités concernant l'agriculture, *précit.*

[39] *Ibid.*, art.12.

pour les Etats parties à la Convention de 2012, d'orienter durablement l'assistance alimentaire vers l'établissement de projets de développement au profit des Etats bénéficiaires.

Du fait de cette restriction annoncée, plusieurs pays en développement ont demandé à l'OMC un assouplissement des règles concernant, cette fois, l'aide alimentaire nationale c'est-à-dire précisément le soutien de l'Etat à l'achat d'aliments auprès de producteurs nationaux en vue de constituer des réserves alimentaires nationales[40]. Sur ce point, les Etats membres de l'OMC, réunis à Bali début décembre 2013, ont réussi à s'entendre sur l'établissement d'un mécanisme provisoire de détention de stocks publics à des fins d'aide nationale[41]. Si cette solution reste provisoire, elle permet à court terme de répondre aux besoins urgents de nombreux pays en développement. L'état des négociations concernant l'assistance alimentaire internationale n'a pas connu ces mêmes avancées. Bien que la Convention de 2012 tente de recentrer les modalités de fourniture de l'aide sur les besoins des bénéficiaires et de préciser les modes d'action en faveur de considérations plus structurelles liées au développement des pays bénéficiaires, cela ne semble pas encore suffisant aux négociateurs de l'OMC pour entamer de nouvelles discussions en vue d'un encadrement assoupli de l'assistance alimentaire[42]. En tout état de cause, l'aboutissement de ces négociations se fera sans doute, comme pour l'aide alimentaire nationale, sur la base d'un compromis *a minima* plutôt que vers l'établissement de réponses ambitieuses au profit d'Etats confrontés à de nombreux défis pour assurer une alimentation adéquate à leur population.

---

[40] OMC, Communication de l'Inde au nom de la coalition G-33, 14 novembre 2012 présentée lors de la réunion informelle du Conseil général de l'OMC le 25 février 2013 [http://www.wto.org].

[41] Projet de décision ministérielle « Détention de stocks publics à des fins de sécurité alimentaire », 6 décembre 2013, doc. WT/MIN(13)/W/10. V. ICTSD, « Un accord historique qui fera avancer l'OMC et l'économie mondiale », *Passerelles*, 7 décembre 2013 [http://ictsd.org/].

[42] Projet de décision ministérielle « Concurrence à l'exportation », 6 décembre 2013, doc. WT/MIN(13)/W/12.

Du droit de l'eau au droit à l'eau ?

Franck DUHAUTOY [*]

L'élément hydrique est un aliment essentiel à la vie[1]. Le droit interétatique de l'eau pourrait permettre de bâtir un droit à l'eau pour les personnes. Il s'agirait de s'inspirer des propos de l'ancien juge de la Cour internationale de justice (CIJ), Hersch Lauterpacht (1897-1960) pour qui : « *L'Etat est fait pour les êtres humains et non les êtres humains pour l'Etat* »[2]. Cependant, la réalisation du droit à l'eau est perturbée par les controverses sur le partage entre Etats de ressources communes (fleuves, nappes phréatiques). De plus, souvent, les instruments positifs du droit de l'eau ne donnent pas de priorités entre les différents usages des réserves hydriques partagées (agriculture, industrie, besoins fondamentaux). En ressort une impression de dischronie, les ensembles normatifs droit de l'eau / droit à l'eau n'avançant pas au même rythme vers une reconnaissance effective d'un droit humain à l'élément hydrique[3]. Ce dernier a, en effet, été reconnu dans une résolution de l'Assemblée générale de l'ONU (28 juillet 2010) même si cette décision n'a pas de valeur juridique contraignante en droit international public[4]. **Dans l'état du droit présent (*de lege lata*), le droit de l'eau interétatique constitue-t-il une porte d'entrée vers un droit humain à l'eau pleinement contraignant ?**

Bien que diverses doctrines s'affrontent au sein du droit international public de l'eau, la théorie du partage sur les ressources communes ne

---

* Docteur en droit public de l'Université de Nantes, Laboratoire Droit et Changement Social (UMR 6297).

[1] Le règlement (CE) 178/2002 définit l'aliment comme « *toute substance ou produit, transformé, partiellement transformé ou non transformé, destiné à être ingéré ou raisonnablement susceptible d'être ingéré par l'être humain* » (art. 2).

[2] LAUTERPACHT (H.), *The Function of Law in the International Community*, Oxford, Clarendon Press, 1933, pp. 430-431.

[3] L'expression de dischronie est issue des travaux de Mme DELMAS-MARTY, professeure au Collège de France.

[4] Résolution A/RES/64/292. L'Assemblée générale « *Reconnaît que le droit à l'eau potable et à l'assainissement est un droit de l'homme, essentiel à la pleine jouissance de la vie et à l'exercice de tous les droits de l'homme* » (§ 1).

cesse de progresser (I). Elle a toutefois des difficultés à accoucher d'un droit à l'eau pour les individus (II).

I.- Vers un souverainisme hydrique limité

Loin d'être perçue comme mobile et partagée, l'eau est assimilée par certaines doctrines territoriales ou historiques à une ressource statique sur laquelle l'Etat traversé exerce un contrôle total. La souveraineté territoriale est pensée comme un droit de propriété sur des eaux pourtant communes car mouvantes (A). Toutefois, l'évolution du droit interétatique de l'eau affaiblit ces logiques exclusivistes (B).

A) Des théories exclusivistes critiquées

Certaines doctrines avantagent les Etats d'amont. Il en va ainsi de la souveraineté territoriale absolue issue d'une controverse entre le Mexique et les Etats-Unis (EU) sur les eaux du Rio Grande (fin du XIXème S.)[5]. Apparentée à cette première doctrine existe celle de la « supra-riveraineté » développée par l'ex-Zaïre (République démocratique du Congo) en 1971. A l'époque ses autorités considéraient le Congo comme un fleuve intérieur car il prend sa source dans cet Etat et y parcourt l'essentiel de son trajet[6]. Une autre doctrine dite de l'intégrité territoriale absolue avantage les Etats d'aval. Elle utilise la notion de débit naturel indiquant qu'aucun Etat ne peut augmenter ou réduire le débit d'un cours d'eau partagé sans l'accord des autres entités étatiques ayant alors un droit de veto sur tout nouvel aménagement.

Une quatrième doctrine étaye sa vision sur la profondeur historique. Les droits étatiques sur des eaux communes y reposent sur un *continuum* temporel avantageant les Etats nés tôt dans l'histoire. Etre le premier utilisateur étatique d'une source d'eau est censé légitimer un exclusivisme

---

[5] Pour cette doctrine, l'Attorney General Judson Harmon (1846-1927) a utilisé un arrêt de la Cour suprême : *The Schooner Exchange v. MacFaddon and Others* (1812) : « *La juridiction de l'Etat sur son propre territoire est nécessairement exclusive et absolue. Ses seules limites sont celles qu'elle s'impose elle-même* » (§ 116).

[6] Voir : MUBIALA (M.), La théorie du riverain léonin, *Afr. J. Int'l & Comp. L.*, 307 (1994) p. 308. Pour mémoire, le Fleuve Congo prend sa source dans la province du Katanga avant de parcourir le Congo démocratique sur 4 700 km. Il ne fait frontière avec un Etat étranger (le Congo-Brazzaville) que sur une longueur de 200 km.

juridique d'accès. Tout usage nouveau ne peut reposer que sur une autorisation du premier usager-propriétaire. L'Accord relatif à la pleine utilisation des eaux du Nil signé par l'Egypte et le Soudan le 8 novembre 1959 semble constituer l'unique traité international en rapport. Cet accord bilatéral leur attribuant l'équivalent de 90 % des débits de ce fleuve parle des « *droits acquis antérieurement* » par ces deux Etats (art. 1)[7]. Nulle part n'y apparaissent les droits des autres entités étatiques riveraines du Nil qui, se développant, commencent à revendiquer.

Ancrées dans « *une approche statutaire rigide s'attachant au concept de territoire* »[8], les doctrines précitées démontrent un caractère extrémiste. Au mieux, elles se désintéressent des droits des Etats voisins, au pire, elles les nient. La ressource hydrique y est perçue comme statique et non comme mobile et partagée. En droit privé français de la propriété, elle s'apparenterait à un immeuble par destination[9]. Cette conception oublie le caractère dual de la souveraineté étatique reposant sur des droits mais aussi sur des devoirs. Ainsi, après avoir affirmé les droits des Etats sur leurs ressources naturelles, la résolution 3281 (XXIX) de l'Assemblée générale de l'ONU indique leurs devoirs : « *Dans l'exploitation des ressources naturelles communes à deux ou à plusieurs pays, chaque Etat doit coopérer sur la base d'un système d'information et de consultations préalables afin d'assurer l'exploitation optimale de ces ressources sans porter préjudice aux intérêts légitimes des autres Etats* »[10]. L'exclusivisme souverain est donc nié. Faute de titre, l'Etat agissant aux dépens du territoire d'autrui se trouve face à un principe d'interdiction générale d'action (de pollution, d'extraction). Un *dominium* absolu des Etats sur leurs ressources naturelles

---

[7] Nations unies, *Recueil des traités,* n° 6519, « Accord entre la République du Soudan et la République arabe unie relatif à la pleine utilisation des eaux du Nil. Signé au Caire le 8 novembre 1959 », p. 65.

[8] SOHNLE (J.), *Le droit international des ressources en eau douce : solidarité contre souveraineté*, Paris, La documentation française, Collection Monde européen et international, 2002, p. 244.

[9] Bien que mouvante entre Etats et donc *a priori* meuble par nature, dans les théories exclusivistes l'eau internationale perd son caractère mobilier et devient accessoire d'un immeuble (le territoire de l'entité étatique).

[10] Article 3 de la résolution 3281 (XXIX) de l'Assemblée générale de l'ONU (12 décembre 1974).

se voit refusé[11], en soi une bonne nouvelle pour les populations des Etats voisins. Pour les eaux communes, il est possible de parler d'une « *évolution expansionniste de l'objet* » remettant en cause l'exclusivisme des Etats[12].

B) L'affirmation d'une solidarité interétatique

La souveraineté caractérise l'indépendance de l'Etat-nation mais rien ne lui interdit de céder une partie de ses prérogatives à une instance transnationale (type organe indépendant de régulation d'un cours d'eau) ou intergouvernementale. Une conscience d'enjeux communs peut en constituer l'élément déclencheur. Ainsi, en 1906, les EU acceptèrent une convention sur les eaux du Rio Grande coulant vers le Mexique organisant une « *equitable distribution* » entre les deux Etats[13] sous forme d'une répartition paritaire entre agriculteurs mexicains et étatsuniens (art. 2).

La CIJ a aussi fait sien l'adage *sic utere tuo ut alienum non laedas*[14] (utilisation non dommageable du territoire)[15]. Ce principe, fondant désormais le droit international de l'environnement, a été utilisé dans un contentieux sur les eaux du Danube. Dans sa décision, la CIJ a insisté sur l'utilisation non dommageable du territoire que chaque partie doit respecter en suivant les « *normes actuelles* »[16]. Elle a précisé que « *la Tchécoslovaquie, en prenant unilatéralement le contrôle d'une ressource partagée, et en privant ainsi la Hongrie de son droit à une part équitable et raisonnable des ressources naturelles du Danube -...- n'a pas respecté la proportionnalité exigée par le droit international* »[17]. Les juges se placent dans la logique d'une communauté d'intérêts menant à un partage, développée dès 1929

---

[11] DAILLIER (P.), FORTEAU (M.), PELLET (A.), *Droit international public,* 8ème éd., Paris, L.G.D.J., 2009, n° 283.

[12] SOHNLE (J.), *Le droit international des ressources en eau douce : solidarité contre souveraineté*, Paris, La documentation française, Collection Monde européen et international, 2002, p. 36.

[13] Voir le Préambule de la *Convention Concerning the Equitable Distribution of the Waters of the Rio Grande for Irrigation Purposes*, 21 mai 1906.

[14] « Use de ta propriété de façon à ne pas endommager celles des autres ».

[15] CIJ, Affaire du Détroit de Corfou (Royaume-Uni c. Albanie), arrêt du 9 avril 1949, CIJ, *Recueil 1949*, p. 22.

[16] CIJ, Affaire relative au projet Gabcikovo-Nagymaros (Hongrie / Slovaquie), arrêt du 25 septembre 1997, CIJ, *Recueil 1997,* § 140.

[17] *Idem,* § 85.

lors d'une controverse sur l'Oder[18]. A cette époque, la Cour permanente de justice internationale (CPIJ) avait déclaré que « *[la] communauté d'intérêts sur un fleuve navigable devient la base d'une communauté de droit, dont les traits essentiels sont la parfaite égalité de tous les Etats riverains dans l'usage de tout le parcours du fleuve* »[19]. Ces propos sur la navigation seront repris par la CIJ : « *Le développement moderne du droit international a renforcé ce principe également pour les utilisations des cours d'eau internationaux à des fins autres que la navigation* »[20]. La règle de « *communauté d'intérêts* » pousse les Etats d'un bassin hydrographique à s'accorder avant de construire de nouvelles infrastructures pouvant changer l'approvisionnement de chaque pays. Indubitablement le droit d'accès à l'eau des personnes a tout à y gagner.

Parallèlement, les travaux de la Commission du droit international (CDI) ont abouti à la Convention (dite de New York) sur les utilisations des cours d'eau internationaux à des fins autres que la navigation (1997). Celle-ci affirme que « *Les Etats du cours d'eau doivent utiliser sur leurs territoires respectifs le cours d'eau international de manière équitable et raisonnable* » (art. 5, § 1). Les principes de solidarité et de gestion responsable sont donc posés. Ceci « *comporte à la fois le droit d'utiliser le cours d'eau et le devoir de coopérer à sa protection et à sa mise en valeur* » (art. 5, § 2). Ces principes de solidarité et de prudence génèrent une souveraineté réduite. Chaque Etat peut créer les projets hydriques qu'il désire à condition de ne pas nuire aux intérêts des autres pays riverains du cours d'eau concerné. Cette coopération entre entités étatiques d'un même bassin vise à assurer un partage équitable et raisonnable du précieux liquide. Naît ainsi une appropriation simultanée et non plus unilatérale. Toutefois, ce point concerne les sujets de droits que sont les Etats dans l'ordre international. Qu'en est-il des personnes ?

---

[18] Il est possible de parler de « *solidarité réalisée par une internationalisation expansionniste de l'objet* » (NB : l'eau) comme indiqué dans : SOHNLE (J.), *Le droit international des ressources en eau douce : solidarité contre souveraineté*, Paris, La documentation française, Collection Monde européen et international, 2002, pp. 91-236 (titre de la 1ère partie).

[19] CPJI, Juridiction territoriale de la Commission internationale de l'Oder, arrêt n° 16, 10 septembre 1929, CPJI série A n° 23, p. 27.

[20] CIJ, *Id,* § 85.

II.- Un droit à l'eau peu soluble dans le droit de l'eau

Les doctrines extrémistes fondées sur une souveraineté étatique sans devoir régressent face à celle revendiquant une utilisation raisonnable et équitable des ressources hydriques communes. Ce droit interétatique de l'eau pourrait-il faciliter l'émergence d'un droit humain à l'eau ? La Convention de New York fournit des éléments de réponse (A), tout comme certains traités régionaux (B).

A) Une convention internationale décevante

Dans l'arrêt Gabčíkovo-Nagymaros, la CIJ a rappelé l'importance du respect de l'environnement pour les Etats mais aussi pour les personnes[21]. La Cour rapproche donc les questions hydriques de l'universalité des droits humains même si la CIJ ne traite pas des cas individuels. La responsabilité des Etats est ici posée dans une perspective anthropocentrique[22].

Dans la Convention de New York de 1997, l'utilisation équitable et raisonnable évoquée (art. 5) ne fixe pas de hiérarchie entre les besoins économiques et sociaux des Etats (art. 6, § 1, al. b)[23]. L'art. 10 poursuit en ce sens. Son paragraphe 1 précise que, sans accord ou coutume, aucune utilisation d'un fleuve international n'est prioritaire. Le paragraphe suivant indique qu'une controverse d'usage doit être réglée en accordant une « *attention spéciale [...] à la satisfaction des besoins humains essentiels* ». Il est possible d'en douter puisque le paragraphe 1 précise justement l'absence d'usage prioritaire[24]. De plus une attention aux besoins humains ne signifie pas priorité et encore moins droit à l'eau. Ajoutons que ce paragraphe 2 de l'article 10 débute par « *en cas de conflit* » excluant ainsi

---

[21] Voir : CIJ, Affaire relative au projet Gabcikovo-Nagymaros (Hongrie / Slovaquie), arrêt du 25 septembre 1997, CIJ, *Recueil 1997*, § 53.

[22] Voir : SOHNLE (J.), Irruption du droit de l'environnement dans la jurisprudence de la CIJ : l'affaire Gabcikovo-Nagymaros, *Revue générale de droit international public*, Tome 102, n° 1, 1998, pp. 85-121.

[23] Toutefois, cette Convention n'est pas encore en vigueur. 35 ratifications sont nécessaires. Au 15/12/2013, seuls 32 Etats l'avaient ratifiée : http://treaties.un.org/Pages/ViewDetails.aspx?src=TREATY&mtdsg_no=XXVII-12&chapter=27&lang=en (page consultée le 15 décembre 2013).

[24] PAQUEROT (S.), *Eau douce. La nécessaire refondation du droit international*, Sainte-Foy, Presses de l'Université du Québec, 2004, p. 143.

l'hypothèse d'un droit permanent consacré par la Convention. D'ailleurs l'expression « *besoins humains* » ne fait naître aucune obligation pour les pouvoirs publics. N'en jaillit aucune prérogative de droit subjecti pour les individus. Ce terme ouvre plutôt la voie à une logique de marché que des sociétés privées peuvent combler (potabilisation, fourniture). La méthode exégétique peut, éventuellement, permettre d'atténuer cette vision. Lors de l'élaboration de la Convention, le Groupe de travail plénier avait explicité les « *besoins humains essentiels* » comme la fourniture d'eau suffisante pour maintenir la vie humaine (boisson potable et ressource pour l'agriculture vivrière)[25]. La contradiction relevée précédemment entre les § 1 et 2 de l'art. 10 n'est toutefois pas expliquée même s'il résulte des débats qu'un Etat ne peut dénier à un autre l'eau assurant la survie de sa population au prétexte des besoins de son développement économique[26]. *In fine,* la Convention de New York est loin de reconnaître un droit à l'eau potable et encore moins un nouveau droit de l'Homme. Ce traité est même contre-productif car, sans priorité claire, il fournit des arguments légaux aux Etats voulant soutenir que d'autres usages priment sur les besoins humains fondamentaux[27]. D'ailleurs, la Convention de New York n'évoque même pas le droit à la vie pourtant coutumier voire de *jus cogens*.

Pour les aquifères, un projet d'article de la CDI énonce le principe d'utilisation « *équitable et raisonnable* » (art. 4)[28]. Là encore, aucune priorité entre usages n'existe même si l'article 5 (§ 2) se clôt par un appel à « *particulièrement tenir compte des besoins humains vitaux* », expression au contenu normatif très faible comme déjà relevé.

---

[25] United Nations General Assembly, doc A/51/869, 11 April 1997, § 8 des considérations préliminaires.

[26] Sur ce dernier point, voir : MC CAFFREY (S. C.), A Human Right to Water: Domestic and International Implications, *Georgetown International Environmental Law Review*, vol. 5, n° 1, Fall 1992, p. 24.

[27] GOLAY (Ch.), *La place des besoins humains essentiels dans la Convention des Nations unies sur le droit relatif aux utilisations des cours d'eau internationaux à des fins autres que la navigation*, Genève, IUHEI, section III. 2.c, 2001.

[28] Voir la résolution A/RES/63/124 en date du 11 décembre 2008.

B) Des traités régionaux tout aussi insuffisants

Des institutions communes de gestion organisant une transmission réciproque d'informations[29] ne se rencontrent pas toujours au sein des traités régionaux hydriques comme l'illustre celui entre l'Union indienne et le Pakistan sur les eaux de l'Indus[30]. Il s'agit pourtant d'un préalable à toute approche liée aux droits de l'Homme.

La Communauté de développement d'Afrique australe (CDAA)[31] a donné naissance à un Protocole (révisé en 2000) sur les cours d'eau partagés entre Etats membres. Il fixe un objectif d' « *utilisation durable, équitable et raisonnable des cours d'eau partagés* » (art. 2, b). L'art. 3 (§ 7, a) précise qu'il s'agit d'obtenir une utilisation optimale et durable respectueuse des intérêts des Etats riverains et des générations présentes et futures. En ratifiant ce Protocole, les Etats de la CDAA consentent à ne plus disposer d'une compétence exclusive sur leur territoire[32]. Les facteurs et circonstances relevant d'une utilisation équitable et raisonnable des cours d'eau communs sont précisés dans l'art. 3, § 8, a) qui nomme les besoins sociaux, économiques et environnementaux des Etats. Ceux-ci « *doivent être considérés ensemble et une conclusion atteinte sur la base d'un tout* » (art. 3, § 8, b). A aucun moment n'est précisé que l'accès à l'eau constitue un droit humain prioritaire[33].

---

[29] Exemple de la Commission internationale des frontières et des eaux Mexique / Etats-Unis au sein du Traité entre les Etats-Unis d'Amérique et le Mexique relatif à l'utilisation des eaux du Colorado, § 211-216.

[30] Traité relatif à l'utilisation des eaux de l'Indus (1960), Karachi, 19 septembre, *In* ONU, *RTNU, vol. 419*, New York, Nations unies, p. 125. [Inde, Pakistan, BIRD]. L'Union indienne n'a pas toujours respecté cette obligation.

[31] 15 Etats en sont membres : Afrique du Sud, Angola, Botswana, Lesotho, Madagascar, Malawi, Maurice, Mozambique, Namibie, Congo démocratique, Seychelles, Swaziland, Tanzanie, Zambie et Zimbabwe.

[32] Ce protocole du traité fondateur de la CDAA a été accepté par tous ses Etats membres (sauf Madagascar).

[33] Simplement, les populations dépendantes du cours d'eau partagé doivent être prises en compte parmi l'ensemble des facteurs relevant d'une utilisation équitable et raisonnable (art. 3, § 8, a, iii).

La Communauté de l'Afrique de l'Est (CAE)[34] s'est aussi intéressée à ces questions avec un Protocole pour le développement durable du bassin du lac Victoria (2003) qui consacre « *le principe d'une utilisation équitable et raisonnable des ressources en eau* » (art. 4, § 2, a). Celui-ci reprend presque mot pour mot (art. 5, § 4) les facteurs et circonstances développés dans le Protocole de la CDAA sur les cours d'eau partagés. Aucune priorité n'est, là encore, fixée entre ceux-ci (§ 5). Une utilisation raisonnable et équitable des ressources hydriques partagées ne fait pas naître un droit à l'eau pour les personnes. Dans un Accord-cadre sur le Bassin du Fleuve Nil signé par l'Ethiopie, le Kenya, l'Ouganda, le Rwanda, la Tanzanie et le Burundi, il est précisé que l'eau « *doit être utilisée en priorité de la manière la plus économique, en tenant compte de la satisfaction des besoins de base de la population* »[35]. Là encore, les nécessités basiques de la population ne sont pas définies comme un droit. Même quand apparaît l'invocation d'un droit comme dans la Charte des eaux du Fleuve Sénégal (2002), il s'agit davantage de normes programmatiques que prescriptives immédiates[36]. Proclamer une utilisation équitable et raisonnable d'un cours d'eau partagé ne constitue donc pas un prodrome pour affirmer un droit effectif à l'élément hydrique pour les nécessités vitales des populations des Etats. Dans des pays souvent pauvres, le développement économique risque de s'imposer sur les besoins domestiques des populations.

L'utilisation équitable et raisonnable des ressources en eau ou l'obligation de ne pas causer de dommages significatifs reflètent désormais la coutume internationale[37]. S'affirme un droit à l'eau pour les Etats qui, par

---

[34] La Communauté de l'Afrique de l'Est (CAE) née le 7 juillet 2000 regroupe 5 Etats : Burundi, Kenya, Ouganda, Rwanda, Tanzanie. En 2010, elle a développé un marché commun des biens, du travail et des capitaux.

[35] Article 3, § 14 de l'Accord-cadre sur la Coopération dans le Bassin du Fleuve Nil.

[36] La Charte des eaux du Fleuve Sénégal a été signée par la Mauritanie, le Mali et le Sénégal. Son art. 4 affirme : « *les principes directeurs de toute répartition des eaux du Fleuve visent à assurer aux populations des Etats riverains, la pleine jouissance de la ressource, dans le respect de la sécurité des personnes et des ouvrages, ainsi que du droit fondamental de l'Homme à une eau salubre* ».

[37] Voir : MC CAFFREY (S. C.), The UN Convention on the Law of the Non-Navigational Uses of International Watercourses: Prospects and Pitfalls, *In* BOISSON DE CHAZOURNES L., SALMAN (S.M.A.) (dir.), *Water Resources and International Law (Report of the 2001 Session)*, Hague Academy of International Law, Centre

ricochet, peut s'avérer positif pour leurs habitants. Cependant, l'affirmation d'un partage des ressources hydriques communes entre Etats riverains est loin de contribuer à la création d'un droit de l'Homme à l'eau. En effet, les concepteurs du droit de l'eau interétatique hésitent à donner une primauté effective aux besoins domestiques des personnes, accaparés qu'ils sont par le développement économique. Promouvoir un droit de l'Homme à l'élément hydrique demeure donc plus que jamais nécessaire, le droit interétatique de l'eau privilégiant une autre logique.

for Studies and Research in International Law and International Relations, Martinus Nijhoff Publishers, 2002, pp. 26-27.

Démocratie alimentaire et agriculture urbaine

Francesco ADORNATO *

Comme l'a écrit Michel Buisson, « la souveraineté alimentaire est indispensable pour la défense et pour le développement de certains types d'agriculture dont la promotion contribue elle-même à la réalisation de la souveraineté alimentaire ». « Cette affirmation – poursuit Buisson – implique de répondre à deux questions : en quoi la situation de l'agriculture dépend-elle de la souveraineté alimentaire, et en quoi certains types d'agricultures confortent-ils la souveraineté alimentaire ? » (Buisson, 2013).

1. Dans quelle mesure l'agriculture urbaine peut-elle contribuer à la souveraineté alimentaire ?

Par agriculture urbaine, on entend une activité agricole localisée à l'intérieur d'une zone urbaine ou périurbaine. Cette activité produit des ressources et distribue une diversité de produits alimentaires et de services « en réutilisant une grande quantité de ressources humaines et matérielles, de produits et de services à l'intérieur et autour de cette zone, en échange de services et de produits » (Mougeot, 2000).

La production de nourriture en milieu urbain n'est pas une pratique nouvelle dans l'histoire des villes. Cette forme d'agriculture était déjà présente lors de l'avènement des premières cités-Etats. Il suffit de penser aux jardins suspendus de Babylone et aux premières cités de Syrie, d'Iran, d'Irak, aux citadelles des Incas du Machu Pichu au Pérou qui étaient composées de zones résidentielles, d'habitation et de terrasses cultivées.

Au Moyen Âge, les villes européennes connaissaient différents types de jardins urbains destinés à assurer la subsistance des familles et des couvents, permettant ainsi aux cités d'être autosuffisantes en cas de siège ennemi.

A la fin du 19ème siècle, avec l'avènement de la bourgeoisie industrielle et de la séparation ville-campagne, l'agriculture urbaine tend à disparaître ; les pratiques agricoles urbaines sont en effet déconsidérées tant du point de vue productif que culturel. La pratique de l'agriculture urbaine de-

* Professore ordinario di diritto agrario, Universita degli studi di Macerata (Italie).

vient non seulement de plus en plus difficile mais aussi illicite : les fonctionnaires zélés des services sanitaires se montrent déterminés à éliminer toute forme de culture ou d'élevage dans les villes. C'est ensuite la diminution des coûts de transport des marchandises qui a joué un rôle décisif dans la disparition de l'agriculture urbaine dans la majorité des villes.

Et plus récemment, le boom économique de l'après-Guerre en Europe et aux Etats-Unis, a libéré les habitants de la préoccupation alimentaire au point de réduire l'agriculture urbaine à un phénomène marginal. En revanche, l'agriculture urbaine n'a pas disparu dans les pays de l'Est comme la Pologne, par exemple.

Dans les années 1970, les « crises pétrolière » ont été source d'un renouveau de l'agriculture urbaine tant dans les pays du Nord que du Sud. Selon un rapport du Programme des Nations Unies pour le Développement (PNUD), l'agriculture urbaine occupe aujourd'hui 800 millions de personnes et 200 millions d'entre elles produisent principalement pour les marchés agricoles. L'Organisation des Nations Unies pour l'alimentation et l'agriculture (FAO) estime que parmi ces 800 millions de personnes, 130 millions se trouvent en Afrique et près de 230 millions en Amérique latine. Il s'agit le plus souvent d'une activité horticole exercée, pour diverses raisons, sur les toits des immeubles. Un exemple particulièrement significatif nous vient de Mumbai : l'*urban farming* sur les toits permet non seulement le développement d'un nouveau modèle économique, d'une « sensibilité environnementale » mais aussi l'émergence de nouveaux espaces de participation et d'expression sociale et politique des femmes.

Dans le monde occidental, ce phénomène d'*urban farming* peut dans certains cas s'analyser comme la manifestation de la faillite du modèle de croissance exacerbée du secteur immobilier dans les métropoles, ou bien encore comme une tentative de conciliation de cette même croissance avec des objectifs d'innovation sociale et de « soutenabilité ».

Les expériences d'agriculture urbaine sont très nombreuses mais deux d'entre elles méritent une attention particulière. A Londres, en plein cœur de la *City*, une ferme urbaine a pris la place d'un gratte-ciel de 48 étages -projeté par le célèbre architecte Richards Rogers- dont la construction a été interrompue en 2010 en raison de la crise immobilière ; les produits de cette ferme urbaine sont commercialisés par un réseau de franchise dans la *City*. A Melbourne, le concours *Growing up* lancé par la municipalité dans le but de reconvertir des gratte-ciel en espaces verts publics a primé un projet prévoyant l'implantation de jardins fruitiers ou vergers (*Urban orchard*) sur les toits. L'économie générale du projet repose sur un système d'autoproduction d'énergie biomasse issue des déchets et sur la vente directe des produits afin d'accroître la « soutenabilité » de la production.

2. Les raisons de cette expansion sont multiples.

Nous devons aujourd'hui affronter des problèmes que nous ne pouvons plus ignorer : la sécurité alimentaire, la raréfaction des ressources naturelles et énergétiques, l'utilisation durable des ressources (et particulièrement de l'eau), le changement climatique, la protection et la valorisation du paysage, la biodiversité, les phénomènes migratoires, la surpopulation urbaine et la cohésion sociale, la gestion des biens communs, l'identité territoriale... on pourrait en citer bien d'autres encore. Autant de défis qui sont aujourd'hui au coeur des débats qui entourent l'avenir de la Politique agricole commune (PAC). En témoigne la communication de la Commission européenne (Com 2010-672) appelant les Etats membres a accordé une attention particulière aux défis de la sécurité des approvisionnements, de l'environnement, du changement climatique et de l'équilibre des territoires. Mais surtout émerge la grave et urgente question de l'anthropisation urbaine qui recoupe des problématiques contemporaines comme celle des flux de populations fuyant la misère et la guerre.

En 1900, seuls 10 % de la population mondiale vivaient dans les villes. Actuellement plus de la moitié de la population est concentrée dans des agglomérations toujours plus denses ; en 2030, ce sont 80 % de la population qui vivront dans les villes.

Pendant longtemps « les populations archaïques ont cherché à se lier au territoire en renonçant au nomadisme et en développant l'économie agricole afin de se défendre contre les ennemis : les villes sont alors devenues des lieux sûrs, protecteurs et fortifiés. Désormais, avec la globalisation, le droit de vivre sur son territoire change de nature dans la mesure où les populations de toute la planète sont à la recherche d'une existence digne et d'un espace permettant de vivre dignement (Bordoni, en Bauman, 2011) : en ce sens, pauvreté, alimentation et migration sont étroitement liées.

Selon les démographes, on estime qu'en 2025 plus de la moitié de la population des pays en voie de développement – soit près de 3,5 milliards de personnes – vivra en zone urbaine, et qu'en 2020 le nombre de personnes pauvres vivant en agglomération urbaine pourrait atteindre 1,4 milliard ; 85 % des pauvres d'Amérique latine et 50 % des pauvres d'Asie et d'Afrique devraient vivre dans des villes. Des villes plus « vertes », avec une agriculture urbaine diffuse, pourraient assurer un accès à l'alimentation, à des aliments sains, sûrs et nutritifs et à des moyens de subsistance.

L'agriculture urbaine peut constituer une réponse efficace et durable à l'expansion constante des villes dans les pays émergents et au développement corrélatif de *slums*, *bidonvilles* et *favelas*. En permettant tout à la fois aux familles de se nourrir et de tirer un revenu de la vente de leurs produits, l'agriculture urbaine peut aussi offrir une voie de sortie de la pauvreté.

3. L'agriculture urbaine met en lumière l'asymétrie et la diversité des rapports économiques, sociaux et culturels entre le Nord et le Sud, mais aussi les relations villes-campagnes, les relations entre catégories sociales et même les rapports entre les personnes.

Il est également important de relever comment, dans le même temps, dans les sociétés occidentales se dessinent de nouveaux rapports écologiques entre villes et campagnes.

Les villes sont devenues « plus diversifiées compte tenu des processus d'individualisation, d'européanisation, de globalisation » (Le Galés, 2006). D'autre part, on constate que le « territoire agricole » s'étend de manière discontinue pour devenir un territoire agricole périurbain (Mininni, en Donadieu, 2006).

Comment protéger l'agriculture des villes ? Comment créer plus de cohésion sociale au sein des villes ?

A ce sujet, l'on peut citer quelques expériences comme celle de New York qui est devenue un des principaux laboratoires de l'*urban farming* à travers divers projets d'urbanisation qui sont socialement très pertinents. On songe à la construction à Brooklyn d'une école avec une annexe composée d'une serre où les enfants (500 en tout, de la crèche au collège) cultivent des aliments qu'ils mangeront le midi à la cantine ; école et serre jouissent d'amples surfaces de panneaux photovoltaïques afin d'éviter la consommation d'énergies fossiles.

Dans cette hypothèse, agriculture urbaine, accès à l'alimentation, éducation alimentaire et cohésion sociale s'entrecroisent et se recoupent.

L'agriculture urbaine semble en mesure de dépasser certaines limites du système alimentaire industriel. En effet, elle peut s'adapter à de nombreuses situations et permettre de s'affranchir de la dépendance des énergies fossiles en utilisant efficacement les nombreuses ressources humaines et matérielles présentes dans les zones urbaines.

On peut, en conclusion, identifier plusieurs avantages de l'agriculture urbaine : en plus de la diminution des coûts (notamment des couts liés à l'augmentation du pétrole) et de la fourniture de produits plus frais, l'agriculture urbaine favorise la redécouverte des bénéfices sociaux et participe à l'augmentation du bien être psychologique procuré par cette pratique.

En définitive, ces phénomènes nouveaux et diffus (*Kleingarten* en Allemagne, *Allotment Gardens* en Angleterre, *Huertos marginales* en Espagne, *Orti urbani* en Italie, *Jardins partagés* en France) qui se développent aux limites de l'agriculture, sont autant de signaux de l'émergence d'une économie civile non exclusivement fondée sur le profit. Le phénomène d'agriculture urbaine permet de mettre en évidence le caractère « pluriel » de l'agriculture tant du point de vue objectif que subjectif (Adornato, 2012). De plus, l'agriculture urbaine montre que l'exercice de l'activité agricole n'est pas réductible au seul modèle de l'entreprise ; bien au contraire, nombre de sujets (personnes physiques ou personnes morales) et qui ne sont pas des « entrepreneurs » contribuent aux activités agricoles. La reconnaissance de la pluralité des sujets qui exercent l'agriculture urbaine participe au renforcement de la démocratie alimentaire et cela devrait conduire à l'adoption de politiques communautaires appropriées. La démocratie alimentaire qui s'exprime à travers l'agriculture urbaine permet à son tour de renforcer la cohésion sociale et de consolider des parcours d'intégration sociale dans les campagnes mais aussi dans les villes : l'intégration des personnes handicapées et la réinsertion de condamnés, la formation des mineurs. Autres services rendus et non des moindres, la transmission des savoirs et des cultures agricoles et rurales à travers les fermes écoles.

De plus, face à l'absence d'une gouvernance « démocratique » globale, l'agriculture urbaine met en œuvre des processus de subsidiarité qui renforcent les pratiques démocratiques et la participation des citoyens, en particulier des plus marginaux, à la vie des institutions.

De la démocratie alimentaire à la démocratie.

Références

ADORNATO, F., *L'agricoltura urbana*, in Agricoltura Istituzioni Mercati, 2012.

BORDONI, C., in Bauman,.Z., *Il buio del postmoderno*, Aliberti, 2011.

BUISSON, M., *Conquérir la souveraineté alimentaire*, L'Harmattan, 2013.

LE GALES, P., *Le città europee. Società urbane, globalizzazione, governo locale*, Il Mulino, 2006. 113.

MOUGEOT L.J.A., *Urban Agriculture: Definition, Presence, Potentials and Risk, in Growing Cities Growing Food*, Ruaf Foundation, 2000.

MININNI, M., in Donadieu, P., *Campagne urbane. Una nuova proposta di paesaggio della città*, Donzelli, 2006, VIII.

Conclusion : Du consommateur mangeur au consommateur citoyen

Quels principes pour un droit des consommateurs citoyens ?

Programme Lascaux *

Introduction

Pour penser une démocratie alimentaire il faut sans doute s'interroger sur la place qu'occupent les consommateurs dans le système agroalimentaire. Dernier maillon de la chaîne de production et de consommation, le consommateur est souvent un réceptacle passif du système libre-échangiste. Pourtant, dans son assiette, il y a une image du monde, et ses choix alimentaires pourraient avoir une influence allant bien au-delà de la qualité des aliments qu'il consomme. Or dans les réglementations actuelles, les aspects sociaux, écologiques, relèvent plutôt des mentions volontaires à faire figurer sur les aliments. Les mentions obligatoires, sur la composition et les apports nutritionnels du produit, rapprochent l'aliment d'un bien de consommation comme les autres. Peu ou pas informé quant à la formation du prix, aux conditions environnementales et sociales de production, de transformation et de distribution des aliments, le consommateur n'est pas en position d'avoir un impact sur le système agroalimentaire. Rien ne lui permet de faire la distinction entre du riz issu d'une agriculture intensive et de l'exploitation de travailleurs sous-payés, et le riz issu d'une agriculture durable. Souvent, c'est le prix qui va le conduire à arbitrer. Quitte à ne rien faire de cette information, n'aurait-il pas le droit de savoir ? Comment replacer le consommateur au centre du système ? Comme lui donner les moyens d'être un citoyen ?

La mondialisation et la généralisation du système agro-industriel ont fait de l'aliment un produit comme les autres, et du mangeur un consommateur, dépossédé de l'habilité à choisir l'alimentation qui lui correspond

* Ce texte est la synthèse de la table ronde « Quels principes pour un droit des consommateurs citoyens ? », à l'occasion des rencontres internationales du programme Lascaux « Penser une démocratie alimentaire » (25-27 novembre 2013). Cette synthèse a été réalisée par Sarah TURBEAUX (Ingénieur d'étude du programme Lascaux), à partir des contributions de Marine FRIANT PERROT, présidente de la table ronde, Gilles FUMEY, Hugo MUNOZ, Charles PERNIN et Christine MARGETIC, intervenants, Catherine DEL CONT, Coralie BONNIN, Nathalie LAZARIC et Jean-Pierre DOUSSIN, discutants.

[Gilles Fumey]. Ce consommateur est-il à même de voter avec sa fourchette ? La satisfaction de ses besoins individuels peut-elle nourrir ses aspirations collectives [Hugo Munoz] ? Quel rôle jouent les associations de défense des consommateurs dans la formulation des règles touchant au produit alimentaire ? L'information du consommateur est-elle la panacée ? [Charles Pernin]. L'agriculture de proximité et la consommation locale sont-elles des pistes de réponse [Christine Margetic] ?

Au travers de ces différents témoignages, de juristes, de géographes, de représentants de la société civile, il s'agira d'interroger le système agro-alimentaire actuel, mais aussi d'envisager des perspectives de solutions et de proposer des principes pour mettre le consommateur au centre du système agro-alimentaire.

Dans un premier temps, où et comment est né le système agro-industriel tel que nous le connaissons aujourd'hui ? Comment l'aliment est-il devenu une marchandise, comment le mangeur est-il devenu un consommateur ?

Ce que nous devons à la mondialisation.

Gilles Fumey, géographe (Université Paris-IV Sorbonne)

Le système agro-industriel tel que nous le connaissons aujourd'hui est né aux États-Unis au milieu du XIXème siècle, en partie pour répondre aux besoins des nouveaux émigrants installés dans les villes. La production agricole a été intégrée dans des filières, qui ont notamment utilisé la ressource animale pour en faire de la viande à consommer. On parle de « système agricole minier », dans lequel la nature est considérée comme un pourvoyeur de ressources. Ce modèle agricole a été transféré après la seconde guerre mondiale en Europe occidentale où les pays affamés par la guerre ont saisi l'opportunité de développer un modèle agro-industriel adossé à un nouveau système de distribution de masse. L'aliment est tombé au rang d'objet de consommation (comme un téléphone ou un produit financier). De mangeur local, l'homme est devenu mangeur global. Mieux (ou pire), il est devenu un consommateur. Un consommateur qui se croit libre de choisir son alimentation, alors qu'en réalité, il a été conditionné par la publicité.

Du fait de la mondialisation de l'agro-industrie, les inégalités produites à l'échelle locale ont été démultipliées à l'échelle mondiale, circonscrivant de vastes zones où sévissent la faim et la malnutrition.

Les aliments ne devraient pas être considérés comme des marchandises ordinaires. Voici un premier principe pour un droit des consommateurs citoyens.

Un second principe est le droit de savoir. De nombreuses crises alimentaires, à l'exemple du récent scandale de la viande de cheval, sont nées du mensonge. Au XVIIIème siècle, peu de gens avaient connaissance des conditions dans lesquelles le sucre arrivant des Antilles était produit dans les plantations utilisant les esclaves, jusqu'à ce qu'un écossais quaker, Thomas Clarkson, arrive vers 1790 à se procurer sur un port un document montrant comment les esclavagistes chargeaient leurs bateaux d'esclaves. Il fait de ce document un dessin qu'il fait reproduire dans toutes les paroisses quakers, puis protestantes de l'époque afin de révéler à ceux qui ne pouvaient pas imaginer, ce qu'était le trafic des esclaves. Cinquante ans après, l'esclavage était aboli.

Aujourd'hui nous avons la capacité d'utiliser l'image. Dans la globalisation actuelle, nous avons grâce à l'image et à internet, la possibilité de fabriquer, de promouvoir une prise de conscience mondiale. Les AMAP sont nées au Japon, sont passées par l'Amérique du Nord et la Grande Bretagne avant d'arriver en France. Le fait de savoir ce que nous mangeons fait de nous non seulement des mangeurs, mais des amateurs (Olivier Assouly, *L'amateur*, IFM/Regard), car nous avons la possibilité de choisir ce que nous voulons manger. Nous sommes mieux informés et nous souhaitons que nos nourritures portent les valeurs qui nous ressemblent.

En tant que mangeur, nous avons donc la possibilité de faire des choix. Pour autant, le consommateur peut-il jouer le rôle de citoyen ? Une décision individuelle peut-elle remplacer une décision collective ?, Hugo Munoz nous apporte un éclairage sur les notions de « consommateur » et de « citoyen », et sur leurs implications.

Le consommateur peut-il jouer le rôle de citoyen ?

Hugo Munoz, juriste (Université du Costa Rica, Costa Rica)

« Consommateur » et « Citoyens » : des notions aux implications différentes.

L'expression « consommateur citoyen » renvoie à l'idée qu'un consommateur puisse avoir une action plus importante, allant au-delà de la recherche du meilleur prix. Cette expression est devenue une sorte de *slogan* pour exprimer justement cette idée d'un consommateur engagé et protagoniste dans la société. Ce rapprochement entre les notions de « consommateur » et de « citoyen » ne doit cependant pas aboutir à une assimilation des deux notions, dans la mesure où elles ont une origine et des implications très différentes.

Le citoyen renvoie à une position à la fois de faiblesse et de force. La citoyenneté permet de protéger l'individu face à la puissance étatique, mais également de le doter du pouvoir de choisir ses représentants. Les élections des citoyens vont légitimer le pouvoir. La notion de consommateur, plus récente, renvoie elle à une position de faiblesse par opposition au professionnel (un autre particulier).

Alors que les citoyens existent et agissent dans un contexte politique, c'est dans le marché que les consommateurs trouvent leur place.

Les décisions du citoyen, individuelles à la base, deviennent collectives une fois qu'il s'est exprimé, au regard de ses droits politiques. Dans le cadre de la démocratie, cette décision collective est normalement la décision de la majorité. Or cette possibilité de s'exprimer collectivement concerne moins le consommateur, dont les choix sont nettement individuels. Les consommateurs s'expriment collectivement par le biais associatif, qui leur permet d'avoir une représentation plus forte, soit lors d'un différend, lorsqu'ils mènent une action de groupe ou « class action », soit lorsqu'ils s'expriment en tant que groupe d'intérêt. Cette dimension collective n'existe que de manière ponctuelle, sur un sujet spécifique, un différend spécifique. Les consommateurs n'ont ni la vocation, ni l'espace institutionnel leur permettant de se prononcer sur des questions d'ordre général ; et en tout cas, leurs prises de position, même sur des sujets amples, reflètent essentiellement des approches corporatistes. En outre, si les avis des consommateurs ne sont pas contraignants, ceux des citoyens le sont en principe.

Enfin, le citoyen obtient son statut de citoyen le plus souvent par des faits juridiques (des faits de la nature), le fait d'être né dans un pays et le fait d'atteindre la majorité. Le consommateur lui, devient consommateur par un acte juridique, dans le cadre d'un contrat, et sous réserve de ses ressources financières.

Les limites du « consommateur-citoyen »

On met de plus en plus aujourd'hui le consommateur à la place du citoyen, mais cela présente des limites qui apparaissent clairement à travers l'exemple des OGM.

Les citoyens européens s'opposent fréquemment à accepter les OGM dans leur nourriture. Les institutions européennes sont contraintes par les États européens, par les collectivités locales qui interdisent fréquemment l'agriculture OGM dans leur territoire, par les citoyens européens, mais également par leurs engagements internationaux relatifs au commerce international.

Afin de comprendre la position de l'Union européenne sur les OGM aujourd'hui, l'affaire de la viande bovine aux hormones est éclairante[1]. L'Union européenne avait interdit l'importation depuis les États-Unis, le Canada et l'Argentine de viande bovine issue d'animaux nourris aux hormones de croissance, en utilisant l'argument d'un risque sanitaire. Condamnée par l'Organe de règlement des différends de l'OMC, l'Union européenne a néanmoins choisi de ne pas modifier les règles sanitaires concernant l'usage des hormones de croissance, et continue de supporter des mesures de rétorsion commerciale.

Les autorités européennes, ayant à l'esprit ce précédent sur la viande aux hormones, et craignant que les pays cultivateurs d'OGM ne portent plainte devant l'organe de règlement des différends à l'OMC, ont décidé de ne pas interdire l'importation d'OGM. A la place, elles ont choisi d'utiliser l'information des consommateurs, et ont consenti à la mise sur le

---

[1] Cette affaire fait l'objet d'un différend entre les Etats-Unis et les Communautés européennes depuis 1996. Voir l'affaire DS26 devant l'Organe de Règlement des Différends (ORD) de l'OMC : http://www.wto.org/french/tratop_f/dispu_f/cases_f/ds26_f.htm

marché d'aliments OGM portant l'étiquette « produit OGM »[2]. En faisant ce choix, l'Union européenne a placé le consommateur à la place du citoyen, et choisi l'information du consommateur plutôt qu'une décision étatique, en supposant que les consommateurs, majoritairement hostiles aux OGM, n'achèteraient pas les produits OGM. Ce faisant, l'Union européenne à remplacé la décision collective par une décision individuelle. Cependant un ensemble de décisions de consommateurs ne peut se substituer, ni valoir décision étatique.

La démocratie alimentaire suppose un renforcement des consommateurs et des citoyens

Une définition claire et précise du « consommateur » et du citoyen » apparaît nécessaire, en fonction de leurs origines, de leur nature, du contexte dans lequel ils agissent, de la façon dont on leur octroie leur statut. En redonnant au citoyen sa place dans la prise de décisions de société, et en instaurant davantage de transparence dans les relations de consommation, on pourra aboutir à un renforcement de ces deux acteurs. On pourrait alors parler de démocratie alimentaire. Les mécanismes démocratiques nécessaires à ces évolutions existent déjà, et c'est un avantage considérable.

[2] V. Règlement CE n° 1830/2003. V. dans cet ouvrage, la contribution de M-A Ngo : Les OGM, illustration des obstacles et des potentialités offertes par le droit pour une meilleure démocratie alimentaire.

Une expérience sud-africaine de renforcement du pouvoir des citoyens

Catherine Del Cont

En Afrique du Sud les règles de concurrence énoncent que le droit de la concurrence a pour finalité de garantir le bon fonctionnement du marché mais aussi le bien commun des citoyens[3]. En d'autres termes, le bien être du consommateur ou « consumer welfare » ne se limite pas à la recherche de prix bas. Cette définition de l'objectif de la concurrence a permis à des consommateurs citoyens et à des petits producteurs de lait de faire condamner des industriels de la transformation laitière[4] qui usaient de leur puissance d'achat pour obtenir des prix bas, et se justifiaient en arguant de la baisse de prix répercutée au consommateur. Or cette politique de prix faisait disparaître les petits producteurs et désertifiait ou paupérisait des territoires.

Le consommateur est-il vraiment maître de ces choix ? Comment se repère-t-il dans le maquis des mentions obligatoires et volontaires qui sont présentes sur l'étiquetage des aliments ? Comment agir, notamment lorsque l'on est une organisation de défense des consommateurs ? Charles Pernin interroge le paradigme informationnel et l'aptitude du consommateur à jouer un rôle citoyen dans la conduite du changement.

[3] La loi sud-africaine de 1998 sur la concurrence a pour objectifs de «promouvoir et maintenir la concurrence dans la République pour [...] c) créer des emplois et améliorer le bien-être social et économique des citoyens [...]; e) garantir l'égalité de chance des petites et moyennes entreprises de participer à l'économie; et f) promouvoir l'élargissement de l'accès à la propriété, notamment accroître celle des personnes historiquement défavorisées (chap. 1, sect. 2).

[4] Plainte à l'encontre de Clover Industries Ltd et consorts, transmise par la Commission nationale de la concurrence au tribunal de la concurrence de l'Afrique du Sud le 7 décembre 2006.

Constats et pistes de réflexion pour un rééquilibrage du rapport de forces entre consommateurs et professionnels de l'agroalimentaire.

Charles Pernin, association Consommation Logement et Cadre de Vie

Le mythe du consommateur souverain

Les professionnels de l'agroalimentaire prétendent répondre aux besoins et aux attentes des consommateurs dans la conception, la manière de commercialiser et de distribuer les produits alimentaires. Pourtant, l'idée que le consommateur serait maître de ses choix et les dicterait au secteur de la production est un mythe. C'est ce que dénonçait JK Galbraith en affirmant : « La croyance en une économie de marché où le client est roi est l'un de nos mensonges les plus envahissants ».

Depuis les années 1960, la diversification de l'offre alimentaire qui a accompagné l'essor de la société de consommation a été perçue comme quelque chose de positif. Mais aujourd'hui, dans certains hypermarchés américains, on peut trouver 285 sortes de gâteaux, 230 sortes de soupes et face à cet « hyper-choix », le consommateur ne peut plus comparer ni choisir. De plus, derrière la profusion des marques, il existe en réalité une très grande concentration d'opérateurs et finalement, c'est un choix en trompe-l'œil qui s'offre au consommateur.

Ajoutons que le rapport entre le consommateur et le fabricant est intrinsèquement déséquilibré : l'industriel en sait infiniment plus sur son produit que le consommateur qui l'achète. Cette asymétrie d'information permet au professionnel de vanter les mérites de son produit, d'en taire les inconvénients et parfois de tromper le consommateur.

Le récent développement du marketing « santé » sur les produits alimentaires illustre bien ce phénomène. Dans le cas d'une barre aux céréales et au chocolat, le professionnel communique sur la présence de calcium et sur les bienfaits du produit sur la croissance osseuse, alors que cette barre chocolatée est très calorique, sucrée et composée de graisses non saines. Ce type de dérives a conduit à l'adoption en 2006 d'un règlement européen destiné à encadrer les allégations nutritionnelles et de santé. Compte tenu du lobbying de l'industrie agroalimentaire sa mise en œuvre n'est toujours pas effective. Face à la complexification croissante du système agroalimentaire et au risque de tromperie qu'elle induit, il est apparu nécessaire de mieux informer le consommateur. En Europe, les dernières décennies ont été marquées par l'adoption d'une série de règles définissant l'information qui doit être fournie au consommateur. Cette réglementation est un enjeu de lobbying intense.

L'étiquetage a remplacé les réglementations contraignantes sur la composition des produits.

Jean-Pierre Doussin

La première réglementation sur les aliments remonte au code Hammourabi. L'étiquetage des produits alimentaires est né en France en 1972-1973[5], au niveau européen en 1978[6] et au niveau mondial avec l'adoption d'une norme générale pour l'étiquetage des denrées alimentaires préemballées par la Commission Codex alimentarius en 1985[7]. A partir de ce moment, l'étiquetage a été magnifié, et dans les instances internationales il a condamné ce que l'on appelait les réglementations « recette ». La dénomination du produit (cassoulet, beurre...) supposait une composition donnée. Ces dénominations ont été abandonnées pour la plupart notamment sous l'action du Codex Alimentarius ou de l'OMC. C'est ainsi par exemple que la dénomination « sardine », qui concernait un petit poisson spécifique : *sardina pilchardus*, renvoie désormais à tous les petits poissons sous réserve d'indication de l'espèce, solution identique pour la coquille Saint-Jacques. La tendance au plan international a été de remplacer toutes les réglementations contraignantes sur la composition des produits par l'étiquetage.

L'expérience de la CLCV en matière de lobbying

L'élaboration des textes sur l'information du consommateur suppose la consultation des parties prenantes : professionnels des différents secteurs de l'industrie agroalimentaire, experts scientifiques et techniques, associations de défense des consommateurs. Mais au-delà des consultations officielles, chacun s'emploie à défendre ses intérêts et à influer sur la rédaction des réglementations.

---

5 Décret du 12 octobre 1972 (JO du 14 octobre 1972) et ses trois arrêtés d'application du 16 novembre 1973 (JO du 21 novembre 1973).

6 Directive n°79-112 du 18 décembre 1978 (JOCE du 8 février 1979).

7 L'Étiquetage des Denrées Alimentaires Préemballées (CODEX STAN 1-1985).

A Bruxelles, il existe 3000 groupes d'intérêt tous secteurs confondus, qui emploient 10 000 personnes. Les ONG représentent 10% de ces groupes d'intérêt, les professionnels 50 à 80% selon les chiffres, les bureaux d'étude et de conseil complètent le tableau. Si le Bureau Européen des Unions de Consommateurs (BEUC), l'ONG qui représente les consommateurs à Bruxelles, emploie trois salariés sur les questions alimentaires, chaque secteur de l'industrie agroalimentaire possède lui son propre lobby, tout comme les grandes entreprises. Le rapport de force est donc très déséquilibré et les représentants des intérêts des consommateurs ont perdu un certain nombre de batailles, relatives à l'étiquetage nutritionnel ou à l'information sur les OGM par exemple.

L'avantage stratégique des associations de défense des consommateurs réside cependant dans leur capacité à mobiliser les médias, relativement plus facilement que les professionnels de l'agroalimentaire.

Pistes de réflexion et perspectives

Si l'on souhaite une meilleure prise en compte des questions environnementales, sociales, de santé, dans les domaines agricoles et alimentaires, l'information du consommateur via l'étiquetage n'apparait pas nécessairement comme la solution la plus adaptée. Un très grand nombre de facteurs entrent en jeu dans le choix d'un produit alimentaire : le prix et le pouvoir d'achat, la publicité, le marketing, les préférences issues de l'histoire personnelle, etc. Tous les consommateurs ne sont pas des experts et face à une profusion d'informations, ils ne seront pas à même d'arbitrer.

Les limites de la surcharge informationnelle

Nathalie Lazaric et Coralie Bonnin

Information n'équivaut pas à connaissance, et la capacité d'absorption du consommateur est limitée. La profusion d'informations via l'étiquetage comporte le risque de produire des inégalités entre les consommateurs, par rapport à leur niveau d'éducation, de revenu, la région dans laquelle ils habitent, etc. Les habitudes sont également un obstacle.

L'affichage environnemental est un exemple de la grande complexité et du coût de l'information des consommateurs. Il n'est en outre pas certain qu'il soit bien reçu des consommateurs et qu'il leur délivre l'information souhaitée.

Face à cette surcharge informationnelle, le bouche à oreille, tout comme les lanceurs d'alerte, apparaissent comme des moyens d'agir intéressants.

L'on ne peut pour autant se contenter d'une opacité sur les produits et les modes de production, nous avons besoin de transparence. L'important est que l'information soit accessible. Cela ne signifie pas que chacun ira regarder toutes les informations au moment où il choisira son paquet de gâteaux. Cela signifie que l'information doit être disponible et que des experts, des autorités indépendantes, des militants, des journalistes pourront y avoir accès et retracer l'histoire, l'origine, les conditions de production de l'aliment. Ces contre-pouvoirs constituent un levier démocratique qui permettrait de rééquilibrer l'asymétrie entre consommateurs et professionnels.

La transparence, oui, mais quid du contrôle ?

Jean-Pierre Doussin

A chaque scandale alimentaire, de nouvelles réglementations émergent. Le cas des lasagnes au bœuf fabriquées à partir de viande de cheval a ainsi abouti à une volonté d'indiquer la provenance de la viande. Or la provenance de la viande est pratiquement impossible à vérifier par la voie de l'analyse. Pour connaître la provenance de la viande, il faut avoir le droit de s'introduire dans les circuits, dans la chaîne alimentaire. Mais le consommateur de base est incapable d'aller chercher ces informations. Qui alors va contrôler la provenance de la viande ?

Par ailleurs, que ce soit au niveau local ou au niveau global, le contrôle est indispensable. La proximité n'empêche pas la fraude, comme dans le cas constaté récemment d'un producteur d'AMAP qui se fournissait chez un grossiste sans que personne ne s'en rende compte pendant plusieurs années. Pour que l'accès à l'information, y compris sur internet, ait un sens, une condition doit être remplie : que cette information soit vérifiable, et que les moyens d'aller la vérifier existent.

Aujourd'hui, on perçoit une attention inédite sur la question alimentaire, dans la presse notamment, et les professionnels en tiennent compte. Les nouvelles technologies peuvent aussi changer la donne. Certaines prises de parole des consommateurs sur le web, à l'instar d'une pétition récente demandant aux pouvoirs publics des informations sur la qualité des saumons, sont intéressantes. Un autre élément concerne les aides à la décision, telles que les applications des smartphones qui permettent de scanner un code barre et d'avoir accès à des notations synthétiques des produits. Ces initiatives ne sont toutefois pas encadrées actuellement. Nous sommes aujourd'hui à un moment charnière, avec un fort climat de méfiance des consommateurs vis-à-vis de l'industrie agroalimentaire, ce qui peut encourager les professionnels à faire évoluer leurs pratiques et à accepter davantage de transparence.

La solution viendrait-elle d'une agriculture de proximité et d'une consommation locale ? Le choix de « consommer local » peut-il être une réponse à la promotion du consommateur-citoyen ?

Les voies d'une relocalisation alimentaire, comment « consommer local » ?

Christine Margetic, géographe (Université de Nantes)

Aujourd'hui nous consommons le monde entier dans nos assiettes à tous moments et d'une certaine manière en tous lieux. Pourtant on assiste depuis quelques années au retour d'un certain nombre de consommateurs vers le « local ». Cette idée de retour au local s'articule autour de deux notions clé : la diversité et le système de valeurs. Consommer local renvoie à la diversité des choix alimentaires, des stratégies d'achat, des formes d'agriculture. En tant que citoyen, mon système de valeurs – mon parcours de vie, mon lieu de naissance, les habitudes de mes parents – impacte le choix des aliments que je vais consommer. C'est pourquoi un aliment ne peut être réduit à un produit alimentaire.

Le choix de consommer local peut-il être une réponse à la promotion du consommateur-citoyen ?

Le « local » renvoie notamment à trois questions :

- Le produit local est-il un bon produit ?

Souvent, les consommateurs présupposent que la proximité géographique est garante d'une certaine qualité du produit. Les Associations pour le Maintien d'une Agriculture Paysanne (AMAP), sont d'ailleurs à l'origine d'une inversion dans la manière de penser la relation agriculteur-consommateur, puisque ce sont des consommateurs qui vont chercher des producteurs. C'est une approche inverse de celle des filières agroalimentaires. Si la proximité géographique n'est pas toujours évidente, les AMAP permettent la création d'un lien social, et sont l'expression d'une adhésion à un système de valeurs. Il en va de même pour l'agriculture biologique.

Favoriser les liens de proximité entre agriculteurs et consommateurs, favoriser les circuits courts, implique toutefois de penser la question foncière. Certains outils juridiques à disposition des collectivités territoriales, comme les Zones Agricoles Protégées (ZAP) ou encore les Périmètres de Protectionet de mise en valeur des Espèces Agricoles et Naturelles périurbaines (PEAN), apportent une partie de réponse. Il en va de même des associations comme Terre de Liens, qui achètent des parcelles pour l'installation d'agriculteurs qui commercialiseront en circuits courts. Pour autant, les terres agricoles disparaissent toujours, mais à un rythme moindre (la surface agricole d'un département disparaît tous les 7 ans en France). Solution pour quelques producteurs et consommateurs, ces circuits courts restent encore des niches, parallèlement aux filières longues qui se maintiennent autour des villes.

- Le produit local est-il réponse à une défense de l'agriculture locale ?

Localement, quel que soit le circuit de commercialisation envisagé, les producteurs sont de plus en plus dans une logique de concurrence même pour conquête de nouveaux marchés comme la vente directe ou la restauration collective à terme. Pour autant, des formes collectives émergent, parfois articulées autour de la promotion d'un produit alimentaire ou d'un territoire. Et cette dynamique conforte certaines agricultures en défense dans des zones à enjeux non agricoles pour la collectivité.

Dans la défense de l'agriculture locale, les industries agroalimentaires jouent aussi un rôle, qui n'est pas toujours connu des consommateurs. Consommer un camembert AOP de Normandie contribue au maintien du bocage et des haies, puisque son cahier des charges spécifie que les agriculteurs maintiennent une certaine densité de haies. Une entreprise comme Bonduelle fonctionne avec des cahiers des charges très stricts, en matière environnementale notamment, etc. Parallèlement, des enseignes de la grande distribution indiquent le nom de l'exploitation et/ou de la commune de l'exploitation d'où proviennent les fruits et légumes. S'il peut y avoir derrière ces informations une stratégie marketing, ces actions contribuent à valoriser l'agriculture locale.

Les villes, les collectivités se réapproprient de plus en plus leur agriculture périphérique, dans une logique de marketing territorial, à l'instar d'Aix-en-Provence. Certaines de ces démarches ne trouvent cependant pas toujours de débouchés économiques.

- Produit biologique ou produit local ?

La question s'est souvent posée au niveau de la restauration collective. Beaucoup de collectivités ont souhaité dans un premier temps privilégier des produits biologiques dans les cantines. Cependant, il n'existe souvent pas assez de productions biologiques autour de tous les établissements pour assurer cet approvisionnement. Ceci explique le glissement du « bio » vers le « local ». Et par « local » on entend généralement le département, une échelle retenue à la fois par les collectivités et par les entreprises de restauration.

Ainsi, un certain nombre d'expériences, de la fourche à la fourchette, se sont peu à peu multipliées et ont conduit à un feuilletage de l'espace, avec des démarches qui ne se recoupent pas forcément mais qui portent sur de mêmes produits et dénotent un changement de mentalité. Changement chez les agriculteurs, en amont mais aussi chez les acteurs qui valorisent un produit alimentaire que les consommateurs dotent de plus en plus de valeurs éthiques. Avec une difficulté permanente, la capacité à éclairer ces consommateurs de la construction de démarches pas toujours labellisées.

Conclusion

La sécurité alimentaire suppose d'avoir accès à une alimentation saine, de qualité et choisie. Parce que l'aliment est un bien vital, il ne devrait pas être considéré comme une marchandise ordinaire. Mais même dans les pays dits développés, le consommateur n'est pas toujours en position de choisir les aliments qu'il souhaite manger. Pourtant, c'est lui qui a le dernier mot. C'est lui qui peut choisir de consommer « bio », local, ou d'acheter un produit issu du commerce équitable. Parce qu'il est le dernier maillon de la chaîne alimentaire, ses choix peuvent avoir des répercussions à chaque échelon des filières.

Permettre au consommateur de connaître les conditions sociales et environnementales de production d'un aliment, son origine géographique, apparaît nécessaire pour qu'il puisse jouer un rôle autre que celui de simple mangeur. Pour autant, les choix des consommateurs restent des choix individuels, qui reposent sur l'éducation, le revenu, les habitudes et les lieux de vie de chacun. Cela ne signifie pas cependant que les consommateurs n'aient pas le droit de savoir, le droit d'avoir accès à une information fiable.

Si le « prix » est aujourd'hui l'un des premiers critères de choix, cela ne signifie pas qu'il doive le rester, ni qu'une prise de conscience ne soit pas en train d'émerger. Les habitudes de consommation évoluent, les scandales alimentaires à répétition et la méfiance croissante des consommateurs vis-à-vis des produits alimentaires industriels poussent les professionnels et les pouvoirs publics à faire évoluer leurs pratiques. Une évolution des règles, nationales et internationales, apparaît nécessaire pour accompagner ce mouvement et pour avancer vers l'objectif de démocratie alimentaire.

Au-delà de l'information du consommateur, viser l'objectif de démocratie alimentaire suppose d'agir tout au long de la chaîne agroalimentaire. En amont, il s'agit d'assurer la préservation mais aussi l'accès aux ressources naturelles agricoles des petits paysans. Pourtant les États, contraints par leurs engagements commerciaux, ne sont pas toujours en mesure, ni de préserver leurs ressources alimentaires tout en en assurant l'accès à ceux qui en vivent, ni, en bout de chaine, de garantir au consommateur une alimentation adéquate.

La première phase du programme Lascaux a consisté à penser une évolution des règles nationales et internationales pour une amélioration de la sécurité alimentaire mondiale tout au long de cette chaine alimentaire. Il s'est agi avant tout de la recherche d'un équilibre. Équilibre dans les investissements internationaux dans la terre agricole, équilibre entre innovation technologique et accès aux intrants agricoles, équilibre entre valeurs marchandes et droits fondamentaux dans les échanges commerciaux internationaux.

Face au constat de la raréfaction des ressources naturelles, alors que nous serons au moins 9 milliards d'individus à nourrir en 2050, il apparaît vital, au-delà de la recherche d'équilibre, de penser la question de l'ajustement des ressources et des besoins alimentaires et même, plus largement, l'ajustement de l'ensemble des ressources naturelles avec les besoins socioéconomiques fondamentaux. Permettre cet ajustement suppose d'en penser l'encadrement juridique, non seulement au plan national, mais aussi au plan international. C'est là l'objet de la seconde phase du programme Lascaux.

Publications du Programme Lascaux

I. – Ouvrages

- Ballar R. et Collart Dutilleul F. (dir.), *Aspectos jurídicos de la valorizacíon de los productos alimentarios – Aspects juridiques de la valorisation des denrées alimentaires*, Actes de colloque international (San José, novembre 2010), éd. Inida, San José, Costa Rica, 2011, 254 pages.
- Collart Dutilleul C., *La propriété industrielle appliquée aux produits agro-alimentaires*, thèse de doctorat en droit privé, sous la direction de C. Bernault, thèse dactylographiée, Université de Nantes, 2013.
- Collart Dutilleul F. et Nihoul P. (dir.), *Code de droit européen de l'alimentation*, éd. Bruylant, Bruxelles, 2012, 694 pages.
- Collart Dutilleul F. and Nihoul P. (eds.), *European food law Code*, Bruylant, Brussels, 2012, 714 pages.
- Collart Dutilleul F., Nihoul P., León Guzman M y Muñoz Ureña H. (dir.), *Código del Derecho Europeo de la Alimentación*, Inida, San José, Costa Rica, 2012, 786 pages.
- Collart Dutilleul F, Nihoul P. en Van Nieuwenhuyze E. (door), *Codex Europees Voedingsrecht*, Bruylant, Bruxelles, 2012, 722 pages.
- Collart Dutilleul F. (dir.), *De la terre à l'aliment, des valeurs au droit,* Actes des colloques internationaux « *L'accès à la terre et ses usages* » (juin 2009, Nantes) et « *De la terre à l'aliment, des valeurs aux règles* » (juin 2010, Nantes), éd. Inida, San José, Costa Rica, 2012, 465 pages.
- Collart Dutilleul F. et Riem F. (dir.), *Droits fondamentaux, ordre public et libertés économiques*, Actes du colloque Lascaux-CDRE (Bayonne, 17 février 2012), éd. Institut Universitaire Varenne, Bayonne, coll. Colloques & Essais, 2013, 306 pages.
- Collart Dutilleul F. et Bugnicourt J.-P. (dir.), *Dictionnaire juridique de la sécurité alimentaire dans le monde*, éd. Larcier, Bruxelles, 2013, 697 pages.
- Collart Dutilleul F. and Bugnicourt J.-P. (eds.), *Legal Dictionary of Food Security in the World*, Larcier, Brussels, 2013, 436 pages.

- Collart Dutilleul F., Bugnicourt J.-P., y Munoz Urena H. A. (dir.), *Diccionario Jurídico de la seguridad alimentaria en el mundo*, éd. Inida, San Jose , Costa Rica, 2014, 598 p.
- Collart Dutilleul F. et E. Le Dolley (dir.), *Droit, économie et marchés de matières premières agricoles*, Actes du colloque Lascaux (mars 2013, Paris), éd. LGDJ/Lextenso, Paris, 2013, 300 pages.
- Collart Dutilleul F. et Parent G. (dir.), *De la souveraineté à la sécurité alimentaire*, Actes du séminaire international Lascaux-CEDE (Laval, Québec, 5-6 septembre 2011), éd. Yvon Blais, Cowansville, 2013, 244 pages.
- Collart Dutilleul F. et Bréger T. (dir.), *Penser une démocratie alimentaire*, vol. 1, éd. Inida, San José, Costa Rica, 2013, 482 pages.
- León Guzman M., *L'obligation d'auto-contrôle des entreprises en droit européen de la sécurité alimentaire*, thèse de doctorat (Université de Nantes), préf. F. Collart Dutilleul, éd. Inida, San José, Costa Rica, 2011, 517 pages.
- Muñoz Ureña H. A., *Principe de transparence et information des consommateurs dans la législation alimentaire européenne*, thèse de doctorat (Université de Nantes), préf. F. Collart Dutilleul, éd. Inida, San José, Costa Rica, 2011, 458 pages.
- Sun J., *The international harmonization of food safety regulation in the light of the American, European and Chinese law*, thèse de doctorat en droit privé, sous la direction de F. Collart Dutilleul, thèse dactylographiée, Université de Nantes, 2013.
- Yamthieu S., *Accès aux aliments et droit de la propriété industrielle*, thèse de doctorat (Universités de Ngaoundéré –Cameroun- et de Nantes –France-), éd. Larcier, Bruxelles, janvier 2014, 394 p.

À paraître

- Collart Dutilleul F. et Sun J. (dir.), 欧盟食品法律汇编, Law Press China, 2014.

II.- Numéros spéciaux de revues

- Collart Dutilleul F. et Del Cont C. (dir.), *La production et la commercialisation des denrées alimentaires et le droit du marché,* Actes des 1res Journées Lorvellec (décembre 2009, Nantes), *Revue Lamy de la concurrence*, octobre-décembre 2010, n° 25, 23 pages.

- Collart Dutilleul F., Del Cont C. et Friant-Perrot M. (dir.) (), *Actualités de droit économique – Aspects de droit de la concurrence et de la consommation et de droit de l'agroalimentaire,* Actes des 2es Journées Lorvellec (septembre 2010, Nantes), *Petites Affiches*, 6 octobre 2011, n° 199, 39 pages.
- Collart Dutilleul F. et Pironon V. (dir.), *Droit économique et sécurité alimentaire*, Actes du colloque Lascaux-CREDECO (Nice, 13 juin 2012), *Revue internationale de droit économique*, 2012, n° 4, 108 pages.

III.– Articles

2009

- Collart Dutilleul F. et Garcia F., « Dans le domaine de l'alimentation : quels "droits à" dans le "droit de" ? », *in Droit économique et droits de l'homme*, sous la coordination de L. Boy, J.-B. Racine et F. Siiriainen, préf. J.-F. Renucci, éd. Larcier, Bruxelles, 2009, p. 497.
- Collart Dutilleul F., « Analyse de la contribution du Secrétariat de la FAO pour la définition des objectifs et les possibles décisions du Sommet mondial des 16, 17 et 18 novembre 2009 sur la sécurité alimentaire », décembre 2009, en ligne [HAL].
- Houdeingar D. (2009), « Les conflits d'usage entre principe de coexistence et principe de responsabilité », Communication au colloque international « *L'accès à la terre et ses usages : variations internationales* » (8-9 juin 2009, Nantes), décembre 2009, en ligne [HAL].

2010

- Annoussamy D., « La faim et ses remèdes dans *Manimegalai* », mars 2010, en ligne [HAL].
- Ballar R., « Derecho, cambio climatico y la produccion agricola en la region de Centroamerica », Communication au colloque international « *De la terre à l'aliment, des valeurs aux règles* » (28-29 juin 2010, Nantes), juillet 2010, en ligne [HAL].
- Boy L., « La confrontation de l'agriculture et du marché : les aspects contractuels – Introduction », Actes des 1res Journées Lorvellec (décembre 2009, Nantes), « *La production et la commercialisation des denrées alimentaires et le droit du marché* », *Revue Lamy de la concurrence*, octobre-décembre 2010, n° 25, p. 112.

- Brégeot G., « Des politiques non agricoles pour développer la production agricole ? », Communication au colloque international « *De la terre à l'aliment, des valeurs aux règles* » (28-29 juin 2010, Nantes), juillet 2010, en ligne [HAL].
- Bugnicourt J. –P., « Le droit spécial de l'alimentation à la lumière du droit privé – Synthèse du séminaire du 29 janvier 2010 », février 2010, en ligne [HAL].
- Bugnicourt J. –P., « Synthèse de la table ronde n° 1 – "De la terre aux aliments : état des lieux des questions, des problèmes, des attentes" », juillet 2010, en ligne [HAL].
- Bugnicourt J. –P., « Synthèse de la table ronde n° 2 – "De la terre aux aliments : qu'en est-il des droits à la terre et à l'alimentation ?" », juillet 2010, en ligne [HAL].
- Bugnicourt J. –P., « Synthèse de la table ronde n° 3 – "Développement agricole et réduction de la pauvreté" », juillet 2010, en ligne [HAL].
- Bugnicourt J. –P., « Synthèse de la table ronde n° 4 – "De la terre aux aliments, des valeurs aux règles : quelles solutions ?" », juillet 2010, en ligne [HAL].
- Bugnicourt J. –P., « "La valorisation des produits agricoles – Approche juridique" - Compte rendu », décembre 2010, en ligne [HAL].
- Collart Dutilleul F., « Échec des négociations de l'OMC, de la FAO et de Copenhague en novembre et décembre 2009 – proposition de "feuille de route" pour le programme Lascaux », janvier 2010, en ligne [HAL].
- Collart Dutilleul F., « Failure of negociations on agricultural trade at the WTO, of the FAO Summit and of the Copenhagen climate change Conference in November and December 2009 - Analysis and "roadmap" proposition of the Lascaux program », janvier 2010, en ligne [HAL].
- Collart Dutilleul F., « Fracasos de las negociaciones en la OMC, de la FAO y de la Cumbre de Copenhague en noviembre y diciembre 2009 - Análisis y proposición de orientaciones del programa Lascaux », janvier 2010, en ligne [HAL].
- Collart Dutilleul F., « Propos liminaires », Actes des 1res Journées Lorvellec (décembre 2009, Nantes), « *La production et la commer-*

cialisation des denrées alimentaires et le droit du marché », Revue Lamy de la concurrence, octobre-décembre 2010, n° 25, p. 96.

- Collart Dutilleul F., Borghetti J.-S. et Bugnicourt J.-P., « Le droit civil de la responsabilité à l'épreuve du droit spécial de l'alimentation : premières questions », *Dalloz*, 6 mai 2010, p. 1099.
- Del Cont C. et Pironon V., « L'affaire de la viande bovine irlandaise », Actes des 1res Journées Lorvellec (décembre 2009, Nantes), « *La production et la commercialisation des denrées alimentaires et le droit du marché », Revue Lamy de la concurrence*, octobre-décembre 2010, n° 25, p. 106.
- Delcourt L., « Crise alimentaire ou faillite du modèle agricole ? », Actes des 1res Journées Lorvellec (décembre 2009, Nantes), « *La production et la commercialisation des denrées alimentaires et le droit du marché », Revue Lamy de la concurrence*, octobre-décembre 2010, n° 25, p. 100.
- Echols M., « Agriculture and contract law », Actes des 1res Journées Lorvellec (décembre 2009, Nantes), « *La production et la commercialisation des denrées alimentaires et le droit du marché », Revue Lamy de la concurrence*, octobre-décembre 2010, n° 25, p. 112.
- Gadbin D. (2010), « La confrontation de l'agriculture et du marché : les aspects concurrentiels - Introduction », Actes des 1res Journées Lorvellec (décembre 2009, Nantes), « *La production et la commercialisation des denrées alimentaires et le droit du marché », Revue Lamy de la concurrence*, octobre-décembre 2010, n° 25, p. 105.
- Garcia F., « L'obligation de collaboration des entreprises en matière de sécurité des produits – Élément d'un renouveau de la responsabilité civile par le droit communautaire », *Revue de la Recherche Juridique - Droit prospectif*, 2010 n° 4, p. 1829.
- Houdeingar D., « De la terre à l'aliment : état des lieux des questions, des problèmes, des attentes », Communication au colloque international « *De la terre à l'aliment, des valeurs aux règles* » (28-29 juin 2010, Nantes), juillet 2010, en ligne [HAL].
- Houdeingar D., « La concurrence des agricultures dans le marché international », Actes des 1res Journées Lorvellec (décembre 2009, Nantes), « *La production et la commercialisation des denrées alimentaires et le droit du marché », Revue Lamy de la concurrence*, octobre-décembre 2010, n° 25, p. 97.
- Parent G., « Le système canadien de gestion de l'offre en lait au Canada : un pont désormais fragile entre agriculture et marché », Actes

des 1res Journées Lorvellec (décembre 2009, Nantes), « *La production et la commercialisation des denrées alimentaires et le droit du marché* », *Revue Lamy de la concurrence*, octobre-décembre 2010, n° 25, p. 114.

- Rajagopal PV, « Agricultural development and poverty reduction in India », Communication au colloque international « *De la terre à l'aliment, des valeurs aux règles* » (28-29 juin 2010, Nantes), août 2010, en ligne [HAL].
- Requillart V., « Agriculture et concurrence : regards économiques », Actes des 1res Journées Lorvellec (décembre 2009, Nantes), « *La production et la commercialisation des denrées alimentaires et le droit du marché* », *Revue Lamy de la concurrence*, octobre-décembre 2010, n° 25, p. 110.
- Riem F., « L'équilibre dans les rapports entre producteurs et distributeurs », Actes des 1res Journées Lorvellec (décembre 2009, Nantes), « *La production et la commercialisation des denrées alimentaires et le droit du marché* », *Revue Lamy de la concurrence*, octobre-décembre 2010, n° 25, p. 115.
- Sidibé I. (2010), « Le cadre institutionnel de la gestion de l'eau du barrage de Sélingué (Mali) », Communication au colloque international « *De la terre à l'aliment, des valeurs aux règles* » (28-29 juin 2010, Nantes), juillet 2010, en ligne [HAL].
- Sun J. and Du G. (2010), « The justification of Chinese traditional thought on the right to adequate food », juin 2010, en ligne [HAL].

2011

- Bugnicourt M., « Les risques biologiques : le point de vue du Microbiologiste - Éléments de synthèse », novembre 2011, en ligne [HAL].
- Bugnicourt M., « Mémento des risques biologiques à l'attention des juristes - Point de vue d'un microbiologiste sur les risques et leur gestion », novembre 2011, en ligne [HAL].
- Collart Dutilleul F., « Préface », *in* M. León Guzman, *L'obligation d'auto-contrôle des entreprises en droit européen de la sécurité alimentaire*, thèse de doctorat (Université de Nantes), éd. Inida, San José, Costa Rica, 2011.
- Collart Dutilleul F., « Préface », *in* H. A. Muñoz Ureña, *Principe de transparence et information des consommateurs dans la législation*

alimentaire européenne, thèse de doctorat (Université de Nantes), éd. Inida, San José, Costa Rica, 2011.

- Collart Dutilleul F., « Le droit au service des enjeux alimentaires de l'exploitation et du commerce des ressources naturelles », juin 2011, en ligne [HAL].
- Collart Dutilleul F., « Law devoted to food issues and natural resources exploitation and trade », juin 2011, en ligne (HAL).
- Collart Dutilleul F., « El Derecho al servicio de las problemáticas alimentarias de la explotación y del comercio de los recursos naturales », juin 2011, en ligne (HAL).
- Collart Dutilleul F., « G faim, G 20, G vain », LeMonde.fr, 29 juin 2011.
- Collart Dutilleul F., « Pour un retour du droit au service de la sécurité alimentaire », *LeMonde.fr*, 6 juillet 2011.
- Collart Dutilleul F., « Les enjeux alimentaires du commerce des ressources naturelles », in *Les ressources*, Études réunies par I. Negrutiu et alii, Publications universitaires de Saint-Étienne, coll. Les colloques de l'Institut universitaire de France, 2011, p. 63.
- Garde A. et M. Friant-Perrot, « La publicité alimentaire et la lutte contre l'obésité infantile en droit français et en droit anglais », *Petites Affiches*, 6 octobre 2011, n° 199, p. 27.
- Jeannin M.-V., « Le déséquilibre significatif ou une atteinte significative à la liberté contractuelle ? », *Petites Affiches*, 6 octobre 2011, n° 199, p. 15.
- Le Goff D., « Le contentieux de l'article L. 442-6 du Code de commerce : premier bilan », *Petites Affiches*, 6 octobre 2011, n° 199, p. 8.
- Pironon V., « Actualités de droit de la concurrence et des pratiques anticoncurrentielles : les groupes de sociétés en droit des pratiques anticoncurrentielles », *Petites Affiches*, 6 octobre 2011, n° 199, p. 3.
- Rochdi G., « Le Rapport Ciolos », Communication au colloque du Réseau Trans Europe Experts (avril 2011, Paris), avril 2011, en ligne [HAL].
- Saas C., « La protection des consommateurs d'aliments : le regard d'un pénaliste », *Petites Affiches*, 6 octobre 2011, n° 199, p. 27.

2012

- Adornato F., « Accès à la terre et globalisation », in *De la terre à l'aliment, des valeurs au droit,* sous la direction de Collart Dutilleul F., Actes des colloques internationaux « *L'accès à la terre et ses usages* » (juin 2009, Nantes) et « *De la terre à l'aliment, des valeurs aux règles* » (juin 2010, Nantes), éd. Inida, San José, Costa Rica, 2012, p. 17.
- Alvarez Hernadez F., « La valorizacion de la produccion agroalimentaria en la comercializacion internacional - Alternativas para el productor agrario costarricense », in *Aspectos jurídicos de la valorizacíon de los productos alimentarios – Aspects juridiques de la valorisation des denrées alimentaires*, sous la direction de R. Ballar et F. Collart Dutilleul, Actes de colloque international (San José, novembre 2010), éd. Inida, San José, Costa Rica, 2012, p. 55.
- Ballar R., « La gestion du sol et le développement durable au Costa Rica : des tentatives institutionnelles aux concrétisations limitées », in *De la terre à l'aliment, des valeurs au droit,* sous la direction de Collart Dutilleul F., Actes des colloques internationaux « *L'accès à la terre et ses usages* » (juin 2009, Nantes) et « *De la terre à l'aliment, des valeurs aux règles* » (juin 2010, Nantes), éd. Inida, San José, Costa Rica, 2012, p. 197.
- Ballar R., « La valorizacion de los productos agricolas y el desaraollo sostenible », in *Aspectos jurídicos de la valorizacíon de los productos alimentarios – Aspects juridiques de la valorisation des denrées alimentaires*, sous la direction de R. Ballar et F. Collart Dutilleul, Actes de colloque international (San José, novembre 2010), éd. Inida, San José, Costa Rica, 2012, p. 135.
- Bengoa Cabello J. A., « Los derechos de los campesinos », in *De la terre à l'aliment, des valeurs au droit,* sous la direction de Collart Dutilleul F., Actes des colloques internationaux « *L'accès à la terre et ses usages* » (juin 2009, Nantes) et « *De la terre à l'aliment, des valeurs aux règles* » (juin 2010, Nantes), éd. Inida, San José, Costa Rica, 2012, p. 19.
- Bernault C. et Collart Dutilleul C., « L'articulation du droit national, communautaire et international des signes de qualité : l'approche européenne », in *Aspectos jurídicos de la valorizacíon de los productos alimentarios – Aspects juridiques de la valorisation des denrées alimentaires*, sous la direction de R. Ballar et F. Collart Dutilleul, Actes de colloque international (San José, novembre 2010), éd. Inida, San José, Costa Rica, 2012, p. 9.

- Bibiane Yoda F., « La sécurisation foncière en milieu rural au Burkina Faso », in *De la terre à l'aliment, des valeurs au droit,* sous la direction de Collart Dutilleul F., Actes des colloques internationaux « *L'accès à la terre et ses usages* » (juin 2009, Nantes) et « *De la terre à l'aliment, des valeurs aux règles* » (juin 2010, Nantes), éd. Inida, San José, Costa Rica, 2012, p. 27.
- Bouget D., « Pauvreté absolue et besoins fondamentaux », janvier 2012, en ligne [HAL].
- Bouhey A., « La société civile et la mise en œuvre du droit à l'alimentation et du droit à l'accès à la terre », in *De la terre à l'aliment, des valeurs au droit,* sous la direction de Collart Dutilleul F., Actes des colloques internationaux « *L'accès à la terre et ses usages* » (juin 2009, Nantes) et « *De la terre à l'aliment, des valeurs aux règles* » (juin 2010, Nantes), éd. Inida, San José, Costa Rica, 2012, p. 33.
- Boucobza X., « La méthode de promotion de la sécurité alimentaire : une application de la *lex publica* ? », *in Droit économique et sécurité alimentaire*, sous la direction de F. Collart Dutilleul et V. Pironon, Actes du colloque Lascaux-CREDECO (Nice, 13 juin 2012), *Revue internationale de droit économique*, 2012 n° 4, p. 71.
- Bouillot P.-E., Collart Dutilleul C. et Garcia F., « La valorisation des produits agricoles par les circuits de commercialisation », in *Aspectos jurídicos de la valorizacíon de los productos alimentarios – Aspects juridiques de la valorisation des denrées alimentaires*, sous la direction de R. Ballar et F. Collart Dutilleul, Actes de colloque international (San José, novembre 2010), éd. Inida, San José, Costa Rica, 2012, p. 191.
- Bouquet-Elkaïm J., « Le droit des peuples autochtones à la terre : de la reconnaissance au règlement des conflits d'usage - Études de cas autour de l'exploitation du nickel calédonien », *in De la terre à l'aliment, des valeurs au droit,* sous la direction de F. Collart Dutilleul, Actes des colloques internationaux « *L'accès à la terre et ses usages* » (juin 2009, Nantes) et « *De la terre à l'aliment, des valeurs aux règles* » (juin 2010, Nantes), éd. Inida, San José, Costa Rica, 2012, p. 39.
- Boy L., « Propos conclusifs », *in Droit économique et sécurité alimentaire*, sous la direction de F. Collart Dutilleul et V. Pironon, Actes du colloque Lascaux-CREDECO (Nice, 13 juin 2012), *Revue internationale de droit économique*, 2012 n° 4, p. 99.

- Boy L., « Valorisation des produits agricoles et régulation du marché - Introduction », *in Aspectos jurídicos de la valorizacíon de los productos alimentarios – Aspects juridiques de la valorisation des denrées alimentaires*, sous la direction de R. Ballar et F. Collart Dutilleul, Actes de colloque international (San José, novembre 2010), éd. Inida, San José, Costa Rica, 2012, p. 105.
- Carretero Garcia A., « La politique espagnole de développement rural », *in De la terre à l'aliment, des valeurs au droit,* sous la direction de F. Collart Dutilleul, Actes des colloques internationaux « *L'accès à la terre et ses usages* » (juin 2009, Nantes) et « *De la terre à l'aliment, des valeurs aux règles* » (juin 2010, Nantes), éd. Inida, San José, Costa Rica, 2012, p. 55.
- Clavier J.-P., « Les dérogations au monopole en droit des brevets », *in Aspectos jurídicos de la valorizacíon de los productos alimentarios – Aspects juridiques de la valorisation des denrées alimentaires*, sous la direction de R. Ballar et F. Collart Dutilleul, Actes de colloque international (San José, novembre 2010), éd. Inida, San José, Costa Rica, 2012, p. 75.
- Collart Dutilleul F., « La problématique juridique des investissements dans les terres agricoles des pays en développement », in La promotion de l'investissement pour la production agricole : aspects de droit privé, Actes du colloque UNIDROIT (Rome, novembre 2011), *Uniform Law Review / Revue de droit uniforme*, 2012, n° 1-2, p. 73.
- Collart Dutilleul F., « Le végétal et la sécurité alimentaire : approche juridique internationale », in *Le végétal saisi par le droit*, sous la direction de W. Dross, Actes du colloque « Le Végétal » (Lyon, décembre 2011), éd. Bruylant, Bruxelles, 2012, p. 47.
- Collart Dutilleul F., « The law pertaining to food issues and natural resources exploitation and trade », *Agriculture & Food Security*, 1:6, 2012.
- Collart Dutilleul F., « Compte-rendu de lecture – O. de Schutter et K. Y Cordes, Accounting for Hunger. The Right to Food in the Era of Globalisation Studies in International Law », *Revue trimestrielle de droit européen*, 2012, n° 3, p. 735.
- Collart Dutilleul F. et Pironon V., « Droit économique et sécurité alimentaire - Introduction », *in Droit économique et sécurité alimentaire*, sous la direction de F. Collart Dutilleul et V. Pironon, Actes du colloque Lascaux-CREDECO (Nice, 13 juin 2012), *Revue internationale de droit économique*, 2012, n° 4, p. 5.

- Collart Dutilleul F., Fercot C., Collart Dutilleul C. et Bouillot P.-É., « L'agriculture et les exigences du développement durable en droit français », *Revue de droit rural*, avril 2012, Étude 5.
- Collart Dutilleul F., « Préface », *in De la terre à l'aliment, des valeurs au droit,* sous la direction de F. Collart Dutilleul, Actes des colloques internationaux « *L'accès à la terre et ses usages* » (juin 2009, Nantes) et « *De la terre à l'aliment, des valeurs aux règles* » (juin 2010, Nantes), éd. Inida, San José, Costa Rica, 2012, p. 1.
- Collart Dutilleul F., « De la terre à l'aliment : Introduction à la problématique juridique de la sécurité alimentaire », *in De la terre à l'aliment, des valeurs au droit,* sous la direction de F. Collart Dutilleul, Actes des colloques internationaux « *L'accès à la terre et ses usages* » (juin 2009, Nantes) et « *De la terre à l'aliment, des valeurs aux règles* » (juin 2010, Nantes), éd. Inida, San José, Costa Rica, 2012, p. 5.
- Collart Dutilleul F., « Entre politique foncière et politique alimentaire : quel droit pour quel développement ? », *in De la terre à l'aliment, des valeurs au droit,* sous la direction de F. Collart Dutilleul, Actes des colloques internationaux « *L'accès à la terre et ses usages* » (juin 2009, Nantes) et « *De la terre à l'aliment, des valeurs aux règles* » (juin 2010, Nantes), éd. Inida, San José, Costa Rica, 2012, p. 71.
- Collart Dutilleul F., León Guzman L. et Hostiou R., « Experiencias en el marco del Programa Lascaux: La construcción de la noción de excepción alimentaria », Communication au colloque de l'Université de Pinar del Rio « Agroécologie et sécurité alimentaire » (octobre 2012, Cuba), décembre 2012, en ligne [HAL].
- Collart Dutilleul F., « Introduction générale », *in Aspectos jurídicos de la valorizacíon de los productos alimentarios – Aspects juridiques de la valorisation des denrées alimentaires*, sous la direction de R. Ballar et F. Collart Dutilleul, Actes de colloque international (San José, novembre 2010), éd. Inida, San José, Costa Rica, 2012, p. 1.
- Collart Dutilleul F., « Conclusion générale », in *Aspectos jurídicos de la valorizacíon de los productos alimentarios – Aspects juridiques de la valorisation des denrées alimentaires*, sous la direction de R. Ballar et F. Collart Dutilleul, Actes de colloque international (San José, novembre 2010), éd. Inida, San José, Costa Rica, 2012, p. 201.

- Doussin J.-P., « Le commerce équitable, instrument de mise en œuvre concrète des droits de l'Homme », *in De la terre à l'aliment, des valeurs au droit,* sous la direction de F. Collart Dutilleul, Actes des colloques internationaux « *L'accès à la terre et ses usages* » (juin 2009, Nantes) et « *De la terre à l'aliment, des valeurs aux règles* » (juin 2010, Nantes), éd. Inida, San José, Costa Rica, 2012, p. 125.
- Del Cont C., « Qualité et valorisation des produits agroalimentaires et marché : signes et démarche de qualité et concurrence », *in Aspectos jurídicos de la valorizacíon de los productos alimentarios – Aspects juridiques de la valorisation des denrées alimentaires,* sous la direction de R. Ballar et F. Collart Dutilleul, Actes de colloque international (San José, novembre 2010), éd. Inida, San José, Costa Rica, 2012, p. 117.
- Delcourt L., « L'avenir des agricultures paysannes face aux nouvelles pressions sur la terre », in *De la terre à l'aliment, des valeurs au droit,* sous la direction de Collart Dutilleul F., Actes des colloques internationaux « *L'accès à la terre et ses usages* » (juin 2009, Nantes) et « *De la terre à l'aliment, des valeurs aux règles* » (juin 2010, Nantes), éd. Inida, San José, Costa Rica, 2012, p. 95.
- Fernandez Fernandez E., « Conflits d'usage des espaces naturels au Costa Rica », in *De la terre à l'aliment, des valeurs au droit,* sous la direction de Collart Dutilleul F., Actes des colloques internationaux « *L'accès à la terre et ses usages* » (juin 2009, Nantes) et « *De la terre à l'aliment, des valeurs aux règles* » (juin 2010, Nantes), éd. Inida, San José, Costa Rica, 2012, p. 143.
- Friant-Perrot M., « Valorisation des produits agricoles et agro-alimentaires et information des consommateurs dans la proposition de règlement européen concernant l'information des consommateurs sur les denrées alimentaires COM 2008 (40) final », *in Aspectos jurídicos de la valorizacíon de los productos alimentarios – Aspects juridiques de la valorisation des denrées alimentaires,* sous la direction de R. Ballar et F. Collart Dutilleul, Actes de colloque international (San José, novembre 2010), éd. Inida, San José, Costa Rica, 2012, p. 163.
- Garcia K., « Existe-t-il un droit à l'alimentation au regard de la Convention européenne des droits de l'Homme ? », in *De la terre à l'aliment, des valeurs au droit,* sous la direction de Collart Dutilleul F., Actes des colloques internationaux « *L'accès à la terre et ses usages* » (juin 2009, Nantes) et « *De la terre à l'aliment, des valeurs*

aux règles » (juin 2010, Nantes), éd. Inida, San José, Costa Rica, 2012, p. 159.

- Gnahoui David R., « Accès à la terre et à l'aliment au cœur de l'éthique des affaires : la situation de l'Afrique francophone », in *De la terre à l'aliment, des valeurs au droit,* sous la direction de Collart Dutilleul F., Actes des colloques internationaux « *L'accès à la terre et ses usages* » (juin 2009, Nantes) et « *De la terre à l'aliment, des valeurs aux règles* » (juin 2010, Nantes), éd. Inida, San José, Costa Rica, 2012, p. 83.
- Golay G., « Les moyens disponibles pour revendiquer le respect du droit à l'alimentation », in *De la terre à l'aliment, des valeurs au droit,* sous la direction de Collart Dutilleul F., Actes des colloques internationaux « *L'accès à la terre et ses usages* » (juin 2009, Nantes) et « *De la terre à l'aliment, des valeurs aux règles* » (juin 2010, Nantes), éd. Inida, San José, Costa Rica, 2012, p. 185.
- Hospes O., « Overcoming barriers to the implementation of the right to food », in *De la terre à l'aliment, des valeurs au droit,* sous la direction de Collart Dutilleul F., Actes des colloques internationaux « *L'accès à la terre et ses usages* » (juin 2009, Nantes) et « *De la terre à l'aliment, des valeurs aux règles* » (juin 2010, Nantes), éd. Inida, San José, Costa Rica, 2012, p. 215.
- Houdeingar D., « L'accès à la terre en Afrique subsaharienne », in *De la terre à l'aliment, des valeurs au droit,* sous la direction de Collart Dutilleul F., Actes des colloques internationaux « *L'accès à la terre et ses usages* » (juin 2009, Nantes) et « *De la terre à l'aliment, des valeurs aux règles* » (juin 2010, Nantes), éd. Inida, San José, Costa Rica, 2012, p. 249.
- Jacquot M., « Le droit à l'alimentation dans le contexte européen et international – Retour d'expérience », *in De la terre à l'aliment, des valeurs au droit,* sous la direction de F. Collart Dutilleul, Actes des colloques internationaux « *L'accès à la terre et ses usages* » (juin 2009, Nantes) et « *De la terre à l'aliment, des valeurs aux règles* » (juin 2010, Nantes), éd. Inida, San José, Costa Rica, 2012, p. 439.
- Jourdain-Fortier C. et Loquin E. (2012), « Droit du commerce international et sécurité alimentaire », *in Droit économique et sécurité alimentaire*, sous la direction de F. Collart Dutilleul et V. Pironon, Actes du colloque Lascaux-CREDECO (Nice, 13 juin 2012), *Revue internationale de droit économique*, 2012, n° 4, p. 21.

- Lascaux, « Les sources africaines des droits fondamentaux : redécouvrir la Charte du Mandé (XIIIème siècle) – table ronde », Conférence de D. T. Niane donnée à Nantes à l'occasion des manifestations internationales Lascaux (novembre 2012) en partenariat avec l'Université Permanente, le Comité pour la Mémoire et l'Histoire de l'Esclavage, le SPIDH et le Mémorial de l'abolition de l'esclavage de Nantes, décembre 2012, en ligne [HAL].
- León Guzmán M., « The ambiguous categorization of risk concerning the traditional foreign products », *in De la terre à l'aliment, des valeurs au droit,* sous la direction de F. Collart Dutilleul, Actes des colloques internationaux « *L'accès à la terre et ses usages* » (juin 2009, Nantes) et « *De la terre à l'aliment, des valeurs aux règles* » (juin 2010, Nantes), éd. Inida, San José, Costa Rica, 2012, p. 277.
- León Guzmán M. et Muñoz Ureña H. A., « Proposition de réglementation spécifique de la production et de la commercialisation de produits agricoles et alimentaires traditionnels en Amérique latine », *in De la terre à l'aliment, des valeurs au droit,* sous la direction de F. Collart Dutilleul, Actes des colloques internationaux « *L'accès à la terre et ses usages* » (juin 2009, Nantes) et « *De la terre à l'aliment, des valeurs aux règles* » (juin 2010, Nantes), éd. Inida, San José, Costa Rica, 2012, p. 459.
- León Guzmán M., « La valorizacio n de los alimentos en Europa y en Ame rica Latina », in *Aspectos jurídicos de la valorizacíon de los productos alimentarios – Aspects juridiques de la valorisation des denrées alimentaires*, sous la direction de R. Ballar et F. Collart Dutilleul, Actes de colloque international (San José, novembre 2010), éd. Inida, San José, Costa Rica, 2012, p. 145.
- Leparoux P., « Limitation de l'accès à la terre et nettoyage ethnique rampant dans la vallée du Jourdain », *in De la terre à l'aliment, des valeurs au droit,* sous la direction de F. Collart Dutilleul, Actes des colloques internationaux « *L'accès à la terre et ses usages* » (juin 2009, Nantes) et « *De la terre à l'aliment, des valeurs aux règles* » (juin 2010, Nantes), éd. Inida, San José, Costa Rica, 2012, p. 443.
- Li E., « Which land property system to ensure effective protection of human rights? The Chinese land property system's example », *in De la terre à l'aliment, des valeurs au droit,* sous la direction de F. Collart Dutilleul, Actes des colloques internationaux « *L'accès à la terre et ses usages* » (juin 2009, Nantes) et « *De la terre à l'aliment, des*

valeurs aux règles » (juin 2010, Nantes), éd. Inida, San José, Costa Rica, 2012, p. 301.

- Malwé C., « L'accès à la terre et à l'aliment dans la jurisprudence de la Cour interaméricaine des droits de l'Homme », in *De la terre à l'aliment, des valeurs au droit,* sous la direction de Collart Dutilleul F., Actes des colloques internationaux « *L'accès à la terre et ses usages* » (juin 2009, Nantes) et « *De la terre à l'aliment, des valeurs aux règles* » (juin 2010, Nantes), éd. Inida, San José, Costa Rica, 2012, p. 315.
- Manciaux S., « Les règles du droit des investissements internationaux s'opposent-elles aux politiques de sécurité alimentaire ? », *in Droit économique et sécurité alimentaire*, sous la direction de F. Collart Dutilleul et V. Pironon, Actes du colloque Lascaux-CREDECO (Nice, 13 juin 2012), *Revue internationale de droit économique*, 2012, n° 4, p. 49.
- Martín López M. A., « The Relationship between the Right to Food and the Trade of Agricultural Products – Reflections after the Food Crisis », *in De la terre à l'aliment, des valeurs au droit,* sous la direction de F. Collart Dutilleul, Actes des colloques internationaux « *L'accès à la terre et ses usages* » (juin 2009, Nantes) et « *De la terre à l'aliment, des valeurs aux règles* » (juin 2010, Nantes), éd. Inida, San José, Costa Rica, 2012, p. 323.
- Matthews Glenn J., « L'accès à l'eau in situ en droit canadien », avril 2012, en ligne [HAL].
- Matthews Glenn J., « Troubles de voisinage législatif : L'exemple de la Loi sur l'aménagement du territoire et de la Loi sur l'eau saine dans l'Ontario, Canada », *in De la terre à l'aliment, des valeurs au droit,* sous la direction de F. Collart Dutilleul, Actes des colloques internationaux « *L'accès à la terre et ses usages* » (juin 2009, Nantes) et « *De la terre à l'aliment, des valeurs aux règles* » (juin 2010, Nantes), éd. Inida, San José, Costa Rica, 2012, p. 169.
- Morales S., « La conciliation en droit international entre l'appropriation du vivant végétal et le système multilatéral d'accès et de partage des avantages élaborés par le Traité international sur les ressources phytogénétiques pour l'alimentation et l'agriculture », *in Aspectos jurídicos de la valorizacíon de los productos alimentarios – Aspects juridiques de la valorisation des denrées alimentaires*, sous la direction de R. Ballar et F. Collart Dutilleul, Actes de colloque international (San José, novembre 2010), éd. Inida, San José, Costa Rica, 2012, p. 21.

- Mousseau F., « Souveraineté sur les ressources naturelles et investissements internationaux », Communication aux rencontres internationales Lascaux « Nourrir le monde : la parole aux citoyens » (novembre 2012, Nantes), décembre 2012, en ligne [HAL].
- Muñoz Ureña H. A., « Les contrats de bio-prospection, des outils pour le développement durable ? », in *De la terre à l'aliment, des valeurs au droit,* sous la direction de Collart Dutilleul F., Actes des colloques internationaux « *L'accès à la terre et ses usages* » (juin 2009, Nantes) et « *De la terre à l'aliment, des valeurs aux règles* » (juin 2010, Nantes), éd. Inida, San José, Costa Rica, 2012, p. 337.
- Muñoz Ureña H. A., « La valorizacion de la inocuidad de los alimentos a partir de la superposicion de los tratados regionales: el caso de los permisos de funcionamiento de las fabricas de alimentos en Centroamerica », *in Aspectos jurídicos de la valorizacíon de los productos alimentarios – Aspects juridiques de la valorisation des denrées alimentaires*, sous la direction de R. Ballar et F. Collart Dutilleul, Actes de colloque international (San José, novembre 2010), éd. Inida, San José, Costa Rica, 2012, p. 179.
- Niane D. T., « La Charte du Mandé, précurseur des droits de l'Homme », Conférence donnée à Nantes à l'occasion des manifestations internationales Lascaux (novembre 2012) en partenariat avec l'Université Permanente, le Comité pour la Mémoire et l'Histoire de l'Esclavage, le SPIDH et le Mémorial de l'abolition de l'esclavage de Nantes, décembre 2012, en ligne [HAL].
- Otis G. et Thériault S., « Inuit subsistence rights in Nunavik: A legal perspective of food security in the Artic », in *De la terre à l'aliment, des valeurs au droit,* sous la direction de Collart Dutilleul F., Actes des colloques internationaux « *L'accès à la terre et ses usages* » (juin 2009, Nantes) et « *De la terre à l'aliment, des valeurs aux règles* » (juin 2010, Nantes), éd. Inida, San José, Costa Rica, 2012, p. 365.
- Paré F., « Pour la sécurité alimentaire : restaurer la responsabilité d'Etat », *in Droit économique et sécurité alimentaire*, sous la direction de F. Collart Dutilleul et V. Pironon, Actes du colloque Lascaux-CREDECO (Nice, 13 juin 2012), *Revue internationale de droit économique*, 2012, n° 4, p. 87.
- Paré F., « Sécurité alimentaire et commerce international », Communication aux rencontres internationales Lascaux « Nourrir le

monde : la parole aux citoyens » (novembre 2012, Nantes), décembre 2012, en ligne [HAL].

- Parent G., « Droit économique et sécurité alimentaire : un couple mal assorti ? », *in Droit économique et sécurité alimentaire*, sous la direction de F. Collart Dutilleul et V. Pironon, Actes du colloque Lascaux-CREDECO (Nice, 13 juin 2012), *Revue internationale de droit économique*, 2012, n° 4, p. 15.
- Quilcue A., « El acceso a la tierra en Colombia », in *De la terre à l'aliment, des valeurs au droit,* sous la direction de Collart Dutilleul F., Actes des colloques internationaux « *L'accès à la terre et ses usages* » (juin 2009, Nantes) et « *De la terre à l'aliment, des valeurs aux règles* » (juin 2010, Nantes), éd. Inida, San José, Costa Rica, 2012, p. 449.
- Quintero Navas G., « Espaces ruraux, conflit armé et accès à la terre en Colombie », in *De la terre à l'aliment, des valeurs au droit,* sous la direction de Collart Dutilleul F., Actes des colloques internationaux « *L'accès à la terre et ses usages* » (juin 2009, Nantes) et « *De la terre à l'aliment, des valeurs aux règles* » (juin 2010, Nantes), éd. Inida, San José, Costa Rica, 2012, p. 383.
- Rajagopal PV., « From land to food: Inventory of questions, problems and expectations by Ekta Parishad, a key witness in India », in *De la terre à l'aliment, des valeurs au droit,* sous la direction de Collart Dutilleul F., Actes des colloques internationaux « *L'accès à la terre et ses usages* » (juin 2009, Nantes) et « *De la terre à l'aliment, des valeurs aux règles* » (juin 2010, Nantes), éd. Inida, San José, Costa Rica, 2012, p. 453.
- Reis P., « Les exceptions au monopole dans le Traité UPOV : le cas des semences de ferme ou du prétendu "privilège de l'agriculteur" », *in Aspectos jurídicos de la valorizacíon de los productos alimentarios – Aspects juridiques de la valorisation des denrées alimentaires*, sous la direction de R. Ballar et F. Collart Dutilleul, Actes de colloque international (San José, novembre 2010), éd. Inida, San José, Costa Rica, 2012, p. 89.
- Rodgers C., « Common property and common space: community, property rights and the environment », in *De la terre à l'aliment, des valeurs au droit,* sous la direction de Collart Dutilleul F., Actes des colloques internationaux « *L'accès à la terre et ses usages* » (juin 2009, Nantes) et « *De la terre à l'aliment, des valeurs aux règles* » (juin 2010, Nantes), éd. Inida, San José, Costa Rica, 2012, p. 395.

- Roman D., « Droits de l'Homme, pauvreté et besoins fondamentaux », janvier 2012, en ligne [HAL].
- Romero Perez J. E. (2012), « Tratados, Acuerdos y Constitucion Politica », *in Aspectos jurídicos de la valorizacíon de los productos alimentarios – Aspects juridiques de la valorisation des denrées alimentaires*, sous la direction de R. Ballar et F. Collart Dutilleul, Actes de colloque international (San José, novembre 2010), éd. Inida, San José, Costa Rica, 2012, p. 37.
- Sun J. (2012), « The evolving appreciation of food safety », *EFFL Review*, Vol. 7, n° 2, p. 84.
- Teller M. (2012), « Sécurité alimentaire et responsabilité sociale des entreprises », *in Droit économique et sécurité alimentaire*, sous la direction de F. Collart Dutilleul et V. Pironon, Actes du colloque Lascaux-CREDECO (Nice, 13 juin 2012), *Revue internationale de droit économique*, 2012, n° 4, p. 63.
- Ulate Chacon E., « El uso del suelo y nuevas formas de usucapion en la propiedad agraria y forestal en Costa Rica », in *De la terre à l'aliment, des valeurs au droit,* sous la direction de Collart Dutilleul F., Actes des colloques internationaux « *L'accès à la terre et ses usages* » (juin 2009, Nantes) et « *De la terre à l'aliment, des valeurs aux règles* » (juin 2010, Nantes), éd. Inida, San José, Costa Rica, 2012, p. 411.
- Yokoyama M., « Le patrimoine culturel immatériel, dit "Trésor humain", au Japon », mars 2012, en ligne [HAL].

2013

- Agbayissah S., « Les matières premières agricoles a l'épreuve du droit des sûretés », *in Droit, économie et marchés de matières premières agricoles*, sous la direction de F. Collart Dutilleul et É. Le Dolley, Actes du colloque Lascaux (mars 2013, Paris), ed. LGDJ/Lextenso, Paris, 2013, p. 251.
- Aubry-Caillaud F., « Gestion des risques alimentaires : la nécessité d'une conciliation durable des approches multilatérale et européenne », *in Penser une démocratie alimentaire*, sous la direction de F. Collart Dutilleul et T. Bréger (coord.), vol. 1, éd. Inida, San José, Costa Rica, 2013, p.347.
- Baccouche T., « Le triptyque Terre-Eau-Développement, une autre histoire sur les origines de la révolution tunisienne », *in Penser une démocratie alimentaire*, sous la direction de F. Collart Dutilleul et T. Bréger (coord.), vol. 1, éd. Inida, San José, Costa Rica, 2013, p. 103.

- Ballar R., « Tres verdades incomodas para la seguridad alimentaria », *in Penser une démocratie alimentaire* », sous la direction de F. Collart Dutilleul et T. Bréger (coord.), vol. 1, éd. Inida, San José, Costa Rica, 2013, p. 243.
- Bareït N., « La liberté contractuelle sous la toise de la Convention européenne des droits de l'Homme », *in Droits fondamentaux, Ordre public et libertés économiques*, sous la direction de F. Collart Dutilleul et F. Riem, Actes du colloque Lascaux-CDRE (Bayonne, 17 février 2012), éd. Institut Universitaire Varenne, Bayonne, coll. Colloques & Essais, 2013, p. 51.
- Barroso L. A., « Child consumption and food (in)security in Brazil », *in Penser une démocratie alimentaire*, sous la direction de F. Collart Dutilleul et T. Bréger (coord.), vol. 1, éd. Inida, San José, Costa Rica, 2013, p. 431.
- Bernard A. (2013), « La guerre des farines », *in Droits fondamentaux, Ordre public et libertés économiques*, sous la direction de F. Collart Dutilleul et F. Riem, Actes du colloque Lascaux-CDRE (Bayonne, 17 février 2012), éd. Institut Universitaire Varenne, Bayonne, coll. Colloques & Essais, p. 153.
- Bernard A., « Le libéralisme et les déchets de l'Occident », *in Penser une démocratie alimentaire*, sous la direction de F. Collart Dutilleul et T.Bréger (coord.), vol. 1, éd. Inida, San José, Costa Rica, 2013, p. 47.
- Bernault C., « La protection et la promotion de la spécificité agricole et alimentaire à partir du concept d'exception culturelle », *in De la souveraineté à la sécurité alimentaire*, sous la direction de F. Collart Dutilleul et G. Parent, Actes du séminaire international Lascaux-CEDE (Laval, Québec, 5-6 septembre 2011), éd. Yvon Blais, Cowansville, 2013, p. 69.
- Bernhard S. et Luguenot F., « Les matières premières agricoles sont-elles une classe d'actifs ? », *in Droit, économie et marchés de matières premières agricoles*, sous la direction de F. Collart Dutilleul et É. Le Dolley, Actes du colloque Lascaux (mars 2013, Paris), éd. LGDJ/Lextenso, Paris, 2013, p. 49.
- Berros M. V., « Alimentos producidos localmente: beneficios de la proximidad », *in Penser une démocratie alimentaire*, sous la direction de F. Collart Dutilleul et T. Bréger (coord.), vol. 1, éd. Inida, San José, Costa Rica, 2013, p. 365.

- Bodea S., « Le Code foncier et domanial du Bénin », Communication dans le cadre de l'atelier Lascaux du Forum mondial des droits de l'Homme organisé par le SPIDH (mai 2013, Nantes), juin 2013, en ligne [HAL].
- Bonnin-De Toffoli C. et Lazaric N., « Le comportement écologique du consommateur, un facteur déterminant de la sécurité alimentaire », *in Penser une démocratie alimentaire*, sous la direction de F. Collart Dutilleul et T. Bréger (coord.), vol. 1, éd. Inida, San José, Costa Rica, 2013, p. 451.
- Bouillot P.-E., « Le développement durable et le droit agroalimentaire », *in De la souveraineté à la sécurité alimentaire*, sous la direction de F. Collart Dutilleul et G. Parent, Actes du séminaire international Lascaux-CEDE (Laval, Québec, 5-6 septembre 2011), éd. Yvon Blais, Cowansville, 2013, p. 203.
- Bouquet-Elkaïm J., « Organismes génétiquement modifiés et démocratie - Pourquoi un contentieux des faucheurs volontaires ? », *in Penser une démocratie alimentaire*, sous la direction de F. Collart Dutilleul et T. Bréger (coord.), vol. 1, éd. Inida, San José, Costa Rica, 2013, p. 421.
- Boussard J.-M. et Nussenbaum M., « Les dérives, outils de couverture ou de spéculation ? », *in Droit, économie et marchés de matières premières agricoles*, sous la direction de F. Collart Dutilleul et É. Le Dolley, Actes du colloque Lascaux (mars 2013, Paris), éd. LGDJ/Lextenso, Paris, 2013, p. 117.
- Brégeot G. et Cheneau-Loquay A., « Le projet de développement au service de la sécurité alimentaire des consommateurs : pour une approche territoriale », *in Penser une démocratie alimentaire*, sous la direction de F. Collart Dutilleul et T. Bréger (coord.), vol. 1, éd. Inida, San José, Costa Rica, 2013, p. 381.
- Bréger T., « Mondialisation, marchandisation des biens essentiels et ordre public », *in Penser une démocratie alimentaire*, sous la direction de F. Collart Dutilleul et T. Bréger (coord.), vol. 1, éd. Inida, San José, Costa Rica, 2013, p. 273.
- Bugnicourt M., « Contribution pour un ajustement du curseur juridique en matière de sécurité alimentaire (une approche de microbiologiste) », *in Penser une démocratie alimentaire*, sous la direction de F. Collart Dutilleul et T. Bréger (coord.), vol. 1, éd. Inida, San José, Costa Rica, 2013, p. 391.

- Capelle-Blancard G., « La hausse des prix agricoles : transmission des prix entre marchés à terme et marchés », *in Droit, économie et marchés de matières premières agricoles*, sous la direction de F. Collart Dutilleul et E. Le Dolley, Actes du colloque Lascaux (mars 2013, Paris), e d. LGDJ/Lextenso, Paris, 2013, p. 175.
- Carretero Garcia A., « Responsabilidad por posibles daños económicos sobre la salud y el medio ambiente derivados del cultivo de OMGs en el Derecho español », *in Penser une démocratie alimentaire*, sous la direction de F. Collart Dutilleul et T. Bréger (coord.), vol. 1, éd. Inida, San José, Costa Rica, 2013, p. 181.
- Collart Dutilleul C., « La propriété industrielle appliquée aux produits agroalimentaires – Problèmes et voies de solutions au regard des concepts de souveraineté et de sécurit » alimentaires », in *De la souveraineté à la sécurité alimentaire*, sous la direction de F. Collart Dutilleul et G. Parent, Actes du séminaire international Lascaux-CEDE (Laval, Québec, 5-6 septembre 2011), éd. Yvon Blais, Cowansville, 2013, p. 183.
- Collart Dutilleul F., Fercot C., Hugou B., Sun J. et Yamthieu S., « Approche juridique des risques alimentaires », *in Le risque*, sous la direction de F. Tripier, Actes des Journées de la MSH Ange-Guépin, éd. L'Harmattan, Paris, coll. Logiques sociales, 2013, p. 275.
- Collart Dutilleul F., « Indigeste viande de cheval », *lemonde.fr* (16 février 2013) et *Le Monde* (17-18 février 2013).
- Collart Dutilleul F., « Cheval : un commerce "déconnecté de la nécessité économique" », *L'Indépendant*, 21 février 2013.
- Collart Dutilleul F. et Diabate A., « La sécurité alimentaire et le droit à l'alimentation à l'épreuve des investissements internationaux en Afrique de l'Ouest : les risques d'une désillusion », juin 2013, en ligne [HAL].
- Collart Dutilleul F., « Les concepts de développement durable et de sécurité alimentaire à la lumière des relations extérieures de l'Europe », *in Le droit des relations extérieures de l'Union européenne après le Traité de Lisbonne*, sous la direction de A-S. Lamblin-Gourdin et E. Mondielli, éd. Larcier, Bruxelles, 2013, p. 261.
- Collart Dutilleul F., « Préface», *in Droits fondamentaux, Ordre public et libertés économiques*, sous la direction de F. Collart Dutilleul et F. Riem, Actes du colloque Lascaux-CDRE (Bayonne, 17 février 2012), éd. Institut Universitaire Varenne, Bayonne, coll. Colloques & Essais, 2013, p. 9.

- Collart Dutilleul F., « Heurs et malheurs du droit fondamental à l'alimentation », *in Droits fondamentaux, Ordre public et libertés économiques*, sous la direction de F. Collart Dutilleul et F. Riem, Actes du colloque Lascaux-CDRE (Bayonne, 17 février 2012), éd. Institut Universitaire Varenne, Bayonne, coll. Colloques & Essais, 2013, p. 119.
- Collart Dutilleul F., « Penser une démocratie alimentaire », *in Penser une démocratie alimentaire*, sous la direction de F. Collart Dutilleul et T. Bréger (coord.), vol. 1, éd. Inida, San José, Costa Rica, 2013, p. 1.
- Collart Dutilleul F., « Proposition pour la reconnaissance internationale d'une "exception alimentaire" sur le modèle de "l'exception culturelle" », *in Penser une démocratie alimentaire*, sous la direction de F. Collart Dutilleul et T. Bréger (coord.), vol. 1, éd. Inida, San José, Costa Rica, 2013, p. 13.
- Collart Dutilleul F., « Investissements interna-tionaux et accaparement des terres : la recherche d'un équilibre », *in Penser une démocratie alimentaire*, sous la direction de F. Collart Dutilleul et T. Bréger (coord.), vol. 1, éd. Inida, San José, Costa Rica, 2013, p. 83.
- Collart Dutilleul F. et Hugou B., « Problématique juridique des marchés à terme de matières premières agricoles », *in Droit, économie et marchés de matières premières agricoles*, sous la direction de F. Collart Dutilleul et E. Le Dolley, Actes du colloque Lascaux (mars 2013, Paris), éd. LGDJ/Lextenso, Paris, p. 3.
- Collart Dutilleul F., Diabaté A. et Sidibé I., « Le respect du droit à l'eau et la sécurité alimentaire dans le cadre des aménagements hydro-agricoles au Mali », *in Penser une démocratie alimentaire*, sous la direction de F. Collart Dutilleul et T. Bréger (coord.), vol. 1, éd. Inida, San José, Costa Rica, 2013, p. 143.
- Collart Dutilleul F., « Les voies d'amélioration de la sécurité alimentaire dans un contexte de mondialisation du commerce », in *Penser une démocratie alimentaire*, sous la direction de F. Collart Dutilleul et T. Bréger (coord.), vol. 1, éd. Inida, San José, Costa Rica, 2013, p. 213.
- Collart Dutilleul F., « Les concepts et les stratégies juridiques – Introduction », *in De la souveraineté à la sécurité alimentaire*, sous la direction de F. Collart Dutilleul et G. Parent, Actes du séminaire international Lascaux-CEDE (Laval, Québec, 5-6 septembre 2011), éd. Yvon Blais, Cowansville, 2013, p. 9.

- Collart Dutilleul F., « Certains moyens juridiques et les de fis qu'ils soulèvent – Introduction », *in De la souveraineté à la sécurité alimentaire*, sous la direction de F. Collart Dutilleul et G. Parent, Actes du séminaire international Lascaux-CEDE (Laval, Québec, 5-6 septembre 2011), éd. Yvon Blais, Cowansville, 2013, p. 143.
- Collart Dutilleul F., « Discussion générale sur les moyens juridiques : défis, priorités et hiérarchie », *in De la souveraineté à la sécurité alimentaire*, sous la direction de F. Collart Dutilleul et G. Parent, Actes du séminaire international Lascaux-CEDE (Laval, Québec, 5-6 septembre 2011), éd. Yvon Blais, Cowansville, 2013, p. 219.
- Cordier J., « Les fondamentaux des marchés de matières premières agricoles », *in Droit, économie et marchés de matières premières agricoles*, sous la direction de F. Collart Dutilleul et É. Le Dolley, Actes du colloque Lascaux (mars 2013, Paris), éd. LGDJ/Lextenso, Paris, p. 19.
- Courleux F. et Depeyrot J.-N., « Négociations du cadre communautaire de régulation financière : quelles incidences sur les filières agroalimentaires ? », *in Droit, économie et marchés de matières premières agricoles*, sous la direction de F. Collart Dutilleul et É. Le Dolley, Actes du colloque Lascaux (mars 2013, Paris), éd. LGDJ/Lextenso, Paris, p. 241.
- Cuq M., « Le droit des investissements étrangers et le droit à une alimentation adéquate », *in Penser une démocratie alimentaire*, sous la direction de F. Collart Dutilleul et T. Bréger (coord.), vol. 1, éd. Inida, San José, Costa Rica, 2013, p. 123.
- Del Cont C., « Une nouvelle articulation entre concurrence et agriculture pour renforcer la sécurité alimentaire et le droit à l'alimentation en Europe », *in Penser une démocratie alimentaire*, sous la direction de F. Collart Dutilleul et T. Bréger (coord.), vol. 1, éd. Inida, San José, Costa Rica, 2013, p. 337.
- Declerck F., « Qualité des prix forme s sur les marchés agricoles », *in Droit, économie et marchés de matières premières agricoles*, sous la direction de F. Collart Dutilleul et É. Le Dolley, Actes du colloque Lascaux (mars 2013, Paris), éd. LGDJ/Lextenso, Paris, 2013, p. 189.
- Després L., « Comment le fonctionnement actuel du système économique mondialisé influence-t-il la sécurité alimentaire ? », *in Penser une démocratie alimentaire*, sous la direction de F. Collart Dutilleul et T. Bréger (coord.), vol. 1, éd. Inida, San José, Costa Rica, 2013, p. 57.

- Diabate A., « L'accès à la terre et le droit des investissements au Mali », Communication dans le cadre de l'atelier Lascaux du Forum mondial des droits de l'Homme organisé par le SPIDH (mai 2013, Nantes), juin 2013, en ligne [HAL].
- Diabate A. et Yamthieu S., « Quel droit pour la sécurité alimentaire en Afrique ? Synthèse des Journées scientifiques de Bamako (4-5 juin 2013) », juillet 2013, en ligne [HAL].
- Doussan I. et Thévenot G., « Le droit de la protection phytosanitaire et l'objectif de protection de la santé et de l'environnement : une intégration à parfaire », *in Penser une démocratie alimentaire*, sous la direc-tion de F. Collart Dutilleul et T. Bréger (coord.), vol. 1, éd. Inida, San José, Costa Rica, 2013, p. 193.
- Doussin J.-P., « Souveraineté alimentaire et agriculture familiale - Réflexions autour d'une de marche volontaire de renforcement de capacité des organisations de producteur : le commerce équitable », *in Penser une démocratie alimentaire*, sous la direction de F. Collart Dutilleul et T. Bréger (coord.), vol. 1, éd. Inida, San José, Costa Rica, 2013, p. 319.
- Drapier S., « Le rôle des agences de notation de l'agroalimentaire dans la fixation des normes internationales », *in Penser une démocratie alimentaire*, sous la direction de F. Collart Dutilleul et T. Bréger (coord.), vol. 1, éd. Inida, San José, Costa Rica, 2013, p. 371.
- Fercot C., « La souveraineté alimentaire : l'alimentation au croisement de la politique et du droit », *in Penser une démocratie alimentaire*, sous la direction de F. Collart Dutilleul et T. Bréger (coord.), vol. 1, éd. Inida, San José, Costa Rica, 2013, p. 285.
- Fernandez Fernandez E., « L'accaparement des terres au Costa Rica : le cas des entreprises productrices d'ananas », Communication dans le cadre de l'atelier Lascaux du Forum mondial des droits de l'Homme organisé par le SPIDH (mai 2013, Nantes), en juin 2013, en ligne [HAL].
- Friant-Perrot M., « Information et qualité des aliments : de l'étiquette à l'assiette, comment garantir au consommateur européen le choix de son alimentation ? », *in Penser une démocratie alimentaire*, sous la direction de F. Collart Dutilleul et T. Bréger (coord.), vol. 1, éd. Inida, San José, Costa Rica, 2013, p. 437.
- Frison-Roche M.-A., « Quelle(s) autorité(s) de régulation pour les marche s de matières premières agricoles ?3, *in Droit, économie et marchés de matières premières agricoles*, sous la direction de F.

Collart Dutilleul et E. Le Dolley, Actes du colloque Lascaux (mars 2013, Paris), éd. LGDJ/Lextenso, Paris, 2013, p. 267.

- Gaudemet A., « Quel encadrement normatif pour les produits à terme ? », *in Droit, économie et marchés de matières premières agricoles*, sous la direction de F. Collart Dutilleul et É. Le Dolley, Actes du colloque Lascaux (mars 2013, Paris), éd. LGDJ/Lextenso, Paris, 2013, p. 215.
- Gaurier D., « Les interdits alimentaires religieux : quel possible rapport avec une forme de sécurité alimentaire ? », *in Penser une démocratie alimentaire*, sous la direction de F. Collart Dutilleul et T. Bréger (coord.), vol. 1, éd. Inida, San José, Costa Rica, 2013, p. 413.
- Golay C., « Le droit a l'alimentation, le PIDESC et les droits des paysannes et des paysans », *in De la souveraineté à la sécurité alimentaire*, sous la direction de F. Collart Dutilleul et G. Parent, Actes du séminaire international Lascaux-CEDE (Laval, Québec, 5-6 septembre 2011), éd. Yvon Blais, Cowansville, 2013, p. 121.
- Godin X. et Legal P., « Propriété privée foncière (XIIIe – XXIe siècles) », mai 2013, en ligne [HAL]
- Grunvald S., « La notion de subsistance au plan collectif et individuel : un éclairage pénaliste », *in De la souveraineté à la sécurité alimentaire*, sous la direction de F. Collart Dutilleul et G. Parent, Actes du séminaire international Lascaux-CEDE (Laval, Québec, 5-6 septembre 2011), éd. Yvon Blais, Cowansville , 2013, p. 109.
- Guilleminot B., Ohana J.-J., Ohana S. et Paumier A.-L., « Les marchés à terme faussent-ils le processus de formation des prix ? », *in Droit, économie et marchés de matières premières agricoles*, sous la direction de F. Collart Dutilleul et E. Le Dolley, Actes du colloque Lascaux (mars 2013, Paris), éd. LGDJ/Lextenso, Paris, 2013, p. 199.
- Guyomard H., « Les déterminants du risque-prix. Problématique générale et impact de la financiarisation », *in Droit, économie et marchés de matières premières agricoles*, sous la direction de F. Collart Dutilleul et E. Le Dolley, Actes du colloque Lascaux (mars 2013, Paris), éd. LGDJ/Lextenso, Paris, 2013, p131.
- Halley P., « Le développement durable, une stratégie pour la sécurité alimentaire ? L'exemple des réformes du droit de l'eau au Québec », *in De la souveraineté à la sécurité alimentaire*, sous la direction de F. Collart Dutilleul et G. Parent, Actes du séminaire international Lascaux-CEDE (Laval, Québec, 5-6 septembre 2011), éd. Yvon Blais, Cowansville, 2013, p. 17.

- Houdeingar D., « L'accès a l'eau des populations du bassin du Lac Tchad », *in Penser une démocratie alimentaire*, sous la direction de F. Collart Dutilleul et T. Bréger (coord.), vol. 1, éd. Inida, San José, Costa Rica, 2013, p. 133.
- Hugou B., « Spéculation financière et sécurité alimentaire », *in De la souveraineté à la sécurité alimentaire*, sous la direction de F. Collart Dutilleul et G. Parent, Actes du séminaire international Lascaux-CEDE (Laval, Québec, 5-6 septembre 2011), éd. Yvon Blais, Cowansville, 2013, p. 169.
- Jourdain-Fortier C. et Pironon V., « La sécurité alimentaire dans le droit de l'OMC : analyse critique et prospective », *in Penser une démocratie alimentaire*, sous la direction de F. Collart Dutilleul et T. Bréger (coord.), vol. 1, éd. Inida, San José, Costa Rica, 2013, p. 255.
- Kastler G. et Brac de la Perrière R., « Position du Réseau Semences paysannes sur la commercialisation des semences et la santé des plantes », *in Penser une démocratie alimentaire*, sous la direction de F. Collart Dutilleul et T. Bréger (coord.), vol. 1, éd. Inida, San José, Costa Rica, 2013, p. 167.
- Lambinet R. et Lautier D., « Le rôle du terme et du sous-jacent dans la formation du prix : analyse économique », *in Droit, économie et marchés de matières premières agricoles*, sous la direction de F. Collart Dutilleul et E. Le Dolley, Actes du colloque Lascaux (mars 2013, Paris), éd. LGDJ/Lextenso, Paris, 2013, p. 87.
- León Guzmán M. et Muñoz Ureña H., « Les sources du droit européen de l'alimentation », juin 2013, en ligne [HAL].
- León Guzmán M., « Une affaire salée : la protection des indications géographiques protégées du sel face aux exigences nutritionnelles de la législation costaricienne », *in Penser une démocratie alimentaire*, sous la direction de F. Collart Dutilleul et T. Bréger (coord.), vol. 1, éd. Inida, San José, Costa Rica, 2013, p. 445.
- Malwe C. et Fernandez Fernandez E., « Re-drawing existing powers over natural resources for food secu-rity at the light of a natural resources constrained world », *in Penser une démocratie alimentaire*, sous la direction de F. Collart Dutilleul et T. Bréger (coord.), vol. 1, éd. Inida, San José, Costa Rica, 2013, p. 201.
- Martín Lopez M. A., « Le droit à l'alimentation comme norme impérative générale et la nullité des clauses des traités le transgressant », *in Droits fondamentaux, Ordre public et libertés économiques*, sous la direction de F. Collart Dutilleul et F. Riem, Actes du colloque

Lascaux-CDRE (Bayonne, 17 février 2012), éd. Institut Universitaire Varenne, Bayonne, coll. Colloques & Essais, 213, p. 239.

- Martín Lopez M. A., « Propuesta para conseguir que el derecho a la alimentacion sea considerado como norma imperativa de derecho internacional general », *in Penser une démocratie alimentaire*, sous la direction de F. Collart Dutilleul et T. Bréger (coord.), vol. 1, éd. Inida, San José, Costa Rica, 2013, p. 409.
- Merville A.-D., « Typologie des contrats à terme », *in Droit, économie et marchés de matières premières agricoles*, sous la direction de F. Collart Dutilleul et É. Le Dolley, Actes du colloque Lascaux (mars 2013, Paris), éd. LGDJ/Lextenso, Paris, 2013, p. 57.
- Modou K. L., « Accès à la terre et aux ressources naturelles et sécurité alimentaire en Afrique centrale », *in De la souveraineté à la sécurité alimentaire*, sous la direction de F. Collart Dutilleul et G. Parent, Actes du séminaire international Lascaux-CEDE (Laval, Québec, 5-6 septembre 2011), éd. Yvon Blais, Cowansville, 2013, p. 197.
- Moiroud C., « Du concept de souveraineté à la souveraineté alimentaire », *in De la souveraineté à la sécurité alimentaire*, sous la direction de F. Collart Dutilleul et G. Parent, Actes du séminaire international Lascaux-CEDE (Laval, Québec, 5-6 septembre 2011), éd. Yvon Blais, Cowansville, 2013, p. 29.
- Morales S., « Adéquation des piliers du TIRPAA aux objectifs de sécurité alimentaire et de développement durable », *in De la souveraineté à la sécurité alimentaire*, sous la direction de F. Collart Dutilleul et G. Parent, Actes du séminaire international Lascaux-CEDE (Laval, Québec, 5-6 septembre 2011), éd. Yvon Blais, Cowansville, 2013, p. 189.
- Mousseau F., « Accaparement des terres en Papouasie Nouvelle Guinée », Communication dans le cadre de l'atelier Lascaux du Forum mondial des droits de l'Homme organisé par le SPIDH (mai 2013, Nantes), juin 2013, en ligne [HAL].
- Muir Watt H., « Politique du droit international privé : réflexion critique », *in Droits fondamentaux, Ordre public et libertés économiques*, sous la direction de F. Collart Dutilleul et F. Riem, Actes du colloque Lascaux-CDRE (Bayonne, 17 février 2012), éd. Institut Universitaire Varenne, Bayonne, coll. Colloques & Essais, 2013, p. 245.
- Munier B., « Spéculation du "*momentum*", spéculation institutionnelle des investisseurs financiers : comment modéliser la volatilité

des cours agricoles ? », *in Droit, économie et marchés de matières premières agricoles*, sous la direction de F. Collart Dutilleul et É. Le Dolley, Actes du colloque Lascaux (mars 2013, Paris), éd. LGDJ/Lextenso, Paris. 2013, p. 157.

- Muñoz Ureña H. A., « Il faut que la maison abritant l'investissement étranger ouvre ses portes au développement durable et à la sécurité alimentaire ! », *in Penser une démocratie alimentaire*, sous la direction de F. Collart Dutilleul et T. Bréger (coord.), vol. 1, éd. Inida, San José, Costa Rica, 2013, p. 111.
- Negrutiu I., « Natural resources, what else? La capital naturel évanescent et le défi 8M », Communication à la 1re séance du Cycle « Maîtrise des ressources naturelles et besoins fondamentaux » (mai 2013, Nantes), juin 2013, en ligne [HAL].
- Pailler P., « Le rôle du terme et du sous-jacent dans la formation du prix : analyse juridique », *in Droit, économie et marchés de matières premières agricoles*, sous la direction de F. Collart Dutilleul et É. Le Dolley, Actes du colloque Lascaux (mars 2013, Paris), éd. LGDJ/Lextenso, Paris, 2013, p. 75.
- Parachkevova I. et Teller M., « Légitimité et utilités de la spéculation », *in Droit, économie et marchés de matières premières agricoles*, sous la direction de F. Collart Dutilleul et É. Le Dolley, Actes du colloque Lascaux (mars 2013, Paris), éd. LGDJ/Lextenso, Paris, 2013, p. 33.
- Paré F., « L'autonomie alimentaire », *in De la souveraineté à la sécurité alimentaire*, sous la direction de F. Collart Dutilleul et G. Parent, Actes du séminaire international Lascaux-CEDE (Laval, Québec, 5-6 septembre 2011), éd. Yvon Blais, Cowansville, 2013, p. 47.
- Paré F. et Perrollaz C., « Pour la sécurité alimentaire, restaurer la capacité d'Etat à réguler les affaires alimentaires : aperçu de l'analyse de la Coalition pour l'identification d'un outil effectif de restauration politique », *in Penser une démocratie alimentaire*, sous la direction de F. Collart Dutilleul et T. Bréger (coord.), vol. 1, éd. Inida, San José, Costa Rica, 2013, p. 297.
- Parent G., « L'objectif de sécurité alimentaire au regard du droit », *in De la souveraineté à la sécurité alimentaire*, sous la direction de F. Collart Dutilleul et G. Parent, Actes du séminaire international Lascaux-CEDE (Laval, Québec, 5-6 septembre 2011), éd. Yvon Blais, Cowansville, 2013, p. 3.

- Parent G., « La diversité agricole et alimentaire et l'OMC », in *De la souveraineté à la sécurité alimentaire*, sous la direction de F. Collart Dutilleul et G. Parent, Actes du séminaire international Lascaux-CEDE (Laval, Québec, 5-6 septembre 2011), éd. Yvon Blais, Cowansville, 2013, p. 89.
- Poirmeur Y. (2013), « Synthèse – Les droits fondamentaux en quête de protection », *in Droits fondamentaux, Ordre public et libertés économiques*, sous la direction de F. Collart Dutilleul et F. Riem, Actes du colloque Lascaux-CDRE (Bayonne, 17 février 2012), éd. Institut Universitaire Varenne, Bayonne, coll. Colloques & Essais, p. 265.
- Quin A., « La "Grande transformation" des semences », *in Penser une démocratie alimentaire*, sous la direction de F. Collart Dutilleul et T. Bréger (coord.), vol. 1, éd. Inida, San José, Costa Rica, 2013, p. 155.
- Racine J.-B., « L'ordre public alimentaire », *in De la souveraineté à la sécurité alimentaire*, sous la direction de F. Collart Dutilleul et G. Parent, Actes du séminaire international Lascaux-CEDE (Laval, Québec, 5-6 septembre 2011), éd. Yvon Blais, Cowansville, 2013, p. 125.
- Reygrobellet A., « Quel contrôle du risque-prix par le marche ? Catégorisation des opérateurs, classification et exécution des transactions », *in Droit, économie et marchés de matières premières agricoles*, sous la direction de F. Collart Dutilleul et E. Le Dolley, Actes du colloque Lascaux (mars 2013, Paris), éd. LGDJ/Lextenso, Paris, 2013, p. 221.
- Riem F., « Droits fondamentaux, Ordre public et libertés économiques – Introduction », *in Droits fondamentaux, Ordre public et libertés économiques*, sous la direction de F. Collart Dutilleul et F. Riem, Actes du colloque Lascaux-CDRE (Bayonne, 17 février 2012), éd. Institut Universitaire Varenne, Bayonne, coll. Colloques & Essais, 2013, p. 13.
- Riem F., « Les droits sociaux fondamentaux dans le "contrat social" européen », *in Droits fondamentaux, Ordre public et libertés économiques*, sous la direction de F. Collart Dutilleul et F. Riem, Actes du colloque Lascaux-CDRE (Bayonne, 17 février 2012), éd. Institut Universitaire Varenne, Bayonne, coll. Colloques & Essais, 2013, p. 33.
- Riem F., « Sécurité alimentaire et commerce international : nourrir la planète par le marché ou sauver le "pacte colonial" ? », *in Penser une*

démocratie alimentaire, sous la direction de F. Collart Dutilleul et T. Bréger (coord.), vol. 1, éd. Inida, San José, Costa Rica, 2013, p. 69.

- Robine D., « Les risques spécifiques aux marchés de gré à gré », *in Droit, économie et marchés de matières premières agricoles*, sous la direction de F. Collart Dutilleul et É. Le Dolley, Actes du colloque Lascaux (mars 2013, Paris), éd. Lextenso, Paris, 2013, p. 145.

- Rosenberg D., « Le droit a la sécurité alimentaire : réponses et non-réponses du droit international », *in Penser une démocratie alimentaire*, sous la direction de F. Collart Dutilleul et T. Bréger (coord.), vol. 1, éd. Inida, San José, Costa Rica, 2013, p. 399.

- Rouaud A.-C., « La faculté de désengagement dans l'opération de marché à terme », *in Droit, économie et marchés de matières premières agricoles*, sous la direction de F. Collart Dutilleul et É. Le Dolley, Actes du colloque Lascaux (mars 2013, Paris), éd. LGDJ/Lextenso, Paris, 2013, p. 103.

- Sozzo G., « La construcción mas local de la seguridad de los alimentos: el caso de la Argentina », in *Penser une démocratie alimentaire*, sous la direction de F. Collart Dutilleul et T.Bréger (coord.), vol. 1, éd. Inida, San José, Costa Rica, 2013, p. 355.

- Sun J., « Le développement de la souveraineté alimentaire pour garantir la sécurité alimentaire », *in De la souveraineté à la sécurité alimentaire*, sous la direction de F. Collart Dutilleul et G. Parent, Actes du séminaire international Lascaux-CEDE (Laval, Québec, 5-6 septembre 2011), éd. Yvon Blais, Cowansville, 2013, p. 165.

- Thériault S., « Réflexions sur la notion polysémique de subsistance comme moyen juridique dans le contexte de la sécurité alimentaire : l'éclairage des perspectives autochtones », *in De la souveraineté à la sécurité alimentaire*, sous la direction de F. Collart Dutilleul et G. Parent, Actes du séminaire international Lascaux-CEDE (Laval, Québec, 5-6 septembre 2011), éd. Yvon Blais, Cowansville, 2013, p. 99.

- Torck S., « Quel contrôle du risque-prix par le marché ? Les manipulations de cours », *in Droit, économie et marchés de matières premières agricoles*, sous la direction de F. Collart Dutilleul et É. Le Dolley, Actes du colloque Lascaux (mars 2013, Paris), éd. Lextenso, Paris, 2013, p. 233.

- Ulate Chacón E. et Fisher González V., « Propuestas para la seguridad alimentaria desde la pers-pectiva regional del Sistema de Integracio n Centroamericana (SICA) », *in Penser une démocratie ali-*

mentaire, sous la direction de F. Collart Dutilleul et T. Bréger (coord.), vol. 1, éd. Inida, San José, Costa Rica, 2013, p. 329.

- Valluis B., « Peut-on réguler juridiquement la spéculation ? Quelle gouvernance pour les marchés dérivés ? », *in Droit, économie et marchés de matières premières agricoles*, sous la direction de F. Collart Dutilleul et E. Le Dolley, Actes du colloque Lascaux (mars 2013, Paris), éd. LGDJ/Lextenso, Paris, 2013, p. 285.
- Vu Q. N. (2013), « Land ownership and land seizure in one-party Vietnam », Communication dans le cadre de l'atelier Lascaux du Forum mondial des droits de l'Homme organisé par le SPIDH (mai 2013, Nantes), juin 2013, en ligne [HAL].
- Yamthieu S., « Propriété industrielle et sécurité alimentaire en Afrique : questionnement autour des notions de souveraineté, d'autonomie et d'ordre public alimentaires », *in De la souveraineté à la sécurité alimentaire*, sous la direction de F. Collart Dutilleul et G. Parent, Actes du séminaire international Lascaux-CEDE (Laval, Québec, 5-6 septembre 2011), éd. Yvon Blais, Cowansville, 2013.

À paraître

- Collart Dutilleul F., « Réflexions conclusives sur le droit de la sécurité sanitaire alimentaire face aux risques », *Revue de droit sanitaire et social*, n° 5.
- Collart Dutilleul F., « De l'exception culturelle à une exception alimentaire », in *Mélanges en l'honneur d'André Lucas*, éd. Litec, Paris.
- Collart Dutilleul F., « La première étape d'une longue marche vers un droit spécial de la sécurité alimentaire », in *Mélanges Gilles Martin*, éd. Frison-Roche, Paris.

IV.– Etudes et rapports

- Butault J., « Les causes juridiques de la crise de la vache folle », février 2010, en ligne [HAL].
- Collart Dutilleul F., Fercot C., Collart Dutilleul C. et Bouillot P.-É. (2011), « L'agriculture et les exigences du développement durable en droit français », Rapport au Comité européen de droit rural de Budapest, septembre 2011.

Photocomposition :
Instituto de Investigación en Derecho Alimentario S.A. (INIDA)

Dépôt Légal : Février 2014

www.ingramcontent.com/pod-product-compliance
Lightning Source LLC
Chambersburg PA
CBHW061229220326
41599CB00028B/5381
* 9 7 8 2 9 1 8 3 8 2 0 9 6 *